families

developing Relationships

MOLLIE STEVENS SMART | LAURA S. SMART

with contributions by RUSSELL COOK SMART and CRAIG M. SZWED

FAMILIES
developing RELATIONSHIPS

MACMILLAN PUBLISHING CO., INC.
New York

COLLIER MACMILLAN PUBLISHERS
London

Copyright © 1976, Macmillan Publishing Co., Inc.

Printed in the United States of America

MACMILLAN PUBLISHING CO., INC.
866 Third Avenue, New York, New York 10022

COLLIER MACMILLAN CANADA, LTD.

Library of Congress Cataloging in Publication Data

Smart, Mollie Stevens.
Families : developing relationships.

Includes bibliographies and index.
    1. Family.   2. Marriage.   3. Sex.
    1. Smart, Laura S., joint author.   II. Title.
HQ728.S57   301.42   74-33101
ISBN 0-02-412020-0

Printing: 1 2 3 4 5 6 7 8   Year: 6 7 8 9 0 1 2

To
GRACE BUSSING SHERRER
and
ELIZABETH CHAFFIN SZWED

pREfACE

This textbook is planned for use in an introductory family and marriage course in which students have a variety of objectives. They want to gain an understanding of their interactions and relationships with the people who are important to them in contexts of love and home. They want to integrate different points of view and value systems for themselves. They need skills in communicating, relating, planning, and carrying on home living. Many students will use such a course in their professional work in fields involving service to people, teaching, and research in human development and relationships. While considering all these purposes, we have also thought about the conditions under which present and future students will be learning. The world is shrinking and changing very fast. How can we learn today in such a way that our efforts will be productive for tomorrow as well? In the past, many students took a "marriage course" in order to learn how to have happy marriages. Perhaps they still do, but a book cannot give them definite directions, nor can a teacher. A book can open up choices to students. We hope that our readers will gain freedom to decide what kinds of persons they become and what kinds of relationships they develop with the people they love.

Throughout time and space, families have been and are organized in an amazing number of patterns. Whatever the structure and function of a particular type of family, it arose in order to fill certain human needs. It exists as long as it fills those needs, and often longer. Human beings are very talented at inventing new forms of everything—languages, clothes, houses, vehicles, foods, gadgets, roles, and relationships. And yet, as someone invents a new pattern and some joyfully adopt it, others are satisfied with the old ways and feel anguish at the possibility of having to relinquish them. Conflict is inevitable because no person is an island. Everyone affects other people in what he or she does. Even when a couple flees to the wilderness or a

vii

South Sea island, they are not merely living their own lives but are influencing the networks of people from which they are trying to extricate themselves. We are all involved in continuity and in change.

This book reports many research studies on the various ways in which human beings interact and some of the results of their behavior. Starting with North Americans, whom we know best, we bring in material from many other cultures. We use many examples from India, a place where we have lived for three years. Some historical material is also used. The purpose of this cross-culture discussion is to consider the many social inventions that human creativity has produced and to show that human problems of love and living can be solved in a multiplicity of ways. North American problems seem very threatening when a person considers divorce, crime, poverty, child abuse, racial conflict, venereal disease, and drug problems. Looking beyond national borders, one sees widespread starvation, war, population explosion, and destruction of the earth's resources. All of these problems represent human failure and cry out for solutions that transcend nationalism and parochialism. In introducing students to modes of living and values that differ from their own, we are trying to prepare them for the near future. They need to be able to think flexibly, to consider many different points of view, to discard what is rendered obsolete by new conditions, and to create better ways of being human.

Through understanding the ways in which individuals interact in family and societal settings, a person can judge what is most worthwhile, change his behavior in a direction he really wants, and communicate more clearly with others. He thus develops a justified feeling of being more in charge of his own life and of being able to cooperate and build with other people. In being more able and more free to decide, he experiences liberation. Thus a student of family life will become freer from the fetters of his own past, even while he builds upon all of his experiences to incorporate new knowledge.

Although this book began as a text on marriage and family, it finished with more emphasis on family than on marriage. For us, *family* has taken on a meaning that defies definition in terms of genes and laws. We think of people as a family when they love each other and make a home together. We also recognize many other kinds of families.

The two of us, mother and daughter, aided by our husbands, have looked at the state of human relationships as we now see them in North America, as we have observed them in other parts of the world, as we have learned of them through our parents, siblings, grandparents, and grandchildren, and as we interpret them from reading research. Because the two of us are of different generations, we have brought to bear two very different life experiences, and yet we have a vast amount in common. In putting this book together, we feel that we have grown. While reading it, we hope that our readers will grow too.

Each chapter is the product of both authors since we planned it together; one of us wrote it and the other added and revised. Laura Smart wrote the first drafts of Chapters 3, 4, 5, 6, 7, 8, 14, and the Appendixes "Premarital Questionnaire," "Basic Sex," "Veneral Disease," and "Glossary." Mollie Stevens Smart wrote first drafts of Chapters 1, 2, 9, 10, 11, 12, 13, and 15. We wrote Chapters 16 and 17 together.

We thank our teachers and our students, too numerous to name, who taught us and stimulated us to think about being persons, living and loving in families. We are grateful to the many colleagues who have helped us to understand and express the subject matter of this book, especially Leon Bouvier, Kathleen Brown, Susan Crawford, Robert Gates, Stella Goldberg, Edward Herold, Joseph Hornick, Dorothy H. Martin, Marianne Panzini, Carl Ridley, Graham Spanier, Kathryn Walker, and Elizabeth Wiegand. The shortcomings of the book are due to us, not to them. The photographs that illuminate the pages are the work of Barbara N. Armstrong and Cynthia Oziomek and their students, Laura L. Baker, Donna Harris, Robert J. Izzo, Halvar Loken, David Reinfeld, Ellen S. Smart, Stanley Summer, Craig M. Szwed, and Robert L. Wilke. Our helpful typists were Barbara Bland, Deborah Clarke, and Deborah Petterson. Liane Armstrong did the drawings for Chapter 14 and Appendix B.

M. S. S.   L. S. S.
Kingston,   Storrs,
Rhode Island   Connecticut

CONTENTS

part ONE introduction

1 THIS IS WHERE YOU START   5

Use of Terms and Frame of Reference   5
Why Study Families?   6
Approaches to the Study of Families   8
Uniqueness   22

part TWO the strands of family life

2 LOVE   29

Evolution of Love   29
A Love Career   31
Lovers in Time and Space   39
Conclusions   48

3 COMMUNICATION: GETTING IT OUT AND TAKING IT IN   54

Some Basic Uses for Communication   54
The Nature of Communication   57

Effective Versus Ineffective Communication   63

Communication in the Family   65

Other Uses for Communication   73

4 THIS GROWS ON YOU: SEX   80

Prenatal Sexual Differentiation   80

Physically Based Sex Differences   81

Interaction of Organism and Environment   84

Gender-Role Learning in Childhood   84

Sex Education in the Family: The Early Years   92

Sexual Behavior   94

Puberty and Adolescence   96

Sex Education in the Family: Pubescence   99

Sexual Response   99

5 IT KEEPS ON GROWING: MORE ABOUT SEX   106

A Cross-Cultural Perspective   106

Premarital Heterosexual Attitudes and Behavior   107

Homosexuality   118

Gender Roles in Adolescence and Adulthood   123

Sexual Standards After Marriage   129

Communication and Sex   131

Aging and Sexuality   132

PART THREE A family is people

6 TWO FIND EACH OTHER   143

Everybody's Business   143

How Do People Meet?   144

Getting to Know You   151

Committed Relationships: The Beginnings of Partnerhood   159

Permanent Versus Temporary Matching   163

"Assortative Mating": Who Marries Whom?   165

Some Theories of Partner Selection   166

7 PARTNERHOOD 174

Variations on Partnerhood   175
Gender Role and Partnerhood   177
Partnership Interaction   178
The Wedding: A Transition Point   185
Chances of Success in Marriage: Marital Stability   188

8 MORE ABOUT PARTNERHOOD 201

Marital Adjustment and Satisfaction   201
Marital Adjustment and Satisfaction: Conclusions   212
Cohabitation   212
Remarriage   214
The Middle and Aging Years   216

9 A MATTER OF CHOICE: PARENTHOOD 222

Major Decisions   222
Transition to Parenthood   225
Joys and Satisfactions of Parenthood   227
The Parent-Child Career   233
Adoptive Parents   237
Single Parents   238
Paths to Rejecting Parenthood   239
Deterrents to Reproduction   240
Reasons Why Parenthood Is Difficult   244
Aids to Parents   246

10 LIVING AND LEARNING WITH CHILDREN 252

Childpower: Some Effects of Children on Parents   252
The Language of Behavior   253
Parents' Effects on Children   254
Success from the Parent's Standpoint   266
Parent Education   268
Parents and Adult Offspring   268

11 SISTERS, BROTHERS, AND ALL THE REST   274

Sibling Relationships   274
Interaction with Grandparents   285
In-Law Relationships   290
Other Kin   293
Quasi-Kin   294

PART **FOUR**   **A family is based on home**

12 DOMESTIC EXECUTIVES   303

The Case of Carol, Danny, Anita, and Jay   303
A Concept of Management   305
The Homemaker   306
The Lineage Family   313
Research Findings and Recommendations   314

13 HEALTH IS MORE THAN BRUSHING YOUR TEETH   318

Health as a Management Problem   319
Definition of Health   319
Nutrition   320
Exercise and Rest   328
Shelter and Clothing   331
Illness and Accidents   334
Hereditary and Genetic Defects and Handicaps   339
Drugs   339
Recreation   342
Health Services   343

14 FAMILY PLANNING: GETTING IT RIGHT   349

Population   349
Birth Control   357
Reproduction   368

15 MONEY, WORK, AND LAWS: UNAVOIDABLE 381

Financial Management 381
Management and the Law 399
Financial and Legal Management Are Related 406
Marriage Contracts: A New Direction in Financial and Legal Management 407

16 THE CRISES OF RELATIONSHIPS 412

Crisis and Problem Solving 413
Individual Disruption 415
Family Dissolution 425
Disorganization at All Levels 432

PART five down the road and around the world

17 DOWN THE ROAD AND AROUND THE WORLD 449

New Orientations to Life 452
New Modes of Living and Relating 457
Strengthening Family Living 470
In Conclusion 475

appendixes

A. PREMARITAL QUESTIONNAIRE 483
B. BASIC SEX 492
C. BUDGET 497
D. A DAILY FOOD GUIDE 500
E. VENEREAL DISEASE 502
F. GLOSSARY 508

AUTHOR INDEX 513

INDEX OF SUBJECTS 521

families

developing relationships

The one chapter in this section of the book explains our point of view and use of terms. We have been more personal than the authors of most textbooks and we hope that our readers will find it acceptable to learn something about our own experiences and values. This chapter also includes some basic material in the study of family relationships.

PART ONE

ONE

INTRODUCTION

CHAPTER 1

THIS IS WHERE YOU START

We, the authors of this textbook, are mother and daughter, members of a family. We use life experiences with families, both our own and others that we have observed, as examples in this book. Most of our readers have also grown up in families (their **families of orientation**), and some may have started families of their own (their **families of procreation**) through marriage, bearing children, or both. Your and our experiences with families are valid starting points upon which to build a more complete knowledge of families.

The family in some form is basic to most, or perhaps all, societies. There are many possible definitions for the family, and we wish to take a broad rather than a restrictive view. Therefore, throughout the book we include many types of families, both in our own society and outside of it, within our conception of the family.

USE OF TERMS AND FRAME OF REFERENCE

Because of our own experiences in countries other than the United States, we include examples from other cultures. We do not dwell at great length upon the many ethnic and class differences within our own society. By "our society" we mean the United States of America and the Dominion of Canada, or for short, North America. We exclude Mexico from our use of the term *North America*, considering it part of Central America instead. Our choice is arbitrary, and we realize that Spanish culture, including Mexican, is very much a part of certain areas in the United States. As with most of life, cultural groups and the geographic areas that they inhabit form a continuum.

Not wanting to overemphasize either the male or female members of families, we have broken with the time-old tradition of referring to an individual who might be male or female as "he." At times, we call such an individual "he" or "him," at other times, "she" or "her." If this choice seems strange, it is only because we were all brought up taking for granted that the use of the male pronoun is correct.

We also break with the tradition of referring to ourselves as "the authors." We are two people, individuals who have had some common experiences and some unique experiences. When we wish to express a common experience or belief, we use the pronoun "we." However, when we wish to speak as individuals, we do so. After the use of the word "I," we often place our initials in parentheses to show which author is speaking. Conveniently, from my (LSS) point of view, my Mother's initial is an M. In this way, you, the reader, may be able to remember more easily which one of us is the elder author (MSS) and which is the younger (LSS).

Values

We believe that is it impossible to write a value-free book, and we do not claim to have done so. However, we have tried to make our beliefs clear. We do not expect you to agree with us on all counts; how dull that would be! We hope to challenge you, not to tear down your beliefs, but to give you a new perspective from which to view them. We see such a challenging of values as a part of our own growth as individuals: this statement in itself is a value-laden statement with which you may disagree!

Tools of the Trade

A person encountering a new experience or environment needs to learn new ways of coping. This may mean adapting old ways, or learning to use new tools or concepts. In this book we use concepts and terms from a number of related fields, including child development, home economics, psychology, sociology, and anthropology. Some students will be familiar with some or all of these terms; to others, the terms will be new. In this chapter we introduce a number of these basic tools of the trade; we bring in more later. For quick reference, the terms may be found in the Glossary (Appendix F) at the back of the book. The learning of new terms may be dull to most students, but once they are understood, they greatly simplify the communication process.

WHY STUDY FAMILIES?

Why are you taking this course? Fulfilling a requirement may be part of your reason. There are, however, other reasons that you might have. The family has been a basic unit in our society, and most societies, for longer than written records go back. Many people today say that the family is dying, and that if it dies, our society will perish as well. Do you think that this is true? What evidence do you have to support or refute it? In this book, you may find evidence on one or both sides of the argument.

A person usually takes the interaction of her family for granted, until she encounters a family that functions in a different way. Can you remember a time when you were surprised or shocked by the way that a friend's family did something? I (MSS) remember being amazed that the mother of one of my friends would cut a piece of cake for each family member, and save the rest for the next day. In my family, my mother would give each person as many pieces as she wanted, even if the entire cake was devoured at one sitting. This is an example of a small cultural difference that existed within one neighborhood at one point in time. Rationing the cake could be seen as being stingy, as evidence that the family was not affluent, evidence of good management of resources, or evidence that the mother was concerned about the health of the family members. By studying families other than his own, a person gains a new perspective from which to view his own family, and himself. He also gains increased understanding of the "family of man" or people throughout the world.

Personal Choices

When I (LSS) was an undergraduate in the early seventies, many girls suffered from Senior Panic. They felt a terrific pressure to become engaged or even to marry. No doubt some of the pressure came from parents who felt that college was the best place for finding a husband. Peers who were already engaged added to the anxiety of those who had not yet found their partners. Some of the steam has been taken out of Senior Panic, since young women have more choice than they have ever had as to what they will do with their lives and when they will do it. Even so, many real and difficult choices must be made. Having to live up to definite expectations produces one kind of pressure (or even panic), but being free to make very important choices can also result in anxiety. The difficult choices include whether to commit oneself to another person; whether to marry; and, if so, when; whether to have children; and, if so, when and how many.

Most people probably still think that "falling in love" is the basic reason for getting married, but the choice whether to marry should be an active one, and not the passive one implied by the concept of falling in love. Where a person will go as an individual, or as one of a couple or family depends upon many factors, including choosing a compatible partner at the right time under the right circumstances. No one can foresee the future, but by investigating what has happened to others in similar circumstances, one has a better idea of her own chances. This book raises questions about human interaction that may give the reader more insight into her own behavior.

Never before has the question of the active development of oneself as an individual been more pertinent to family relationships. The human liberation movement, born of women's liberation, has caused many individuals to question their goals. Men are giving up responsible, high-paying jobs in order to learn a trade or profession that they believe will be more personally satisfying. Women are venturing forth from their homes, and some men are returning joyfully to theirs. For others, traditional roles continue to provide sources of satisfaction. Human liberation means that the individual can search for what is right for him or her. But it may mean the painful giving up of other parts of himself that were or are important. We do not advocate the abolition of traditional roles, but the *right* of people to do so if their development is fostered by so doing. In order to choose, a person has to know what the choices are.

These choices are not equally available to all persons. Although discrimination is not as all-encompassing as it was a decade or two ago, it still exists and will continue to do so for years to come. Advances made by women and minority groups have made some persons think that the battles are won. They have not been. We believe that equal opportunity should be extended to all persons, so that the poor and the "different" can make the same choices that the richer, mainstream people can.

APPROACHES TO THE STUDY OF FAMILIES

Although one's own life experiences are a valid starting point, they are very limited. Research done by social scientists provides a way of distilling the experiences of many persons. The scientific method of study is a value orientation not shared by all persons. It forms the core of this book, because what we have written here is in large part based upon social scientific research. There is considerable room for error on a number of counts, the most important of which is the errors that can be made by the researcher. We have tried to interpret research as accurately as possible.

The following sections of this chapter describe different types of families, starting with the kind most familiar to North Americans. Although this plan may seem like a roundabout way to get to the personal and family questions that most concern students, we think it the soundest route. While the traditional extended family or the polygamous family may look unconnected with present-day life, these structures serve some of the same purposes for which the most modern forms of living are designed.

The Structures of Families

Every society has its own particular regulations and expectations that show people how to behave in different situations. Each person acquires a set of behavior patterns or **roles** that go with the **positions** he occupies. In each position, his behavior dovetails with that of the other person in that position. In the mother-daughter position, a girl is in the role of daughter to the woman in the role of mother. In one **sibling** position, the girl plays the role of sister to the boy who is playing the role of brother to her. The type of family in a society is the result of the way the positions and role are defined. When we speak of the **structure** of a family, we mean the pattern of positions and roles in it.

Whatever the structure of the family in a particular society, it seems natural and right to most of the people living within it. At first glance, the family structures of other societies may look peculiar, wrong, or inferior. Every form of the human family, however, demonstrates solutions to human problems and represents human creativity. Occasionally students of family and marriage can deepen their awareness by examining nonhuman family forms. Humans are primates, and the other primates, their closest animal relatives, also live in a variety of family forms. These range from promiscuous troops to more limited pairings of males and females to raise their young [6, p. 250].

Nuclear. Father, mother, and children make up a unit found in almost all societies, known as the **nuclear family.** When this unit is called the **conjugal family,** it means that the husband-wife relationship is of primary importance. The nuclear

BARBARA N. ARMSTRONG AND CYNTHIA A. OZIOMEK, THE UNIVERSITY OF AKRON

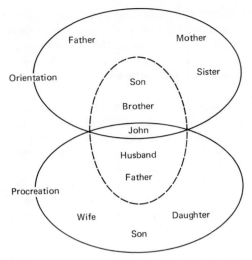

FIGURE 1-1   John's two nuclear families. John plays roles of son and brother in his family of orientation; husband and father in his family of procreation.

family is established and regulated by marriage. There are many different ways in which the nuclear family is attached to other family units and members, sometimes being part of an intricate large family structure and in other times and places as an isolated unit. Throughout Western Europe, the United States, Canada, Australia, New Zealand, and in many other parts of the world, the nuclear unit of a married couple and their children is the most important and usual family form. Even where nuclear families are the norm, there are many family units with a structure other than just the married couple and their children. The last census in the United States showed 9,478,000, or 13.5 per cent of children under 18, living in one-parent families. Only about 70 per cent of United States children under 18 were living with both natural parents who have been married only once [5a]. Six per cent of families had an adult other than the mother or father living in the home [16]. Although a resident grandparent is not usual, neither is it surprising. Many people have had the experience, however temporary, of living at home with people who were not members of their nuclear families of orientation or procreation.

A nuclear family has connections with individuals and other units called the **kin.** Included under kin are grandparents, grandchildren, uncles, aunts, nephews, nieces, cousins, grown brothers and sisters, and their spouses. North American society exerts little, if any, pressure on nuclear units in regard to how much attention they pay to uncles, aunts, nieces, nephews, and cousins, although it is expected that parents and children and brothers and sisters act and feel in certain ways toward each other.

A nuclear family lives only as long as its two focal members, the husband and wife, since the conjugal relationship is what holds the group together. Sometimes a nuclear family is called a *broken family* when one of the conjugal pair dies or leaves the family through divorce or desertion. There is some disagreement as to whether **nuclear** should be applied to a family consisting of one parent and a child or children. The term *one-parent* family makes it quite clear. When children move out of their family of orientation and marry, they start new nuclear units.

Extended. When nuclear units are integrated into more complicated family structures, however, the resulting families may last for generations. The traditional family of Asia, the **extended** family exemplifies this type of family. An extended family includes two or more nuclear units living in one home, most often an older parent couple with their married sons and the sons' wives and children. Or it may consist of several brothers, their mother, and their wives and children. Many extended families live in India today, especially in rural areas and in the more traditional, smaller cities; the extended family is the ideal, but not the most common, type of family. A recent study of family types in Ahmedabad, one of the most modern industrial cities, showed about 20 per cent to be extended families [7]. Because 80 per cent of Indians live in rural areas, the total percentage of extended families in India must be considerably larger. About a third of families in Thailand are extended families [12]. An investigation of childrearing in extended Indian families dealt with families that ranged in size from 10 to 28 members, with an average number of 16.5 [1]. We have visited a joint family consisting of more than 40 members. In an extended family, the emphasis is on parent-child bonds, and relationships between siblings, especially brothers. Since "blood ties" hold the family together, it is called the **consanguine** family.

Extended families are similar to communal families in that they are more complex in structure and can perform more functions than the nuclear family. An extended family is usually organized, as some communes are, around a business or occupation that provides work and income for everyone. For example, the Patel family of India owns a textile manufacturing business, in which three adult sons divide the responsibilities of personnel, technology, and sales. Their father, although titular head of the business and the family, has retired from active work. The mother devotes herself to volunteer work while one daughter-in-law runs the household, another is responsible for all the children, and another is a graduate student. In the large, rambling Patel house, each nuclear unit has some private space, but all cooking is done in one kitchen and all eating in one dining room. Thus husbands and wives have some time alone together at night, but during most of the daytime hours, they are with several members of the consanguine family, sharing work, leisure, and food. The conjugal relationship is diluted in concentration and intensity, in contrast to the husband-wife relationship in the nuclear family, where much of daily life is shared by only the pair. Childrearing is different, too, in both aims and methods.

Most extended families are **patrilineal,** with a father at the head and descent going through the male, as in the Patel family. (Many long-lasting communes are also headed by a strong man.) **Matrilineal** families, those headed by mothers and descended through the female line, also exist in India, Africa, and other places. Since relationships along blood lines (either patrilineal or matrilineal) are very important, terms for relatives are much more exact and numerous than those available in the English language and other Western European languages. In Hindi, one does not say merely, *aunt,* but *bua, thaii, chachi, masi, ma,* or *mami,* depending upon whether the woman is on the paternal or maternal side, whether she is a blood relative or not, and whether she is younger or older. Here there is not merely one role of *niece* but six.

Extended families also exist among lower-class ethnic groups in North America where several generations may live in one house. Although they may not live in one house, upper-class extended families often have joint property. They may build their houses in a cluster, particularly summer houses. On the seacoast of Rhode Island, there are still clusters of nineteenth-century cottages in which large extended families used to spend their summers and a few still do. Upper-class North American families share some characteristics with Asian extended families. Blood relations are important and the conjugal pair less central than in the middle-class nuclear family. The upper-class family traces its ancestry far into the past and includes present, secondary, and even tertiary members as important. The child in this family would have little choice as to whether he associated with his cousins and behaved warmly to his aunts and uncles. Older members have power and status. Since women normally outlive men, the leader or highest status member of an upper-class family is likely to be a woman with considerable financial power. To the children, it may be a grandmother, great-grandmother, or even a great aunt. The upper-class family controls the choice of marriage partners much more than does a middle-class family, although not as completely as does an Asian extended family. With any extended family, a marriage is a family affair, since it is a link between two ongoing families.

Polygamous. When one person has plural spouses at the same time, the marriage is polygamous. The most common form of polygamy is **polygyny,** in which a man has more than one wife. **Polyandry,** wherein a woman has more than one husband, is practiced by only a few societies. Polygamy, of course, makes for a family larger than the monogamous, conjugal nuclear family.

Common in Africa and the Middle East, polygyny most often occurs in places where the Islamic religion and culture dominate. The Bible records some polygynous families, such as Jacob's. Polygyny was practiced in pre-Communist China and by Hindus in India before 1957. In the United States, the Mormons used to be polygynous. There are still some polygynous families in North America. Even so, many North Americans have little understanding of polygyny; perhaps its being illegal makes it seem immoral. Probably the most common concept of a polygynous family is based on a visual image of an oasis, a harem, a handsome sheik, and a large number of beautiful young women in filmy, full trousers and floating veils. We ourselves admit to surprise and disappointment on first entering the harem (women's quarters) of a Muslim family in India. Secluded from the entrance and the rest of the house, it was an ordinary courtyard with ordinary rooms opening off it. The women's clothes were no different from those of women on the street, just everyday cotton saris. Rather than dancing and playing instruments, the women in the harem were preparing the next meal and taking care of the young children.

In polygynous families, wives are friends, sometimes sisters, often with close, affectionate feelings toward each other. The first wife is likely to have status and authority. Although there are sure to be some disagreements, clashes, or even jealousies when people live together, in the polygyous family there is nothing like the intense jealousy or sense of failure that many a North American wife feels when her husband takes a mistress. In a society where there is a great deal of housework to be done by women and where pregnancies are frequent, it may be much easier to share the wife's role with sisters and friends than for one woman to do it alone. There is also the matter of companionship. In polygynous and extended families, women enjoy talking while they work and knowing that a loved one is always there.

Among the polyandrous tribal people in the Himalayas, the ideal type of family consists of one woman with several husbands. Often the husbands are brothers. This custom occurs also in South India and among some Eskimo tribes. Where life is very hard and earning a living takes a great deal of effort, it may work out best to have several men supporting one woman and her children. Thus, the population is controlled, since one woman can bear only a certain number of children, no matter how many husbands she has. Female infanticide is often built into the polyandrous family system since the sex ratio will be upset if some women have plural husbands.

Communal. About the only generalization to be made about communal families is that they consist of cooperating groups of people who are committed to their group [9]. Members are not necessarily, but may be, related by blood or marriage. Communal families have lived in various parts of the world in times past, often as Utopian societies. The Oneida Community of New York State, established in 1846, is an American example that has been studied extensively. Much has been written about communal childrearing in the U.S.S.R. and in kibbutzim, communes that have flourished in Israel for half a century. Information on Chinese communes is now available. We briefly discuss communes in Chapter 17.

One-Parent. Since nearly 11.6 per cent of families in the United States and 8.9 per cent of Canadian families are one-parent families, a large number of North American parents and children are represented in this type of structure [11, 14]. Although many one-parent families are the result of death, marital breakup, and unwed motherhood, there are also single women and even a few single men who choose to become parents and to live in one-parent families. When we discuss them in Chapter 17, we call them **spousefree parents.**

Although many people view one-parent families as merely incomplete or deviant *conjugal* families, a look at the structure reveals something quite different. One adult performs the functions usually shared by two, including earning money, keeping house, and caring for children. The great majority of single parents are women, and many of them are poor. An analysis of United States poor families showed that women headed 39 percent of white units and 61 percent of black ones

[2]. Families headed by single women make up more than one quarter of all the families classified as poor. Because one person must do the work of two, the economic liability of this type of structure is serious, to say nothing of the limitations on affection, communication, emotional support, helping and teaching. On the other hand, there are a few one-parent families with adequate income and in which friends and other adult family members give love, support, and help.

Homosexual. When two people of the same sex live together, they may consider themselves a family. Although it seems fairly certain that the majority of North

Americans do not think of homosexual pairs as families, this kind of living arrangement makes possible many of the functions and relationships carried out in the conjugal family. Of course, reproduction is not possible, but some homosexual pairs do bring up children. These couples thus perform the nurturant socialization of the newborn, the one function that Reiss (see page 60) considers the universal function of the family. Homosexual behavior occurs in all parts of the world among human beings and also among other primates. Of the 76 societies studied by Ford and Beach, 49 societies, or 64 per cent, considered homosexuality acceptable. Some of these societies have an institutionalized form that is a homosexual marriage. Resulting families are structured according to the norms of society. For example, the Kodiak, of Alaska, rear some of their baby boys to play the female role [5, p. 131]. These boys learn women's crafts and wifely homemaking skills, eventually becoming wives of important members of the community. Such a wife is given great respect.

The Functions of Families

Just what does a family do that makes it a family? Since sociologists have written a great deal about this topic, a group of our students set out to find out what ordinary people thought to be the functions of a family. They tried to secure equal numbers of men and women, distributed between three age groups, under 30, 30 to 60, and over 60. They got answers from 117 people to the questions, "Why do you think people live in families? What are the important things that families do for their members?" Most people (101 out of 117) mentioned *love, affection,* and *emotional security.* All but two of the under 30's mentioned love, as did all of the women between 30 and 60. The next most frequently mentioned function had to do with children, their protection, care, and socialization or upbringing.

Many Possible Functions. The number of functions a family might perform are almost unlimited. In fact, one of the marvelous and unique characteristics of the family is that its fields of action are not strictly defined and it can specify new roles, duties, rights, and actions as needed [17]. A list of functions performed by families in various places and times includes the following: love and affection, sex, reproduction, childrearing, education, religion, recreation, production, consumption, and status-giving.

Sometimes all of these functions are performed by a nuclear family. Pioneer families and other isolated families, such as sheep ranchers in New Zealand, must do almost everything for themselves. Sue and Ross, who are in their twenties, live on 120 acres of mostly wooded land in northern Maine. They live in a one-room house without plumbing or electricity. They built this themselves from timber taken from fallen-down barns. Their only source of cash income is ten colonies of honey bees. They have a small garden, an apple orchard, and several hens. In the winter, they are entirely snowed in, and must snowshoe three miles to pick up their mail.

Many functions are more easily carried out by an extended family or a communal family than by a nuclear unit. Where the *conjugal* family is the usual type, other institutions take over a large part of education, religion, production and recreation, and security. In North America, where kin relationships are often optional and nuclear families are largely on their own, families use schools, churches, stores, factories, and recreation facilities. Not long ago families did more and other institutions did less. When faced with modern social problems, a number of people suggest solving them by returning to an older era of multiple family functions. With this mind set, people often complain that the schools are usurping parents' rights, the parents should teach their children to work and be productive in the home, that family religion should be given more attention and that parents should be able to control their children's bad behavior. Letters to the editor still place the blame for delinquency on parents. Public school sex education programs are still hotly debated.

Universal Functions. A generation ago, Murdock [8] claimed that the nuclear family is universal and that it always has four functions. Ever since that time, sociologists have been looking for exceptions. Although they have discovered a few, it is still true that the nuclear family can be found in almost all human societies and that it almost always fulfills four functions. These are sexual relations, economic cooperation, reproduction, and **socialization.** One could argue, then, that a celibate commune is not a family, or even that a childless married pair is not a family. The truth is that definitions of family and marriage vary with place, time, and the orientation of the person stating them. Sociologists try to define the family as an institution, in terms that can be tested scientifically. For example, Reiss [10, pp. 18–26] having disproved Murdock, stated the only universal function of the family (nuclear, extended, or otherwise) to be the **nurturant socialization** of the newborn. The group that **nurtures** the newborn, the family, does not have to be biologically related in any particular way, but the society defines its relation to the newborn and views it as right, proper, and obligatory that this group nurture and socialize its infants. The Bureau of the Census, in contrast to the sociologist, defines family in concrete terms that American census-takers can use to decide whether a group of people should be counted as a family.

Looking at North American families, it is obvious that the conjugal family predominates and that a large proportion of such families do provide for sexual relations, economic cooperation, bearing children, and bringing them up. Our students were pleased to see that their findings on the most frequently mentioned family function were in agreement with what their textbooks said about the major function of the family in the United States, the provision of love, affection, and emotional security. Discussing the family, Udry [15] stated, " . . . it has become the only major focus of emotional life in the society," and, "Marriage is the longest and most significant relationship in life" [15, pp. 15–16]. There are, however, other structures through which people relate to each other in ways that are very important to the participants. Very often love and emotional security are involved, but one or more of the four "universal" functions may be lacking. Some of these structures are legal and socially accepted; some are not. Some are changing status, such as the custom of living together before marriage, which is becoming more and more accepted by society.

Developmental Approach

Family development usually refers to the changes that take place in individual nuclear families over time. A nuclear family begins with marriage and ends with the death of one member of the couple. Studies of two or more generations are also done. There are at least two other ways in which **family development** might be used. It could be applied to an ongoing family to study generation after generation. Or, the term could refer to changes in the family as an institution in a given culture or society, as is done in the historical study of the family.

Nuclear Family Development. A family goes through different stages, each of which has its particular tasks, problems, hazards, and rewards. Thus, families in the same stage of development share many similar conditions and concerns. Researchers usually divide the life of a nuclear family into stages according to the coming, growing up, and departing of children. Evelyn Duvall [3, pp. 113–114], who has written a great deal about family development, points out that there are two main divisions, the *expanding family stage* and the *contracting family stage*. The expanding stage lasts from marriage until all the children are grown; the contracting stage begins when the first child leaves home and ends when one of the pair dies. These two main stages can be split into smaller and smaller stages. The couple without children must be considered in different terms. The family development framework is not so suitable for them.

Lifetime and Lineage Families. Because the word *family* has several meanings, Margaret and Harold Feldman [4] have suggested the terms *lifetime family* and *lineage family*. The lifetime family of any individual begins at her birth and ends at her death. During that time she moves into and out of various positions and roles. She is a daughter until her parents die. She may become a sister, niece, cousin, wife, mother, aunt, and grandmother. Movement is always forward in time, never backward and hence the individual does not experience cycles. *Careers* is the term used to describe the forward movement. Just as in an occupational career, where events are not repeated, in the parent-child career (one of the family careers), the mother experiences child A's infancy only once. He then becomes a preschoolchild and a schoolchild, and is never a baby again. The marital career progresses onward, even though the couple may joke about having a second or third honeymoon. The lifetime family career includes, in addition to the marital career and the parent-child career, two more careers, the sexual experience career and the adult-parent career.

The *lineage family* is the family that lasts through time, going on and on through generation after generation. When the family is viewed in this way, the positions remain, but different people move into and out of them as they live their individual careers. "The Heyward family has lived in this house for 7 generations!" The

Heyward family is a lineage family whose members were born in a particular house. The first male born in each generation lived his lifetime family careers and his occupational career in the house and the surrounding fields. When his lifetime career ended, he went to a nearby cemetery, while the lineage family continued in cycles of births, careers, and deaths. The term *cycle* is appropriate to use with the lineage family, because the events of family living occur over and over again, as new casts of characters play the old roles of baby, sister, brother, father, and so on up to great-grandmother. The best-known lineage families are royal or very wealthy families. Everyone belongs to lineage families whose cycles stretch back endlessly.

In Europe and North America the patrilineal line forms the base for a family life cycle investigation. In Africa, the matrilineal line is often the base of the family life cycle, as it is among the Akan people of Ghana [8a].

Usefulness of the Developmental Approach. The developmental approach is useful for doing research on family and individual behavior, changes, crises, strengths, and weaknesses. The practical uses of this approach are great. A young couple can look ahead in order to plan wisely, knowing something of the demands they will encounter in future stages or categories. In teaching college students, we have found that the concept of family life stages helps young women to look beyond finding a husband and living happily ever after. Both sexes learn that the role of parent-of-young-children requires a special set of skills, knowledge, attitudes, and strengths. They come to realize that the parents of school-aged children take on new social roles in regard to the community, that vocations and careers outside the home have their ups and downs in relation to the various family careers. Appreciating how much of life goes beyond the wedding, they tend to see some of their studies as potentially important to later vocations and others as useful in specific aspects of family living. Individuals can gain self-understanding and be better understood if the ebb and flow of their various careers is considered [13]. Persons grow and change with the development, interaction, and decline of careers in family, community, vocations, recreations, religion, and so on. In fact, another example of a helpful developmental point of view is that of a family facing problems peculiar to a certain stage. Even though the solution may be hard to find, it helps to know that other families in their stage face similar dilemmas or that families grow beyond such difficulties.

The Family as a System

A family can be thought of as a complex system, an organization of people who interact with one another and influence one another in many ways. Their communications with one another are very important in their interactions. A large part of the concern of this book is with interactions within the nuclear family, especially between the husband and wife. Interactions between nuclear family and kinship system are also of interest. The family is only one social system, however, and it operates in connection with many other systems, social and nonsocial.

The Family's Connection with Nonsocial Systems. Although we are mainly interested here in the family's interaction with human social systems, we should mention some of the other systems that are significant to family functioning. The survival of the family, in fact human life, is threatened because the ecological system of the world has been changed by man. The family function of reproduction has had a lot to do with upsetting the ecology. And now, food shortages, energy problems, crowding, and pollution are affecting families. One can even go outside the earth to note a system that affects the family system. The solar system affects the family interactions of all who believe in astrology or of all of us, if the believers are correct. The configuration of the stars at the moment of birth is thought to affect the child's personality and his potentialities. Astrologists assert that the stars influence the person continually. Marriages must therefore be made between couples whose horoscopes fit auspiciously and weddings must be performed at the proper moment for heavenly powers to work benignly upon the pair. (Although we ourselves do not use the principles of astrology, we believe that there is something valid in it that remains to be identified scientifically.)

The Family's Relation to Other Social Systems. Families are deeply affected by the following: the economic system that determines their level of living and its

Consider all the differences between the families of these Indian children and adolescents with the girls shown in the picture on page 21.

stability or instability; the occupational system that may dictate where they live, when they move, and how much self-esteem the husband and wife derive from their jobs; the education system that directs learning and self-concepts; the religious system that influences their philosophy of life, morals, social involvement, and perhaps their number of children; the legal system that defines the responsibilities of parents, children, community, and state; the health care system that makes for more or less freedom of choice on family limitation, methods of childbirth, and use of hospitals. Families also affect these other social systems through their interactions with them. Sometimes families organize into a new social system for the purpose of influencing another system. For example, a group of parents formed an organization that changed a hospital's pediatric department by adding a play program and liberalizing visiting regulations.

Influence of Social Stratification System: Caste and Class. Almost all societies organize their members so that some rank higher than others socially and thus have more power and influence. The type of work that people do and the amount of income they receive are often the basis for their social positions. Caste and class are two modes of social organization through which statuses are assigned and maintained. Some differences between class and caste are shown in Figure 1-2.

A **caste** system locks certain people into a particular kind of work or function through inheritance or birth. The Indian caste system still operates to a large extent even though Gandhi and his followers have tried to get rid of it. A child born in a caste of leatherworkers is most likely to become a leatherworker and a child of cloth merchants will most likely go into the family business, each child retaining the same

FIGURE 1-2   Schematic representation of class system and caste system. Dotted lines between class divisions indicate that individuals can move from one class to another. The upper class is smallest and hardest to enter. Closed lines around castes indicate that movement is impossible or extremely difficult. There may be a great many castes of varying size. Outcastes are people not included in any caste.

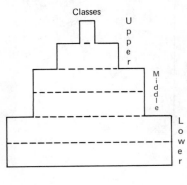
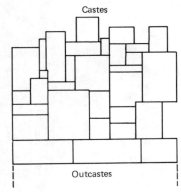

social standing as their *community,* as caste is now called. Most likely they will marry within the community. Some people are outcastes, placed below all the castes. In a caste system, there is often some distinguishing feature of the various castes that enables people in the society to tell one caste from another. Skin color may be such a feature. It has been argued that black people have been in the position of a caste in the United States, since they have been held to a certain status and they can be distinguished physically from the rest of the people.

A **class** system places people into higher and lower groups within the society, giving the higher people more rewards. Older societies, such as the British, are quite strict about keeping individuals in the classes into which they were born, although some movement takes place. In the United States, it is easier to move from one class to another, but not as easy as many people think. New Zealand and Australia are less class-bound than the United States, having fewer divisions and fewer restrictions on social mobility. Class structure also differs from one region of the United States to another, being more rigid and complicated in New England and more open in the

West. The class system goes against the ideals of democracy and restricts the opportunities of many people. The class system, however, is a reality, *although unjust,* by democratic standards.

A family's class and caste are very important in determining the structure and function of that family and its relation to the other social systems. A great deal of recent American research has been concerned with contrasts between lower- and middle-class families, their marriage patterns, sex behavior, childrearing patterns, nutritional intake, learning behavior, and intelligence. The upper class is relatively untouched by social and psychological research, since it is not easy to get upper-class people to submit to scrutiny by sociologists and psychologists. Research on black-white differences has met a lot of resistance by blacks because previous research of this nature often gave results that they considered inaccurate, unjust, and insulting.

Class and caste can be broken down into a number of more precise components. Instead of trying to compare, for example, middle- and lower-class behavior in general terms, the trend now is to ask the relation of a certain income level to a certain childrearing practice or to study how families in a certain occupational situation solve a particular problem. Class and caste are too vague and inclusive to be useful as research variables.

The Systems Approach to Family Study. We have mentioned some of the systems outside the family that influence it and the individuals that comprise it. The systems approach to the family is a theoretical approach developed at great length elsewhere [10]. In this book, we do not follow one theoretical orientation to the exclusion of others. We use an approach when it seems to best explain what we are trying to say.

UNIQUENESS

Every family is special, even though there is much that can be said about families in general. Since every human being is different in some way from all others, the married pair and their family must be a unique combination. Each family is unique in the expectations of the people in various roles, in its patterns of interaction, its history of development, and its relationships with other systems.

Because each family is special, there are no formulas for coping with its crises and problems. A marriage counselor cannot simply turn to page X of his manual and tell his clients to follow prescriptions 5, 8, and 14. A family is continually creating new ways of coping with the situation of the present. When problems are too difficult and a friend or professional is called in to help, that person draws upon what he knows about families and people in general and also creates something new when he applies it to this particular family.

A sense of uniqueness makes a pleasurable bond between family members. Newlyweds, or newlybondeds, often make a big thing out of their uniqueness, having secrets, sending coded messages, communicating with private looks and gestures. As the family life careers progress for a pair, they and their children may develop solidarity through a private communication system with invented words, family rituals, or jokes that are not funny to outsiders. Our family has many cherished special words that we use in private conversations and letters to each other. Thus we laugh, we remember shared incidents, we acknowledge past immaturities, and we affirm our membership in our own very special family.

SUMMARY

Personal experiences, observations, and research are all valid sources of information about families. This book is primarily concerned with persons and families living in the United States and Canada, but draws upon supplementary information from many parts of the world. We have chosen and defined certain terms, approaches, and values. Family studies lead to understanding of self and others, promoting personal liberation by extending the individual's choices.

Families consist of persons acting toward each other in certain expected ways, with some leeway in creating new interactions. Although every family is unique, certain types predominate in various parts of the world and in various positions in each society. The most common or basic unit is the nuclear family, consisting of a married couple and their children. Nuclear units are, in some places, incorporated into extended families. Monogamy and polygamy are variations in marital customs. Communal families include many different types, organized in a variety of ways, but committed to their groups and working together in some way. One-parent families, also varied in structure and behavior, constitute a sizable proportion of North American families. Homosexual pairs may be considered families.

Families perform few or many and varied functions, according to the demands on them and the opportunities for action. Changes in family functions reflect changes in the whole society.

The developmental approach to the study of the family focuses on changes that take place in a family and its members, over a span of years. Stages are defined according to the birth, maturing, and departure of children. The careers concept is helpful in studying individual development. Cycles refers most accurately to the generational or lineage family. The family can be thought of as a social system, related to the other systems in society and also to biological and physical systems. Ecology and astrology are of concern to many people today as they face problems facing individuals and families.

The status and power held by each family bears some relation to the whole society of which that family is a part. A class system organizes social placement, but allows some movement from one class to another. A caste system is more closed.

REFERENCES

1. Ames, E. W. Family structure and childrearing in India. Paper presented at meeting of the Society for Research in Child Development, Minneapolis, 1971.
2. Chilman, Catherine S. Families in poverty in the early 1970's: Rates, associated factors, some implications. *Journal of Marriage and the Family,* 1975, **37,** 49–60.
3. Duvall, Evelyn M. *Family development* 4th ed. Philadelphia: Lippincott, 1971.
4. Feldman, Margaret and Harold Feldman. The family life cycle: Some suggestions for recycling. *Journal of Marriage and the Family,* 1975, **37,** 277–284.
5. Ford, Clellan S. and Frank A. Beach. *Patterns of sexual behavior.* New York: Harper, 1951.
5a. Glick, P. C. A demographer looks at American families. *Journal of Marriage and the Family,* 1975, **37,** 15–26.
6. Jolly, Alison. *The evolution of primate behavior.* New York: Macmillan, 1972.
7. Khatri, A. A. The Indian family: An empirically derived analysis of shifts in size and types. *Journal of Marriage and the Family,* 1972, **34,** 725–734.
8. Murdock, George P. *Social structure.* New York: Macmillan, 1949.
8a. Oppong, Christine. *Marriage among a matrilineal elite.* Cambridge: Cambridge University Press, 1974.
9. Ramey, James W. Communes, group marriage, and the upper-middle class. *Journal of Marriage and the Family,* 1972, **34,** 647–655.
10. Reiss, Ira L. *The family system in America.* New York: Holt, 1971.
11. Schlesinger, Benjamin. The one-parent family in Canada: Some recent findings and recommendations. *Family Coordinator,* 1973, **22,** 305–309.
12. Smith, Harold E. The Thai family: Nuclear or extended. *Journal of Marriage and the Family,* 1973, **35,** 126–141.
13. Spence, Donald L. and Thomas D. Lonner. Career set: a resource through transitions and crises. *Aging and Human Development,* 1975, in press.
14. Sudia, Cecilia E. An updating and comment on the United States scene. *Family Coordinator,* 1973, **22,** 309–311.
15. Udry, J. Richard. *The social context of marriage.* Philadelphia: Lippincott, 1971.
16. U.S. Census of population, marital status and living arrangements. Series P-20, #225 (November 1971).
17. Zimmerman, Carle C. The future of the family in America. *Journal of Marriage and the Family,* 1972, **34,** 323–333.

Part II is about the personal growth and interactions between persons that lay the foundations for adult love, intimacy, marriage, parenting, and homemaking. The development of loving is traced from infancy into adulthood. Many meanings and contexts of love are presented through the use of examples from other times and other places. Communication is the subject of the next chapter because of its importance in understanding oneself and others, in developing loving relationships, and in carrying on the work and business of family living. The last two chapters in Part II describe the development of the individual as female or male, feminine or masculine, including body, personality, and social interactions.

PART TWO

THE STRANDS OF FAMILY LIFE

CHAPTER 2

LOVE

The word *love* has too many meanings. It is surprising that the English language does not provide a larger vocabulary for dealing with such an important topic. Eskimos have many words for the different types of snow, since snow in all its variations is important in their daily life. Speakers of Hindi have several words for rice, which is a very important food for them, that indicate whether the rice is raw, cooked, or combined with other foods. The Greeks had three words for love: *philos* ("brotherly"), *agape* ("spiritual"), and *eros* ("sexual"). Since love *is* important to North Americans, and essential in a textbook on family life, we struggle along with the word *love,* describing different aspects of it and analyzing some of its components.

Being **in love** is one kind of love, important in itself and in forming partnerships on which families are established. Love is important at every age and stage, since everyone needs to love and be loved. Love is different at each age and stage, since it expresses what a person has learned and experienced. Love is viewed differently in various places and at various times. By describing its development in several settings, we hope to give a perspective from which the reader can better understand himself and his love relationships. A broad understanding of love is basic to gaining insight into the significance of love in finding and choosing a partner and building a marriage or a lasting, meaningful relationship.

EVOLUTION OF LOVE

Love includes actions and feelings or inner experiences. Some of the behavior characteristics of human love can be observed in many living things. Attachment and care behavior are ways in which human love is expressed and developed.

29

Attachment

When one creature makes repeated efforts to gain and keep the proximity of a certain other creature, he is **attached** to that creature. When the attempts are mutual, there is an **attachment** between the two. Attachment is a part of love, a basic, essential part, but not all of it.

Attachments occur in nonhuman creatures as well as in people of all ages. Lorenz [14, pp. 32–36], an ethologist, tells about a chichlid fish that seemed to be attached to a special female. Geese and gannets mate monogamously for life. Beach has shown that dogs show preferences for specific individuals as mates, retaining these attitudes for as long as 66 months [2]. Attachment in dogs and people does not have to be sexually based. Nick, a dog we had while I (MSS) was a child, had a dog friend called Mac, who lived across the street. As soon as Mac was let out in the morning, he came to our front steps and sat on his hind legs, watching the door until Nick was let out. The two dogs played and stayed close together all day.

Primates show a large variety of attachments between individuals [13, p. 254]. A chimpanzee, Flo, who has been studied in her natural habitat for many years, maintained close relationships with her four children. A family photograph shows

Flo grooming eleven-year-old Faben while four-year-old Fifi plays with the new baby, and Figan, age seven, sprawls nearby. Studies of Japanese macaques have revealed extended families. In one, a mother and her brother lived in close proximity and the brother helped to take care of his nieces and nephews.

Care

Mammals and birds take care of their young, feeding, grooming, warming, and protecting them from injury. Mates perform some of these functions for each other, too. Monkeys, especially young females, enjoy baby-sitting, taking care of infants belonging to other females. If a mother dies, her infant may be adopted.

Attachment and care behavior are elements of human love that combine with other behaviors and feelings. Through growth and learning, the individual develops complex modes of loving that are distinctively human.

A LOVE CAREER

The subtitle of this section is how the individual learns to love through the people in his life. The human baby is born with great potentialities for loving, some of which he shares with animals, birds, and fish, others of which are especially human.

The life of an individual starts in a very small social world and expands to include more and more people, more types of social interaction, more ways of loving, learning, and growing. Figure 2-1 is a diagram that shows seven stages in the expansion of life and love. A dot at first, the self, becomes a cone that expands as the individual interacts with other people. The mother is the first of the other people, represented in a heart-shaped space with the baby's self filling the top of the heart. Concentric hearts represent the significant people as they are added to the child's social world. As his world expands, he interacts with more people and more categories of people. In this process, he and they learn to love. The following sections deal with the first six stages.

Infant-Mother

Under ordinary circumstances, the baby's first relationship is with his mother. She cares for him and they become attached to each other.

Attachment. A newborn is equipped for building an attachment to another person. Since there is another person especially equipped to build an attachment to this baby, the result is certain, unless something goes wrong with the natural process. The infant and mother become attached to each other through their own actions,

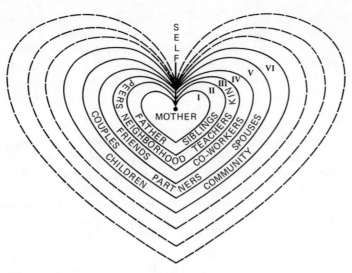

FIGURE 2-1   Stages in the expansion of life and love.

pieces of behavior that fit together like keys and locks. (This process is described in detail by the ethologists, particularly Ainsworth.)

Ainsworth defines attachment as "an affectional tie that one person forms between himself and another specific person, binding them together in space and enduring over time" [1]. Bowlby, the originator of the use of *attachment* in this sense, says, "No form of behavior is accompanied by stronger feelings than is attachment behavior. The figures toward whom it is directed are loved and their advent is greeted with joy" [3, p. 209].

The newborn infant can root (move his head to find the nipple) and suck, thus taking part in finding his mother's breast and obtaining milk from it. When held against another person's chest, with his head at the shoulder, the baby cuddles. He looks at faces more than at other objects and at eyes more than at any other part of the face. He listens to sounds, especially to voices. He cries. Within the early weeks, he smiles and vocalizes, soon doing so to particular people and in response to particular actions. Human infants also grasp and cling, although not as strongly as do other primates. All these behaviors serve to bring the mother close to the baby, to make her respond to him, care for him, feel pleasure in him, and become attached to him. As they respond to each other, their attachment grows stronger.

A baby shows that he is attached to his mother (or to another person) by crying when she leaves, trying to follow her and looking for her. When a baby is with his mother, he derives security that enables him to explore strange places and toys and to allow strange people to come close to him. Perhaps this security is a reflection of his experience of *care,* his knowledge that his mother cares for him.

PHOTO BY ERIKA, PHOTO RESEARCHERS, INC.

Respect. There is another aspect of infant love that Ainsworth and her associates have demonstrated. By one year of age, babies tend to obey and to cooperate with the people to whom they are attached. The more harmonious the infant-mother relationship during the first year, the more the baby tries to do what he perceives his mother as wanting him to do [25].

In infant obedience and cooperation, we can see the origins of *respect*, one of the elements of love. Respect involves realizing that the other person is an individual with needs and wants, letting the other person be himself, helping him to grow in his own ways [10, pp. 26–29]. In suppressing his impulses and trying to cooperate with what his mother asks him to do, the baby is respecting her as a person with wishes separate from his own. Thus, the care and respect that a baby receives in the first budding of love is in the attachment process, which is biologically based and set to go at birth. In the context of attachment, the mother's care and respect for the infant give rise to respect in him.

The Home Circle

Section II in the diagram (Figure 2-1) includes father, siblings, and any other members of the household.

Fathers. A father may or may not have a close relationship with his infant. Male langur monkeys pay very little attention to babies, whereas marmoset males carry their young all the time except when the mothers are feeding them [13]. So it seems to be with human fathers, varying from culture to culture and individual to individual. A study of middle-class Boston fathers' interactions with young infants

This Sikh father, descendant of generations of warriors, was willing to be photographed in a public place in India with his nestling child.

showed that the men spent an average of 37.7 seconds daily in talking to their babies [20]. In contrast, Arapesh fathers, in New Guinea, were seen to share child care equally with their wives [16, p. 39].

Men do not have all the biological equipment for interlocking with the infant's attachment behaviors, although they have some of it. An infant can cuddle on a man's chest, look at his face and eyes, listen to his voice, coo to him, cry when he leaves, and search for him. A biologically based interlock is the appearance of babies and young children and the "cute response" [13, p. 227]. People, as well as animals, feel attracted to creatures that have large heads and eyes, small chins and mouths, and arms in a more advanced state of development than legs. Along with the feeling that such creatures are "cute" often goes an impulse to take care of them and an inhibition against hurting them.

Siblings and Others. If there are older children in the family, the baby ordinarily becomes attached to them as well as to her father and to other household members or people who come in and out often. She is most likely to build attachments with people who play with her and pay attention to her, offering her interesting stimulation.

Self. The diagram shows a wedge that represents the self as part of the individual's development in love. This portion begins as a small part of the infant-mother circle and increases as the child grows and encounters more and more of the social world. Love of self includes *knowledge, respect,* and *care* [10, p. 26]. The infant comes to know herself through her own senses and actions and through the ways in which her parents and siblings see her. If they show her that she is lovable through their enjoyment, care, and respect, she knows she is lovable. Through testing her own powers of mind and muscle, making some decisions that turn out well, she comes to *know* herself as a person in her own right, an autonomous, lovable person.

The Neighborhood Circle

Peers, kin, and teachers make up Section III. Much of the action is outside the home but is still closely related to it. Grandparents, aunts, and uncles may give *unconditional love,* acceptance of the child for who she is (grandchild, niece). Peers and teachers are more demanding and selective, rewarding her when she fits their expectations, punishing her when she does not.

At home and in the neighborhood, the young child explores love relationships through play, pretending to be mommies, daddies, and children sorting out ideas and feelings. In doll play and dramatic play with her peers, the child rehearses attachment behavior, care, and even respect and knowledge of the beloved. Sex play between peers is common at this age, because of a desire for knowledge of self and others and of the processes of life itself. *Care* is shown in efforts to help at home and to give to friends and family. *Respect* for the wishes of others (parents, teachers, siblings) shows in cooperation. Love-oriented behavior can be dampened by shame, guilt, and feelings of powerlessness.

Friends and Co-Workers

Section IV corresponds to the school age and early adolescence. The personnel of previous stages continue to interact with the child but now her important new influences are friends and work. Both help her to develop that part of loving that is knowledge.

Friends. At this age, friends are likely to be the same age and the same sex. The strength of attachment between the pair determines the closeness of the friendship. Attachment behavior is not so biologically based as it is in infancy, but rather depends upon proximity, shared activity, and communication.

Through long talks with close friends, a child reaches into the deeper parts of the human personality and gets new insight into love. The love is for himself as well as for others, because his most pressing task at this point is to understand himself better. The problem is to develop a strong sense of identity, as Erikson has explained and most young people well know [9]. The adolescent has to recognize himself as the child he was, anticipate himself as the adult he will be, and accept himself as he now is, to feel that his family, friends, and community are worthwhile and that he fits into the whole scene. Thus, he needs to know and respect himself in connection with all the people in his life and to know, respect, and care for them too. Through his attachments to a few friends, he works on these problems.

Work. Through work, both at school and in jobs, the young person learns *responsibility* for himself and others. He *responds* to social needs by becoming competent and producing. He also contributes to his self-knowledge and self-respect and to his feelings of being an important part of his society. Teachers are key figures in helping him to be a worthy worker, both in the way they see him and in the skills they teach. Parents and other adults do likewise. And although the student does not feel love from teachers in the same sense that he feels it from family and friends, he knows respect, care, and knowledge to the extent that teachers offer them.

Lovers and Spouses

By the time a person can become a committed member of a pair, he has loved his way through four sections of our diagram and has piled up a good deal of experience. He has formed attachments to parents, siblings, kin, and friends, in addition to a mother. Within the context of his various attachments, he has cared for other people, respected them, responded to them, taken responsibility for them, and sought to know and understand them. Books addressed to lovers usually begin here, often with the question, "How do you know you are in love?"

In Love. Being in love is usually easy to recognize. It includes the very strong feelings that Bowlby (see page 32) recognized as accompanying attachment behavior, efforts to attain and keep proximity to the loved one (attachment behavior), and sexual response. The combination of all these strong feelings often blocks out other perceptions, feelings, and actions, even affecting breathing and heart rate.

> How does Love speak?
> In the faint flush upon the telltale cheek,
> And in the pallor that succeeds it; by
> The quivering lid of an averted eye—
> The smile that proves the parent to a sigh
> > Thus does Love speak.
> > How does Love speak?
> By the uneven heart-throbs, and the freak
> Of bounding pulses that stand still and ache,
> While new emotions, like strange barges, make
> Along vein-channels their disturbing course;
> Still as the dawn, and with the dawn's swift force—
> > Thus doth Love speak. [28, p. 9]

The state of being in love is often temporary. The word *infatuation* is often used to refer to what we have called being in love, but we object to this word because it implies deception, or that the relationship is shallow and will remain shallow, and is therefore doomed. Rather, some couples who are in love progress to a more stable, less exhilarating kind of love; others "fall out of love" or cease to be in love with each other. When looking back upon their now defunct love, many couples declare that they never really loved each other; it was only infatuation. The next time they feel the same way about a new person, they again say that they are "in love."

What we have called being "in love" is not enough to build a lifelong relationship upon, but it is a beginning. Furthermore, as the years progress, the excitement, desire for closeness, and sexual response that one feels in the early stages of being "in love" add sparkle to a relationship that has become more concerned with day-to-day life than with the excitement of courtship.

For some couples, the "in love" feelings appear to give way completely to another kind of love.

> After the fierce midsummer all ablaze
> Has burned itself to ashes and expires
> In the intensity of its own fires,
> There come the mellow, mild, St. Martin days
> Crowned with the calm of peace, but sad with haze.
> So after Love has led us, till he tires
> Of his own throes and torments and desires [28, p. 21]

Being in love usually involves two people of opposite sexes, since the sexual behavior system is activated, along with attachment behavior. After the arousal of attachment behavior and sexual response, what happens depends upon both the loved one and the social setting. Sometimes only one person is in love and the other person does not respond in like fashion. Mutuality is essential for the development of a relationship and unrequited love usually fades away, though not without pain. Many popular songs deal with the sadness of one who was loved but is no longer, such as the classic "Smoke Gets in Your Eyes." Trying to hide his tears, the singer pretends that the dying flame of his love has enveloped him in smoke.

The role of family, kin, friends, and society is so important that we devote the next section to it, under the heading *Lovers in Time and Space*. First we must discuss the next step in the love career—partnership love.

When couples ask, "How do we know we are really in love?" what they often mean is, "Do we love each other enough to get married or to set up housekeeping together or to make some sort of commitment to each other?" They are not asking whether their hearts are beating fast enough or whether they are sufficiently breathless. They wonder about whether their desire to be with each other will last and if it will be satisfying for them to live as partners.

Partnership love includes being *in love* (attachment plus sexual response) and the elements that Fromm [10, pp. 7–38] has called *care, responsibility, respect,* and *knowledge*. In previous stages of growth, the individual has learned something of these aspects of love, through receiving them from other people, through practicing them in simple ways and rehearsing them in dramatic play. If the childhood and adolescent learning of love have gone well, the person in love has some substance with which to anchor ephemeral feelings.

Partnership love is obviously mutual. Each feels that together they are a couple. They are **pair-bonded,** Fromm says. Two people care for each other and take care of each other. Respect is reciprocal. Both are responsible and responsive to one another. Each continually seeks to know the other. Fromm suggests that man's need to love and be loved in this full sense arises from his feeling separate and alone. The only way to escape continually from aloneness is to love. In knowing another person deeply, one feels united. "Love is the only way of knowledge, which in the act of union answers my quest. In the act of loving, of giving myself, I discover us both, I discover man" [10, p. 31].

Erikson's concept of the **sense of intimacy** is a similar insight into knowing as loving. The main problem of growth for the older adolescent or young adult is to learn how to know another person deeply and to be known by him. The process is a two-way interaction, in which each person tries to experience the other person deeply, to know and understand his thoughts and feelings, and in turn to allow the partner to experience, to know and understand him. Lack of intimacy means *isolation* [8]. Much of this book is concerned with the development of the sense of intimacy, with knowing and responding. The chapter on communication is about the process of knowing and being known. The theme of knowing and intimacy as emphasized in this book also runs through discussions of family interaction, sex relationships, family problems, and therapy.

A mature person establishes intimate interactions with the people he loves, close (intimate) friends, as well as family. When a sex relationship is part of love, the intimacy is more complete. Fromm [10, p. 33] goes on to say that man and woman are aware of sexual polarity, division along sex lines, and also know that each carries both male and female characteristics. Union between a man and woman therefore carries a sense of unity that yields the deepest knowledge of others and self. Erikson [8, p. 265] also regards heterosexual mutuality as the deepest sort of intimacy. ". . . . the total fact of finding, via the climactic turmoil of the orgasm, a supreme experience of the mutual regulation of two beings in some way takes the edge off the hostilities and potential rages caused by the oppositeness of male and female, of fact and fancy, of love and hate."

To return to the question of what kind of love is adequate for marriage or commitment in Western culture, we suggest that partnership love is the right kind. Since nobody is perfect in ability to feel and give care, respect, responsibility, and knowledge, partners keep working at all this. But love is not enough. Love-partners interact with other people, and families with other social systems.

We discuss the process of selecting a partner further in Chapter 6, and the process of maintaining the partner relationship is discussed further in Chapters 7 and 8. Love plays an important role in both processes, but can neither explain the processes or keep them functioning by itself, as we show.

LOVERS IN TIME AND SPACE

People fall in love everywhere. They have done so since, and perhaps before, the beginning of recorded history. The development of the love affair depends very much on where and when it takes place. The behavior, feelings, and beliefs of the pair are heavily influenced by the beliefs and values of the people around them, by the customs and laws of their community and society. All cultures recognize the situation of attachment-and-sexual-response that we call being in love. It may be regarded as universal or exceptional, delightful or deplorable, sweet or sick. In the examples that follow, we start with our own culture and go on to some others that illustrate various attitudes toward lovers and the functions of being in love.

Here and Now

In North America it is commonly believed that everyone, child or adult, is entitled to love. As mentioned in Chapter 1, love is thought to be the most important function of the family. The state of being in love is also highly esteemed. Being in love is the basis on which to choose a marriage partner. Although it is acceptable to give thought to other considerations, such as moral character and religion, to marry for money is considered despicable. Of course, there are exceptions to this general

A Moghul prince and princess are depicted smoking (hashish?) together in this sixteenth century Indian miniature.

picture. Property and lineage are important in the upper class, where parents and the extended family have considerable control over partner selection. Some ethnic groups also permit parental control and stress mate selection factors other than being in love.

Being in love is also the basis for continuing a marriage, as the high divorce rate suggests. There is some difference of opinion on whether a marriage should be broken if the couple fall out of love, but it is acknowledged as highly desirable that

CRAIG M. SZWED

the in-love state should be maintained throughout a marriage. Attachment and sexual response are not the only salient aspects of love and marriage, as shown by columnists such as Ann Landers, and by articles in popular magazines that deal with partnership love and the technologies of family living. The in-love state is nevertheless of tremendous importance, since it is stimulated and sustained at a high pitch by the romantic love complex.

Romantic Love. Americans and Canadians believe strongly in romantic love, although, of course, there are differences between individuals and groups. Reiss[21], using a scale for measuring romantic love, found females higher than males, high school students higher than college students, and blacks higher than whites. When 255 college students were questioned about their experiences with romantic love, the women reported having fallen in love more frequently than did the men [7].

Romantic love is based on a complex of beliefs, attitudes, and values that have been handed down for centuries in the Western world. To fall in love is beautiful, wonderful and mysterious, magical, and not really understandable.

> That old black magic has me in its spell
> That old black magic that you weave so well
> Those icy fingers going down my spine
> The same old witchcraft when your eyes meet mine.*

For each person, there is a perfect mate. The song goes on:

> For you're the one that I have waited for,
> The mate that fate had me created for.

Some people are lucky and find their intended mates. Others have to wait and wonder if and when it will happen.

> Will I ever find the girl of my mind,
> The girl who is my ideal?
> Maybe she's a dream, and yet she may be
> Just around the corner, waiting for me.
> Will I recognize the light in her eyes
> That no other eyes reveal?
> Or will I pass her by
> And never know that she is my ideal.‡

Romantic love is blind. It thrives on not perceiving reality and is therefore enhanced by beautiful clothes, makeup, moonlight, candlelight, firelight, perfume, music, and strange places. Participants remain mysterious and therefore attractive by holding back information about themselves or even deliberately creating false impressions. Each can then believe what she (he) wants to believe about the other, creating the person in the image of the ideal.

Exploitation of the Romantic Love Complex. Other systems in our society impinge upon the courtship and marriage system at the point of falling in love and on the basis of staying in love. The economic system zeroes in on lovers through the advertising industry and the entertainment industry. Both industries play shamelessly and successfully upon themes from the romantic complex.

Advertisements proclaim that attachment and sexual response will reward those who groom and adorn themselves with certain products, including tooth paste, tooth

*"That Old Black Magic," by Johnny Mercer and Harold Arlen. Copyright © 1942 by Famous Music Corporation. Copyright renewed 1969 by Famous Music Corporation. Reprinted by permission.
‡"My Ideal," by Leo Robin, Richard Whiting, and Newell Chase. Copyright © 1930 by Famous Music Corporation. Copyright renewed 1957 by Famous Music Corporation. Reprinted by permission.

polish, mouthwash, soap, deodorants, razors, shampoo, hair rinse, hair dye, face creams, moisturizers, cuticle cream, and nail polish; medicate themselves with aspirin, stomach-settlers, laxatives, appetite depressants, vitamins, and sleep-inducers; consume or make use of soft drinks, cigarettes, cars, and mattresses. There is some validity to claims that beauty and health will make a person more fall-in-lovable, but it is farfetched to say that a particular shampoo will make a person irresistible to the opposite sex. Therefore, advertisers cleverly refrain from saying just that, but build up a picture that strongly suggests it. Linking a mattress with sexual response is more easily credible. There is necessarily more innuendo in regard to soft drinks and cars, since direct statements about inducing attachment and response would be even more absurd than in the case of tooth paste. I (MSS) can remember back to adolescence when an ad for a beauty mask parted me from a week's allowance, giving me hope of enchanting the boy who sat across the aisle from me.

The entertainment industry shapes everyone's ideas about love, through songs, films, and television. The desirability of being in love is stressed, with directions on how to achieve it and how to feel when things go right or wrong, when it does not happen, and when a love affair breaks up.

Counter Themes. Although romantic love is a strong influence, there are contemporary themes that do not fit the romantic picture: equality between the sexes; honest communication; emphasis on the immediate present; the importance of individual development and self-expression. There seems to be a growing acceptance of ideas such as being in love can be very temporary, monogamy is too restricting, and everyone is entitled to entertainment through sex, either as observer or participant.

Another theme in North American concepts of love is a realistic view of marriage as a partnership. The ideal is a strong love of the type we have described as partnership love. Cooperation, communication, and application of homemaking knowledge are seen as keys to satisfying family interaction and personal development. Romantic love contributes important threads to the fabric of a marriage. This is the point of view shown in some magazines and newspaper features.

Studies on Attraction. Psychologists and sociologists are doing research to find out what makes a person like, love, dislike, or hate certain other individuals [4]. This topic is discussed further in Chapter 6. Here we are especially interested in what makes people fall in love. If falling in love is romantic, then, according to definition, it has little to do with knowing and understanding the other person, but is much concerned with an attractive exterior. Although research has shown that similarity in certain personality characteristics, attitudes, and opinions stimulates liking, studies also show that physical attractiveness is indeed important in choices made by both men and women.

Some insight into loving as different from liking can be gained by looking at the items in a scale that measures loving and liking [23]. The scale was derived from answers given by college students who checked the questions once in reference to a girlfriend or boyfriend and once in reference to a platonic friend of the opposite sex. In the following questions from the love scale, the respondent marks in one of 9 points, from *not at all true; disagree completely* through *definitely true; agree completely*. The girlfriend's or boyfriend's name is to be put into the blank. Some of the items from the love scale are:

I feel that I can confide in ____ about virtually anything.

I find it easy to ignore ____ 's faults.

I feel very possessive toward ____ .

If I were lonely, my first thought would be to seek out ____ .

I would forgive ____ for practically anything.

I feel responsible for ____ 's well-being.

When I am with ____ , I spend a great deal of time just looking at her (him).

Scores on the love scale were highly related to the respondents' reports on whether they were in love and whether they expected to marry the person. Liking scores were only moderately related to being in love and intending marriage.

Another attempt to distinguish between loving and liking met with some success [18]. College students checked statements referring to another person whom they identified as being the object of dating, friendship, or love. The love group indicated that they felt more attachment, altruism, and physical attraction for their partners than did the friendship group. The love and friendship groups were about the same in their expressions of respect for the other person.

Studies such as these indicate that careful questioning can distinguish between loving and liking. Such questionnaires can help individuals to judge the depth of their feeling for potential partners. The questionnaire in Appendix A in this book is intended to stimulate discussion between couples, not to help the individual to decide whether his feeling is loving or liking.

Evolution of Love in the West

The study of the history of the family is in its infancy. Available research has little to say about love, but plenty to say about sex and marriage [6, 12, 22]. Other cultures have provided varying amounts of information regarding love. In this section, we briefly trace the development of love in Western culture. Then we look at three contrasting cultures, Samoan and ancient and modern Indian.

The Ancient World. The Old Testament tells some stories about couples falling in love, but on the whole, it treats being in love as of little importance. The Song of Solomon is a romantic expression, but the biblical focus is usually on God and upon playing one's proper role in human affairs. The New Testament teaches much about spiritual and brotherly love, but little about falling in love or erotic love. The Greeks and Romans were interested in love, including romantic love and homosexual love. They contributed some ideas that survive today.

The Middle Ages. Romantic love developed to a high degree in Europe, beginning in the twelfth century, as courtly love. Love was a favorite topic of conversation at court. The *Treatise on Love,* by Andreas Capellanus, is a report on what Queen Eleanor of France (later of England) and her courtiers thought to be the nature and proper conduct of love. Love affairs were not preludes to marriage, nor were they between spouses. They were extramarital affairs. The woman was married to someone else and sometimes the man was also married [5].

Capellanus starts with a definition of love that includes several romantic notions. "Love is a certain inborn suffering derived from the sight of and excessive meditation upon the beauty of the opposite sex, which causes each one to wish above all things the embraces of the other and by common desire to carry out all of love's precepts in the other's embrace" [5, p. 28].

Attachment was explained by Capellanus. The very word *love,* in Latin *amor,* comes from the word *amus,* meaning "hook" or "capture." Thus, the attachment aspect of love is contained in its name. " . . . the man who is a captive of love tries to attract another person by his allurements and exerts all his efforts to unite two different hearts with an intangible bond. . . ." [p. 31].

The treatise includes a list of 31 rules on how love is to be conducted. In the rules can be seen many of the romantic ideas that persist today: it is possible to fall in love with someone other than one's spouse; lovers are always jealous, and jealousy stimulates love; everyone is entitled to love; no one can love two partners at once and a true lover does not seek other partners; greed and love are incompatible; love fades when made public and changes easily anyway; frustration enhances love; seeing one's lover causes paleness, heart palpitations, lack of appetite and sleeplessness; being in love means thinking constantly about the beloved and trying to please him. Courtly love was definitely for the royalty and nobility. Capellanus tells just how a would-be lover should approach someone from a class lower or higher than his own and what she should answer. As for peasants (farmers), they should not be instructed in the theory and practice of love, lest they neglect their work. However, if a nobleman should be so foolish as to fall in love with a farmer's daughter, Capellanus' advice was, " . . . be careful to puff them up with lots of praise and then, when you find a convenient place, do not hesitate to take what you seek and embrace them by force."

The Puritans. In contrast to the nobility of the Middle Ages, the Puritans who settled this continent did not have the time or resources to make an art out of love. They certainly did not leave great treatises on love for us to read. Their religion emphasized work in the service of God, and there was much work to be done. Love was probably taken for granted as one small part of life. Sex was to be enjoyed within the confines of marriage, but neither sex nor love in marriage was supposed to infringe upon man's or woman's love for God. " . . . Husband and wife must not become 'so transported with affection, that they look at no higher end than marriage it self'" (sic) [17].

Some sermons published in Boston in 1712 mention the duties of husbands and wives to each other.

> They should love while detailing endeavor to have their affections really, cordially and closely knit, to each other. . . . (God) requires Husbands and Wives to have and manifest very great affection, love and kindness to one another. They should (out of Conscience to God) study and strive to render each other's life easy, quiet and comfortable; to please, gratify and oblige one another, as far as lawfully they can . . . yet let this caution be minded that they dont (sic) love inordinately, because death will soon part them. [26]

The Victorians. Historical material from the nineteenth century, the Victorian period, shows a very different attitude toward the relationships between men and women. Prudery and double talk were the order of the day. Women were supposed to be pure (sexually), strongly virtuous, weak, inferior to men, superior to men, competent, incompetent, and pious. Writings of women and about women of this period show that the love of her husband and the privilege of loving were supposed to be full and sufficient rewards for all sorts of self-denigration and self-suppression on the part of the woman. Women's duty was to resist men's sexual advances before marriage and to submit to them quietly after marriage [27].

The romantic theme dominant in the Victorian era is that of idealizing the woman, of putting her on a pedestal, and never viewing her as a person. Probably women did not really see men as persons either. Each sex maintained a large fiction about the nature of the other. Although women were supposed to provide the utmost in care and respect for men, there was little chance for mutual response and knowledge, for true intimacy to develop. The honest communication of today's partners must have been very rare in the Victorian couple.

On the other side of the ledger, the Victorians believed that romantic love was very beautiful and that true lovers had a special, unique experience. Poems, music, and art were created in the expression of love. One of the legacies from this period is the high regard for love that exists. The present belief in the uniqueness and value of a love relationship owes some of its foundations to the Victorian attitude toward love.

The South Seas: Source of Romantic Fantasies

To a North American couple, Samoa looks like a perfect setting for romantic love. Cocoanut palms shade silken sands. Warm, clear water covers coral reefs where millions of bright fish swim. Giant ferns fringe the mountains. It is easy to assume that the beautiful Samoan youths and maidens, in their colorful lava-lavas, hibiscus flowers behind their ears, are involved with love that is overpowering, idealistic, monogamous, faithful, and jealous. Samoa is a perfect setting for Samoan love affairs, too. Margaret Mead made observations here in the 1920s [15]. We use it as a contrast, making no guesses as to whether Samoans are the same today. Like Western-world romantic lovers, the Samoans sing love songs, write love letters, and call upon the moon, stars, and sea in their talk of love. However, they see nothing amiss in carrying on more than one love affair at a time. Teen-agers usually have a number of casual love affairs that include sexual intercourse. The only girls who are to be virgins at marriage are the daughters of chiefs. "Samoans rate romantic fidelity in terms of days or weeks at most, and tend to scoff at tales of life-long devotion. (They greeted the story of Romeo and Juliet with incredulous contempt)" [15, pp. 155–156].

The South Sea islands have long been regarded as a sexual paradise by the Western world, and with good reason. There is little restraint on young people's choice in love affairs, although marriage is controlled. Boys are expected to learn techniques that will make them proficient lovers. Sex is considered an art. " . . . there are no neurotic pictures, no frigidity, no impotence, except as the result of severe illness, and the capacity for intercourse only once in a night is counted as senility" [15, p. 151].

Shallowness, lack of deep feeling, is the key to the difference between Samoan romantic love and the Western type. The young people fall in love easily and often, conducting their affairs with beauty and grace, but attachments are weak. From infancy, an individual learns not to *care* greatly, not to expect much from any particular relationship [15, p. 199]. Problems of interpersonal relationships are simple and easily solved. The individual does not experience an urgent need to establish identity and intimacy. The whole culture, then, makes casual sex appropriate.

The Exotic East: India Then and Now

Ancient India is intriguing to everyone interested in love because of the records that are available, both written and graphic. Present-day India is interesting as a contrast to Western romanticism.

Ancient India. The Kama Sutra, written around 400 A.D., has become well-known to American students who are fascinated by its explicit instructions on how to perform sexual acts in ways that produce the most pleasure. Similarly, American tourists in India are eager to see the erotic sculpture on the temples at Kajuraho and Konarak. These artistic works, verbal and visual, are expressions of the unity of religion, love, and sex in Hinduism. The Kama Sutra is not only a book of instructions on how to enjoy sex but on how to show love in sexual expression. *Kama* means both love and pleasure. Love and the enjoyment of all the arts are believed to contribute to the well-rounded personality. Love is a basic sentiment and its expression is an art. The longing of lovers for each other was used by Sanskrit poets and artists to depict the love of God. In fact, a whole system of human relationships and behavior was designed in terms of religion. Very little was left to spontaneity or to chance. Every role, including those of husband and wife, had its obligations, and the performance of those duties had religious overtones.

Lovers were supposed to be married to each other. The joy and goodness of love expressed through sex were not permitted to be sampled before marriage. Grooms, as well as brides, were expected to be virginal at marriage. There was allowance for the possibility of a young couple falling in love and wanting to get married for love. Eight forms of marriage were known, a love marriage being sixth in desirability. The most approved forms, the first four, brought purification to ancestors, but the sixth form did not [19, p. 152].

Modern India. Dating and casual contacts between young Indian men and women are rare, and generally disapproved. Adolescents are usually segregated by sex in schools and in social life. Since families exert firm control over the choice of marriage partners, it is necessary to keep boys and girls from becoming strongly attached to partners of their own choice. Occasional love marriages occur, and the attitude toward them has not changed since ancient times. Unless parents approve the match, general social disapproval ensues. Because women are expected to be virgins at marriage, and sex urges are recognized as powerful, young people rarely find opportunities to be alone together. Gossip and social disapproval are strong forces that keep them in line, even when they would like to go off in pairs.

Among traditional Indian families, the love between mother and son may be stronger than the husband-wife bond. The young wife has very low status until she has borne a son. She pours out affection on the baby who becomes very attached to her. Religion and social approval strengthen the tie between mother and son and maintain it throughout life. An example is Ramdas, a young man who came from the head family in a village. His first absence from home was a business trip of two months, which meant leaving his parents, wife, and five children. He described his return, "As I came in, the whole family was there. I went to my mother and put my arms around her. All I could say was 'Mother.' We both stood there, crying."

Love between a man and woman is supposed to develop after marriage, when courting begins. Traditionally, the groom does not see the bride until the wedding. However, a procedure sometimes followed today is for the parents to set up matches for the boy and girl to accept or reject. They might then start to fall in love when the match had been arranged and approved. The assumption is that love will naturally follow if the important conditions are right, horoscopes matching, families in proper relationship as to caste and affluence, the couple adequate in health, character, competence, and good looks. It often works out as intended.

CONCLUSIONS

Universal Aspects

Falling in love can happen anywhere, and it often does. The in-love condition is biologically based behavior that is shaped by the culture in which it occurs. The most mysterious aspect of falling in love is the question of why a specific person is chosen rather than any other person. The romantic complex promotes the notion that for each individual, there is only one other with whom the best in-love relationship could be established. Where the *one ideal lover* concept is lacking, as in Samoa, people also fall in love but there they are very free to change the love object. The *one ideal lover* seems to be losing ground with youth today, as evidenced in more frequent and agreeable divorces, more premarital love affairs, more extramarital sex. Not all lovers believe in monogamy, faithfulness, permanence, or jealousy.

Attachment behavior has a biological base in youth and adulthood, as it has in infancy. Looking and clinging are common to both stages. Infants gaze at their mothers' faces, especially their eyes; lovers gaze at each others' faces, especially their eyes [23]. In fact, a study on looking showed that both men and women preferred individuals who maintained eye contact with them. What is more, they liked opposite-sex individuals with wide dilated pupils better than those with small pupils [24]. Girl babies look at faces and eyes more than do boy babies; women look at men more than men look at women [23]. Puberty brings development of secondary sex characteristics, which become additional focuses of lovers' gazing. We need no research to prove that men tend to look at breasts and hips, and women at broad shoulders, slim waists, and long legs. Lovers put their arms around each other and cling to each other, just as infants cuddle and cling. The term *lovemaking* is very apt, because sexual intercourse often (but not always) creates powerful bonds of attachment between lovers.

Societal Regulations

Cultures set forth a variety of ways of expressing love. Every society regulates lovemaking, not only because sexual intercourse produces children but because of the bonds it creates between couples. Thus, the Puritans were supposed to keep the joy of loving within bounds lest it interfere with the society's greater duty to God. Ancient India, also concerned with duty to God, emphasized joy in lovemaking because it was thought to be a manifestation of universal love and energy. Three main areas of social shaping of love behavior can be seen.

Choice of a Lover. Freedom to choose a lover varies enormously from one society to another. In the examples given here, Samoa is very free and modern India is very restricted. Capellanus' writings showed the role of a strong class system in regulating love, denying instruction in love behavior to the workers.

Attachment Behavior. A society may teach its young attitudes toward lovemaking and techniques for it. The Victorians taught the beliefs of the romantic complex and taught attitudes but not techniques relating to sexual intercourse. They, like the courtly lovers of Europe, concentrated on how to behave during the first stages of falling in love. In contrast, the Kama Sutra taught every detail of lovemaking. The present situation in North America is similar in the availability of vast information on how to conduct sexual behavior. Sex therapists concentrate on enhancing sexual pleasure, the ultimate goal usually being orgasm through sexual intercourse.

Importance of Heterosexual Love. In contemporary American society, tremendous emphasis is placed upon fulfillment through heterosexual love. It is doubtful if any society has ever taken love more seriously. Although in the days of courtly love, royalty and nobility were much involved with love, romantic love was not considered appropriate for the lower classes. The Indian attitude, both ancient and modern, is that love has its place and that sex is important, but man and woman have many duties to perform and life involves a great deal more than lovemaking.

Fulfillment of the Individual versus Welfare of the Group

Our society is greatly concerned with the rights and fulfillment of the individual. This emphasis can be seen in the freedoms guaranteed by the Constitution of the United States. Interest in individual fulfillment is just as great today, or even greater. This attitude stands in contrast to that of most Asians and Africans, who consider family and group welfare as more important than the individual.

American youth have embraced Kahlil Gibran because he expresses the notion that one can have a marriage that is based on being in love and loving, and at the same time, individual development is possible. "Let there be spaces in your togetherness . . . eat not from the same loaf . . . the oak tree and the cypress grow not in each other's shadow" [11, pp. 15–16].

Carl Rogers also maintains that a couple can be in love, married, and growing.

> When a person is making progress, in all the ways I have described, toward becoming his own separate self, then he/she is a worthy partner—not a slave or slave-owner, not a shadow or an echo, not always a leader nor always a follower, not a person-to-be-taken-for-granted . . . it is so rewarding to be in process of becoming one's real self, that it is almost inevitable that you will permit and encourage your partner in the same direction, and rejoice in every step that he or she takes. It is *fun* to grow together, two unique and intertwined lives. [21a, p. 208]

We, too, believe that it is possible for two people to be in love, to show mutual care, respect, responsibility, and knowledge and to grow as individuals. Probably a limited number of couples actually achieve all this. It is much more difficult to build and maintain this dynamic relationship than to play the wife-husband roles as prescribed by society. The dilemmas involved include the following.

Permanence and Stability. Is the marriage to last "as long as we both shall live" or "as long as we both shall love?" What degree of in-loveness must be maintained in order to keep the partnership?

50   THE STRANDS OF FAMILY LIFE

Dependency versus Self-Sufficiency. How can two people be a team and yet be individuals?

Exclusiveness. How much can this relationship dominate the emotional lives of the pair? Can there still be love and loyalty for children and kin? For friends? For other loves?

Synchronized Growth. How can two committed people continue to grow at the same rate and change in the same direction? Two people brought together by similar circumstances may find that as their experiences become more different, they no longer grow as a pair. This has been common when one partner works to support the other through school, or when one partner works exclusively outside of the home and the other stays at home and cares for children.

SUMMARY   Concepts of love vary between cultures and between individuals. Attachment, an element of love, is an affectional bond that ties one person to another, making him try repeatedly to gain the presence of the loved one and to stay near her. Attachments are seen in animals and birds, as well as among human beings. Care, another element of love, also occurs in subhuman forms of life. Through care, a person tries to promote the well-being of another.

At birth, an infant has behavior patterns through which he builds an attachment to his mother, at the same time stimulating attachment behavior in her. The result is a bond between the pair. The infant also builds attachments with other people. Fathers vary greatly in the amount and quality of their interactions with infants.

As his social world expands in people and space, the young child experiences love expressed in different modes, conditional and unconditional love. The child explores and rehearses love through play. Friends play important roles in the adolescent's identity and intimacy, both of which require knowledge of himself and others. Friends also give opportunities for care, respect, and response.

The state of being in love includes very strong feelings, efforts to gain and keep the presence of the beloved person, and sexual response. Heart rate, breathing, and perception are affected. An intense level of being in love is usually temporary. Couples in love often wonder if their love is sufficient for commitment of a somewhat permanent sort.

Partnership love (love appropriate for commitment to a partnership) includes being in love plus care, responsibility, respect and knowledge. Love that comprises these elements offers the experience of intimacy and some escape from loneliness. When sex is included with the other elements of love, the possibility for deep intimacy is especially great.

Falling in love occurs everywhere, but the conduct and meaning of a love affair are shaped by the culture in which the couple live. At present in the United States and Canada, being in love is highly valued and considered to be the main factor in mate selection. Romantic love is cherished. Based on centuries-old ideas, romantic love is a complex of beliefs, attitudes, and values. Romantic love is exploited by industry, especially the advertising and entertainment industries.

As an example of historic American views on love, the Puritans held marital love and sex in great esteem. They insisted, however, on keeping mortal love under control so that it would not interfere with the love of God. Another era, the nineteenth century, embraced romance, prudery, and the double standard. Expectations of women were contradictory. Greeks and Romans were interested in romantic love. Courtly love, a flowering of romantic love, began in the twelfth century.

The nonwestern world has not and does not incorporate the romantic complex. In Samoa, sex is an art, jealousy is muted, and commitment is weak and temporary. In ancient India, love and sex were blended in designed expression of religious love. In modern India, most marriages are arranged by parents, and falling in love is not considered an adequate method of choosing marital partners. Love is supposed to come after marriage. In traditional Indian families, the strongest love bond is between the mother and son.

Sexual intercourse is an adult equivalent of attachment behavior, being biologically based upon complementary behavior patterns in two people. Thus, lovemaking is an appropriate term.

Every society regulates lovemaking because of its bonding properties as well as its reproductive role. The regulations often differ from one social class to another and in subcultures. Regulations are placed upon the choice of a lover, upon the when and how of attachment behavior, and upon the degree of importance accorded to heterosexual love and to self-expression and development. The fulfillment of the individual has always been important to Americans and is becoming even more so. The modern approach to love and marriage includes the notion that the bonds of love not only permit freedom to the individual but that a full partnership love actually promotes growth in both partners. Dilemmas of modern love partnerships include permanence and stability, dependency versus self-sufficiency, and exclusiveness.

REFERENCES

1. Ainsworth, Mary D. Salter. The development of infant-mother attachment. In Bettye M. Caldwell and Henry N. Ricciuti (eds.). *Review of Child Development Research,* Vol. 3. Chicago: U. of Chicago, 1973.
2. Beach, Frank. Beagles and locks. *American Psychologist,* 1969, **24,** 971–989.
3. Bowlby, John. *Attachment and loss.* Vol. I. *Attachment.* London: Hogarth, 1969.
4. Byrne, Donn and William Griffitt. Interpersonal attraction. *Annual Review of Psychology,* 1973, **24,** 317–336.
5. Capellanus, Andreas. *The art of courtly love.* Trans by John J. Parry. New York: Norton, 1941.
6. Carlier, Auguste. *Marriage in the United States.* New York: Arno, 1972. (Reprinted from the 1867 edition.)
7. Dion, Kenneth L. and Karen K. Dion. Correlates of romantic love. *Journal of Consulting and Clinical Psychology,* 1974 (in press).

8. Erikson, Erik H. *Childhood and society.* New York: Norton, 1963.
9. Erikson, Erik H. *Identity and the life cycle.* New York: International Universities, 1959.
10. Fromm, Erich. *The art of loving.* New York: Harper, 1956.
11. Gibran, Kahlil. *The prophet.* New York: Knopf, 1965.
12. Gordon, Michael (ed.). *The American family in social-historical perspective.* New York: St. Martin's, 1973.
13. Jolly, Alison. *The evolution of primate behavior.* New York: Macmillan, 1972.
14. Lorenz, Konrad Z. *King Solomon's ring.* New York: Crowell, 1952.
15. Mead, Margaret. *Coming of age in Samoa.* New York: Morrow, 1928.
16. Mead, Margaret. *Sex and temperament in three primitive societies.* London: Routledge and Kegan Paul, 1935.
17. Morgan, Edmund S. The Puritans and sex. In Michael Gordon (ed.). *The American family in social-historical perspective.* New York: St. Martin's, 1973.
18. Pam, Alvin, Robert Plutchik, and Hope Conte. Love: A psychometric approach. *Proceedings, 81st Annual Convention, American Psychological Association,* 1973, 159–160.
19. Prabhu, Pandharinath H. *Hindu social organization.* (3rd ed.). Bombay: Popular Book Depot, 1958.
20. Rebelsky, Freda and Cheryl Hanks. Fathers' verbal interaction with infants in the first three months of life. *Child Development,* 1971, **42,** 63–68.
21. Reiss, Ira L. *The social context of premarital permissiveness.* New York: Holt, 1967.
21a. Rogers, Carl R. *Becoming partners: Marriage and its alternatives.* New York: Delacorte, 1972.
22. Rothman, David J. and Sheila M. Rothman (ed.). *The colonial family in America.* New York: Arno, 1972.
23. Rubin, Zick. Measurement of romantic love. *Journal of Personality and Social Psychology,* 1970, **16,** 265–273.
24. Stass, A. W. and F. N. Willis, Jr. Eye contact, pupil dilation and personal preference. *Psychonomic Science,* 1967, **7,** 375–376.
25. Stayton, Donelda J, Robert Hogan, and Mary D. Salter Ainsworth. Infant obedience and maternal behavior: The origins of socialization reconsidered. *Child Development,* 1971, **42,** 1071–1082.
26. Wadsworth, Benjamin. The well-ordered family: or relative duties. Boston: B. Green, 1712. In David J. Rothman and Sheila M. Rothman (eds.). *The colonial family in America.* New York, Arno, 1972.
27. Welter, Barbara. The cult of true womanhood: 1820–1860. In Michael Gordon (ed.). The American family in social-historical perspective. New York: St. Martin's, 1973.
28. Wheeler, Ella W. *Poems of passion.* Chicago: W. B. Conkey, 1883.

CHAPTER 3

COMMUNICATION: GETTING IT OUT AND TAKING IT IN

In the previous chapter, we discussed knowledge as one of the basic elements of love. Knowing one's beloved and letting oneself be known are essentials of loving, of developing an intimate, caring relationship. And how does a person know another person and be known? By communication, sending messages and receiving them. Vital though communication is to lovers, it is not their monopoly. Every living creature communicates. In fact, every system does. In this book, we are especially concerned with communication between lovers and between family members and, to some extent, between all human beings.

SOME BASIC USES FOR COMMUNICATION

Without a good communication system, human society would fail utterly in many processes.

Socialization

Through communication, the infant and child become a part of the culture into which the baby is born. No newborn knows how to speak the language of his parents and community, but no one is surprised when within a year or two the child begins to use it. The infant arrives into a setting in which the older members speak with each other. They talk to the baby in this language and use it when addressing each other in the baby's presence. When the child reaches a certain level of mental and physical maturity, she begins to speak the language.

Exactly how a child acquires language is not known. What is important for our purposes is that in normal children, this learning takes place without causing much trouble to those who do the "teaching." When a child cannot hear, see, or both, he has more problems than a normal child in learning the language, and in becoming a part of the family and community. Such a child's tremendous need to communicate is illustrated by the story of Helen Keller, who became deaf and blind at the age of 19 months because of illness. Helen remembered feelings of terrible frustration because she was unable to communicate with those around her. At the age of six, she made the discovery with the help of her teacher, that every thing has a name. Having learned this, the rest of the world opened up to her, although it was difficult for her to grasp the meaning of abstract concepts such as "love" and "think" [16].

A newborn baby could fit equally well into an American, Indonesian, or Nigerian family, or any other human family. He becomes a member of a particular society through the content and style of communication he experiences. He becomes socialized into that society. What the child sees and understands will be largely conditioned by the language. In Chapter I, it was stated that the Hindi-speaking child has six different kinds of aunts, depending upon the age of the aunt, relation to his parent, and whether or not the aunt is a blood relative. This child would find it hard to understand how North Americans can lump together six totally different types of relative into one category.

A Vehicle for Adaptation and Stability

Communication is necessary if a given society is to survive, because it allows both change and stability. Any society (or person) must be able to change if it or he is to live. If life were completely unpredictable, however, nobody could function. Most social interaction is probably concerned not with change but with the ordinary demands of daily life in a group. Communication between people thus maintains equilibrium, or a relatively steady state [3, p. 14].

Change, rapid or slow, is always with us. Changes in technology, the economy, and the political structure all exert an influence upon each of us. Social change has become more rapid since the beginning of the industrial revolution. In former times a boy would grow up to resemble his father in occupation and philosophy of life; a girl knew that her life would most likely center around her husband and her children. The girl might marry someone whose occupation differed somewhat from her father's. She might be a butcher's wife rather than a tailor's wife, as her mother had been. But the girl would have learned how to cook, sew, keep house, and care for children.

In earlier eras, when a couple married, each had ideas about what a husband and wife should be like, both in terms of what each should do to keep the family functioning, and in terms of how each should feel about their interaction, their tasks, and their children. Most of the other people of the same social class in the community felt the same way. Discussion of the woman's and man's role in the family was not important, because it was understood by all.

In a society that is undergoing technological and social change, more communication becomes necessary. First, it is not as likely that all persons, particularly those of different generations, will have the same expectations concerning what life should be like, what a man should do and feel, what a woman should do and feel, and so on. A girl may get some ideas of what it is like to be a woman from her own mother, but she can no longer model herself on her mother as closely as did a girl of a century or two ago. Furthermore, a girl has more diverse models today, for example, her teachers and television personalities. Her mother may have spent more years bearing and raising children and fewer years working outside the home than the modern girl wishes to do. Jobs that did not exist twenty or thirty years ago may appeal very much to the young woman and man of today.

Compared with their counterparts in former generations, a young couple at the present time needs more discussion of their desires and expectations. We do not wish to imply that communication was unimportant in the past, but only that it is more necessary now, because roles are less clearly defined.

Communication is increasingly significant for another reason as well: Our society is tremendously complex, made up of many different groups with varying interests. In order to maintain a degree of cohesiveness, groups separated by geography or philosophy must be able to air their views before each other. Through communication, a society (or small group, such as a family) is able to adapt to new situations, while maintaining some sense of cohesion and continuity.

In a very real sense, we are evolving toward becoming a global society.

Worldwide communication systems already exist, but need to be improved. The actual existence of human life may depend upon adequate worldwide communication.

THE NATURE OF COMMUNICATION

Communication refers to the sending and receiving of messages through both words and nonverbal behavior that occur in a social context.

Verbal and Nonverbal Communication

When North Americans think of communication, we usually think of *verbal* communication, that which is written or spoken. The *nonverbal* elements of communication are, however, much more important than one might at first think. For example, it is sometimes easy to tell how a friend is feeling just by looking at him. If he approaches with a grin on his face, his posture erect, and his steps bouncing, the person who is "tuned into" these nonverbal cues readily assumes, *without even thinking about it,* that her friend is in a good mood. If he walks slowly, eyes downcast, posture slumped, the perceptive friend assumes that he is unhappy or perhaps tired. The person who picks up her friend's nonverbal cues will react to him differently in each case.

People do not always have to speak to communicate how they are feeling; they can do so nonverbally. *When two or more people are interacting, it is impossible for them not to communicate.* Even silence can send a message from one person to another [18, p. 99].

Not all persons are equally sensitive to nonverbal cues. I (LSS) was once sitting in a tight circle with two friends, talking about a problem and trying to keep from crying. A third friend, Fred, came up to us, sat down, and started talking about a small aggravation of his. The three of us looked at him in disbelief, but Fred kept right on talking. I found out later that this is characteristic of Fred: he is unable to pick up nonverbal cues that other people notice.

Usually, human beings use a wide assortment of cues given off by a person with whom we are conversing. We hear the words, listen to the tone of voice and the emphasis placed on words, and observe the speaker's facial expression, focus of eyes, body postures, and gestures. When an author wants to report the context in which words are spoken, he must do so with more words. Note the difference in the meaning in the following sentences:

"You're a good friend!" she snapped, her eyes blazing with anger.
"You're a good friend!" she said, smiling and reaching over to touch his arm.

We can distinguish between the two sentences on the basis of the *nonverbal cues* accompanying the words (ex. 1: blazing eyes; ex. 2: touching the listener's arm); and also on the basis of the *tone of voice,* that one only can infer from the way words are written. The nonverbal cues that accompany the first example imply a lack of sincerity: the speaker does *not* think the listener is a good friend. But the sentence implies even more than that: it suggests that the speaker had expected the listener to be a good friend, but had been disappointed. In the second example, the touching of the listener's arm implies that the speaker really *does* think the listener is a good friend and that she wants to emphasize this point.

Another kind of nonverbal communication is through the use of *symbols.* Meaning is communicated to people in this culture by halos, hearts, and skull-and-crossbones. Falling in love is a stimulus to all sorts of creative expression, as lovers try to communicate with each other in attractive, original, and artistic ways. "I love you" and "You are beautiful" may seem inadequate, and a love poem or song may seem more appropriate. Flowers, gifts, special settings, and music are all used to communicate "I love you." Some symbols carry generally recognized meaning, for instance, a diamond ring. Other symbols may be invented by the pair to carry messages that are not put into words. For example, Dick expresses special tenderness by ordering the kind of wine he and Helen drank on their first date.

Congruent and Incongruent Messages

When nonverbal cues that a person is giving are relaying the same message as the verbal cues, we say that his message is **congruent.** If a mother picks up her child and hugs him, and says, "I love you," the two messages sent by the mother are the same, or congruent. But if a mother hits the child and says, "I love you," the message is **incongruent.** It may be that the mother is hitting the child in order to make him stop doing something that is dangerous, such as running out into the street. By keeping him from running into the street, she is showing her love for him. Saying "I love you" at that time might be accurate. However, the actual feelings that the mother has *at that time* are probably feelings of *fear* that the child will be hurt by running into the street, or perhaps *anger* that she has been disobeyed again. A more congruent message to say to the child at that time would be, "I am afraid that you will get run over! And I am angry that you keep running into the street when I have told you many times that you must not!"

The following examples further clarify the distinction between congruent and incongruent messages:

1. Congruent message: Sam says to Joan, "I love you, darling," and draws her close, kissing her.
2. Incongruent message: When her husband tells her that he won't be home for dinner that night, Gloria says curtly, with tight lips, "Oh, that's all right."
3. Incongruent message: George, who is trying to diet but loves to eat good food, says while gulping his second helping of pie, "Mom, why are you such a terrible cook?"

Gloria may or may not want her husband to know that she is angry at him for planning to be out for dinner. If he wishes, he can ignore her nonverbal message and insist to himself and to her that she had told him it was all right to stay away. George, on the other hand, wants his mother to know that she is a good cook, but his feelings of discomfort about eating pie when he knows he should not are also evident in what he says.

An incongruent message may also be used when a person wants to convey a negative message through the use of sarcasm. Gloria might also say to her husband, "I can tell you really care about me," with tones of sarcasm that make the words mean, "I can tell you *don't* care about me." Should her husband get defensive, and reply, "What do you mean, 'I can tell you really care about me!'" (repeating her intonation), "I *do* care about you!" Gloria then can repeat her message, using intonation which removes the sarcasm: "All I said was, I can tell you really care about me. You're giving me warning that you won't be home for dinner" [22, p. 41].

A person may be unaware that he is sending nonverbal messages that are not congruent with his verbal messages. The young woman who wears a short skirt and tight top, with no bra, may be unaware that she is sending a message of sexual availability to a particular man. If he makes sexual advances, she may be incensed at his forwardness, and say something to that effect. The man, meanwhile, may be confused and angered himself by her messages that *he perceives* as conflicting.

On the simplest level, when communication occurs between two individuals, A sends a message (verbally, nonverbally, or both) and B receives it. However, as indicated by the above example, the message that A intends to send may not come through to B as A had intended. The young woman did not intend to be sexually provocative to the man; from her point of view, her clothes were comfortable and perhaps stylish. He understood her physical appearance to be an invitation for his advances. When he slid his hand around her waist, he gave her the chance to clarify her message to him. Had she accepted his advances, he would have been assured that his assumption was correct. However, her rebuff showed that he had interpreted her appearance incorrectly.

Within the context of the family or some other close relationship, we usually have more information about the person with whom we are communicating than we do when we are relating to a stranger or acquaintance. A husband might know from previous experience that when his wife puts on a certain negligee, it means that she would like to make love. However, on a particular night she might put on the negligee only because all her other nightclothes are dirty.

Representations of Reality

Verbal and nonverbal communication is a representation of reality. If I describe to you a person throwing a ball, you will form a mental picture of someone engaging in that activity, based on your previous experiences. You do not actually *see* a person throwing a ball, however: you only conjure one up in your mind. The description is only a representation of the event: Each event is unique, even when we are watching a pitcher practice his curve ball over and over again.

Virginia Satir, an experienced family therapist, has seen the problems that can be caused when a person fails to realize that words are representations of reality. She may assume that something which occurs once is an example of all instances: a young woman is mistreated by a man whom she loves and so assumes that all men mistreat women. Or, a person may assume that all people think the way she does: I like carrots, so everyone must like carrots. Or, she may think that what she perceives is final, and will not change: I don't like Sandy because she seems selfish. Instead of observing her in other situations, or finding out why she is behaving the way she is, I will write her off as a lost cause.

Another problem encountered by the person who does not realize that words are abstractions, or representations of reality, is that she tends to think in terms of "black and white." Such a person believes that each individual is either good or bad, and not a combination of the two. For example, she may believe that it is not possible to love and hate the same person. The person who does not realize that words are abstractions assumes that the characteristics that she names in things or people represent the complete reality of the thing or person. By calling a person a name, such as coward, bully, devil, sexpot, or pollyanna, one may give the impression that the particular name describes the whole person, all of him. For instance, Joe calls Sally a *cripple*. He might have said that Sally is crippled or disabled. The term *a cripple* suggests that Sally is just that and no more. In reality, Sally is a person with many attributes, abilities, and assets. She cannot walk smoothly and cannot run at all, because one leg is shorter than the other. Joe saw Sally's limited locomotion, gave the condition a name, applied the name to Sally as an individual, and left the impression in himself and perhaps in others that Sally's disability was a total picture of Sally. When Sally hears herself called *a cripple,* it makes her think that others perceive her as nothing but a person who can't walk well and it diminishes her concept of herself.

Another source of misunderstanding is the assumption that another person can understand what is going on inside the speaker's head and that the speaker also knows what the listener is thinking. A wife asks her husband, "Did you bring the whachamacallit?" If he asks her what she means, and she gets annoyed, she was assuming that he could read her mind [26, pp. 66–67].

The person who realizes that words represent reality will be more able to express herself meaningfully to her listener. She will understand that there is room for a tremendous amount of error in the sending of messages and their comprehension. She will also more readily understand the complexity of communication and of the world.

Different Kinds of Meanings

Clarity of communication suffers because words often have two kinds of meanings: a literal, or **denotative** meaning, and a **connotative** meaning. If you look up a word in a dictionary, you will find its different denotative meanings listed. For example, the word *bail* has a number of different denotative meanings, including the following:

1. Security given for the due appearance of a prisoner in order to obtain his release from imprisonment.
2. To deliver (property) in trust to another for a special purpose and for a limited period.
3. A device for confining or separating animals.
4. To clear water from a boat by dipping and throwing over the side [31].

We can usually tell which denotative meaning is intended by the context in which the word is found. Misunderstandings can and do occur when the context does not make the meaning clear.

Another kind of meaning that words have is the *connotative* meaning, which is a more personal meaning. What kind of reaction do you get to the word *liberation?* Liberty is a basic value in our society; if this were the only association of the word liberation, one would expect that only positive (good) feelings would be aroused by the word. For some, the word liberation is associated with women's liberation or black liberation. Such connotations might stimulate feelings of anger, pride, anxiety, or hopefulness.

Not a Simple Two-way Process

It is tempting to think of communication between two persons as a simple, two-way process, in which one person sends a message, the second one receives and processes it, and sends one back. We tend to think that people in real life talk and communicate in turns the way people do on television or in a novel [3, p. 12].

> Speech communication is a two-way process, not to be conceived as one where a verbal ball is being tossed back and forth, but as one where at least two, and often many, balls are being tossed in both directions at the same time [5, p. 51].

Even though we are not usually aware of it, when we are conversing with another person, we are constantly giving off cues to which the other responds. We smile, look surprised, our eyes widen, we grimace, we move closer or farther away, we cross our arms or legs, or relax our bodies completely. The person with whom we are talking may interpret our nonverbal cues correctly or incorrectly, but whichever is the case, an effect has been made upon the interaction.

Imagine, for example, that you are talking with a friend about an issue that is emotionally laden and difficult for you to discuss. You are concerned about your friend's reaction: will he *accept* you and what you are saying, or will he think you wrong, odd, immoral, and so on? As you are speaking, you see your friend stiffen a bit. He is trying to look unruffled, but you detect tension. How do you feel? Would

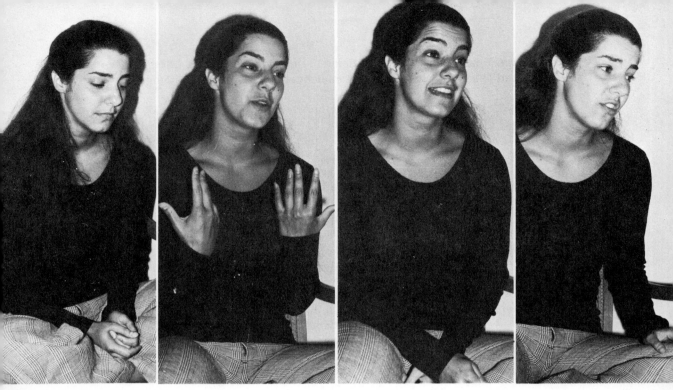

Jane is talking about her boyfriend. Can you tell how she feels by looking at each photo?

you have a different reaction to a response that is decidedly warm and accepting? To *accept* what another person does or says is not the same as *agreeing* with it, *condoning* it, or *wanting it for oneself*. Debbie, a woman with a career, accepts her sister's wanting to be a housewife as right for her sister, but not for herself. Ted feels that he is incompetent. Kevin accepts his feelings, but does not agree with Ted's evaluation of himself when he says, "I know that *you* think you're not doing a good job, but *I* think you're doing fine."

Interference from Within. The message that is sent to us by another can become garbled by interference from our own needs and desires, and by our anxiety. The man who wants to get to know a woman better may think that her casual, "Hello, how are you?" means that she is interested in him the way he is in her. Perhaps the most harmful interference to communication is feelings of anxiety and fear [5, pp. 70–71]. Negative feelings about the person with whom we are attempting to communicate can distort our perceptions and understanding. Mutual distrust between whites and blacks or chicanos is a barrier to communication and cooperation. A "straight" person is afraid of the "freaks," and a "longhair" fears the

THE STRANDS OF FAMILY LIFE

"straights." Individuals on each side of the chasm may label their feelings as dislike or hatred, but behind these feelings are likely to lurk anxiety, fear, and misunderstanding.

EFFECTIVE VERSUS INEFFECTIVE COMMUNICATION

Just because a message is sent does not mean that the same message is received by the listener. Both the speaker and the listener need particular skills if effective communication is to take place.

Empathy versus Sympathy

In order for effective communication to take place, the listener must be able to "put himself in the psychological shoes" of the speaker [6, p. 318]. In other words, the listener must have **empathy** for the speaker. The listener must not, however, lose himself in the words of the speaker, and forget that it is the speaker who has a particular feeling and not himself. The person who experiences real empathy has been described as a pendulum that swings between his own identity and feelings and identity with the speaker [15]. Although the empathic listener can feel and understand the emotions expressed by (or behind the words of) the speaker, he understands that he is a separate person from the speaker.

When we were in India, we were told by a person whose first language was Hindi that "Hindi is the sweetest language." At that point, we were struggling with Hindi lessons five days a week, and found many of the sounds impossible to articulate, and the grammar troublesome because it was so different from English grammar. One of us replied that perhaps Hindi was the sweetest language to him, but to us, it was difficult. A look of disbelief crossed the face of our acquaintance, and he repeated: "Hindi is the sweetest language." At that moment our acquaintance was entirely lacking in empathy. He could not put himself in our shoes; he could not believe that even a foreigner would not immediately recognize Hindi, which he had learned at his mother's knee, as the sweetest language in the world.

If he had responded instead, when we insisted that Hindi was difficult, "Oh, goodness, I meant that Hindi is the sweetest language to *me* because it's my mother tongue!" he would have given an indication that he realized that we might feel differently. If he had also said, "I can understand how Hindi might be difficult for you, because the sounds and grammar are different from English," his response would have been empathic.

In contrast to empathy, a person who feels **sympathy** cannot distinguish his own feelings from those of the speaker. This frequently happens when the listener's experience is similar to the speaker's. Dennis is telling Jerry about his feelings concerning his (Dennis') divorce. Jerry was recently divorced, and still has a lot of tumultuous feelings concerning his own divorce. As Dennis becomes more emotional, so does Jerry. Jerry finally says, "I can really understand what you're saying, man, but I don't think I can help you sort out your feelings. This is hitting too close to home for me—it makes me think about Barbara and me." Jerry recognizes that he is feeling sympathy, not empathy.

Suppose that Jerry does not have disturbing feelings about his own divorce and says instead, "Wow, man, you're really making me feel sad. Seeing you upset like this really affects me, too. You really feel torn by this whole thing. You're glad to be rid of the pressure of living with Tish, but you still feel that you have failed." In this case, the feelings behind Jerry's words are empathic ones, because Jerry recognizes that the problem of the divorce is Dennis' problem and not his. Jerry's understanding of Dennis' feelings may have come in part because of Jerry's own divorce, but Jerry can keep the two events and the accompanying feelings separate in his own mind.

The Problem of Not Hearing

Very frequently a breakdown of communication occurs when two people do not "hear" each other. "Nonlistening" is unfortunately a very common practice in our society; parents don't listen to their children, so the children do not learn how to listen to their parents. Nonlistening can also come from a kind of verbal sparring in which each person is more concerned about what *he* is going to say next rather than what the other person is trying to communicate [18]. Preschool children will often hold a mock conversation, each one speaking in turn, but the second child's sentences have nothing to do with the first child's. Adult conversations can be remarkably similar.

> *Ken:* "Guess what! I got the promotion! Just one other guy and I got it!"
> *Mark:* "Yeah, well my boss says some of us will be coming up for a promotion soon. I think I've been doing a pretty good job."
> *Ken:* "With the raise in pay, we'll be able to get out of the financial hole we're in. But the best part of it is that he finally recognizes that I've got something to offer."
> *Mark:* "Yeah, well it's been a long time coming for me. I've been putting in extra hours for over a year now."

How do you feel when another person cuts you off in the middle of a thought, or starts each of his sentences with a quick "yes" and then goes on to tell his own story? When their own needs are overpowering, even the most skilled listeners trangress in this way at times, but to do so frequently is bound to frustrate the speaker, to make him feel unimportant and unheard. This can happen when one or both people are playing a game of one-ups-manship (who can tell the funniest story? who had the worst experience? who caught the longest fish?), or it can happen when one or both conversants feel threatened by what the other is saying.

In contrast, a person who really listens to another is at the same time communicating that he cares about the speaker as a person. At times, we all need simply to talk about a problem with another person; sharing the burden somehow makes it lighter. The listener need not always have a verbal response: a concerned facial expression, or a calm, warm hand may say to the speaker, "I hear you, and I care."

Not hearing can also occur because the listener is too close to the problem, or too emotionally involved in it. Alice R. is pregnant by mistake and not married. When she tells her mother, who is a social worker, her mother's response is, "How can you do this to me?" Instead of supporting her daughter when her daughter has a difficult problem, Mrs. R. ignores Alice's feelings. Because she is a social worker, Mrs. R. frequently deals with women who have problem pregnancies. As a professional, she is effective, but when her daughter needs help, she is unable to give it because she is overwhelmed by her own feelings. The problem is too close to home.

Clarification of Messages. Even when two conversants are attending to what the other is saying, they may not "hear" each other. Because of the different denotative and connotative meanings of words, and because of interference from anxiety and one's own needs, the message sent may not be the same message that is received. If one person is not sure what the other means, he may ask for clarification by saying, "Do you mean———?", "What I hear you saying is———. Is that right?" or, "What does 'it' refer to?" Sometimes, putting what another person has said into one's own words, and saying these words back to the original speaker, can help clarify for both parties what the first speaker was trying to say. Doing this exercise for each thought expressed by each party in a conversation would take up an extraordinary amount of time, and would probably confuse rather than clarify. But if a particular statement is difficult for the listener to grasp, putting it into his own words *out loud* can save time and confusion in the long run.

COMMUNICATION IN THE FAMILY

Because of the nature of the family, communication between family members has some special characteristics.

Roles and Expectations

The kind of communication that exists in a family is intimately bound up with the kinds of roles and expectations in the family. In a family in which the members relate to each other mostly in accordance with the status of each member, the members will communicate in a much more restricted way than will families in which the members relate as persons [4, pp. 95–96]. If a person's role is clearly set out for him, then his relationship to other people does not have to be discussed. If the father makes all the decisions about how the family will function, and the other family members accept him as the decision-maker, he will do more talking than listening. Thus, if a family is more *status-oriented* than *person-oriented,* then members are treated according to the positions they occupy. A child is supposed to act in certain ways simply because he is a child, and very often those role prescriptions include being obedient, polite, and quiet. The eldest child may be required to mind the younger ones and wash the dishes simply because he or she is the eldest. Likewise, a wife has her slot to fill and a husband his.

In status-oriented families, children, in particular, are not permitted to express their feelings. When the child in this kind of a family asks why he must do something or may not do something, he is more likely to be told, "Because I said so," rather than be given an explanation. Such an explanation does nothing to clarify for the child the reason an act is demanded or forbidden, but it does clarify for the child what his relationship to his parent is and who is more powerful.

In contrast, the person-oriented family makes opportunities for each member to act as a unique person. The feelings of each member are important to the others, as means of understanding and planning appropriate actions for each. Person-oriented families carry on much discussion. Everyone talks and everyone listens.

Honesty

"Open and honest communication" seem to be bywords of the young generation. Turned off by what they see as hypocrisy in their parents, many young people want to do away with what their parents see as tact and good taste. Having taken an introductory course on counseling skills, James decided that he should tell his parents that he was having sexual relations with Maria, whom he wanted to marry. To James and Maria, their sexual experiences together were good, and terribly important. James' instructor had stressed the importance of honesty in communication. Therefore, when James went home from college, he told his parents about himself and Maria, and let them read some passionate letters that Maria had written to him.

Instead of loving Maria as much as James did, his parents were horrified. To his parents, Maria was a slut. Girls who have intercourse before marriage could be nothing else. The marriage of James and Maria has done nothing to change their opinion of Maria.

James later realized his mistake. Honesty does not always require that hurtful realities be laid bare. James' and Maria's sexual relationship was not something that his parents needed to know. The knowledge wounded his parents, and their rejection of Maria hurt her very much.

Honest and Direct Questions. The issue of honesty is concerned not only with the kind of answers one gives but with the kinds of questions that one asks. An honest question is one to which the person asked can respond without penalty. A dishonest question, in turn, must be answered the way the asker wishes, or the person asked will be penalized in some way. For example, if a person asks me, "Do you mind if I smoke?" and I respond, "Yes, I do," and the smoker gets annoyed or lights up anyway, he asked a dishonest question. Dishonest questions unfortunately are very much a part of our everyday life. The words "Do you mind if . . ." very frequently preceed a dishonest question. Other examples are, "Are you busy?" "Is it all right if we are half an hour late for dinner?" "May we bring the children?" The person asking a dishonest question often has an answer in mind [20].

Related to honest and dishonest questions are direct and indirect questions. A direct question "asks it like it is"—there is no hidden meaning. "Would you like to have dinner with me Saturday night?" is a direct question. An indirect counterpart, so frequently used, is "What are you doing Saturday night?" The problem with an indirect question is that the listener can never be sure what is really on the asker's mind. If a husband asks his wife, "Are you tired tonight?" when he really wants to know if she would like to make love, the wife can't be sure whether her husband is really concerned whether or not she is tired, or if he has something else on his mind watching the late show? going out for a drink?).

Communication Codes

It is possible for a group of people to develop an elaborate code that is mutually understandable. For instance, the Lacey family has a hospitality code that can result in sadly overstuffed guests among those who do not understand. Conversations like these are common:

> Mrs. Lacey: Do have some more strawberry shortcake.
> Harriet: No, thank you.
> Mrs. Lacey: Oh come on. You had such a small piece to start with.
> Harriet: Really, I've had plenty.
> Mrs. Lacey: I'll think you don't like my shortcake!
> Harriet: You make the best strawberry shortcake of anyone I know, and I just love it. But I simply can't eat another bite.
> Mrs. Lacey: Oh, all right Harriet. Now Horace, let me give you some.
> Horace: No thanks, Mrs. Lacey.
> Mrs. Lacey: Why Horace, you had such a small first course. I thought surely you would like the dessert.
> Horace: I've had plenty of everything, thank you.
> Mrs. Lacey: Surely a big man like you can eat more than such a small dinner. Let me give you just a sliver.
> Horace: Well, all right, just a wee bit.

Harriet obviously understood the code and Horace did not. Mrs. Lacey had to keep pushing food until she had exhausted all possibilities of having the guests accept more. She may even have hoped that there would be a piece left for tomorrow, but hospitality required her to make sure that her guests were not refusing from politeness rather than satiation. Harriet properly reassured Mrs. Lacey that she was a marvelous cook and hostess. Horace, not understanding the true meaning of Mrs. Lacey's comments, did not elaborate enough on his pleasures, satisfaction, and approval concerning the meal. For his ignorance of the code, Horace was punished by an overloaded stomach.

Planned Communication

Fruitful communication requires *respect* for the other person's integrity and feelings.

Ben Ard, a marriage counselor, underscores the need for careful communication between parents and children, and others who are close to one another. He writes:

> In many serious marital discussions, considerate, thoughtful, and even planned communication can frequently be more helpful than merely saying whatever one "feels" like saying. When important matters are being discussed between married couples, I would go so far as to suggest . . . that some thought be given to the questions raised, to possible alternative positions and why one "feels" the way one does. I have even suggested something akin to "position papers" being written out before an important discussion (e.g., whether or not to get a divorce, or have another child, or indulging in a bit of wife-swapping, or moving one's mother-in-law into the family home, or moving to another state, etc.) [1]

Too frequently people treat those close to them in a way in which they would not treat an acquaintance or a stranger. Intimacy is seen as a license to be rude or cruel in the guise of honesty. The harried mother, who has asked her child many times to clean her room, finally explodes in anger: "Why do I have such a slob for a daughter? Your room is always a pig pen!" This kind of character defamation is not likely to motivate the child to change her habits. If a guest breaks a dish, a hostess will usually respond (perhaps untruthfully) that the guest shouldn't worry; it is nothing. But the same woman, when her child breaks a dish, accuses the child of carelessness.

Miller, et. al. [22a] point out that honest and skillful communication is not sufficient for the building and maintaining of relationships. A person can use communication skillfully with the intent of damaging her partner's self esteem. Esteem for self and partner is built when each partner takes responsibility for what she says, how she says it, and in which context. Each partner also needs to be in control of the way he responds to what the other partner says. According to Miller, et. al., "This is a critical choice point which, over time, distinguishes esteem building partnerships from esteem diminishing relationships."

Timing of communication is important. Children learn at a young age to make requests of their parents at times advantageous to the child. When the parent is busy and doesn't want to be bothered by the child, the parent is likely to say "yes" to a request that will keep the child occupied. When tired and hungry, it is usually best to avoid topics of discussion that are likely to cause disagreement, unless one wants a fight! A particular time of day may be an impossible time for a certain individual to communicate effectively; for example, before breakfast. Nonverbal cues are important aids to determining a time for fruitful communication. The slamming of a door that is usually closed gently can alert the listener to the possibility that the person entering or leaving is in a bad mood. A furrowed brow, slumped shoulders, or a frown can signal that now is not the best time to begin discussion of certain topics.

Handling Disagreements

Unnecessary blowups can be avoided through the use of tact and good timing. Conflict and disagreements are not always harmful to relationships, and, in fact, may be necessary for continued growth in the relationship. Some couples who remain married to each other even seem to thrive on continued conflict [7]. One of our students, when asked why people live in families, replied with a sparkle in her eye, "So they'll have someone to fight with."

Bach and Wyden wrote a book devoted to the subject of marital fighting. They maintain that since fighting is inevitable in marriage, couples might as well learn to do it effectively [2]. What they are really talking about, however, is communication in marriage, more than fighting. Disagreements are inevitable between people who are truly intimate and can be used to deepen the relationship and the intimacy. Problems and disagreements should be aired regularly, and not stored away in a "gunny sack" and later dumped upon the hapless partner when the burden becomes too great. Bach and Wyden recommend honesty during marital "fights." However, when extramarital sex, real or fantasized, is discussed, they recommend that extreme tact be used.

Marital Adjustment

A number of studies have indicated that communication is positively related to marital adjustment [12, 14, 19, 23]. A recent study found that high marital satisfaction was reported by couples who used high disclosure in their communication [6a]. However, there is some evidence to the contrary; that is, that for some couples free communication is not necessary for marital adjustment, or that it can be detrimental to adjustment [8]. In her intensive study of working-class families in the 1950s, Komarovsky found that her subjects did not expect or desire communication between marital partners. Because her respondents believed that men and women were unable to communicate effectively, they were not distressed by the lack of deep, honest communication with their partners [17].

From reports of college students of behavior of their parents Straus found that "gut-level communication" between spouses was associated with *more* rather than less physical violence. However, couples who used a "rational" approach to verbal communication (similar to what we have called planned communication) were less likely to resort to physical violence. Rational communication was found to be even more important for working-class couples than for middle-class couples [28].

The amount of communication necessary for good marital adjustment, and its revealingness and honesty, depends upon the expectations and desires of the people involved. Wendy and Charlie have a mutual understanding concerning their extramarital affairs. Wendy is aware that Charlie has had them from time to time and she accepts his need for them, as long as he spares her any direct knowledge of them. Charlie doesn't want to know about Wendy's extramarital adventures, either. For Charlie and Wendy, open discussion of extramarital interests is too threatening to dwell upon. Each accepts the other's need for outside relationships as a matter of right, but does not want to know about them. For some couples, this kind of agreement would be impossible, either because extramarital relationships are taboo, or silence about them is taboo.

As our readers must know by now, we have strong personal values concerning communication between married partners. We believe that deep communication is necessary for pair intimacy and for the growth of partners as a pair and as individuals.

Tactile Communication

Verbal communication is not the only important kind of communication between marriage partners and others in close relationships. Sensual or tactile communication can be an important vehicle for the communication of positive feelings. Nonsexually oriented touching—the stroking of a cheek, a hug, a hand clasp—can be a source of strength for a downcast mate or friend. Sexual intercourse and the accompanying lovemakings are often a way to express love and closeness. The amount of and importance of tactile communication vary tremendously among couples and families, and by ethnic group and nationality. The roots of tactile communication seem to be deeply embedded within the human spirit, if one accepts the idea that the human being shares many characteristics of the lower primates.

> Tactile communication plays a major part in primate life. . . . Mothers carry the young for long periods on their bodies. Adults frequently sit or even sleep together in furry clumps. Above all, primates groom each other. [13, p. 153]

> There is a huge repertoire of patting and nuzzling lumped as greeting behavior—as well as the agonistic contact of cuffs and bites and even kicks. Chimpanzees, particularly, pat each other's hands, faces, and groins, lay a hand on each other's backs in reassurance, and kiss in affection. [13, p. 155]

PHOTO BY DONNA J. HARRIS, THE MERRILL-PALMER INSTITUTE

Childrearing

The kind of communication used in a family will have a profound effect upon a child growing up in it. The language spoken will shape the child's reality. Although it is possible for a human being to learn without knowing any verbal language, the use of the language is extremely important in human learning.

Parents need to have an idea of their child's level of comprehension, which is related to her age and experiences. A young child may not be able to understand something that is clear to her older sibling or to her parents. If a child does not understand what is being said to her, the adult speaker should rephrase the statement or request in more simple, concrete terms. This does not mean that ''baby talk'' should be used, or that more complex words should not be introduced as the child becomes ready to grasp them. The parent needs to be alert to whether or not the child has grasped the meaning of what was said [9].

Communication patterns in the family are intimately bound up with the kind of expectations family members have for one another, and with the kind of people existing in a family. The parent of a small child has a great deal of power over the child, by virtue of his being an adult. Within certain legal limits, the parent has the right to shape his child's behavior by any means that he wishes. If the child does something that the parent does not like, he can ignore the act, or reprimand the child nonverbally (by withdrawing affectionate attention from the child, or leaving her physically); verbally (by calmly talking with the child and explaining her transgression); rebuke the child; threaten her; or punish her (hitting, whipping, spanking, and so on).

Physical punishment is a form of communication: It communicates displeasure or anger from the giver to the receiver. Rewards may also be given through communication, both verbally and nonverbally. Telling a child when he has done a good job helps the child to feel positively about himself and his abilities. The use of reasoning (verbal communication) has been found to increase the effectiveness of accompanying physical punishment [24].

The child who is given information about the cause and effect of what she has done will be more able to transfer her learning to similar situations. In other words, reasoning with a child helps her to control her own behavior in the future, instead of having to rely on external punishment (a tongue-lashing or a spanking from a parent, for example). Reasoning alone, without some kind of negative sanction, does not help the child to develop socially responsible behavior as effectively as does reasoning that occurs with some kind of punishment. The punishment does *not* have to be physical, however [2a].

If a delay occurs between the misdeed and the punishment, the punishment will be more effective if the misdeed is described to the child when the punishment is given [30]. Therefore, if a child has to wait "until father gets home" for her punishment, mother would do well to explain the misdeed to father in front of the child.

Popular literature as well gives support to the idea that reasoning with the child increases the parent's effectiveness in socializing the child. Harris, the author of *I'm O.K., You're O.K.*, recommends rational discussion, paying attention to the facts involved [11a]. Although it differs in content from that of Harris, Gordon's book *Parent Effectiveness Training* also underscores the importance of reasoning with a child [9a]. Instead of jumping to conclusions about what a child has done, a parent should listen acceptingly to what the child has to say, and encourage the child to explore his feelings. Both Harris and Gordon are therapists who have developed programs for working with parents and children.

How early can parents start using reasoning with their children? Common sense suggests that before a child can understand explanations, the use of them will be ineffective. Punishment may possibly be effective in controlling the behavior of the young child who continues to play in the street in spite of being told not to. A very young child, however, is capable of inhibiting her own behavior after she has been told not to do something. Becky at 11 months was a very active child who vigorously explored her environment. She crept up to a Christmas tree and reached for an ornament hanging a few inches away from her head. Her mother said, "No, Becky." Becky stopped reaching. And until the Christmas tree was taken down a few days later, Becky did not touch the ornaments or the tree. She would approach the tree and stare at the shiny ornaments, but she did not touch them.

Why did one firm "no" from Becky's mother inhibit Becky from touching an attractive, available object for a period of several days? A study by Stayton, Hogan, and Ainsworth suggests an explanation [27]. Of 25 white middle-class infants age nine to twelve months, those infants whose mothers were most sensitive to their needs, and who were accepting the infant and cooperative with him, were most able to comply with the commands and prohibitions of the mothers. A few of the more intelligent babies who had been given freedom to explore their environments and whose mothers were responsive to their needs also showed evidence of having internalized controls, as Becky had. In other words, if the mother is concerned with the needs of the infant in her daily interactions with him, the infant will respond more readily to prohibition placed upon him by the mother. The authors suggest that it is not punishment that inhibits undesirable behavior at this early age but the infant's trust that the mother is looking out for his best interests. The infant develops this trust to a high degree only if the mother behaves in specific ways toward the infant, communicating to the infant that the mother respects his needs to a reasonable degree.

There is evidence that thirteen years later, when the child is a young teen-ager, the same principles operate. In a study of fourteen-to-sixteen-year-old males, it was found that boys whose mothers discussed their sons' misdeeds with them, seeking the boy's explanation before deciding whether or not to punish, were more able to resist temptation in an experimental situation [17a]. Allowing the child a chance to discuss the infraction and possible reasons for it apparently made the punishment more legitimate in the eyes of the child, and therefore more effective in curbing prohibited behavior in subsequent situations.

The self-esteem of adolescents was shown in another study to be related to family communication patterns when parents, as well as boys and girls of fourteen and fifteen, answered questions about parent-adolescent communication, marital communication, and adjustment. Adolescents with high self-esteem reported significantly more effective communication with mothers and fathers than did adolescents with low self-esteem. In addition, the parents of high self-esteem adolescents saw themselves as communicating better with each other than did the other parents, and also rated their marriages as more satisfying [21]. The study suggests that within the family, positive interpersonal skills are associated with positive individual development and interpersonal adjustment. The topic of discipline is elaborated upon in Chapter 10, pp. 260–265.

OTHER USES FOR COMMUNICATION

Processing

Not only do people need to communicate with others; they need to communicate with themselves. Sometimes, the two uses of communication may be fused, and at other times, separated. Frequently, when I (LSS) am confused about my feelings about a particular person at a particular time, I write what I call an "imaginary letter" to the person. I try to express all of my feelings on paper, pretending that I am going to send the letter to the person, but knowing that I will not. Putting the words down on paper helps me to clarify what I feel, and frequently when I read the letter over a few times the feelings of stress and confusion go away. While pretending to communicate with another person, I hold a deep conversation with myself. A diary may serve the same purpose as an "imaginary letter."

At other times, a person may need to talk about a problem with other people, not so much for the purpose of conveying the information to someone else, but in order to sort things out much as I do when I write "imaginary letters." Talking about a problem helps the speaker to clarify what happened that is now troubling him. It may be hard for the person with the problem to put a sequence of events in order in his mind and attach labels to the feelings that the events evoked. Talking to another person who listens acceptingly can begin this sorting-out process.

Even thinking, or talking to oneself, can be helpful in processing events and feelings. A person who cannot communicate adequately within himself—that is, label his own feelings and be honest with himself about what he is thinking and feeling—will have a hard time communicating with those outside himself. The young child talks to himself out loud, and gradually he becomes able to talk silently to himself—to think [29, pp. 16–24].

Tension Release

When a person feels angry, an outpouring of angry words can sometimes release some of the tension. If angry feelings are not released through words or action, but kept inside, they may intensify in a spiral of emotion.

> Emotionally poisoned speech often floods through our being in waves. We seldom say, "Oh, how I hate him" just once to ourselves; we say it again and again. We almost hypnotize ourselves with the refrain. Like Tam O'Shanter's wife, we "nurse our wrath to keep it warm." The circling statements intensify as they spiral. Irritation turns to anger and anger into fury as the hypnotic self-suggestion dulls our critical powers. . . . [5, p. 24]

A vocal expression of anger can serve as a tension release.

In a study done on a college campus, a thousand samples of emotionally toned utterances were collected by students in dormitories. Over 70 per cent of them expressed anger. Slightly more than 10 per cent reflected anxiety. One per cent expressed guilt, and 19 per cent had to do with happy or joyful experiences. Rather than indicating that college students feel angry 70 per cent of the time, the findings in this survey indicate that it is more acceptable to express negative, angry feelings than it is to express other feelings in our culture. These angry feelings were most frequently expressed in terms of ejaculations rather than verbalizations. Subjects showed anger more through cries or groans than in words. "Even the curses were colorless, trite, and without real meaning or pertinence . . ." [5, pp. 24–25]. If the angry *words* meant little, how, then, did the researchers get such a clear picture of anger? From the cries, groans, and accompanying gestures. These human behavior patterns are understood universally. They are more primitive than words, less intellectual, more emotional, emitted spontaneously, and understood immediately.

Straus's findings, however, caution us concerning the use of angry words within the family as a tension release. Since he found that uncensored outpourings were associated with violence in the family [28], we suggest that it is a safer, more effective release to sound off to a disinterested party who can be trusted not to tell. Blowing up in front of the source of one's frustration can lead to more conflict. It is better to wait until the subject can be discussed rationally.

An alternative way of expressing angry feelings to one's partner is to make a "contract" that it is all right to let feelings come out in an uncensored form. When Tasha is angry at Jake, she sometimes will say to him, "What I want to say to you isn't entirely rational. I would like your permission to tell you how I feel, and then I'll try to sort things out." Not all couples would find Jake and Tasha's way of handling angry feelings to be acceptable or helpful. In order for this method to work, it is essential that both partners feel that it is acceptable.

Discovery of Others

It is through communication that one learns about other people, and in so doing, learns more about himself. Communication is an antidote to isolation and loneliness.

> Communication . . . has a creative power. It gives self-awareness to each speaker in the reciprocal relation with the other. . . . Each . . . recognizes the other and receives from him that same recognition without which human experience is impossible. For, reduced to himself, man is much less than himself; whereas, in the light of openness to the other, the possibility of unlimited growth is offered to him. [10, pp. 67–68]

It is through the exchange of information that people get to know each other in the first place, and if the relationship is to continue to grow, communication must continue. Letters to "Dear Abby" from socially unsure individuals ask the question, "How do I get to know———?" The reply is, "Take an interest in him (her)." Get the person talking about himself.

There must be a certain amount of reciprocity in such communication, however. I (LSS) spent the evening with a young woman who would tell me nothing of personal interest about herself, although she was skilled in keeping me talking. When a pause would come, I would try to find out some information about her, but she would cleverly turn things around and get me talking once more. The one-sided flow of information was apparently comfortable for her, but it was not for me.

Defining a Relationship

Related to the discovery of others is the use of communication to define a relationship. When two people begin interacting, they have a wide choice of behaviors from which to choose. The kinds of behaviors they select will define the kind of relationship that develops. The "agreement" concerning the kind of relationship is in a constant process of development [11]. One does, however, get clues concerning how she should interact with another person from the way he dresses (a postman's or nurse's uniform, faded blue jeans and t-shirt, a conservative business suit), or wears his hair, or the way he speaks (his accent and grammatical structure), his skin color, and so on. Some of these clues put the individual in a particular category that is more reliable than others: the uniform of a postman or nurse clearly identifies a role for us about which we have certain expectations that are more likely to be proven correct. When in uniform, certain behaviors can be expected from these individuals in relation to others. For a religious ceremony, one goes to a priest or minister; if injured, one calls a nurse or a doctor.

> The roles and status of receivers and senders in a network of communication indicate to the participants how a message ought to be interpreted. . . . In communication theory, therefore, roles have a double function: they identify the participants, and they represent silent messages about communication which constitute instructions of the receiver to the sender about the way he should be addressed and from the sender to the receiver about the way his message ought to be interpreted. [25, p. 223]

The role and status of a person with whom we are communicating help us to interpret what the person is saying, and help us know how to respond. We get an idea of whether the conversation is one between equals, or between unequals; of how similar we are to the other person; and of how intimate the communication should be. Nonverbal as well as verbal communication plays a part here. Jones is sitting in his office with his feet on his desk, smoking a cigarette as he looks over an intraoffice memorandum. A man walks in. Jones keeps his feet on the desk, and says, "Hi, Charlie, have a chair." Is Charlie of the same or lower status as Jones, or a higher status?

Control

Communication is also used to manipulate and control others. The child learns this quite early in life: when he cries, someone will usually attend to him. Later, when he learns how to use words, he has even a greater tool with which to control the actions of others. Instead of crying in order to get a drink of milk, he says the word *milk*—and milk is given to him. A bit later in his life, his mother asks him if he would like to go outside, and he says "No"—not because he doesn't want to go out, but merely to have control of the situation. Words have a magical quality, because they give him a power far beyond his small size.

Most people are not aware of how often they use speech to control or persuade others. Some control speech is a part of most human interactions. Any request that is made has the potential of controlling. The tone of voice, or nonverbal behaviors accompanying speech, can influence the behavior of the listener. At the more extreme end, speech can be used to whip up strong feelings, such as political speeches or sermons. Control speech can be used for good or ill [5].

SUMMARY Essential on many levels, communication is important in love relationships and thus in marriage and family relations. The child is socialized as parents and other people communicate to him in in the context of their culture. The language used constitutes a particular interpretation of reality.

Communication is basic to social adaptation, permitting both change and stability. The more rapid the change taking place, the greater is the need for communication between people in the society. Partnership roles between men and women undergo social change and thus require increased communication in order to maintain the relationship.

Communication involves sending and receiving verbal and nonverbal messages. Nonverbal (neither spoken nor written) messages include facial expression, looking behavior, gestures, posture, and other aspects of physical appearance, as well as tone of voice. Symbols are shared carriers of meaning that may be understood by a group or privately by a pair or a few people.

Congruent messages are messages that agree. Sometimes verbal and nonverbal messages are incongruent, making it difficult for the receiver to know just what the sender meant. Sometimes the sender is not aware that he is sending incongruent messages. When he communicates, a person is sending a message about what he thinks is real. The recipient may be confused because he has a different interpretation of reality. Confusion may come from an individual's thinking that all other people share his values or that an interpretation he has made is true for all people. Sometimes people assume that they can read each other's minds.

Communication is complicated, since many messages are sent and received in one social encounter. Thus, there may be confusion in the sending, in sorting what is sent and also in distractions arising within the recipient. Anxiety and fear and preoccupation interfere with the individual's ability to receive the messages that others are trying to send. Communication can be made more effective when the listener uses empathy. Then he imagines himself into the place of the other person but still remembers that he is himself. In contrast, in feeling strong sympathy, a person may lose his sense of self. Nonlistening is another detriment to communication. A speaker can tell when the other person is really listening by the attentive expression on his face and by his not interrupting, as well as by comments that show he is trying to understand. Communication is improved when participants try to clarify their interpretations.

The role orientation of a family strongly influences the kinds of communication patterns that develop. Less effort is required when status and role determine interaction; more communication is needed when each family member is regarded as a unique person. Honesty does not always require the *whole* truth, since other considerations must also be weighed. Questions, as well as answers, can be either honest or dishonest, depending upon the intention. Sometimes a communication code appears dishonest to an outsider but is, in reality, understood by the participants. Positive communication involves respect as well as honesty. Family members may fail to respect each other's feelings, often because they do not plan the content and timing of what they are trying to communicate. Disagreements can be used constructively to deepen understanding. The depth of communication required for marital success depends upon the couple's expectations of marriage and of each other.

Tactile communication is a mode of expressing feelings within the family and among people who are close to each other.

In the context of childrearing, communication is used for teaching and learning. Communication style is related to what family members expect of each other.

Communication with oneself promotes self-knowledge, as well as problem-solving. Tension and angry feelings can be released through words and perhaps even more, through vocal and nonverbal expression. Self-knowledge increases with deepening knowledge of others, the reciprocal process of communication contributing to both. Responding and caring are aspects of this process. Communication is also used to define roles and to control people and situations.

REFERENCES

1. Ard, Ben N., Jr. Communication in marriage. *Rational Living,* 1971, **5,** 220–22.
2. Bach, George and Peter Wyden. *The intimate enemy.* New York: Morrow, 1968.
2a. Baumrind, Diana. Socialization and instrumental competence in young children. 1970, **26,** 16–37.
3. Birdwhistell, Ray L. *Kinesics and context: Essays on body motion communication.* Philadelphia, U. of Pa., 1970.
4. Britton, James. *Language and learning.* London: Penguin Books, 1970.
5. Brown, Charles T. and Charles Van Riper. *Speech and man.* Englewood Cliffs, N.J.: Prentice-Hall, 1966.
6. Brownfield, E. Dorothy. Communication: Key to family interaction. *Marriage and Family Living,* 1953, **15,** 316–319.
6a. Corrales, Ramon. The influence of family's life cycle categories, marital power, spousal agreement, and communication styles upon marital satisfaction in the first six years of marriage. Unpublished doctoral dissertation, University of Minnesota, 1974. Cited in Sherod Miller, Ramon Corrales and Daniel Wackman. Recent progress in understanding and facilitating marital communication. *Family Coordinator,* 1975, **24,** 143–152.
7. Cuber, John and Peggy Harroff. *The significant Americans.* New York: Appleton, 1965.
8. Cutler, Beverly and William Dyer. Initial adjustment processes in young married couples. *Social Forces,* 1965, **44,** 195–201.

9. DeForest, Edgar. Communication in the family. *Journal of Communication*. 1957, **7,** 103–110.

9a. Gordon, Thomas. *Parent effectiveness training.* New York: Wyden, 1970.

10. Gusdorf, Georges. *Speaking.* Evanston, Ill.: Northwestern U. P., 1965.

11. Haley, Jay. An interactional description of schizophrenia. In Don Jackson (ed.). *Communication, family and marriage.* Palo Alto, Calif.: Science and Behavior Books, 1968.

11a. Harris, Thomas. *I'm O.K., you're O.K.* New York: Avon, 1973.

12. Hobart, Charles and William Klausner. Some social interactional correlates of marital role disagreements and marital adjustment. *Marriage and Family Living,* 1959, **21,** 256–263.

13. Jolly, Alison. *The evolution of primate behavior.* New York: Macmillan, 1972.

14. Karlsson, Georg. *Adaptability and communication in marriage.* Totowa, N.J.: Bedminster Press, 1963.

15. Katz, Robert, cited in Charles T. Brown and Charles Van Riper. *Speech and man.* Englewood Cliffs, N.J.: Prentice-Hall, 1966.

16. Keller, Helen. *The story of my life.* New York: Grosset, 1904.

17. Komarovsky, Mirra. *Blue-collar marriage.* New York: Random, 1962.

17a. LaVoie, Joseph C. and William R. Looft. Parental antecedents of resistance-to-temptation behavior in adolescent males. *Merrill-Palmer Quarterly,* 1973, **19,** 109–116.

18. Lederer, William J. and Don D. Jackson. *The mirages of marriage.* New York: Norton, 1968.

19. Locke, Harvey, Georges Sabagh, and Mary Margaret Thomes. Correlates of primary communication in empathy. *Research Studies of the State College of Washington,* 1956, **24,** 116–124.

20. Madsen, C. cited in David Knox. *Marriage happiness: A behavioral approach to counseling.* Champaign, Ill.: Research Press, 1972.

21. Matteson, Roberta. Adolescent self-esteem, family communication, and marital satisfaction. *Journal of Psychology,* 1974, **86,** 35–47.

22. Mehrabian, A. *Silent messages.* Belmont, Calif.: Wadsworth, 1971.

22a. Miller, Sherod, Ramon Corrales and Daniel Wackman. Recent progress in understanding and facilitating marital communication. *Family Coordinator,* 1975, **24,** 143–152.

23. Navran, Leslie. Communication and adjustment in marriage. *Family Process,* 1967, **6,** 173–184.

24. Parke, Ross D. Effectiveness of punishment as an interaction of intensity, timing, age, nurturance, and cognitive structuring. *Child Development,* 1969, **40,** 213–235.

25. Reusch, Jurgen. Synopsis of the theory of human communication. *Psychiatry,* 1953, **16,** 215–243.

26. Satir, Virginia. *Conjoint family therapy.* Palo Alto, Calif.: Science and Behavior Books, 1967.

27. Stayton, Donelda, Robert Hogan and Mary D. S. Ainsworth. Infant obedience and maternal behavior: The origins of socialization reconsidered. *Child Development,* 1971, **42,** 1057–1069.

28. Straus, Murray. Leveling, civility and violence in the family. *Journal of Marriage and the Family,* 1974, **36,** 13–29.

29. Vygotsky, Lev S. *Thought and language.* Cambridge: The M.I.T. Press, 1962.

30. Walters, R. H. and D. Andres. Cited in Ross Parke. Social development and interpersonal relationships. *Young Children,* 1968, **24,** 225–240.

31. *Webster's seventh collegiate dictionary.* Springfield, Mass.: Merriam, 1965.

CHAPTER 4

This GROWS ON YOU: SEX

Males and females are not exactly alike. Just how much they differ, and whether these differences are innate, learned, or both, is a hotly debated subject today. Some people believe that all sex differences are predetermined by biology or God; others believe that all sex differences beyond the anatomical are learned. There is much argument, even among those who believe that the differences between the sexes develop from the interaction of heredity and environment.

In this chapter and the next, we describe the sexual development and behavior of the individual, both female and male, and explain some of the known differences and similarities between them. We have chosen a predominantly chronological sequence in organizing these chapters. We hope to show the amazing complexity of the processes that interact to make an individual male or female.

Because prenatal development and sexual anatomy may be unfamiliar to some students, we explain these very briefly in Appendix B.

PRENATAL SEXUAL DIFFERENTIATION

Although each new individual is "programmed" from conception to become either male or female, the developmental process is subject to error. In the vast majority of cases, the individual who is genetically male is easily recognized as male at birth, and likewise with the female. We include a very brief, simplified discussion of sexual *anomalies* (abnormalities) in order to show the delicate balance that initially determines maleness or femaleness.

Prior to the sixth week of prenatal development, the male and female sex glands or **gonads** are the same, or undifferentiated. The undifferentiated gonad of the early **embryo** consists of a rind and a core, and at this stage it is impossible to tell the difference between a male and female embryo by looking at it. Around the sixth week, however, in the XX embryo the rind begins to develop into an **ovary,** and the core becomes vestigial. At the same time in the case of the XY embryo, the core becomes a **testis** (plural: testes, also known as testicles) and the rind becomes vestigial [24].

At about eight weeks, the embryo has developed into what is called a **fetus.** Until birth this organism cannot be identified as a male or female without analyzing the chromosomes to determine whether or not the fetus' chromosomes bear a Y chromosome. During the third month of prenatal development, differentiation of the external sexual organs takes place. The male's testes produce **testosterone,** the predominantly male hormone. Under the influence of this hormone, the male's external genitals develop. If the testosterone level is very low, as in the case of the normal female fetus, female external genitals and the female duct system, through which the egg will eventually pass, develop.

Although in most cases an individual who is genetically male is born with male genitalia (a penis, scrotum, and testes), and the genetically female individual is born with female genitalia (a vulva, vagina, uterus, and ovaries), the process sometimes goes awry. If for some reason the male fetus does not produce testosterone, his gonads will differentiate as female and he will be born looking like a female, although he will be sterile. If the female fetus is in contact with male hormones, as happened in the 1950s when pregnant women were given progestin (a male hormone) to prevent miscarriage, she will be born with external male genitals, and normal, unaffected female internal organs. Masculinization of a genetic female may also occur as the result of a genetic defect that causes the fetus' adrenal gland to produce too much testosterone. The fetus in this case also is born with male-like external organs but normal female internal organs [8]. Both conditions require surgical correction, since menstruation will occur when the child reaches puberty. The individual who suffers from an overactive adrenal gland requires lifelong hormonal treatment, in addition to early surgery.

Although the most dramatic influence of the presence or absence of testosterone on the growing fetus is the development of male or female genitals, there is evidence that brain organization is also affected [7, 15].

PHYSICALLY BASED SEX DIFFERENCES

More males are conceived than females (120 males per 100 females), but males have a higher mortality rate from conception on than do females. For every 110 males born, 100 females are born. But for every 106 live male births, there are 100 live female births. Throughout life the male's higher vulnerability to disease slowly chips

away at this ratio. By age 60 or 70, women exceed men in prosperous countries. In environments of extreme poverty, childbirth takes a great toll of women.

At birth, males as a group are heavier and longer than females as a group, but they are less developed. A newborn female functions as maturely as a four-to-six-week-old boy. At puberty, the average girl's growth is about two years ahead of the average boy: her bones ossify earlier. Girls learn to walk and talk before boys do. The male newborn exhibits more spontaneous movement, consisting of larger bodily movements than the female, whose movements are finer, concentrating around the facial area [15].

Sex differences in brain organization have been demonstrated in children and adults by tests of differential use of the right and left hemispheres. Boys and men, as compared with girls and women, make more use of the right hemisphere in processing spatial information. Women are more likely to use some of the verbal processing system, located in the left hemisphere, when they try to solve spatial problems. On the average, females are more fluent then males, suggesting more use of the left hemisphere [19]. However, these sex differences in brain organization are only differences between group averages, and very slight differences at that. There are many women who exceed the average male score on spatial tests and many men who are more fluent than the average woman. In the case of most characteristics, individual differences are larger than group differences. Even with the timing of puberty, where the difference between the averages of boys and girls is larger (about two years), the range in timing in each sex is greater than the sex differences. Thus, 11-year-old John, who has reached puberty, and 14-year-old Gladys, who has not, are both normal. Figure 4-1 shows distributions of heights of boys and girls at ages 12 and 17. At 12, the girls' mean height is slightly greater than the boys', but there are still some girls who are shorter than the average boy. At 17, the boys' mean height exceeds the girls', but there are still some boys who are shorter than the average girl.

The important point in the discussion of genetic sex differences is that most of them overlap in distribution. Especially in the realm of psychological differences, the average differences between the sexes are so small that they are completely useless in predicting what any individual can do. There is thus no basis in reality for restricting women or men from any occupation on the grounds of sex differences.

FIGURE 4-1a   Frequency distribution of heights of a sample of 12-year-old American youths.

Source: Health Services and Mental Health Administration. Height and weight of youths 12–17 years. United States DHEW Publication No. (HSM) 73–1606. Rockville, Maryland: U.S. Department of Health, Education, and Welfare, 1973. Table 1.

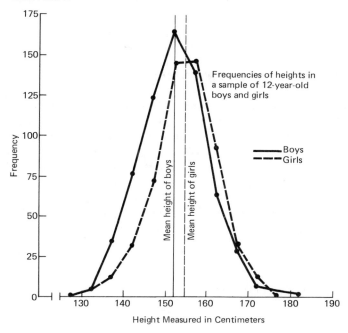

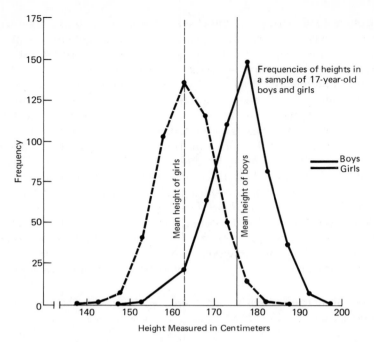

Figure 4-1b   Frequency distribution of height of a sample of 17-year-old American youths.

Source: Health Services and Mental Health Administration. Height and weight of youths 12–17 years. United States DHEW Publication No. (HSM) 73-1606. Rockville, Maryland: U.S. Department of Health, Education, and Welfare, 1973. Table 1.

INTERACTION OF ORGANISM AND ENVIRONMENT

The anatomical and behavioral differences that have been observed in very young infants account for a part of male-female differences in childhood and adulthood, but most certainly do not tell the whole story. Hormonal levels may influence behavior [15]. For example, a study of college women indicated that during the week preceding their menstrual periods, most of the women were least likely to feel self-confident and self-assured [23].

The environment interacts with the organism's genetic substructure, and may change it (or reinforce it) within a range. The child and its socializing agents influence each other from birth on. This point is elaborated in Chapter 10, on parent-child interaction.

GENDER-ROLE LEARNING IN CHILDHOOD

Only gradually does the young child become established as a boy or a girl, as he or she learns to feel, think, and act in these terms. Different theories have been developed to explain the process of gender-role learning. We first describe psycho-analytic theory briefly and then elaborate more on social learning theory, since to us the latter seems to explain more. The two theories do not really contradict each other and may even complement each other. Our presentation of the theories does not mean that we believe that either is totally correct. Psychoanalytic theory especially has been under attack by many social scientists. The fact remains, however, that it has been a tremendous influence upon the thought of social scientists and the public as well.

Psychoanalytic Theory

According to psychoanalytic theory, the infant begins life seeking pleasure through his mouth (through suckling). The first year of life is called the *oral* stage, and both male and female infants have as their love object their mother. However, the infant cannot at this stage distinguish himself from his mother, whom he views rather as an extension of himself. Around the beginning of the second year, the child becomes focused upon the anus and eliminatory functions as a source of pleasure (the *anal* stage). During this stage the child must learn to control his elimination of urine and feces. Beginning around age three, the third stage is the *phallic* (from *phallus,* meaning penis) stage, when the child focuses upon his or her genitals as a source of pleasure.

It is during the phallic stage that the child has important experiences in regard to sex-role learning. The girl becomes aware that she has no penis, and the boy, noticing that females lack a penis, becomes fearful that he will lose his (the "castration complex": It is called this in spite of the fact that true castration does not involve the removal of the penis, but the removal of either male or female gonads). During the phallic stage the boy develops the Oedipus complex, and the girl develops the Electra complex: He or she sexually desires the opposite-sexed parent. For the boy, the Oedipus complex also involves a fear of his father, whom he thinks might harm him physically. The boy manages to overcome his fear of his father by identifying with him. The girl learns to substitute for her desire for a penis the wish for pregnancy and the child that results.

According to the theory, around age six the child's interest in sexuality drops off, and he enters the *latent* period that lasts until puberty. During this stage, the child is not interested in sex, nor is he interested in friends of the opposite sex. As the child begins to mature sexually, he enters the *genital* stage, when once again the pleasure zone becomes the genital area. During the genital stage, the child becomes interested in members of the opposite sex.

Social Learning Theory

A second theory of gender-role learning is social learning theory. The child learns appropriate feelings, thoughts, and behavior through interaction with other people, who instruct, reason, reinforce, and act as models. For the young child, parents are the most powerful of the social influences on gender-role learning. However, siblings are also important as are peers. Teachers and other adults also may have an effect.

Parents as Socializers. The first important milestone is the establishment of **gender identity.** The baby learns, "I am a boy" or "I am a girl." This piece of learning is normally a firm conviction. *Myself, a girl* or *myself, a boy* becomes incorporated into the self-concept. The lesson is so thoroughly learned by 18 months of age that when a mistaken sexual assignment needs to be corrected, authorities urge that it be done no later, and preferably several months earlier [22, p. 13].

Parents begin at the birth of their children to treat them differently, as boys or as girls. The differential treatment is due to both the behavior of the infant and to the parental perception of the child as male or female. Mothers and fathers do not consciously plan to teach their babies to feel like boys or girls. Parents themselves learned when they were very young that boys and girls are different in important ways and that they should be treated differently. Part of every cultural heritage is an interpretation of what it means to be male and female. When parents stray far from their culture's usual ways of teaching babies to regard themselves as male or female, those infants may grow up with some disturbance in gender identity. The classic example is the longed-for boy who turns out to be a girl but is treated as a boy, especially by the father. Her conviction of being a girl is likely to be weak.

Initial socializing for gender identity consists largely of speaking to and of the baby as *she* or *he,* attaching words and tones of approval to sex-defining terms (my good boy, our clever daughter). Dressing the child as a boy or girl probably contributes to the establishment of gender identity, but in the cultural context. In 1895, my (MSS) father and his peers went to kindergarten in Canada dressed in blouses and pleated skirts, their hair in curls. They apparently had no problems of gender identity, because everybody knew who was a boy and who was a girl, even though the current fashions did not differentiate between male and female clothes for young children.

As the child grows from infancy, parents continue to affirm gender identity, or, as it is also called, gender-role orientation. Theories of identification hold that young children strive to incorporate some of the essence of their parents into themselves, a process that is both conscious and unconscious. In acting and feeling as she (he) perceives her (his) mother (father) to feel, the child becomes more firmly a girl (boy). Different theories impute various motives to the child's efforts to imitate parents.

Parents call attention to the ways in which Sam looks and acts like Daddy and Katie looks and acts like Mommy. Older brothers and sisters or kin may also be held up as models for Sam and Katie. Many studies on father absence, summarized by Biller [3] indicate that fathers' influence on boys' gender-role orientation is profound. When fathers were absent or unavailable during the boys' first five years, and especially during the first two years, boys later showed less masculine self-concepts, as well as inadequate personalities in other aspects. Fathers also exert considerable influence on girls' gender-role orientation, as studies of father absence and unavailability have shown [3, pp. 110–114].

Research generally agrees that fathers are more interested and active than mothers in differentiating between boys and girls, seeing that each sex behaves appropriately [4]. Mothers seem merely to go along with fathers, supporting them in their efforts to make boys be boys and girls be girls. And so it is reasonable that father absence has a crucial effect on the child's gender-role development.

After the young child has established a firm gender identity, there is still much to do in sex-role development. *Gender-role adoption* is the acquiring of behavior patterns that are culturally accepted as sex-appropriate. Both parents, of course, define to children what is masculine and feminine behavior. They make it clear by what they *do,* as well as by words, rewards, and punishment, serving as models of male and female in clothing, grooming, coordination, tone of voice, work, play, interests, sensitivities, attitudes, and values. The parents' interactions with each other show children a powerful model of male-female interaction. The young child ordinarily goes along with much of what his parents ask of him. He incorporates some of the demonstrated behavior and rejects some, in favor of other models and other behavior that gratifies him more. Siblings, peers, and other adults are also models. In fact, preschool children's knowledge of culturally accepted adult male and female roles seems to be little affected by father absence, social class, race, and sex. Using appropriate pictures, young children were asked questions about who performed certain roles in a pretend family and in their own families. Father-absent children knew very well that fathers ordinarily earned wages, exerted power, and made decisions, even though they were not observing their own fathers doing so [1].

It is in *motivation* to use the knowledge that fathers exert special influence on children. Boys are generally pushed toward masculine gender-role adoption and preference for the male gender role by fathers who are warm, nurturant, and involved with the boy, and who are strong decision-makers [3].

An example of the meaning of these words was provided by a man who has written extensively about the father's role, Henry Biller [3, 3a]. He came to see us at the end of a working day, bringing his five-year-old son. Cameron had spent the whole day with Henry, playing in the office while his father worked. Cameron played with our blocks while we talked and then sat on his father's lap in blissful relaxation. Cameron told us that he had spent two days and two nights at a professional meeting with his father, eating meals with Henry and his colleagues and playing with other children, swimming and watching television while Henry worked. The Billers' two older sons also have turns going to meetings with Henry and the two-year-old has his special times, too. These boys not only see what their father does but they have a good time doing it. Each son has his father's full attention for long periods of time. Their father is not only a warm, nurturant male model but a reasoning, sharing, enjoying participant with the child.

A mother reinforces masculine behavior by direct approval and also by defining the father to the son as worthwhile, whether he be present or absent. Girls seem to be motivated to adopt gender-typed behavior by fathers who offer nurturance, acceptance, interaction, and approval for that behavior [11]. For instance, he tells her how attractive she looks in ruffles and smacks delightedly when she offers the cookies she made. Studies of father-absent girls suggest that the most important area of father influence is in the girl's relationships with the opposite sex. Father-absent adolescent girls have been found likely to show either sexual anxiety, shyness, and discomfort around males, or "promiscuous, inappropriately assertive behavior" with boys and men [14]. It seems that the father teaches the girl how to act in relation to men, and probably also how to feel in relation to men. Thus, both gender-role orientation and gender-role adoption are affected.

A woman's ability to attain orgasm seems to be related to her trust in the important men in her life. Since consistently orgasmic females were found likely to have had strong, stable fathers, it is likely that trust in their sexual partners was built upon early trust in their fathers [5].

Siblings and Other Kin. Gender-role learning is, of course, influenced by other family members, in addition to parents. A younger child is affected by the sex of the older siblings. When fathers are absent, older brothers' influence is likely to be heightened. (The teaching and learning functions of siblings is discussed further in the chapter on siblings.) In cases of father absence, a grandfather or an uncle sometimes takes on more responsibility with children, especially with boys. The purpose, of course, is to supply the male influence that seems to be essential for smooth gender-role development.

Teachers. Both purposefully and unintentionally, teachers also play a part in gender-role learning. Like everyone else, teachers have concepts of appropriate masculine and feminine behavior. They are also either men or women, chiefly women in North America. In all the other countries where we have worked and observed in schools, the proportion of men teachers was higher in the grades and high school. In nursery schools and kindergartens the world over, women are in charge. When fathers are absent, as they are from six or seven million American families, children have a highly feminine environment. Even when fathers come home at night, many or most are away all day, and few take their children for an occasional day at work with daddy. Therefore, both younger and older American children are likely to be under the influence of women much more than of men.

A nursery-school observational study revealed that young children are more likely to imitate teachers of their own sex. In the predominantly feminine school world, young girls can see more congruence between their sex roles and school goals than can young boys [17]. Women nursery school teachers have been found to reinforce feminine behavior in both girls and boys. (Feminine behavior was defined as the play activities preferred more by girls than by boys [9].)

A few years later, however, a replication of this study yielded different results [29]. Although gender preferences in the children's choice of activities were evident, and children reinforced like-sexed peers, the teachers did not differentially reinforce

boys and girls. Neither did they make reinforcement contingent upon sex-appropriate play. Perhaps these teachers had consciously eliminated sex biases from their behavior with children.

A third observational study revealed nursery school teachers responding more to boys than to girls, giving boys more reprimands for aggression, and twice as much praise, hugging, and instruction as they gave to girls [27].

When nursery school teachers attempted to promote selection of sex-inappropriate toys, as they did in an experiment, young boys resisted more vigorously and *anxiously* than did girls. This finding was consistent with earlier research that has shown boys to be under greater pressure than girls to assume sex-appropriate behavior patterns [25].

There is abundant evidence that the school experience is structured very differently for boys and girls. In the later elementary grades, boys receive more than their share of low marks, grade retention, special class placement, referral to specialists, and teacher disapproval [17]. It is not suprising that boys respond with more aggression and negativism.

In a comparison of male and female teacher behavior, observations and pupil interviews were analyzed. Boys did indeed receive more disapproval than girls, but although both men and women disapproved more of boys, the men were less disapproving than the women. When choosing leaders, teachers more often chose children of their own sex. Boys saw themselves as closer to male teachers, but girls had similar feelings of affiliation toward both male and female teachers. The experimenters concluded that male teachers established a classroom atmosphere that was more congenial to boys than was that established by a woman teacher. Having a male teacher was little or no detriment to girls, and an advantage to boys [17].

The Media. Gender-role learning is also influenced by toys, books, television, films, and similar experiences. Since adults design and control the media, their ideas of gender role are translated to the children by these means. Toys intended for boys are mechanical and spatial, stimulating the boy to take them apart, put them together, and fix them. Girls' toys are oriented toward "domestic development" and learning to be nurturant and social [21]. Girls often want to play with boys' toys and are usually permitted to do so. Because pressures on boys are greater, they are not often so eager to play with girls' toys. Although many books portray rigid sex roles to chidren, there is a trend toward humanly oriented books. *William's Doll* is a refreshingly different story of a little boy who wants a doll to love and care for, so that he can practice being a father. He gets one in the end, thanks to an understanding grandmother. But it wasn't easy [31].

On many children's television programs, women are not even portrayed. Those programs that do portray females show them as being deferent to the wishes of males, and more likely to be punished for action than are males. Males are portrayed as both good and evil, but females are almost always shown as good. Females are more likely to use magic; it seems that only through magic can they achieve anything. Males are shown as not deferring to the wishes of others, and not expressing admiration for others [28].

Changing Attitudes Toward Rigid Gender Roles

The weight of evidence makes it clear that young children are pressured to behave within gender-role restrictions. Young boys receive more severe pressure than young girls, but at later ages, girls are more restricted than boys. Boys are urged to compete and achieve, girls to develop social skills and sensitivity. Within the field of child development, there have always been some adults, often nursery school teachers, who believed that all children should be allowed and encouraged to explore activities and materials freely, to develop all their talents, and to grow fully as human beings. Women's liberation and other social forces have sought to rescue women from the bondage of strict gender roles and in so doing have raised questions for men and women, boys, and girls. At least one author has suggested that men may be more restricted than women in terms of the range of emotional behavior allowed them and the choice between paid employment and homemaking [10].

Sex-appropriate behavior is no longer clearly stated in the Western world, or even in the world as a whole. Who can now say with certainty that it is masculine to be aggressive and feminine to be sensitive? Along with the loosening of stereotypes of gender-role behavior, we see more emphasis on individuals as human persons, rather than as women or men. There is increasing latitude for all persons to acquire executive competence and assertiveness that used to be considered masculine, and attitudes of caring, knowing, and responding that used to be considered feminine. Concrete indications of these changes include unisex clothing and hair styles, men sewing and knitting, and women fighting for financial and occupational equality. In the face of these changing attitudes and practices, we wonder how many parents continue vigorous efforts to promote clear sex-role adoption by saying, "Boys don't cry," or "Little ladies don't swear," or, later on, by encouraging girls to be nurses, not doctors, and boys to be doctors, not nurses.

Because the terms *feminine* and *masculine* are emotionally tinged and associated with notions of propriety and restrictions, it is difficult to think about all persons having both masculine and feminine characteristics (as indeed they do). Therefore, the more objective terminology of Bakan [2] is helpful in learning to think about and accept the wide ranges of behaviors that are truly human and possible for both sexes. Bakan suggests that all living forms have a balance of two fundamental modalities, *agency* and *communion*. Agency has to do with the organism as an individual and is manifested in the protection, assertion, and expansion of the self. Communion has to do with the organism as a part of a larger whole, and is manifested in the sense of being one with the larger whole. Agency is what has been traditionally conceived as

"masculine traits"; communion is "feminine." By getting away from the terms *masculine* and *feminine,* however, it is easier to conceive of these traits as being fundamentally human.

Bakan emphasizes that in the normal person, agency and communion are tempered or mitigated by each other, and that unmitigated agency or communion is pathological. The wholly agentic individual would think only of himself, and obviously could not function as a social being. The wholly communal person would be equally at a loss socially, because he would always defer his needs to the needs of others.

Cognitive Theory

Through his own thinking and reasoning, the child structures his sex role, just as he is active in building other parts of himself. Cognitive theory complements social learning theory, which focuses on the ways in which other persons influence the child's learning. Since growth and development are results of interactions of the child with his world, his own actions, as well as the actions of others, are salient in sex role development.

The crucial establishment of gender identity, discussed under the previous topic of social learning, depends not only upon what parents and other people tell the child, but upon the child's cognition. Before three years of age, probably between one and two years, the toddler thinks something like, "I am a girl" or "I am a boy." Then she and he try to fit their behavior to what they perceive as girl behavior and boy behavior, respectively. They get the necessary information from direct statements by family and others, by observation and reinforcements for appropriate behavior. It can be as subtle as physical teasing and rough play, followed by smiles and laughs when the baby boy participates, or as an approving nod when the baby girl hugs her doll. Although the smiles and nods may act as rewards, they also act as feedback that informs the baby that the behavior actually was girl behavior or boy behavior.

As the child grows up, even after gender identity is firmly established and irreversible, she continues to observe, discuss, and reason about the gender roles in her family, community, and society. Eventually, if she goes to college, she learns about gender roles in other cultures. She thinks about those too and about her own self, her behavior and relationships, She develops moral values of which sex and gender role behavior are a part. She makes goals and plans for reaching them. Thus the individual exerts control and direction over her own self development, through interaction with other people and through her own thinking.

SEX EDUCATION IN THE FAMILY: THE EARLY YEARS

When an infant is born, he begins to learn about his environment. He cannot at first distinguish himself from the things that surround him, including the person who cares for him. However, he begins to learn lessons about himself at an early age. He is quick to sense whether the person holding him is tense or relaxed.

The sex education of the child cannot be held off, as many North American parents believe, until the child is ten or eleven. It begins when the child is still an infant, and is nonverbal in the beginning. A baby enjoys being touched and tickled, and it enjoys being bathed gently. When the infant's genitals are washed, it responds with pleasure. If the person bathing the infant responds with displeasure to his squirms of delight, the baby begins to learn that he is doing something wrong.

As the child grows, her parents continue to give her an education in sex, whether or not they intend to do so. Parental acceptance of family nudity, whether or not parents kiss and cuddle in front of the children, adult and child toileting practices, parental acceptance of child masturbation, and other sex exploration

By watching, Kisandra learns that her parents believe that loving and touching go together.

practices, all begin to form the child's ideas about sexuality. The little girl pictured on page 93 is learning how her parents express their love for each other. When the child starts to ask questions about himself and his world, he will include questions that the parent may interpret as being sexually oriented. The parent's reactions to these questions will also shape the child's sexual attitudes. If the child senses that the parent gets upset or nervous when certain topics are brought up, the child will invariably feel that there is something wrong with these topics.

The parent, of course, is not the only socializing agent. I (LSS) suffered from an early age because of my knowledge of sexual matters. At the age of three or four, I informed my four-year-old boyfriend that his "piddler" was really called a penis. His mother was horrified at my "dirty talk" and said that I could no longer play with him if I did not stop. I was perplexed. Why did my mother and father tell me to say something that upset my friend's mother so much? Parents need to be sensitive to the reactions of their children to such situations.

If the parents and child have a trusting relationship with each other, the child will probably continue to bring questions to the parent who has answered them (or honestly tried to) in the past. The child may eventually pick up the cultural taboos concerning sexual activity and development and stop asking questions of the parent, especially around adolescence. We return to the subject of sex education in the home later in this chapter (see page 99).

SEXUAL BEHAVIOR

In our society, a great deal of emphasis is placed on sex. Advertising, movies, the theater, television, and novels use sex as a lure to gain the individual's attention. At the same time, religious organizations, parents, teachers, and other groups often warn the individual that sex before marriage is bad, and will lead to disaster. There is no one correct answer to the question, "Is sex good or bad?" Certainly, some sex is necessary if the human race is to continue, but if the only purpose of sex is the creation of new life, sexual intercourse can be limited to very few occasions in a person's lifetime. The mature individual must decide for himself what role his sexuality will play in his life. What he has learned about sex in his family will probably influence his decision, but other factors as well will enter into his decision-making.

Cross-Cultural Comparisons

In all societies, expression of sexuality is restricted in some ways. What is and is not permitted, however, varies widely from one society to the next. A person is not born with sexual attitudes; these must be developed as he grows up. Ford and Beach's description of the sexual behavior of 190 societies throughout the world illustrates how many variations there can be in beliefs about what is proper and right regarding sex for human beings [12]. In the United States, for instance, a man is permitted by custom and by law to have only one wife at a time; a wife is permitted to have only one husband. Westerners tend to think that monogamy is normal and natural for all human beings. Ford and Beach, however, found that less than 16 per cent of 185 societies studied prohibited all members from having more than one spouse. Most of the societies that permit marriages of more than two individuals permit only the husband to have more than one spouse, and he is allowed this privilege only if he can afford to support them. Only two societies studied by Ford and Beach permitted a woman to have more than one husband.

Societies also take different stands concerning premarital and extramarital sexual relations. In some societies, children are given no information at all about sex; in others, adults instruct children in sex play; in still others, children engage in considerable sex play when adults are not present. Only about five per cent of the 185 societies for which this information was available wholly disapproved of premarital and extramarital sex relations. This does not mean that all individuals in the permissive societies could have intercourse with whomever they pleased; most societies place restrictions on which people are available sexual partners.

Early Childhood

In some societies, parents will kiss or stroke their infant's genitals in order to comfort him or her. Whether or not the young child is stimulated by those older than himself, he will discover his own genitals just as he discovers his fingers and toes. However, the American baby is likely to learn from his parents that it is considered wrong for him to play with his genitals. Some parents may slap the child or say, "Don't do that!" in a desperate tone of voice; others may give the child a toy to play with instead. For some children, the mere fact that the parent does not respond with a comment such as, "That feels good, doesn't it?" is enough to give the child the idea that all is not right.

The child's feelings of shame may or may not stop him from sexually stimulating (masturbating) himself. Girls as well as boys **masturbate,** although they may not be aware that they are doing so. The male usually masturbates by moving his hand up and down the shaft of his penis, but he may also stimulate himself by pressing his penis against a bed or other object, or by rubbing it on his thigh. A female's self-stimulation techniques may vary widely. Some females masturbate by pressing their legs together, or by rubbing against a pillow, bed, and so forth. Others stroke, tickle, or press their vulvas with their hands. Some tickle or press directly on or next to the clitoris in a rhythmic motion, either gently or with more vigor. Another method is to insert an object in the vagina and simulate sexual intercourse.

It used to be thought that masturbation caused a number of maladies, including insanity and acne. It is now known that masturbation does not become harmful to the individual unless he (or she) experiences a large amount of guilt, or masturbates to the exclusion of all interpersonal activities. Masturbation can be an extremely useful way to release sexual frustrations at times when other releases are not available or are not appropriate.

Children also play sex games with each other, in like-sex and opposite-sex groups. They examine each other's genitals and may attempt and succeed at sexual intercourse—without ejaculation on the part of the prepuberal male. Depending upon the attitudes of his society or parents, the child will be encouraged, ignored, or punished for his sexual behavior.

Later Childhood

By the time a child enters school, he has a clear idea of himself as either a boy or a girl. During the primary grades, the sexes may play with each other less and less (the "latent period" in psychoanalytic theory). The reason for the decrease in interaction between boys and girls around the age of ten may be that by playing more exclusively with same-sexed friends, the child is able to increase his feelings of being a boy or a girl. Children of this age may develop feelings of scorn for their opposite-sexed age mates. In so doing, each sex is able to reinforce its own feelings of maleness or femaleness. The rejection stage may also help the child to learn cooperative behavior [6]. The period of like-sexed play and friendship is more pronounced in many other countries, such as England, New Zealand, and India, where adults arrange to keep boys and girls separated a good deal of the time.

On the other hand, not all children "hate" members of the opposite sex at this age, as indicated by a series of studies done in Georgia, Pennyslvania, and Missouri. In these studies, about 55 to 60 per cent of ten-year-old boys, and 80 per cent of ten-year-old girls, stated that they wanted to get married some day. At age twelve, these figures rose to 65 to 70 per cent for the boys, and 90 per cent for the girls [4a]. Usually, children of these ages who are interested in getting married some day choose a "sweetheart" who in most cases is not aware that he or she has been chosen. Crushes on adults, movie stars, singers, and so on are also common at this age. The child is able to role-play (much as he did at a younger age when he played house) what it is like to be in love, and no one need find out.

PUBERTY AND ADOLESCENCE

The stage of development at which sexual maturity is reached is **puberty.** A series of bodily changes called **pubescence** lead to the point of puberty. Pubescence lasts about two years, on the average, but some children reach puberty in less than two years, while others take longer. There is evidence that pubescence begins when the body reaches a critical weight. **Menarche,** the first menstruation, is commonly taken

as the indication of puberty in a girl. Boys have no event that corresponds to menarche, but male puberty is indicated when a boy first produces sperms. The timing of puberty is genetically controlled, but is influenced by nutrition and possibly by other factors.

The term **adolescence** refers to a cultural invention, a time of life that is socially defined. It begins with pubescence and ends, vaguely, at adulthood. Since adulthood has many definitions, even within North American culture, it is hard for an individual to know whether he graduates from adolescence to adulthood when he gets his driver's license, when he graduates from high school, when he gets a job, or when he gets married.

Female Physiology

The average age of menarche for American girls is around 12.5 years, which means that pubescence begins around 10.5. A group of malnourished American girls began to menstruate at 14.4 years [13], although their weight, 43.5 kg., was almost the same as the menarchal weight of the well-nourished girls (44.6 kg.) who were 12.5 years old. Critical weights for menarche are different in different races, the Japanese weight, for instance, being about 6 kg. less than the American. The age of menarche has declined throughout the Western world for over a century, most likely because better nutrition has made girls bigger at an earlier age.

Pubescence usually begins with the appearance of the breast bud, although sometimes the pubic hair is the first sign [30]. The uterus and the vagina develop further at the same time. The height spurt begins and picks up speed, reaching its greatest velocity at about six months before menarche and then slowing down. About two years after the first pubic hair appears, circumanal hair and then axillary hair begin to grow. The internal organs also spurt in growth, each having its characteristic timing of the peak in growth velocity.

Menarche is marked by the appearance of menstrual blood. When a girl has her first menstrual period, she generally is not capable of conceiving a baby. Her menstrual periods may be erratic for a year or two, and she may skip periods altogether.

In a mature female, the tissue within the uterus is built up each month prior to **ovulation,** the release of an egg from one ovary. Rich in blood vessels, this lining is sloughed off each month if the egg is not fertilized. This sloughing-off of the blood-rich uterine lining is called **menstruation.** Menstruation occurs generally every twenty-eight days and lasts from two to seven days. However, it is considered normal for women to menstruate every twenty days, or every forty days. Each woman has her own individual cycle, which may vary as much as ten days (five days early or late) and still be considered a normal cycle. It is quite common for women to have emotional ups and downs connected with the menstrual cycle. The few days before menstruation are likely to be difficult ones for those women who experience cyclic effects. Around age fifty, the woman experiences a change in physiologic functioning that is known as **menopause,** the **climacteric,** or the "change of life." Her ovaries gradually stop producing eggs and hormones over a period of about two years. When menopause is complete and no ova are being released, the woman may no longer become pregnant. We discuss menopause further in the next chapter, pages 132–134.

Male Physiology

Pubescence begins, on the average, at about age 12, with the testes and scrotum increasing in size [30]. Pubic hair may also begin, but its growth is slight until the time when the penis begins to grow fast. Height also spurts at this time. About two years after the first pubic hair, circumanal, then axillary and facial hair appear. The voice begins to change, because of the enlarging larynx, at the time when penis growth is nearly finished. Strength spurts when height is nearly complete. About midway through the series of changes, about a third of boys have some breast development, which lasts about a year. The pubescent growth spurt lasts longer in boys than in girls, resulting in greater average height in men than in women. Although the sequence of pubescent growth is quite consistent, the timing varies considerably from one boy to another. There is great variation in a group of thirteen and fourteen year olds, ranging from prepubescence to maturity.

A few months after the beginning of pubescence a boy will experience his first ejaculation, either through self-stimulation or when he is asleep (a "wet dream"). From infancy, he has been capable of having an erection and probably also an orgasm [12], but no ejaculation has occurred. Ejaculation is made possible at puberty when the male begins to produce sperm.

SEX EDUCATION IN THE FAMILY: PUBESCENCE

When the child's body begins to mature, she (or he) has to adapt her self-concept to her changing form. How she reacts will depend in part upon her family's attitude toward the changes. The girl who is told nothing in advance about menstruation, or the boy who has been told nothing about ejaculation, may be frightened when the evidence first appears. Not all parents understand their own sexual "plumbing" and its workings, but there are ways for parents to find out: through books, from the family doctor, Planned Parenthood, or a local family service agency. Sexual anatomy and reproduction are taught to children in many schools, but the basic attitudes and feelings about sex are acquired long before pubescence. The biological changes that herald sexual maturation make sex information even more important at this time.

SEXUAL RESPONSE

In order for a woman to become pregnant, she does not have to be sexually aroused. All that is necessary is that a man become sexually aroused enough to have an erection and an ejaculation in or very close to her vagina. The female's contribution to the new life depends upon her own biological clockwork. For the male to contribute to a new life, a complicated series of responses must take place.

Male Response

When a male becomes sexually aroused, the spaces in the spongy tissue of his penis become engorged with blood, making the penis firm and erect. Arousal may be caused by fantasy, by viewing a person or object, by touching another person, or by being touched by someone. The erection may be lost if the individual is startled in some way, by a sudden noise, change in lighting or temperature, or other environmental changes [18].

Once the penis is erect (the *excitement* phase), it may be inserted into the female's vagina or other means of manipulation may be employed in order to induce orgasm. During sexual intercourse, the penis is plunged into the vagina, drawn partially out again, and then plunged in again. This in-and-out activity may last only a second or two, or many minutes. Many men learn to delay the completion of their response cycle, increasing the likelihood of their partner's reaching orgasm. After the penis has become erect, the male experiences a *plateau* stage that is a time of high sexual excitement. Usually, the plateau stage is followed by the *orgasmic* phase, when ejaculation occurs. At times, however, a man may not be able to reach the orgasmic phase; instead, his penis will gradually lose its hardness.

When an individual is about to have an orgasm, he or she knows that it is imminent, much as a person knows when a sneeze is coming. The exact mechanisms that trigger an orgasm are not known. A simple explanation, however, it that neuromuscular tension is released [20]. A normal orgasm may be mild or extremely intense.

Immediately following orgasm, the male ejaculates, releasing about a teaspoonful of semen, which is thick and milky and contains millions of sperm. The ejaculate may spurt from the end of the penis or it may dribble out. After ejaculation, the penis returns to its flaccid state. Before a male can be sexually stimulated again, he must pass through a refractory period that may last for a few seconds to any number of hours. Unlike the male, the female does not have to experience an orgasm in order to contribute her part to the creation of new life. She is, however, capable of *multiple* orgasms, whereas the man must undergo the refractory period before he may experience a second orgasm (See Figure 4-2).

Female Response

Freud made a distinction between a woman's having a clitoral orgasm, through stimulation of the clitoris, and a vaginal orgasm, through sexual intercourse. The former was his definition of an infantile woman, and the latter he defined as a mature woman. Masters and Johnson's laboratory research has demonstrated that there is no physiological difference between these so-called types of orgasms. There is only one kind of orgasm, triggered by direct or indirect stimulation of the clitoris. The orgasm is located and *experienced* by the woman in or around the vagina [15a]. Some women require direct stimulation of the clitoris in order to reach orgasm; for other women, such stimulation is painful. Similarly, women vary in the amount of vaginal sensitivity that they report.

Many women fear that they are abnormal if they do not easily achieve orgasm through coitus. Recent clinical evidence indicates that many, perhaps most, women who are able to reach orgasm are *not* orgasmic through coitus alone. A surprising number of women who complain of never having reached orgasm are able to climax when they are given sufficient stimulation, either through masturbation or from their partners [15a].

The first sign that a female is becoming sexually excited is the "sweating" of the vagina: ten to thirty seconds after the beginning of effective sexual stimulation,

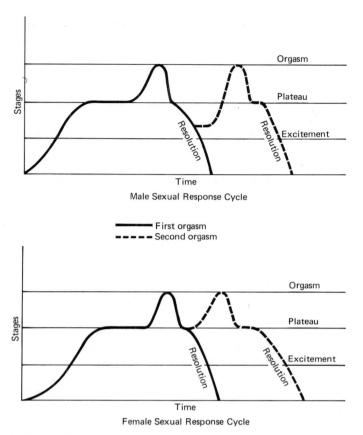

FIGURE 4-2   Male and female sexual response cycles, showing that the female is capable of multiple orgasms, whereas the male must undergo a refractory period before experiencing a second orgasm.

Source: Adapted from William H. Masters and Virginia E. Johnson. *Human sexual response.* Boston: Little, Brown, 1966, p. 5.

vaginal lubrication appears within the vagina, preparing the vagina for penetration by the penis. Although the early embryonic development of the clitoris is parallel to that of the penis, and although in some ways the clitoris resembles a miniature penis, it does not respond to sexual stimulation in the same way as does the penis. The glans (head) of the clitoris will engorge with blood, but this engorgement may not be noticeable. The clitoris does *not* "erect" the same way as does the penis [18].

As the female becomes sexually aroused, during the excitment stage, her vagina, which is normally shaped like a tube, balloons out at the top so that it looks more like an inverted pear. As she proceeds to the plateau stage, the width and depth of her vagina increase a bit more. When a female experiences an orgasm, rhythmic contractions occur in her uterus and vagina. Unlike the male, who can experience only one orgasm before he must go through a refractory period, the female can experience a series of orgasms before dropping into the resolution stage [18]. (See Figure 4-2.)

Kinsey found that women increased in sexual responsiveness (ratio of orgasms per coital contact) up until around age thirty, and then dropped off somewhat [16]. Part of the reason for this increase may be that in our society a woman has to overcome her girlhood socialization that sex is wrong. She has to learn full sexual responsiveness. Another reason is that her body becomes more responsive with more sexual experience.

When a man becomes sexually aroused, his penis becomes engorged with blood. Similarly, when a woman becomes aroused, the tissue surrounding her sex organs become full of blood. The clitoris has aptly been described as "the tip of the iceberg" [26]. During sexual excitement, it takes longer for the woman's network of blood veins to engorge with blood, partly because there are more veins. Sexual activity and pregnancies increase the complexity of this network, and increase a woman's sexual capacity [26].

Individual Differences

Sexual responsiveness is highly complex. It depends upon a person's anatomy, innate capacity, and experiences. In the nineteenth century, it was thought that men had a greater sexual capacity than women; today opinion is swinging in the other direction. Because women can have more orgasms in a shorter period of time, it is said that they have greater capacity than men.

Not all persons have an equal interest in, or desire for, sexual activity. A male or female may feel inadequate or disabled sexually because he or she does not feel able to measure up to a standard of sexuality, or feels that he or she has exceeded it. The girl who was interested in sex used to feel abnormal, as did the boy who was not interested in sex. Today, the girl who can't have multiple orgasms may feel that she is different. It should be remembered that there is a wide range of normal behavior, and that individual differences are much greater than the differences between averages of two large groups.

Some couples may find that they are instantly compatible sexually, but for most couples, sexual adjustment takes time. North Americans are not trained in sexual techniques, as are the Mangaians of Polynesia. The young Mangaian male learns about female sexual anatomy and learns the difference between a fully covered clitoris and an exposed clitoris, a high clitoris and a low clitoris, differently shaped labia, and so on. Different types of anatomy require different kinds of stimulation, and the Mangaian youth learns these techniques expertly [26]. By contrast, the Western male and female have to discover their own idiosyncracies by themselves, and may worry when they appear to differ from a standard set forth in their marriage manual.

In the next chapter, we discuss sexuality in adolescence and adulthood. It should be underscored that the development of sexuality, as with other aspects of the individual, is a continuous process. Although pubescence is an important milestone in the development of sexuality, the individual has been capable of orgasm since infancy. The difference now is that sexual activity can result in a new life. Sexual activity becomes more socially oriented in adolescence and adulthood, and less self-centered. Pleasure-seeking for one's own satisfaction does, of course, normally continue throughout life.

SUMMARY   Differences between the sexes are rooted in physical structure and elaborated by interaction between the individual and sociocultural forces. Chromosomal content, fixed at conception, determines sex. The individual is an embryo from the time of attaching to the mother's uterus until eight weeks of age, when it becomes a fetus. At birth, the fetus becomes an infant, or, in informal terms, a baby. During embryonic life, the reproductive system, as well as other systems, differentiates. The genitals and other parts of the body, perhaps the brain, are responsive to hormones circulating in the mother and in the embryo and fetus.

Conceived in greater numbers than females, males are more vulnerable to destructive influences in the environment, both before and after birth. Females mature more rapidly, both physically and psychologically. Although sex differences in brain functioning have been demonstrated, the differences between averages are so small as to be meaningless for individuals. The most salient of sex differences is that between the reproductive systems, since the two are complementary. During the embryonic period, the undifferentiated gonad develops into either a testis, whose endocrine secretions direct the development of male external genitalia, or an ovary.

Through learning, the young child develops a self-concept that includes being a girl or a boy. Both psychoanalytic theory and social learning theory contribute to understanding how individuals develop the psychological aspects of femininity and masculinity. The former theory bases learning more strongly on bodily experiences and emotional interaction with parents. The latter stresses more cognitive and social interaction, with reinforcement as an influence and modeling an important process. Gender identity or sex-role orientation (thinking of oneself as a male or a female) seems to have a critical period for establishment, during the first two or three years. Gender-role adoption, or acting like a male or female, is a longer, more gradual process. Both processes are strongly influenced by fathers, who are likely to take more interest than mothers in motivating children toward sex-typed behavior. Siblings, teachers, and the media also influence sex typing. Cultural definitions of gender roles are loosening at present, with an increasing focus on a range of behavior that is *human* rather than "male" or "female."

Cross-cultural comparisons reveal great variety in the patterning of sexual expression. Childrearing methods are articulated with societal norms of sexual behavior. Masturbation and sex play in childhood are interpreted in various ways, and thus restricted or encouraged. In later childhood, when growth is slow and the reproductive system is immature, some societies keep boys and girls quite separated. Pubescence is the period during which the body grows fast, changing in all its systems while the genital system matures. Adolescence is a socially defined, culturally variable period between childhood and adulthood. Although sex education in early childhood is largely handled by parents, adolescents often need sex education beyond what is offered in the home.

Sexual interaction involves responses that are both physiological and psychological. Erection, the male physiological response, is essential for intercourse, but female arousal is not. Ejaculation marks the completion of the male physiological response, and orgasm is its psychological counterpart. Female response also includes genital enlargement and orgasm. Interaction involves mutual stimulation. There are wide cultural and individual differences in sexual techniques, since learning, teaching, and natural endowment are all factors in performance.

REFERENCES

1. Aldous, Joan. Children's perceptions of adult role assignment: Father-absence, class, race and sex influence. *Journal of Marriage and the Family,* 1972, **34,** 55–65.
2. Bakan, David. *The duality of human existence.* Chicago: Rand McNally, 1966.
3. Biller, Henry B. *Father, child and sex role.* Lexington, Mass., Heath, 1971.
3a. Biller, Henry B. and Dennis Meredith. *Fathers and children,* New York: McKay, 1975.
4. Block, Jeanne Humphrey. Conceptions of sex roles: Some cross-cultural and longitudinal perspectives. *American Psychologist,* 1973, **28,** 512–526.
4a. Broderick, Carlfred. Normal sociosexual development. In Carlfred Broderick and Jessie Bernard (eds.). *The individual, sex, and society.* Baltimore: Johns Hopkins, 1969.
5. Chilman, Catherine S. Some psychosocial aspects of female sexuality. *Family Coordinator,* 1974, **23,** 123–131.
6. Cox, Frank D. *Youth, marriage, and the seductive society.* Dubuque, Iowa: Brown, 1967.
7. Dawson, John L. M., Y. M. Cheung, T. S. Lau, and F. Yue. The neonatal sex hormone reversal of cognitive skills in rats and men. U. of Hong Kong, 1972. (Mimeo.)
8. Ehrhardt, Anke. Maternalism in fetal hormonal and related syndromes. In Joseph Zubin and John Money (eds.). *Contemporary sexual behavior: Critical issues in the 1970s.* Baltimore: Johns Hopkins, 1973.
9. Fagot, Beverly I. and G. R. Patterson. An in vivo analysis of reinforcing contingencies for sex role behaviors in the preschool child. *Developmental Psychology,* 1969, **1,** 563–568.
10. Farrell, Warren T. Growing up male in America. In *World Year Book.* Chicago: Field Enterprises Educational Corporation, 1974.
11. Fish, K. D. and Henry Biller. Perceived paternal relationships and college females' personal adjustment. *Adolescence,* 1973, **8,** 415–420.
12. Ford, Clellan and Frank Beach. *Patterns of sexual behavior.* New York: Harper, 1951.
13. Frisch, Rose E. Weight at menarche: Similarity for well-nourished and undernourished girls at differing ages, and evidence for historical constancy. *Pediatrics,* 1972, **50,** 445–450.

14. Hetherington, E. Mavis. Effects of father absence on personality development in adolescent daughters. *Developmental Psychology,* 1972, **7,** 313–326.

15. Hutt, Corinne. Sex differences in human development. *Human Development,* 1972, **15,** 153–170.

15a. Kaplan, Helen Singer. *The new sex therapy.* New York: Brunner/Mazel, 1974.

16. Kinsey, Alfred, Wardell Pomeroy, Clyde Martin, and Paul Gebhard. *Sexual behavior in the human female.* Philadelphia: Saunders, 1953.

17. Lee, Patrick C. and Annie L. Wolinsky. Male teachers of young children: A preliminary empirical study. *Young Children,* 1973, **28,** 342–352.

18. Masters, William and Virginia Johnson. *Human sexual response.* Boston: Little, Brown, 1966.

19. McGlone, Jeanette and Andrew Kertesz. Sex differences in cerebral processing of visuospatial tasks. *Cortex,* 1973, **9,** 313–320.

20. Melton, Alfred. Human sexual response. In Carlfred Broderick and Jessie Bernard (eds.). *The individual, sex, and society.* Baltimore: Johns Hopkins, 1969.

21. Mitchell, Edna. The learning of sex roles through toys and books: A woman's view. *Young Children,* 1973, **28,** 226–231.

22. Money, John and Anke A. Ehrhardt. *Man & woman boy & girl.* Baltimore: Johns Hopkins, 1972.

23. Patty, Rosemarie A. and Marcia M. Ferrell. A preliminary note on the motive to avoid success and the menstrual cycle. *Journal of Psychology,* 1974, **86,** 173–177.

24. Rosenzweig, Saul. Human sexual autonomy as an evolutionary attainment: Anticipating proceptive sex choice and idiodynamic bisexuality. In Joseph Zubin and John Money (eds.). *Contemporary sexual behavior: Critical issues in the 1970s.* Baltimore: Johns Hopkins, 1973, 189–230.

25. Ross, Dorothea M. and Sheila A. Ross. Resistance by preschool boys to sex-inappropriate behavior. *Journal of Education Psychology,* 1972, **63,** 342–346.

26. Seamans, Barbara. *Free and female.* Greenwich, Conn.: Fawcett, 1972.

27. Serbin, Lisa. Sex sterotyped patterns of social reinforcement in the preschool classroom. Paper presented at meetings of the Society for Research in Child Development, Philadelphia, 1973.

28. Sternglanz, Sarah H. and Lisa A. Serbin. Sex role stereotyping in children's television programs. *Developmental Psychology,* 1974, **10,** 710–715.

29. Stewart, Mollie K. Sex-typed behaviors of boys and girls in preschool activities and the reinforcements of these behaviors by peers and teachers. M. S. thesis, U. of Rhode Island, 1973.

30. Tanner, James M. The adolescent growth spurt and developmental age. In Russell C. Smart and Mollie S. Smart (eds.). *Readings in child development and relationships.* New York: Macmillan, 1972.

31. Zolotow, Charlotte. *William's doll.* New York: Harper, 1972.

CHAPTER 5

it keeps on growing: more about sex

In the previous chapter, we discussed the individual's sexual development from conception to puberty. In this chapter, we follow male and female sexual development and behavior through adolescence, adulthood, and old age.

A CROSS-CULTURAL PERSPECTIVE

By the time a person reaches puberty, he or she already has acquired many feelings and ideas about the culturally accepted manifestation of sexuality. The body is seen as something to be covered up or displayed in various types of social situations. Members of the opposite sex and the same sex may or may not touch in public, and if they do touch, the contact may be approved or disapproved. An American man living in India scandalized the citizens of a medium-sized city by wearing short-shorts and kissing his wife good-bye at the train station. An Indian holy man, naked or wearing a loincloth, was "decent" but an American in short-shorts was not. In our society, a bathing suit is "decent" when worn at the beach but not in the office.

Some societies permit children to engage in sexual play before puberty, because of the belief that if a child does not experiment, he will never function adequately in the sexual realm as an adult. Others forbid sex play until puberty, but permit limited or relatively unlimited sex play after puberty has been reached. Other societies restrict full sexual activity until marriage [15]. Whatever the correct childhood behavior in a particular society, the members of that society believe that the behavior contributes to proper adult attitudes and behavior [15].

In many preindustrial societies, adulthood follows quickly on the heels of childhood. Before menarche, a female is a girl, and afterwards, she is a woman. She may, however, have to go through ceremonies known as **puberty rites** in order to be fully admitted to womanhood. This usually means that she is secluded from most of the people in her group, especially the men. She may receive special instruction from older women regarding sex and marriage. In some societies, she is tattooed, or her ears are pierced, or her hair is cut off. Generally, at the end of her time of seclusion, she is bathed or goes through a ritual purification, after which she dons the clothes of a mature woman.

For the male in such societies, puberty rites may be even more important than for the girl, because he does not have the dramatic beginning of menstruation to mark his passage from childhood to manhood. His puberty rite may be very simple: on the island of Truk, when a male's facial and pubic hair become noticeable, he puts on a red loincloth and goes to live in the men's dormitory.

Some societies pay attention to the appearance of facial or body hair or to the boy's first ejaculation as an indication of his manhood. In other societies, boys are initiated in groups when enough boys in an age group have become sufficiently mature. In many societies, male puberty rites include seclusion of the boy and a test of his endurance through ordeals of some kind. He may undergo circumcision or other bodily mutilation [15]. If he successfully completes the initiation rites, it is proclaimed to the world that he is a man.

In modern industrial societies, it is extremely difficult to pinpoint exactly when an adolescent becomes an adult. There are a number of occasions that may serve as **rites-de-passage,** such as graduating from high school, becoming 18 or 21 years old, joining the military, graduating from college, or getting married. However, some grown-up children are still dependent upon their parents in some way for support, perhaps even after military service is over, or when college has begun and ended, or even after the children have married and borne children of their own. Likewise, some "children" who are still in school or who have dropped out of school before age 18 are full-fledged members of the working force, supporting themselves and perhaps their parents or brothers and sisters as well.

Adulthood, then, cannot be easily defined in our society as it can in a society where there is a recognized break between childhood and maturity. The end of adolescence, the time between the end of childhood and the beginning of adulthood, comes at different times for different people. For this reason, we have chosen to combine adolescence and adulthood in our discussion of more mature sexuality.

PREMARITAL HETEROSEXUAL ATTITUDES AND BEHAVIOR

The question of the existence of a "sexual revolution" may be approached in two ways. One may look at changing attitudes toward sexual behavior, or one may look at changes in behavior. Both sexual attitudes and behavior have changed rapidly in recent years.

By premarital heterosexual behavior, we mean sexual behavior between members of the opposite sex that occurs between puberty and the first marriage. (We realize, of course, that not all persons marry.) Sexual behavior includes kissing, touching, petting, and coitus. Coitus has been the most frequently used index of premarital sexuality, but more recent studies have taken into account the fact that amount and kind of sexual experience varies widely even among virgins.

Four Sexual Standards

In 1960, Reiss wrote a book that dealt with the major sexual standards in the United States as he saw them [49]. These standards are *abstinence, permissiveness-with-affection, permissiveness-without-affection,* and the *double standard.*

The sexual standard that is upheld by many religious organizations and by the law in most states is *abstinence before marriage;* that is, no sexual intercourse prior to marriage for either men or women. The traditional sexual standard of our society, abstinence, is losing ground to the permissive standards, described below. Some people who hold the abstinence standard think that sexual intercourse is too cherished and intimate an act to be performed outside of marriage. However, there are various subdivisions of this standard which allow differing degrees of intimacy. A person who believes that coitus before marriage is wrong may believe that only kissing is acceptable, or may believe that petting is acceptable.

Of course, not all virgins hold the abstinence standard. There are reasons for refraining from intercourse other than feeling that it is wrong before marriage. For many, the time has not yet come, for a number of reasons. Unfortunately, growing numbers of sexually inexperienced young women and men are feeling socially pressured into having premarital coitus, or are feeling abnormal if they are abstinent. Virginity is seen as a burden instead of something worth saving for the right time and person.

Research on college campuses indicates that among college students *permissiveness-with-affection* is becoming the dominant sexual standard [7, 26, 26b, 39, 45a]. For persons who hold this standard, premarital intercourse is acceptable for both men and women as long as the couple feels mutual affection. This standard is the traditional standard in Sweden [49] and Denmark. The Danish standard, however, may be changing toward promiscuity, as the American and Canadian standards become permissiveness-with-affection [10].

Permissiveness-without-affection has traditionally been the least commonly held standard in the United States, but there is evidence that it is becoming more popular [45a]. Adherents of this standard feel that both sexes are entitled to indulge in premarital coitus for the pleasure that it brings. Couples need not be in love.

Like the abstinence standard, the *double standard* is losing ground as the permissiveness standards gain acceptance among college students. The traditional double standard holds that premarital sexual relations are permissible for males but not for females. Because men were considered to be more in need of sex than were women, not all men were expected to remain abstinent before marriage. In order to save the chastity of their sweethearts, double standard men engage in premarital coitus with permissive women. Traditionally, double standard men would go to prostitutes, but in the late nineteenth century more women who were not prostitutes began to have premarital intercourse. At that time, most men probably considered these permissive women to be "bad."

Newer Approaches to Sexual Permissiveness

In more recent writings, [50, 50a] Reiss has elaborated his method of measuring premarital sexual permissiveness and the theoretical explanation of it. Within any one of the standards previously mentioned there is room for a great deal of variation. As defined, an abstinence standard individual may believe that only kissing is permissible before marriage, or may believe that everything except penile-vaginal intercourse is permissible before marriage.

Furthermore, Reiss reasoned that sexual permissiveness would vary for individuals not only in the amount of physical activity, but also in the conditions under which such activity would be acceptable. Kissing, petting, and coitus were the physical acts that Reiss studied, and the conditions of affection were no affection, strong affection, love, and engagement. Reiss also asked his respondents whether they thought that a certain act under one of the conditions was acceptable for females, and also for males. For example, respondents were asked whether their agreement or disagreement was strong, medium, or slight to the following question: "I believe that kissing is acceptable for the male before marriage even if he does not feel particularly affectionate toward his partner." Both men and women answered this question and eleven more that dealt with the three physical acts under the four conditions of affection. Then, men and women answered the same questions again, only the word "female" was substituted for the word "male" in each case. By comparing an individual's answers on the male and female questions, it could be determined whether a person held a double or single standard, as well as how permissive he or she was under various conditions [50].

If one defines a permissive sexual standard as referring only to premarital coitus, then those who engage in petting but not intercourse would be considered nonpermissive. It seems more realistic to conceptualize as permissive individuals who engage in genital petting. Certainly the person who believes in petting is more permissive than the person who does not.

Choosing a Sexual Standard

In some societies, traditional standards are still upheld by the majority of people. The person who deviates from the rest of the group is likely to be punished in one way or another. Because virtually everyone that he knows upholds the traditional standards (at least in public), the deviant will be cut off from all his friends and family if he does not live by their standards. In North America, however, there are many different groups of people holding different standards. If a person wishes to change his attitudes and beliefs, he can often find another group of people willing to accept him even if his family refuses to associate with him. Although changing basic attitudes is often a long and painful process, it can be done.

During the teen-age years, the individual's friends become increasingly important to her; their opinions often mean more to her than those of her family. Eventually, if the individual becomes fully an adult, she is able to make up her own mind about what is right and wrong for herself. She may choose traditional values handed down from her parents, or she may choose some new values and keep some old ones. As an adult, she is responsible not only for her own actions but also for the welfare of the people whom her actions affect. A responsible individual will carefully consider all of the possible consequences of her actions, both for herself and for other people.

Sexual Decision-Making. Choosing a sexual standard for oneself is rarely easy in the United States. Because of the varying opinions and standards, it is difficult to put sex into perspective. Is sex something dirty or disgusting? Is it the most wonderful thing in the world, but only in marriage? Is it bargaining currency for getting what you want from another person? Is it a way to prove your adulthood? Is it fun? Is it sacred? Is it a lasting bond between two people? Is it a moment's pleasure?

A person looking for the answers to these questions would do well to consider the possible consequences, positive and negative, of either engaging in or refraining from sexual intercourse before marriage. He should weigh each consequence in terms of his own personal beliefs regarding right and wrong. Some consequences, however, are unforeseen. No person can predict his own reactions perfectly.

The most commonly noted consequence is pregnancy. Premarital pregnancy has traditionally been seen by middle-class persons in our society as an entirely negative consequence. Some groups in our society have not viewed it in this way, and it is becoming less of a source of shame among the middle class as well. What used to be seen as almost entirely the woman's problem, how to deal with the problem pregnancy, is now being shared by more men [24].

The premaritally pregnant woman, whether or not she is supported by her man, has a number of choices open to her. She may choose to terminate the pregnancy. She may marry, either the father of the expected child or someone else. Or, she may decide not to marry, or perhaps be unable to marry. In this case, she may continue the pregnancy and bear the child, either in a distant location or, with increasing frequency today, in her own community. She may give up the baby for adoption. (In some states, the father's consent is required.) Or, she may keep the baby, or perhaps the father will keep the baby. A healthy, normal infant will be readily adopted, especially if it is white.

In the black, slum subculture, unmarried parenthood has not been viewed as negatively as it has been in the white, middle-class subculture [23, 54]. Sexual activity begins at a much earlier age for black ghetto children. Although the mother or parents of the pregnant black teen-ager may regret the girl's having to drop out of school and the lowering of her chances for advancement, the girl herself may be pleased: pregnancy is a sign of womanhood. A child would give her a feeling of responsibility, because the child would be dependent upon her [23].

Whether the responsible individual with an unplanned premarital pregnancy decides to terminate the pregnancy or bear the child, the decision is not a simple one to make. Both men and women very often have unhappy feelings later on regarding their choice, regardless of what it is. Parents who give up their child for adoption wonder about the child's welfare. Those who keep their child may wonder at times if the child might have been better off adopted by someone else. Some who have abortions (or whose partners have them) feel guilty later on. The man may worry that he did not support his woman enough, and the woman may later feel that she did not give enough consideration to her man's feelings.

The consequence of conception, of course, can usually be avoided by the scrupulous use of contraceptives. A problem arises when a couple does not plan in advance for the eventuality of sexual intercourse, or when the person using the contraceptive is careless. Some people think that by planning for a possible sexual encounter, they are ruining its spontaneity. Some women may be able to keep their feeling of innocence only if they allow themselves to be swept off their feet by their partners. To think about contraception would spoil purity. A resulting conception, however, reveals the fallacy of such thinking.

Even if an individual or a couple does think about contraception before the occasion for its use arises, he or they may be reluctant to obtain the contraceptive. Nonprescription contraceptives are available in drug stores, but they are sometimes kept behind the counter. In some areas a girl under a specified age must have parental consent in order to obtain prescription contraceptives. If in doubt about her legal rights, she should contact the local family planning center or Planned Parenthood clinic. Her inquiry will be kept in confidence by the people in these agencies.

Venereal disease is a very real possible consequence of premarital intercourse. It, too, may usually be prevented by the careful use of a prophylactic. Some double-standard men protect themselves from venereal disease by the use of a condom ("rubber") and consequently protect their partner from pregnancy as well [49]. Venereal disease is discussed further in Chapter 13 (see pages 335–337), and in Appendix E.

A third consequence of premarital intercourse is social condemnation. This consequence usually is felt more keenly by the female than by the male. For the double-standard male, premarital intercourse is a cause for boasting to his friends. A way to avoid social condemnation is to make sure that no one finds out. The female who has intercourse with a double-standard male will usually find that he does not respect her request for secrecy. For couples with an egalitarian permissive standard (permissiveness with or without affection), it may be easier to keep their activities a secret. To maintain secrecy, care must be taken to prevent pregnancy and venereal disease, for if either of these conditions is discovered, it will provide proof of sexual activity, and a basis for condemnation.

A fourth consequence may be guilt feelings. If the individual is acting against his own sexual standard, it is very likely that he will feel guilty. In our society, women are especially susceptible to guilt feelings, but men are certainly not immune either. A person who forces or encourages another to engage in activities that are contrary to the second person's values may do that person a great injustice. In a moment of passion, a person may agree to do something that he will later regret. This is why communication between possible sexual partners is important, and why issues of "how far to go" are best discussed before the passions begin to boil. Such cool-headed discussions are probably rare, because our popular culture puts such an emphasis upon being swept off one's feet.

Premarital sex can lead a couple into premature commitment to a partner or to concentration on heterosexual relationships at a time when friendships with the same sex would be more growth-promoting. In societies where boys and girls are kept apart during middle childhood and early adolescence, individuals build close friendships with members of their own sex, usually have a few "best friends," and belong to a group of like-sex friends. It is at this time of life that the sense of identity is developing fast. Friendship contributes to identity by providing a noncritical person who shares the same experiences, doubts, puzzlements, and projections to the future. A friend listens to confidences. In the very process of *expressing* to a sympathetic, trustworthy person, the adolescent gains insight, solves problems, and gets a feeling of connection to the social group and to the past and future. All this is more possible when sexual activity is not part of the picture [14]. Although it is conceivable that boys and girls help one another to establish the sense of identity, it is much more likely that the very exciting emotional experience of sex prevents or shatters the cognitive and mildly emotional progress of identity development through discussion. In terms of time, it is reasonable that the boy and girl who are together daily are not going to be spending hours with like-sex friends. When a pair-involvement results in a teen-age marriage, the boy and girl (or one of them) may still be involved in establishing a sense of identity and therefore be unable to develop the intimacy that a partnership requires. Thus they fail with each other, perhaps because they are not suited as partners or possibly because they simply are too immature in their personality development.

There is widespread belief that premarital coitus may lead to marital infidelity. Although a higher percentage of people who engage in premarital intercourse also engage in extramarital intercourse, it is not known whether the first condition causes the second [49]. Another fear is that if a person is allowed to have coitus before marriage, he won't marry. The argument is that if a person can have sex (the bait), why should he fall into the trap of marriage? Marriage statistics, however, show that over 90 per cent of Americans do marry at some time during their lives.

People who favor premarital intercourse point out the advantages. The most obvious is physical satisfaction. An additional advantage is what Reiss calls "psychic satisfaction—non-sexual, lasting, emotional rewards [yielded by] a sexual relation-ship . . . such as security, warmth, and emotional satisfaction" [49, p. 18]. However, both physical and psychic satisfaction are possible only insofar as the individual does not feel guilty about his activities. Premarital coitus may help sexual adjustment in marriage. Women who experience orgasm in premarital sexual intercourse are more likely to experience orgasm through intercourse after marriage than women who have not had premarital intercourse. However, premaritally orgasmic women may be more capable of orgasm than those who did not experience premarital inter-course, and orgasmic women probably would have experienced orgasm sooner or later regardless of their premarital activity [49].

When considering numbers of sexually active young people, the number of virgins is likely to be forgotten. Preliminary results from a 1975 Canadian study show over 70 per cent virgins among students (both male and female) between 16 and 19 years of age [26a]. College students, age 20, in the same study indicated that 54 per cent of the women and 32 per cent of the men had not had sexual intercourse. A United States college group in 1970 included 63 per cent of the women as virgins, and 35 per cent of the men [51]. These figures suggest that the student who chooses to abstain from coitus before marriage will be among a majority, except in the case of college men. Therefore, the young person who feels pressured by friends to partici-pate in sexual activity need not feel like an exception or a freak by sticking to standards of abstinence. Although society used to support premarital chastity unequivocally, social pressures are by no means aligned on the side of premarital sex. Standards vary among different groups and different individuals.

When deciding whether to choose a permissive or restrictive standard for oneself, the individual should carefully consider his motivations for choosing a particular standard, and the consequences of each. Will he go against beliefs that are important to him? Is he motivated by a desire to be popular, or to prove his autonomy? Will sexual involvement increase the emotional intensity of his relationship to levels that he cannot or is unwilling to handle? Will sexual involvement be a meaningful addition to the relationship, from which both partners will benefit? Do both partners agree on the meaning of the relationship? What about contraception? If a pregnancy results, what action will be taken? Also, the possibility of contracting venereal disease should not be overlooked. Although the careful and well-informed person's chances of causing a pregnancy or contracting or giving venereal disease are very small, and although medical intervention is possible in both cases, the individual should not dismiss either consequence as being impossible for himself.

Female Sexual Revolutions

Kinsey's data showed that women born before 1900 were half as likely to experience premarital coitus as those born in subsequent decades. Of women born before 1900 who were unmarried at age 25, 14 per cent had experienced premarital coitus. The women born in the first decade after 1900 reached sexual maturity between 1915 and 1925, and during these years a rise in female premarital coitus took place. Of those women born between 1900 and 1910, 36 per cent who were unmarried at 25 had premarital coital experience. The increase continued at about the same rate until 1929, and then leveled off [35, pp. 298–299]. The first female sexual revolution, in terms of a rise in premarital coitus, took place between approximately 1915 and 1929. During this time, the male premarital intercourse rate showed virtually no increase.

Premarital coital rates for males and females stayed about the same from the early 1930s until the late 1960s. Studies done in the late 1960s and early 1970s have shown changes in premarital sexual behavior and attitudes, particularly of females.

Increased Frequency of Premarital Coitus. A number of studies have indicated that more female college students, and perhaps high school students as well, are engaging in premarital coitus [3, 10, 26, 26a, 33a, 39, 51, 53, 58a].

Increased Acceptance of Premarital Coitus. Females in larger numbers are approving of premarital coitus [10, 51]. (See Table 5-1.) As stated previously, there appears to be increasing acceptance of the permissive standards as well [26, 45a].

TABLE 5-1   Percentages of College Students Taking Liberal Positions on Sex Questions, 1958, 1965, 1968, 1970

	Acceptance of Nonvirginity*		Approval of Premarital Coitus*		Premarital Intercourse Is Not Immoral†	
	1958	1968	1958	1968	1965	1970
Intermountain*						
(Mormon country)						
Males %	5	20	23	38	—	—
Females %	11	26	3	24	—	—
Midwest U.S.A.*						
Males %	18	25	47	55	—	—
Females %	23	44	17	38	—	—
Denmark*						
Males %	61	92	94	100	—	—
Females %	74	92	81	100	—	—
Georgia U.S.A.†	—					
Males %	—	—	—	—	67	86
Females %	—	—	—	—	30	66

*Source: Harold T. Christensen, and Christina Gregg. Changing sex norms in America and Scandinavia. *Journal of Marriage and the Family*, 1970, **32**, 616–627.

†Source: Ira E. Robinson, Karl King, and Jack O. Balswick. The premarital sexual revolution among college females. *Family Coordinator*, 1972, **21**, 189–194.

Increased Enjoyment of Premarital Coitus. Females are reporting more enjoyment of premarital coitus, both in general [39], and in the enjoyment of their first premarital coitus [59].

Increased Number of Coital Partners. Females are not only more likely to have premarital intercourse than they were a generation ago, they also appear to be having it with more partners [7, 58a]. Nonvirginity and the number of sex partners that a college girl has appear to be related to her physical attractiveness. In one study, 56 per cent of the most attractive girls, 31 per cent of the medium-attractive, and 37 per cent of the low-attractive girls were nonvirgins. The most attractive girls had the largest number of sex partners [32].

Sex and Love. Although the behavior of women is becoming more liberal, a number of studies have found that women tend to equate sex with love, whereas for men, love and sex are more easily separated. For example, in a study of Canadian high school students it was found that 74 percent of the females and 36 per cent of the males reported that they had been in love with their first coital partner [26a]. There is evidence that even women living in communes that allow sexual freedom tend to fall in love with *one* of their sex partners [8]. There are, of course, exceptions to these findings.

Male Evolution

Until very recently, male premarital coital rates had been stable since the early 1900s [7, 9, 26, 51, 59]. However, studies done in the early 1970s indicate a rise of male premarital intercourse at the college level [26a, 26b]. Two American studies indicate a rise in high school male premarital coital behavior [53, 58a] although the sampling method of one of these studies has been called into question [34]. A study of Canadian high school students age 16 to 19 found almost identical percentages of males and females to have had coital experience, 27.1 per cent of the males and 28.8 per cent of the females [26a].

Males have apparently become more permissive in terms of attitudes toward premarital sex. (See Table 5-1.) More males in one study approved premarital coitus in 1968 than in 1958 [9]. A second study found a decrease between 1965 and 1970 in the percentages of males who said that premarital sexual intercourse was immoral [51]. It can be seen that female attitudes changed more, on the whole, than did male attitudes, but that both sexes became more permissive, as measured here.

Other Group Differences

Males and females, of course, are not the only groups that differ in sexual behavior and attitudes. Premarital coital behavior varies by region of the country [7], by race, and by social class. In one study, blacks were found to have a more permissive sexual code than whites. Black males were the most permissive group, and white females the most restrictive. Blacks were found more likely than whites to require affection as a prerequisite for kissing and petting [48]. Although one study found no relationship between sexual permissiveness and social class [50], lower-class persons do have sexual experiences at an earlier age than do middle-class persons [54].

Influence of Peer Group. The adolescent peer group is thought to have a tremendous influence upon the adolescent individual. In the sexual realm, there is evidence that the perceived behavior of the peer group is related to the individual's behavior. Studies have found that the adolescent's sexual behavior was consistent with that of her friends [44, 57]. Using as subjects patients at a venereal disease clinic in New Zealand, investigators found that similarity between the individual's sexual activity and his friends' varied by the age of the respondent. Forty-four per cent of those persons who had their first coitus at age 14 or under reported that their friends were sexually active at the time, as compared with 80 per cent of those age 15 and 16, and 64 per cent of those age 17 and older. The author suggests that the media are a potent socializing force for some individuals, and that their influence has not been adequately researched [11]. Certainly, television, advertising, movies, and magazines do exert a tremendous influence upon our behavior in many ways, and sexual behavior is no exception.

Society as a Whole

Most sexual attitude and behavior studies are done on college students. A national poll sampling persons of all ages, however, also supports the contention that sexual attitudes are becoming more permissive. In 1969, 68 per cent of those sampled in a Gallup poll said that they thought that premarital intercourse was wrong. In 1973, 48 per cent said that they thought it was wrong. See Table 5-2 for a breakdown by age. In both 1969 and 1973, more women than men said that they thought that premarital sex was wrong. In 1969, 74 per cent of the women and 62 per cent of the men, and in 1973, 53 per cent of the women and 42 per cent of the men condemned premarital coitus [17].

The Impact of Sexual Relations

A very important question regarding premarital sexual relationships is how do they affect the individual, both at the time of the relationship and in later years? Feelings of regret and remorse have been reported by some nonvirgins, but there is evidence that these feelings are becoming less prevalent [9, 10].

Over time, however, people tend to become more conservative in their sexual values. Parents who engaged in premarital intercourse themselves were nonetheless unlikely to be permissive about their sons, and even less likely in the case of daughters [2, 60]. Permissiveness reaches a high point during the premarital years, and then declines with the onset of marriage, reaching a low point when the children are teen-agers and young adults [50]. It will be interesting to see if this trend continues with the present generation of young parents. There is indication from one study that some cohabiting couples will become more conservative when they have

TABLE 5-2   **Percentage of Americans Disapproving of Premarital Intercourse, 1969 and 1973**

Age	1969	1973
All ages	68%	43%
Under 30	49	29
30–45	67	44
50 and over	80	64

Source: G. Gallup. Attitudes of Americans on sex seen undergoing a profound change. Press release, August 1973. *Family Planning Digest*, 1974, **3**:1, 3.

children. Results showed that only a third of female cohabitors and just under half of male cohabitors would approve if their children cohabited [26b].

On Self Esteem. Whether a person who engages in premarital intercourse will have high or low self esteem appears to depend upon the values of the reference group of the individual. An earlier study done on a conservative campus indicated that among conservative individuals, those who refrain from premarital coitus will have higher self-esteem [55]. A study done more recently on two campuses, a moderate Canadian campus and a liberal New York state campus, indicated that there was no significant relationship between sexual permissiveness and self-esteem at either campus. At the liberal campus, however, individuals who reported having had more coital partners had *higher* self-esteem than those who reported having had fewer partners [45a]. What these studies suggest is that self-esteem is related to the way a person sees her behavior in relation to the dominant values in her group.

On the Marital Relationship. As stated in Chapter 8, premarital coitus is associated with higher sexual satisfaction in the case of females [22], but also with a higher rate of extramarital intercourse [38]. Older studies found that the sexually conservative had lower divorce rates, but other indexes of conservatism are also associated with lower divorce rates. Premarital chastity does not *cause* greater marital stability [6].

How much residual feelings of guilt and remorse over premarital encounters affect the marital relationship has not been determined. Case studies reported in studies of premarital intercourse (and letters to Ann Landers) indicate that some people are greatly bothered. Such feelings could perhaps affect the parent's ability to cope with his child's developing sexuality.

HOMOSEXUALITY

Homosexuality may be defined as feeling sexual attraction to the same sex. It may or may not be accompanied by the overt expression of these feelings. Kinsey defined a homosexual as an individual who had at least one homosexual experience at some time in his life [36]. Even a person who had had one homosexual experience in childhood would be considered a homosexual by this very broad definition.

Some individuals are attracted to members of both sexes, and these may be termed **bisexuals** or **ambisexuals.** To further clarify the distinction between hetero-, homo-, and bisexuals, we make the distinction between them as follows: a **heterosexual** is a person who, throughout all or most of his adult life, is sexually attracted to and possibly has sexual relations only with members of the opposite sex. A **homosexual** is a person who throughout all or most of his adult life is sexually attracted to and possibly has sexual relations only with members of the same sex. In either case, an occasional "switch" to the other sex would not change the individual's basic sexual preference orientation. A *bisexual* is an individual whose erotic and love interests are divided between men and women. The bisexual may have concurrent relationships with men and women, or may change back and forth throughout his or her life.

Our definitions would not be accepted by all clinicians, social scientists, heterosexuals, homosexuals, or bisexuals. There is much controversy as well regarding the causes of homosexuality, and whether it is a disease or a normal condition. In 1973, the American Psychiatric Association's board of trustees voted to remove homosexuality from the mental illness category. Not all psychiatrists agree with this decision, however. This move by the American Psychiatric Association reflects a softening of public opinion in this country regarding homosexuality.

Causes of Homosexuality

The ancient Greeks believed that each person was originally created from the splitting of another individual. Some persons came from an all-male whole, others from an all-female whole, and others from a half-male, half-female whole. The resulting mortal searched for his "other half," an idea kept alive in our society today in the romantic notion that people are made for each other. We have tended to forget about the homosexual pairs, thinking only about the heterosexual. The Greek explanation of homosexuality, of course, is not accepted today. But it has not been replaced by a completely adequate explanation.

Freud's Explanations. Freud never developed a coherent theory of homosexuality, and his writings on this subject have been subject to many interpretations by other psychotherapists. Freud considered all persons as having both male and female qualities but did not regard homosexuality as normal. The child's failure to resolve the Oedipal conflict could be manifested in a number of ways, including homosexuality. Homosexuality wasn't thought by Freud to be treatable by therapy, because it was a "perversion" and not a "neurosis" [20].

Disease Theories. A number of psychiatrists still view homosexuality as a disease. Some claim that there is no such thing as a happy homosexual, that all homosexuals are depressed, guilty, and fearful of the opposite sex. The family is sometimes seen as the cause; in the case of the boy, the father is detached, absent, or brutal, and the mother is overprotective or domineering. The female homosexual (Lesbian) may come from a similar family, or the girl's mother may regard all men as brutal or no good, and teach this attitude to her daughter. Other explanations for homosexuality include a deep fear of assuming adult responsibility, extreme competitiveness with one's own sex, the child's awareness that her or his parents wanted a child of the opposite sex, or, in the case of the male, a search for maleness that the individual feels that he lacks [20].

Normality Theories. Other psychiatrists view homosexuality as a normal variant of the human behavior spectrum. They note that not all homosexuals come from disturbed families, and that not all persons from father-absent, mother-dominated families become homosexuals. Some argue that homosexual behavior is normal for mammals. Several studies have found groups of homosexuals to be as psychologically healthy as matched groups of heterosexuals. The homosexuals who go to psychiatrists for help are troubled people, but psychiatrists rarely see the "invisible" nontroubled group of homosexuals [20]. Members of the Gay Liberation movement who lobbied to have homosexuality removed from the mental illness category have pointed out that nothing makes a person feel mentally sick more effectively than constantly being told that he is sick. They contend that now that the "sick" label is being lifted, more and more homosexuals will come "out of the closet" and declare themselves to be homosexuals. This appears to be happening.

Influence of Hormones. There is some evidence that hormonal imbalances may be a part of the explanation for at least some homosexuality. The Masters and Johnson Sex Research Institute reported in 1971 that young men who were predominantly or exclusively homosexual had lower levels of testosterone than did normal men. A very small group of Lesbians was found in England to have lower estrogen levels than normal women. These findings have not been consistently supported by other researchers, and in some cases have been refuted. Administering testosterone to male homosexuals does not change the orientation of their sex interests, but does increase their sex drive [20].

It is possible that prenatal influences of hormones could influence an individual's later sexual orientation. Severe prenatal protein deficiency has been found to cause estrogen feminization of human males, resulting in enlarged breasts, atrophied testes, and a more feminine cognitive style, with higher verbal ability and lower spatial skills [12]. Whether or not the individual's sexual orientation was also affected was not determined by this study. However, prenatal effects have not been ruled out as yet.

Some Tentative Conclusions. Homosexual behavior cannot be explained by one factor or one series of events [37]. Robert Gould [20], a psychiatrist, suggests that there are three types of homosexuals: "Those who are disturbed and whose homosexuality reflects that disturbance symptomatically," for example, those persons with an intense fear or hatred of the opposite sex. Such fear, however, need not be manifested in homosexual behavior, but can also be manifested in sadomasochistic heterosexual behavior (that is, enjoying inflicting pain on one's partner or enjoying having pain inflicted on oneself).

A second type of homosexual is the disturbed individual "for whom homosexuality is not related to the psychiatric problem" [20]. The disturbance in this case is not sexual, but has to do with some other aspect of the personality.

The third type of homosexual is the well-adjusted kind, who is not a psychiatric patient. This kind of individual lives a comfortable, productive, and happy life, and is often committed to long-lasting, intimate, one-to-one relationships, as is the normal and healthy heterosexual.

Changing Attitudes Toward Homosexuality

The decision of the board of trustees of the American Psychiatric Association mentioned previously is an indicator of the change of opinion that is occurring in this country. Other countries have been more tolerant to homosexuality in the past, and some are more tolerant now. In ancient Sparta, love between men was considered to be the ideal, and wives merely fulfilled the needed function of providing new citizens for the state. A man would have sexual intercourse with this wife for this purpose, but he lived with and loved his male companions.

In France, the *Code Napoleon* of 1810 allows all homosexual (and heterosexual) behavior between consenting adults [37]. The same has been allowed in England and Wales since 1971, and Illinois led the way in this regard in the United States [52].

Some persons still hold strong convictions, religious or otherwise, that homosexuality is unnatural, wrong, or sinful. The individual who is concerned about being homosexual and wishes to change can usually be helped to adjust [37]. However, it

CRAIG M. SZWED

should be emphasized that one or two feelings of attraction to same sex, or even homosexual acts, do not mean that a person is a homosexual. During childhood and adolescence there is a developmental stage in which homosexual feelings and acts are normal.

It is our belief that feelings of love and attraction for the same sex are normal throughout the lifespan. In our society it is permissible for women to show affection for one another, to hug and kiss. Most men hesitate to express their feelings in this way, although in Europe such behavior is considered natural. Body contact is essential for human life. Infants and children need to be held and cared for, and most adults feel the need for close contact with another human being. In our society, this need usually is fulfilled through heterosexual contact, but as we have seen, this has not always been the case in all societies.

Many homosexual groups have called themselves "homophiles," which means "one who loves the same sex." By putting the emphasis upon emotions rather than the genitals, they believe that they portray themselves more accurately.

Changing Behavior

Male homosexuals have been more promiscuous than Lesbians, at times restricting their encounters to casual "quickies" in men's rooms (called "tearooms"). The Lesbian is more likely to seek a stable relationship. There is evidence that the male homosexual scene is changing [27]. On the one hand, the "tearoom trade" seems to be increasing, with more men who consider themselves heterosexual in orientation becoming the passive partners in oral-genital sex. These men rationalize their behavior by saying that they aren't homosexuals because they never put some one else's penis in their mouth, or engage in anal intercourse.

At the other end of the spectrum, more homosexuals claim to be seeking stable relationships with other men. The "gays" who have "come out of the closet" and are no longer ashamed of their homosexuality are also more likely to have women lovers as well, that is, to be bisexual.

Women and Homosexuality

Lesbian behavior has received less attention from society and social scientists as well. The most basic reason for this omission is that male behavior has long been considered to have more of an influence upon society than female behavior. Lesbians have been studied and ostracized less because as women they were considered less important. Perhaps their behavior is less offensive than male homosexual behavior because it is less genitally oriented and likely to be less promiscuous.

It is not known how many women are homosexual or bisexual, although Kinsey [53] estimated the number to be about half of the number for male homosexuals. (Kinsey defined a homosexual as a person who had had at least one homosexual experience as an adult.) Recent evidence indicates that bisexuality among women is increasing even more than among men [5]. It is known for certain that most women swingers (see pages 130–131 in this chapter and pages 460–461 in Chapter 17) engage in homosexual activities at parties, whereas male homosexual behavior among swingers is almost nonexistent [1].

The partnerships of 34 white female "married" homosexuals were studied in order to see whether their role relationships were differentiated [31]. The terms *butch* and *femme* commonly referred to those who played masculine and feminine roles, respectively. Results showed that in many ways, the long-lasting, quasi-marital unions of these female homosexuals resembled heterosexual marriages in straight society.

GENDER ROLES IN ADOLESCENCE AND ADULTHOOD

In the previous chapter, we described how early gender-role learning takes place. By the age of two or earlier, the child has a conception of herself or himself as female or male. As the child progresses through childhood, she continues to learn her culture's conception of the proper gender role. This learning continues through life.

The Question of Malleability

Some feminists argue that *all* sex differences beyond the anatomical are learned. It is our belief, however, that one's maleness or femaleness provides broad ranges for behavior, but that there are some differences beyond genital differences [30, Parts I and II]. Socialization has a large influnce upon the innate differences, in most cases enlarging upon them.

The case of the transsexual indicates that this socialization process occasionally does not occur. A *transsexual* is an individual, usually male (we use the male example), who believes that he was born into the wrong body. From early childhood, he identifies strongly with women, and is very unhappy as a boy. He wants to have relationships with men, but not man-to-man. Rather, he sees himself in the female role. The homosexual, by contrast, sees himself as a man, a man attracted to other men. The only solution for the true transsexual is a sex change operation; the body is more easily changed than the mind.

Studies of male transsexuals suggest that an individual can be effectively socialized as a member of the opposite sex [21]. However, the role of altered brain states upon transsexualism has not been ruled out [13].

In the normal individual, as we have stated before, heredity sets the stage for environmental influences. Sutton-Smith put it this way: "Masculinity and femininity are . . . forms of adaptation towards which the individual is assisted by inheritance and training" [56].

Continued Learning of Gender Roles. Individuals throughout their lifetime are rewarded by others for gender-appropriate behavior, but more importantly, they are punished for behavior that is considered inappropriate [58]. Such reward and punishment is usually subtle, but potent. The individual seeks to maintain a feeling of consistency between himself and his reference group or groups, and a feeling of differentness from those with whom he does not identify. A woman who becomes involved in the women's liberation movement may experience a change of reference group, from that of other women who accept traditional roles to the other women in the movement. She learns a different conception of sex roles and is rewarded and punished by her new reference group for different behaviors. We now turn to the growth of the women's movement, and then to its effects upon women and men.

The Women's Movement: A Brief "Herstory"

More than a century and a quarter has passed since the first Women's Rights Convention, held in Seneca Falls, New York, in 1848. The women who met there wanted to be released from bondage to men, who controlled their lives as husbands and fathers. The movement to free the slaves was growing in the United States, and some women clearly saw the parallels between their condition and that of the slaves. A woman belonged to her husband, who could abuse her as he wished. She could not be a minister, a doctor, or a lawyer. She could not vote. A different moral code existed for women.

The opening of the West also had an effect upon women's rights. Women were scarce in the West, and this gave them a bargaining power that they did not have in the "civilized" East. It was impossible for women to be sheltered and protected in the West the way they had been in the East. They often had to do the work of men. It is significant that Wyoming led the way in 1869 in giving the women the vote.

During the 1800s, women began to go to college in greater numbers, and more women also began to earn their own living, largely due to the industrial revolution. Women were paid less than men; working conditions and wages were deplorable; but women began to gain another bit of bargaining power that was previously denied them. Groups of feminists fought for equal rights for females, with varying degrees of success, but did not receive the right to vote until 1920. About the same time, the first revolution in female sexual behavior was taking place. During World War I, the services of women had been needed in the labor market, and their working experience changed their lives and status in a way that could not be completely undone.

Following World War I, more women went to college and entered the professions than ever before. During World War II, they worked in huge numbers. But after the war was over, drastic changes occurred for women. Women's place suddenly became the home once again. Books and articles in women's magazines promulgated the idea that the ideal woman stayed at home, making and caring for lots of babies and keeping her husband happy. It was all right for her to go to college, but she should not consider having a career unless she were unfortunate enough to remain single.

The Rebirth of Feminism. In 1963, Betty Friedan published *The Feminine Mystique* [16]. It tells the rise and fall of the first women's movement, and it helped to start a new movement. The National Organization for Women (NOW) was founded in 1966. Since that time many other women's rights organizations have been founded, some of them highly structured, such as NOW, and others at the grass-roots level. Women want equal pay for equal work; they want equal job and educational opportunity; many want day care facilities for their children. Before the 1973 Supreme Court decision that struck down the antiabortion laws, many women lobbied for the individual right to choose whether or not to end a pregnancy.

In 1967, an amendment to the Constitution made it unlawful for a person to be discriminated against on the basis of race or sex. At the time, some legislators took the "sex" part as somewhat of a joke, but women took it very seriously.

Consciousness-Raising Groups. The work of the women's movement is carried on in part through discussion groups known as consciousness-raising groups. Women meet in order to discuss their experiences and their thoughts and feelings concerning what it means to be a woman. Men are often excluded from these sessions.

Black Feminism: Some Contrasts. The early feminists saw their position as being similar to that of the slaves. Although some black women today join the feminists, others believe that they can have no true liberty until all blacks have real equality. They feel that black women should not join with white women in the white woman's struggle against male dominance, because black women are not dominated by black men. The black man is even more controlled by white society than is the black woman, who has traditionally been more able to get work than has the black man [43].

Requirements for Women's Self-Esteem. Before we assess some of the changes that the women's movement has made on the lives of both men and women, we would like to note some requirements for woman's best functioning and self-esteem, as proposed by Whiting [61]. She studied family life in simple subsistence societies in which women still participate in the production of goods, and/or control resources. Female economic roles complement male roles.

In such societies, the men are herders and women usually tend gardens that are close to the house, but when gardens are far away they become the male's responsibility. In this case, the woman stays at home and tends the fire. Women sell excess produce, cooked food or cloth if there is a market nearby. When the woman goes to the market she may take her babies or leave them at home with a relative or an older child.

In societies that are changing from pastoralism to agriculture, woman's work is usually heavy. As land becomes scarce and herds dwindle, the man's work becomes less and the woman's responsibility becomes greater. Men fail to help in agriculture if it is considered "woman's work."

In these societies, whether or not the man still has a viable economic role, the woman is contributing to the welfare of her family. Her role is not limited to cooking, cleaning, and child care. She controls economic resources, and this gives her power and prestige. Furthermore, there are relatives nearby with whom to interact and to take care of her children; she never spends the entire day in housework and child care. When children reach the age of five to seven, they begin to care for younger siblings and help with other family tasks. This gives the children a sense of being worthwhile and gives them direct experience in adult roles.

Whiting proposes that in order for a woman to be happy she must have self-esteem, and in order to have self-esteem she must (1) "be involved in productive work—cooking, cleaning, and childrearing is not sufficient." (2) She needs to have control of some resources so that she is not totally dependent upon her husband for material goods. (3) "She needs to be away from her children four or five hours a day and at some period to be in the company of other adults." (4) She needs a flexible schedule and a work day no longer than five hours. (5) She needs other women nearby to help her in emergencies.

The American housewife spends more time than ever before in child care and housework. Housework "expands to fill the time available" [16, Chap. 10]. Although children do need the attention of their parents, too much parental attention can be damaging. The feminine mystique that extolled the glories of full-time housewifery and motherhood is apparently on the wane. Not all women should work outside the home; many really are fulfilled as homemakers. Nor are paid jobs essential to all. But Whiting's research supports and explains Friedan's thesis that many women are discontent in the homemaker role.

Women's Reactions to the Women's Movement

Women's self-attitudes, and conceptions of their own present and future roles, are changing. Between 1968 and 1971, women college students in New England and the Midwest changed toward seeing themselves as more aggressive, independent, objective, dominant, competitive, rational, logical, with less need for security. All of these qualities had previously been delegated almost exclusively to men [25]. Another study done in 1971 asked students to compare themselves with members of the opposite sex on twelve personality qualities. Many students did not ascribe gender to the traits. Sixty-five per cent of the females and 55 per cent of the males said that they were no more or less intellectual than the opposite sex. Both males and females, however, did agree that independence, aggressiveness, ambition, and objectivity-rationality were more characteristic of men than of women. Passivity, however, was not seen as a feminine trait [39].

While their mothers play productive roles outside the home, these children learn to do the same, through imitating and helping.

In this same study, it was noted that women in the 1960s were already beginning to question existing gender roles and the subordination of individual needs to that of the family. The questioning became more profound in the 1970s. Fewer children were desired in the 1970s than in 1965, with 10 per cent wanting no children.

Gallup and Harris polls have tapped the opinion of the public at large, rather than relying solely on college students. In 1970, 69 per cent of females and 58 per cent of males said that they would have less respect for a man who stayed home with his children while his wife worked. More men (58 per cent) than women (49 per cent) said that they would vote for a qualified woman president, according to the 1969 Gallup poll. In a 1970 Harris poll, 91 per cent of the women and 85 per cent of the men said that a woman can be successful at a career and feminine at the same

IT KEEPS ON GROWING: MORE ABOUT SEX

time. This finding, at least, is encouraging. Some confusion does exist regarding the condition of women and what should be done about it. A Harris poll in 1970 reported the following:

> Fifty-two per cent of women *disagreed* with the statement: "It's about time women did something to protest the real injustices they've faced for years."

> Sixty-six per cent of women *agreed* with the statement: "If women don't speak up for themselves and confront men on their real problems, nothing will be done about these problems." [25]

Role Strain. Role strain, as distinguished from role conflict, has been defined as the feeling of stress in fulfilling the demands of one's role obligations [19]. In a study of males, females, and transsexuals, it was found that females experience the most role strain, men a medium amount, and transsexuals the least [33]. It isn't easy being a woman today.

Men's Reactions to the Women's Movement

But then, it isn't always easy to be a man, either. Men who are intimately involved with women who are changing cannot help being changed as well. The adjustment process can be difficult. Men are responding to two kinds of changes in women: women are challenging male instrumental dominance, and they are becoming less willing to serve male emotional needs at the cost of their own needs and ambitions [58]. Some men are very happy to have their wives work, if only for the reason that it increases the family income. For others, the fact that they no longer bring home all the "bacon" is a threat to their masculinity and sense of self-worth. These men are used to being the instrumental leader of the family, and find it hard to give ground.

Traditionally, women have been socialized to be more expressive; that is, to be caring, giving, feeling creatures who serve the needs of their men and children. Men, on the other hand, have not been taught how to express their feelings, or even to know what their feelings are. The skillful woman would help her man to experience himself at the emotional level. Just as the woman in a traditional relationship would live vicariously through her man's achievement in the world of work, the man would live his emotional life vicariously through his woman's [58].

Some men today are struggling with the task of becoming more expressive. Men's consciousness-raising groups are meeting to discuss the problems and possibilities of being a man in a world that is becoming more woman-oriented.

Men's role-conceptions are changing. One study found that among some college men, the norm of male superiority appears to be giving way to "an ideal of intellectual companionship between equals." However, nearly a third of the males in this study still felt some anxiety over not living up to the old standard of male superiority. These men had ambivalent feelings toward the idea of working wives.

The ideological supports for the traditional way of life are weakening, but among some men the emotional commitment to the old ways is still strong [38]. In a second study, college men characterized their ideal woman as being more competent, adventuresome, and independent than they characterized themselves [44a]. Young men do appear to be moving away from the idea of a strongly male-dominated family [25].

Implications of the Women's Movement

Although we have been referring to the women's movement, many of its members think of it in terms of human liberation rather than just the liberation of women. It is not just the black woman who cannot be free until her man is; this truth applies to all women. As long as men and women live together, their lives and roles will be intertwined. The man who allows his wife to be a person is freed from the responsibility of providing a vicarious life for her. Instead, they can share in each other's lives.

SEXUAL STANDARDS AFTER MARRIAGE

The Christian marital vow usually includes the words "forsaking all others." These words are a promise of emotional and sexual fidelity to one's partner. But as we all know, the formal standard of marital fidelity is not adhered to by all persons in our society.

Nor do all societies require marital sexual fidelity. In polygamous societies, individuals (more usually men than women) are permitted to have more than one spouse. In other societies, sexual liasons are permitted for married persons. In some cases, "wife-lending" or "wife exchange" is encouraged as a part of the hospitality code. Among the Chuckchee of Siberia, the host offers his wife to a man who is traveling away from home, and has the favor returned when the guest is in turn in the host's role. Other societies lift the restrictions on extramarital sex on specific festive occasions [15].

Illicit Extramarital Sex

Traditionally, extramarital sex in our society has equaled "the affair." An affair is an extramarital sexual involvement that is carried on without the knowledge or consent of the spouse of at least one of the parties to the affair. Both persons involved in the affair may be married, or one may be married and the other single. An affair may be a one-night stand, or it may continue for years.

It is not possible to say how many people actually engage in extramarital affairs, but some of the older studies estimated that between 25 and 50 per cent of men have at least one affair [15]. The figures for women were thought to be lower. No doubt more people have a desire for having an affair at times during their married lives than actually carry through with their fantasies. In his book *The Affair,* Morton Hunt [28] claims that nearly every married person has the desire for an affair at least once during his marriage.

Consensual Extramarital Sex

Not all persons who engage in extramarital sex do so without their partner's knowledge or approval. *Swinging* and *sexually open marriages* are lifestyles that condone sexual infidelity. We deal more with these lifestyles in Chapter 17. We are concerned here with them as sexual behavior.

> Swinging generally involves two or more pair-bonded couples who mutually decide to switch sexual partners or engage in group sex. Singles may be included either through temporary coupling with another individual specifically for the purpose of swinging or as a part of a triadic or larger group sexual experience. [47, p. 436]

A sexually open marriage is a marriage or marriage-type relationship in which the partners agree that each has the right to form intimate relationships with others that may involve sex. The spouse's other partners may or may not be personally known.

The line between swinging and sexually open marriage appears to be blurring. Swinging started out as purely sexual activity, with emotional involvement taboo [1]. Some swingers would avoid any conversation that might induce social intimacy. The feeling among such swingers was that sex that was "just sex" would not disrupt the marital relationship, and would probably enhance it, but that emotions were dynamite to be avoided.

More recently, some swingers have been turning to more of a sexually-open marriage-type relationship. Ramey calls this relationship intimate friendship, "an otherwise traditional friendship in which sexual intimacy is considered appropriate behavior" [47, p. 436]. Swingers make friends with some of their swinging partners, and then drop out of the larger swinging circuit [46].

Swinging is not the only route to sexually open marriage. A couple may decide, before or after (or even without) marriage, that sexual fidelity is not important to them. For some but not all couples, a sexually open marriage may be part of a larger lifestyle, open marriage, which the O'Neills described in their book of that name (see pages 461–462 in this text) [45]. Allowing one's partner sexual freedom does not guarantee that one is looking out for his or her best interests, however. We have known couples who seemed to use what they called a "sexually open marriage" to cover up a troubled relationship, or to allow a time-out period while they tried to decide whether or not to separate.

Postmarital Sex

What happens to the person who loses his partner through death or divorce? Sexual needs do not end because the relationship ends. Postmarital sex has not been adequately studied. Hunt [29] estimates that of divorced and separated people (what he calls the Formerly Married), almost none of the men and only 20 per cent of the women have had no sexual intercourse since the breakup of their marriages. Five out of six begin having coitus within a year of the marital breakup. Among the sexually active, sex without love is common, but certainly not universal. Some Formerly Marrieds break up one relationship in order to begin or legalize a new one, and these pair-bonded individuals would not differ much from other such couples.

The sexual needs and activities of the widowed are virtually unresearched. Those persons widowed early in life, or while still sexually active with their partners, would suffer more sexual deprivation than those not interested in sex. The widow(er) who was deeply in love at the time of separation by death would probably have a harder time adjusting sexually to a new partner, or even looking for a new partner.

COMMUNICATION AND SEX

Sexual behavior that occurs between two people is itself a form of communication. The same message, however, is not always inherent in all acts of sexual intercourse (or breast-fondling or oral-genital intercourse) even between the same people. A specific sex act may mean, "I love you" or "I enjoy you" or "You turn me on," or "I abuse you." It can, of course, mean one thing to one partner and something else to the other. Sexually intimate behavior can be an expression of feeling that already exists, or it can cause a feeling to grow larger or smaller. Verbal communication is needed to clarify the development of feelings.

Communication about sex is important for the enhancement of the sensual and sexual aspects of the relationship, as well. Masters and Johnson [41] emphasize the importance of each partner letting the other know what feels good. What is most enjoyable to one person may be dull, painful, or repulsive to another. The quality of communication is important: saying "You're clumsy—stop it" would not be as helpful as asking for a gentle touch.

Communication about sex can also avert unwanted pregnancy. Before the invention of highly effective and nonvisible female contraceptives (that is, the Pill and the I.U.D.), the careful male used a condom. Now, many males assume that their female partners have protected themselves. After all, the men reason, it *is* the female who gets pregnant. Both may be reluctant to discuss contraception before coitus. The female may fear that if she mentions that she is unprotected, intercourse will not take place. If pregnancy results, it is the fault of both.

AGING AND SEXUALITY

The work of Masters and Johnson [42] has refuted the myth that sex is only for the young. Kinsey [36] noted a decline in male coital rates, starting from the time of marriage and continuing throughout the man's lifetime. A similar decline was noted for females [35], but it was concluded that the decline in female behavior was a reflection of a decline in male capacity, rather than that of the female.

Supporting the contention of Kinsey and his colleagues, Masters and Johnson [42] found in their clinical laboratory experiments that men past sixty were slower to be aroused sexually, slower to develop an erection, and slower to reach orgasm than were younger men. As the female ages, her capacity to reach orgasm does not diminish, especially if she receives regular stimulation. Masters and Johnson place great emphasis upon the monotony of sexual experience as a cause of the male's waning capacity.

Menopause

The cessation of menstruation is called **menopause.** Menstruation does not merely pause, however. It stops, usually after some irregular periods, but sometimes with no warning. Since most women have a span of a few months or a year or two during which menstruation signals its approaching end, menopause is commonly considered to be a period of life. *Change of life* is often a term for it. Some of these signals are menstrual periods are shorter and then longer; periods are less frequent; periods are skipped; bleeding is profuse; hot flushes or hot flashes, sudden waves of heat with perspiration and then chilling, lasting from a few seconds to half an hour and occurring once or several times a day; emotional disturbances of irritability, nervousness, depression, frigidity, lack of memory, and problems in concentrating.

Menopause occurs when the estrogen level sinks to a certain point. A woman's ovaries produce estrogen from before she is born until she dies. Her ovaries are especially active during her prenatal life and during the period between menarche and menopause. Estrogen production begins to decrease in the late twenties and continues to decrease. Menopause may occur any time between the ages of 35 and 60, the average age of menopause being around 47. Removal of both ovaries will bring on the physical symptoms of menopause. Being the result of a lack of estrogen, menopause is like a deficiency disease [18]. (Not all physicians would agree with us.) The simple technique of supplying estrogen usually relieves troublesome symptoms of menopause.

An occasional complication of menopause is pregnancy. It is rare for a woman to become pregnant one year after her last menstrual period, but it has happened. In the beginning stages of menopause, when periods are merely lengthened or skipped, pregnancy can occur. Healthy children have been born to women of 60 or even 70, but the odds of a menopausal woman producing a mongoloid or deformed child are high [4].

Postmenopause

Most women live for many years after the menopause. After menstruation has finally stopped, many discomforts disappear, including the hot flashes and many emotional complaints. If a woman has had a hard time with heavy bleeding or painful periods, she usually welcomes freedom from these burdens. Why, then is this time of life considered problematic by some people?

Some of the symptoms of insufficient estrogen continue to be annoying and even debilitating [4]. The vagina becomes less acid, increasing the likelihood of infections. Its walls lose elasticity and may bleed because they are easily eroded. Thinness and dryness of the vagina may make intercourse painful. General skin tone slackens. Breasts shrink and droop. Bones become porous and brittle, because of a loss of calcium. There is an increased risk of coronary heart disease and cancer. Numerous physical problems include insomnia, headache, fast-beating heart, vertigo, loss of appetite, and weight gain. Estrogen therapy often improves or even removes these problems. In the case of loss of bone tissue, however, estrogen therapy may prevent deterioration but will not reverse the process.

Treating the Symptoms of Menopause and Postmenopause. As simple as it is to swallow an estrogen pill, a physician's skill is needed in interpreting the tests that show the woman's natural estrogen level and then fitting the dose to her individual

needs. The doctor also chooses the type of preparation that she can tolerate best, since some women experience side effects from hormone therapy. For instance, if she has nausea from one medication, the doctor can most likely find another one that does not bother her. Regular and adequate medical care is very important in keeping an older woman in good physical condition.

Emotional Aspects of Menopause and Postmenopause. The hormone-related emotional problems should, of course, be controlled through hormone therapy. Other problems stem from the self-concept and its relation to the parent-child, marital, and occupational careers. Since menopause often coincides with the children's departure from home, the mother may be then faced with problems of how to occupy herself in ways that seem worthwhile to her. Feeling useless and low in self-esteem, she may attribute her problems to menopause. Another example comes from the sexual career. If a woman has not had a satisfactory sex life up to this time, she may use menopause as an excuse for avoiding sexual intercourse. If untreated menopausal symptoms are also making intercourse unpleasant, then she will be thoroughly convinced that she should not participate.

Emotional aspects may be very positive. Some women report no negative symptoms at all and many more have no symptoms when they have adequate medical supervision. Many such women comment that it is wonderful to be relieved of the nuisance of monthly periods. Some report improved sexual relations because they no longer have to worry about getting pregnant. Even women with mild negative symptoms may think that the benefits of menopause outweigh the problems. Since menstruation no longer serves any useful purpose to the woman who does not want to have any more children, menopause may be especially welcome to women who are eager to get on with their jobs and occupational careers. Menopause marks the beginning of a period of life that can be very fulfilling in terms of companionship in marriage and advancement in personal development.

SUMMARY   Cultures vary widely in their interpretation of sexuality and their regulation of its expression. The timing and conduct of a person's passage into adulthood is related not only to cultural interpretation of sex but also to an interpretation of the whole course of human development. Adulthood is not clearly defined in modern industrial societies, since adolescence is a long and important period.

Premarital heterosexual activity varies widely between groups and individuals. American premarital sexual standards have been classified into the following four: abstinence, permissiveness with affection, double standard, and permissiveness without affection. In deciding upon the choice of a standard, the probable consequences of various courses of action (and inaction) are pertinent. Pregnancy, a possible result of sexual activity, is almost entirely preventable and also terminable, but when pregnancies are neither prevented nor terminated, the resulting babies must be cared for. And any one of these results of sexual activity may have a profound effect upon one or both of the couple involved. Another consequence, often preventable, is venereal disease. Guilt feelings may result. When heterosexual activity crowds out like-sex friendships in adolescence, development of the sense of identity may be curtailed.

Advantages of premarital intercourse include physical and psychological satisfaction. Premarital intercourse may also provide helpful experience and testing for compatability. Some groups look down upon virgins, although there are indeed many who do just the opposite. Before beginning a sex relationship, it is wise to think over possible consequences and plan to prevent undesired ones.

The twentieth century has seen a great change in women's sexual behavior in terms of acceptant attitudes and premarital intercourse, and in the frequency and number of partners. Although men have not changed as greatly as women in terms of frequency of premarital sex, their experiences must have changed because women have changed. Different behavior and attitudes have been noted in regard to social class, regions, and race. Adolescent peer groups exert strong influence on sexual practices.

Attitudes toward premarital sex change as persons grow older, being most permissive before marriage and becoming more strict after marriage, especially when their children are adolescents.

Homosexuality is the sexual attraction to persons of the same sex. Bisexuals are attracted to both sexes. Homosexuality is interpreted variously as abnormal and a disease or as a normal variation of human behavior. Some but not all homosexuals are troubled about their condition. Some are well adjusted, leading productive, happy lives. Increasing numbers of men and women are declaring themselves homosexual. Transsexuals feel like members of the opposite sex and wish to be so, in every way. Sex-change surgery can be a satisfactory solution.

Gender roles continue to be developed throughout life, with cultural forces molding the individual. When a person changes reference groups, as when a woman joins a women's group, there is a change in the forces influencing gender role development. In the nineteenth century, women gained some rights, some freedom from men, and a new point of view on gender roles. They suffered a setback after World War II, when the cultural ideal for women was focused on homemaking and having many children. The female role expanded again in the 1960s, through women's liberation, the Equal Rights Amendment, and the ecological threat of population explosion. Women are seriously concerned now with working out appropriate new roles. Changes in women's roles have profound effects upon men's and children's roles, and hence upon the quality of life in the society. While women expand their roles and influence, their self-esteem, and dignity, men are trying to retain their masculinity and feelings of self-worth. One avenue of growth for men is in emotional expression and freedom to sample and enjoy activities that were formerly restricted to women. Companionship, cooperation, and equality between men and women are sought as ways of fulfilling both.

Extramarital sex, although generally illicit, has always been carried on to some extent in the Western world. Swinging and sexually open marriage are new trends in which partners agree to having sex relations outside their marriage. Postmarital sex relations occur among the majority of divorced and separated people. Old people continue to be interested in sex and to enjoy it when they have the opportunity to engage in it.

Verbal communication is important in sexual interaction, for clarifying perceptions and feelings and improving techniques. It is also essential for planning contraception and preventing venereal disease.

Menopause, the cessation of menstruation, marks the end of fertility but not of the enjoyment of sex. Lowered estrogen levels may bring on bodily aging changes and perhaps emotional upsets, but hormonal therapy can do much to retard these changes. Many women have no problems with menopause. Some welcome it.

REFERENCES

1. Bartell, Gilbert D. *Group sex: An eyewitness report on the American way of swinging.* New York: American Library, 1971.
2. Bell, Robert and Jack Buerkle. Mother and daughter attitudes to premarital sexual behavior. *Marriage and Family Living,* 1961, **22,** 390–392.
3. Bell, Robert and Chaskes, Jay. Premarital sexual experience among coeds, 1958 and 1968. *Journal of Marriage and the Family,* 1970, **32,** 81–84.
4. Boston Woman's Health Book Collective. *Our bodies, ourselves.* New York: Simon & Schuster, 1971.
5. Brody, Jane. Bisexual life-style appears to be spreading and not necessarily among swingers. *New York Times,* March 24, 1974.
6. Burgess, Ernest and Paul Wallin. *Engagement and Marriage.* Philadelphia: Lippincott, 1953.
7. Cannon, Kenneth and Richard Long. Premarital sexual behavior in the sixties. *Journal of Marriage and the Family,* 1971, **33,** 36–49.
8. Chilman, Catherine. Some psychological aspects of female sexuality. *Family Coordinator,* 1974, **23,** 123–131.
9. Christensen, Harold and George Carpenter. Timing patterns in the development of sexual intimacy. *Marriage and Family Living,* 1962, **24,** 30–35.
10. Christensen, Harold and Christina Gregg. Changing sex norms in America and Scandinavia. *Journal of Marriage and the Family,* 1970, **32,** 616–627.
11. Davis, Peter. Contextual sex saliency and sexual activity: The relative effects of family and peer group in the sexual socialization process. *Journal of Marriage and the Family,* 1974, **36,** 196–202.
12. Dawson, John L. M., Y. M. Cheung, T. S. Lau, and F. Yue. The neonatal sex hormone reversal of cognitive skills in rats and men. U. of Hong Kong, 1972. (Mimeo.)
13. Epstein, Arthur. The relationship of altered brain states to psychopathology. In Joseph Zubin and John Money (eds.). *Contemporary sexual behavior: Critical issues in the 1970s.* Baltimore: Johns Hopkins, 1972, 297–310.
14. Erikson, Erik. *Identity, youth, and crisis.* New York: Norton, 1968.
15. Ford, Clellan and Frank A. Beach. *Patterns of sexual behavior.* New York: Harper, 1951.
16. Friedan, Betty. *The feminine mystique.* New York: Norton, 1963.
17. Gallup, G. Attitudes of Americans on sex seen undergoing a profound change. Press release, August, 1973. *Family Planning Digest,* 1974, **3**:1, 3.

18. Gifford-Jones, W. *On being a woman: The modern woman's guide to gynecology.* New York: Macmillan, 1971.

19. Goode, William J., Cited in Thomas Kando. Role strain: A comparison of males, females, and transsexuals. *Journal of Marriage and the Family,* 1972, **34,** 459–464.

20. Gould, Robert E. What we don't know about homosexuality. *New York Times Magazine,* February 24, 1974, 12, 13, 51+.

21. Green, Richard. Twenty-five boys with atypical gender identity: A behavioral summary. In Joseph Zubin and John Money (eds.). *Contemporary sexual behavior: Critical issues in the 1970s.* Baltimore: Johns Hopkins, 1972, 351–358.

22. Hamblin, Robert and Robert Blood, Jr. Premarital experience and the wife's sexual adjustment. *Social Problems,* 1956, **3,** 122–130.

23. Hammond, Boone and Joyce Ladner. Socialization into sexual behavior in a Negro slum ghetto. In Carlfred Broderick and Jessie Bernard (eds.). *The individual, sex, and society.* Baltimore; Johns Hopkins, 1969, 41–51.

24. Harrison, Norma. The adolescent father: Coming of age. *McCalls,* April, 1974, 40.

25. Hartley, Ruth E. Role models and role outcomes. Paper presented at *Women: Resource for a changing world.* Conference held at Radcliffe Institute, Radcliffe College, Cambridge, Mass. April 17, 18, 1972.

26. Hobart, Charles W. Sexual permissiveness in young English and French Canadians. *Journal of Marriage and the Family,* 1972, **34,** 292–304.

26a. Hornick, Joseph. Premarital sexual attitudes and behavior: A reference-group contingent-factor theory. Unpublished PhD Dissertation, University of Waterloo, 1975.

26b. Huang, Lucy Jen. Research with unmarried conhabiting couples: Including non-exclusive sexual realtions. Paper presented at the annual meetings of the National Council on Family Relations, St. Louis, October, 1974.

27. Humphreys, Laud. New styles in homosexual manliness. In Helena Z. Lopata (ed.). *Marriages and families,* New York: Van Nostrand, 1973, 354–362.

28. Hunt, Morton. *The affair.* New York: American Library, 1971.

29. Hunt, Morton. *The world of the formerly married.* New York: McGraw-Hill, 1966.

30. Hutt, S. J. and Corinne Hutt. *Early human development.* London: Oxford U. P., 1973.

31. Jensen, Mehri S. Role differentiation in female homosexual quasi-marital unions. *Journal of Marriage and the Family,* 1974, **36,** 360–367.

32. Kaats, Gilbert R. and Keith Davis. The dynamics of sexual behavior in college students. *Journal of Marriage and the Family,* 1970, **32,** 390–399.

33. Kando, Thomas. Role strain: A comparison of males, females, and transsexuals. *Journal of Marriage and the Family,* 1972, **34,** 459–464.

33a. Kantner, John. Teenage sexual and reproductive behavior. Speech presented to the American Psychological Association, New Orleans, 1974.

34. Kantner, John. Teens and sex: A national portrait? *Family Planning Perspectives,* 1973, **5,** 124–125.

35. Kinsey, Alfred C., Wardell B. Pomeroy, Clyde E. Martin, and Paul H. Gebhard. *Sexual behavior in the human female.* Philadelphia: Saunders, 1953.

36. Kinsey, Alfred C., Wardell B. Pomeroy, and Clyde E. Martin. *Sexual behavior in the human male.* Philadelphia: Saunders, 1948.

37. Kogan, Benjamin. *Human sexual expression.* New York: Harcourt, 1973.

38. Komarovsky, Mirra. Cultural contradictions and sex roles: The masculine case. *American Journal of Sociology* 1973, **78,** 111–122.

39. Lozoff, Marjorie. Changing life styles and role perceptions of men and women students. Paper presented at *Women: Resources for a changing world.* Conference held at Radcliffe Institute, Radcliffe College, Cambridge, Mass. April 17, 18, 1972.

40. Maslow, Abraham and James Sakoda. Volunteer error in the Kinsey study. In J. Himeloch and Sylvia Fava (eds.). *Sexual behavior in American society.* New York: Norton, 1955, 119–125.

41. Masters, William and Virginia Johnson. *Human sexual inadequacy.* Boston: Little, Brown, 1966.

42. Masters, William and Virginia Johnson. *Human sexual response.* Boston: Little, Brown, 1970.

43. Mayo, Julia. The new black feminism: A minority report. In Joseph Zubin and John Money (eds.). *Contemporary sexual behavior: Critical issues in the 1970s.* Baltimore: Johns Hopkins, 1973, 175–186.

44. Mirande, Alfred. Reference group theory and adolescent sexual behavior. *Journal of Marriage and the Family,* 1968, **30,** 572–577.

44a. O'Leary, Virginia and Charlene Depner. College males' ideal female: Changes in sex-role stereotypes. *Journal of Psychology,* 1975, **95,** 139–140.

45. O'Neill, Nena and George O'Neill. *Open marriage: A new life style for couples.* New York: Avon, 1972.

45a. Perlman, Daniel. Self-esteem and sexual permissiveness. *Journal of Marriage and the Family,* 1974, **36,** 470–474.

46. Palson, Charles and Rebecca Palson. Swinging in wedlock. In Helena Z. Lopata. (ed.). *Marriages and families.* New York: Van Nostrand, 1973, 203–215.

47. Ramey, James W. Emerging patterns of innovative behavior in marriage. *Family Coordinator,* 1972, **21,** 435–456.

48. Reiss, Ira. Premarital sexual permissiveness among Negroes and whites. *American Sociological Review,* 1964, **29,** 688–698.

49. Reiss, Ira. *Premarital sexual standards in America.* New York: Free Press, 1960.

50. Reiss, Ira. *The social context of premarital sexual permissiveness.* New York: Holt, 1967.

50a. Reiss, Ira and Brent C. Miller. A theoretical analysis of heterosexual permissiveness. *Technical Report No. II.* Minnesota Family Study Center, University of Minnesota, 1974.

51. Robinson, Ira, Karl King, and Jack Balswick. The premarital sexual revolution among college females. *Family Coordinator,* 1972, **21,** 189–194.

52. Rosenzweig, Saul. Human sexual autonomy as an evolutionary attainment, anticipating proceptive sex choice and idiodynamic bisexuality. In Joseph Zubin and John Money (eds.). *Contemporary sexual behavior: Critical issues in the 1970s.* Baltimore: Johns Hopkins, 1973, 189–230.

53. Sorensen, Robert C. *Adolescent sexuality in contemporary America.* New York: World, 1973.

54. Staples, Robert. Research on black sexuality: Its implication for family life, sex education, and public policy. *Family Coordinator,* 1972, **21,** 183–188.

55. Stratton, John and Stephen Spitzer. Sexual permissiveness and self-evaluation: A question of substance and a question of method. *Journal of Marriage and the Family,* 1967, **29,** 434–441.

56. Sutton-Smith, Brian. Sex differences in development. In Lee C. Deighton (ed.). *Encyclopedia of Education,* Vol. 2., New York: Macmillan, 1971, 59–65.

57. Teevan, James, Jr. Reference groups and premarital sexual behavior. *Journal of Marriage and the Family,* 1972, **34,** 283–292.

58. Tresemer, David and Joseph Pleck. Maintaining and changing sex role boundaries in men and women. Paper presented at *Women: Resource for a Changing World.* Conference held at Radcliffe Institute, Radcliffe College, Cambridge, Mass. April 17, 18, 1972.

58a. Vener, Arthur and Cyrus Stewart. Adolescent sexual behavior in middle America revisited: 1970–1973. *Journal of Marriage and the Family,* 1974, **36,** 728–735.

59. Vener, Arthur, Cyrus Stewart, and David Hager. The sexual behavior of adolescents in Middle America: Generational and American-British comparisons. *Journal of Marriage and the Family,* 1972, **34,** 696–705.

60. Wake, F. R. Attitudes of parents toward the premarital sex behavior of their children and themselves. *Journal of Sex Research,* 1969, **5,** 170–171.

61. Whiting, Beatrice. Work and the family: Cross-cultural perspectives. Paper presented at *Women: Resource for a changing world.* Conference held at Radcliffe Institute, Radcliffe College, Cambridge, Mass. April 17, 18, 1972.

Part III is concerned with interactions between intimates, most of whom are related to one another through marriage or blood (more accurately, genes). "Two Find Each Other," a chapter on partner selection, is concerned with the ways in which people find and choose each other to live as couples, usually, but not always, as a married pair. We have used the term **partner selection** instead of **mate selection** because we did not wish to imply that all partners would necessarily have children. The word **mate** connotes

PART THREE

A family is people

reproduction. Similarily, the next two titles use the word **partnerhood** *rather than the more usual term,* **marital relationships,** *because some couples are committed couples without being married. As partners, they have many, perhaps most, of the experiences and relationships of married couples. The topic* **parenthood** *includes the pros and cons of becoming a parent instead of remaining childfree. This choice was less open to previous generations. Its availability has many implications. New national and global situations are significant in regard to choosing or rejecting parenthood. Parent-child interaction is viewed more from the parent's point of view than from the child's.*

CHAPTER 6
TWO find EACh OTHER

Wherever one travels in the world, people are interested in who marries whom. In this chapter, we discuss how partner selection takes place. We include semipermanent nonlegal unions as well as legal marriages in our definition of partnership.

EVERYBODY'S BUSINESS

Why is mate selection of interest and importance in all societies? Why are engagement and wedding pictures published in the newspapers, and why is the latest match of such interest to the town gossips? In most societies, marriage and children go together. It may be considered proper for the wedding to take place before a child is conceived, or after the woman knows that she is pregnant, or perhaps after a child is born. But traditionally, matches have been made with the expectation that a child would at some time be born to the couple.

Society in General

Society's stake in a match involves the making of a stable marriage that will produce and maintain healthy children who will become good citizens. Laws are set up with these purposes in mind. Through gossip, gifts, parties, and outright approval and criticism, friends, neighbors, and acquaintances encourage promising matches and discourage poor ones.

Now that more couples are deciding not to have children, perhaps society should have less concern regarding the matching of these couples. In her article "Marriage in Two Steps," Margaret Mead suggested that the first step of marriage, individual marriage, should be easier to enter into and get out of than the second step, parenthood marriage [27]. In other words, since society has less to lose if a childless couple breaks up, such a couple should be allowed more freedom to get married, break up, and rematch than the couple with children. The couple that wants to have children should more carefully consider whether or not to marry, or enter the second step of marriage. We agree with Mead. However, her plan has not been legally institutionalized.

Families' Concern

Parents almost always care tremendously about having their children make suitable matches, although definitions of good matches vary from one culture to another. Parents consider some or all of the following: child's happiness, family reputation, money, social position, continuity of family, health, and potential of mate for various kinds of development. Parental influence on mate selection varies throughout the world from absolute control to no control, but in most places, parents share control with their children, kin, and community.

Siblings usually have something to say about a match, as critics or even as matchmakers. We know a young man who married against the wishes of his parents, siblings, and grandparents. However, the parents and grandparents attended the wedding, but the siblings expressed opposition until the end, refusing to go to the wedding.

The Couple

"Of course it is the couple's business," most of our readers would say. Some might go on to say that choosing a partner is their business and nobody else's. However, if nobody helps a person to get acquainted with potential partners, the question of *choosing* may not come up very often.

HOW DO PEOPLE MEET?

Marriages may or may not be made in heaven. The actual process of making the acquaintance of a suitable partner is a bit more complicated. Because of the importance of partner selection, each society has developed a way to get marriageable people together.

Propinquity

Propinquity usually means "closeness" in spatial terms. When applied to partner selection, it means that people tend to marry those who live close to them. In our society, marriage between two people who have not met is rare, although this custom was common on the frontier, where there was a shortage of women. In societies in which young people are allowed a degree of freedom of choice, marriages tend to take place within the community. By contrast, arranged marriages are usually made between families living in different communities [40].

In terms of propinquity, the campus is a kind of community. Individuals who go to college often marry someone who comes from a different town or state, but from the same college "community." Similarly, the place of work may provide a place for meeting potential marriage partners. Propinquity not only determines who will *meet* whom; it apparently has an effect upon the continuance of relationships as well. Catton and Smircich suggest that the closer together a couple lives, the less time and energy must be expanded for them to get together. They found that marriage rates among couples in Seattle decreased as a function of distance between the couple's residences [10].

Matchmaking

"Matchmaker, matchmaker, make me a match . . ." sing the daughters in *Fiddler on the Roof,* a musical play set in czarist Russia. They assume that their match will be

TWO FIND EACH OTHER

someone handsome, kind, and a good provider. When their eldest sister reminds them that they could be married off to someone old and fat, or cruel, the younger girls decide that they would be better off single for a while. Matchmaking probably takes place in all societies. It may be formal, or informal.

Traditional Matchmaking. In societies such as India or traditional China, marriages are arranged by the families. The purpose of a marriage is to carry on the family name, and to build or strengthen an alliance between two families. The young couple is not supposed to get too close to each other, because a strong dyadic attachment would work against the cohesiveness of the family rather than for it. A prospective marriage partner is selected on the basis of qualities that would benefit the family: a beautiful girl with a large dowry, who is submissive and has learned the arts of homemaking and child care, would be the ideal bride. She would have to be of the same social standing as the boy's family. In traditional China, the aristocratic family would not consider a girl whose feet had not been bound when she was in infancy, making her unable to walk, but erotically beautiful and demonstrating that she was of high enough social standing to be carried about.

In a patriarchal society, the woman's family has less bargaining power than the man's. In order for a girl to marry well, the traditional Indian bride's father must provide her with a dowry of money and goods that goes to the husband's family at the time of marriage. (However, it is illegal to *ask* for a dowry.) The bride's parents would hope to find a man of the same social standing, who was handsome, and who would be able to provide a good standard of living.

The matchmaking that takes place in India may be done by the families themselves, or through a village matchmaker who knows of a suitable young person in a neighboring village. Or, advertisements may be made in the paper. Figure 6-1 includes an example of such marriage advertisements. Beauty, caste, and education are all important bargaining points. But before a match can be made, an astrologer must determine whether or not the horoscopes of the young people fit together.

At times, matchmaking may be done by the whole community. Tara and Deepak were two young people of marriageable age in a modern Indian city. They met at a party, and Deepak was greatly taken with Tara. He thought about her a great deal during the several months that separated their first and second meetings. Meanwhile, many people in the community were starting to talk among themselves, saying how suitable a match the young couple would make. After their second encounter, Deepak was even more determined to "get things going" with Tara. He spoke to his mother, saying that he would like to marry Tara. Deepak was overjoyed when his mother replied that she had been thinking the same thing. We attended their wedding, which was a cause for great celebration for all.

The idea of marriages arranged by parents or an outsider goes against the feelings of people in our society. My (LSS) friends in India who attended a college in a large city had ambivalent feelings about arranged marriages. One girl sighed, "I do not know whether I will be happy or sad. My parents will try to find a good husband for me, but there is no way that I will know for sure before I marry him. They will let

WANTED for a 24 years old beautiful, good-natured Varshney girl, educated up to M.A., height 1.60m, fully accomplished in household affairs, a well-established, capable match of the same or Aggarwal caste. Preference to Engineer, Doctor or Industrialist. Girl's father and brother industrialists. Early decent marriage. Write to Box 000, Hindustan Times, New Delhi-1.

Source: New Delhi, *Hindustan Times*, January 20, 1974.

BERLIN—"Attractive mother, 30, of a seven-year-old boy who needs a daddy is seeking a warm, modern-thinking partner not under five feet seven inches. Marriage not excluded. Send photo."

Source: Providence, Rhode Island, *The Providence Evening Bulletin*, December 12, 1973.

WANTED tall, charming, fair Medico match from respectable well-placed family for Army Captain Doctor, Punjabi Khatri, 26 yrs., 170 cm. tall, smart, getting Rs. 1350/-P.M. Girl's merits main consideration. Box 000, Hindustan Times, New Delhi-1.

Source: New Delhi, *Hindustan Times*, January 20, 1974.

RENO, NEVADA—"Male writer, 29 years old, 5 feet 11 inches, 140 lbs., brown hair (but losing it). Never married. College graduate (with honors). Had vasectomy. Well off. Seeks unattached woman with no dependents, age 21–33, any weight, for meaningful relationship and possibly childfree marriage. Write . . . . . Care of NON."

Source: National Organization for Nonparents. Newsletter #9, October, 1973.

FIGURE 6-1   Examples of marriage advertisements.

me meet him, and talk with him for fifteen minutes, but what can you learn about someone in that length of time?" And yet, these girls knew that they would marry *someone,* and that their parents would *try* to find them a suitable match. Furthermore, they insisted that their parents, being older and wiser, would probably be able to make a better choice of a mate than they could themselves.

Modern Matchmaking. Figure 6-1 also includes newspaper advertisements from Europe and from the United States. The American example is from a new and very modern association, NON, devoted to people who want to have no children. The European advertisement, from an East German newspaper, is one of thousands that are published weekly in central and eastern Europe.

Friends are often unsolicited matchmakers. "How come a nice girl like you isn't married?" is a cliché, but the single woman is likely to hear it often. Amy, a career woman in her midforties, says that ten years ago her parents finally gave up trying to to match her up with "nice boys" when she went home to visit them. Similarly the newly widowed man finds himself besieged with dinner invitations from well-meaning friends; when he gets there, there is invariably a single woman there for him to be nice to.

Not all single people resent being matched. Indeed, some people go to considerable trouble and expense in order to be matched with a stranger for an evening. Computer dating services abound in urban and college communities. These services are used more frequently by women than by men, because men still have the edge over women when it comes to initiating relationships. Computer dating services require that the applicants fill out questionnaires having to do with **demographic information,** the applicant's personality, interests, and preferences in a date.

A preliminary study of computer-matched marriages investigated the differences between the married individuals and others with whom they had been matched and had dated but had not married. All pairs of individuals, whether or not they eventually married, had been matched as closely as possible on forty variables having to do with personality and interests. The married group differed significantly from the nonmarried group on only six of the items. The most important variable was the expressed desire to marry; that is, if a couple that had been matched dated but did not marry, it was likely that one of them had a low desire to get married (to anyone) [42]. This important issue has not been given much attention in studies of mate selection: does one or both partners have a high desire to marry at the present time or in the near future?

Interpersonal Attraction

In a partner selection system that allows a degree of autonomy to the participants, mutual attraction obviously plays a role in determining who selects whom. Our culture places a great deal of emphasis upon the importance of being attractive, particularly to the opposite sex. It is important to have clean, shiny hair; white teeth, a body that is neither too fat, nor too thin; a handsome or pretty face; a glowing, blemish-free complexion; acceptable clothing. One's breath and body odor should not be offensive. The myth is that if a person complies with these regulations, she will be attractive, or even irresistible to the opposite sex.

How attraction between people really takes place is a bit more difficult to ascertain. A number of studies in recent years have tackled the question, although more have dealt with same-sex subjects rather than opposite-sex pairs.

Physical Attractiveness. Physical attractiveness does appear to play an important role in initial attraction. In one experiment, students were asked to rate same and opposite-sex individuals on a number of characteristics, having been shown photographs of these individuals. The photographs had previously been rated according to physical attractiveness by other students at the same university. Both male and female subjects preferred attractive to unattractive strangers, regardless of the stranger's sex. Physical attractiveness was slightly more important to the male subjects than it was to the females. Attractive male strangers were perceived as being less intelligent and less moral than those who were unattractive, whereas attractive female strangers were seen as more intelligent and more moral than were those females who were unattractive [8].

Probability of Rejection. Other researchers wondered whether the subject's chance of being rejected would influence his choice in a computer-dating situation.

The subjects were 177 male and 170 female students randomly selected from those freshmen and sophomores who had bought tickets for a computer dance at the University of Minnesota. The subjects were assessed by student accomplices for their level of physical attractiveness, and the subjects filled out a questionnaire about themselves, giving estimates of a number of their personal attributes and accomplishments, such as their own level of physical attractiveness and the number of dates that they had had in the past year.

The subjects were divided into two groups: those who were told that the person whom they selected as a date would definitely go out with them; and those who were told that their dates could refuse to go out with them after a brief meeting, and that about 50 per cent of dates in the past had made such refusals. The subjects were asked which qualities in a date were most important to them. Results showed that a person's chances of rejection did not influence his choice in a date. The more physically attractive the subject was, the more socially desirable a date he or she requested. Physical attractiveness was an important and desired characteristic.

The results of a second experiment indicated that " . . . physically attractive women . . . report more satisfaction with their general popularity, their leadership ability, and their degree of self-consciousness" (than did unattractive women) [2, p. 188]. It does help to be attractive!

Attitude Similarity. Attitude similarities also appear to play an important role in attraction, although one's attitudes are not as readily apparent as is one's physical appearance. Experimental studies dealing with attitude similarity as related to attraction have generally been done on same-sex individuals. In one such study a campus living situation was set up for research purposes. Attraction patterns within a small (17 students) all-male house developed in accordance with preacquaintance similarity in a number of attitudes, but more importantly, in accordance with agreement in assessing others living in the house [34]. Another investigator found that subjects evaluated a bogus stranger more positively if he responded similarly to the subject on a personality scale [7]. A considerable number of studies have shown attraction to be related to similarity in attitudes or personality variables [6, 11, 16, 35a, 39].

Machiavellianism, or the tendency to exploit and manipulate other persons, is the result of lack of respect for the integrity of another individual. In being attracted toward a person, Machiavellianism might be expected to exert some influence. A test was used to separate college students into groups of high and low Mach, indicating tendency to manipulate or not to manipulate others. The subjects then got acquainted in encounter groups. When asked which persons they would enjoy as romantic partners, all men preferred low Mach women, but high Mach women preferred high Mach men, and low Mach women preferred low Mach men [35].

Perceived Liking. In order to determine the relative importance of attitude similarity and perceived liking upon attraction, 40 undergraduate psychology students were paired with other students [1]. The subjects were told that the other students were from another section of the course, when in reality they were confederates. The ostensible purpose of the study was to measure decision-making. The experimenter administered an attitude scale to each pair. The subject, and then the confederate, gave reasons for his response. The confederate's response in one condition was similar to the subjects, and in another condition it was dissimilar. After the interaction, the subject and confederate wrote a few sentences concerning their reactions to the experiment and to their partner. In some cases, the confederate wrote that although he felt he was similar to the subject, he did not like him. In other cases, he wrote that he felt that they were similar, and that he did like the subject. In the remaining two cases, he wrote that he felt dissimilar to the subject, but either liked him or did not like him.

If the confederate indicated that he liked the subject, the subject responded by saying that he liked the confederate, whether or not their attitudes were similar. If the confederate did not like the subject, attitude similarity did not increase the subject's opinion of the confederate. In sum, results indicated that perceived liking was a more important determinant of attraction than was perceived attitude similarity.

Other Variables Related to Attraction. A considerable body of research supports the idea that interpersonal responses are determined in part by such variables as voice quality, quality of clothing, and race [8]. One's opinion of oneself also has an effect on interpersonal attraction [2]. Males apparently find it easier to become attracted to the opposite sex than do females, especially during the initial encounter [31]. Males have traditionally been socialized to be the initiators of heterosexual relationships [21], and so it is to their advantage to be more sensitive to feelings of attraction in the early stage of a relationship [12].

GETTING TO KNOW YOU

How well should two people know each other before they marry? The answer to this question depends upon societal norms and individual goals. If the new spouse is supposed to fit into a pre-existing family structure without disrupting it, little previous knowledge of each other by the partners is expected. If the newlyweds are expected to form a relatively tightly knit and self-sufficient unit, interaction during courtship is likely to be intense, in order to allow the young couple to test their relationship.

A Few Examples from Other Societies

If partner selection is controlled by persons other than the couple themselves, acquaintance before marriage will be kept at a minimum. The amount of outside "interference" in partner selection, and the length and quality of the premarital acquaintance, should be looked at not as absolutes but as points along a continuum. Figure 6-2 illustrates this point.

Tara and Deepak, the urban Indian couple described earlier, had met and talked only twice, at parties several months apart, when Deepak decided that he wanted to marry Tara. However, he knew a considerable bit more of what to expect from her than would an American college boy who met a girl twice at a fraternity party. Tara's and Deepak's families were from the same community and had similar values. The members of the community saw the young couple as a good match even before Deepak took an interest in Tara. After Tara and Deepak became engaged, they went on dates alone together, and it would have been possible for one or both of them to terminate the relationship before the marriage ceremony.

Susheela, another modern Indian girl, went a step further than did Tara and Deepak. She lived in the dormitory of a girls' college in a large Indian city, and went out with a boy from a nearby college. She was not engaged to him, although she told

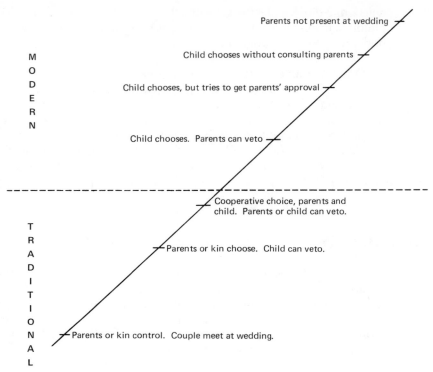

MODERN

Parents not present at wedding

Child chooses without consulting parents

Child chooses, but tries to get parents' approval

Child chooses. Parents can veto

Cooperative choice, parents and child. Parents or child can veto.

TRADITIONAL

Parents or kin choose. Child can veto.

Parents or kin control. Couple meet at wedding.

FIGURE 6-2   From family control to couple autonomy in partner selection.

us that they were in love. When she was discovered holding hands with him in a public place, Susheela was expelled from the dormitory and had to commute to college from her parents' home. A public display of affection or commitment is not permissible even in a modern Indian city.

In Spain, young men may court the young women of their choice. However, if they go out for the evening, the girl's mother comes along. If a young man and woman are found alone together, it is assumed that sexual intercourse has taken place, since a young man and woman are regarded as being irresistible to each other; no further proof is required. Therefore, it is necessary that they be chaperoned in order to preserve the girl's reputation.

If a person is poor or lower class, respectability may, of necessity, lose some of its importance. Temporary or semipermanent liaisons are entered into more frequently. Guillermo was a poor Mexican peasant with several children who wanted a woman who could not have children. His courtship of Julia was brief.

> When he invited her to go bicycle riding she accepted, and after one or two walks together in the Villa they agreed to join in free union. Guillermo and his three children, the youngest then aged two, thereupon moved into Julia's room. . . . [23, p. 141]

Dating in the United States: The History of Dating

What is dating? How did it develop in our society? Is it changing, and if so how? These questions are examined in this section and the next.

For our purposes, *dating* refers to heterosexual social interaction entered into for one or more of the following purposes: fun, recreation, self-exploration, mutual-exploration, status-enhancement, exploitation, sex, and mate selection. This list, while not exhaustive of reasons for dating, is examined later. The possibility of homosexual dating is excluded from this definition in order to distinguish dating from friendship, but doubtless many of the same needs operate when homosexuals get together. Dating may involve groups of people, but these people are very often "paired off" in a way that is recognized by the group. Frequently, a date involves just two people.

Dating for the purpose of recreation is a relatively recent phenomenon in the United States and Canada. Dating was widespread in the 1920s. My (LSS) Canadian grandparents and their friends dated in 1910, although they did not call it that. Previously, heterosexual interaction had more "serious" intentions and overtones; a young man and young woman who spent time alone together were on the road to marriage, assuming that the young man's intentions were "honorable." Relationships without the intent of marriage did, of course, occur, but almost always between a relatively upper-class male and a lower-class female. The double standard allowed such exploitation to take place with little cost to the young man's reputation.

A fascinating account of family life in the nineteenth century in the United States is gleaned from the accounts of European travelers at that time [14]. Many of the reports pictured young Americans as having astonishing amounts of freedom—before they married. However, a great deal of self-restraint was expected at the same time, especially on the part of young women, who were expected to remain chaste until marriage. Adolescents were permitted to be alone together; young women were permitted to travel alone. Some of the travelers complained that the freedom-with-restraint produced women who were cold. The travelers also noted that the age of marriage was extremely early, which could have been the result of the freedom-with-restraint.

Young people apparently had a great deal of freedom in choosing mates as well. In the 1830s, the dowry system was rare in the United States, and parents did not have much to say in the choice of a mate for their child. Mere lip service was paid to the parents' opinion, although it was formally required [14]. However, geographic mobility limited the choice of partners.

Evidence collected from the Hingham, Massachusetts, town records for the period 1635–1880 indicates a distinct shift from parental control of marriage in the seventeenth and early eighteenth century, to a stable, participant-run system in the nineteenth century. The transitional period occurred sometime around the turn of the nineteenth century, shortly after the American Revolution [43]. At this time, increased geographic mobility because of military service and college attendance helped to decrease parental control of marriage.

When marriage occurred, however, women apparently lost whatever bargaining power they once held, resulting in greatly curtailed freedom. Women had little opportunity to venture forth from their homes; they were tied to their kitchens and children. Some of the travelers noted that the women quickly lost their attractiveness: "' . . . they are charming, adorable at fifteen, dried up at twenty-three, old at thirty-five, decrepit at forty or fifty'" [29].

Bundling. In Colonial New England and Pennsylvania there existed a fascinating courtship custom that literally kept young lovers warm on a wintry night. This custom was bundling. There were actually two kinds of bundling: (1) the bundling of travelers, and (2) the bundling of lovers. Because of a shortage of beds, a stranger who stopped at a village or farmhouse to spend the night would usually be invited to sleep with one or more members of the host's family. This invitation was literal; the guest was expected to do no more than share the bed of the family member. The second kind of bundling is what concerns us here.

Travel was slow in the early days of the Colonial period, and farmhouses were far apart. A young man who was courting a woman would have to walk through the snow on a winter's evening in order to visit his sweetheart. Shortly after the evening meal the family would prepare to go to bed, and if he were expected to leave, the young man would have had only a few minutes alone with the person whom he had walked miles to see. Fuel for warmth and light was scarce, and it would have been too costly and wasteful for a young courting couple to burn fuel just for their own comfort and convenience. And so, shortly after the parents and other family members went to bed, the couple would also retire. Frequently, all family members slept in the same room, but the daughter might have her own room. Outer garments, such as shoes, coats, and dresses, would be removed hurriedly, because the air was cold, and the couple would slip into bed beneath the blankets. There, they could talk softly late into the night.

A poem of the period shows the attitude of the country folk toward bundling:

Nature's request is, give me rest
    Our bodies seek repose;
Night is the time, and 'tis no crime
    To bundle in our clothes.

Since in a bed, a man and maid
    May bundle and be chaste;
It doth no good to burn up wood
    It is a needless waste.

Let coat and shift be turned adrift,
    And breeches take their flight,
An honest man and virgin can
    Lie quiet all the night. [13, p. 26]

Samuel Peters, writing in 1781, said that the custom of bundling had prevailed for 160 years in New England, and that it produced fewer "natural consequences" than did lovers courting on the sofa, which had been introduced into the cities of Boston, Salem, Newport, and New York in 1756 [36, p. 225]. He continues in defense of bundling:

> The custom prevails among all classes, to the great honour of the country, its religion, and ladies. Why it should be thought incredible for a young man and woman innocently and virtuously to lie down together in a bed with a great part of their clothes on, I cannot conceive. . . . Upon the whole, had I daughters now, I would venture to let them bundle upon the bed, or even on the sofa, after a proper education, sooner than adopt the Spanish mode of forcing young people to prattle only before the lady's mother the chitchat of artless lovers. [36, p. 228]

The beginnings of bundling on this side of the Atlantic are traced from the influence of various Germanic peoples [13]. The Pilgrims stayed in Holland for a number of years before coming to these shores, and their young people were doubtlessly familiar with *questing,* an early form of bundling that allowed betrothed couples to bed together. Secondly, when the Dutch settled in New Amsterdam they brought *questing* with them. This practice spread up the Atlantic coast, and up the Hudson and Connecticut River valleys. And thirdly, the Germans who came to Pennsylvania in the 1670s and became the "Pennsylvania Dutch" most certainly practiced bundling, and when Doten wrote in 1938, the custom still prevailed. It probably does today among the plain folk in Pennsylvania, although the "bundling board" has in more recent times kept the young people from having too much bodily contact. (A "bundling board" is a piece of wood that is placed between the bundling couple to prevent bodily contact. It apparently was not used in the early years of bundling).

As the country became more urbanized, the practice of bundling began to wane, although it remained in the rural regions for a much longer time than it did in the more urbanized regions. The prudery of the mid and late nineteenth century managed to stamp out most of the memories of bundling.* Bundling was simply not necessary if the young man could easily return to his own home, and if fuel was no longer at a premium. Courting moved from the bedroom to the parlor in the nineteenth century. In the twentieth century, modern dating developed.

Factors Contributing to the Development of Dating. Industrialization was the main factor that led to the modern dating system. Increasing numbers of women working outside the home gave impetus to the Feminist movement. For the first time, women in the industrializing nations had an option other than becoming economically dependent upon men, and although the women were paid less than men, they had a bit of bargaining power that had previously been denied them. Industrializa-

---

*For an interesting and brief account of a similar process at work in Victorian England, see Edward Brecher, *The Sex Researchers,* Boston: Little, Brown and Co., 1969, pp. 7–9.

tion also led to the development of the mass-produced automobile, which gave people, including lovers, a mobility that they had not had before. The automobile provided a sofa—or a bundling bed—on wheels.

A young man would now drive up to his sweetheart's door, park his car, and go inside to get her. Off they would drive for some form of entertainment. This was, and in many cases still is, the date. Dating of this kind began in colleges after World War I and spread into high schools in the following decades. It was viewed with alarm by some researchers, the most noted of whom was Willard Waller.

The Dating—Rating Complex. Waller studied dating at the end of the 1920s at Pennsylvania State University [48]. It was the heyday of the fraternity house, and men outnumbered women six to one. Because of the university's geographic isolation, importing dates was difficult. These factors contributed to a system of competitiveness for dates, and what Waller called the dating-rating complex. Freshmen males simply did not date. After the freshman year, a man's ability to get high-prestige female dates depended upon the status of his fraternity, whether he had a "good line," was a good dancer, was prominent in school activities, had good manners, and was attractive, had plenty of money and access to an automobile. A popular girl was one who was attractive, had good clothes, a "smooth line," and could dance well.

Waller saw the dating system at Penn State as a departure from the formal courtship code, and as placing a tremendous emphasis upon thrill-seeking, exploitative (Machiavellian) relationships that could scarcely prepare the daters for marriage. Pretending that one was in love with one's partner was an important part of the game; each person wanted his partner to feel more involved with him or her than did she or he with the other.

Waller's study was done at the end of the Roaring Twenties, at a particular university that might well have been unique, or at least different from other universities at the time. Since Waller's time, a number of other researchers have retested his ideas, both at Penn State and other places.

About twenty years later, Smith replicated Waller's study at the same campus. The male-female ratio had changed from six to one in the late twenties to three to one in 1950. When Waller did his study, almost half of the males lived in fraternities; at the time of Smith's study only a quarter did. The students were asked to agree or disagree with the 28 characteristics included in Waller's study. He found that his women subjects were less concerned than were Waller's as to whether men belonged to one of the better fraternities, or whether they had a great deal of spending money and access to a car. Eighty per cent of the men said that it was important for a woman to have good manners and be attractive. Smith concluded that a dating-rating complex still existed, but that the priorities had changed since Waller's day [44].

In the 1950s Blood tested Waller's and Smith's findings at the University of Michigan, using an instrument that included some factors that Smith had found to be significant, as well as some of Waller's items. About half of Waller's items were not supported by a majority of the sample. Blood's findings suggest that personality aspects were becoming more important than the more materialistic items that Waller had found in 1929 [3].

Dating at the Present Time

Heterosexual interest has increased for children aged 10 to 17 since 1942 [22]. Different samples of sixth, ninth, and twelfth graders from the same school were questioned in 1942 and 1963. A sociometric test was given in which the subject chose a person in his grade with whom he would like to participate in nine activities. There was a significant increase in cross-sex choices over the 21-year span of the study [22].

Broderick studied the sociosexual development of children aged 10 to 17 in a suburban Pennsylvania community, as well as children the same age in rural and urban Pennsylvania communities [5]. He had previously studied children of the same age in a white, middle-class Georgia community, with which he compared his Pennsylvania samples. He found that 28 per cent of the 10 to 11 year old suburban Pennsylvania boys had begun to date. The majority of boys and girls in both groups claimed to have a sweetheart, although around 80 per cent of these relationships were not reciprocal. The child might not tell his or her sweetheart about his feelings.

Around 60 per cent of the 12 and 13 year olds had begun to date. There was more reciprocity in the sweetheart relationships at this age. Of the 14 and 15 year olds, 84 per cent had begun to date. Fewer of this age group reported having a sweetheart than did the previous groups, but 55 per cent of the sweetheart relationships were mutual.

Only 4 per cent of the 16 and 17-year-old boys, and 3 per cent of the girls, had not begun dating. In the rural Pennsylvania sample, about 25 per cent of the boys and 15 per cent of the girls were still not dating at this age.

Although Broderick's studies, done in the early 1960s, indicate a trend toward very early dating in a particular suburban community in Pennsylvania, and early heterosexual interest in that community and one in Georgia, his results cannot be interpreted as being applicable to all communities. Regional, rural-urban, and other differences exist. Very early heterosexual interest and activities have been documented in the black urban ghetto [17].

Dating as Multipurposed Behavior. Although a young person in our society is likely to marry someone whom he or she has dated, rather than someone selected by a third party, dating is not thought of as mainly a way of finding a marriage partner. The modern dating system has replaced the old courtship system, in which young people did not keep company with the opposite sex unless there was a distinct possibility of marriage. There are many other reasons for dating, which we listed previously and which are now discussed.

An important reason for dating is fun and recreation. It is perfectly acceptable to

CRAIG M. SZWED

date a person for enjoyment only, even if there is no chance of "getting serious," as long as each person understands the intentions of the other. People who are committed to the single life need not separate themselves from the opposite sex. Another reason for dating is status-enhancement. The dating-rating complex will probably continue to have some validity; it is important to virtually all people to have friends. Dating an attractive person makes one feel attractive. Status-enhancement can be carried to extremes and become exploitation, another reason for dating. Traditionally, the man was supposed to "pay" his date in expensive entertainment, and she was expected to "pay" him in some form of sexual favors: kissing, petting, or perhaps sexual intercourse. This kind of bargaining still goes on. When it stops being a game, the rules of which are understood and accepted by the players, exploitation of one by the other is difficult to determine.

Dating may be entered into as a way of getting to know others, or finding out about oneself. Certainly if dating is to function in a way that promotes the growth of those involved, as individuals and perhaps as partners, mutual and self-exploration must occur. In order to make a wise choice concerning one's lifestyle, a person needs to know whether or not he wants to become deeply involved with another person, and, if so, what kind of person can best meet his needs. Unfortunately, little emphasis is placed on this aspect of dating. According to the myth, when one "meets the right person" one decides to marry. But how can a person tell who is right?

Another reason for dating is for sex, or, to put it another way, in order to express one's sexuality. Because sex is a part of human relationships, it is very closely tied in with mutual and self-exploration. Unfortunately, it is often tied in with status-enhancement and exploitation as well. In the past, girls were taught that boys were always ready to use them sexually, and that they, the girls, should resist. At all costs one should save oneself for marriage—if one was female. Today, the double standard is still in force, but there are other themes as well. Women are now being told that their sexual capacity is much greater than men's; women are demanding sexual equality. The result is a much more complex picture; it is reasonable to imagine young women who date at least in part for the traditionally "male" reason of sexual satisfaction.

And finally, we come full circle to partner selection as a reason for dating. Some confirmed singles fall in love with their dates and marry; other daters who want to marry never seem to "find the right one." Dating for the purpose of finding a mate doubtless increases with the age of the daters. One would not expect a thirteen year old to be dating in order to marry.

This list of reasons for dating is not meant to be exhaustive, or mutually exclusive. If the reader is presently dating, we ask you, why do you date?

Is Dating Changing? There is some evidence from research that at the college level, dating is becoming less important as a way for men and women to get to know each other. The coed dorm allows men and women to get to socialize without pairing, and may be a help particularly to shy individuals [24]. It appears that among high school students as well, it is no longer as important that the older, more rigid dating codes be followed. A girl no longer has to worry that if she accepts a date at the last minute, the boy will think that she is unpopular. Indeed, she is free to extend invitations to boys, something that was frowned upon or even forbidden when we were growing up in the early 1930s and the early 1960s.

The women's liberation movement is doubtless responsible for this breaking down of traditional customs and roles. We think that the new dating is a good example of how men, as well as women, can benefit from the new freedoms accorded to women. Certainly many of the men that I (LSS) knew in college complained bitterly that they had to spend their money on women who never reciprocated. The women complained that they could not ask a man out without risking his scorn—and they were probably right. Today, it is still risky in some circles for a woman to play the "man's role"; but this is changing. Just how widespread and enduring these changes are remains to be seen.

COMMITTED RELATIONSHIPS: THE BEGINNINGS OF PARTNERHOOD

When two people tell each other, "I love you," they make some sort of commitment. Whether they say it or not, recognition of love means that the pair realize that they are attached to each other. Usually at this point, they redefine the way in which they are going to behave toward each other. Perhaps they know, from the social rules within which they operate, that when a couple love each other, they should date steadily or be engaged or get married or be exclusive sex partners or ask their parents if they may carry on any of these pair activities. Perhaps they have to talk it out, to find out what the other expects and what would be acceptable to both.

Since modern Western society is still essentially monogamous, the first form of pair commitment is usually steady dating. For many couples, casual dating gives way to steady dating while they are still quite young.

Going Steady

Going steady usually means an agreement between a couple not to date others. This agreement is known by the peer group, and generally supported by it. In some cases, it is a kind of preengagement; the couple moves from going steady to engagement and then to marriage. In other cases, it is more a matter of convenience and security [18].

Interestingly, the idea that one must be in love to go steady was found to be more prevalent at the younger ages rather than the older ages in Broderick's [5] Pennsylvania study. Between the ages of 10 and 15, 40 and 50 percent of the sample thought that one had to be in love to go steady, but at the ages of 16 and 17 only 20 per cent thought so. The remaining 80 per cent apparently thought that going steady was a "desirable social arrangement that need not involve any deep emotional attachment." When a deep emotional attachment is involved, and the couple thinks of themselves as a couple, they are said to be **pair-bonded.**

Going steady has been criticized on the grounds that it limits the number of people that a person can get to know. The counterargument is that it allows the young person to get to know a person on a deeper level than is allowed in the casual dating relationship. Parents and clergy are often concerned that going steady will lead to sexual involvement that casual dating will not.

Commitment to More Than One Person at a Time

An alternative to going steady with one person is "going steadily" with more than one person at a time. The college student who dates one person on campus and another at home is an example of a person with dual commitments. It is certainly possible, however, for an individual to date more or less seriously more than one person in the same locale. This kind of dating gives the advantages of both casual and steady dating, in that it allows a deeper knowledge of more than one person at a time.

Pre-engagement

The business world has stepped in to assure that no young couple in love need be without symbols for their attachments. The exchange of high school and college class rings by going-steady couples is an old custom. The fraternity pin is still worn as a sign of commitment. More recently, the "pre-engagement" or "promise" ring has been pushed on adolescents, as a way of showing a level of commitment deeper than going steady, but not as deep as engagement.

Engagement

Engagement usually involves a formal announcement by a couple or by her parents that they intend to marry. The man's parents usually acknowledge the engagement in some way, too. Sometimes the announcement is made at a party given for the purpose. A notice in the newspaper is often accompanied by a photograph of the

161   TWO FIND EACH OTHER

prospective bride. A growing custom is to picture the prospective bride and groom together. The period after the decision to marry and before the wedding is the engagement period. Testing, planning, and preparation are the main purposes of engagement.

Purposes of Engagement. The relationship is *tested,* both privately and publicly. How do we get along as a couple? How do people see us and react to us as a couple? Do I want to go through with it? If a couple decides not to marry, provided they do so within a reasonable amount of time before the wedding date, no disgrace is involved. When the wedding day draws near, however, few parents will truthfully tell their children that if they have changed their minds, they may back out. This is unfortunate, because some people do change their minds at the last minute, but marry anyway and end up getting a divorce.

The second main purpose of engagement is *planning*. This function can cover a great deal of ground, especially in a religiously, racially, or ethnically mixed marriage. Since to a greater or smaller extent *any* marriage is a mixed marriage, partners have certain differences to come to terms with. Many differences do not even come to light until revealed by the planning activities of the engagement. If the pair come from different social-class backgrounds, different ethnic groups, or different religions, they will likely look for modes of living that will satisfy both as to types of food, ways of serving meals, celebrating holidays, religious participation, earning and spending money. No matter how similar their backgrounds, they need to find out what the other thinks and feels about sex roles, division of housework and family business, responsibilities to parents and in-laws, having children, contraception, and community obligation and relationships with friends and lovers after marriage. It takes a long time to explore these topics and others. It may take even longer to resolve important misunderstandings and conflicts that arise during the exploration. During both the exploration and the resolution, modes of communication and problem-solving are developed.

Along with exploring differences and solving problems goes specific planning for how life together shall be lived. The pair look forward to what they want to achieve, thus establishing goals. Thus they begin the process of family management, of which we say more in Part IV of this book.

Some of the preparation for marriage consists of finding a place to live and collecting some furnishings for it. In earlier times, much more was made of this phase of preparation. The bride traditionally assembled a trousseau, consisting of household linens and clothing for herself. She, her mother, and other women relatives embroidered the pillowcases and monogrammed the napkins. Today's bride-to-be does not feel the necessity of amassing textile goods to last a lifetime, realizing that storage will be a problem, styles change, and she can buy what she needs when the time comes. However, family and friends still give engagement and wedding presents that may amount to a substantial part of the furnishings for the new home. An avalanche of advertising descends upon the publicly announced bride, urging her to manage the gift-giving process in such a way that she receives a useful, prestigious collection and the stores make a good profit.

A third type of preparation, highly recommended, but often neglected, is *physical assessment* and *health planning*. Since health is strongly related to personal adequacy and partner relationships, a thorough premarital physical examination is an important way of determining the resources and liabilities that each partner brings to the family. The state requires a blood test for syphilis, but surely the absence of syphilis is not sufficient assurance of good health. Highly desirable as additional tests for venereal disease would be, ruling out gonorrhea and other venereal diseases, they would scarcely be adequate proof of physical health. In addition to a general physical examination that included venereal disease tests, we would recommend some exploration of the hereditary defects that each individual can be expected to carry. If the two people's genetic inadequacies match in such a way that their offspring would have increased chances of suffering from, say, hemophilia or phenylketonuria (PKU), then surely their premarital planning should include some joint decisions about these liabilities.

The premarital physical examination is an occasion when partners may get some sex education and information, although other opportunities also exist. Even if young people have enjoyed good sex education and an easy access to information, the prospects of marriage or living as a couple will bring up some new questions. Contraception will probably be one of them. Even if the physician is not able to do all of the education needed, he can make a contribution and can also direct his patients to other sources.

In Appendix A, we have provided the reader with a Premarital Questionnaire, to be filled out by the reader and her/his prospective partner, preferably prior to engagement. Use of this questionnaire should help the couple to determine possible areas of conflict that often remain undiscovered prior to marriage.

PERMANENT VERSUS TEMPORARY MATCHING

An engagement used to be considered more of a permanent commitment than it is today. The breaking of a betrothal was a grave social, even legal, offense. "Better now than later" is a common modern attitude. In fact, marriage itself is less of a permanent commitment than it used to be. It has been said that all persons in our society, whether married or not, are available for marriage. Divorce, while not approved by everyone, does not incur the degree of censure that it did a generation ago.

For Now or Forever?

The traditional marriage vow includes the promise to stay together "until death do us part." In spite of making this promise, many people get divorced. Many unmarried partners also vow to remain together. How many such promises are broken? Nobody knows.

The present generation of young people appears to be placing less of an emphasis upon the "foreverness" of marriage, or of marriage-type relationships. Over a decade ago, Hillsdale interviewed couples drawn at random from those who applied for marriage licenses at the city hall of a large Midwestern city. He wanted to find out how many people " . . . bind themselves in a personal, existential commitment to *absolute marriage*, and how many to a *trial marriage*" [19, pp. 138–139]. He found that Catholics were overwhelmingly opposed to the idea of civil divorce and remarriage, and that noncatholics were 84 per cent in favor of them. However, only 19 per cent of the males and 21 per cent of the females had considered the possibility of divorce for themselves [19].

It would be interesting to know whether any of the individuals interviewed by Hillsdale had previously considered the possibility of divorce, or if they thought of it later (for example, the night before the wedding ceremony). It would also be interesting to see if similar couples today have given more thought to the possibility of divorce. We suspect that they would.

Certainly, there are many engaged couples today who still believe that marriage can be broken only by death. Mormons choose between marrying for eternity and marrying only for life on earth. Even so, the divorce rate is again rising to new heights, and half the states have changed to no-fault divorce, removing the stigma of guilt from one of the parties involved. The trend toward more and easier divorce reflects a more permissive attitude toward it by society.

We suggest that the question raised by Hillsdale is an important one that should be explored by couples who are considering marriage. How does each partner feel about the possibility of breaking up? Certainly, few people anticipating marriage would look forward to the demise of their relationship. But if one person believes that marriage is sacred, and that to break the marriage vow would mean an unpardonable breach of faith, and the other person believes that personal happiness and freedom is more important than a vow made at an earlier time, then perhaps the couple should reconsider their decision to marry.

Breaking up and Rematching

Breaking up with a former intimate is not an easy thing to do. The ideal situation is one in which the estranged couple part as friends, but those who do so are probably rare. No-fault divorce makes a friendly separation more possible than it is when one party is "guilty" and the other "innocent" of wrongdoing. More common now than in former years is the feeling of personal failure that comes with divorce. Because the guilt is not placed so much upon one person, each person is likely to feel some responsibility.

People who have been married previously are apparently even more eager to tie the knot (again) than are those who have not been married. In 1960, the marriage rate for divorced men was 171 per 1,000 men, compared with a rate of 72 per 1,000 single men. The rates for women were 124 per 1,000 divorced women, and 90 per 1,000 single women [9].

"ASSORTATIVE MATING:" WHO MARRIES WHOM?

How do people sort themselves out into couples? There are some principles that guide the forming of pairs.

Homogamy

Homogamy means "like marries like." It is easy enough to document that in terms of demographic variables, people tend to marry those who are similar to themselves. Hollingshead provides a bibliography and research demonstrating homogamy with respect to race, age, social class, and religion [20]. The principle of homogamy operates for intelligence, since high correlations are found between IQ's of spouses [46b].

Mixed Matches

All marriages represent mixed matches to one degree or another. Except for marriages between persons who grew up in the same household, which are extremely rare, each partner brings into the union a different cultural background, since no two families are exactly alike. Furthermore, individuals differ from each other in other ways: constitutionally ("night" people versus "day" people; persons who can eat anything without getting fat versus those who must count calories; people who like to live in a temperature of 78 degrees versus those who swelter unless it is below 68 degrees, and so on); politically; geographically; and in terms of values. And yet, interracial and interreligious marriages are what come to mind when one thinks of mixed marriages. Social class may also come to mind, but it is not considered as problematic. It is not unusual for a woman to marry "up" in terms of socioeconomic class, although it is somewhat deviant for a woman to marry "down."

Mixed marriages, of the religious and racial type, have long been considered a social problem in our society. Judaism, Catholicism, and Protestantism have all disapproved of mixed religious marriages. Americans appear to be intermarrying at an increasing rate, nonetheless, and a Gallup poll indicates increasing tolerance for mixed religious and racial marriages [33].

Within a community, interfaith marriage rates are influenced by the ratio of one religious group to another. For example, in Providence, Rhode Island, where a large, prestigious Jewish community exists, the intermarriage rate for Jews was only 4.5 per cent, whereas in Iowa, where the total Jewish population is only 10,000, the intermarriage rate was 50 per cent [41].

It is hard to find out how many marriages are religiously mixed. Only in Iowa and Indiana is information about religion required of persons applying for marriage licenses. Furthermore, a Protestant-Protestant marriage may be an interdenominational marriage that could actually be considered a mixed religious match. If one member of the couple converts to the religion of the other, it is difficult to say whether the marriage is mixed or not. It would depend upon the commitment of the convert to his new and old faiths.

Racially mixed marriages are still regarded less favorably than are religiously mixed marriages. For one thing, they are more visible. The United States has a history of racism; as late as 1958 more than 30 states prohibited interracial marriages between blacks and whites. In many of these states a white was forbidden to marry an American Indian, a Chinese, a Hindu, a Japanese, or a Malaysian, as well. A few of these states maintained their laws until a 1967 Supreme Court decision struck them down [15].

The number of black men marrying white women has increased significantly since the 1950s and 1960s, although the number of white men marrying black women has not increased. The 1970 census showed more than twice as many black men marrying white women as did the earlier censuses [37a].

Motivations for Mixed Marriages. Rebellion against parental authority is frequently stated as a reason for marrying a person of another religion or race. This reason may be applicable in some cases, but to us it indicates a great deal more about our society than it does about the reasons for mixed marriages. In some cases, the ratio of available men and women within one's own group is a relevant factor. If, for example, there are few eligible men in one's own religious group (eligible here meaning men of slightly higher social and educational standing, and slightly older, since women tend to marry "up" in regards to these variables), a woman may marry outside of her religion [47]. Servicemen stationed overseas are much more likely to marry members of another race (and probably of another religion, as well) simply because of propinquity [15]. Drawing upon his extensive studies of intermarriage, Monahan says that motivation and circumstances of interracial marriages are varied and complex and that the situation is changing rapidly. He recommends waiting for further information before coming to definite conclusions [28].

In most cases, the mixed marriages occur because the partners are in love. Certainly this is the reason that most of them would give. And although mixed marriages have a higher divorce rate than do "homogamous" marriages, their success rates are higher than their failure rates.

SOME THEORIES OF PARTNER SELECTION

How does partner selection take place? And how can a person who is looking for a partner find "the right one?" Unfortunately, we do not know for sure. Many researchers have formulated theories to answer these questions, but none of the theories has proven entirely satisfactory. A theory may provide a partial explanation for certain situations, or for certain parts of the selection process.

Ideal Mate Theory

As mentioned previously, Waller and others investigated the qualities that college students considered important in a date. Other studies have sought to find out what young people desire in a mate: the same qualities as a date, or different ones? And what are these qualities? Although the results of the many studies vary, women generally wanted a mate of good character and intelligence, who was attractive, had religious affiliations, wanted a family, and had a good occupation. Men wanted a woman who was attractive, had good homemaking abilities, was intelligent, and who was not selfish. Both men and women wanted to marry someone of the same race and religion [25, 26, 37, 45].

In a more recent study, both students and their parents were found to be far more tolerant of the idea of the student's marrying a person with a slight physical handicap than someone who is addicted to drugs or alcohol. The students were more selective for marriage partners than they were for dates. For example, 75 per cent would not date a drug addict; 85.1 per cent would not marry one. Approximately 39 per cent would not date a person who favored extramarital sex; about 72 per cent would not marry such a person [46].

In a recent study of American and Canadian college students, it was found that most students desired a mate with what the author called "Boy Scout characteristics"—that is, a person who is clean, honest, open, and reverent. The Americans made more direct reference to physical or bodily characteristics. American women, in particular, made specifications such as, "aggressive in lovemaking," "sensual," and "a good lover" [49].

Family Structure Theory

Sutton-Smith and Rosenberg, well-known for their studies on siblings, have evidence that both men and women tend to marry spouses from the same size families as the families in which they grew up [46a]. Men with brothers are likely to marry women with sisters, whereas men with sisters tend to marry women with brothers. In regard to age, men marry women of the position they are used to, those with older sisters marrying first-born women and those with younger sisters marrying laterborns. The authors suggest that males with brothers make more use of cultural stereotypes in choosing mates, since they have no experience with girls in the family. The influence of the stereotype is indicated in their choosing girls with sisters, who may represent the most feminine type of woman to the naïve male. Trends in women's choices were in similar directions, but not so clear.

Astrological Theory

The most ancient theory of mate selection is the astrological theory. It is used today in India to assure that partners will be compatible. The correctness of fit between marriage partners is determined by the position of the stars at the moment that the individuals were born. We do not want to dismiss this as mere superstition, in spite of the lack of research evidence to support it.

Developmental Theory

As we showed in the chapter on love, a person goes through several stages of learning to love before she falls in love and becomes a lover. The love career is strongly dependent upon the culture in which it develops. The selection of a partner, in any culture, consists of a series of steps, not just one event. In Figure 6-3, we sketch some of the important steps in feeling and thinking that go into partner selection in our culture, bringing together some of the content of the *love* chapter

FIGURE 6-3   Partner selection: Steps in feeling, thinking, and action; three paths to marriage.

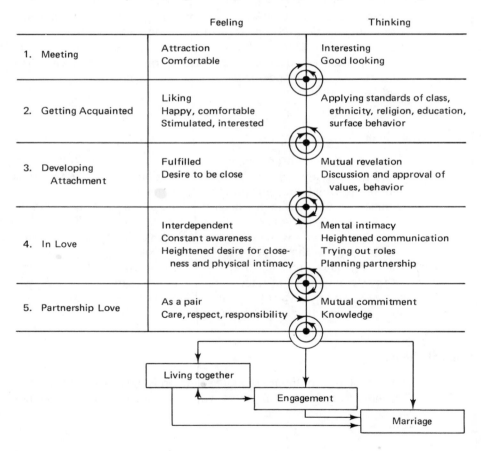

	Feeling	Thinking
1. Meeting	Attraction Comfortable	Interesting Good looking
2. Getting Acquainted	Liking Happy, comfortable Stimulated, interested	Applying standards of class, ethnicity, religion, education, surface behavior
3. Developing Attachment	Fulfilled Desire to be close	Mutual revelation Discussion and approval of values, behavior
4. In Love	Interdependent Constant awareness Heightened desire for close- ness and physical intimacy	Mental intimacy Heightened communication Trying out roles Planning partnership
5. Partnership Love	As a pair Care, respect, responsibility	Mutual commitment Knowledge

Living together

Engagement

Marriage

with this chapter. Although a couple may become committed (select each other) without taking all of these steps, research and theory suggest that the processes pictured here are functional in selecting a compatible mate in our culture.

Potential pairs obviously have to meet each other, which they may do by chance or arrangement. At that point, perceptions of self and other are important. Whether or not he approaches her depends partly on how she looks and partly on whether he sees himself as attractive to the opposite sex [31]. The feelings that lead one toward partner selection include being attracted and being comfortable. At the same time, the person is thinking that this is an interesting person and is planning to find out more. The next step is getting acquainted, possibly dating, or perhaps talking at work. They exchange information about themselves, their values, beliefs, experiences, group memberships, interests, abilities, and achievements. They observe each other in different situations and roles. They feel happy together and stimulated by each other. If all this continues, they become attached to each other. The thinking side of the relationship involves further self-revelation and mutual understanding and approval of what the other person is perceived to be, to do, and to believe. The feeling side involves a desire for closeness and efforts to stay together. The fourth step in this series is being in love, feeling it and knowing it. Feelings include a constant awareness of being in love, a strong desire to be close, interdependence, and physical intimacy. Thoughts include concentration on the partner, making plans for and as a pair, trying out pertinent roles, and striving for mental intimacy. The fifth step, partnership love, is marked by commitment to each other, feeling and knowing themselves to be a couple, establishing the attitudes and actions that constitute partnership love: care, respect, responsibility, and knowledge.

Progress from step to step is affected by pair interactions. The relationship may move forward or backward or even stay in the same spot. Reiss conceptualizes the development of love as a wheel that turns forward or backward as couples develop rapport, reveal themselves, become interdependent, and feel fulfillment [38]. Borrowing the symbol of the wheel from Reiss, we have placed a wheel at the junction of each step with the next and with the thinking and feeling parts of each step. Positive interactions between the pair, their feelings and thoughts, turn the wheel forward and they progress into the next stage. A setback may occur, such as in Stage 2, a discovery by her that his family is of lower social class than hers, or he learns that she has had a venereal disease and may be sterile. The wheel turns backward and they break up. A setback in Stage 3 might be a quarrel that reduces self-revelation and increases disapproval. The wheel backs up, reducing feelings of fulfillment and desire for closeness.

When step by step the wheels turn forward, the couple's love career progresses to partnership love and commitment. They may express the commitment as living together, becoming engaged, or marrying. As Figure 6-3 suggests, engagement may come before or after living together and either may lead to marriage. What triggers the decision to marry? Two people do not marry simply because they are compatible with each other, or even because they love each other; they have to feel ready to marry. When this readiness will occur depends on many variables. At age 80, my

(LSS) grandfather stated while smiling at my grandmother: "When you find the right one, you're ready." Many pressures external to the individuals operate, however. Becoming a senior in college (or high school) leads some couples to get engaged. The death of a parent, pressures to marry from family or peers, or a personal crisis may actually be more important in crystallizing the decision to marry than other variables that have previously been identified [4].

Our review of theories of mate selection is not inclusive of all that have been formulated. It would certainly make finding a partner easier if we knew exactly how partner selection does take place. It is unlikely that we will ever have an all-inclusive theory, because of the tremendous variations in individuals. The best that we can do is set up a few basic guidelines that seem to apply to the majority of couples.

SUMMARY

The selection of a marriage partner is not a private affair, but is significant to society. Parents and kin are often or usually involved. When the pair choose each other, they are likely to come from the same geographical community, whereas with arranged marriages, the man and woman often come from different communities. Traditional matchmaking serves the families more than the couple, but the parents usually take into account their children's needs and characteristics. Modern matchmaking uses advertising and computers.

Interpersonal attraction is obviously important in personal choice. Physical attractiveness is a big factor. Other salient variables are attitude similarity, perceived liking, and self-esteem. When couples have little control of selecting each other as partners, they usually have little opportunity for getting acquainted. Conversely, when selection is by the pair, the process of getting to know each other is elaborated. Dating is a twentieth-century form of interaction that serves the partner-selection function as well as other functions, including recreation. Bundling was an earlier form of courtship that bore some similarity to dating. Modern dating developed as women gained personal freedom through industrialization and job opportunities. The automobile gave impetus to dating as couples found mobility and privacy in it. Among college students and also high school students, dating became a game and an instrument of status enhancement and social mobility. By the 1960s, dating had spread to the preadolescent years. Current social changes are influencing dating customs, giving women more right to initiate and influence activities directly.

When a couple acknowledge love to each other, they are expressing commitment and recognizing the bond of a mutual attachment. Exclusive dating may be agreed upon as the first commitment, even before saying "I love you." Some individuals are committed to more than one person at a time. Engagement is a formal commitment to marry, which is usually made public. The breaking of an engagement brings little social disapproval in modern society. However, breaking an engagement or a marriage is usually painful to the couple, even though the permanence of marriage is not so stringent a requirement for social acceptability.

Marital choice is influenced by homogamy, or *like marries like*. Choice is likely to be homogamous as to race, age, class, religion, and personality characteristics. Every marriage is mixed, to a greater or lesser degree, since every individual is unique and so is every family of orientation. The incidences of interracial and interreligious marriages are increasing, as is public tolerance for mixed marriages. Different religious mixes have different rates of success prediction. Mixed marriages are encouraged by unavailability of homogamous partners and by propinquity of other partners, but a mixed couple perceives their union as "because we are in love."

Other influences on marital choice are the ideals held, experiences in the family of orientation and, perhaps, the stars. Developmental theory traces the events, feelings, and thoughts of a couple in the course of their meeting, getting to know each other, developing bonds of attachment, being in love, and becoming partners. From this point, the path to marriage can be direct or through one or both of living together and engagement.

REFERENCES

1. Aronson, Elliot and Philip Worchel. Similarity versus liking as determinants of interpersonal attractiveness. *Psychonomic Science,* 1966, **5,** 157–158.
2. Berscheid, Ellen, Karen Dion, Elaine Walster, and G. William Walster. Physical attractiveness and dating choice: A test of the matching hypothesis. *Journal of Experimental and Social Psychology,* 1971, **7,** 173–189.
3. Blood, Robert O. A retest of Waller's dating-rating complex. *Marriage and Family Living,* 1955, **17,** 41–47.
4. Bolton, Charles D. Mate selection and the development of a relationship. *Marriage and Family Living,* 1961, **23,** 234–240.
5. Broderick, Carlfred. Sociosexual development in a suburban community. *Journal of Sex Research,* 1966, **2,** 1–24.
6. Byrne, Donn and William Griffitt. Similarity and awareness of similarity of personality characteristics as determinants of attraction. *Journal of Experimental Research in Personality,* 1969, **3,** 179–186.
7. Byrne, Donn, William Griffitt, and Daniel Stefaniak. Attraction and similarity of personality characteristics. *Journal of Personality and Social Psychology,* 1967, **5,** 82–90.
8. Byrne, Donn, Oliver London and Keith Reeves. The effects of physical attractiveness, sex, and attitude similarity on interpersonal attraction. *Journal of Personality,* 1968, **36,** 259–271.
9. Carter, Hugh and Paul C. Glick. *Marriage and divorce: A social and economic study.* Cambridge, Mass.: Harvard U., 1970.
10. Catton, William R. and R. J. Smircich. A comparison of mathematical models for the effect of residential propinquity on mate selection. *American Sociological Review,* 1964, **29,** 522–529.
11. Cavior, Norman and Paul R. Dokecki. Physical attractiveness, perceived attitude similarity, and academic achievement as contributors to interpersonal attraction among adolescents. *Developmental Psychology,* 1973, **9,** 44–54.
12. Combs, Robert H. and William Kenkel. Sex differences in dating aspirations and satisfaction with computer selected partners. *Journal of Marriage and the Family,* 1966, **28,** 62–66.

12a. Dobrin, Arthur and Kenneth Briggs. *Getting married the way you want.* Englewood Cliffs, N.J.: Prentice-Hall, 1974.

13. Doten, Dana. *The art of bundling.* New York: Farrar, 1938.

14. Furstenberg, Frank R. Industrialization and the American family. A look backward. *American Sociological Review,* 1966, **31,** 326–337.

15. Gordon, Albert I. *Intermarriage.* Boston: Beacon, 1964.

16. Griffitt, William. Personality similarity and self-concept as determinants of interpersonal attraction. *Journal of Social Psychology,* 1969, **78,** 137–146.

17. Hammond, Boone and Joyce Ladner. Socialization into sexual behavior in a Negro slum ghetto. In Carlfred Broderick (ed.). *The individual, sex, and society.* Baltimore: Johns Hopkins, 1969.

18. Herman, Robert D. The "going steady" complex: a reexamination. *Marriage and Family Living,* 1955, **17,** 36–40.

19. Hillsdale, Paul. Marriage as a personal existential commitment. *Marriage and Family Living,* 1962, **24,** 137–143.

20. Hollingshead, August B. Cultural factors in the selection of marriage mates. *American Sociological Review,* 1952, **17,** 146–150.

21. Kephart, William. *The family, society, and the individual.* Boston: Houghton Mifflin, 1966.

22. Kuhlen, Raymond and Nancy Bryant Houlihan. Adolescent heterosexual interest in 1942 and 1963. *Child Development,* 1965, **36,** 1049–1052.

23. Lewis, Oscar. *Five families: Mexican case studies in the culture of poverty.* New York: Basic Books, 1959.

24. Lozoff, Marjorie. *Changing life styles and role perceptions of men and women students.* Prepared for *Women: Resource for a changing world.* Conference held at Radcliffe Institute, Radcliffe College, Cambridge, Mass. April 17, 18, 1972.

25. McCormick, Thomas and Boyd Macorory. Group values in mate selection, in a sample of college girls. *Social Forces,* 1943–44, **22,** 315–317.

26. McGinnis, Robert. Campus values in mate selection: A repeat study. *Social Forces,* 1959, **37,** 363–373.

27. Mead, Margaret. Marriage in two steps. *Redbook,* July, 1966.

28. Monahan, Thomas P. Marriage across racial lines in Indiana. *Journal of Marriage and the Family,* 1973, **35,** 632–640.

29. Moreau de St. Mary, Mederic. Voyage aux Stat-Unis de L'Amerique, 1793–1798. Quoted in Frank R. Furstenberg, Industrialization and the American family: A look backward. *American Sociological Review,* 1966, **31,** 326–337.

31. Murstein, Bernard I. Stimulus-value-role: A theory of marital choice. *Journal of Marriage and the Family,* 1970, **32,** 465–481.

33. *New York Times.* Gallup study finds greater tolerance of mixed marriages. November 19, 1972.

34. Newcomb, Theodore M. *The acquaintance process.* New York: Holt, 1961.

35. Novgorodoff, Bernard D. Boy meets girl: Machiavellianism and romantic attraction. Paper presented at meetings of the American Psychological Association. New Orleans, 1974.

35a. Nowili, Stephen. Ordinal position, approval motivation and interpersonal attraction. *Journal of Consulting and Clinical Psychology,* 1971, **36,** 265–267.

36. Peters, Samuel. *General history of Connecticut.* New York: Appleton, 1877.

37. Prince, Alfred J. Factors in mate selection. *Family Life Coordinator,* 1961, **10,** 55–58.

37a. Providence Journal-Bulletin. More black men wed to whites. February 14, 1973.

38. Reiss, Ira L. *The family system in America.* New York: Holt, 1971.

39. Reitz, Willard, J. Douey, and Geoffrey Mason. Role homogeneity and centrality of attitude statements. *Journal of Experimental Research in Personality,* 1968, **3,** 120–125.

40. Rosenblatt, Paul and Paul Cozby. Courtship patterns associated with freedom of choice of spouse. *Journal of Marriage and the Family,* 1972, **34,** 689–695.

41. Rosenthal, Erich. Studies of Jewish intermarriage in the United States. *American Jewish Yearbook,* 1963, **64,** 3–53.

42. Sindberg, Ronald, Allyn Roberts, and Duane McClain. Mate selection factors in computer matched marriages. *Journal of Marriage and the Family,* 1972, **34,** 612–614.

43. Smith, Daniel. Parental power and marriage patterns: An analysis of historical trends in Hingham, Massachusetts. *Journal of Marriage and the Family,* 1973, **35,** 419–428.

44. Smith, William M. Rating and dating: A re-study. *Marriage and Family Living,* 1955, **17,** 41–47.

45. Strauss, Anselm. The influence of parental images upon marital choice. *American Sociological Review,* 1946, **11,** 544–559.

46. Sullivan, Joyce A. *Selection of dates and mates: An intergenerational study.* Office of Educational Services: Ohio State University Libraries, 1972.

46a. Sutton-Smith, Brian, and Ben G. Rosenberg. Sex differences in the longitudinal prediction of adult personality. Paper presented at meetings of the Society for Research in Child Development. Philadelphia, 1973.

46b. Vandenberg, Stephen G. Assortative mating, or who marries whom? *Behavior Genetics,* 1972, **2,** 127–157.

47. Vincent, Clark E. Interfaith marriages: Problem or symptom? In Lloyd Saxton (ed.). *The individual, marriage and the family: Current perspectives.* Belmont, Calif.: Wadsworth, 1970.

48. Waller, Willard. The rating and dating complex. *American Sociological Review,* 1937, **2,** 727–734.

49. Whitehurst, Robert N. Comparisons of ideal spouse conceptions of American and Canadian university students. Paper presented at meetings of the American Psychological Association, Montreal, 1973.

CHAPTER 7

PARTNERHOOD

In the previous chapter on partner selection, we explored how a couple moves from being strangers to considering themselves as a couple, or being *pair-bonded*. Pair-bonding is a special kind of attachment between two people who see themselves as a couple, whether or not the union is formalized in some way (for example, a going-steady couple, a married couple).

Partnerhood involves being pair-bonded, but cannot be explained entirely by saying that a couple sees themselves as a couple. For partnerhood as we define it to exist, there must be love between the participants, there must be an effective communication system, and there must be a kind of *reciprocity* [32]; that is, a mutual exchange, or a give-and-take. For reciprocity to exist between two people, they must remain separate entities; the notion that when two people love each other they "become one" means an end to reciprocity. (See Chapter 2, page 50.)

Partnerhood also implies a sense of commitment, but not a static kind that swears loyalty to the other person "right or wrong" or at any cost to the committed person. It involves instead a commitment to the other person, to the relationship, and also to one's own growth. Carl Rogers suggests the following definition of the relationship that we call partnerhood: "We each commit ourselves to working together on the changing process of our present relationship, because that relationship is currently enriching our love and our life and we wish it to grow" [27, p. 20].

This kind of partnerhood is probably achieved by only a tiny proportion of all the couples who become pair-bonded. Some couples may achieve it for a while, and then move on to another kind of relationship. Because of economic and other inequalities in our society, many couples never have the chance to form a partnership, because they are concerned with day-to-day survival. A starving person or one whose survival is constantly threatened is not able to expend the time and energy necessary to develop an intimate, reciprocal relationship [19].

VARIATIONS ON PARTNERHOOD

Different kinds of partnerships are appropriate in different kinds of cultural environments. Mr. and Mrs. Kavoori, who live in India, perform *pujas* (ritual prayers) together each morning and have a special kind of religious partnership, each receiving spiritual benefits from the cooperative participation. Because he is a married Hindu, Mr. Kavoori cannot perform *puja* alone. The Kavooris have a type of closeness that is not felt by the more secularly oriented.

A few attempts have been made by persons interested in family therapy to classify marriages into types. These types of marriages could conceivably apply to other relationships as well. A basic distinction set forth by Burgess and Locke was that of the *institutional* versus *companionship* marriage [5]. In institutional marriage, roles are clearly differentiated along sex lines, and the husband's status is higher than the wife's. By contrast, companionship marriage is democratic, innovative in respect to roles, and permissive; the emphasis is on personal happiness rather than on fulfilling one's duty.

An Upper-Middle-Class Typology

In a study of upper-middle-class marriages, Cuber and Harroff identified five types of stable (not divorced or separated) marriages [10].

1. The conflict-habituated marriage that revolves around constant bickering and fighting.

2. The devitalized marriage in which the partners at one time were in love, but now have only memories of these more exciting times. Some devitalized couples accept the change in their relationship; others wish they could bring back the good old days.

3. Passive-congenial couples are very similar to the devitalized, except that their relationship has been that way from the beginning. Theirs was and is a marriage of convenience: for example, a business executive needs a charming, socially adept wife, and she wants the comfort and security of a man's salary. Affection may exist between them, but the "bells have never rung."

4. The vital relationship exists when the partners are involved in each other's lives, both in what they do and how they feel about each other. It is a vibrant, growing relationship, but does not exclude certain separate spheres in their lives.

5. The total relationship is like the vital, only more so. Some of these couples are so wrapped up in each other that they have no separate lives or identities. There are no serious differences, although there may have been in the past.

A Black Ghetto Typology

Schulz distinguishes between four different kinds of relationships between black ghetto *boyfriends* and their women and the woman's children [30].

1. The quasi-father gives financial and emotional support to a woman and her children over a period of time, getting in return his meals, washing and ironing, sexual satisfaction, and familial companionship.

2. The supportive biological father supports his children economically, but he may be married to someone other than their mother.

3. The supportive companion provides a woman with weekends away from her children. He does not support her children and would be very unlikely to support a child conceived as a result of their relationship.

4. The pimp lives off the labors of one or more prostitutes.

Many other typologies of relationships could be drawn up. We present several in order to give the reader the idea that stability and adjustment (which are not the same, and are explained in this chapter and the next) can exist in different types of relationships. Not all persons have the same expectations for a close relationship, or the same needs or capabilities.

GENDER ROLE AND PARTNERHOOD

As cultural structuring of relationships becomes looser, there is less need for the adherence to strict definition of gender roles. In many parts of our society today, women are feeling more able to challenge the traditional ideas concerning woman's place and are striving to enter professions that were previously closed to them. Some men are involved in the equally difficult process of becoming more able to feel and express tenderness and caring toward their women, their children, and their male friends.

In many families, one partner is more willing and/or able to meet the challenge of gender-role flexibility than is the other partner. More usual is the man who has held onto the family reins for so long that he is angered and perplexed at his wife for the new demands that she is placing on him. *She* wants to develop her own creative and expressive talents, and to help him to become a more accepting person, both of her and of the changes that she sees going on around them. *He* thinks that he has too much to lose, and he feels outraged by her impudence. But there certainly are families today in which the man perceives how he and the whole family could benefit from a less structured situation, and the woman does not want to change because being supported by a man is too comfortable a situation to exchange for the unknown.

Rogers sees the dissolution of gender-stereotyped roles as a necessary ingredient of partnerhood, and we agree that this is necessary for some people. For others, however, roles provide varying degrees of structure security and predictability to their lives and relationships. We see the dissolution of roles as an evolutionary process that can be hastened by thoughtful effort and facilitated by the cooperation of women and men. We have discussed this controversial issue more fully in Chapter 5.

PARTNERSHIP INTERACTION

The development of a partnership takes place across a span of time. It may begin when two people are attracted to each other, or it may have a more formalized beginning, for example, when a traditional Indian couple (who have not met before) are married. In our society, partner selection is part of the process of developing a partner relationship. Once the selection is mutually made, and the couple are pair-bonded, partnership may exist. But in order for it to continue, it must develop and not stagnate or "unwind." In this chapter, we examine the interaction of partners, both married and unmarried.

Love

In Chapter 2, we discussed the individual's lifetime experience with love. In order for love to exist, there must be *attachment* between the two. Attachment is a special kind of *bond,* or tie between people. We elaborate further on bonds in a later section. *Care,* the promotion of the loved one's life, growth, and well-being, is another essential of love. *Respect,* also a part of love, involves the realization that the loved one is a separate person with his own needs and wants. Love involves *knowledge* of the other person, and a *responsibility* toward him or her.

Love is greatly emphasized in our society as an essential ingredient of marital and family life. Although the choice of a partner is influenced by such mundane things as propinquity, perceived attitude similarity, social homogamy, and so on, most of those who marry are convinced that they marry for love. When love no longer exists, many believe that there is no point in continuing a relationship.

As we have seen, love comes in many colors and markings. The definition of love depends upon the cultural environment and specific experiences of the person who defines it.

Bonds

A group such as the family or even a couple are kept together by **bonds.** "A bond, or tie, exists when a value of the individual—shared or unique—is felt to be fostered by association or interaction with some other person or group" [37, p. 41]. In other

words, if I feel that something important to me is allowed to exist and grow because I am involved with a particular person (I like having a companion; my husband is such a companion) or group (a political party; a bowling league), then I feel *bonded* to that person, or that group. A bond can be one-way, such as when an adolescent has a crush on a movie star.

Many bonds hold a couple together. Indeed, the more bonds there are, the less chance there is that the couple will break up. Some bonds exist only momentarily; two strangers in a crowd lock eyes briefly and then go their separate ways. Others may exist for a short time and then dissipate: two recent divorcees may have much in common while they are still having a hard time adjusting to their divorces, but when they are readjusted the bond breaks easily. A couple on their first date may be amazed by the similarity of their outlooks: they both love basketball and hate baseball; they like the same music; they love Italian food. These bonds may endure, or they may later prove superficial.

The kind of bond that continues to grow, a **crescive bond** [37], is the most flexible and strongest bond of all. If the bonded individuals believe that something that they share (their special way of communicating, for example) is growing or "getting better," then that shared "something" is a crescive bond. It is essential for the continued functioning of a group (even a two-person group) that at least some of the bonds that exist continue to grow.

As Chapter 2 showed, love includes bonds of attachment between people. Attachment is a very durable, often permanent, bond by which one person (or animal) is tied to another. If both are tied to each other, the attachment is mutual, which is the case in pair-bonding. An attachment is built through the exercise of biologically based behavior patterns in which some mutuality is involved, such as the suckling and sucking of mother and infant, and talking, looking, touching, and sexual intercourse of adults. In the presence of the attachment object (the person to whom one is attached), an individual has a feeling of security, well-being, and happiness. The infant or child is more able to explore and to face frightening situations. The adult, also, can face crises and threats better in the company of the attached partner. When attached persons are apart, they keep in contact by whatever sort of communication they can devise, whether it be looking across the room at each other, waving from the train window, telephoning, writing letters, or attempting extrasensory perception. They plan to get back together again, to regain the presence of the beloved. When love declines, it is because the bonds of attachment that hold the lovers together have become ineffective.

When people interact, bonds develop. For this reason, the jealous husband does have reason to fear his wife's interaction with her co-worker; the jealous wife has reason to fear her husband's interaction with fellow members of his Players group, as they rehearse for the play. Whether or not such bonds will replace the marital bonds depend upon many factors.

The chart on page 168 in Chapter 6 depicts partnership love as developing as bonds of attachment are built, as the couple feel themselves to be in love and as they feel like a pair. As partnerhood develops, all sorts of mutual experiences and interaction contribute new sources of bonding. Their attachment grows stronger. In the beginning of a relationship, the bonds are not as many or as strong as they may be later on. The widowed bride is tragic, but it is easier for her to go on with her life than it is for the person who is widowed after many years of interaction. Even the person who reports his marriage as not particularly satisfying may be unable to function without his spouse, because over the years he has become dependent upon his spouse to play certain roles in relation to him. For example, each week before he did the grocery shopping, Mr. Alpert used to ask his wife if there was anything she felt like having for dinner. She would always say, "you buy whatever looks good to you." He became so dependent upon her reassurance that he had a very difficult time shopping after she died. A woman who kept her house neat and clean because her husband liked it that way may be unable to do so when he is no longer there to chide her when it begins to get messy.

Sex. The sexual relationship is usually, but not always, a bond between partners. Its importance in a marital or quasi-marital relationship depends upon the sexual needs of the partners, and the relative strength of other bonds. Desire for sexual activity and frequency of participation vary from one stage of life to another. For the newly in love, living together, engaged, or married couple, sexual activity may be a consuming passion. Or interest and pleasure in sex may grow with time, decline temporarily, and then experience a renaissance. We explore that subject further in the section on marital adjustment and satisfaction.

Jealousy

Traditional monogamous marriage has long been buttressed by jealousy [12], the fear of losing one's partner to a rival. Jealousy is experienced as well by persons in nontraditional relationships such as group marriages and sexually open marriages (see pages 459–461), although such feelings do not support these new kinds of marriage. Although the popular press has dealt with the subject of jealousy, social scientists are just beginning to study it. In a study of 80 undergraduate couples at the University of Connecticut who had been dating for at least two months, Teismann [36] found no sex differences in the way that men and women behave when dealing with a jealousy issue with their partners. He found that couples who role-played a discussion of a jealousy issue were more rejecting of their partners and used more guilt-induction than couples who role-played a discussion of a relationship issue that did not involve jealousy. The relationship-issue group used more cognitive, reconciling, and appealing acts.

However, when it came to conceptualizing jealousy, Teismann did find a sex difference. Females tended to be jealous of the time that their partners would spend with another woman, or attention that the men would pay to her. The men conceptualized jealousy in terms of sexual contact that their partners might be having with other men. A possible explanation for this sex difference is that men are taught to see their partners as their sexual possessions, whereas women are not.

Bargaining

Bargaining begins early in a relationship. When looking for a dating partner, for example, a person does not usually choose someone who is perceived as "too good" in relation to himself. Each person has an idea of what he or she has to offer, and although dreams are free, the cost of rejection often seems high enough to inhibit acting on one's fantasies. The individual's self-conception may or may not be accurate, however. A person with a low self-concept may not play all the cards he has, because he is unaware that he has them!

Quid Pro Quo. As two people associate closely with one another over a period of time, reciprocal behavior patterns develop, although in most cases each person is unaware of how predictable his behavior is. Lederer and Jackson call these reciprocal behavior patterns **quid pro quo,** which means "something for something." The *quid pro quo* pattern becomes a set of ground rules for interaction. As such, it provides predictability and security for the persons who share the response pattern [17].

On an elementary level, a *quid pro quo* held by many spouses is that the husband provides the income and the wife raises the children. On a smaller level, the wife may bake her husband's favorite dessert (which takes considerable time and effort), and he may respond by offering to clean the car, which is something that his wife usually does. He is probably not aware that the extra effort on his wife's part motivated him to do something that pleases her.

Bargaining behavior that is not immediately time-bound provides for the smoothest transition in a relationship. In other words, each partner needs to recognize that if one spouse does something for the other, the act need not be returned immediately. However, the repayment of the debt must not be postponed indefinitely, or the relationship will lose its balance.

Bargaining operates when rules are broken, as well as when extra kindnesses are given. When an unwritten, unspoken rule is broken, the other person may retaliate in kind. The violated individual is likely to feel betrayed without knowing why. Retaliation can lead to a negative cycle of more retaliation.

Another kind of bargaining may also be used by one or both persons in a relationship. When one person consciously attempts to make a deal, bargaining is brought from a nonconscious to a conscious level. It may be done with the intention to assure that a fair balance of give-and-take is maintained, or it may be used as a power weapon or as retaliation. "If you buy that camera, I'm going to get the stereo." The husband who finds out about his wife's secret affair consciously seeks out a lover for himself.

Conflict

Marital conflict has often been regarded as entirely destructive to a relationship. We believe that conflict, when engaged in with respect for one's "opponent" (as one must when playing football or tennis) can contribute to the growth of the relationship. No two people are exactly alike, and it is highly unlikely that two people will ever agree on everything, unless one person submerges his identity and needs to those of the other person.

Action-Oriented versus Personality-Oriented. Conflict, although not inherently bad or harmful, is also not inherently good. The two people may differ over a course of action and engage in a struggle in which one person wins and the other loses a certain amount (action-oriented conflict). On the other hand, the conflict may take the form of hurting the other person, in an effort to protect one's own self-image (personality-oriented conflict). In the second case, the opponents use "dirty fighting": "You're sick!" "Your parents sure did a lousy job in raising you!" The digs may be much more subtle, however, perhaps having a double meaning. Action-oriented conflict may produce positive solutions; personality-oriented conflict is almost always destructive [29].

One study of intact couples who were parents of college students found that "gut-level communication" often escalated into physical violence, but that "rational" or planned communication (see Chapter 3, pages 70, 75) did not. These findings were especially true for working-class couples [33].

Basic and Nonbasic Conflict. Conflict may also be seen as basic or nonbasic [29]. Basic conflict involves changing basic rules in the game: one member of a previously monogamous couple decides that they should both be free to have deep, possibly sexual relations with other persons. If the basic values of the other partner are challenged by this change in the rules, basic conflict results. Or, if a husband in a traditional marriage decides that he will no longer provide for the family, the result is basic conflict. For many couples, a wife's decision to have a career in addition to her family results in basic conflict.

Nonbasic conflict takes place within a shared set of values, or frame of reference. A husband may agree that it is his wife's right to have a job that she enjoys, but he may object to her working late several nights a week because it means that they cannot eat together. Or, to borrow an example from Scanzoni, the partners may agree that sexual intercourse is good and necessary for their relationship, but may disagree on how often it should take place.

Basic conflict represents a more serious challenge to a relationship than does nonbasic conflict, although the "tremendous trifles" of nonbasic conflict can be extremely irritating if not resolved. Both kinds of conflict can be positive to a relationship, if they are brought into the open and dealt with at the action-oriented level rather than the personality level. As we said in Chapter 3, problems should not be stored away or "gunnysacked" and then dumped on the unknowing partner when the burden becomes too much to bear.

Habituated and Situational Conflict. A third distinction that may be made is between *habituated conflict,* an established interaction pattern, and *situational conflict,* which arises because of a situation or event [29]. Some individuals and couples get feelings of fulfillment from conflicting and expressing negative feelings. The "conflict habituated" couples described earlier may pick a fight or resort to violence such as hitting each other or their children. Rose, a young bride married to an easygoing man, habitually picks fights with her husband, explaining that "things were going too smoothly" before the fight.

Situational conflict results, for example, when a couple disagrees concerning whether or not to take a vacation, or how to discipline a child. Systems outside of the relationship can cause or tremendously influence situational conflict: the family that is forced to live in a slum tenement, and has little income to meet its needs, lives in a stress situation that is likely to generate situational conflict.

Bonds and Conflict. In order for conflict to exist, the sparring parties must care enough to continue the relationship. Disagreement, even basic disagreement, will not result in conflict if one person disengages from the other. If there are no bonds between two people, holding them together in the same arena, there can be no fight. For the conflict habituated, conflict itself is a bond; personality needs are fulfilled by conflict. For most people, however, conflict alone is not a strong enough bond to hold them together. Persons who love, or hate, are kept in conflict by these bonds.

Communication

Conflict and communication are intimately related, but they are not the same. A person may have conflicting feelings within himself, but this is not what we mean by conflict. Communication may take place in which there is no element of conflict; that is, when two people agree with each other. A difference of opinion that is communicated, however, is conflict.

In Chapter 3, we discussed the elements of effective communication. Nonverbal communication, when it is incongruent with the verbal messages, can deepen conflict by confusing the listener. A message that is too threatening to the listener's self-image, whether or not it is intended to be so by the speaker, can cause the listener to *not hear* what the speaker is really trying to say. By repeating what the speaker has said in his own words, the listener can clarify the message both for himself and the speaker, facilitating communication. Although honesty is important in communication, if tact is not used as well, conflict can be escalated, perhaps becoming destructive.

Learning how to communicate, and how to engage in constructive conflict, is not a simple matter. A couple who engage in nonconstructive conflict can be taught how to "fight positively" if their differences are not basic, or if these differences can be resolved. For the couple who need therapeutic help, as well as the couple who already communicate and conflict fairly effectively and want to improve their effectiveness, the learning and working process takes time and dedication. Fictionalized accounts of problem-solving, such as are seen on television, give the viewer the idea that relationship problems can be solved in an hour. This is not usually the case.

Through effective communication, conflict can be used for the growth and enrichment of the relationship, and of the individuals as well. By bringing differences out into the open, conflict that is adequately communicated can cause positive change. Adaptability is basic to life; it is the key to survival. It is especially important in cultures experiencing rapid cultural change, such as ours. It is important to individuals, because as they grow up, mature, and age, their own needs, their associates, and their environment all change.

Growth of Partnership

Change is an inherent part of growth. And yet, threads of stability run through the growth of an organism. I am a different person from the one I was five years ago, and yet I am still the same person. Likewise, threads of stability run through a relationship, although the relationship may change radically from one time to the next. As long as crescive bonds continue to grow, or if new bonds are formed that replace the old (with the same person), a relationship will continue.

Just as no two persons are exactly the same, no two relationships are exactly the same. Basic to close relationships are the existence of bonds, bargaining, and (with perhaps a few rare exceptions) conflict. Love, which is a special kind of bond, serves as a mediator for the bargaining and conflict that occur in a relationship.

A partnership is a special kind of relationship between pair-bonded individuals. Although conflict may be rare or not basic, partners do not fear either the idea of conflict, or handling it when it exists.

THE WEDDING: A TRANSITION POINT

A wedding is a ritual and a celebration, with a promise at its core. The promise may be called a vow, bargain, contract, or pledge, according to its context and meaning. Essentially, though, two people, usually a woman and a man, commit themselves to each other in an enduring relationship that is spelled out in the presence of their kin and community. A wedding has layer upon layer of meaning. No matter how sincerely a young couple might try to make it a straightforward declaration of theirs alone, eons of human culture have produced weddings. The particular culture in which this wedding occurs determines whether it is expected to last for eternity, for life, or as long as they shall love, whether the ceremony is holy or purely legal, whether it is primarily a union of a couple or of two families. Even in modern North American society, the meaning of a wedding varies considerably. When a young couple start to plan their wedding, they are often surprised at the complexities they encounter. Many reach a point of bewilderment at which one, usually the man, says, "This is supposed to be *our* wedding, but everybody is trying to run it. Why don't we cut out all this big fuss and just go off by ourselves to get married?"

Older studies have indicated that the couple who wed in church have a greater chance of surviving in marriage than a couple married in a judge's chambers. Four out of five brides still choose a traditional, formal wedding [26]. Of course, a church

wedding does not guarantee permanence, or even harmony. It is possible for a couple to live in genuine partnerhood without ever having had a formal ceremony. The wedding ceremony does, however, have important influences that are both psychological and sociological.

Social Meaning

A wedding to which friends, relatives, and members of the community are invited serves the purposes of publicly sanctioning the marriage and establishing the couple in new roles and statuses in the community. Approval is given to the match and the gifts given by the guests help the couple get started in setting up a home of their own. The marriage of a woman and man unite their families, although this is less important in our society, with the exception of the upper class.

To the middle and working classes, the wedding provides a time to be extravagant, to live beyond one's means, to have a good time with all the people who have social meaning to the family [31]. It appears to serve a similar function in India, where the father of the bride saves for years for the wedding ceremony, and may go very heavily into debt. In both countries, the bride's family wishes to impress the community with how generous and wealthy they are, whether or not they really have the money. The American or Canadian bride has been fed on dreams of a magnificent wedding since early childhood, and may desire such an occasion. The parents of the bride certainly have opinions as well, which in some cases run contrary to the bride's. We have known many young women who have complained that their weddings were really "their mothers'." It was the mother who wanted the bride to have a fancy wedding gown and three hundred guests. In the end, it was the parents' friends who were invited, and not many of the young couple's.

Psychological Meaning

Ideally in our society, the ceremony of the wedding expresses the love that the two people have for each other and the plans that they have for conducting their future life together. If it is a religious ritual, and both are in harmony with the religion, then the ceremony unites them as a pair and also integrates them with philosophy and beliefs, their God or gods, their ancestors, descendants, and fellow human beings. Thus the wedding strengthens the pair relationship by weaving it into a larger spiritual existence.

What about those couples who do not belong to a particular religion? Many of them go part way, perhaps enlisting the services of their parents' church, a friend who is a clergyman, or a nondenominational chapel. Even though unfocused, they have some feeling of their love and partnership being related to a religious, mystical, unifying force. Some couples turn to nature for the beauty that will make their wedding meaningful. Their processional is a walk down a beach or through a forest of autumn leaves, their music from a guitar or a flute, their ceremony written by themselves, with help from Gibran or a friend. The personalized, do-it-yourself wedding has become popular enough to inspire the writing of books such as *Getting Married the Way You Want* [13a].

A wedding ceremony serves as an important **rite-de-passage,** especially for the bride. Traditionally in our society the bride has changed her last name to that of her husband. In some states at the present time she may keep her maiden name, but often this may take permission from a court. It is becoming increasingly frequent for the couple to change their name to a hyphenated form of both names (Anne Michalski and James Sander become Anne and James Michalski-Sander. . . . or Sander-Michalski). Not all names sound harmonious together, and two long names wedded can make for nightmares when one has to sign checks. Besides, what name should their offspring, Brian Michalski-Sander and his bride, Penny Vierra-McLaughlin choose? Instead of using a hyphenated name, some couples choose a completely new last name.

The woman who takes her husband's last name has a change in identification and identity. It implies that she is "his" more than he is "hers." The couple who uses a combination name share their old identities, and their new. The couple who choose a new name dissociate themselves from either of their families of orientation and make it hard for old friends to keep track of them. No method is perfect.

Marriage may mean the granting of adult status to young people who before were previously thought of as adolescents. In this way, also, it can be important psychologically.

Legal Meaning

A wedding involves a contract, as well as a promise and an expression of a relationship. In fact, a marriage may be performed without invoking any sort of religious or loving sentiments, on a pure contractual basis. In France, the two ceremonies are separated and may even be carried out on different days.

The legal basis of marriage varies from one nation to another, and within the United States, from one state to another. We discuss family law further in a later chapter.

A couple or their families can make a contract at marriage. Although such a custom is not common in North America, it is growing in popularity. Influenced by women's liberation, a number of couples have decided that it would be sensible to spell out ahead of time the rights and responsibilities of each person. Sometimes contracts are made for definite time periods, with the plan that they will be reviewed and renegotiated at the end of that period. This arrangement represents a type of management that may compensate for some of the diverse expectations that many couples have. As sex roles, age roles, and other roles become more flexible, people have to work harder at communicating their expectations, understandings, and plans. Disappointment, disillusionment, and severe conflict could be minimized by the interaction involved in making a contract and by having the contract to refer to. The Premarital Questionnaire in Appendix A could form the basis of such a contract.

Homosexual Weddings

Although no legal sanction is given to marriage between members of the same sex, the fact that some homosexual couples wish to marry shows that a desire for deep, sanctioned commitment is not limited to the "straight" world. For the homosexual and her or his associates, the wedding has social and psychological meaning.

CHANCES OF SUCCESS IN MARRIAGE: MARITAL STABILITY

What is a "successful" marriage? Does it mean that the persons involved must feel a certain way about each other; that they must not argue in loud voices; or merely that they do not divorce, no matter how unhappy each spouse might admit to being?

Although a clear differentiation is not always made in family study literature, marital stability has traditionally meant the last definition given: that a stable marriage is an *undivorced* marriage. More recently, separated couples have been included in this definition by some researchers, but this addition creates a problem when it comes to counting the numbers of stable versus unstable couples. Statistics on legal separations are available, but not on nonlegal separations. If Mrs. Leonard runs home to mama for an average of a week out of each month, is her marriage stable? It would have to be counted as so, even though her behavior indicates that it is not.

In this section, we discuss the findings regarding differential chances for "success" (nondivorce) in marriage.

Overall Chances of Divorce

There is no doubt that the divorce rate has been rising in our society over the past hundred years. Exactly what a person's chances are of being divorced, on the average, cannot be safely predicted for a number of reasons. One reads almost everywhere that one in three, or perhaps one in two, marriages end in divorce. These figures, however, are misleading. They are arrived at by comparing the number of marriages in a given registration area (or the entire nation) with the number of divorces during the same time period.

For example, last year in a given city 1,000 persons married, and 400 persons obtained a divorce. The figures 400/1,000 equals two-fifths, or two divorces per five marriages. However, the 400 persons who obtained a divorce represent marriages that began many years earlier, two years ago, five years ago, fifteen years ago, and perhaps even fifty years ago. These marriages from previous years represent a different population (group) of people from the marriages of last year, and cannot be compared with each other.

To further illustrate this point, Plateris suggests the following: Last year in our hypothetical city, 1,000 persons were married, 400 marriages were dissolved by divorce, and 250 marriages were dissolved by the death of one of the spouses. In all, 650 marriages were dissolved. From these figures, we can conclude that for every 1,000 marriages, 650 are dissolved by divorce or death. What happens to the other 350 marriages? Do they go on forever? Of course not [25].

A more accurate way of determining the probability of divorce is to follow each person through her various marriages, counting the times the person is married and divorced. When the person dies, we will know her marital record. Unfortunately, we cannot accurately predict for other persons from this person's record, because the group of persons who married for the first time in 1910, most of whom are dead by now, cannot be compared with this year's crop of brides and grooms. Those married in 1910 were culturally different from the new spouses of today, and experienced different events, such as World Wars I and II and the Depression.

Some studies have counted the number of marriages and divorces among a group of persons who were married a given number of years. A 1971 study found that of persons married at least twenty years, four out of five had been married only once. Ninety per cent of the men and 80 per cent of the women were still married after at least twenty years of marriage.* About 15 per cent of the men, and 17 per cent of the women under 70 who had been married at some point had also been divorced [15]. These figures cannot be used with accuracy to predict the present generation's probability of getting a divorce, but they can be used to show the danger of predicting divorce with the present divorce to present marriage ratio.

Another way of reporting divorce statistics is number of divorces per 1000 population. We cannot predict future number of divorces from such statistics, but we can observe past trends. Table 7-1 shows the number of divorces per 1000 population from 1935 to 1974. The 1935 figure, 1.7 divorces per 1000 population reflects the low divorce rate during the Depression, and the 3.5 figure in 1945 reflects the high divorce rate following World War II.

TABLE 7-1   **Number of Divorces per 1000 Population, United States, for Reporting States and Divorce Registration Areas**

Year (12-month period ending August)	Divorces per 1000 Population
1974*	4.5
1973*	4.4
1972*	3.7
1970†	3.5
1965†	2.5
1960†	2.2
1955†	2.3
1950†	2.6
1945†	3.5
1940†	2.0
1935†	1.7

*Source: Paul C. Glick. A demographer looks at American families. Burgess Award Address presented at the annual meeting of the National Council on Family Relations, St. Louis, October 25, 1974.

†Source: U.S. Department of Health, Education, and Welfare and Public Health Service Vital Statistics of the United States.

*The difference in the numbers of still married persons results from the fact that men tend to die before their wives.

Age at Marriage

It has been well established by research that persons marrying below the national average age (about twenty for women, twenty-two for men) have lower chances of success in marriage than those who marry when older. Figure 7-1 represents the percentage of divorces in 1969 by age of the husband and wife at the time of their marriage. Because women tend to marry men slightly older than they, the longest bars come in different five-year periods.

A nationwide survey made for the Office of Economic Opportunity in 1967 reported that 27 per cent of women who married in their teens, as compared with 14 per cent who married after they had reached their twenties, were divorced within twenty or more years of marriage. The comparable figures for men were 28 per cent who married before the age of twenty-two, versus 13 per cent who married after age 22 [16].

FIGURE 7-1   Per cent distribution of divorces by age of husband and wife at marriage: divorce-registration area, 1969.

Source: U.S. Department of Health, Education, and Welfare, Public Health Service. Divorces: Analysis of changes, United States, 1969. Rockville, Maryland, National Center for Health Statistics, 1973. Table 9.

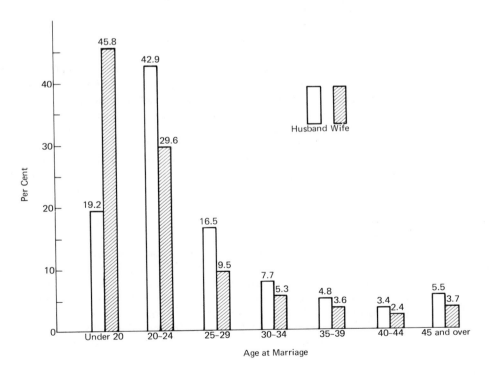

Reasons for the Failure of Young Marriages. It is not the age of the spouses at marriage per se that causes divorce. Those who marry young are more likely to be premaritally pregnant, or are more likely to cut short their educations before graduating from high school or college. Not all premaritally pregnant couples are doomed to failure, of course, but some marriages that would not have taken place otherwise are forced by an unplanned pregnancy. Furthermore, it is not education that appears to be a crucial factor in determining chances for divorce, but income, which is usually (but not always) linked to the amount of education of the spouses, particularly the male [15].

Teen-age marriages, particularly those begun in high school, are not generally given much social support. Although it is less prevalent today than formerly, married or pregnant students may be forced out of daytime school. Families may give some financial support to the young couple (for example, providing room and board), but if the families of orientation are limited in financial resources, the new family of procreation can only be an added strain. One exploratory study of high school marriages in rural Pennsylvania noted that the young spouses saw themselves as nobodies in the community. They were seldom in trouble with the law, but they just didn't matter much [13].

Early marriage is more prevalent among lower socioeconomic groups than it is among groups of a higher socioeconomic level. Those individuals who go on to college and graduate school are more likely to defer marriage than are those who terminate their formal educations with high school. Deferred marriage gives the couple more time for varied dating experience, which may be a factor in marital success [3].

In Figure 7-2, forty-four states are ranked in order of percentages of marriages involving teen-agers. The variation is considerable, with 6.3 per cent of the District of Columbia grooms included and 47.4 per cent of Kentucky brides [16]. When United States teen-age marriages are compared with the frequencies of such marriages in other industrialized countries, the United States ranks high. The men's rate was highest of all twenty-three comparison nations, the women's rate was fifth highest. Canadian ranks were thirteenth for women and ninth for men. Japanese rates ranked lowest for both men and women [16, p. 14].

Timing of the First Birth

Couples who conceived their first child before marriage have been found to have a higher divorce rate than those who were not pregnant at the time of marriage [8]. In addition, those who waited to marry for several months after the pregnancy was known had a higher divorce rate than those who married as soon as the pregnancy was confirmed [6]. Those who conceived immediately after marriage had a higher divorce rate than those who waited for several months or years. The longer the interval between marriage and the first birth, the less was the probability of divorce [8].

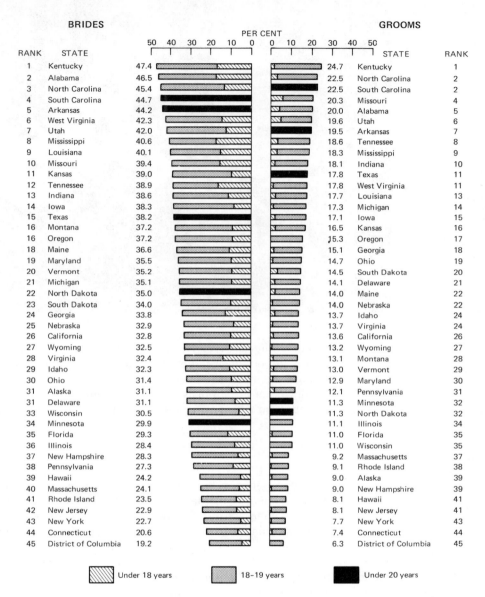

FIGURE 7-2   State rankings by per cent of all marriages involving teen-age brides and grooms, by age: 44 reporting states and the District of Columbia, 1969.

Source: U.S. Department of Health, Education, and Welfare. Teen-agers: Marriages, divorces, parenthood, and mortality. Vital and Health Statistics Series 21-No. 23, 1973 DHEW No. (HRA) 74-1901. Figure 4, p. 11.

The long-term effects of early pregnancy (pre- or postmaritally conceived) appear to be less important in terms of whether or not the woman in question is married. Although she may have been divorced and remarried, a mother of a child conceived out of wedlock is about as likely as other mothers to be married and living with her husband, who may or may not be the father of her first child [11a].

Length of Engagement

Older studies, done between the 1930s and the 1950s, found that the length of engagement was related to marital success. Couples with no engagement, or an engagement of less than six months, were found to be more likely to have poor marital adjustment if married, or to be divorced, than those who were engaged for over six months [34, pp. 179–180]. Unfortunately, these studies did not control for income level. It is likely that many of those couples who had short engagements also had low incomes, and we cannot be certain which variable (length of engagement or income) had a greater effect on marital stability.

Purposes. The purposes of an engagement in our society are to give test to the relationship, both publicly and privately, and to plan and prepare for marriage (see Chap. 6, pages 161–162). Such testing does go on before the formal engagement, but is intensified as the couple moves closer to marriage. Perhaps it is the intensity of the interaction that matters more than the formal engagement. If this is the case, then we speculate that the couple who publicly live together before marriage would achieve the testing purpose, as long as the length and quality of the relationship were adequate. Some planning would be done on the spot, or perhaps omitted. Preparation would also be curtailed. Physical examinations *could* be made a part of the living together period. Heredity counseling, also, could precede any decision about childbearing.

Social Homogamy

In Chapter 6 we noted that like tend to marry like in terms of social characteristics. When marriages do occur across religious and racial lines, are the chances for marital stability affected?

Religious Intermarriage. Since a religion prescribes ways of behaving, as well as interpretations of life, it is logical that spouses from different religions would have more disagreements, conflicts, and problems than a pair of the same religion. Older studies on mixed marriages seemed to bear out this common sense point of view, generally showing lower survival rates in mixed marriages than in homogamous unions. Nevertheless, mixed religion marriages have increased in frequency and acceptability. More recent and more carefully controlled studies have shown *slightly* higher divorce rates among interfaith marriages in contrast to intrafaith ones, but factors other than religious differences are seen as operating through association with mixed marriage [7]. The following conditions, which are more frequent in interfaith marriages, are also associated with above-average chances of divorce: youth of bride and low income [4], premarital pregnancy, civil marriage ceremony and urban residence, and previous divorce [7, 28]. On the other hand, some people in mixed marriages were older and had higher occupational status. These two characteristics are associated with lower divorce rates. Thus, it would seem that many of the people who enter into mixed marriages are different in background and personality from those who marry within their religion.

Racial Intermarriage. Since the 1967 Supreme Court decision that declared miscegnation laws unconstitutional, there has been a rise in marriage across race lines [1]. The rise in interracial marriages has been especially great for couples consisting of black husbands and white wives. In 1970 there were more than twice as many such couples than there were in 1960 [2].

Divorce rates for black-white marriages are higher than for white-white marriages [24], although a study in a Midwestern state indicated that black-white marriages were more stable than black-black marriages [21]. Once again, however, we need to know the income levels of the couples involved before we can attribute the relative instability to racial combination alone. If we could compare black-black marriages with black-white marriages of the same income level, we might find that their success rates are similar, or, we might not. It may be that black-white couples give more consideration to the suitability of their match than do racially homogamous couples. The interracial couples may "try harder," too.

Hawaii has the highest proportion of interracial marriage in the United States, about 20 per cent. It also has the highest rate of divorce among interracial marriages, also 20 per cent [24]. Since space does not permit a adequate discussion of the dynamics of interracial marriage, the interested reader is referred to two books on the subject [12a; 35].

Previous Marriage Record

Monahan reported that for marriages in his Iowa study, there were 17 divorces to 100 marriages when both the husband and wife had not been divorced before, 35 divorces to 100 marriages when both had been divorced before, and 70 divorces to 100 marriages when both had been divorced two times or more, suggesting that a person's risk for divorce increases the more times he is married [22]. Glick and Norton's data, however, suggest a slightly greater stability for second marriages [15] (see Table 8-2, page 215).

It takes two people to make or break a marriage, although there certainly are cases in which one person contributes more to the breakdown of a relationship. However, it is possible that a quality in a husband that would cause one woman to want a divorce would make another woman happy. The individual who is contemplating marriage with a divorcé should take into consideration the financial and emotional strain that might be caused if the divorcé has another family. On the bright side, remarriages of older persons have been found to be more successful than first marriages, in part because the spouses know what to look for when they choose each other [20].

Income and Education

Income appears to be more closely related to marital stability than is education. Cutright suggests that education plays a role in determining the amount of income that a family will have, and that the higher the income level, the less likely are the chances for divorce [11]. The actual interrelationship is, of course, more complex than what was suggested previously. Low income does not cause marital instability, but it does make life more difficult.

Plateris [24] found that men with very little education have a relatively low chance for divorce, but the chances for divorce grow as education increases to a high point among the group of men that has attended or completed high school, and then declines again for those who have a college education. No comparable pattern was found for wives.

Family of Orientation's Influence

The child who comes from a home broken by divorce is more likely to also be divorced than is the child from an unbroken home. Individuals who report having had happy parents, and little conflict with their parents, are also less divorce-prone than those who report the opposite [14, p. 509].

Number of Children

The divorce rate for couples with no children under eighteen is higher than the rate for couples with children. The more children a couple has, the less likely it is that they will get divorced [15]. This should not be interpreted to mean that having more children rather than less will help to guarantee that a divorce will not occur. Most marriages that fail in the early years do so before children are born. And others are merely endured until the children are "old enough."

Traditional Values

Persons who actively practice their religion, and who have traditional values, were found in the older studies to be less divorce-prone. Formal weddings were associated with greater marital stability than civil weddings, for example [18]. Values are changing today, more rapidly among some groups than among others. In a society that is moving away from some old traditions, it may be that such old values are no longer as important in determining marital stability. There is evidence that flexibility in the marital relationship is associated with marital *satisfaction,* at any rate [9].

Adversity

Between 1930 and 1933, during the Depression, divorce rates dropped off sharply. Following the Depression, the gradual rise began again, peaking shortly after World War II, dropping off again and then rising gradually once more. The crisis caused by the 1973 Yom Kippur war in the Middle East apparently had an influence on the divorce rate in Israel. Half of the divorce files opened before the war were dropped between October and January [23]. The Depression and Yom Kippur War evidence suggest that during a crisis, families stick together. In the Depression, few people could afford the cost of a divorce. Perhaps the war in Israel made some couples realize that they were lucky to be alive and intact, or perhaps disruptions caused by the war made getting a divorce inconvenient. A crisis external to a family (or any group) can often serve to make them work together, at least for the duration of the crisis. Clinical evidence suggests that a family that survives a crisis comes out strengthened [17].

Chances of Success: Conclusions

What causes a marriage to go "on the rocks?" In this section we have briefly noted a number of factors that are associated to varying degrees with broken marriages. Clearly, few if any marriages break up as a result of just one of these factors. There are countless "tremendous trifles" that, when added up, become intolerable to some persons. There is extramarital involvement, which may be a cause or a symptom of marital discord.

The factors that we have described do not necessarily *cause* divorce; no one has proved that they have. They are merely "associated with" divorce: persons who divorce may also happen to be of a different race (or the same race), or have had unhappy childhoods (or happy childhoods). One or the other does nothing to guarantee success or failure. Keeping a marriage afloat takes a great deal of work, caring, and communication on the part of both partners, although again, even these factors do not guarantee success!

In the next chapter we continue our discussion of the partner relationship. Marital adjustment and satisfaction, cohabitation, remarriage, and the middle and aging years are the major topics.

SUMMARY   Partnerhood is achieved when a pair-bonded couple have mutual love, effective communication, reciprocity, and commitment to growth of their relationship and of themselves as individuals.

Some of the partner typologies that have been conceived by American researchers are the following: institutional-companionship; middle-class types of conflict-habituated, devitalized, passive-congenial, vital and total; ghetto types of boyfriends, quasi-father, supportive biological father, supportive companion, and pimp.

Gender-role stereotypes may block the development of partnerhood, if the two people vary greatly in flexibility. Some satisfactory partnerships are organized around traditional sex roles, but for extensive freedom, considerable loosening is needed.

In our society, most people agree on the importance of love in the formation and duration of marital partnerships. Attachment, a component of love, is a special kind of bond. Many different bonds hold couples together. Crescive (growing) bonds, resulting from pair interaction, give strength to a partnership. The presence of an attached partner contributes to feelings of security and courage to face threats. When strong, longstanding bonds of attachment are disrupted, the individual has difficulty in many areas of functioning.

Bargaining, or give-and-take according to understood rules, is part of pair interaction. Violation of rules may result in retaliation and the beginning of a series of negative interactions.

Marital conflict is inevitable if both people are free to react and express. Action-oriented conflict focuses on issues resolutions; personality-oriented conflict tears down the other person. Basic conflict threatens values and previously agreed upon procedures; nonbasic conflict involves small issues within a shared value system. Conflict may be habitual or situational. Conflict can be constructive when communication is honest.

A wedding is a ritual commitment of two people to a bonding that has social and legal sanction. The particular ideals and expectations of the culture are embodied in the ceremony, for both the pair and the community. The social function includes a celebration and a happy time for all. Religion, either traditional or personal, is usually invoked. A change in social status occurs, often more for the bride than for the groom. The legal aspects of marriage may include a contract.

Marital stability means sticking together as a pair. Sometimes *success* is also applied to marriages that have not resulted in divorce or separation. Divorce frequency is expressed in various terms. A meaningful approach is to count the number of divorces among a group of persons married a certain number of years previously. Predictions of permanence are lower than average for teen-age marriages, premaritally pregnant couples, those who conceive early after marriage, low-income couples, and childless couples.

REFERENCES

1. Aldridge, Delores. The changing nature of interracial marriage in Georgia: A research note. *Journal of Marriage and the Family,* 1973, **35,** 641–642.
2. Anonymous. More black men wed to whites. *Providence Journal-Bulletin,* February 14, 1973.
3. Bayer, Alan. Early dating and early marriage. *Journal of Marriage and the Family,* 1968, **30,** 628–632.
4. Burchinal, Lee G. and L. E. Chancellor. Survival rates among religiously homogamous and interreligious marriage. *Social Forces,* 1963, **41,** 353–362.
5. Burgess, Ernest and Harvey J. Locke. *The family, from institution to companionship.* New York: American Book, 1945.
6. Christensen, Harold T. Scandinavian and American sex norms: Some comparisons, with sociological implications. *Journal of Social Issues,* 1966, **22,** 60–75.
7. Christensen, Harold T. and Kenneth E. Barber. Interfaith versus intrafaith marriage in Indiana. *Journal of Marriage and the Family,* 1967, **29,** 461–469.
8. Christensen, Harold T. and Hanna M. Meissner. Studies in child spacing: III. Premarital pregnancy as a factor in divorce. *American Sociological Review,* 1953, **28,** 641–644.
9. Crouse, Bryant, Marvin Karlins, and Harold Schroder. Conceptual complexity and marital happiness. *Journal of Marriage and the Family,* 1968, **30,** 643–650.
10. Cuber, John F. and Peggy B. Harroff. *The significant Americans.* New York: Appleton, 1966.
11. Cutright, Phillips. Income and family events: Marital stability. *Journal of Marriage and the Family,* 1971, **33,** 291–306.
11a. Cutright, Phillips. Timing the first birth: Does it matter? *Journal of Marriage and the Family,* 1973, **35,** 585–595.
12. Davis, Kingsley. *Human society.* New York: Macmillan, 1950. Ch. 7.
12a. Day, Beth. *Sexual life between blacks and whites.* New York: World, 1972

13. deLissovoy, Vladimir. High school marriages: A longitudinal study. *Journal of Marriage and the Family,* 1973, **35,** 244–255.

13a. Dobrin, Arthur and Kenneth Briggs. *Getting married the way you want.* Englewood Cliffs, N.J.: Prentice-Hall, 1974.

14. Duvall, Evelyn. *Family development.* Philadelphia: Lippincott, 1971.

15. Glick, Paul C. and Arthur J. Norton. Frequency, duration and probability of marriage and divorce. *Journal of Marriage and the Family,* 1971, **33,** 307–317.

16. Hetzel, Alice and Marlene Capetta. *Teenagers: Marriages, divorces, parenthood, and mortality.* Rockville, Maryland: National Center for Health Statistics, Series 21, Number 23, 1973.

17. Lederer, William and Don Jackson. *The mirages of marriage.* New York: Norton, 1968.

18. Locke, Harvey J. *Predicting adjustment in marriage: A comparison of a divorced and a happily married group.* New York: Holt, 1951.

19. Maslow, Abraham. *Motivation and personality.* New York: Harper, 1970.

20. McKain, Walter. A new look at older marriages. *Family Coordinator,* 1972, **21,** 61–69.

21. Monahan, Thomas P. Are interracial marriages really less stable? *Social Forces,* 1970, **48,** 461–473.

22. Monahan, Thomas P. The changing nature and instability of remarriages. *Eugenics Quarterly,* 1958, **5,** 73–85.

23. *New York Times,* January 13, 1974.

24. Plateris, Alexander. *Divorce: Analysis of change.* Rockville, Maryland: National Center for Health Statistics, Series 21, Number 22, 1973.

25. Plateris, Alexander. *Divorce statistics analysis, United States, 1963.* Rockville, Maryland: National Center for Health Statistics, Series 21, Number 13, 1967.

26. Porter, Sylvia. Year-round marrying boom. *Providence Journal,* November 24, 1972.

27. Rogers, Carl. *On becoming partners: Marriage and its alternatives.* New York: Delacorte, 1972.

28. Rosenthal, Erich. Divorce and religious intermarriage: The effect of previous marital status upon subsequent marital behavior. *Journal of Marriage and the Family,* 1970, **32,** 435–440.

29. Scanzoni, John. *Sexual bargaining: Power politics in the American marriage.* Englewood Cliffs, N.J.: Prentice-Hall, 1972.

30. Schulz, David. *Coming up black: Patterns of ghetto socialization.* Englewood Cliffs, N.J.: Prentice-Hall, 1969.

31. Seligson, Marcia. *America's way of wedding.* New York: Morrow, 1973.

32. Sprey, Jetse. On the management of conflict in families. *Journal of Marriage and the Family,* 1971, **33,** 722–731.

33. Straus, Murray. Leveling, civility and violence in the family. *Journal of Marriage and the Family,* 1974, **36,** 13–29.

34. Stroup, Atlee. *Marriage and the family: A developmental approach.* New York: Appleton, 1966.

35. Stuart, Irving R. and Edwin A. Lawrence. *Interracial marriage: Expectations and realities.* New York: Grossman, 1973.

36. Teismann, Mark. Jealous conflict: A study of verbal interaction and labeling of jealousy among dating couples involved in jealousy improvisations. Unpublished doctoral dissertation, University of Connecticut, 1975.

37. Turner, Ralph. *Family interaction.* New York: Wiley, 1970.

CHAPTER 8

MORE ABOUT PARTNERHOOD

In this chapter, we continue with the theme of partner interaction begun in the previous chapter where we noted that partnerhood involves being pair-bonded and a sense of commitment to one's partner. Although we believe that the most rewarding kind of partnerships involve reciprocity and a commitment to growth, we recognize many other possible kinds of relationships that are also partnerships.

The last section of Partnerhood I was a discussion of marital stability, or success in marriage. As we have defined it, a stable or "successful" marriage is a marriage that is intact, not divorced or separated. We now discuss marital adjustment and satisfaction.

MARITAL ADJUSTMENT AND SATISFACTION

Adjustment is an interaction process that, when successful, leads to satisfaction or happiness. Marital adjustment also serves other related purposes: to reduce marital differences, to reduce tensions between the spouses, and to increase the cohesion of the couple and their agreement on matters that affect their marital functioning [44]. **Marital success** is sometimes used to mean the same thing as adjustment; at other times it means "stability" as we have defined it.

Although it has not always been treated as such by researchers, we consider marital adjustment to be a process, and not a state of perfection to be achieved. It is bound up in the interaction between the partners, and is not the responsibility of one person or the other, although there is evidence that the wife usually changes, or adjusts, more than does the husband [48]. As women and men become more equal, men are being expected to share more of the burden of adjustment.

201

Different Kinds of Adjustment

Just as there are different kinds of relationships that can remain stable, there are different kinds of relationships that satisfy different people. An outsider cannot look at a marriage that would make her unhappy and decide that the wife is unhappy. Some researchers have concluded that women were maladjusted in their marriages because the women did not fit into the researchers' preconceived molds of what a wife should be [24]. Therapists at times have made the same mistake, calling women who opt for a career rather than homemaking maladjusted, cold, or "masculine." Today, even the homemaker is not immune from being called names by some feminists who refuse to believe that being a mother is a satisfying career for many women.

The relationship between a man and woman does not exist in a vacuum. The woman who has had a hard day may not take it out on her husband, but her interaction with him will be different from the way it is when she has had an

exhilarating day. The middle-income couple face different problems from lower-income couples. Children greatly influence the marital relationship.

Legal Marriage: Does It Make a Difference?

Throughout the book, we have been concerned with the *marriage-type* relationship and have not limited our discussion to legal marriage. Although nonlegal unions have, in recent years, become a legitimate target for research, much less is known about them than about legal marriage. Many, perhaps all, of the factors that influence marital satisfaction would influence nonmarital partnership satisfaction. It is obvious, though, that a cohabitation can be dissolved more quickly and simply than can a legal marriage. The living-together couple leaves the door open. Since no public records of nonlegal unions are kept, there is no way of determining their dissolution rate. Thus, the *stability* measure cannot be applied, as it can be to marriage. Interaction between the couple and other social systems are different for the unmarried couple as compared with the married.

Social supports and sanctions are not merely abstract ideas but real actions that affect their recipients. When landlords object to nonmarital cohabitation, as many do, they may refuse to rent to an unmarried couple. Income tax laws may be more favorable to married couples. For the unmarried, health insurance is less likely to cover the cost of childbirth or abortion. Their children may be stigmatized. Not having had a wedding, the couple missed the financial benefits of gifts that help to furnish a home. Parents may express disapproval and try to keep the knowledge from grandparents. It must be a real rebuke when a parent says, "It would hurt Grandpa and Grandma too much if they knew what you are doing, so let's try to keep it quiet."

Such sanctions must be strains on the individuals involved. The results of these strains on pair interaction are not known. Are bonds strengthened, as they seem to be in adversity? Or do the satisfactions of cohabitation simply counterbalance the dissatisfactions? Nonmarital living together seems to be increasing in frequency and in social acceptability [18a, 29]. We discuss this form of partnerhood later in this chapter and further in the last chapter, as a family form of the future.

Working

Most persons spend a significant portion of their waking hours engaged in some kind of work, either in the home or outside. Although we certainly consider housework and much of child care as real work, we are here referring to work outside the home.

The traditional male role has been to provide for the family, and research strongly indicates marital satisfaction is associated with the husband's adequate role performance [19]. If the husband is a good provider, marital satisfaction is usually higher.

Working Wives. The evidence concerning the relationship between employed wives and marital satisfaction is not clear-cut. Women who work full time appear to have lower satisfaction than those who work only part-time, but women who work by choice do not appear to have lower satisfaction than those who stay home [19]. If the husband disapproves of his wife's working, marital satisfaction is generally lower [1].

The woman who works outside the home usually has two full-time jobs: her "outside" job, and her job as homemaker (or homemaker-mother). The working woman's husband who protests that he "helps around the house" is revealing that he still considers housework as being her main responsibility. When a woman leaves the home to work, she has several options open to her regarding house and child care. If she is wealthy enough, she can hire help. Her husband and/or children can do all or most of the work. She and her husband can split the work. She can lower her housekeeping standards, but continue to do most or all of the housework. Or she can hold down two full-time jobs as just described.

Expecting the husband to increase his work load when the wife works appears to be wishful thinking. One study found that husbands contributed an average of eleven hours per *week* to household work (in contrast to the employed wife's four to eight hours per day, and the unemployed wife's five to twelve hours per day.) Whether or not his wife had or got a job outside the home, the husband in this sample did not increase his household work time [49].

Unless she is wealthy enough so that cost is no problem, any of the options listed is likely to affect marital interaction. The husband who is unhappy with the new arrangement will surely find a *quo* for her *quid*.

Job Satisfaction and Marital Adjustment. Is the person who likes his job more likely to like his marriage than the person who dislikes his job? This important question has been virtually ignored by researchers. In a study of teachers and their employed husbands, it was found that the husband's job satisfaction, but not the wife's, was related to marital adjustment. Low job involvement was related to medium-to-high marital adjustment [41]. The relationship between job satisfaction and marital adjustment has not been adequately explored. Does the husband's job satisfaction influence the nonworking wife's marital satisfaction? Is job satisfaction more or less influential upon the marital satisfaction of persons of professions other than teaching? What is the relationship among income, job satisfaction, and marital satisfaction?

Income and Education

Persons with low incomes and little education are more likely to report low marital satisfaction. The depressing effect of low income on marital satisfaction is stronger for blacks than it is for whites [19], probably because of the various types of discrimination that blacks endure. Cutright's findings regarding the relationship of *stability* to income and education (that is, that income is more important) would probably apply to satisfaction as well: it is not education that fosters marital satisfaction, but income [9a].

Children

The effects of children on parents are discussed further in Chapters 9 and 10. Although it is often assumed that children are gratifying, several studies have shown an association between having children and lower marital satisfaction. Renne found that people who were rearing children were more likely to report low marital satisfaction than were those who had never had children or whose children had left home, regardless of race, age, or income level [39].

Husband-wife companionship has been found to decline with the advent of children and to increase as children enter the teen years, and afterwards [42]. Likewise, communication and adjustment were seen as decreasing throughout the preschool years and just before the years of childrearing and increasing when the children left home and later [12]. These findings should not be taken to mean that children are nothing more than a source of marital discord. As we show in Chapters 9 and 10, parent-child relationships, like all human relationships, are varied and complex. Children themselves may be sources of satisfaction at the same time that their presence puts strains on marital interaction.

Sexual Experience

Lovemaking is adult (and adolescent) attachment behavior. Sexual interaction per se may or may not be attachment behavior. Physical sharing and tenderness can be a temporary bond, or it can become crescive. What both partners think at the time is a "one night stand" can become a lifelong sharing; what both think will last "forever" may quickly fade.

Good sex will not ensure that a relationship will continue; bad sex will not ensure its demise. In this section we discuss some of the research findings regarding the association of premarital sexual experience with later marital adjustment and the association between sexual adjustment and marital satisfaction. We again caution the reader that one factor does not "cause" the other.

Premarital Sexual Experience. Although older studies report that wives who engaged in premarital coitus had better *sexual* adjustment in marriage [16], those husbands and wives who married as virgins were a bit more likely to achieve high marital adjustment and stability [8, 47]. It was not concluded from these studies that premarital sexual experience *caused* (or causes) sexual adjustment in marriage;

rather, it is thought that women who had premarital coitus were more likely to be interested in sex, and more responsive, than those who resisted. Those persons who refrained from premarital intercourse had another characteristic that contributed to their later marital-adjustment: responsivity to social requirements and expectations. For example, engaged couples who attended church regularly were less likely to be premaritally sexually experienced than were nonregular attenders [22].

Whether or not these findings would hold true today remains to be tested. We cannot say for sure if premarital sexual experience today is associated with more or less sexual adjustment in marriage. Among some groups today, a person who is responsive to social requirements and expectations would engage in premarital sexual activity, rather than refrain from it as she would have a generation or two ago.

Many, although not all, societies place a premium on female virginity. A virgin is worth more in the "marriage market." Americans, however, have found a way to circumvent the issue of virginity by "doing everything but" have coitus. From the traditional Danish point of view, the American who pets with many partners, but does not have intercourse, is more promiscuous than the Dane who has intercourse with a partner with whom he or she is serious [9].

The definition of virginity has been shown to be a variable concept; that is, not all persons agree that the absence of a hymen, or penetration of the vagina by the penis, marks the end of virginity. When asked if the concept of virginity made sense, 47.4 per cent of the female respondents and 40.5 per cent of the males said "no." The concept of male virginity did not make sense to 57 per cent of the female respondents and 56.2 per cent of the males. [2]. This study suggests that virginity is becoming less important in our society, but it does not support the idea that it is becoming totally irrelevant.

Marital Sexual Adjustment. Marital satisfaction studies have found a strong association between sexual and marital satisfaction. However, the woman's sexual satisfaction and adjustment has usually been measured by asking how frequently she has orgasms from coitus. The possibility of sexual satisfaction from other forms of lovemaking was ignored. Furthermore, a basic assumption underlying most discussion of marital sexual adjustment has been that the male's sex drive is higher, or more pressing, than the female's. That sexual maladjustment can result because the woman desires more sex than the male has, until recently, been ignored [11].

Esteem for Self and Partner

Persons who have high esteem for their partners report higher marital satisfaction than those who do not [19]. There is some support for the idea that persons with high self-esteem have higher marital adjustment [30], although another study did not find a significant relationship between the wife's self-esteem and her marital satisfaction [23].

Health

The relationship of health and marital satisfaction has not been given much attention by researchers. In a large area probability sample survey in California, it was found that unhappy marriage was correlated with poor health, social isolation, emotional problems, and low morale. Marriage was associated with better health only when the respondent reported a satisfactory relationship. Divorced persons were, on the whole, healthier than those who remained in an unhappy marital relationship [40].

Companionship

Companionship means enjoying each other's company, having good times together, sharing activities, and being friends. A person who enjoys companionship with a spouse sometimes comments, "He (she) is my best friend." Companionship has the elements of love that we have discussed as attachment response and knowledge. Care and respect may also be involved in helping one another to enjoyment and in recognizing the individuality of each other. The in-love element is not part of the meaning of companionship, but companions can certainly be in love. Many happily married couples and unmarried partners, also, are companions in love.

It is commonly assumed that families that share many activities and interests are happy families. In terms of marital adjustment, one study found that shared activities in leisure time were associated with marital satisfaction, but not equally for husbands and wives, and not equally at all stages of the life cycle. The husband's satisfaction was associated with shared activities during the first five years of marriage, and the wife's between the eighteenth and twenty-third years of marriage [33].

Companionship in marriage has been found to be correlated with high levels of health, health care practices, and health knowledge [38]. Since health and marital satisfaction have been shown to be associated [40], this finding suggests that all three factors, companionship, health, and marital satisfaction, are related.

In contrast, another study found that marital satisfaction was more strongly related to the absence of hostility than to the presence of companionship. That is, marital satisfaction was negatively correlated with hostility, defined as "the degree of mutual expression of overtly hostile activity, angry outbursts aimed at deflation of [the other's] status and self-regard, and dramatic acts aimed at symbolizing the breakdown of solidarity" (what we have called *personality conflict*). Marital satisfaction was positively correlated with companionship, defined as "the degree of mutual expression by the spouses of affective behavior, self-revelatory communication, and mutual participation in other informal non-task recreational activities" [17]. In other words, in this study hostility accompanied low marital satisfaction more consistently than companionship accompanied high satisfaction.

A third investigation indicated that personal involvement with the partner was associated with marital happiness. Those who reported happy marriages concen-

trated on the relationship aspects of the marriage, whereas those who were less happy in their marriages focused on situational aspects (children, home, social life) as the sources of happiness in their marriages. When asked about sources of unhappiness in their marriages, those who reported happier marriages focused on the situational aspects and those who were less happy in their marriages cited relationship aspects as the source of unhappiness. It was found that those who were satisfied with the relationship aspects were satisfied with the marriage [15].

Class Differences. When divorce applicants were questioned, middle-class spouses reported themselves as more concerned with the quality of their emotional and psychological interaction, whereas lower-class divorce applicants saw their problems as stemming from financial problems and their partner's unstable physical interaction [25].

Roles

Good marital adjustment is associated with congruence between role perception and performance. In other words, if a man performs his role in the way that his wife thinks he should, and she performs her role in the way that he thinks she should, they will report high marital happiness. It appears to be more important for the husband to perform his work role adequately [19]. As women become dissatisfied with their roles, and strive to have more egalitarian roles in relation to their husbands, role strain may result. The husband who does not think that his wife is performing her role in the way that she should (perhaps, the way she used to) will feel dissatisfied with the relationship.

Low sex-role differentiation (that is, husband and wife roles that are similar rather than very different) has been found to be associated with high health, high companionship, and egalitarian power in the marital relationship [38]. It is to the question of power that we now turn.

Power

Although marital power has been studied for a long time, methodological problems have limited the value of what has been found. Many researchers interviewed only the wives, and assumed that the wives' perceptions of power would be accurate, when it has been shown that even when both husbands' and wives' perceptions are used, they do not measure up to their actual behaviors [32]. Relying only on the wife's perceptions compounds this error. But an even more basic problem is that "power" has been defined and measured in a number of different ways. Usually, the respondents have been asked to tell who makes particular decisions, such as what job the husband should take, or who plans family vacations. Possible answers might be husband always, wife always, sometimes wife, and sometimes husband.

Thorough criticism of power studies is not our purpose here. However, "power" covers a lot of territory. Results from different studies are not always strictly comparable, nor are all aspects of family power tapped by available studies.

A More Comprehensive Typology. Many different kinds of power exist in a family. Children, as well as parents, have power, and coalitions are often formed among family members to counterbalance the power of another person or coalition.

Safilios-Rothschild suggests the following typology to explain family power [43]. We present it here in an oversimplified form, in order to give an idea of the complexity of family power.

1. Legitimate power or authority is entrusted to a family member by societal norms, such as legal codes. In the United States and most Western societies, it is entrusted to the husband.
2. Decision-making power is held by the individual who makes decisions.
   (a) Major decision-making power, usually entrusted to the husband, concerns major issues that affect the family's life style; for example, the kind of job that the husband has.
   (b) Everyday decision-making power is usually entrusted to the wife, and involves routine decisions such as what to cook for dinner.
3. Influence power is the degree to which pressure, either covert or overt, is successfully used by one spouse so that his or her view is imposed on the spouse, in spite of the spouse's initial opposition. Influence power, although thought of as being more the woman's realm than the man's, was found in a study by Safilios-Rothschild to be used by both men and woman, but along sex-stereotyped lines. Men relied more on persuasion and discussion, whereas women used "sweet talk and affection . . . anger, crying, pouting. . . ."
4. Resource power is power held by a person because he offers the other a highly desirable or necessary resource. The homemaker's resource power is low, because the resource of being a homemaker is not highly valued. On the other hand, a woman whose job has about the same prestige as her husband's has resource power. In subsistence societies, or even in most traditional societies, women hold power through their control over two important resources, food and the birth of children. Mead has pointed out that in industrialized nations, especially in the United States, women no longer control food and birth. Men have taken over the leading positions in the food industry and in obstetrics, making women's power subject to theirs [31].
5. "Expert" power is granted to a spouse who has special expertise. A woman accountant may be given power to make major financial decisions, even though this is normally the husband's realm.
6. Affective power is yielded by the spouse who has more to lose in terms of affection. The spouse who is less "in love" has more power. The woman who does not work outside the home is more dependent upon her husband for affection than he is on her, because she has fewer relationships than he.
7. Dominance power belongs to the more physically powerful spouse who uses violence or the threat of violence. This resource is more available to men than to women because of the greater physical size and strength of men.
8. Tension-management power is obtained by the spouse who can manage existing tensions and disagreements, even if these cannot be solved. In a family with children, one child may become the peacemaker among family members, or a clown who can get the others to laugh in spite of their problems.
9. Moral power may be claimed by a spouse who takes recourse to more

"legitimate" and "respectable" set of norms. For example, a wife may be able to obtain more equitable division of labor by taking recourse to the norms of the women's liberation movement. This power exists only to the extent that the other spouse agrees.

Most kinds of power can be exercised at different levels. If one person decides who will make all the other decisions, she has a great deal of power even though much of the routine decision-making is carried on by someone else.

It is difficult to assess who has power in a family situation for a number of reasons. Different kinds of power do not have the same weight. Also, it is often difficult to assess who has the power in a given situation because of the time lag between the decision making and the enactment, but also because different family members may be using different kinds of power simultaneously. Perceptual distortions further complicate the picture: the wife may believe that she has little or no power, when she really has as much as or more power than her husband.

Findings of Power Studies. Keeping in mind that the power studies have not included all of these dimensions of power, we now briefly summarize some of the findings regarding marital power.

The husband usually has more power than the wife, in that he makes the more major decisions. Even when an egalitarian power distribution is espoused, family power is not evenly distributed. Stereotyped ideas restrict the realms of men and women [6, 34, 43]. The husband's greater power comes from his greater worth as viewed by society [13], and he is seen as more useful by society in part because he works outside the home. The working wife has more power than the nonworking wife [5]; this is more true for the working-class wife than for the middle-class wife, probably because the former contributes proportionately more to the family income [18]. In one study black women were found to have more decision-making power than their husbands, but these women had better jobs than their husbands [4]. Other researchers have found that intact black families varied from egalitarian (working and middle class) to patriarchal (lower class) [21]. Black women who want love and companionship may lose power in relation to their men because of the relative scarcity of black men [45]. Egalitarian power is associated with high companionship and low sex role differentiation [38].

Power and Bargaining. If one person wields a disproportionate amount of power over the other, the situation may become intolerable for the dominated spouse. The spouse who finds the marital situation intolerable often has recourse to the last "card" of bargaining: threatening to leave, or simply leaving. But in many cases, even if one spouse obviously has a great deal more power than the other, the subordinate spouse does not leave, and may not even actively object, because the subordinate spouse supports the idea that the dominant spouse has *legitimate power*. The subordinate spouse may feel that the bargain is even, because even though she doesn't have a great deal of power in the family situation, she also has less responsibility. Sometimes, when we have to make a decision, I (LSS) let my husband make it so that if things do not turn out well, I'm not to blame! (If I can force him to make the decision, then in that situation I have more power!)

MARITAL ADJUSTMENT AND SATISFACTION: CONCLUSIONS

Many factors contribute to how well each person adjusts to being married to his spouse, and how satisfied each spouse is with the relationship. Social support to the relationship affects not only stability but adjustment and satisfaction as well. Adjustment and satisfaction are highly personal and usually cannot be defined effectively for an individual or couple by an outside observer.

A person's satisfaction with other aspects of his life is likely to affect his satisfaction with and adjustment to his marriage, although the relationship is not always clear-cut. We would expect that a person who is happy with his job and children would be more satisfied with his marriage, but the opposite might be true in some cases.

Marital satisfaction is not static, even within a short time period such as a few weeks or months. Studies of marital satisfaction have been concerned with differences in satisfaction by stages in the marital career or parent-child career. Most couples, however, do experience minor fluctuations in the amount of satisfaction that they feel in their marital relationships. Just as some individuals fluctuate more in their feelings of life satisfaction, so do some couples change more in their relationship satisfaction than do other couples.

Low income is associated with less marital satisfaction. Children can be sources of disagreement and sources of pleasure in a marriage, even at the same time. Sexual adjustment is associated with marital adjustment, but we cannot be certain which causes which. Most likely, sexual and marital adjustment interact. Health and marital satisfaction have been found to go together. Absence of hostility is associated more closely with marital satisfaction than is companionship.

Role conflict in marriage, such as household task division, is a very common source of conflict even in "happy" marriages. The relationship of power to marital satisfaction is highly complex and has not been adequately determined.

In sum, many complexly interrelated factors contribute to the smooth working, or adjustment, of a marriage, and to the happiness, or satisfaction, felt by the partners as a result of the marriage.

COHABITATION

Living together without legal marriage is a growing phenomenon among college students [35], but it is not restricted just to that age group. In the 1970 census, more than 18,000 couples over sixty-five listed themselves as unmarried and living together, and this figure probably is much lower than the true figure [27].

Cohabitation, like other relationships, means different things to different people. Aging cohabitors usually do not marry because it would mean the loss of income; the female cohabitor would lose her dead husband's pension or Social Security check. Some older cohabitors want very much to marry, and may seek out religious formalization of their union, even though ministers are not permitted to perform such a nonlegal, religious wedding [27]. The middle-aged children of aging cohabitors are often shocked by their parents' behavior.

The same middle-aged individuals whose mother or father is "living in sin" may not even know that their college-age children are also cohabiting. Studies indicate that only about a quarter of college students who cohabit tell their parents, or their partner's parents, about the arrangement [29, 35].

Among College Students

Cohabitation involves varying degrees of commitment, from "friend" relationships, to dating relationships, to trial marriage [35]. A relationship that starts out casually may end quickly, or it may progress to marriage. Among college freshmen and sophomores, and especially males, cohabitation does not involve much commitment to permanency, but as the end of college nears, cohabitation comes closer to the nature of trial marriage [35].

Exactly how widespread cohabitation is, even among college students, cannot be said with certainty. At Arizona State, 18 per cent of females sampled, and 29 per cent of males, said that they had experienced cohabitation. Of those who had not cohabited, 35 per cent of the females and 57 per cent of the males said that they would like to [18a]. At Penn State, 32.8 per cent of males and females had lived with a member of the opposite sex. Table 8-1 shows the breakdown of cohabitors by sex and class standing. The high number of freshman women who had cohabited even before the end of their first year in college indicates that college cohabitation is on the increase [35].

Half of the cohabitors in the Penn State study had had more than one such experience. Males reported more repeats, and shorter experiences, than did females.

TABLE 8-1   **Per Cent of College Students Who Have Experienced Cohabitation, by Sex and Class Standing**

	Freshman	Sophomore	Junior	Senior
Male	19%	25%	34%	47%
Female	25%	26%	32%	45%

Source: Dan J. Peterman, Carl A. Ridley, and Scott Anderson. A comparison of cohabiting and noncohabiting college students. Journal of Marriage and the Family, 1974, **36**, 344–354.

85 per cent of the males, and 75 per cent of the females, had cohabited for no more than six months with any one partner. However, in terms of interpersonal growth, cohabitation was usually seen as fulfilling. Eighty-three per cent of the males and 86 per cent of the females described their relationships as "love" or "intimate."

In contrast, a study of 70 cohabiting couples at another university found that few of the individuals involved professed love for each other. When asked why they were living together, a very common answer was that cohabitation is convenient and that it is cheaper than living alone [20].

Cohabitation and the Future of Marriage. Cohabiting women tend to be more marriage-oriented than are men [28, 35]. Marriage after college is a highly popular choice, especially for women, but cohabitation is preferred by many, especially men. Group living arrangements were rejected by both cohabitors and noncohabitors in the Penn State study. Whether or not cohabitation will become a threat to legal marriage remains an open question.

Many Questions Unanswered

Indeed, relatively little is known about cohabitation. We do not know its effects upon later relationship stability and adjustment. We do not know how widespread it is among groups other than college students. We do not know the effect that cohabitation has on the families of orientation: how accepting are parents of college-age cohabitors? We have known such parents who were extremely relieved to find out that their children were not the only ones who were living together. The studies indicate that few parents know about their children's cohabiting arrangements, but more parents may know than are willing to discuss it with their children.

REMARRIAGE

Marriage itself is an extremely complex subject, about which it is risky to generalize. Remarriage, involving one or more persons who were previously married, is even more complex. Former spouses, whether dead or alive, exert an influence upon the new union. When children exist from a former marriage, they too exert an influence upon the new marriage. We can give only a brief description of remarriage, and will not dwell upon the special problems involved.

Remarriage Rates

The marriage rates for divorced persons, especially those in their early twenties, are considerably higher than are the rates for singles [36]. Widowed persons are less likely to remarry than are the divorced. Table 8-2 shows the annual probabilities of divorce, remarriage, and widowhood per 1,000 persons age 14 to 69 in the United

States, 1960–1966. For example, for every 1,000 men in this age range during a given year, six ended their first marriage in divorce and three ended it in widowhood. Seven women out of 1,000 ended their first marriage in divorce in the same year, and eight ended it in widowhood. Of those men whose first marriages had ended in divorce, 169 out of 1,000 remarried. It can also be seen that more men remarry than do women [14].

Second Marriages: Stability and Happiness

Earlier studies reported a higher divorce rate for second marriages than for first marriages [3, 31a], but Glick and Norton's data do not indicate a large difference in

TABLE 8-2　Average Annual Probability of Divorce, Remarriage, and Widowhood per 1,000 Persons Age 14 to 69 Years Old, United States, 1960 - 1966

	Men Under 70 Years Old			Women Under 70 Years Old		
	All Races	White	Negro	All Races	White	Negro
Probability of divorce after first marriage	6	6	10	7	7	10
Probability of widowhood after first marriage	3	3	7	8	8	10
Probability of remarriage after first marriage ended in divorce	169	170	173	139	141	128
Probability of remarriage after first marriage ended in widowhood	94	94	92	27	27	26
Probability of divorce after second marriage	5	5	*	9	10	*

*Extremely small number of events.

Adapted from: Paul C. Glick, and Arthur J. Norton. Frequency, duration, and probability of marriage and divorce. *Journal of Marriage and the Family,* 1971, **33,** 307–317.

the chance for divorce in a second marriage. In her thorough study of many aspects of remarriage, Bernard points out that the higher divorce rate among remarrieds in the late 1940s served to weed out the less happy among them, leaving as a residue a *more happily* married population than the once-married population. Remarriages of widowed persons were happier than were those of divorced persons, but over half of the remarried persons in her study reported that they were happy or very happy in their second marriages.

For some individuals, having gone through a divorce makes subsequent divorces seem easier and more available, but for others, having been divorced once makes them want to try extra hard on their second marriages. Since marriages between the very young are more likely to end in divorce than later marriages, it is likely that for these individuals their second marriages are more stable simply because the individuals have matured.

The Third Marriage and More

Over 70 per cent of divorcing persons are ending their first marriage; 20 per cent are ending their second marriage, and about 6 per cent are ending their third or more marriage [37]. The risk of failure of a second marriage is about the same as for a first marriage [14]. An older study indicated that with a second divorce, a person's chances for marital stability decreased and continued to go down with each subsequent marriage [3].

THE MIDDLE AND AGING YEARS

The excitement of being in love calms down as the years go on, even though it recurs at memorable times. Although a good sex life can continue into old age, frequency of desire usually decreases with passing years. Companionship, however, need not diminish at all. In fact, middle-age and older couples may have more fun and enjoyment as a couple than they have had during many previous years. With more leisure, perhaps more money, and years of experience in knowing each other and responding to one another, the stage is set for better companionship. This is the time to rework old interests, to develop new shared activities, and to build more satisfying patterns in life.

The term *empty nest* has been applied to the home from which children have departed, leaving only aging parents (who may actually be in their forties). This period is sometimes considered a crisis, since the mother no longer has children to care for. Instead of a time of gloom, it is often an opportunity for new creativity, loving companionship, partner activities, and enjoyment of freedom. The launching of children is not always abrupt and not always a crisis [10]. In fact, some parents may even be delighted to find themselves "alone at last!"

Satisfaction

Several studies have found the postparental period to be as satisfying as earlier periods, although other studies have noted a general decline in satisfaction [19]. One recent national study found that women in the postparental stage reported more marital happiness than those women who had children still at home [13a]. Among lower socioeconomic groups, and among marriages with small amounts of companionship and satisfaction in the early years, satisfaction declines in the later years. Persons whose marriages are satisfying in the later years have usually had satisfying marriages since the beginning. Those persons whose needs continue to be satisfied in marriage in the later years report high levels of morale and activity in the later years [46].

Roles and Power among the Aging

After the husband's retirement, the husband and wife experience a shift in roles, as the husband becomes more involved in homemaking tasks. This shift in roles has

MOLLIE S. SMART

been found to be associated with more companionship [26]. Because of the relative scarcity of men in the aged population, husbands in intact couples tend to gain power. Patriarchal control in the aged population exists because old people have been affected less by cultural change than have younger people [6]. Many old widows possess money that could be a source of power to them, but they often give over its management to a male relative or a trust company run by men.

Problems Associated with Aging

For many aged persons after retirement, money becomes more of a problem. It may be difficult to find adequate housing on a limited budget. Poor health is often troublesome [46]. Widowhood, which is more likely to happen to women but appears to have a more devastating effect upon men [7], will almost always be a problem for one spouse or the other. Although widowhood is usually a crisis of great significance, steps can be taken prior to its occurrence to make the transition less difficult. We elaborate further on this subject in Chapter 16, pages 426–427.

"The Golden Years"

For the couple, or individual, with good health and adequate income or savings, the years after 60 or 65 need not be "declining" years. Forced retirement can be a problem for the individual whose entire life revolved around a job, or it can be a time to develop old and new interests. Even individuals with health problems, such as stroke and coronary victims, can learn new skills and make new friends through geriatric day care centers that are available in some communities. By loving and being loved, along with doing something that seems worthwhile, an older person has a good chance of maintaining an adequate sense of self-esteem.

SUMMARY

Adjustment is interaction that reduces differences and tensions and increases cohesion and satisfaction. Nonmarried cohabiting couples live in a different relation to social institutions, incurring a variety of pressures.

The effect of work and jobs on marital satisfaction depends upon the attitudes of the spouses toward them. When the wife has a job, marital satisfaction is greater if she has it by choice and if her husband approves. Sharing of housework can be a problem. Marital satisfaction changes throughout the parent-child career, decreasing and then increasing.

Sexual and marital satisfaction are positively related. So also are premarital sexual experience and sexual adjustment in marriage. Virginity is variously defined and esteemed. Marital satisfaction is associated with good health. Companionship is related to satisfaction, health, egalitarianism, and low sex-role differentiation.

Power is exerted in different forms and contexts: authority or legitimate, decision-making (major and everyday), influence, resource, expert, affective, dominance, tension-management, and moral. Balances tend to occur in favor of husbands versus wives and working versus nonworking wives.

Nonmarital cohabitation is increasing among college students and among the elderly. Remarriage is more frequent among the divorced than among the widowed and is also more frequent among men than women. Remarriages of the widowed are more often happy than remarriages of the divorced. With each divorce after the first, chances for marital stability decrease.

The postparental years are satisfying maritally for those who had satisfaction in earliest periods. A shift in roles, with the husband becoming more involved in homemaking, is associated with companionship. Money and health are often problems in later years.

REFERENCES

1. Arnott, Catherine. Husbands' attitude and wives' commitment to employment. *Journal of Marriage and the Family,* 1972, **34,** 673–684.
2. Berger, David and Morton Wenger. The ideology of virginity. *Journal of Marriage and the Family,* 1973, **35,** 666–676.
3. Bernard, Jessie. *Remarriage: A study of marriage.* New York: Dryden, 1956.
4. Blood, Robert O. Negro-white differences in blue collar marriages in a northern metropolis. *Social Forces,* 1970, **48,** 347–352.
5. Blood, Robert O. and Robert Hamblin. The effect of the wife's employment on the family power structure. *Social Forces,* 1965, **43,** 59–64.
6. Blood, Robert O. and Donald Wolfe. *Husbands and wives.* New York: Free Press, 1960.
7. Bock, E. Wilbur. Aging and suicide: The significance of marital, kinship, and alternative relations. *Family Coordinator,* 1972, **21,** 71–79.
8. Burgess, Ernest and Paul Wallin. *Engagement and marriage.* Philadelphia: Lippincott, 1953.
9. Christensen, Harold and Christina Gregg. Changing sex norms in America and Scandinavia. *Journal of Marriage and the Family,* 1970, **32,** 616–627.
9a. Cutright, Phillips. Income and family events: Marital stability. *Journal of Marriage and the Family,* 1971, **35,** 244–255.
10. Deutscher, Irving. Socialization for postparental life. In Arnold M. Rose (ed.). *Human behavior and social processes.* Boston: Houghton Mifflin, 1962.
11. Ehrlich, Carol. The male sociologist's burden: The place of women in marriage and family texts. *Journal of Marriage and the Family,* 1971, **33,** 421–434.
12. Figley, Charles. Child density and the marital relationship. *Journal of Marriage and the Family,* 1973, **35,** 272–282.
13. Gillespie, Dair. Who has the power? The marital struggle. *Journal of Marriage and the Family,* 1971, **33,** 445–458.
13a. Glenn, Norval A. Psychological well-being in the postparental stage; some evidence from national surveys. *Journal of Marriage and the Family,* 1975, **37,** 105–110.
14. Glick, Paul C. and Arthur J. Norton. Frequency, duration and probability of divorce. *Journal of Marriage and the Family,* 1971, **33,** 307–317.

15. Gurin, Gerald, Joseph Veroff, and Sheila Feld. *Americans view their mental health*. New York: Basic Books, 1960.

16. Hamblin, Robert and Robert O. Blood. Premarital experience and the wife's sexual adjustment. *Social Problems,* 1956, **3,** 122–130.

17. Hawkins, James. Associations between companionship, hostility, and marital satisfaction. *Journal of Marriage and the Family,* 1968, **30,** 647–650.

18. Heer, David. Dominance and the working wife. *Social Forces,* 1958, **36,** 341–347.

18a. Henze, Lura and John Hudson. Personal and family characteristics of cohabiting and noncohabiting college students. *Journal of Marriage and the Family,* 1974, **36,** 722–727.

19. Hicks, Mary and Marilyn Platt. Marital happiness and stability: a review of the research in the sixties. *Journal of Marriage and the Family,* 1970, **32,** 553–574.

20. Huang, Lucy Jen. Research with unmarried cohabiting couples: Including non-exclusive sexual relations. Paper presented at the annual meetings of the National Council on Family Relations, St. Louis, October, 1974.

21. Jackson, Jacquelyne Johnson. Marital life among aging blacks. *Family Coordinator,* 1972, **21,** 20–27.

22. Kannin, Eugene and David Howard. Postmarital consequences of premarital sex adjustments. *American Sociological Review,* 1958, **23,** 557–562.

23. Klemer, Richard H. Self-esteem and college dating experience as factors in mate selection and marital happiness: A longitudinal study. *Journal of Marriage and the Family,* 1971, **33,** 183–187.

24. Laws, Judith Long. A feminist review of the marital adjustment literature: The rape of the Locke. *Journal of Marriage and the Family,* 1971, **33,** 483–516.

25. Levinger, George. Sources of marital dissatisfaction among applicants for divorce. *American Journal of Orthopsychiatry.* 1966, **36,** 803–807.

26. Lipman, A. Role conceptions and morale of couples in retirement. *Journal of Gerontology,* 1961, **16,** 267–271.

27. Lobsenz, Norman. Sex and the senior citizen. *New York Times Magazine,* January 20, 1974, 8–9+.

28. Lyness, Judith, Milton Lipetz, and Keith E. Davis. Living together: An alternative to marriage. *Journal of Marriage and the Family,* 1972, **34,** 305–311.

29. Macklin, Eleanor. Heterosexual cohabitation among unmarried college students. *Family Coordinator,* 1972, **21,** 463–472.

30. McIntire, Walter and Gilbert Nass. Self-actualizing qualities of low and high happiness stable marriages. Paper presented at meetings of the National Council on Family Relations, Toronto, 1973.

31. Mead, Margaret, Speech to the College of Home Economics, University of Rhode Island, Kingston, Rhode Island, 1969.

31a. Monahan, Thomas P. The changing nature and instability of remarriages. *Eugenics Quarterly,* 1958, **5,** 73–85.

32. Olson, David. The measurement of family power by self report and behavioral methods. *Journal of Marriage and the Family,* 1969, **31,** 545–550.

33. Orthner, Dennis. Leisure activity patterns and marital satisfaction over the marital career. *Journal of Marriage and the Family,* 1975, **37,** 91–103.

34. Parsons, Talcott and Robert Bales. *Differentiation in the nuclear family*. New York: Free Press, 1955.

35. Peterman, Dan J., Carl A. Ridley, and Scott Anderson. A comparison of cohabiting and noncohabiting college students. *Journal of Marriage and the Family,* 1974, **36,** 344–354.

36. Plateris, Alexander. *Divorce statistics analysis, United States, 1963*. Rockville, Maryland: National Center for Health Statistics, Series 21, Number 13, 1967.
37. Plateris, Alexander, *Divorces: Analysis of changes, United States, 1969*. Rockville, Maryland: National Center for Health Statistics, Series 21, Number 22, 1973.
38. Pratt, Lois. Conjugal organization and health. *Journal of Marriage and the Family,* 1972, **34,** 85–89.
39. Renne, Karen S. Correlates of dissatisfaction in marriage. *Journal of Marriage and the Family,* 1970, **32,** 54–66.
40. Renne, Karen S. Health and marital experience in an urban population. *Journal of Marriage and the Family,* 1971, **33,** 338–348.
41. Ridley, Carl A. Exploring the impact of work satisfaction on marital interaction when both partners are employed. *Journal of Marriage and the Family,* 1973, **35,** 229–237.
42. Rollins, Boyd and Kenneth L. Cannon. Marital satisfaction over the family life cycle: A reevaluation. *Journal of Marriage and the Family,* 1974, **36,** 271–282.
43. Safilios-Rothschild, Constantina. The dimensions of power distribution in the family. In Jacob Christ and Henry Grunebaum (eds.). *Marriage problems and their treatment.* Boston: Little, Brown, 1972.
44. Spanier, Graham. Toward clarification and investigation of marital adjustment. Paper presented at the meetings of the National Council on Family Relations, Toronto, 1973.
45. Staples, Robert. The myth of black matriarchy. In Robert Staples (ed.). *The black family: Essays and studies.* Belmont, Calif.: Wadsworth, 1971.
46. Stinnett, Nick, Linda Mittelstet Carter, and James Montgomery. Older persons' perceptions of their marriages. *Journal of Marriage and the Family,* 1972, **34,** 665–670.
47. Terman, Lewis M. *Psychological factors in marital happiness.* New York: McGraw-Hill, 1938.
48. Uhr, Leonard Merrick. Personality changes in marriage. Unpublished Ph.D. dissertation, Ann Arbor, Michigan, U. of Michigan, 1957. Cited in J. Richard Udry. *The social context of marriage.* Philadelphia: Lippincott, 1971.
49. Walker, Kathryn. Household work time: Its implication for family decisions. *Journal of Home Economics,* 1973, **65,** 7–11.

CHAPTER 9

A MATTER of choice: PARENTHOOD

Some of life's greatest joys and worries come from having children. As the parent of three children, I (MSS) can truthfully say that I would not have missed it for anything! I can think of nothing more interesting and more growth-producing (for me) than being a parent. Even so, I would never urge people to have children if they did not want to do so. There are many ways of growing and many interesting activities in life that others may find more satisfying than parenthood. What is more, children bring many problems and sorrows to parents and in some cases, the pain seems to outweigh the joy. Having children is a very personal choice to be made, in North American society, by partners or couples, or sometimes by single people.

Since antiquity, human beings have made efforts to control the birth of children, but only recently has birth control technology become highly effective and widely available. Parenthood is no longer taken for granted as the result of marriage. Although there are some pressures on a young couple to have children, other pressures make them think it over carefully.

MAJOR DECISIONS

The biggest decision regarding parenthood is whether or not to become a parent. Dropping birth rates in Canada and the United States indicate that individuals are becoming more reluctant to enter the parent-child career or to add children to those they already have. In 1973, the birth rate in both countries was the lowest it had ever been, 15.5 per 1000 population in Canada and 15 in the United States [11; 9]. Quebec had the lowest rate of the provinces, 13.8, and Newfoundland the highest,

222

22. Increases in childlessness were greatest among the most educated women. Among ever-married United States women age 25 to 39, 22 per cent were childless, in contrast to seven percent childless among those the same age who had not finished high school [10].

If a person does not enter the parent-child career, no further decisions about parenthood are necessary. If the parent-child career is chosen, the next question is *when* to begin it. After the first child is born, the parents then face the question of whether to have another and, if so, when, and when to stop having children. Leaving the first question for a later section, we now discuss the questions of when to have children and how many children to have.

When to Start the Parent-Child Career

There are many different ways of being ready for parenthood. First and foremost is *wanting it*. Easiest to understand, perhaps, is *physical readiness*. A girl is not ready to be a mother until she completes her own growth and lives a few years longer. The most favorable age for childbearing (as judged by infant mortality rates) is between 20 and 24 years of age, although the years between 19 and 35 are adequate [16]. Physical readiness also requires being in good health, including a state of excellent nutrition. Although couples rarely consult doctors for preconception advice, to do so would be to give their baby the best chance for a good start.

Costs of prenatal care and birth have to be paid. Resources for caring for the baby require some financial planning and home management. It requires money to buy space, furniture, equipment, and clothing, and having a child often means a rearrangement of ways of earning, spending, and living. If both partners hold jobs, then the woman has to plan to stop her career for at least a few weeks or months, if not years. How will the family get along with less money? How will the new mother feel about giving up her occupational career to a greater or lesser degree? Will the new father take time off, too, in order to share the transition to parenthood and child care? Are grandparents going to help? What other sources of help will be used? In planning for parenthood, a person will have some individual problems to be solved, as well as these more general questions. If she is going to be a single mother, she will need a set of resources different from those of a wife. If one of the couple has a particular disability or if they carry a special responsibility, then plans for having a child are affected. These are questions of readiness for having a baby, since plans must be made to answer them.

How Many Children?

Should we have another child? And another? Intended numbers, as well as actual births, have decreased. A U.S. Government survey in 1974 found that among wives between 18 and 39 years of age, every 1000 of them intended to have 2,550 children, in contrast to 3,118 intended children in 1967 [10]. Intended numbers were higher among older women and black women. Across age levels, women's expectations for numbers of children were smaller than they had ever been [16a].

Sometimes couples have a second child out of a sense of duty and obligation, rather than because they really want another. A persistent myth says that there is something wrong with having an only child. Part of the myth is that only children are spoiled, selfish, and lonely. Another part of it says that parents are selfish if they do not provide a playmate for their first child. As we read the research literature, there are advantages and disadvantages to each position in the family. It is doubtful whether the advantages of having a younger sibling generally outweigh the advantages of being an only child. It is highly questionable whether the advantages of giving the older child a playmate outweigh the costs to parents who do not really want another child or who do not have personal and financial resources adequate for a second (or third) child. There are many other ways of finding playmates for one's child. It hardly seems fair to the second child to be given birth for the good of the first one, and not because of being wanted for himself. In fact, if people gave birth only to children *they* really wanted, many human problems would be prevented, perhaps even the population explosion.

Fortunately, the number of offspring does not have to be decided when the partnership is set up. If marriage required a contract specifying the number of children, there would probably be more mistakes in childbearing than there are today! When a couple first declare their love for each other and begin making plans for marriage, they often say something like this: "Let's have six children. They'll all be beautiful with you for a father (mother)." At this stage of life and love, an expansive statement about the number of desired children is often just a way of saying, "I love you very, very much and I want to share the rest of my life with you."

Couples differ in the number of children that may be appropriate for them. Before making any major change in life, it is wise to take stock of the present situation and weigh possible courses of action in regard to aims and goals. Because most couples would plan carefully before changing jobs, buying a house, or even buying a car, it makes sense for them to give even more thought to conceiving a baby. The baby causes bigger, more permanent changes and greater responsibilities than do most other new steps in life. Therefore, questions about the present and the future need to be considered each time a child is planned.

Sometimes couples disagree as to having a baby, or another baby. For the sake of the child herself, it seems to us that the veto power should be stronger, because we think a baby should be wanted by *both* parents. However, some such conflicts are solved by having the baby for the sake of the one parent who wants it, as in the case of Rob, who very much wanted a son, even though he had four girls, and Jean, who felt that she had already more than enough children. Rob told Jean that if she would try again, with the use of new techniques for controlling the sex of the fetus, he would change his mode of life to help a great deal more in caring for all the children. (In this family, income was more than adequate.) Jean wanted Rob to be fulfilled. The two of them discussed ways of rearranging their mode of life in order to keep from overtaxing Jean. They had a son. Now, five years later, the seven of them are doing well, although Jean is more tired than she would like to be. Rob has kept up his part of the agreement. Both Jean and Rob put a great deal of time and energy into parenting. One of their minor problems is social disapproval for having so many children in an overcrowded world. They do not believe they have done wrong, however, because they planned for all their children, they love them dearly, and they do a good job as parents.

The question of population trends is discussed in Chapter 14. Readers may question whether Jean and Rob should have had five children. The situation could be viewed from the standpoint of the couple, the family, the community, the United States, or the world.

TRANSITION TO PARENTHOOD

The process of reproduction is described in Chapter 14. This section is concerned with taking on parental roles, how people respond to their children, how it feels and what it means to become parents.

Parenthood as Crisis

Becoming a parent involves many changes in behavior. Whether it is actually a crisis is debatable. When the individual is unprepared or unable to make the necessary changes, then a great deal of stress occurs. New parents, especially mothers, usually need some help from other people in taking on their new roles and responsibilities. Becoming a parent is both biological and social, since other people help the biological process to go along smoothly. The educator teaches the pregnant pair about the bodily changes they are feeling and seeing. The doctor or midwife helps the mother to deliver the baby (and perhaps the father helps, too). A nurse-educator shows the mother how to help the baby in his efforts to find, suck, and swallow his food. In learning to care for and educate infants and young children, parents receive inputs from many sources, including kin, friends, professionals, and the media. Some of these inputs are truly helpful. Much of the outcome depends upon the personal resources of the couple and the use that they are able to make of the proffered help.

The other important person in this picture is the baby herself. What kind of baby is she? She makes the transition easy for her parents if she takes her food easily, rarely regurgitates, sleeps continuously for several hours, seldom cries, and responds to comforting. When 296 first-time mothers and 272 first-time fathers answered questionnaires about their young infants, 8 per cent of the women and 5 per cent of the men said that the baby interrupted their sleep and rest very much [29]. Physical tiredness and fatigue were felt somewhat by 64 per cent of mothers, and very much by 14 per cent. The majority of babies, then, were not very troublesome at night, but caused some fatigue to mothers, whereas a small minority placed considerable physical strain on the parents.

The ease and difficulty of making the transition to parenthood was studied, as mentioned, by looking for conditions associated with the parents' perceptions of bothersome change [29]. Transition to parenthood was found to be less stressful for both women and men when the child was planned, and when the child had not been conceived before marriage. The longer the woman had been married, the better her health, and the easier her pregnancy, the less was she likely to report a crisis. Relatively little stress was felt by men who were older rather than younger and who reported that the role of father was important to them, as compared with other roles. Less than average crisis was experienced by women and men who had quiet babies who were healthy and ate and slept well.

In summary, people can get along better as parents if they prepare themselves for it and begin it at a suitable time. Satisfactory parenthood also depends upon social supports and upon the children themselves. When parents have a hard time, it is not always the result of something they did or did not do.

JOYS AND SATISFACTIONS OF PARENTHOOD

When a group of Californian women rated benefits and costs of parenthood, the chief positive items were enjoying children's activities, observing development, liking children, and watching children achieve. The costs rated highest were loss of freedom and mobility, foregoing opportunities, worrying about children's health and well-being, and economic costs [1].

In another exploration of the satisfactions that new parents experienced, 12 items were used:

Pride in the baby's development
Less boredom
Closer relationships with relatives
More appreciation of family and religious tradition
More interaction with neighbors
More to talk about with spouse
Closer to spouse
Fulfillment
Appreciation of own parents
Fun playing with baby
Purpose in life
Enjoyment of baby's company

Certain characteristics distinguished parents who felt more or less of these gratifications with their babies. The less educated the parents, the more pleasure they indicated. Men in occupations of lower prestige indicated more pleasure. This finding is hard to interpret. Perhaps it means that the less educated parents had fewer opportunities for interesting, pleasant experiences and therefore enjoyed their babies more fully. Or possibly, the more educated people were more aware of problems and worried more about being parents and about their children's development. Other findings were that women under age 23 reported more maternal pleasure the longer they had been married, whereas women over 23 reported less pleasure the longer they had been married. Women's gratification was associated with placing high importance on the mother's role, high marital adjustment, and improved marriage. Men's pleasure in the baby was associated with having gone to parent classes and read books or cared for young children, placing the father role high in importance, and seeing a positive change in the marriage [29].

Many of the pleasures mentioned could apply to later stages in the parent-child career, when children are older. Playing with the child and enjoying his company may increase as children are more able to share activities with parents. Many fathers have more gratification from playing ball, boating, and camping with children than they do from playing with infants. Mothers, too, may enjoy sharing their work and recreation with children more than they enjoy the interaction with babies. If parents have to work very hard, and opportunities for recreation are limited, then they may not have many experiences of enjoying play with their children.

Even so, there are still many ways of being gratified by parenthood. We turn, now, to some of these satisfactions that do not come from parent-child interaction, but that still constitute some of the reasons why people have children. In thinking about these reasons for childbearing, we hope that our readers will evaluate them and decide for themselves whether they are good reasons.

Doing What Comes Naturally

Growing up in a family, a young child sees family living as the way life is. A boy learns that he will be a daddy and a girl learns that she will be a mommy. What else could they expect other than to act like this daddy and this mommy? There has to be a baby, or several, to complete the picture. In imaginative play, the young child pretends parenthood, rehearsing future roles, being daddies and mommies, having babies, nursing, diapering, bathing, feeding, hugging, kissing, singing, spanking, scolding.

As the child grows older, he forgets many of the details of his preschool years, but he retains feelings about his experiences in the parent-child relationship and as a family member. College students remember the school-age period very well, however. Their memories of parental care and devotion have been found to be related to their attitude toward becoming parents [18]. Undergraduate men and women were divided into a group having highly positive attitudes toward having and rearing children and a contrast group with moderate to low attitudes toward parenthood. They were asked, "How much energy did your mother devote to your care and well-being (when not at work)?" and the same question in regard to their fathers. Highly positive attitudes toward childbearing and childrearing were more typical of students, both male and female, who remembered mothers and fathers as highly nurturant.

Thus, the child is oriented toward parenthood because his first experience shows him family life as the only way of living. The anticipated rewards are then influenced by the extent to which his parents are concerned and nurturant toward him. During the adolescent years, experiences outside the family make their impact. The young person talks with friends, reads, and views television. Expanded intellectual powers permit reasoning and thinking about parenthood. Even when careful thought points to one conclusion about childbearing and childrearing, the thinking is overlaid upon a core of emotional experience as a young child. And the most common attitude in young adults is, "Of course I want to have children. It's the natural way to live."

Proving Oneself

Many people feel great satisfaction in knowing that they have made a baby and knowing that other people know it. Perhaps it is a special kind of competence, biological or reproductive competence, the exercise of certain bodily powers. The existence of the baby shows that its parents are sexually mature, fertile and competent biologically. Sometimes one child is enough to prove this point for the parents, but there are people, probably more men than women, who like to prove it repeatedly. The Spanish word *macho* means a "virile, strong, brave man." The machismo pattern means that the male repeatedly seeks sexual conquests and, when married, tries to prove his continuing virility by siring many children. (Machismo is by no means confined to Latin cultures, nor is it universal in Latin countries [17].)

There are many good reasons for keeping the lid on machismo and letting one or two children prove the point. However, in thinking about reasons for having children, machismo is a powerful one. To a person whose self-esteem depends upon demonstrated virility, the rewards of reproduction are good feelings about himself.

New Roles and Privileges. The role of new mother looks highly desirable in the enchanting pictures of mothers and babies shown in American magazines. Soft pink cheek rests on soft pink cheek. Shimmering golden hair trails over peach fuzz. Tiny fingers rest on a round breast. The scene gives promise of a new starring role that rivals the joys of a bride walking down the aisle. A romantic picture with slightly less impact is that of new parents standing beside the crib, watching their beautiful baby sleeping. It is almost as good as cutting the cake.

"When I am a mother (or a father), I'll be *really* grown up." Western civilization has no consistent way of conferring adult status. Is a child to consider himself a man, herself a woman, upon confirmation or Bar Mitzvah, on getting a driver's license, graduating from high school or college, voting, getting married, getting a job? (A Melanesian boy becomes a man when he moves into the men's clubhouse.) It is rewarding to know definitely that you have become an adult. If having a baby makes you feel grown up, then having a baby is rewarding. (In actuality, having a baby may or may not launch an individual into adulthood.)

Parenthood sharply changes the status of individuals in some societies. In India, a bride occupies a very lowly position in the family. Her status rises markedly when she bears her first baby, especially if it is a boy. Subsequent births improve her position. Her power increases enormously when her son marries, and this increase in power is implied in the birth of that first son. A new Indian father also advances in status, although the change in his position is not as marked as the mother's. The father does gain social approval for developing in the approved direction, in the stage of the householder. In Western society, there is a similar but weaker version of status advance through parenthood. The young couple usually feel social approval of their taking on parental roles and "settling down" into homemaking, childrearing, and community participation. Social approval and increased esteem are rewarding.

Doing One's Duty

Family Duty. Parents of young marrieds are often eager to be grandparents. The paternal side wants its name carried on. Both sides want their genes passed along. They think it will be rewarding to have grandchildren to watch, care for, give to, boast about, and eventually perhaps leave some money to. The young couple may feel the pressure exerted subtly, or their parents may simply urge them to have children. In bearing a baby, many a young woman feels that she is giving her mother a gift, perhaps giving all four grandparents a gift. Sometimes it is an offering with which she hopes to obtain more love than she has heretofore had from her mother.

To a Hindu, family duty is also a religious duty. In order for the dead male ancestors to advance from one stage of being to a higher stage, they must have the prayers of their male descendants. A father needs a son to pray for him and for his father and grandfather. The male line must keep going, and as it flows on unbroken, the wives receive spiritual benefits as part of the husbands' salvation. Therefore, bearing a son, or enough sons to surely have one who will discharge the religious duty, is a solemn family duty for a young couple. They understandably feel fulfilled when they perform this essential service to the husband's father, all his male ancestors and their wives.

Duty to Church or State. Duty toward a group can also motivate reproduction. When a minority group wants more power, or perhaps just to maintain its position, an obvious way is to increase its numbers. A steady increase can be assured by convincing members that their duty is to reproduce. "Be fruitful and multiply" is a command from the Lord, recorded in the book of Genesis, first spoken to Adam and Eve and later to Noah. Since that time, the same command has been given by various religious bodies. A young modern couple may feel satisfaction in doing their duty as Catholics, Jews, or Mormons when they produce another baby to join the church or temple. The group may be a racial minority. Many American blacks oppose birth control for black people because they want their numbers to increase. Nations, especially in wartime, have often promoted childbearing as a patriotic duty. Hitler exhorted "Aryans" to reproduce as a duty to Germany and to a particular physical type of German. Sometimes a political, religious, or racial group rewards mothers for repeated childbearing by giving them medals and public notice, or designating them as "Goldstar Mothers" or "Heroines of the Republic." Long ago in French Canada, it was the custom to give a couple a farm for every dozen offspring. Thus, doing one's reproductive duty to the group can bring all sorts of rewards, from satisfaction and recognition to substantial material benefits.

Immortality

Less specific than the Hindu reason for wanting sons, but still powerful, is the notion of living on through one's children. It may be in terms of genes being passed along in

A Navajo child and her grandmother.

an endless chain, or it may be influence, in terms of knowledge and behavior patterns passed from parent to child.

A Source of Help and Support

Children help with the work on farms and in other family businesses. To an American pioneer family, the rewards of childbearing were economic, as well as personal and emotional. Parental assessments in Panama, the Dominican Republic, and Yugoslavia led to a conclusion that when children are economic assets, they raise their parents' regard for themselves [2]. In addition to feeling satisfaction with their child helpers, such parents would look ahead to their own old age, when children's efforts in the family business will provide security for them. The Indian joint family

231   A MATTER OF CHOICE: PARENTHOOD

described on page 11 is an example. When Mr. Patel retired from managing the family's textile mill, he continued to live from the income it produced while his sons ran the business. Indian college women expressed a long-term time orientation when asked to finish sentences concerned with the satisfactions of having children. They talked mainly about the time 25 years hence, when adult children would offer pleasure, help, and support [21].

An analysis of parental evaluation of children in six countries (Japan, Korea, the Philippines, Taiwan, Thailand and the United States) showed the economic value of children to be strongest in rural areas and weakest among the urban middle class [14].

Intergenerational help, economic and otherwise, is given in the United States, as shown by a study of 85 sets of three-generation families in Minnesota [13, pp. 64–66]. All the help given and received was analyzed as to sources, which included immediate and extended kin, peers, church, social agencies, private specialists, and commercial sources. The grandparent generation received 65 per cent of its help from the other two generations; that is, their own children and grandchildren. For the parent generation, familial help was 53 per cent of all help received and for the married child generation, it was 44 per cent. Of total help given, the percentage given to the other two generations was 47 per cent for grandparents, 44 per cent for parents and 28 per cent for married children. These proportions of help given and received within three-generation families show a high level of transactions between generations. A young adult, aware of all the cooperation between his parents and grandparents, would be realistic in thinking that by having children, he was producing a future source of help and support for himself.

Another situation in which financial aid comes to parents through children is when welfare assistance is given to parents who cannot earn enough to support their families. Since public assistance is given in proportion to the number of dependent children in the family, each child actually does increase the family income, small though it is.

Pride and Vicarious Satisfaction

One of the pleasures of parenthood is, beyond a doubt, being proud of one's offspring. What does it take to make a parent proud? It varies with the parent. One may be bursting with pleasure over a normally developing infant or a child who learns to read at age seven and passes each grade at the end of the year. Another parent may require the child to win a medal, get the highest marks, or look like a fashion model before that parent is proud. Similar to feeling proud is living one's life over through the child. Many parents seek pleasure in having their children do well where they failed, solve problems that stumped them, or win the recognition that was withheld from them. Even successful adults enjoy all over again the particular delights of stages that they have passed through and that their children are now living.

As with other anticipated pleasures of parenthood, pride and vicarious satisfaction may or may not be realized, depending on the child and on what pleases the parent. The desire for these pleasures is neither good nor bad. The way in which these desires are expressed can be either positive or destructive to the child.

THE PARENT-CHILD CAREER

Since children grow up and parents grow, too, any parent-child relationship is constantly changing. Not only is it changing within itself but also in relationship to the other careers of the parent and the child.

Ups and Downs

The best way to get a true picture of the parent-child career would be through a longitudinal study in which the same parent-child pairs were observed throughout life. Lacking this, we turn to several studies of portions of the parent-child career. First is a comparison of changes in attitudes of students who had become parents of children with changes in attitudes of their classmates who had not become parents. All subjects were studied before they graduated and five to seven years later, using a measure of attitudes of rejection toward children. Respondents who had not become parents made virtually no change in strength of negative attitudes. Those who were parents had become more negative. Parents with the largest numbers of children had increased most in attitudes of rejection of children [15]. This particular study sampled parents who were in the early stages of the parent-child career. Several others have dealt with parents in a wider range of stages.

In interviews with middle-class mothers of children from prenatal up to 18 years, questions were asked about the advantages and disadvantages of various ages. Pregnancy and adolescence were seen as worst stages, the times with fewest advantages and greatest number of disadvantages. The time from six to eleven was rated highest. The age from two to four was seen as less advantageous than the first year or the elementary school stage [23]. Another study of satisfaction with children throughout the life span showed a steeper decline in the school age than in adolescence [3].

As adults look forward to parenthood, they may expect some stages to be more or less rewarding than others, but like childbirth itself, they cannot be sure until they get there. Whether or not children turn out to be sources of pleasure, most prospective parents surely hope that they will be so, and they look upon that pleasure as a reward of parenthood. The extent of the pleasure, its timing, and its balance with pain are all very difficult to predict.

It is commonly believed that having children makes a marriage stronger and more lasting. When ethnic differences were measured in a working-class sample, it was found that 70 per cent of the black group agreed strongly with this belief, whereas 58 per cent of the chicanos and only 28 per cent of the whites did so [12].

The research evidence on this question does not lead to a yes-or-no answer. It may be that children strengthen some kinds of marital relationships and weaken others. There is no good reason to think that children will improve a poor marital relationship. Research has shown, however, that children may be the only source of pleasure in an unhappy marriage [19]. Sometimes divorce statistics are used to support the notion that a marital relationship will be improved if the couple have a child or another child. The argument will be advanced that there are more divorces among childless couples and couples with few children than among couples with larger numbers of children. Actually, divorce is more common in the early years of marriage, when couples obviously have no or few children, as compared with later years. It is likely that couples who are not getting alone well together do not have children, or do not add to the children they already have, rather than that the absence of children causes the breakup. However, some unhappy couples do stay together "for the sake of the children" until the children are old enough to leave home.

Many researchers have tried to find out what effects children have on parents. Because there are so many ways of approaching this broad question, the results of the research do not give a clear answer. A parent can experience problems and satisfactions at the same time, stemming from the same child. The results of children upon the marital relationship can be quite different from the satisfaction felt with the child. Several studies examined marital satisfaction in relation to stages of family life (defined according to ages of children). Using middle-class samples, two United States interview studies [3, 27], one United States questionnaire study [26], and one New Zealand questionnaire study [31] showed general satisfaction to be high in the beginning of marriage and parenthood, declining as the children got older, and increasing as the children left home. In a sample with above-average educational level, marital communication and adjustment were found to decrease as children were born and to increase when children left home [7]. Correlates of dissatisfaction in marriage were examined in a large sample that included the proportions of social classes existing in one county. Results showed childless marriages to be more satisfactory. In contrast to nonparents, parents, especially those currently raising children, were less likely to be satisfied with their marriages. This was true regardless of sex, race, age, or income [25].

A brighter view of parenthood emerges from a questionnaire study of a random sample of urban couples that included working-class and middle-class couples. The subjects were all first-time parents whose babies were less than a year old. When asked about changes in their marriage since the birth of the baby, 42 per cent of the respondents said that the marriage had improved, 43.5 per cent said that it had stayed about the same, and 7.5 per cent of the women and 5.5 per cent of the men said that the marriage had deteriorated [29]. The same question was approached with a middle-class urban sample by interviewing parents during pregnancy and after the birth of the baby. Only 18 per cent indicated increased satisfaction, whereas 39 per cent remained the same, and 43 per cent decreased [6]. One possible source of the difference in these two studies is that the first study included all social classes, whereas the second involved only middle-class subjects. As mentioned earlier, the more highly educated the men and women were, the fewer gratifications they reported in regard to their infants.

Growth Through Parenthood

Another common belief is that persons increase in self-esteem through being parents. Research has confirmed this notion for men but not for women. The study of parenthood in Panama, the Dominican Republic, and Yugoslavia showed that for married people between 20 and 40, self-esteem was higher for childless women than for women with children, but that the opposite was true for men [2]. Apparently, men were built up by parenthood and women were not. Similar findings were reported in the United States by a review of literature on the transition to parenthood. In the early and middle adult years, women decreased in self-esteem and personal development whereas men increased [28]. Although these results may look like a large black mark for motherhood, the responsibility for them need not fall on the children. Quite possibly the role of homemaker and mother is held in low social esteem and the woman, therefore, sees herself as unworthy while performing in that role. It is at this time of life that many women are cut off from the occupational career that formerly gave them status and satisfaction. The homemaker role is often very burdensome, with little help in doing the dull and hard tasks. As the next chapter shows, parenting is an activity in which tremendous creativity and all sorts of talents can be used to the great advantage of children. Quality of care-giving, socializing, and teaching has direct effects on the child's physical, social, emotional, and intellectual development. Surely, if women and the rest of society appreciated these facts, women would derive more self-esteem from being competent mothers. However, some of the best educated women may reject motherhood because they do not understand all that goes into doing it well, and they do not wish to put out all that effort in the face of a general lack of appreciation.

Children do cause a great deal of work, but, at the same time, they stimulate parents to grow. Different stages of child growth call for different kinds of development in parents. During pregnancy and at birth, as we have already discussed, transitions to new roles mean a shakeup of established routines and attitudes. Such growth is both painful and pleasant. Having a baby means knowing something one did not know before, having a special experience that makes a person different. Being parent to an infant, for most people, is the first time for being primarily responsible for a completely dependent person. It is a matter of life and death! First-time parents may feel overwhelmed when this thought hits them. It is suddenly very important to understand nonverbal communication and to communicate through physical channels. The baby offers chances for having new feelings and new transactions. It may be difficult to realize that the new baby is a unique and separate individual.

Early Childhood. As the child develops his conviction of being a distinct person and agent, the parent has to seek a balance between setting him free and providing the nurturance and limits that will keep him safe. This complicated process requires empathy, vigilance, patience, planning, and inventiveness. The toddler tackles problems of learning to walk, and talk, to manage for himself at table and toilet, to manipulate his toys. As he grows older, he explores, asks questions, starts new tasks, intrudes, and imagines. If the parent is open-minded and ready to grow, he will see some of what the child is trying to do and be. Again, the child's growth needs make pressures on the parent, and if the parent can respond to these needs, she finds new ways of being creative. By this time, parents, most likely now deeply attached to their children, want to help the children develop. Hence they try to change their own behavior in ways that will be good for the child. In the process, the parents themselves grow.

School Age. The process of letting go, of course, continues when the child goes to school. As he learns skills and rules, parents teach him and learn from him. For all parents, but especially for immigrant parents, the child teaches them new things that he has learned in school, from his friends, and from other contacts that the parent does not have. I (MSS) learned the states and capitals of the United States with my children. Later, living in India, the two of us (MSS and LSS) learned the geography of the country together.

Children push and pull their parents into community involvement that requires parents to learn and develop. Girl Scouts, Boy Scouts, parents' and teachers' (PTA) meetings, Sunday School, and so many more expect some commitment from parents. One does not have to be a parent in order to participate in such organizations, but for parents, the pressure is turned on. And, reluctant or eager, parents find themselves in new worlds where they have to adapt. Beginning in the school years and continuing even throughout life, children enlarge their parents' social contacts, bringing home friends, instigating contacts between families, showing parents new places to go for fun, and getting involved with social agencies. When a family moves to a new community, as does the average American once in five years, children are often the first links between the family and the new neighbors. At this stage of life, parents are most likely to learn more about children, in general, and to be able to see their own children in relation to others.

At the time that children are opening new worlds of activity and interest to parents, they also are more independent and may even contribute some help with housework. Thus, parents gain in freedom and also have more choices of activity open to them. There are possibilities for new friends, new social organizations, new skills, and new work.

Adolescence. While the adolescent is struggling with his problem of separating himself further from his parents, alternating between wanting to be close and wanting to be independent, his parents suffer, too. Even when they realize that the child is ambivalent, and normally so, it is hard to keep trusting and loving, letting him make mistakes, neither hanging onto him nor pushing him out. The patience, self-control, and empathy needed are like the demands of preschool years, but new in scope. There is also a new pleasure, the adult thinking of which adolescents are capable. In spite of their sometimes babyish emotions, teen-agers are capable of logical thought. They have interesting ideas on all sorts of problems that adults are also interested in, and discussions between the generations can be stimulating and rewarding to parents.

Adulthood. Grown children can be tremendously growth-promoting to their parents, especially if they are friends who enjoy each other's company. Adult children have all the advantages of adolescents and none of the disadvantages. They are like close friends, if parents realize that they actually are adults. But they are friends who have access to another universe of ideas, people, and experiences, all of which they can share with their parents. Thus, adult children represent a very important pathway of communication with the changing world as parents grow old and encounter the dangers of rigidity. With the shared past and long-standing intimacy and affection as a background, adult children are well fitted to know their parents' needs and potentialities, and to offer opportunities for growth that parents can use.

When parents grow old, they are likely to become more dependent upon their children than they have ever been before. They may need and receive economic aid, as well as assistance in planning and making decisions, in everyday tasks such as shopping and home maintenance. Grown children are very important sources of care, respect, and response. Since old people in Western society occupy a marginal position, with respect and recognition hard to obtain, the esteem of their grown children can contribute enormously to the parents' feelings of being worthwhile.

ADOPTIVE PARENTS

When people want to be parents but cannot give birth to children, they may acquire offspring through adoption. More rarely, parents adopt children for other reasons, as they do when they feel needed by a child who has no parents or whose parents cannot care for her. Parents may add to the children they already have by adopting another child. Sometimes a man adopts children belonging to the woman he marries, in order to feel completely a father to them and to have the same legal obligations as a biological father.

Adoptive parents are definitely parents by choice, since it usually takes a great deal of persistence to get a child from an agency. They may also be able to choose some of the genetic, physical, and mental characteristics of their children. Adoptive parents can receive most of the ordinary rewards and pain of parenthood, although they miss out on the pleasure of proving themselves biologically and thinking about their genes being passed on indefinitely. One of the drawbacks of adoptive parenthood (although some people think it an advantage) is not experiencing pregnancy, delivery, and the postpartum recovery period. As mentioned earlier, these physical experiences serve to break up routinized behavior patterns, to focus the parents on the new child, and to provide a setting in which parent-child bonds can most readily be established. As one adoptive father put it, "For months, I could hardly realize that we had a daughter. Suddenly, one day, she was here in the midst of us and we never really got ready for her. When she cried at night, I was always surprised."

Adoptive parents are not always married couples. Single people adopt children, often older children. Occasionally, homosexual pairs act as parents. Adoptive agencies used to insist upon the utmost conventionality in would-be adoptive parents, but now the agencies have relaxed on many of their regulations.

SINGLE PARENTS

The old term *unmarried mother* implies something lacking or wrong with the single woman who brings up her child. The newer term *single mother* suggests the acceptability of choosing to be a mother but not a wife. (Our term for unmarried parents-by-choice is **spousefree parents.** We discuss spousefree parenthood as a life style on pages 464–466.) Of course, there are still women who would like to marry the fathers of their children. In separating sex from parenthood, it has become more feasible to have parenthood without marriage. The women's movement has also given women courage to choose to do as they wish. Since financial support and help in raising a child are usually contributed by fathers, single mothers have to find alternatives. Many single mothers live in small group homes or boarding homes [5]. Usually in these arrangements the mother and child sleep in their room or small apartment and share dining and living quarters with the larger family unit. Single fathers are also known. Most children of single parents experience multiple caretakers and group care. Parents often belong to clubs or associations that recognize their special needs. For example, *Parents Without Partners,* the largest organization for single parents, has over 70,000 members. In it, members find support systems responsive to their special problems [34].

PATHS TO REJECTING PARENTHOOD

If people choose parenthood for its expected rewards, then they reject it because they do not expect it to be rewarding or not rewarding enough to offset the disadvantages. Although social pressures still impel many young couples toward parenthood, counterforces have been at work, starting in 1963 with Betty Friedan's blast, *The Feminine Mystique* [8]. Since that time, many feminist writers have pointed out the disadvantages of parenthood, especially motherhood.

Childlessness has increased recently among better-educated women but not among those who have not finished high school. [10] The difference between 22 per cent and 3 per cent suggests that more than 19 per cent of United States college women have chosen to be childfree. The rate of involuntary childlessness is around 2 or 3 per cent, based on an estimate of childless wives counted in the 1970 Canadian census [32]. Veevers [33] interviewed 52 Canadian wives who were childless by choice. Two paths to the childfree state were observed. About a third of the subjects had entered marriage with an agreement by the couple that they would have no children. These women, in general, had made their decision in early adolescence, but were unable to say why they had done so. A few women had made the decision after meeting the men they were to marry, being convinced by the men. Over two-thirds of the subjects were childless because they had repeatedly postponed childbearing. The usual experience was a series of four steps to permanent childlessness. At marriage, most of these women had thought little about motherhood, either pro or con. They practiced birth control carefully. In this stage, they seemed no different from many, or most, young couples.

The second stage consisted of an indefinite postponement of childbearing, rather than the usual plan of newlyweds to wait until they are settled, or have enough money, or are adjusted to marriage. The childless couple in the second stage became increasingly indefinite about when they would enter the parent-child career although they did not consider themselves to be against it. In the third stage, they admitted the possibility that they would never have children. They had experienced the advantages of childlessness and had seen the restrictions and struggles incurred by their friends with children. The fourth stage was an acknowledgement that they would never have children. Usually what happened was a recognition that they were now committed to childlessness, that the decision had taken place without their knowing just how or when.

DETERRENTS TO REPRODUCTION

The burdens of motherhood have received a great deal of attention lately and many disadvantages may apply somewhat more to mothers than to fathers. However, offspring bring disadvantages to men, too, as some of the following will show.

Restrictions

Children tie you down! Nobody doubts it. Even partners who are sure they want children will postpone pregnancy for a few months or years. They want to be free to have fun together, to advance in their work, to assemble a pleasant place to live, to travel. Society generally approves of a period of freedom for newlyweds. As Veevers has shown, some couples enjoy their freedom so much that they keep postponing restrictions.

If the first baby brings an end to carefree recreation, travel, and spending and severely limits the mother's job potential, then can the second be even more restricting, and the third . . . ? Yes. Each child adds to the work load of the parents, using an additional portion of their time, energy, and opportunities for being alone together. Figure 9-1 shows the total hours of daily household work done in families with none to nine children. It is harder to get an adequate baby-sitter for two children than for one. A friend or relative may be willing to mind one child but not two. Whereas a couple might take one small child backpacking or bicycling, two are likely to be backbreaking, and three impossible. One child can sleep on a cot in a motel room or in the grandparents' spare bedroom; two might squeeze in; three would spill over. For a women who wants to have a job or to study, every additional baby poses more problems.

Expenses

Everyone knows that children cost money, but nobody knows just how much each one is going to cost before he reaches the point of earning his own living. Partners contemplating parenthood will note that the mother will have to give up her job at least temporarily and that child care will cost something either in lost income or hired services. Medical care will also cost, but it may be scaled to their income. If the prospective parents do not look beyond the first year or two, they may think that

FIGURE 9-1   Total hours of daily household work by all workers in families where the homemaker is not employed outside the home.

Data from Katherine E. Walker. Household work time: its implications for family decisions. *Journal of Home Economics*, 1973, **65** (7), 7–11.

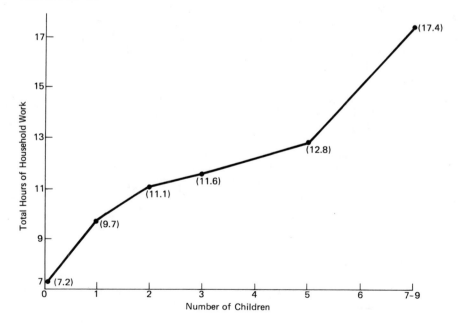

A MATTER OF CHOICE: PARENTHOOD

babies don't eat much and that many of their clothes will come from presents. When a child approaches adolescence, however, he needs *more* food than an adult. His clothes cost more because he grows out of them quickly and also gives them hard wear. And actually, new babies do cost a great deal in terms of medical fees, housing, equipment, loss of income, and increased need for insurance.

Using data gathered by the U.S. Department of Labor, a study of expenditures per family member shows the following: a family with a disposable income between $10,000 and $15,000 spent $840 per person on food when it consisted of two members (a family total of $1680) but only $462 per person when there were five members (a total of $2310). For housing and utilities, the two-member family spent $1219 per person ($2438, total), the five-member family $535 ($2675, total). Figures for the three-member family were $549 for food and $875 for housing, per person [4]. Each addition to a family in a given income bracket thus means less spent on basic items for each individual in it. Any projection of costs over the next 18 years would of course be in today's dollar values. However, let us take a modest estimate of the average yearly cost of a present-day child, $4000. Multiply this figure by 18 years and it can be seen that the child costs $72,000. Send the child to college and you will add 4 × $6,000 or $24,000, for a total cost of $96,000. Give her a fancy wedding or buy him a car and the investment approaches $100,000.

Children Not Enjoyed

As mentioned previously, it is hard for parents to know whether they will enjoy their children or not, and whether they will enjoy them at all ages and stages. If a person feels definitely negative toward children, including potential offspring, it surely will be a deterrent to reproduction. But social pressures from family and friends being what they are, some child-dislikers succumb and produce children.

Women's liberation and other social forces are making it more comfortable for those who wish to resist pressures toward parenthood. Books and magazine articles analyze these pressures, urging women (rarely men) to be individuals and do what they themselves really want to do. For example, *Life* magazine published the following:

> The eight years before we had children were glorious. I had an enjoyable career, an idyllic home life. But friends pitied us, undoubtedly worried that we would continue living hedonistic, meaningless but terribly comfortable lives until we became parents. . . . You don't have to justify being childless. It's no one's business but your own if your ovaries don't work or if they do. If you are pressured to "prove yourself," take it from one who has been there. [24].

Fear of Being a Bad Parent

A person can like children and yet feel that he is not suited to being a parent. He (or she) may not want the restrictions on time, money, and freedom to move. She may feel physically inadequate for pregnancy, labor, and child care. Noncommitment to permanent marriage may look like an obstacle to being a good parent. She may wish to remain single. A history of depression or emotional instability can make a person cautious about his potential as a parent. One of the pair may worry that the other one would not be a good parent, even though quite *self*-confident.

Fear of Effect on Marriage

A couple may want to keep their pair relationship just the way it is, not risking it with the introduction of a third member. If they know something of the research on childbearing as a crisis, they may choose to avoid that crisis.

Concern with Population

A few years ago a young woman received national notice for her valedictory speech at a college graduation. Pretty and talented, the very picture of an ideal American girl, she announced that she had regretfully given up any plans to bear children. Her reason was her worry over the population explosion. At present, there is nothing remarkable in young women and men rejecting parenthood because they believe that the earth already has too many people. It is all too obvious that the increasing population is an important cause of food shortages, crowding, pollution, and the ravaging of land and sea.

There are, however, many couples who are not directly influenced in their reproductive behavior by the threat of overpopulation. Perhaps those who give it as a reason for childlessness are using it to rationalize, or more likely, as a valid additional reason to support their decision.

Social Disapproval

Although all the voluntarily childless wives studied by Veevers [33] felt social disapproval directed against them, a growing number of people do not disapprove of childlessness but rather disapprove of people who bear many children. In crowded parts of the world, such as Indonesia, Tonga, and India, government officials post signs saying that two children are enough. In the United States and Canada, voluntarily childless people support each other and are approved by many individuals and some organizations, such as NON, the National Organization for Nonparents. An example of NON's positive approach is their use of the attractive term *childfree*, instead of the negative *childless*.

REASONS WHY PARENTHOOD IS DIFFICULT

In addition to the reasons implied in the previous section, "Deterrents to Parenthood," are some others that make parenthood less than blissful.

Complication of Relationships

As Figure 9-2 shows, the husband-wife dyad involves only one relationship. When one child is added, the relationships are represented by a triangle instead of a straight line, because they include husband-wife, father-child, and mother-child. With the birth of the second child, the number of relationships jumps from three to 6, because the newcomer relates to three people. A family with four children includes 15 different relationships. If one adds groups, such as Child 1 and Child 2 in relation to Child 3 and Child 4, the relationship network becomes ever so much more complex. Often parents will notice that when just one family member is absent, the whole atmosphere changes, sometimes for the better, sometimes for the worse, but usually in the direction of tranquility.

Permanence

There is no acceptable way to terminate American parenthood. If incompatible parents and children could divorce each other, the situation would be quite different. There are cultures where it is all right for children to wander off and live with relatives or friends for indefinite periods, which they may well do when things get tough at home. Or it may be permissible for parents to give out some of their children for adoption, as did the parents of an Indian friend of ours. In this case, the motivation was not to get rid of their lovely daughter, but to share their children with a brother who had none. In contrast, in the United States, there is practically no reason that would justify a couple giving up a child, except a serious abnormality of the child. Even parents who do not wish to shoulder the burden of caring for a retarded child are often told that the child will be better off at home and they should devote themselves to making the best possible life for him.

The state rarely steps in to rescue a child from inadequate parents, even though the parents' behavior is really a cry for help. Legally, and by custom, the rights of parents have been held to be more important than the welfare of children. Hence, child abuse often reaches extreme levels before a neighbor tells the authorities or the parents themselves take the child for treatment. Even then, the parent is not routinely given the chance to undo parenthood, but efforts are made to rehabilitate the person as a parent.

A number of fathers, and some mothers as well, try to escape parenthood by deserting. They may thus shift most of the burden to the other parent, but the deserting parent will still be required to pay for the support of children to the extent to which he possibly can.

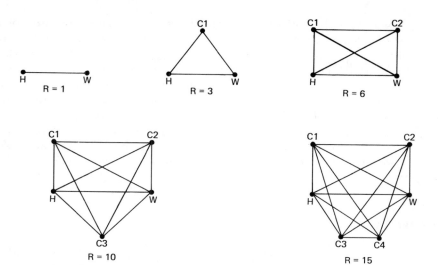

FIGURE 9-2 Number of pair relationships in families of 2 to 6 members. H = husband. W = wife. C = child. R = number of 2-person relationships.

No Choice

In discussing reasons why people choose to be or not to be parents, we assumed that people actually were choosing. It is true that birth control technology is available in all parts of the world, but it is not available to all people. There are still many women who conceive without wanting to do so and men who impregnate without wishing to become fathers. A survey by the International Planned Parenthood Federation showed that only one-third of the world's adult population knows enough about birth control to plan their families [20].

Even the willing parent has little choice beyond being or not being. Technology that is basic to choosing the sex of one's child is not yet developed for ordinary use. There is as yet no way to choose a pretty, clever child, big or small, fair or dark, quiet or noisy, outgoing or inward oriented. Children affect parents in different ways, as every parent of two children knows. Parenthood can be a delight to the willing parent who gets a compatible child; it can be frustrating and disappointing with a child who does not fit the parent's capacities and expectations.

Social Nonsupport

In comparison with some other countries, the United States does little to assist parents in preparation for parental roles, in making choices as to becoming parents, or in performing as parents. For one reason, there is no overall family policy. States and local communities do as they see fit. The limited offerings in school are confined

A MATTER OF CHOICE: PARENTHOOD

largely to girls, and in some school systems, to girls who are not very talented academically. Controversies rage regularly over whether sex education belongs in the schools, even though it is the only place where many future parents will ever have a chance to learn basic facts and technologies and to discuss implications intelligently. Education for child care and development has low status, is often dismissed as mere baby-sitting, is pinched on fundings, and its teachers are paid less than teachers of physics and computer science. Public provisions for health care, nutrition, and family-centered recreation are abysmal. But why go on with negatives? The following section illustrates some supports to parents that are offered in various parts of the world, including some enclaves in the United States.

AIDS TO PARENTS

The following are examples from our reading and experience and are not at all exhaustive of the ways in which various societies support parenthood.

Supports to Latin American mothers have been required by law ever since the 1920s [17]. Privileges and protections include paid maternity leave, free medical care for mother and child, a layette and milk for the baby, a cash allowance for breast feeding, time off during work hours for nursing the baby, nurseries for infants located in factories and firms where women work.

Children's allowances are given to all mothers in Canada in amounts graduated to the age of each child. Although there is a question as to the wisdom of encouraging childbearing, it is still true that cash payments to mothers make it easier for women to carry on in the maternal role. Government-supported low-cost medical and hospital insurance are widely available, making it possible for most parents to get health care for their children.

The Swedish government set up the Royal Commission on Sex Education and paid for a comprehensive study of the Swedes' sexual knowledge, behavior, and attitudes. The results gave information on what had been accomplished to date by the official sex education program and how it might be made more practical. The study showed that 98 per cent of Swedes wanted unmarried mothers to have all the rights of married mothers, a situation that largely prevailed [22].

Free contraceptive services are provided for all who accept them in China, India, England and other countries. In China, a local health worker makes monthly visits to each woman of childbearing age, checking on her use of contraceptives and her satisfaction with them [30]. Although population control is an important aim of most government-sponsored birth-control services, the quality of family life is also enhanced by family planning.

Milk and dairy products are subsidized by the New Zealand government, to the extent that everyone can afford them. Thus, the nutrition of children is underwritten. Government subsidies make physicians' fees very low, prescriptions free, and hospital care almost free. Financed by a combination of government payments and voluntary efforts, parent education is offered to all, not just in groups and classes but on an individual basis as well. Marriage counseling is available. Recreation facilities are within geographic and financial reach of almost all urban dwellers. Business and work hours are planned to permit maximum use of the many parks, swimming pools, courts, beaches, and playing fields.

College and university education is free in Sri Lanka and the U.S.S.R. for students who qualify for higher education and competition is fierce for the few positions. In the kibbutzim of Israel, all the work and responsibilities of parents are shared by the whole communal group. The parent-child relationship is one of enjoyment and emotional closeness. Parents are not involved with providing food, clothes, education, medical care, and discipline to their own children any more than they are in providing for all children in the kibbutz. Child care and responsibility are also shared widely in China [30].

On the island of Bali, villages put on dance dramas in the temple courtyards. In the village where we visited, the young mothers go together to these affairs, enjoying each other's company during the performance. The babies and toddlers go, too, as does everyone in the village, but the grandmothers, not the mothers, are in charge of the young children for the evening.

In Chapter 1, we wrote about how work is shared in joint families, as is common in Asia. Although many restrictions may be, and often are, placed upon young adults, the responsibilities and work of parenthood are shared, and loneliness is not a problem. Parents never experience the depths plumbed by the North American parents who believe that their children's shortcomings are the result of their own inadequacies as parents and as persons.

There are, of course, supports to American parents. The federal Department of Health, Education and Welfare disseminates information, sponsors research, and funds assistance programs within the limitations of its budget. Private voluntary agencies make many important contributions. For example, the Vanier Institute in Canada and the Child Study Association of America educate parents and parent educators. The Family Service Society provides a variety of programs, including group and individual counseling, day care, and family planning services and educates both clients and leaders.

Parental Support in New Family Forms. Utopian societies are both old and new in the United States. They have come up with many imaginative and ingenious arrangements for sharing the burdens of parenthood. A longitudinal study of alternate family forms in California offers some concrete examples of efforts to relate practice to theory [5]. The 50 families in the study included unmarried couples and single mothers, many living in groups, and communal families. Perhaps the first sharing of parenthood is in giving birth, which is usually done at home, with the help of other members of the community and with the attitude that the new baby is a treasure to all. Infants are held, carried, and breast fed for warmth, closeness, and "naturalness." Nursing mothers switch babies for feeding, sharing their gift of milk, caring for more than their own, and thus teaching the babies to trust adults in general. When infants reach two and a half or three years of age, they become members of children's groups, who do much to care for one another. Mothers are then freed from intense child care. Adults, as well as children, are seen as having rights.

SUMMARY Figure 9-3 summarizes the two opposing sets of pressures on persons as potential parents.

Gratifying to some but not to others, parenthood is not the only path to challenge and growth. Having children is a personal choice, even though many outside pressures for and against childbearing are often exerted. After choosing to be a parent, the questions *when* and *how many* must be answered.

Readiness for parenthood involves many areas of life, including physical, financial, emotional, and occupational ones. Plans for each conception require evaluation of the whole family situation at that particular time.

The transition to parenthood may be a crisis, depending upon how difficult it is to make the necessary changes and adjustments. Degree of difficulty depends upon the parents themselves, their own resources, the social supports, and the baby. Pleasures with children vary between persons and from one time of life to another. Other satisfactions through parenthood involve meeting all sorts of expectations, proving oneself in various ways, discharging duties, achieving new status, religious values, pride, and vicarious satisfaction.

FIGURE 9-3 Pressures toward and against parenthood.

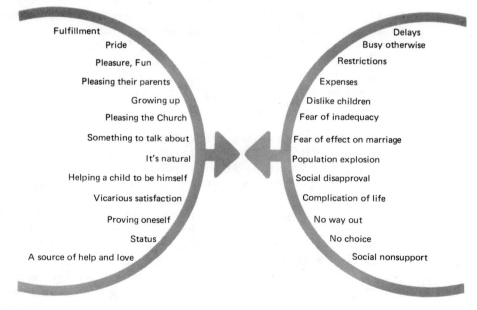

Fulfillment
Pride
Pleasure, Fun
Pleasing their parents
Growing up
Pleasing the Church
Something to talk about
It's natural
Helping a child to be himself
Vicarious satisfaction
Proving oneself
Status
A source of help and love

Delays
Busy otherwise
Restrictions
Expenses
Dislike children
Fear of inadequacy
Fear of effect on marriage
Population explosion
Social disapproval
Complication of life
No way out
No choice
Social nonsupport

The parent-child career goes up and down in satisfactions, as does the marital career, also. The middle stages of both the parent-child and marital careers tend to be relatively low. Some of the pain of being a parent is associated with personal growth. Various demands for parental development are typical of different periods of child development. Although women's self-esteem tends to decrease in the middle years and men's to increase, it is not certain that parenthood is the reason.

Adoptive parents are parents by choice. They miss some of the experiences of biological parenthood but their responsibilities to children are the same as those of all parents. Some single parents are parents by choice and single by choice. They often get together in groups to help each other to meet the demands of parenthood.

A third of voluntarily childless women enter marriage with an agreement not to have children. The rest go through stages of postponement, often reaching commitment to childlessness without realizing it. Deterrents to reproduction include restrictions on freedom to work, play, and travel; increased housework and hours spent in child care; the financial burden imposed by children; dislike or nonenjoyment of children; fear of parental inadequacy in self or partner; desire to keep the partnership relation as it is; awareness and concern with world population problems; social disapproval of childbearing, a recent reality for people who have more than two or three children.

Being a parent is often difficult. The addition of each child complicates the relationships in the family group. No matter how incompatible a particular child-parent dyad may be, Western society offers no acceptable way of severing the relationship. Even parents who have made a true choice of childbearing have little or no choice as to the characteristics of their child.

In many countries, including the United States, support offered to children and parents is not very substantial. In other countries, for example China, childrearing is shared and parents are aided. In some of the new types of families, as well as in some of the older and rarer experimental forms, parents are assisted by the community.

REFERENCES

1. Beckman, Linda J. Relative costs and benefits of work and children to professional and non-professional women. Paper presented at meetings of the American Psychological Association, New Orleans, 1974.

2. Bortner, R. W., Claudia J. Bohn, and David F. Hultsch. A cross-cultural study of the effects of children on parental assessment of past, present and future. *Journal of Marriage and the Family,* 1974, **36,** 370–378.

3. Burr, Wesley R. Satisfaction with various aspects of marriage over the life cycle: A random middle class sample. *Journal of Marriage and the Family,* 1970, **32,** 29–37.

4. Cutright, Phillips. Income and family events: Family income, family size, and consumption. *Journal of Marriage and the Family,* 1971, **33,** 161–173.

5. Eiduson, Bernice T., Jerome Cohen, and Jannette Alexander. Alternatives in child rearing in the '70's. Paper presented at meetings of the American Orthopsychiatric Association, New York, 1973.

6. Feldman, Harold and Michael Rogoff. Correlates of change in marital satisfaction with the birth of the first child. Unpublished study. Cornell University. (Mimeo.)

7. Figley, Charles R. Child density and the marital relationship. *Journal of Marriage and the Family,* 1973, **35**, 272–282.

8. Friedan, Betty. *The feminine mystique.* New York: Norton, 1963.

9. Glick, Paul C. A demographer looks at American Families. *Journal of Marriage and the Family,* 1975, **37**, 15–26.

10. Globe and Mail. U. S. couples plan fewer children. Toronto, October 2, 1974.

11. Globe and Mail. '73 birth rate lowest ever across Canada. Toronto, October 24, 1974.

12. Heath, Linda L., Brent S. Roper, and Charles D. King. A research note on children viewed as contributors to marital stability: The relationship to birth control use, ideal and expected family size. *Journal of Marriage and the Family,* 1974, **36**, 304–320.

13. Hill, Reuben. *Family development in three generations.* Cambridge: Schenkman, 1970.

14. Hoffman, Lois W. A cross-cultural study of the value of children. Paper presented at meetings of the American Psychological Association, New Orleans, 1974.

15. Hurley, John R. and Robert L. Hohn. Shifts in childrearing attitudes linked with parenthood and occupation. *Developmental Psychology,* 1971, **4**, 324–328.

16. Illsley, Raymond. The sociological study of reproduction and its outcome. In S. A. Richardson and Alan F. Guttmacher (eds.). *Childbearing: Its social and psychological aspects.* Baltimore: Williams & Wilkins, 1967.

17. Kinzer, Nora S. Priests, machos and babies: Or, Latin American women and the Manichaean heresy. *Journal of Marriage and the Family,* 1973, **35**, 300–312.

18. Lott, Bernice E. Who wants the children? *American Psychologist,* 1973, **28**, 573–582.

19. Luckey, Eleanore B. and Joyce K. Bain. Children: A factor in marital satisfaction. *Journal of Marriage and the Family,* 1974, **32**, 43–44.

20. McDonald, Corbett. Quebec birth rate drop "remarkable." *London* (Ontario) *Free Press,* October 24, 1973.

21. Mead, Robert D. and Labh Singh. Motives for child-bearing in America and in India. *Journal of Cross-Cultural Psychology,* 1973, **4**, 89–110.

21a. Metropolitan Life Insurance Company. Trends in expected family size in the United States. *Statistical Bulletin,* 1975, **56:** 1: 8–11.

22. Moskin, J. Robert. Sweden: The contraceptive society. In Arlene S. Skolnick and Jerome H. Skolnick (eds.). *Family in Transition.* Boston: Little, Brown, 1971.

23. Pohlman, Edward. Mothers' perceptions of relative advantages and disadvantages of children at different ages and of various characteristics. *Perceptual and Motor Skills,* 1967, **24**, 1311–1314.

24. Radl, Shirley. Mother's day is over. *Life,* May 19, 1972.

25. Renne, Karen S. Correlates of dissatisfaction in marriage. *Journal of Marriage and the Family,* 1970, **32**, 54–67.

26. Rollins, Boyd C. and Kenneth L. Cannon. Marital satisfaction over the family life cycle: A reevaluation. *Journal of Marriage and the Family,* 1974, **36**, 271–282.

27. Rollins, Boyd C. and Harold Feldman. Marital satisfaction over the family life cycle. *Journal of Marriage and the Family,* 1970, **32**, 20–28.

28. Rossi, Alice S. Transition to parenthood. *Journal of Marriage and the Family,* 1968, **30**, 26–39.

29. Russell, Candyce S. Transition to parenthood: Problems and gratifications. *Journal of Marriage and the Family,* 1974, **36**, 294–302.

30. Sidel, Ruth. *Women and child care in China.* Baltimore: Penguin, 1973.

31. Smart, Mollie S. and Russell C. Smart. Present, past, and projected satisfaction in stages of the family life cycle in New Zealand. *Journal of Marriage and the Family,* 1975, **37,** 408–415.

32. Veevers, J. E. Factors in the incidence of childlessness in Canada: An analysis of census data. *Social Biology,* 1972, **19,** 266–274.

33. Veevers, J. E. Voluntary childless wives: An exploratory study. *Sociology and Social Research,* 1973, **57,** 356–366.

34. Weiss, Robert S. The contributions of an organization of single parents to the well-being of its members. *Family Coordinator,* 1973, **22,** 321–326.

CHAPTER 10
living and learning with children

Parent-child relationships resemble a two-way street with plenty of traffic. Whereas there is a big flow in the direction from parent to child, another stream moves from child to parent. Traffic feeds in and out from other streets that represent other persons and groups. If a person stands on one sidewalk and watches the whole scene, it may seem pretty confusing. He cannot take in everything at once and yet if he looks at one small portion of the traffic, he misses a great deal of the street action. In a previous chapter we discussed the experience of choosing parenthood and taking on parental roles. In this chapter we focus mainly the ways in which parents influence children. First, however, we briefly show that the traffic is also moving in the other direction; that children constantly influence parents. At the same time, we acknowledge the complex network of forces acting upon parents, causing them to behave in one way or another with their children [31].

CHILDPOWER: SOME EFFECTS OF CHILDREN ON PARENTS

Sheer weight of numbers affects parents. Intensive interviews with parents of 39 families revealed that mothers from larger families gave more reports of reacting to child aggression [31]. Fathers of large families often saw themselves as coping with problems of obedience and problems relating to mealtimes. Research generally shows that as the size of the family increases, parents become more authoritarian and parent-child communication decreases [33].

When the mother has intense, continuous interaction with her children, she is likely to feel fatigued and irritated, just as anyone would with any long-lasting, un-

252

relieved responsibility. A review of world-wide anthropological literature concludes that children are more likely to be rejected when mothers and children are alone together all day than when fathers and grandparents are present [32a].

Parents are affected by many child behaviors that are not intended. In the following examples, children do not plan to do anything to influence adults. Infants are born with built-in behaviors that influence parents in consistent ways. Mothers and fathers have been seen reacting differently to boys and girls and to passive and alert babies [8a, 22]. Experiments have shown that women react differently to stubborn behavior, dependence, and independence on the part of school-age girls [21]. Fathers' willingness to admit anxiety, sensitivity, and similar feelings was affected by the sex of their children [24]. A man with a son and a daughter was more likely to say he had such feelings than was a man with either two sons or two daughters.

Often a parent will find one child particularly satisfying and another especially irritating, without knowing why. ''Mother always jumps on me when there's any trouble,'' Polly complains. ''Nick can get away with everything. He knows just what to say to her so that she'll laugh or feel sorry for him. She'll tell me Nick didn't understand what he was doing and I know that he knew very well.''

Sometimes children manipulate their parents, shaping their behavior intentionally. Tactful, understanding, diplomatic behavior is the stuff of which social skills are made. Children may also acquire the techniques of warriors and politicians, such as dividing and conquering, exploiting weaknesses, and harrying to exhaustion.

THE LANGUAGE OF BEHAVIOR

As we pointed out in Chapter 3, communication is sometimes nonverbal. The younger the child, the more he tells through his actions rather than in words. Even after infancy, when the child can talk, he cannot always express in words what he is thinking and feeling. When three-year-old Sunny went with her parents to visit a favorite family friend, she was surprised to find a mother, father, and their two young children also visiting. Sunny's special friend was the grandmother of Peter and Donna, the visiting children. Sunny's father told her to go and play with Peter and Donna, instead of playing with their grandmother. Peter and Donna were very bossy. Sunny could not find anything to do. When the children were standing beside the newcomers' car, Donna said, ''This is our car. You can't get in it.'' Sunny found a sharp stone. She scratched as hard as she could, making circles on the shiny red car. Donna ran to where the adults were talking and reported, ''Sunny's scratching our car.''

When Sunny's parents saw what she had done, they were very embarrassed and her mother said, ''She has never done such a thing before. I can't imagine what got into her.''

After Sunny's parents had thought it all over, they were able to imagine what got

into her. They realized that Sunny was jealous of Donna and Peter and disappointed that she did not receive the attention she usually got from her friend. Her conscience was developed enough to keep her from hitting Donna, but the car made an appropriate (to Sunny) target for her anger.

The language of behavior is often less elaborate than scratching a car. It can be a drooping posture, a facial expression, or sitting indoors instead of playing outside with the other kids. All such behavior carries meaning that is helpful in understanding children, especially when they do not or cannot tell parents how they feel and think.

PARENTS' EFFECTS ON CHILDREN

We are looking at parents as caregivers, socializers, and teachers. The three functions overlap. Parents often perform two or three of the functions at the same time.

Our dividing them up is simply a way of untangling the web of family interaction in order to make it easier to understand.

Parents as Caregivers

Care is one of the components of love. Taking care of children is, in almost all societies, considered the duty of parents. Sometimes parents get a great deal of help from servants, kin, or community. An extreme example is the Israeli kibbutz, where the bulk of care is given by adult members *(metaplot)* who specialize in the caregiving function.

Child care means providing for safety, health, and growth through shelter, food, clothing, regulation of stimulation, sanitation, medical attention, and protection from noxious influences. To a very large degree, the child's health is a measure of the care given by his parents. A healthy child is not only free from illness and wounds but also has weight proportionate to his height, lively skin and eye color, shiny hair, firm muscles, balanced posture, abundant energy, curiosity, concentration, and resilient emotions.

In the area of child care, the family system has important interaction with the physiological systems of the child, on one hand, and on the other, with educational, economic, and political systems of the nation and the world. For example, poor children throughout the world are smaller than children whose families have adequate incomes. When income is adequate, then the educational and occupational level of parents shows up as an influence, as seen in a Danish study of the skeletal maturity of children seven to 18 years old [2]. Thus if parents do not have the money to buy food, children will be undernourished; but even when money is available, educated parents will supply a better diet. The same point could be made in the area of keeping children free from infections. Where poverty prevails, children are often invaded by bacteria, viruses, worms, amoebas, bacilli, and toxic chemicals, because their parents have little power to keep hookworms out of bare feet, amoebas out of the drinking water, or lead paint off the walls. When parents can pay for better living conditions, their knowledge of child care makes an obvious difference in their children's health. If parents know how infections are carried, they can prevent them through cleanliness techniques and teaching. Parents can help the ill child to recover with minimal stress because they know that rest and high protein food will aid the child's resources in overcoming infection.

Neglect and Abuse: the Negation of Care. The problem of child abuse is growing throughout the Western world. Every day many parents fail to give care. They hurt their children by beatings and other forms of attack, by giving insufficient or improper food, or by failing to protect them from cold, dirt, and irritating substances. Although one parent, more often the mother, actually does the battering or starving, the problem is really one of family interaction and of the interaction between the family and the other systems in the society [10].

The victims of abuse are often infants and young children, but children of all ages, including teen-agers, are abused by their parents. Many of these children who are abused are unwanted, often conceived out of wedlock by parents of low socioeconomic status. Some child abuse occurs at all socioeconomic levels, however. A nationwide survey of abused children revealed 29 per cent of them as deviant in social interaction and general functioning, 14 per cent with physical deviations, and 8 per cent with intellectual deviations [11]. Although lack of care may have produced the deviations in the children, the fact remains that the abused children presented great problems to their parents, in their undesired births and in problems of functioning. A substantial number of the parents were themselves unwanted and abused babies. Thus the parents already knew family violence, having experienced it from their own parents. When they became parents, they already had violent, aggressive behavior patterns available to use. When these parents met frustrations, often from being poor and having few resources of any kind, their difficult children made it all the harder to cope with their multitudes of problems. Not knowing how to get the baby to stop crying or the toddler to stay out of the way or the child to stop wetting the bed, the parent hurt the child instead of giving him care.

Child abuse is a family problem in the sense that the whole family interaction results in the attack or neglect. Although one person may be the attacker, all share in it by being afraid to interfere, by not caring, and not giving care enough to prevent it. Society shares in the attacks on children in the interactions of many other social systems with the family. For example, political and economic systems create poverty for some families. The educational, religious, and medical systems permit the birth of unwanted children. The educational system does little to prepare adolescents for parenthood, especially those who have the least potential as parents. One of the important problems facing our society is to learn to give care to all of its children, through their parents and in other ways as well.

Parents as Socializers

Parents teach children how to function as members of their family, community, and society. The process of socialization is the acquisition of the behavior patterns, values, beliefs, attitudes, knowledge, and skills of a particular culture. Through socialization, the child builds a concept of herself as worthy or worthless, competent or incompetent, able or unable to control herself and events outside herself. Socialization orients her to present, past, and future, determining to a large extent her willingness to delay immediate pleasure for future gains, as well as her evaluation of the past. Parents perform many socializing functions in regard to their children, but they obviously do not do the whole job. Nor does the family do it all. The younger the child the more the parents are likely to be the main socializers. Of course, there are exceptions, such as upper-class families who employ nurses and teachers as care-givers and socializers.

Strictly speaking, all teaching is socializing, but we plan to use the term *teaching* for parents' functions in purposefully helping their children to acquire intellectual and motor competencies. Under *socializing,* we are concerned with shaping the child's social and emotional behavior, his attitudes and values, and his assumption of the roles defined by his culture. Of all the roles that everyone must learn, sex role is one of the roles most strongly influenced by parents. Parents also act as socializers in the contexts of emotional expression and control and moral development.

Outside Influences on Socialization. In socializing, just as in caregiving, parents' behavior is influenced by social systems outside his family. The occupational and economic systems are linked to the family in modes of parent-child interaction. For example, observations of black parents with their fifth-grade sons revealed the more *educated* mothers as encouraging their children's autonomy more and as using more words [7]. When fathers came from higher *occupational* levels, mothers encouraged sons' autonomy. The more educated the fathers, the more love they expressed and the more words they used.

Race differences may be important in the socializing practices of parents. When black and white high school students of the same socioeconomic level were questioned, the black students reported more close relationships with both fathers and mothers than did the white students [30]. In an extensive study of the effects of parental authority patterns on preschool children, the black girls seemed to respond differently from white girls to authoritarian parental practices [3]. The black parents enforced directions firmly, did not encourage individuality, and often one of the pair was rejecting. Compared with white girls whose parents behaved in this manner, the black girls were more domineering, independent, and very much at ease. The author suggests that since black women, as compared with white women, have outstanding competencies, their socialization practices most likely prepare their daughters for survival in a difficult world. "Perhaps the black girl admires and seeks to emulate her aggressive mother whose forcefulness assures her security." Thus the daughter, although made to conform as a child, would learn the adult role by watching her mother's performance and successes.

Gender Role. Parents are the primary socializers in gender-role learning. This topic has been covered on pages 84–90.

Emotional Expression and Control. Parents' personalities and childrearing practices are related to children's personality characteristics and emotional behavior. Parental warmth, nurturance, supportiveness, acceptance, and love are all associated with healthy development of children [33]. Extroversion has been found characteristic of school-age boys and adolescents who perceived their parents as loving, and introversion and withdrawal in those who saw their parents as punishing and rejecting [26].

A review of many studies of father-absent children brought out the important influence of fathers on their sons' emotional expression and self-control [5]. As a preschool-child, the father-absent boy is likely to be more dependent, anxious, less aggressive, less masculine, and less mature than other boys. Studies of school-age father-absent children have revealed a high rate of behavior problems in regard to school adjustment [5, p. 77]. During the school years and adolescence, father-absent boys are more likely than other boys to be weak in peer relationships, conscience, impulse control, and delay of gratification, and thus to have problems in handling their aggressive impulses [5, pp. 63–68]. Some studies of father-absent girls have shown them as more dependent on their mothers and as having more difficulty in dealing with their aggressive impulses than girls with fathers at home [5, p. 111].

The mother is seen as an important influence on boys' self-control in several studies concerned with resistance to temptation. Interviews and family interaction observations were conducted with adolescent boys and their parents discussing typical discipline situations [19]. The boys were also tested on yielding to the temptation of touching objects that they had been punished for touching. Self-control was related to the degree of mothers' communicativeness, but not to that of the fathers, and not to general measures of discipline. The important contribution of the influential mothers was most likely their asking for information about the problem and then discussing and interpreting it. In other words, they reasoned with their sons.

Moral Development. Children's goodness has been measured in terms of what they know and what they do. Tests of moral knowledge and judgment, such as Kohlberg's, use stories that present moral problems [18]. The subject's solutions form the basis for locating him in a stage of moral development, of which Kohlberg has defined six. The moral judgment of middle-class, eighth-grade boys and girls was examined in relation to their parents' levels of moral development [13, 14]. Sons' levels were significantly related to mothers'. Warm, nurturant, high-level fathers tended to have high-level children, but the moral level of cold, distant fathers were not related to the moral level of their children. This study shows what many others have shown about the importance of love and support in making a father influential in his children's development. After interviewing the parents and children in regard to the moral problems, the family was asked to discuss two of the stories in which they had made different choices. Observation and analysis of these family discussions showed that high-level parents were more likely to encourage their children to discuss and that high-level moral judgment in children was associated with parental encouragement to discuss. The importance of the mothers' moral level and influence was brought out in another study, in which the same test was given to groups of delinquent and nondelinquent boys and their mothers [15]. The mothers of nondelinquent boys, as well as the normal boys themselves, showed higher levels of moral judgment than the mothers of delinquent boys and their delinquent sons.

A cross-national study also points up the mother-son relationships [27]. Preadolescents in New Zealand answered questions about their parents and, at the same time, took a moral orientation test. Results were compared with those from similar studies done in England and the United States. Of the three, the New Zealand children averaged highest in choosing adult-approved or "good" solutions to moral problems involving honesty, kindness to other children, and cooperation with parents and teachers. The New Zealanders, as compared with the other two groups, also saw their parents as high in giving support, control, and punishment. Support was indicated by agreeing with statements such as, "I can count on him to help me out if I have some kind of problem," control by, "She is very strict toward me if I don't do what is expected of me," and punishment, "He won't let me do something with my friends when I do something he doesn't like." Most of the difference between New Zealand children and English and American children was the result of differences between the boys. The New Zealand mothers' patterns of socializing varied more from the English and American than did the fathers' from the other two. New Zealand mothers gave especially strong support and control, both of which were associated with their sons' high moral orientation.

The importance of mothers in moral teaching is thus seen in several studies and the influence of fathers has also been noted. It is likely that children's moral development is promoted by both parents when both are active and by either parent when only one is available.

The action part of moral behavior includes doing what one knows to be right: telling the truth, helping, giving, being kind and generous, not hurting others, and respecting the rights and belongings of others. Studies concerned with moral action have examined some of these behaviors. Generosity and helping are of special interest. Research on all sorts of moral behavior shows that it is influenced by age, experience, and conditions of the experiment. Although much of the research on altruistic behavior has been done in laboratory experiments, the results have some implications for parents. Experiments have shown that in such situations as giving to charity or sharing treats with friends, children are most likely to do what a model does and to say what he says [6]. That is, if an adult makes a donation, so does the child, but if he tells the child it is nice and kind to give but does not give himself, the child will not give but will be able to say later that giving is good. The warmth shown by the model will increase the child's imitative actions, but only if given when the child imitates. Otherwise, the model's warmth is likely to make the child self-indulgent. The hypocrite, who practices selfishness and preaches generosity, loses ability to influence children as they grow beyond about nine years of age. When a selfish model praised children's donating, they gave less than when they were praised by a generous model or even by a neutral model [20]. The implications for parents are clear. If they want their children to be kind and generous, they will have to show them, as well as tell them, and it will help if they respond with warmth and praise when the child is doing right.

Research on helping or rescuing others from pain and peril suggests that children, as well as adults, are held back from action by fear that they will break rules or that other people will think poorly of them. For instance, when children were told that it was all right for them to leave the room, they were more likely to go to the aid of a child crying in the next room [28]. Sympathy for the person in distress probably plays an important part in a child's rescue attempts, since in so doing, he is trying to relieve his own upset feelings. It seems likely that parents promote children's helping behavior when they demonstrate it themselves and when they appear to get satisfaction out of doing so [6].

Discipline: Practical Implications of Research on Socialization

The word *discipline* is sometimes understood as *punishment,* unfortunately. Like the word *love,* discipline has many meanings. To us, it means "teaching the child to control himself and to behave and feel as a cooperating member of his family and his society."

Discipline is closely related to love, since children want to please the people they love. Therefore, there is more power in a reason, rebuke, or reward from a loved one than from a person with no emotional meaning for the child. By being warm and loving, having good times with the child and meeting his basic needs, a parent lays down the foundation for discipline.

Setting Limits. Good discipline includes making clear what kind of behavior is permitted and what is not. Mrs. Katz has arranged her kitchen cupboards with nesting pots, wooden spoons, clothespins, and plastic milk bottles in a large lower section. All foods and cleaning material are kept in high cupboards. Jerry, age one and a half, goes to his cupboard and plays with his toys. The kitchen is a place where the choices open to Jerry are mostly between one piece of "good" behavior and another piece of "good" behavior. At an older age level, say ten years, an environment that promotes good behavior might be a back yard with a basketball hoop and a tree, but no flower beds.

The child also needs to be told what he may do and what he may not do. It is not enough to say just *no* or *don't,* but it is necessary. *Limits* are a line drawn around something that is right. "You may go out, but be home by 10 o'clock." "You can buy a jacket by yourself, but $— is all we can afford." "Yes, you can read to the end of the chapter before you turn the light out." In setting limits such as these, parents give children some freedom but they use their own wisdom and exert their authority in making decisions that their children are not mature enough to make.

Reasoning and Talking It Over. There are two strong reasons for communicating with children as to why the parent sets certain limits or makes certain demands. First, the child is much more likely to cooperate when she knows the reasons. Second, reasoning helps her to develop her own conscience and moral code, to make the good behavior truly a part of herself. In communicating reasons and explanations, frankness about feelings also helps. If the parent is a skilled listener, he will help his child to express what he feels along with what he thinks. "It was wrong to tell Joey to crawl out on the roof and then to shut the window so that he couldn't get back into the bedroom. Do you want to tell me anything about what happened before that?"

In expressing their own feelings to a child, parents accomplish several important ends. They make the present issue more understandable. They make themselves more understandable, as human beings with feelings. They show children how to express feelings and imply that it is all right to do so. We are assuming here that the parents are not expressing themselves violently or explosively, but rather along these lines, "I'm feeling pretty upset, too. When I saw Joey up on the roof in his pajamas, I was afraid that he would slip on the ice and fall off, or at least that he would catch cold. And then when I saw you holding the window shut, it made me very angry. Being so frightened made me more angry than if you had done something wrong but not dangerous."

In Chapter 3, we have discussed ways of communicating with children and within the family. All of this material is important in connection with discipline.

Rewards, or Positive Reinforcement. Children, like other people and animals, tend to repeat acts that are rewarded. What is a reward? The approval of a loved person is one of the strongest rewards, even if it is only expressed in a smile or a pat. A child will work, control himself, and try to do "right" for expected approval. Feedback, or information about results of one's actions, also acts as positive reinforcement, leading the child to repeat his successful actions or to take the next step.

Concrete rewards, such as money, candy, stickers, or even elaborate ones such as watches and cars, may be effective in themselves or for their symbolic value. Unless the reward has some value other than the immediate pleasure it brings, it may soon wear out as a motivator of good behavior. Gold stars or candies may continue to move children to learn and act as desired because they give feedback and symbolize approval.

Good discipline includes rewarding the child for "good" behavior and not rewarding him for "bad" behavior. It sounds simple, but it is hard to carry out. When Dylan was sitting quietly in his room, hooking up wires to his dry cell, he got no positive reinforcement from his father, but when he enticed Joey onto the roof and shut the window, he received a great deal of attention. Sometimes any kind of attention, even disapproval, feels better to a child than getting no response.

Punishment and Negative Reinforcement. Punishment is an action or occurrence that hurts or makes a person unhappy. If he learns from it, he learns *not to respond*. Thus he does not make the unpleasant stimulus occur. Negative reinforcement is an event leading to a response that ends the event or makes its recurrence less likely. Suppose that Dylan saw his father acting very angry and upset while Joey was out on the roof. If he had been negatively reinforced by his father's emotional behavior, he would have tried to terminate it, to make his father feel better. In order to end his father's anger, he would have opened the window and let Joey come in. Not wishing to make his father angry again, Dylan might never again close the window after suggesting that Joey climb out onto the roof. The negative reinforcement would be continuing to affect Dylan.

Withholding a reward can be negative reinforcement. The child does something in order to change the situation of no reward to reward. She cleans up her room in order to be able to go out to play. Often punishment is used intentionally as negative reinforcement. When parents punish by scolding, spanking, withdrawing privileges or giving tasks, they are often trying to change a child's behavior from "bad" to "good." When they withhold approval and ignore, however, they often are just not thinking about the child and not intentionally applying negative reinforcement. Very often, intentional punishment does not get the desired results, and neither does ignoring improve the child's behavior. Are punishment and negative reinforcement useless? It depends on the kind of punishment and the circumstances under which it is given. Intense punishment makes a person afraid and anxious. He is likely to resent and fear the person who punishes harshly and will not try to please him or imitate him. Mild punishment may be effective when given with reasons and explanation by a loved parent, especially if the parent also shows the child how to do right instead of wrong. Sometimes ignoring bad behavior acts as negative reinforcement, especially if desired behavior is rewarded.

Setting a Good Example. Since children model their own behavior on that of people they love and admire, of people who seem to be powerful, and of people they see rewarded, parents stand a good chance of being imitated. Not only will a child do what his parents do, but he will also say what they say, even though the words do not agree with the actions. It can be very disconcerting to a parent to have his insincerity or bigotry reproduced. Sometimes children act as mirrors to parents who see their own weaknesses reflected. Luckily, reasoning can repair some of the damage. Overhearing Melinda saying, "Shut up, you old bat" to her grandmother, Glenna took her daughter aside, slapped her lightly on the seat, and said, "How dare you be so rude to your grandmother! What ever has got into you?"

"I didn't think you'd care, Mother! I know you say I should always be polite, but I heard you telling Dad on the phone that Grandma made you sick and tired and that you weren't going to listen to her talking and talking and talking."

Glenna suddenly saw herself being just as rude as Melinda had been. She explained, "I do care about Grandma. She is my mother and I love her even though she does talk a lot. I'll try to be more patient with her. Will you try with me?"

Putting It All Together. In teaching a child to behave in the right ways and to gradually take responsibility for his own behavior, parents use various methods, in various combinations. Parenting is an art, not a science, since every child is his own unique self and every situation is a new one. It is important to love the child and let her know it, to make clear what is approved and disapproved, to give opportunities for good behavior rather than bad, to listen to the child and encourage her questions and expression, to explain and reason, to be firm and yet flexible, to admit mistakes, to be consistent in words and actions, to reward frequently, especially with praise and approval, to punish lightly and with explanation. No parent has ever done all of this all of the time, since parents are not perfect. Like children, they are still learning and growing. In fact, helping a child to grow into a responsible adult is in itself a growth-producing process.

Parents as Teachers

Even in the early years, parents are teachers in the sense of stimulating their children's development. The kind of physical and social environment they provide will make a difference in the mental development of the child. For example, Yarrow and associates found that six-month-old-infants' scores on mental and motor tests and on measures of goal-directed behavior and exploratory behavior all correlated with the quality of the stimulation from toys and people [37]. When parents (or anyone else) respond to what infants do, and when they arrange for babies to play

Learning the family business in South India.

with toys that they can manage and control, then the infants grow mentally and socially [34]. A study of adoptive mothers and their babies showed that infants' IQs tended to be lower when mothers were highly restrictive, talked little to their babies, and gave them little physical contact [4].

Many studies show that preschool children's intelligence, language development, learning style, and general competence are related to their mothers' methods of teaching them and guiding their daily lives. Children's competence and mothers' adequacy vary with socioeconomic level, but there are some excellent mothers in all levels. A vivid description of what these mothers actually do is given by Burton White, the coordinator of a complex longitudinal study of competence in young children [35, pp. 242–244]. White holds that the action of the mother directly to and with her child of one to three, especially two to three years, is the most important formative factor in his development; that the results of these actions form the basis for the child's behavior and success in school; that a good job of mothering can be done without a father in the home. The competent mothers talk a great deal to their children, most often in response to the child, encouraging, helping, stimulating his interest, setting limits as to what he may do and not do, and making suggestions that will expand his play. The mothers are busy people, doing their other work while they also meet the needs of their children, pausing in other tasks briefly but sufficiently. They design environments for play that contain many interesting things to see, manipulate, climb, explore, and use imaginatively. They can say *no* without feeling guilty or anxious. They have high levels of energy. (This is a composite picture. Probably no individual woman is such a paragon.)

Father-availability has been found related to sons' cognitive functioning and school competence [5, pp. 55–63]. A study of father-son interaction indicated that fathers' methods of teaching, like mothers', affect the development of sons' IQs and related competencies. Paternal nurturance, support, expectations, and direct teaching all had positive relations to sons' intellectual development.

Class and ethnic differences in measured IQ, achievement, and cognitive style may arise largely from differences in parents as teachers of their young children. Many studies have shown class differences in mothers' interactions with infants and preschool children. Middle-class mothers generally exceed lower-class mothers in talking more responsively, asking questions that focus the child on the task, giving more praise, watching the child and returning his glances, and giving him more things to play with [23]. Both ethnic and class differences were demonstrated in a comparison of teaching styles of Anglo-, Mexican-, and Chinese-American mothers [29]. Each mother taught a bean bag toss game and a color sorting game to her three year old. The Chinese mothers gave a high proportion of enthusiastic positive feedback and also fitted their responses very carefully to the child's demand for help. Mexican mothers gave much negative feedback and many nonverbal instructions. The differences were consistent with the mothers' concepts of their own parental roles. The Chinese mothers saw their instruction of young children as an important part of the mother's responsibilities. The Mexican mothers considered teaching to be

This father is available for play, instruction, and protection.

the teacher's job, in the school. The Anglo mothers said that they were uncertain as to what they should be teaching.

Even though competence in teaching is more typical of mothers in higher socioeconomic positions and in certain ethnic groups, *anyone can learn* these competencies. Presumably fathers, as well as mothers, can learn to teach young children. The sort of excellence described by White and implied in these other studies is a human potential. Since the link between children's intellectual competence and parental teaching behavior is well established, many intervention programs are now in progress. Parents are learning how to be teachers [25].

SUCCESS, FROM THE PARENT'S STANDPOINT

Successful parenthood is defined differently by different societies, but from the viewpoint of parents themselves, a feeling of success comes from a good fit between their goals for their children, their own resources, and the development of the children.

Parents' Values and Goals for Children

Goals might include physical attributes, such as strength and beauty, and achievements, such as earning a million dollars. However, available information on parents' goals is mostly in terms of the behavior and personality characteristics that they try to develop in their children. Records from seventeenth-century France, for example, show parents as being very concerned with making their children obedient and dependent [16, pp. 146–158]. Obedience or "breaking the will" was also a big issue with parents in the seventeenth-century Plymouth Colony [8, pp. 80–191]. An observer wrote, "And surely there is in all children . . . a stubbornness, and stoutness of mind arising from natural pride, which must, in the first place, be broken and beaten down; that so the foundation of their education being laid in humility and tractableness, other virtues may, in their time, be built thereon . . . " [8, pp. 182–183].

In modern North America, obedience is still a goal of parents, but the issue is not so clear-cut. Surveys and analyses of parents' goals show them to be numerous, complex, and variable [9, 31]. Stolz in her comprehensive study of parents of children age eight months to 14 years, found 55 categories of basic values. Most parents mentioned 20 per cent of them, of which mothers and fathers agreed on these eight: independence, family unity, manners, getting along with people, obedience, religion, responsibility, and morality. Mothers also included freedom from anxiety, family love, and enjoyment. Fathers added knowledge, safety, and justice [31, p. 84]. Emmerich queried parents of preschool children about a more limited range of parental goals that were important in socialization and interpersonal relationships. Of the positive goals Emmerich identified, parents ranked them in this order of importance: trustingness, obedience, friendliness, assertiveness, independence. Negative goals, or attributes that parents wanted their children not to have, were, in this order of importance: avoidance, aggression, submissiveness, overfriendliness, and dependency.

In daily life, parents set goals for small pieces of behavior, as well as broad goals of socialization. Mrs. A. tries to get Joe to wipe his feet before he enters the house. Mr. B. urges Leon to swallow that mouthful of food before he takes a drink of milk. Mrs. C. insists that Lisa greet people by name, instead of just saying, "Hi."

Problems Seen by Parents. In addition to rating goals in order of importance, Emmerich's subjects told which goals were problematic by showing where they most wanted changes in their preschool children's behavior [9, pp. 28–30]. An increase in obedience was desired by 97 per cent of the parents, a decrease in aggression by 91 per cent, a decrease in dependency by 89 per cent, and an increase in independence by 75 per cent. When a parent values a certain kind of behavior highly and also wants his child to change in regard to this kind of behavior, then this behavior is a problem to the parent.

Parents' Resources

Resources include everything that parents can bring to bear upon their children in order to impel them toward the goals they have for them. As mentioned previously, nations and communities vary greatly in how much help they offer to parents. The extreme example is the kibbutz, where nation and community have similar aims, and where parents participate in setting goals and working toward them for all children. In many times and places, schools and churches are resources for parents, but sometimes parental goals do not jibe with those of the social institutions. Resources also exist in the family as a whole, in the parents as a pair, and in the individuals. Since mothers' and fathers' resources tend to strengthen and complement each other, the single parent usually needs to find some source for supplementary resources.

No matter how strongly one might believe in a particular method of teaching children, one must be *able to apply it* before it can work. Most parents felt able to give positive reinforcement but unable to ignore undesirable behavior, even when they thought that negative reinforcement or nonintervention might be effective. They also found it difficult or impossible, often, to modify the situation in ways that they believed would be helpful. For instance, a different neighborhood or a room for each child could reduce behavior problems but might be unattainable. In such cases, the parents' limited *resources* make it impossible to apply the learning theories that they hold.

Child Development and Behavior

The proof of the parents' success is the child himself, or so it is to the parents, and, to a large degree, to kin and community. The child's health and growth show parental care; her manners and character reveal parental socializing; her intelligence and achievement reflect the parents as teachers. When they judge their child adequate, satisfying, or excellent in all these ways, then parents feel that their theories were valid, that they applied them correctly, and that they did right as parents. Thus there is a fit between the development of the child and the parents' goals and resources.

Rarely do the child, the goals, and the resources dovetail perfectly. Many parents feel somewhat unsuccessful and some feel that they are failures. Some parents are judged failures by the community.

PARENT EDUCATION

In traditional societies, families teach children to be parents. In complex, rapidly changing cultures, children's early experiences in family living are not sufficient to equip them for parenthood [36]. Potential parents have to learn from other systems in addition to the lessons they learn from their parents and kin.

Ideally, education for parenthood is both preparental and on the job. Some girls and very few boys are fortunate enough to have high school courses that prepare them for parenthood. During pregnancy, many couples have some instruction on the care of infants. When the baby is born, the time when the sudden change is made from nonparent to parent, much day-to-day education could be used, and often none is available. Hospital personnel, midwives, or baby-care nurses can be very important teachers at this time. In New Zealand, specially trained nurses offer their services to new mothers, 95 per cent of whom accept. The Plunket nurse goes to the home for the first few weeks, giving advice and support to the mother. Later the mother takes the baby to the nurse's office for individualized service during the first five years of life.

Parents of preschoolchildren may be educated in connection with the day care centers or nursery schools that their children attend. Parent-teacher organizations sometimes offer courses for parents. Social agencies are also sources of education. *Parents' Magazine* publishes sound articles for parents and also provides guidance in setting up and conducting study courses. Authorities speak to parents through books and television.

Classes and study groups provide support that only personal interaction can give. Many types of courses are offered, each reflecting the theories of learning and development held by its originator. A course may stress *behavior modification* or *communication* or *self-development*. Since parents can help each other to grow and learn, parent educators usually structure the group in such a way that sharing is most helpful. Some parent-run groups operate for years, with members contributing ideas, leadership, information, materials for discussion, and support for one another as they develop parental competencies and philosophy.

PARENTS AND ADULT OFFSPRING

Attachments or ties of love continue to bind grownup children and parents in many, probably most, cases. A study of young adults' kinship relations revealed them as feeling that relationships with their parents were closer than relationships with their siblings and best friends. They also felt more obliged to parents [1, pp. 78–83, 114].

Women tend to feel kinship ties more strongly than men, or at least to take responsibility for maintaining relationships [32]. The mother-daughter attachment in adulthood is usually stronger than the mother-son attachment, and the sister-sister attachment tends to be stronger than attachments involving brothers. There may even be a biological basis for mother-daughter closeness, since the mother-daughter attachment is strong in many adult mammals, including sheep as well as primates.

Some young adults find it a problem to establish satisfactory relationships with their own parents. In some cases, a parent tries to dominate the adult child. In other cases, the young adult has not taken the steps necessary to achieve emancipation. This situation seems to happen more frequently with mother-daughter pairs, although it can also occur in father-daughter, mother-son, or father-son pairs. Since the younger person is usually the one who perceives the relationship as problematic, it is most often up to the younger one to try to solve the problem. Sometimes it is necessary to cut ties by going away, perhaps just by moving out of the parental home or by going to a distant place to live. In other cases, a changed attitude is enough. With 35-year-old Meg, deepened insight into her mother was enough to give her a feeling of independence. ''My mother is always telling me what to do and what she

An Indian woman is protector to her blind, dependent mother.

STANLEY SUMMER

thinks about everything I do. She keeps giving me stuff, buying clothes for me, and even wants to help my friends. If only she wouldn't phone me every day!"

In discussing Meg's mother, Meg was able to give some reasons for her annoying behavior "I'm all Mother has. Dad died when I was 12 years old and she had to work to take care of me. We were very close while I was growing up and we didn't have the usual adolescent-parent conflicts. I just can't hurt her feelings now."

Meg was helped to see that her mother had potential for growth, just as she herself had, and that the two of them could continue to love each other while changing. She also came to realize that she must accept her mother as a human being, with imperfections, instead of expecting her to be completely competent and adequate (which she seemed to be to the 12-year-old Meg). Meg decided that she must make certain decisions in order to be her own self and that she could trust her mother to accept her as an adult instead of as an adolescent or little girl.

Parents continue to give care to their grown children and also to receive care from them. Thus, there is mutual dependence in many parent-offspring pairs. One-directional dependence usually occurs only when the parents are very old. The Minnesota study of three generations showed that the oldest and youngest generation turned to each other for help with problems more than did the middle generation [12, pp. 63–67]. The kinds of help given and received included economic, emotional gratification, household management, child care, and illness assistance. Parents gave the most economic aid and married grandchildren received the most.

Caregiving patterns might be expected to vary from one culture or subculture to another. A study of family and friend relationships among older black women revealed patterns of children's giving to married and spouseless mothers [17]. Gifts were given to about 64 per cent of all the women but the spouseless mothers received more economic and health assistance. Younger children gave more care to spouseless mothers than to married mothers. Eldest children gave care equally.

SUMMARY   Family and other social systems affect the ways in which parents and children influence one another. Children, especially young ones, communicate much through nonverbal behavior.

Children's health is largely the result of care given by parents, whose caregiving capacities are limited by both economics and education. When parents abuse, neglect, and injure their children, family pathology is indicated, as well as pathological interaction between family and society.

As socializers, parents teach children to function as members of their culture and to think, believe, and feel in appropriate ways toward other people and toward themselves. Healthy child development is associated with parental love, warmth, nurturance, and support. Parents' level of moral development is related to children's, with mothers' reasoning being an important influence, especially with boys. Helping and giving are stimulated when parents help, give, and appear to feel good about doing so.

Discipline is the operation of teaching a child to control himself, to behave responsibly, and to cooperate with his fellow beings. A loving relationship is a good foundation from which to discipline a child. Methods include setting limits verbally and environmentally, reasoning and explaining, expressing feelings and encouraging the child to express hers, giving frequent rewards, especially approval, giving information about success, punishing seldom and lightly, with explanation, setting a good example, being consistent in words and deeds, admitting mistakes, and not expecting perfection in child or self.

Mental development is influenced by parents' teaching and guidance. Although there is a class difference in adequacy of teaching style, competence as a teacher can be taught and learned.

Parents feel successful when they are able to implement the goals they have for their children and when the children develop and behave in accordance with the parents' goals. A problem exists when a parent wants a child to change his behavior in regard to a highly valued goal. All parents hold learning theories that they try to apply. Parent education can be done before people become parents and at any time during parenthood. Parents can help each other to develop competencies and philosophies.

When children grow up, friendship and enjoyment of companionship with parents is possible but not inevitable. Interdependencies are common between generations, with the middle-age generation contributing the largest share of help, but the older generation still giving.

REFERENCES

1. Adams, Bert N. *Kinship in an urban setting.* Chicago: Markham, 1968.
2. Andersen, E. Skeletal maturation of Danish school children in relation to height, sexual development and social conditions. *Act. Paed. Scand.* Supplement 185, 1968. (Quoted in *Dairy Council Digest,* 1969, **40:** 2, 10.)
3. Baumrind, Diana. An exploratory study of socialization effects on black children: Some black-white comparisons. *Child Development,* 1972, **43,** 261–267.
4. Beckwith, Leila. Relationships between attributes of mothers and their infants' IQ scores. *Child Development,* 1971, **42,** 1083–1097.
5. Biller, Henry B. *Father, child, and sex role.* Lexington, Mass.: Heath, 1971.
6. Bryan, James H. Why children help: A review. *Journal of Social Issues,* 1972, **28,** 87–103.
7. Busse, Thomas V. and Pauline Busse. Negro parental behavior and social class variables. *Journal of Genetic Psychology,* 1972, **120,** 280–294.
8. Demos, John. Infancy and childhood in the Plymouth Colony. In Michael Gordon (ed.). *The American family in historical perspective.* New York: St. Martin's, 1973.
8a. Duchowny, Michael S. Interactional influences of infant characteristics and postpartum maternal self image. Paper presented at meetings of the American Psychological Association, New Orleans, 1974.
9. Emmerich, Walter. The parental role: A functional-cognitive approach. *Monographs of the Society for Research in Child Development,* 1969, **34:**8.

10. Gelles, Richard. Child abuse as psychopathology: A sociological critique and reformulation. *American Journal of Orthopsychiatry,* 1973, **43,** 612–621.

11. Gil, David G. Violence against children. *Journal of Marriage and the Family,* 1971, **33,** 637–648.

12. Hill, Reuben. *Family development in three generations.* Cambridge, Mass.: Schenkman, 1970.

13. Holstein, Constance E. Personal communication, 1973.

14. Holstein, Constance E. The relation of children's moral judgment level to that of their parents and to communication patterns in the family. In Russell C. Smart and Mollie S. Smart (eds.). *Readings in child development and relationships.* New York: Macmillan, 1972.

15. Hugins, William and Norman M. Prentice. Moral judgment in delinquent and nondelinquent adolescents and their mothers. *Journal of Abnormal Psychology,* 1973, **82,** 145–152.

16. Hunt, David. *Parents and children in history.* New York: Basic Books, 1970.

17. Jackson, Jacqueline J. Comparative life styles and family and friend relationships among older black women. *Family Coordinator,* 1972, **21,** 477–485.

18. Kohlberg, Lawrence. *Stages in the development of moral thought and action.* New York: Holt, 1969.

19. LaVoie, Joseph C. and William R. Looft. Parental antecedents of resistance-to-temptation behavior in adolescent males. *Merrill-Palmer Quarterly,* 1973, **19,** 107–116.

20. Midlarsky, Elizabeth, James H. Bryan, and Philip Brickman. Aversive approval: Interactive effects of modeling and reinforcement on altruistic behavior. *Child Development,* 1973, **44,** 321–328.

21. Osofsky, Joy D. The shaping of mothers' behavior by children. *Journal of Marriage and the Family,* 1970, **32,** 400–405.

22. Osofsky, Joy D. and Barbara Danzger. Relationships between neonatal characteristics and mother-infant interaction. *Developmental Psychology,* 1974, **10,** 124–130.

23. Pytkowicz, Ann S. and Helen L. Bee. Mother-child interactions and cognitive development in children. *Young Children,* 1972, **27,** 154–173.

23a. Rohner, Ronald P. *They love me, they love me not: The worldwide study of parental acceptance and rejection.* New Haven: HRAF Press, 1975.

24. Rosenberg, Benjamin G. and Brian Sutton-Smith. Family interaction effects on masculinity-femininity. *Journal of Personality and Social Psychology,* 1968, **8,** 117–120.

25. Schaeffer, Earl S. Parents as educators: Evidence from cross-sectional, longitudinal and intervention research. *Young Children,* 1972, **27,** 227–239.

26. Siegelman, Marvin. Loving and punishing parental behavior and introversion tendencies among sons. *Child Development,* 1966, **29,** 985–992.

27. Smart, Russell C. and Mollie S. Smart. New Zealand pre-adolescents' parent-peer orientation and parent perceptions compared with English and American. *Journal of Marriage and the Family,* 1973, **35,** 142–148.

28. Staub, Ervin A. A child in distress: The influence of age and number of witnesses on children's attempts to help. *Journal of Personality and Social Psychology,* 1970, **14,** 130–140.

29. Steward, Margaret and David Steward. The observation of Anglo-, Mexican-, and Chinese-American mothers teaching their young sons. *Child Development,* 1973, **44,** 329–337.

30. Stinnett, Nick, Sharon Talley, and James Walters. Parent-child relationships of black and white high school students: A comparison. *Journal of Social Psychology,* 1973, **91,** 349–350.

31. Stolz, Lois M. *Influences on parent behavior.* Stanford, Calif.: Stanford U. P., 1967.

32. Troll, Lillian E. The family of later life: A decade review. *Journal of Marriage and the Family,* 1971, **33,** 263–290.

33. Walters, James and Nick Stinnett. Parent-child relationships: A decade review of research. *Journal of Marriage and the Family,* 1971, **33,** 70–111.

34. Watson, John S. and Craig T. Ramey. Reactions to response-contingent stimulation in early infancy. *Merrill-Palmer Quarterly,* 1972, **18,** 219–221.

35. White, Burton L. and Jean C. Watts. *Experience and environment: Major influences on the development of the young child.* Englewood Cliffs:, N.J. Prentice-Hall, 1973.

36. Whiting, Beatrice B. Folk wisdom and child rearing. *Merrill-Palmer Quarterly,* 1974, **20,** 9–19.

37. Yarrow, Leon J., Judith L. Rubenstein, Frank A. Pedersen, and Joseph J. Jankowski. Dimensions of early stimulation and their differential effects on infant development. *Merrill-Palmer Quarterly,* 1972, **18,** 205–218.

CHAPTER 11
sisters, brothers, and all the rest

Suppose a young adult looks back over his life and asks, "What made me the way I am today?" No doubt he will give some credit to his parents. If he has brothers and sisters, or only one sibling, he will probably see them as having been a great influence upon him. He may realize that a brother or sister, or several of them, are closely connected with many of his feelings about himself, his estimates of what he can do, his knowledge, skills, and interests.

Grandparents also may be seen as having played a part in the personality development of the growing person, especially if they lived near enough to him to have frequent contact. In sheer number of hours spent together, however, grandparents and other relatives have much less opportunity than siblings to be important influences. The network of kin may be small or large or strong or weak in regard to the nuclear family and its members.

SIBLING RELATIONSHIPS

Siblings are the closest of relatives, since all of their genes come from the same two people. Not only do they draw upon the same sources of heredity but they also live in very similar environments and tend to spend a great deal of time together, sharing the intimate experiences of daily living. Siblings do not have the *same* sets of genes unless they are identical twins, nor do they have the same environments, even if they are identical twins. Each child contributes part of the family environment of every other child. Granted their similarity in heredity and environment, it sometimes seems surprising that siblings turn out as differently as they do.

Ordinal Position

The child's position in the family is often thought to be important in shaping his personality. Everyone has her own experience of being in the particular spot of eldest, middle, or youngest, and in a special arrangement of boys and girls or all boys or all girls, or even in being an only child. It is easy to assume that one's own experience applies to all the other people in a similar position. Many psychologists have studied ordinal position with many different results [35]. One finding that often appears in American studies is the difference between eldest children and others. Especially among girls, firstborns have often been seen as more anxious, fearful, sensitive to pain, and desirous of love and friendship [10, 24, 28, 34].

In their cross-culture study of child behavior, the Whitings found that only in their United States sample did the eldest child differ in these ways from middle children. Among their subjects in Africa, India, Okinawa, the Philippines, and Mexico, the youngest's personality was different. American eldest children were more anxious and sought attention more; non-American youngest children sought attention more [45].

The Whitings' study suggests that differences in child rearing affect the patterning of ordinal positions. A sample of thirty-nine societies revealed many differences in the ways that firstborns are treated. The birth of the first child, which frequently gave parents greater status and their marriage more stability, was often recognized in elaborate birth ceremonies. Firstborns were likely to have authority over their younger siblings and to be more respected by them in childhood and adulthood. In contrast, the North American ideal is to treat all children "fairly," dividing property and privileges equally among them. In practice, it often does not work out that way. For instance, in our family, as in many, the first child's baby book is bulging with photographs, whereas the last child's book is rather thin.

Sibling Interaction

Sometimes I love you, sometimes I hate you! These feelings are true of most close relationships, but especially of siblings. They did not choose each other, and yet they live in the closest proximity, often sharing a room, sometimes even a bed. They play with the same toys. One wears another's outgrown clothes. They have the same surname, parents, relatives, and family reputation. There are many chances for them to play together, to have fun with each other, to help each other, and to conflict, fight, and resent each other. In addition to loving and hating, siblings switch easily from cooperating to trying to control and trying to resist. The following discussion treats siblings in the various roles that they play with each other.

Playmates and Companions. Even though we said earlier that we think it unfair to have a child for the main purpose of being a playmate, it is still fun to have a playmate! One of the great advantages of having a sibling is to have someone to play

with at any time of the day or night, while working, eating, going to school, or doing just about anything. It takes two or more to play games of chance and skill, to throw and catch a ball, to turn a rope for jumping, and to take roles in imaginative play. Two or more can think up new things to do much better than only one. Sometimes it is important to have a sibling for company, just to be together without doing anything in particular. It keeps a person from feeling lonely and alone. Since adults are bigger and stronger than children, a child companion often feels more comfortable and more like oneself. Even siblings who often quarrel may seek each other's companionship frequently, as do Rachel and Pat. They have many conflicts over toys, being first, sitting in the front seat, and so on, but when Pat takes a long afternoon nap and Rachel wakens early, she keeps asking, "Can I wake Pat up? I want to play with him. I have nothing to do."

Much important learning takes place through play, especially in young children. Before the age of six or seven, imaginative play, especially dramatic play, is the means through which children reflect upon their experiences, interpret them, and place them in meaningful contexts. Siblings are likely to resemble each other on tests of creative thinking. [31]. Through play, children develop motor coordination and intellectual skills. Thus, sibling play is an important mode of learning and one in which children teach each other. Enjoying play together and realizing the necessary

Brothers are playmates at hide and seek.

contributions of others, siblings strengthen their attachments to each other and prepare for later group interactions.

In their study of families with six or more children, Bossard and Boll found that almost all of the informants reported a great deal of play between siblings. Excerpts from the interviews represent playing together as one of the best parts of living in a large family. An example follows:

"We rarely had outside company and did not feel the need of it. We had good imaginations and played many games, which were joined in by two dogs and a cat. This life continued for some years, and, as far as we children were concerned, it was the closest thing to heaven" [5, p. 168].

When Sutton-Smith and Rosenberg [42, p. 50] interviewed children in grades 3, 4, and 5, they asked, "How do you have fun with your sibling?" Over half of the answers involved playing games together. Girls, more than boys, mentioned a variety of pursuits including working, helping, teaching, reading, and going places.

Children's preferences in playmates were affected by the sex of siblings, according to Koch's findings on five and six year olds from two-child families. Children generally preferred like-sex playmates. The child in a two-sex sibling pair was more likely than the child of a like-sex pair to prefer opposite-sex playmates or to be indifferent as to the sex of his playmates [22]. Thus, the sibling inclined the child to increased acceptance of playmates of the same sex as the sibling.

Facilitation and interference by siblings were also examined in the study of power and influence of siblings ages five and a half to thirteen and a half [4]. A facilitating comment was, for example, "You did that very well." An interfering comment was, "Give me that." Older siblings were seen very much more as facilitators than as interferers, and the overall perceptions assigned more facilitation than interference in sibling interaction. This result is heartening, when one considers the great attention paid to power and control by researchers and writers, and the few articles to be found on positive relationships between siblings.

Does sibling companionship last throughout life? Observation of extended families in India suggests that it does when adult brothers live and work together. In the American family system, where siblings do not live together after they grow up, there is also some evidence that friendship and companionship are still alive. Although siblings were not usually available for interaction in a metropolitan area, it was found that they were likely to turn to each other when their marriages were disrupted [33]. The sister-sister tie is especially strong. Thus, kinship is seen to operate in a compensatory manner. We were interested to see our own experience reflected in this study. My (MSS) sister lived hundreds of miles away in Canada. When her marriage broke up, she and her sons came to live with us for a year. We renewed the companionship of our girlhood. Figure 11-1 shows six-year-old Laura's interpretation of this situation.

Teacher-Learner. Siblings teach one another purposefully and also unintentionally. Common experience, as well as research, shows that older siblings are often in the position of teaching younger ones, both by acting as models and by controlling

My Family

FIGURE 11-1   When I (LSS) was 6 years old, I drew this picture of "My Family."

through dispensing all sorts of reinforcements. The eldest girl is most likely to be a teacher to younger siblings, not only in North America but also in many cultures. Among high school girls in South India, the eldest of several sisters was likely to have a position of honor, with minimal household work assigned to her. Her chief task was to be teacher to the younger children [12].

Facilitation is part of teaching, as well as of playing. The good teacher arranges an environment and tasks that make the pupil free to learn. Since younger children often perceived older siblings as facilitators, it seems likely that the latter were thus in their roles as teachers. Teachers also use control as a technique for focusing the learner's attention and efforts.

Firstborn girls, especially, show preference for teaching as an occupation, most likely reflecting their childhood experiences as teacher of younger siblings [42, p. 115]. Many studies have revealed firstborns as being more adult-like than later borns, more anxious, achievement-oriented, affiliative, conservative, and controlling of subordinates. Firstborn girls were found to exceed other girls and boys in offering to help a child in distress [40]. These characteristics fit with the firstborn taking on an active role in teaching siblings. An analysis of scores on a college entrance examination showed higher results for closely spaced girl pairs than widely spaced girl pairs, and higher for girls with sisters than for girls with brothers. Results were different for boys, with secondborn boys scoring higher when widely spaced than when closely spaced. This study and others have shown the firstborn of a male pair to score higher than the second on tests of intellectual abilities [26, 32].

Teaching, learning and conceptualizing of school-age sibling pairs were analyzed with older siblings present or absent while younger siblings sorted objects and attained concepts. Results confirmed the studies just mentioned, by showing girl siblings to be more effective teachers than boy siblings or nonrelated girls. (Boy and girl teachers were equally good with nonrelated children.) Not only did girl siblings learn better and attain more mature concepts but the girl siblings also exceeded the other child-teachers in the use of these techniques: reasoning from a general principle, explaining, defining, describing, demonstrating, illustrating, and selecting examples [7]. Boy siblings seemed to be more influential as models than as teachers. Children attained more mature concepts when siblings were four years older than when they were two years older [7a].

Sex-role learning is strongly influenced by siblings in that secondborn children's behavior patterns resemble those of their older siblings, whereas firstborn children develop less of the behavior typical of the sex of their younger siblings [42, p. 154]. The mechanisms of these learnings are complex, no doubt including modeling, operant conditioning, and environmental factors, such as the presence or absence of gender-typed play materials (dolls, footballs, and the like).

When fathers are absent, older brothers have special significance for boys. Black, father-absent children between four and six years of age were assessed for aggressive and dependent behavior. Boys, but not girls, with older brothers were found to show more aggression and less dependency than boys without older brothers [46].

Protector-Dependent. When Susan and Ellen were getting ready to go to school in the morning (to second grade and kindergarten, respectively), Susan would often assume a teacher role, telling Ellen to hang up her pajamas and showing her how to read a word or two. Then they might be playmates for a few minutes with the piano or the trapeze, scuffling as rivals when their desires conflicted. But when they walked up the street to school, Susan was the protector against teasing boys who threw snowballs, and Ellen was the dependent. Almost any mother of two or more children could tell such a story. The elder sibling typically defends the younger ones from outside attack, even though she may use aggression and control at home.

In non-Western cultures, older siblings often care for younger ones and may be literally burdened with them. When we met some children on a mountainside in Nepal, one little girl was carrying a baby. We asked the children to dance for us by first dancing for them. The child nurse put the baby down and did a lovely dance but stopped reluctantly as her little sister kept creeping into the dance and clutching at her. The role of the child nurse is also prominent in Africa. In Acholi, the *lapidi* or child nurse is usually a girl but may be a boy, between six and ten years of age. The *lapidi,* who starts to take care of the baby when he is as young as one month of age, follows the baby's mother to the fields. The young woman giving the information said that she had greatly enjoyed being *lapidi* for her cousin until he was a year old, when another cousin took over as *lapidi* and the first one went to school [2].

In Bossard and Boll's study of 100 large families (with six or more children), 91 of the families were reported to have sibling participation in childrearing, especially in discipline [5]. Of these, 82 families indicated that siblings were important as childrearers. There were three main types of delegation of responsibility: because of abdication or incapacitation of parents, siblings carried on the whole childrearing function; parents gave over a certain supervision and protection of younger children

A child nurse, with her dependent.

to older children; one or two older children functioned as assistants to parents. The reactions of the younger children to siblings' discipline was favorable on the whole. Comments indicated that 57 per cent considered the discipline satisfactory, or very satisfactory, whereas only 11 per cent said that they resented it. What happens to the overburdened eldest child is another story. Bossard and Boll [5, pp. 262–284] found that these children were often reluctant to have children. As one of their informants put it, "By the time I was 18, I had changed so many diapers and blown so many noses that I wanted to do other things than marry and keep on doing more of the same." Apparently, the children in the dependent role like it, as they look back, for Sutton-Smith and Rosenberg found that youngest girls from large (four or more children) families were most likely to want to have many children [41].

When the dependent sibling is handicapped, the burdens carried by the protector are even heavier. Studies of the families of mentally retarded children have shown special kinds of personality development in the normal siblings. When normal girls had many interactions with retarded siblings, their mothers saw them as having more neurotic or negative traits than comparable girls outside the family. Normal boys and girls with retarded siblings were relatively disinterested in achieving personal success and more concerned with dedication, personal sacrifice, and contributing to the welfare of mankind [14, 15].

Adversaries. Rivalry and jealousy are common among siblings, even among playmates and good companions. Julia and Jack have always been exceptionally good friends, but their father recalls this incident. One day he came home with two identical trucks, except that one was red and one was blue. He said to two-year-old Julia, "You take first choice, dear. Do you want the red truck or the blue truck?"

Julia sized up the situation for a moment and then firmly announced, "I want Jack's."

Children's quarrels with their siblings were explored in interviews with kindergarteners [23]. Twenty-eight per cent of the subjects said that they quarreled often and severely, 36 per cent said they quarreled occasionally, and 36 per cent said that they rarely quarreled. Although the exact extent of it may not be known, there is evidence that older siblings quarrel, too. The most ancient literature records conflicts between brothers. More modern literature, including research studies, shows that sisters also fight, but in styles that differ from the mode of brothers.

The firstborn has about a year, at the very least, in which he does not have to share his parents' attention with other children. Although he may displace his father somewhat in his mother's attentions and later (according to psychoanalytic views) see his father as a rival to be displaced, no rival sibling threatens his early months. The birth of the second child is very significant, often disturbing, to most firstborns. In many cultures this event signals the end of his infancy. It may mean that he is weaned and must stop sleeping with his mother. Balinese mothers tease toddlers by paying attention to new babies. In Western cultures, mothers may try to ease the emotional shock of having a young sibling but they still give much time, attention, and energy to the new family member because she is physically dependent. The firstborn is likely to feel jealous as he sees the baby receiving a share of what used to be his alone.

A laterborn child has at least one sibling who is bigger, more powerful, and more able than herself. She does not know how it feels to be the only focus of parental attention but she soon realizes that her sibling is more powerful and influential than she is. Here, according to Adler, is an important source of the feeling of inferiority [1].

The importance of the adversary roles is supported by studies of the ways in which children employ power tactics [42] and their perceptions of power and influence in siblings' interactions [4]. Sutton-Smith and Rosenberg asked questions about power relationships of sibling pairs at preadolescence and at college age. At both age levels, firstborns perceived themselves, and secondborns also saw them, as more bossy and exercising higher power. Firstborns commanded, reprimanded, scolded, and bossed, used more physical restraint and physical attack, gave more rewards, and deprived the sibling of more privileges. The secondborns pleaded, whined, sulked, harassed, pestered, bothered, asked for help and sympathy, got angry, and acted stubborn [42, p. 57]. Sex differences in children's use of physical power were significant. Boys were more inclined to hit, beat, wrestle, and chase, whereas girls scratched, pinched, and tickled. In general, boys more often used attack and offense; girls most often used reasoning, defense, and making the sibling feel obligated. Thus, boys behaved in more physical ways, girls behaved more symbolically. In same-sex sibling pairs, offense, sulking, and teasing were more frequent. In opposite-sex pairs, defense and making up occurred more often. The polite behaviors of explaining, asking, and taking turns were used much more by firstborn girls than by firstborn boys.

In their study of college students' use of power in two-child families, Sutton-Smith and Rosenberg did a factor analysis of siblings' answers to items on an inventory. A *factor analysis* gives, in order of importance, the factors constituting the kind of behavior being studied [42, pp. 59–63]. The first of the six factors for males combined commanding, making the other feel guilty, physical restraint, flattery, reprimanding, and physical attack. This factor represents the sort of power that goes with *ascribed* status, such as that of hereditary rules. It is typical of political and military leaders who rule by charisma, strategy, and force. This factor was more typical of firstborns than of secondborns, and was more typical of males than of females. The first of the six female factors was summarized as negativism, trickery and anger, and called the *trollop factor*. The whole analysis showed more use of strategy by girls, and of more socially desirable strategies by girls than by boys.

Perceptions of older and younger siblings' power and influence were studied in 498 girls and boys from 5½ to 13½ years of age [4]. Shown pictures of children in various age and sex combinations, performing social actions, the subjects were asked, "Who would say . . . ?" Examples of items indicating high power were, "You can have it" and, "Stop doing that." Low power was shown by, "Can I have this?" and, "No, I won't do it." Results showed that the older sibling was generally assigned high power and the younger sibling was assigned low power. Children with older male siblings saw higher power in the older sibling than did children with older female siblings.

Products of Sibling Interaction

From the research quoted previously and from other studies too numerous to mention, these conclusions follow: sibling interaction is one of the basic ways in which personality is shaped and culture is passed on; patterns of reaction and motivation are established; philosophies of life are begun; sibling interaction ordinarily takes place in conjunction with parent-child interaction, modifying, supplementing, and occasionally replacing it.

Self-Concept. The ways in which a person sees herself (or theories about herself) are, in part, products of the roles she has played with siblings and reflections of siblings' perceptions of her. Self-concepts of kindergarten children were more positive when they came from small families. Older and only girls had more positive self-concepts or self-esteem than did middle and youngest girls [37]. It seems reasonable that an individual would think better of herself as a teacher than as a pupil, as protector than as dependent, and as the more powerful of adversaries.

Yet another aspect of self-theory is *locus of control*, or the extent to which one feels able to influence events versus the extent to which influence seems to reside in the world outside the self. Since siblings give each other frequent, repeated experiences with controlling and being controlled, the results of these encounters are bound to affect the child's convictions as to the degree to which he himself is in charge.

Another component of the self-concept is gender identity, the conception of oneself as female or male. Interactions with siblings have been shown to influence sex-typed behavior in general.

Orientation to Family of Procreation. Experiences in the family of orientation shape not only the individual's behavior as a member of one sex or the other but also his notions of how family life should be conducted. The choosing of wives and decisions about how many children to have are influenced by the numbers and sexes of siblings. Apparently, people try to repeat social patterns that they are familiar with, other things being equal.

Skills and Competencies. Siblings influence the choice and development of all sorts of competencies, cognitive, creative, motor, and social. Even in infancy, the presence of an older sibling made a difference in exploratory and social skills. As compared with only children, babies with siblings explored toys more, made more responses to toys, laughed and smiled more, and initiated more play with a stranger [9].

The interests and skills siblings learn together often have a direct bearing on occupational choice, as shown by the relationship between ordinal position and certain jobs and professions. In many ways, interactions in the wider world are reflections or outgrowths of the behavior patterns and interpretations that children learn in the home-based world of sibling interaction.

INTERACTION WITH GRANDPARENTS

Even though grandparents are unlikely to live in the same house with adult children and their offspring, the grandparent generation in North America is not isolated. Many studies have shown that intergenerational contacts are kept up through visiting, telephoning, and all sorts of mutual helping [43].

Grandparenthood may be reached in the forties. Even when grandparents are in their fifties and sixties, they are usually vigorous and active, busy with work and interests. Grandmothers, as well as grandfathers, are likely to have jobs and careers. During the years of great-grandparenthood, living with adult children becomes more frequent. Of people over eighty, 25 per cent of the men and 47 per cent of the women live with their children. Of those who do not live in the same household, the

DALV JONES

majority of people over eighty live within ten minutes' travel time of an adult child [39].

Availability

Most children have some experience with grandparents. Most grandparents of young children are alive and living within a distance that permits some interaction.

Chances of Having Living Grandparents. Compared with the situation of 50 years ago, today's children are much more likely to have grandparents. In a recent year, 97 per cent of white ten year olds had at least one living grandparent and 74 per cent had all four living grandparents. Of 20 year olds, 78 per cent had at least one and 7 per cent had four grandparents. Fifty years previously, the corresponding figures at age ten were 79 per cent and 11 per cent, and at age 20, the corresponding figures were 51 per cent and less than 1 per cent [29].

In contrast to such high grandparent availability, consider the situation in poor countries where life expectancy is short. In Gabon, West Africa, where life expectancy for men is 25 years of age and women 45, there must be little opportunity for children to know their grandfathers [44, p. 746].

Place of Residence. When grandparents live nearby, they are likely to have closer affectional ties with grandchildren [6]. There is some evidence that young nuclear families are likely to live farther from the grandparents than are older nuclear units [43]. However, persons over 65 in six countries (Denmark, Britain, United States, Poland, Yugoslavia, and Israel) were found to have frequent contact with their children. About 50 per cent of those interviewed had seen one of their children within the past 24 hours and about 75 per cent had seen one of their children within the past week. It seems likely, then, that geographic factors do not keep the majority of grandparents and grandchildren from seeing each other regularly. A sizable minority of grandparents, however, live far apart from their grandchildren [38].

Patterns of Relationships

Although all grandparents and grandchildren are unique persons, studies have shown some of the general ways in which they relate to each other. Age is one important factor. There are, of course, ethnic and class influences. If a social group holds grandparents as authority figures, then it is not likely that they will have free and easy relationships with their grandchildren [3]. On the other hand, if people believe that parents and/or teachers should assume responsibility for children, then grandparents can relate to them in other ways.

Styles of Grandparents. Interviews with 70 pairs of middle-class grandparents revealed a variety of styles in which the subjects saw themselves as operating. Five types of grandparents are described. The *formal* do what they think grandparents are supposed to do, showing interest in the children, giving them special treats, and baby-sitting occasionally, but being careful not to intrude on the parent by interfering and giving advice. This traditional type of grandparent was represented by a third of the men and women, with twice as many of them over 65 as under 65. the *fun seekers,* 29 per cent of the women and 24 per cent of the men, play with their grandchildren and expect mutual satisfaction from the relationship. Fun seekers were usually younger grandparents. The *surrogate parent,* who takes care of grandchildren while the mother works, was rare in this sample. Only 14 per cent of grandmothers, and no grandfathers, were surrogate parents. The *reservoir of family wisdom,* was another rare type, an authoritarian figure who dispenses special skills or resources. The *distant figure* is benevolent but remote, having little contact with grandchildren. Nineteen per cent of the grandmothers and 29 per cent of the grandfathers were distant figures. They were more often younger, rather than older [30].

Black Grandparents. A comparison of kin relationships in black and white families showed that the black families had more contact with kin, received more help from them in childrearing, and were more likely to have them living in the home. Although this study does not discuss grandparenting in particular, it does suggest that black grandparents exceed white grandparents in interacting with grandchildren and helping parents in child care [17].

Age Effects. Just as the age of the grandparent seems to make a difference in the interaction with children, so does the age of the child matter. Whereas fun seeking with or caring for a preschool child requires a grandparent strong of wind and limb, being responsible for an adolescent may involve less bodily activity and more mental and moral fiber.

From the standpoint of children, perceptions of grandparents have been found to differ from age to age. Three age groups of white, middle-class children were interviewed and questioned. All groups reported more contact with maternal grandparents than with paternal grandparents. Of the four grandparents, the maternal grandmother was most often chosen as favorite, especially by the four- and five year olds. (The fact that grown daughters are likely to maintain close relationships with mothers is consistent with closeness between maternal grandmother and grandchildren.) The youngest children saw their favorite grandparents almost entirely in terms of what the grandparents gave to them in the way of love and presents. The middle group (eight and nine year olds) gave some egocentric responses like those of the younger children, but also mentioned mutual enjoyments, such as playing games. In addition, the middle group told some of the good qualities of the grandparents. The oldest group (11- and 12 year olds) also gave egocentric reasons and did not mention

mutuality as much as did the middle group. There was some indication that the older children did not feel as close to the grandparents as did the youngest and middle groups [21].

A Special Case. Although studies such as these give insight into overall trends, individual cases show some of the potentialities of the relationship. One case in point is a grandmother-granddaughter pair, Jane and Jean. Jane resembles Jean, her grandmother, physically and psychologically. Both have brown eyes and brown hair, whereas Dora, the mother, has blue eyes and blonde hair. Jean has always been a radical and a rebel, whereas Dora is a conservative, married to Charles, an establishment man. As a young child, Jane often visited Jean. The two went on long trips together. They have always written letters to each other regularly. When Jane dropped out of college to join a counterculture community, Dora and Charles were so shocked and hurt that Jane felt she could not communicate with them. Having always dreamed about having such experiences herself, Jean was open to all that Jane wanted to tell her. Jane and Jean are as close as ever and Jean is Jane's only anchor to her family of orientation.

Emotional and Social Meanings

Of the 70 pairs of grandparents mentioned previously, the majority enjoyed those roles, but 36 per cent of the grandmothers and 29 per cent of the grandfathers felt uncomfortable or disappointed. Some found it hard to think of themselves as grandparents, probably disliking the implications of age. Some conflicted with the parents as to how the children should be reared. Others felt indifferent and guilty about their indifference [30].

In addition to being potential sources of mutual pleasure, love, and security, grandparents and children can help each other with developmental problems. Through their experiences with grandparents, children form concepts of what old

The Seder, a time when a Jewish family blends feelings of warmth, security, continuity of life, and renewal.

age is like and attitudes toward it [18]. In playing the role of grandchild, the child learns the grandparent role, in anticipation, and therefore prepares himself for later life, just as he also learns how to be a parent by being a son or daughter.

The **sense of integrity,** according to Erikson, is "the acceptance of one's one and only life cycle and of the people who have become significant to it as something that had to be and that, by necessity, permitted of no substitutions" [13, p. 139]. It means feeling good about the time, place, conditions, and conduct of your own life, a feeling of belonging to a particular part of the human order, and that the whole and the part are worthwhile. Some of the grandparents studied said that their grandchildren helped them to feel biological renewal and to see themselves as going on into the future. Quite often, grandfathers expressed satisfaction in the emotional fulfillment of being with grandchildren, doing for them, giving to them, and teaching them.

The continuity of life can be enhanced for grandchildren, too. Although the study of grandparents showed that only a few thought of themselves as reservoirs of family wisdom, grandchildren might see them as playing such a role more frequently. I (MSS) recall many satisfactions when my grandmother was my reservoir of wisdom. She was in her seventies when I was born and could, therefore, remember events that I studied in history classes. Most excitingly, she sometimes spoke of Ontario as *Upper Canada,* because she could remember Confederation, when Canada became a nation. Grandma even provided a link with England, because she remembered her own mother going back to her home in Devon to visit my grandmother's grandmother. These reminiscences gave me a great feeling of belonging in the history of my family and my country when I was around ten years old.

IN-LAW RELATIONSHIPS

In-laws are widely recognized as potential sources of trouble. Many non-Western societies take care of the mother-in-law problem by *mother-in-law avoidance,* a requirement that a man keep from meeting his mother-in-law. In traditional Indian families, in-law conflicts are avoided by having the bride guided and taught by the mother-in-law. The bride must learn to cook, keep house, and generally behave in the manner of the groom's family. The daughter-in-law must also show respect to the father-in-law and older brothers-in-law by careful avoidance behavior. According to the family, it may be by not being seen at all, by covering the face, or by covering the head. When one of my (MSS) daughters was ill in an Indian village home, she judged the seriousness of her condition by the fact that the wife of the middle son, while caring for her, did not realize that her sari had slipped off her head in the presence of Older Brother.

In modern Western societies, such as in North America, there are no firm rules for behavior with in-laws. We have mother-in-law jokes that depict her as troublemaker. Indeed, studies of in-laws have shown mothers-in-law to be the most difficult of all in-laws [25, p. 228; 11, p. 117]. The sister-in-law was consistently revealed as the second most difficult. Interestingly, in Duvall's study, most of the women who were judged difficult as mothers-in-law were not considered troublesome grand-mothers, since only 7 of the 1,337 respondents mentioned grandparents as being difficult, whereas 491 named mothers-in-law. This finding points up the fact that in-law relationships differ at different times in the marital career of the couple.

Premarital Stage

"I've just got a new son-in-law, if they ever get married." So said a middle-aged man in a recent cartoon. With living together more frequently preceding marriage, the term *son-out-law* might be considered, except for the fact that most cohabiting couples probably do not consider themselves committed to marriage. Of the 86 Cornell University women queried about the relationship, 60 per cent considered that cohabitation should be based initially on a strong, affectionate, and exclusive dating relationship. Only 8 per cent thought that tentative engagement was neces-sary. To the cohabiting students, parents were a major problem area. The majority had tried to conceal their relationships from their parents, for fear of disapproval. About half thought that their parents did not know of their cohabitation, whereas the others thought they might know. The young man's parents were more likely to know than were the young woman's. The cohabiting couple were likely to feel guilt and sadness at possibly hurting their parents and being unable to share with them [27]. It seems likely that as cohabitation becomes more usual, it will be more acceptable to parents. Parents will be at a loss for a while to know how to behave as pre-in-laws or out-laws or whatever they may be called, since there are at present no such roles in our society. Although we cannot provide research data, I (MSS) can say from experi-ence that when middle-aged parents get together with their close friends, a topic of conversation is how to feel, think, and act in regard to one's cohabiting children.

Engagement is the traditional time for in-law relationships to get started, and established customs are available to guide the participants. The form may vary from an elaborate engagement party to simply telling the news, but parental approval of the match is a positive support. For many couples, engagement is the time for getting to know one another's family of orientation and much of the kin network. Although the broad outlines of in-law roles are sketched, much of each relationship has to be worked out between the people involved. The more mixed the match, the more communication will be necessary for creating satisfying interaction.

Early Marriage

Although Western culture generally holds the husband-wife relationship as being of primary importance, most people believe that a young couple has duties to parents-in-law. In the Minnesota study of three generations, only 14 per cent of the young married couples disagreed with the statement, "A young couple has a real responsibility for keeping in touch with parents-in-law" [19, p. 60]. The two generations usually help each other, the parent generation giving more [8, 19].

Age of Couple. The age of the bride was found to be related to the amount of in-law difficulty reported by young couples [25]. Of 544 women, excellent adjustment to in-laws was reported by 45 per cent of those who married between 17 and 19, and by 63 per cent of those married at 24 or older. This finding fits with the fact that the establishment of adult relationships with parents is a task of the late teens and early twenties. The younger the married couples, the more they would be engaged in the adolescent process of becoming independent financially and emotionally. Parent-adolescent problems would become in-law problems as well.

The Mother-in-Law Problem. Since the women complained more about mothers-in-law than did the men in Duvall's study, the husband's mother is implicated as the greatest troublemaker of all in-laws. Or could it be that the daughter-in-law is the problem? It is more likely that each contributes to the conflict. Women have more at stake than men in homemaking and childrearing. The husband's mother must give over the product of her parent-child career to a young, inexperienced woman who is likely to be less competent than herself. The younger the bride, the less competent she will seem, and the more she might learn and improve through advice and supervision. The young wife probably is not very good at homemaking and knows it. She may feel that she has to compete with her mother-in-law in homemaking and for her husband's esteem. Another factor may be that homemaking standards and techniques have changed since the time when the parents were first married.

Although each case is unique, some general principles often hold. The situation may be eased by making real attempts to communicate (see Chapter 3) and by showing respect through gaining knowledge of the other person as an individual. Since self-esteem is basic to being able to ask for help, to give and accept help, and to share a loved one, both the young woman and older woman would profit from facing problems of self-esteem. The young husband usually plays a crucial role in conflicts between his two important women. To make both feel loved and esteemed is ideal. To choose the wife, if choice is necessary, is to solidify the pair relationship and to give it primary importance. If the young husband is extremely attached to his mother and dependent on her, then his wife and his mother are very likely to have trouble with each other. On the other hand, if the young couple live far away from their parents, many of the troublesome conflicts will never occur. At the same time, mutual aid and loving contacts will also be reduced.

The Middle Years

When a couple become parents, then in-law relationships involve relations with their children's grandparents. As the generation in the middle, the parents strongly influence the ways in which children and grandparents can relate to each other. Parents largely control the contacts that the younger and older generations have and they interpret them to each other. If Mother and Mother-In-Law are still locked in competition to be most esteemed by Father, then Mother is likely to set the stage for her children to dislike Paternal Grandmother. Happily, though, the most usual course of events seems to be for parents to accept the help and love that grandparents offer in this stage of life and to work out ways of getting along together. The mother has learned how to keep house and has developed her own style of homemaking, community activities, and perhaps a job. The father has had some experience and hopefully some success in his vocation. Some couple solidarity and nuclear family identity are established. Thus, many of the trouble spots of early marriage have disappeared, as far as in-law relationships are concerned.

When children reach adolescence, the parent couple often feel squeezed between the demands of their children and their parents. The financial cost of children goes up astronomically at this point, and grandparents may need support, too. Emotional demands may be even greater than economic, since the normal struggles of adolescents are fraught with difficulty for parents, whereas the adjustments required by aging grandparents may place additional burdens upon the parent generation.

In cultures where the grandparent generation retains strong authority in the family, the situation is, of course, quite different. In the extended family, the parent generation continues to defer to the elder generation and the mother-in-law can still direct the daughter-in-law, even when she is the mother of adolescent children. The middle-aged husband may quite properly continue to esteem his mother above all women.

OTHER KIN

Since **kin** usually means all the relatives other than the nuclear family in which a person is living, we have already discussed some of the kin, for some nuclear members become kin. When a child grows up, leaves his family of orientation, and forms his family of procreation, then his parents may become "relatives" or kin to him, although he remains a child to them. He and his siblings are adult kin to each other.

Basic Family Units

The importance of kin varies inversely with the importance of marriage, for the society and for the individual. Where the marriage relationship is considered to be of primary significance, then kin relationships are not so important[16]. However, even in a society that stresses marriage, such as middle-class America, kin usually provide basic family relationships for those who have not married and those who are widowed or divorced. Sibling relationships are especially strong among older, unmarried people, with sister-sister ties being the strongest. Cousins, aunts, uncles, nieces, and nephews also serve as sources of help, love, and security for people who are not in nuclear units.

Mutual Aid

Kin might be likened to a savings account, something to fall back on when the more usual arrangements or resources fail. In poor countries and in economically deprived ethnic groups, kin are often more important than among financially prosperous people. As mentioned previously, black Americans generally have more kin interaction and mutual helping than do white Americans. A prevalent pattern in India is that kin have privileges and responsibilities to each other that seem incredible to a Westerner. For example, young Indian friends of ours live in a one-bedroom apartment with their two children. Whenever either set of grandparents wishes, they come and stay for two or three months. Grown siblings also visit freely.

Belongingness and the Sense of Integrity

An interesting kin behavior pattern is the family reunion. In this sense, the family is the large, ongoing entity that really does have cycles. (See page 17 for a distinction between cycles and careers.) Many families have reunions at weddings, anniversaries, and funerals. My (MSS) parents recently celebrated their sixtieth wedding anniversary, and 150 to 200 people came to greet them. Second and third cousins drove 200 miles to the event. Some families have formalized family reunions that are exactly that. Figure 11-2 illustrates such a reunion. Most large family groups, the kind that have reunions, boast of at least one family historian, who gathers vital information, records it, saves clippings and photographs, and serves as a clearinghouse for kin communications.

Family reunions and family historians promote emotional security and the sense of integrity in all the members. Just as my (MSS) grandmother's true family stories did for me as a child, so does kin solidarity give individuals a feeling of belonging to present, past, and future.

QUASI-KIN

"You are just like a sister to me!" "I feel as though you were my own parents." "A brother couldn't have done more." Most of us have such experiences. In our family,

38 Kinfolk Hire Bus For Visit

LANSING, MICH.–(AP)–The 38 Michigan members of the Harr clan believe the energy crisis may keep them from driving to Wisconsin for their family Christmas dinner. So they've chartered a bus.

The Lansing branch of the family will be lead by Edwin Harr, in his 60s, when they board the bus next Saturday morning for the trip to the home of his daughter, Edna Huggett, and her husband, James, in Marshall, Wisconsin.

"The men are real happy about not having to drive. Everybody's real tickled about it. We can all sing and talk together. It wouldn't be as close if we took separate cars," said Doris Feldpausch about the trip to her sister's.

The charter with Indian Trails Bus Co. will cost $520, or $13.68 per person, Mrs. Feldpausch said.

The bus will leave Dewitt, just north of here, early Saturday morning to start the 600-mile trek. The family is to arrive at the Huggetts just in time for dinner.

FIGURE 11-2   The family reunion is still very much alive.

Source: Providence Evening Bulletin. December 18, 1973.

there are three biological daughters, plus an Indian daughter and a fourth American daughter. People use kinship terms to express love and closeness to those who are not biologically related but to whom they are attached.

Fictive Kin

Sociologists have studied the use of kinship terms in addressing nonrelatives. *Fictive kin term* is what they call it [20]. Fictive kin terms have been noted in Japan, Latin America, India, and the United States. It seems likely that they are used in most societies. In interviews with 115 American wives, 70 per cent reported that they or members of their family used fictive kin terms, some with only one or two people, some with a great many. *Uncle* and *aunt* were the most frequently used. More female than male terms were used. About 75 per cent of fictive kin were close family friends. Often the parents of the user were the ones who suggested the term, and children were the most frequent users. Fictive kin probably substitute somewhat for real kin or for kin living far away. Use of the terms also seems to strengthen friendships.

Sororities, Fraternities, and Fraternal Orders. Quasi-sibling relationships are the core of sororities, fraternities, and fraternal orders. Members call themselves and others brothers and sisters. They have duties and responsibilities to each other, such as offering aid for studies or business, reflecting glory upon the group through personal achievements, refraining from disgraceful behavior that would bring shame to the group, and contributing to the financial support of the group. Sororities and fraternities have also regulated mate selection for their members [36].

Utopian and Religious Societies, Communes, and Others

Quasi-family describes many of the organizations in which unrelated individuals live, work, and love in close relationships. Family terms are often used. A commune may be "a family" and the leader a father or a mother to the group. In the Utopian societies of the past, the leader was often a strong, authoritarian man. Nuns are *sisters,* and heads of convents or orders are *mothers.* The *father,* of course, is God.

An even looser, more comprehensive use of fictive kin terms occurs among oppressed and/or militant people who feel kinship through devotion to a cause. Blacks may call one another *brother* and *sister* in order to express racial solidarity. Women call each other *sister* in the context of women's liberation.

SUMMARY

Age and position differences showed firstborns as more bossy and exercising more power, whereas secondborns did more pleading, whining, and harassing. Boys used more physical means, whereas girls used more symbolic means.

As playmates and colleagues, siblings have good times together. Preference in friends is affected by experiences with siblings. Adult siblings, especially sisters, often turn to each other in times of stress. Siblings teach each other and learn from one another. Firstborn girls are likely to be good teachers and to help other children. Sex-role learning and marital choice are related to ordinal position and composition of the family. Siblings protect and care for younger siblings, who depend upon them. Playing a protector role often influences children later in their social and family behavior. Sibling interaction affects an individual's self-concept in terms of self-esteem, locus of control, and gender identity. Other results include orientation to family living, skills and competencies, and choice of occupation.

Four-generation families are now common in North America. Young parents and their children do not ordinarily live with the grandparents, but the various generations usually keep in touch. Types of grandparents show considerable variation including the formal, fun seekers, surrogate parents, reservoirs of family wisdom, and distant figures. Black grandparents help more with care of grandchildren than white grandparents. From their interaction, grandchildren may prepare themselves by anticipating roles in later life, whereas grandparents may develop the sense of integrity.

Female in-laws cause more trouble than males, since the mother-in-law, especially the paternal one, ranks first and the sister-in-law second as sources of difficulty. Early marriage is the time when in-law problems loom largest, because of the young couple's establishing new relationships and their immaturity. If conflicts are solved at this stage, the middle years are likely to be easier. Grandparents are usually appreciated by parents.

Kin are very important in cultures where the conjugal bond is not emphasized, and, in North America, to persons without partners. Kin usually provide aid in cultures and situations of stress and deprivation. Belongingness and the sense of integrity are enhanced by kin gatherings, family history, and symbols of family continuity. Kin can be secured by means other than biological connections. Quasi-kin include those referred to as "just like" kin, adopted kin, those called by kin names, members of organizations that use kin names, and devotees to a cause who express solidarity through kin terms.

REFERENCES

1. Adler, Alfred. *Understanding human nature.* New York: Premier, 1959.
2. Apoko, Anna. At home in the village: Growing up in Acholi. In Lorene Fox (ed.). *East African childhood.* New York: Oxford U.P., 1967.
3. Apple, Dorian. The social structure of grandparenthood. *American Anthropologist,* 1956, **58,** 656–663.
4. Bigner, Jerry J. Second borns' discrimination of sibling role concepts. *Developmental Psychology,* 1974, **10,** 564–573.
5. Bossard, James H. S. and Eleanor S. Boll. *The large family system.* Philadelphia: U. of Pa., 1956.
6. Boyd, Rosamonde R. The valued grandparent: A changing social role. In Wilma Donahue, et al. (eds.). *Living in the multigenerational family.* Ann Arbor, Mich.: Institute of Gerontology, 1969.
7. Cicirelli, Victor G. The effect of sibling relationship on concept learning of young children by child-teachers. *Child Development,* 1972, **43,** 282–287.
7a. Cicirelli, Victor G. Relationship of sibling structure and interaction to younger sib's conceptual style. *Journal of Genetic Psychology,* 1974, **125,** 37–49.
8. Clark, Alma B. and Jean Warren. *Economic contributions made to newly married couples by their parents.* Cornell Agriculture Experiment Station Memoir 382, 1963.
9. Collard, Roberta R. Social play and play responses of firstborn and laterborn infants in an unfamiliar situation. *Child Development,* 1968, **39,** 325–334.
10. DeFee, John F. and Philip Himelstein. Children's fear in a dental situation as a function of birth order. *Journal of Genetic Psychology,* 1969, **115,** 253–255.
11. Duvall, Evelyn. *In-laws, pro and con.* New York: Association Press, 1954.
12. Elder, Joanne F. Family patterns and adolescent girls in South India and the United States. Unpublished M. A. thesis. Oberlin, Ohio: Oberlin College, 1955.
13. Erikson, Erik H. *Identity, youth and crisis.* New York: Norton, 1968.

14. Farber, Bernard. Family organization and crisis: Maintenance of integration in families. *Monographs of the Society for Research in Child Development,* 1960, **25.**

15. Farber, Bernard. Interaction with retarded siblings and life goals of children. *Marriage and Family Living,* 1963, **25,** 96–98.

16. Gibson, Geoffrey. Kin family network: Overheralded structure in past conceptualizations of family functioning. *Journal of Marriage and the Family,* 1972, **34,** 13–23.

17. Hays, William C. and Charles H. Mindel. Extended kinship relations in black and white families. *Journal of Marriage and the Family,* 1973, **35,** 51–57.

18. Hickey, Tom, Louise A. Hickey, and Richard Kalish. Children's perceptions of the elderly. *Journal of Genetic Psychology,* 1968, **112,** 227–235.

19. Hill, Reuben. *Family development in three generations.* Cambridge, Mass.: Schenkman, 1970.

20. Ibsen, Charles A. and Patricia Klobus. Fictive kin term use and social relationships: Alternative interpretations. *Journal of Marriage and the Family,* 1972, **34,** 615–620.

21. Kahana, Boas and Eva Kahana. Grandparenthood from the perspective of the developing grandchild. *Developmental Psychology,* 1970, **3,** 98–105.

22. Koch, Helen. The relation in young children between characteristics of their playmates and certain attributes of their siblings. *Child Development,* 1957, **28,** 173–202.

23. Koch, Helen. The relation of certain formal attributes of siblings to attitudes held toward each other and toward their parents. *Monographs of the Society for Research in Child Development,* 1960, **25:** 4.

24. Landers, Daniel M. and Rainer Martens. The influence of birth order and situational stress on motor performance. *Psychonomic Science,* 1971, **24,** 165–167.

25. Landis, Judson T. and Mary G. Landis. *Building a successful marriage,* (5th ed.). Englewood Cliffs, N.J.: Prentice-Hall, 1968.

26. Lunneborg, Patricia W. Birth order and sex of sibling effects on intellectual abilities. *Journal of Consulting and Clinical Psychology,* 1971, **37,** 445.

27. Macklin, Eleanor. Heterosexual cohabitation among unmarried college students. *Family Coordinator,* 1972, **21,** 463–472.

28. Mealiea, Wallace D. and Frank H. Farley. The relationship between ordinal position in females and the expression of extreme fear. *Journal of Social Psychology,* 1973, **90,** 333–334.

29. Metropolitan Life Insurance Company. This age of grandparents. *Statistical Bulletin,* 1972, **53** (September), 8–10.

30. Neugarten, Bernice L. and Karol K. Weinstein. The changing American grandparent. *Journal of Marriage and the Family,* 1964, **26,** 199–204.

31. Olive, Helen. Sibling resemblances in divergent thinking. *Journal of Genetic Psychology,* 1972, **120,** 155–162.

32. Rosenberg, Benjamin G. and Brian Sutton-Smith. Sibling age spacing effects upon cognition. *Developmental Psychology,* 1969, **1,** 661–668.

33. Rosenberg, George S. and Donald F. Anspach. Sibling solidarity in the working class. *Journal of Marriage and the Family,* 1973, **35,** 108–113.

34. Schachter, Stanley. *The psychology of affiliation.* Stanford, Calif.: Stanford U.P., 1959.

35. Schooler, Carmi. Birth order effects: Not here, not now. *Psychological Bulletin,* 1972, **78,** 161–175.

36. Scott, John F. Sororities and the husband game. *Trans-Action,* 1965 (September–October), 10–14.

37. Sears, Robert R. Relation of early socialization experiences to self-concepts and gender role in middle childhood. *Child Development,* 1970, **41,** 265–289.
38. Shanas, Ethel. Family-kin networks and aging in cross-cultural perspective. *Journal of Marriage and the Family,* 1973, **35,** 505–511.
39. Shanas, Ethel, Peter Townsend, Dorothy Wedderburn, Henning Friis, Paul Milhhoj, and J. Stehouwer. *Older people in three industrial societies.* New York: Atherton, 1968.
40. Staub, Ervin. The use of role playing and induction in children's learning of helping behavior. *Child Development,* 1971, **42,** 805–806.
41. Sutton-Smith, Brian and Benjamin G. Rosenberg. Sex differences in the longitudinal prediction of adult personality. Paper presented at meetings of the Society for Research in Child Development, Philadelphia, 1973.
42. Sutton-Smith, Brian and Benjamin G. Rosenberg. *The sibling.* New York: Holt, 1970.
43. Troll, Lillian E. The family of later life: A decade review. *Journal of Marriage and the Family,* 1971, **33,** 263–290.
44. *United Nations Demographic Yearbook.* New York: United Nations Publishing Service, 1972.
45. Whiting, Beatrice B. Folk wisdom and child rearing. *Merrill-Palmer Quarterly,* 1974, **20,** 9–19.
46. Wohlford, Paul, John W. Santrock, Stephen Berger, and David Liberman. Older brothers' influence on sex-typed, aggressive, and dependent behavior in father-absent children. *Developmental Psychology,* 1971, **4,** 124–134.

Homemaking, in a broad sense, is the subject of Part IV. In providing for the needs of its members, a family works, sets goals, plans, and solves problems. Caring for one another is an expression of love. Communication is an essential process in carrying on the work and business of the group. Concepts of gender roles and consequent freedoms and restrictions are highly significant to the ways in which work is assigned and done. The family even plans its own

PART four

a family is based on home

structure and functions. In deciding whether and when to have a child and subsequent children, a couple carries on family management in one of its most crucial areas. At the time of life when persons are soon to form partnerships and create new families, the topics of health, finances, and law have special significance. The solving of personal and family crises is a recurrent demand, for which knowledge and preparation are helpful. Homemaking includes a mass of detailed skills and actions, along with small and large goals and plans. Each family is continually creating, making its own home. Some of its most creative processes are described here, although detailed directions for homemaking are too voluminous to include. The human liberation movement, influential in almost all parts of the world, is presently affecting relationships between homemaking and gender roles.

CHAPTER 12
dOMESTIC EXECUTIVES

The incident of a conversation between an effective manager and a mediocre one makes a good beginning for a chapter on management. This is a true story, but, of course, it is disguised.

THE CASE OF CAROL, DANNY, ANITA, AND JAY

"You're so lucky to be able to go to Europe for the summer! I wish something nice like that would happen to our family, but Jay and I will never be able to afford the things you and Danny have," Anita complained.

"*We* made it happen," Carol explained. "Danny and I aren't any luckier than you and Jay. Luck has nothing to do with our trip this summer. We've been planning it for a long time and we had to cut a lot of corners to save enough money for a big trip."

"Well, I don't know how you do it, unless you inherited some money or won a lottery. Jay and Danny have the same kind of jobs and what you and I earn doesn't amount to much."

Carol could have gone on to explain that she and Danny gave a great deal of thought to deciding what they most wanted to do and figuring out the most effective ways of reaching their goals. Even before they married, both were skilled in getting the most for their money and allocating their time to the tasks that really had to be done, learning new skills that would help them to achieve what they wanted to do. Throughout his high school days, Danny was in demand as an odd-job man because he was such a satisfactory worker. He earned enough money for his clothes, books,

303

and recreation, and saved some for college. Carol, as a teen-ager, earned money from baby-sitting. When they married, they used their personal budget records to set up a family budget. Plans were made for the use of all earnings, and money was set aside for travel.

With little previous experience in earning and budgeting, Anita and Jay decided after they were married to use Jay's earnings to live on and Anita's for emergencies and fun. A surprising number of emergencies occurred. The Fun-Fund was rarely large enough to meet the demands on it. The Fun-Fund never grew big enough to cover the costs of a trip to Europe. More serious, however, was their constant anxiety over not having enough money and Anita's envy of friends who seemed to have more money than they did.

Carol and Danny *were* lucky in having childhood experiences that taught them how to be effective managers. Anita and Jay were unfortunate in that they knew so little about management when they were married and that they learned practically

nothing about it afterwards. However, most of Anita's and Jay's adult years are still ahead of them. They could learn to think and talk with each other about what is most important, least important, and in between (their values). Then they could set goals that reflected what they knew to be important. The goals would also be realistic ones that could be reached by effective use of the resources available to them. Suppose that Anita and Jay communicate honestly with each other and agree that they place a high value on gaining new experiences through travel. They might consider a trip to Europe as a goal, but upon figuring out what it would cost and how long it would take them to save enough money for the trip, they might set a goal that would be more attainable, such as a trip to Niagara Falls. Then they would have to use their resources in order to take a satisfying trip to Europe or Niagara Falls. They must save money. How much? Can they get time off from their jobs? Should they use a tent some nights, instead of motels? If they plan well ahead, could they get a charter flight or a package deal at a hotel? After they arrive, what shall they see and do? How much will it cost? How can they get the most interesting experiences for their money?

If Anita and Jay find information on all these questions and then communicate fully about their findings, thoughts, wishes, and feelings, they can make some wise decisions that will help them reach their goals. In addition to the rewards of successful management, they will reap benefits in their relationship to each other. Their partnership will be strengthened from communicating, solving problems together, and enjoying the results of their joint efforts. Pair bonds grow. They feel that they love each other more.

A CONCEPT OF MANAGEMENT

Management is knowing where one is going and using some effective means of getting there. Very often, a person needs to think about her values, about what is important, and what directions she wants her life to take. Goals are set in accordance with the values held, some goals taking precedence over others. Ways and means of reaching the goals are explored, chosen, and employed.

Management and relationships are two sides of the coin of family living. No matter what type of family structure is involved, when people live together they are involved with some sort of homemaking that uses time, effort, and money or things to produce some sort of creature comforts. Together, the family members have a variety of resources that can be put into homemaking. (In homemaking, we include house-keeping and everything else that makes a home a comfortable, comforting place.) Resources are also put into familymaking, which means much more than bearing children and bringing them up. Under familymaking, we include the supports for personal development of all members and for solidarity of the family group.

In the study of family management, four types of variables are used: *Situational,* the available physical and social objects that can satisfy or constrain needs, such as income, ages and numbers of members, and productive capacities; *affective,* the preferences, beliefs, values, and psychic needs; *decision making,* the way in which members control events; *welfare,* the level of family functioning that results from the interaction of the first three types of variables and in turn influences them, level of living, financial security, health, and educational status [6].

The Focus of Management

The processes of management are carried out by individuals. A person manages her own affairs. At the same time, she may also take part in managing the affairs of the lifetime family of which she is a member. In addition, she may manage some of the business of the lineage family. For example, during one day, Mrs. Bonaventura took some money out of her regular savings account and put it into a high interest account, planned the coming week's meals around the specials listed in the paper, and gave her daughter a tablecloth that her own mother had monogrammed.

A person may manage as an individual or as a member of a group that is working together. In some ways, it is easier to function alone but in other ways it is more satisfying to manage as a member of a team. Discussion is often helpful in clarifying values, setting goals, and organizing resources. As for carrying out actual work, two or three pairs of hands will do it faster than one.

THE HOMEMAKER

In cultures where sex roles and position-related roles are sharply defined, responsibility for home management is also made clear. In many places, women must cook, wash, clean, and care for children, whereas men must earn money or grow and hunt food. The most common arrangement is for the wife-mother to organize and direct most of the production and consumption that occur in the home. She, then, would be the home manager.

The home manager is also an individual with some private, personal goals, resources, and problems. Herein lies the source of many family conflicts and partner disagreements. Sometimes the individual's wishes and resources dovetail perfectly with the problems and goals of the family group. Father just loves refinishing old furniture and the family needs a dining table. Mother wants to try her new Chinese cookbook, and the children are eager to learn more about the Chinese way of life. But at other times, one person wants something that does not fit with what looks to be good for the family in general. It could happen to anyone. Gigi wants the car in order to take her friends to the concert, but the rest of the family needs it for a trip to the beach. Rex has made an elaborate block structure in the living room and he wants it left standing for a few days. Very often, however, the wife experiences some conflicts in how she would like to manage as an individual and how she thinks that she should manage as a homemaker. She would like to be better dressed, more educated, to have more time to herself, perhaps with the larger goal of gaining more self-esteem and self-confidence. She also wants to achieve family goals. If she diverts some money from food to a new outfit for herself, she may diminish nutrition, health, and mealtime pleasure. Before the days of women's liberation, many women tried to find total personal fulfillment in working toward family goals. I (MSS) remember one such woman who said, "Even when I am peeling a potato, I feel happy because I think of the larger contribution I am making to my family."

In the North American atmosphere of today, most young women and men think that they have rights as individuals within the family, and that good management includes balancing personal and group needs and goals. Homemaking and home management are thus more likely to be shared by a couple than to be the job of the woman only. They share the goal-setting and planning, as well as the action and work necessary for carrying out the plans. She tells what she wants for *herself*. So does he. They try to fit both sets of personal goals into what they see as family goals. It's an old story that behind every successful man stands a helpful woman. A modern sequel is that today, many successful women credit their husbands with giving them the respect and support that enabled them to do a personal job along with a family job. We are not maintaining that housework is shared equally by most husbands and wives. The study quoted on page 204 shows that it is not. We believe, however, that both men and women are increasingly aware that women, as well as men, need personal fulfillment in addition to fulfillment as homemakers.

Long before becoming a partner or a parent, the individual **manages.** Far-reaching, long-term decisions are made about education, occupation, and whom and when to marry. The early planning of life careers has effects that can be seen throughout life, such as greater economic achievement of those who are better educated, marry later, and have fewer children [4, pp. 331–332]. Management and work skills, too, are begun early.

Everyone has to do something about managing her own money, health, nutrition, clothing, and living quarters. The family of orientation teaches these skills to its children. Schools and other social systems also contribute. When two people become a couple, they often find that their individual management skills are not sufficient. Differences in values and goals may cause conflicts between them. Quarrels may arise over who should do various tasks and how work should be done. Communication and love are both necessary for solving such problems. Not only does each person have to find out what the other feels and thinks, he also has to care about those feelings and thoughts and to respect the person who has them. Care and respect are basic to being willing to work at unpleasant tasks and to give up some of one's personal goals.

One aspect of management is the seeking and using of new information. As the chapter on health shows, for instance, nutrition research frequently yields new information. All family members benefit when the homemaker keeps up-to-date in nutrition knowledge and puts the new findings to work in planning, buying, and preparing food. Homemakers, both male and female, need continuing education. As they learn, they develop new goals and new plans for reaching them.

Since the development and maintenance of loving families is our primary interest, much of the section is concerned with the efforts of small family groups to manage themselves. However, even when all group members participate to the extent of their abilities and resources, some members contribute more than others. In the majority of North American families, as in the rest of the world, the wife-mother is the leader in home management, spending more of her time and energy in this activity than any other family member. Most homemaking decisions and actions are delegated to her, or fall to her by default. Much as liberationists would like to see housework and management shared equally between the sexes, such is not the case in other than a few exceptional families. More equal participation in management would surely facilitate more equal distribution of work loads.

Managing

Management questions that have to be answered are of three main types: what the group wants to achieve, or *goals;* what methods or strategies will be used in trying to achieve the goals, or *problem-solving;* how satisfactory were the solutions used in reaching the goals, or *evaluation.* Many goals require little or no discussion because they are imbedded in the family's value systems, strongly established, and taken for granted. For instance, in many families, there is no disagreement over wanting community respect and seeing a neat front yard or entranceway as a goal connected with respectability. When goals are mutually exclusive, however, priorities have to be established. Is it more important to have the house look acceptable to the neighbors by having it painted or to have a vacation?

When goals of individuals conflict, then the group may try to define a more comprehensive goal that will ease the problem of priorities. Father wants to take a job in another part of the country. The children want to stay where their friends live. Mother does not want to leave her job. Can they identify an overall family goal that will make it possible to solve the problem?

When goals are clear, plans for reaching them have to be made. The group examines ways of using what they have in order to get what they want. A family's resources include all the material things they own, or are available to them: their time, energy, knowledge, skills, and strengths. A good solution to a problem means not only that the action would achieve the goal but also that the family members commit themselves to the action. As an example, the goal may be a neat, clean house, serving the larger goals of looking acceptable to the neighbors and being pleasant and well organized for the family. The problem is that the house is dirty and untidy. The group considers solutions that include various members collecting trash, repairing steps, painting, scrubbing, putting up shelves, and buying furnishings. Decisions are made as to who shall do what. All go about their agreed-upon tasks and finish them. The step of evaluating is now easy. It takes little effort to decide that the goal was reached. Suppose, though, that one or more members did not really think it was a good idea to do all that work to clean up the house. They agreed

verbally because they felt pressured or because they thought that others would agree with them on some other issue if they acquiesced now. They are not committed to the decision. They do not pick up the trash or wash the windows, even though they agreed to do so. Then another person sees them slacking on their jobs and feels that he, therefore, does not have to do what he promised to do. This sort of thing happens when the solution to the problem does not involve a real commitment to action on the part of all members.

Planning Over Time. *Satisfaction now* has to be weighed against possible greater benefits to be gained by waiting. Hill [4, p. 321] speaks of "family life cycle management" as being the timing of changes in the various careers that contribute to the family's life style. Examples of such changes are taking a new job, moving, having a baby, and sending a child to college. Effective management means timing changes in such a way that they bring maximum benefit over the family's life span. The question of the father's new job, mentioned previously could be considered in these terms, as well as in terms of individual wishes.

Real differences were found in a series of studies contrasting decision-making of normal and abnormal families [10]. The abnormal group consisted of families with a child who had been diagnosed as schizophrenic, delinquent, or aggressive, acting out. The child in question and his parents were tested in making decisions as a group. Families in the control group had no history of emotional or criminal problems or receiving psychotherapy and were considered normal by the person referring them. The normal families showed more agreement prior to discussion, took less time in arriving at group decisions, and made decisions that better fulfilled the choices of the individuals in them. Such studies do not tell whether poor decision-making leads to family problems or whether family problems cause poor decision-making. Most likely there is a reciprocal effect. A similar study that used father-mother-son triads showed that the normal families exceeded the abnormal families in father-son agreement, maternal influence, and mothers' tendency to overrate her husband and underrate herself [10]. Another investigator showed that in normal family triads, the mother and father spontaneously agreed more frequently than in abnormal family triads [9].

The relation of family decision-making style to psychological health of individuals has been analyzed in forty three-person families consisting of wife, husband, and a son or daughter between the age of fourteen and eighteen [8]. Each family played a decision-making game designed for its socioeconomic status, either middle class or working class. Persons scoring high in a test of self-actualization (thought to indicate psychological health) were more often in families that placed more emphasis on human relations and growth than upon tasks. These families, also, seemed to make decisions without a leader. In the contrast families, who placed more emphasis on getting the "right" answer, the husband exercised much power over the wife but relatively little control over the children. In the first families, wives were often employed and the educational level of husbands and wives were high; in the second families, wives were seldom employed and their educational levels were lower.

The Importance of Communication and Decision Making

Communication is basic to the sharing of family management, since participants will have to do so in order to make joint decisions as to what their problems are, what they wish to achieve, and how they will go about solving and acting.

As we have pointed out in previous chapters, as two people fall in love and define themselves as a couple, they tell each other much about their interests, goals, and beliefs. Agreements on values draw them together as a pair. At this point in the development of the love career, a beginning, perhaps unintentional, is made in sharing family management. When a couple goes through a formal engagement, impetus is given to management through planning, deciding, and preparing all sorts of home furnishings and arrangements, talking and learning about budgets and legal arrangements, learning homemaking skills in anticipation of new roles, discussing whether and when to have children, planning conception control, having physical examinations and discussing their implications, planning the wedding, and discussing occupational careers for both. Most of this type of planning and anticipatory management may also be done by couples who marry without formal engagement, although it does take time, and a hasty marriage will not have the benefit of previous communication on a variety of important topics. And it may be that before marriage, the setting up of a good communication system is more important for future family management than are the actual solutions chosen. Chapter 3 deals with communication in detail.

Making Decisions Effectively

When faced with making a decision, the group considers all the information that the members can produce, each person trying to express himself in such a way that the others can understand exactly what he means. Every member also is responsible for listening carefully and asking questions when he does not understand. They continue to express, listen, and question as they think of various courses of action, and the probable results of each. The process goes on as they agree upon the course of action. This type of family communication has been called *supportive,* in contrast to *defensive,* when participants are not open to each other. Supportive family communication systems are most likely to produce constructive decisions and actions and to promote positive social behavior in children [1].

Influences on Management: Love and Power

As the examples of research on decision-making have suggested, the motivation and emotional interactions of family members are important influences on the management process. Here we consider the far-reaching effects of love and power.

Love. All of the elements of love will contribute to democratic family management, in which children as well as parents are involved. The bonds of *attachment* supply motivation, in making individuals want to be with the group and to care for its members. Providing *care* of all sorts is one of the functions of management. *Respect* for others means that each member regards each other member as a worthwhile individual, with his own special needs, talents, and contributions to make. If each member is respected, then he gets a chance to voice his ideas while others listen and respond, trying to accommodate to them. Even an infant is listened to in the sense that the others try to interpret his behavior and adjust family life to the baby's requirements. *Knowledge* of one another, which each tries to achieve, contributes to setting up family goals that will serve all, and to recognizing the talents and potentials of each person in order to develop and use these resources.

Power. When one person is more able than others to promote the particular solution he favors, he is *dominant.* When he dominates more often than others, he has greater power. *Authority* is legitimate power, the power held by a person when the group believes that he holds power and that it is right for him to hold it. Thus, one individual may dominate group decisions occasionally or habitually.

The power situation in one family may be quite different from that in another. In the same family, the dominance patterns change over time in both the long run and the short run.

The individual characteristics and resources of each member will combine with those of others and with many other factors to produce a unique power pattern in each family. However, certain general conclusions about power patterns can be drawn from research. For example, age of child and social class differentiated between dominance patterns in 44 families consisting of mother, father, and son of either 11 or 16 years of age [5]. The lower-class and middle-class families were not different in size, child's IQ, father's age, mother's age, family religion, and birth order of participating child. The individuals first filled out a questionnaire about their families and then, as family groups, filled it out again so as to represent the family's opinion. These data yielded scores of dominance, interruption, disagreement, and talking time. In summary, the power pattern was similar in both classes when the son was younger, with relatively equal parents, both more powerful than the son. With an adolescent son, the middle-class father retained his dominant status but the mother became more nearly equal with the son, whereas in the lower class, the common pattern was egalitarian between father, mother, and son.

If power relationships were considered in families with several children, the results would be even more complicated than those stated in the paragraph above. Children often form coalitions against other siblings and/or parents. One child may line up with one or both parents. And alliances change in time and in situations. Everyone develops and changes in the resources she brings to the family group and in the demands she makes upon it. The more immature a family member, the more limited the decisions she can make independently. The parents of an infant hold great authority, which they exercise constantly in caring for the baby. Power-based interactions, especially those between partners, are discussed on pages 209–212.

Childrearing as Family Management

The whole process of childrearing could be thought of as a family's creation and development of its own resources. The children themselves are active in their own development, in cooperation with parents who guide management democratically. Such parents give their children freedom to make decisions that they are capable of making successfully. They encourage children to take part in family decisions, respecting their contributions to discussions, trying to understand what children are thinking and feeling, and trying to make their own messages clear. But these parents also exert authority appropriately in places where children's decisions would be destructive to children and/or family. Parents of this sort have been called "authoritative" in contrast to "authoritarian." As shown in an earlier chapter, children's self-control and moral development are associated with parental support, encouragement in communication, and involvement in interaction with children [2]. The development of children's skills and talents is a more easily observed creative family process.

Children's health practices were found related to parents' use of "developmental" childrearing methods [7]. Over 500 children between nine and 13 years of age were interviewed about how they took care of themselves in regard to their teeth, exercise, cleanliness, nutrition, elimination, and smoking. Interviews with the mothers, fathers, and children gave information on childrearing. Good self-care by children was related to parents' reasoning, rewarding, and granting autonomy.

THE LINEAGE FAMILY

Research on management in the lineage family is new, although it is not new to think of the ongoing family, with cycles that extend through time. When asked for an example of a lineage family, many people would think of a royal family, or perhaps the Kennedys or Rockefellers. Everyone has a family that goes back in time, however, even though childfree people may not refer their families forward.

The research that revealed the realities of lineage family management is that of Reuben Hill and his associates at the University of Minnesota. The purpose was to explain the success or failure of families in planning and controlling the future, through analyzing their behavior through time, in earning, saving, buying, and planning [4, p. 15]. The subjects were 120 three-generation families, or 360 nuclear families, 120 of whom were grandparent families, 120 parent families, and 120 young married children families. Data were collected in a series of interviews with each family, over the span of one year. Questions elicited information on values, plans, actions, interactions, achievements, and satisfactions.

Linkages and interactions between generations were found to be very important to the functioning of the nuclear families and the individuals in them. Continuity between generations was seen in transfers of goods, transmission of behavior patterns, including managerial ones, and expressive behavior such as religious, various competencies, helping, advising, visiting, and contacting. The middle or parent generation had greatest contact with the other two generations, often serving as a bridge between them. The intergenerational exchanges of help and resources served to even out the inequities caused by the unequal resources available to nuclear families at different points in the life career. The middle generation usually had more resources than their old parents or their married children, and gave more money, goods, and services to both than either gave to them. The middle generation both gave and received much emotional support. Presumably, when these middle agers become old and their children reach middle age, the same intergenerational helping pattern will hold. The resources of the whole lineage family will continue to be evened out as the needs of the nuclear units change.

In timing the important actions of nuclear families, or family life career management, the parent generation is often consulted by the younger one and can be very helpful. Hill [4, p. 331] suggests that parents should point out the great economic advantages of finishing college before marrying, gaining occupational experience before childbearing, limiting the number of children, and spacing them so that they will not all be going to college and getting married at the same time. Of course, many other important matters exist on which generations can give each other important information and advice, such as business affairs, social competencies, homemaking, travel, and recreation. Although the flow of help from parents to married children was greatest, it was by no means one-sided. The same was true between parents and grandparents.

RESEARCH FINDINGS AND RECOMMENDATIONS

As it becomes clear that the lineage family gives strength and advantages to its member nuclear families, we wonder about the individuals and family units who do not belong in ongoing families. Are they disadvantaged by having no parent generation to turn to for resources and counsel or no grandparent generation with whom to exchange emotional support? Do they plan their major life changes as satisfactorily as do those who can mull it over in a large family group? When we consider newer family forms, in Chapter 17, we examine some of the ways in which innovators substitute for the support and exchanges offered by the lineage family.

The results of Hill's research have implications for individuals, nuclear families, and lineage families. The authors have summed up some of their practical findings as follows [4, pp. 350–351]:

1. Plans are more likely to be carried out if a time is set for doing so.
2. When a major change is going to be made, plans should be thought out carefully for all the other changes that will be entailed, and the budget for everything should be figured out in advance.
3. When changes are made according to a family policy, then family members are more likely to be satisfied with the change than they are when no policy governs the action. Therefore, it is helpful to make policies.
4. Many families do not plan much for buying expensive durable goods, particularly automobiles. They would probably be more satisfied if they did.
5. The families most satisfied with their decisions tend to be those who first discuss among themselves and also talk with people outside the family, and who do more shopping around.
6. Close kinship ties are associated with families' financial success, even when little financial help is accepted from kin.

Hill's recommendations for social policy changes included; financial support that would help children to get more education; encouragement of wives to work in the labor force by providing day care, maternity leaves, part-time jobs, and home-making services; recognition of the extended family network as a resource for problem-solving and strengthening it by rewarding intergenerational cooperation through tax deductions.

Educational programs were outlined for three stages of the family life career, in order to help families to manage resources and careers better. In the newly married, childfree stage, couples would learn short-run planning, better searching for information, and sharper evaluation. Childrearing families would try to improve communication with children and to involve children in planning and evaluating. Policies of life career management, especially educational plans, would be developed. Families in the launching and postparental stages would take up a new set of consumer problems. They would also study their roles in keeping contacts between the generations and in giving help and counsel.

Areas of Family Management

The following chapters focus on some of the areas in which management is especially important to family living. Although books have been written on each of these topics, we hope to show some of the decisions that must be made, their far-reaching effects, and their relations to goals and family welfare. We summarize some of the information that is most basic to management in these areas, hoping to lead the reader to seek more details when they are needed. In order to make a particular decision, a family may have all the necessary information within its members, and a discussion session can bring it out for all to consider. In another case, a book or a professional expert might supply the information. Or, a community agency, religious organization, or other system might be the source of information and/or management counseling.

Management is a topic of study in itself, pursued in relation to business, home, or the individual. A textbook on management, such as *Management for Modern Families,* by Gross, Crandall, and Knoll, goes deeply into the processes of communicating, decision-making, goal setting, planning, and implementing. The study of management complements the study of relationships [3].

SUMMARY Management, the employment of resources in order to reach goals, is used by individuals and groups, both within and outside the family. In management research, the variables studied include situational, affective, decision-making, and welfare. Foundations for management are laid in childhood and cultivated throughout life. Each of the steps leading to marriage has its own significance for later family management.

The homemaker, female or male, solves personal problems, as well as family problems, through management processes. Conflicts between self-goals and family goals are not uncommon.

When a family manages as a group, the members work together to set up goals that they agree upon, to make plans for achieving the goals, to carry out the actions decided upon, and to evaluate the whole process. Goals can be long term or short term. Management includes planning over time to guide important changes.

Communication is essential to managing as a group. Responsive listening and honest expression are supportive to group problem-solving. Abnormal families differ from normal in communication. Love facilitates family management in providing motivation and attitudes that improve communication and identification of resources. Power patterns determine which family members exert most influence at various times. These patterns, especially parent-child power patterns, change over time.

In childrearing, a family develops its own resources. The type of authority exerted by parents has important results in children's development and behavior.

The lineage family is the ongoing family in which cycles occur. Management processes are carried on by two, three, or more generations in cooperation with each other. All generations benefit from these transactions and interactions. An outstanding result is the equalization of resources, making help available at times when it is greatly needed. Another important benefit is shared planning of life cycle management, bringing to bear wide resources on planning for important career changes.

Practical results of research recommend improving family management practices. Social policy changes are needed, as well as programs of education designed for at least three stages of the family life career.

REFERENCES

1. Alexander, James F. Defensive and supportive communication in family systems. *Journal of Marriage and the Family,* 1973, **35,** 613–626.
2. Baumrind, Diana. Will a day care center be a child development center? *Young Children,* 1973, **28,** 154–169.
3. Gross, Irma H., Elizabeth W. Crandall, and Marjorie M. Knoll. *Management for modern families.* New York: Meredith, 1973.
4. Hill, Reuben. *Family development in three generations.* Cambridge, Mass.: Schenkman, 1970.
5. Jacob, Theodore. Patterns of family conflict and dominance as a function of child age and social class. *Developmental Psychology,* 1974, **10,** 1–12.
6. Nichols, Addreen, Catherine R. Mumaw, Maryann Paynter, Martha A. Plonk, and Dorothy Z. Price. Family management. *Journal of Marriage and the Family,* 1971, **33,** 112–118.
7. Pratt, Lois. Child rearing methods and children's health behavior. *Journal of Health and Social Behavior,* 1973, **14,** 61–69.

8. Price, Dorothy Z. Relationship of decision styles and self-actualization. *Home Economics Research Journal,* 1973, **2,** 12–20.
9. Schuham, Anthony I. Activity, talking time, and spontaneous agreement in disturbed and normal family interaction. *Journal of Abnormal Psychology,* 1972, **79,** 68–75.
10. Winter, William D. and Antonio J. Ferreira (eds.). *Research in family interaction.* Palo Alto, Calif.: Science & Behavior Books, 1969, pp. 110–127.

CHAPTER 13

HEALTH IS MORE THAN BRUSHING YOUR TEETH

Healthy people can function on high levels of work, play, and love. They have abundant energy to use in daily living, in problem-solving, and in the pursuit of happiness. Since health deficits place burdens upon individuals and their relationships, it is worthwhile to plan and work for optimal health. In building partnerships, creating homes and family units, the *care* dimension of love is expressed in management for family health. In this way, love contributes to its own growth.

Statistical studies provide evidence that married partners definitely contribute to each other's health as measured by mortality [20]. In both Canada and the United States, death rates were lower among the married, both men and women, than among singles, widowed, and the divorced. When causes of death were analyzed in the Canadian study, it was apparent that suicides showed the greatest difference between married people and those whose marriages were dissolved. For women, the increase in deaths from accidents was as great as the increase from suicides, in moving from married to dissolved marriage categories. Table 13-1 illustrates the Canadian differences in mortality between single, married, and dissolved marriage categories, according to age levels.

Good health can make a big difference in the way a person handles crises and solves problems. When feeling good, with plenty of energy, it is easier to cope with hard times. This principle was illustrated in a reporting of crises by 500 women who had recently become first-time mothers [27]. The young mothers who said that they were in excellent health were less likely to report high levels of crisis than were those who said they were in less than excellent health.

HEALTH AS A MANAGEMENT PROBLEM

Management includes deciding what one wants (goal setting), with priorities specified, and then using available resources most efficiently in order to achieve the goals. How high a level of health does a couple want for themselves and for their children? Defining this general goal together is part of the family management process and a function of partners. If the family includes children, then management includes interaction of all members in deciding just what level of health is worth working for. In order to make such decisions, the members need information on which to base these decisions. The culture in which they live and their educational experiences will determine whether they accept information from science, from a religion, such as Zen or Hinduism, or from the advertising industry.

In setting health goals, decisions are made by weighing the cost of achieving them and imagining whether the satisfactions would be worth the cost. Although money is part of the cost, other considerations are effort, time, and giving up of conflicting goals. Would it be worthwhile to start jogging and stop smoking, for example?

After deciding upon goals, the next step in management is to figure out the best use of resources in order to achieve the goals. Health management includes a great many aspects of family living: nutrition and all that it involves; the rhythms of work, rest, and recreation; prevention of infections and treatment of them when they occur; shelter and clothing; control of drug use; obtaining professional health services. Resources include all the competencies and assets that the family can muster in working toward the goals involved. *Competencies* are skills and abilities of all sorts. *Assets* include money, material objects, credit, and available services from kin and community.

DEFINITION OF HEALTH

Health refers to mental, emotional, and social functioning as well as to physical aspects of persons, but in this chapter, we focus on physical health and the relationship of physical health to other parts of personhood. Health is much more than absence of disease and illness. It is optimal functioning of the whole organism plus optimal development throughout the life span. The word **optimal,** meaning the best that can be, indicates that standards of health and growth have to be decided upon by people.

The standards of health that we accept are those of science. A working definition of a healthy individual, or criteria that anyone can apply in practical daily life, includes the following: firm muscles; clear skin and eyes, shiny hair; body balanced when moving and at rest; abundant energy and enthusiasm for work and play; ability to sleep and relax; quick recovery from irritation and tension-provoking experiences.

TABLE 13-1

Canadian Mortality According to Marital Status, by Sex, Death Rate per 100,000 During 1969 - 70

	Male			Female		
Age Group	Single	Married	Widowed and Divorced	Single	Married	Widowed and Divorced
15 and over	1,527.7	1,045.7	2,347.3	848.6	581.0	1,167.0
15–24	163.2	95.8	516.1	57.6	41.7	466.7
25–44	350.4	180.5	724.6	196.9	104.9	350.8
45–64	1,837.8	1,086.8	2,823.3	759.1	557.6	944.8
65 and over	7,579.1	5,811.2	10,469.5	4,878.5	3,345.4	5,846.1

Reprinted by permission from Metropolitan Life Insurance Company. *Statistical Bulletin,* 1973 (August), p. 5.

For a child, normal growth must be included, and for adults, normal age-related bodily changes (development).

NUTRITION

The body is part of the person. The body is built out of substances contained in food, its construction directed by organizers contained in the genes. What could be more important, then, than supplying the quantity and quality of building materials that the organizers can use to greatest advantage? The body is continually being built and rebuilt. The supply of building materials is always critical to the quality of the body and hence of the person. Nutrition is thus important every day and in all stages of life. However, some stages are more critical than others.

In this brief section, our purpose is to draw attention to the contribution that good health makes to family living and the necessity for family management that provides good nutrition for all members. We believe that nutrition education is appropriate for everyone, and not just in school, but continuing throughout life. A daily food guide is provided in Appendix D.

Some Critical Periods for Nutrition

Prenatal and Infant. The materials that go into the foundation of any structure are especially important, since the underpinnings are there permanently. So it is with human bodies (animals, too). Because the embryo and fetus are hidden and perhaps even secret, the pregnant parents may be unaware of the far-reaching importance of what they provide at this time for their child-to-be.

Nutritionists from many different countries have agreed that malnutrition during prenatal life and infancy had harmful effects on birthweight, survival, illness, growth, and behavior [6]. Prenatal malnutrition has been shown by animal experiments to produce structural and biochemical abnormalities in the brain, lungs, thyroid, liver, kidney, pituitary, skeleton, and lymph system. Even minor nutritional defects during pregnancy have been shown to affect the later development of the offspring. For instance, adding sugar to the mother's diet was related to later obesity in the infant. Insufficiencies in minute quantities of trace elements, such as zinc, have been shown to produce abnormal offspring.

Survival and absence of physical and mental defects in human infants are related to birthweight. Prematurity and malnutrition of the mother are frequently noted when newborns weigh too little. Quality of nutrition is an important factor in the production of larger babies, who are more likely to survive and have better health [1]. Since the brain develops early in life, it is especially affected by prenatal malnutrition. The most rapid brain growth takes place prenatally and during the first

Brother shields his mother and baby sister from the hot Mexican sun.

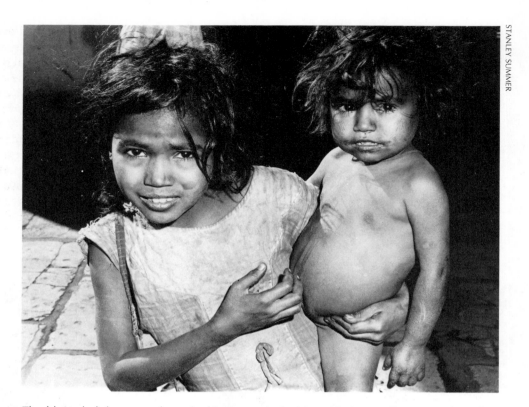

The bloated abdomen and rough skin are typical of kwashiorkor, a disease resulting from protein deficiency.

six months after birth, the time when new cells are added. The brain reaches 90 per cent of its adult size by three or four years of age. From the evidence available, it is likely that learning ability and various brain functions are depressed by prenatal malnutrition [33].

Growth during infancy is very rapid, although slower than before birth. Malnutrition is one of the chief contributors to high infant mortality rates among poor people. The time between weaning from the breast and being able to eat adult food is a time of great risk for the infants of the poor, and the earlier the weaning takes place, the greater is the risk to life and health. Damage results from infections as well as from inadequate nutrients. In Western nations, where breast-feeding is infrequent, specially prepared infant food is available to those who can afford it. A study sponsored by the Gerber Baby Food Company, which did not include families with very low incomes, showed only 17 per cent of infants being breast-fed. Most of the babies received adequate nutrients, with the exception of iron in which 58 per cent were deficient. The deficiencies found were in the babies who got little variety in their diets [26]. In contrast to this group of fortunate infants are 300 million malnourished children living throughout the world, some of them in North America [14]. Varying degrees of deprivation of calories, proteins, minerals, vitamins, and trace elements have resulted in a range of deficits in physical and mental growth, as well as susceptibility to infection. Figure 13-1 shows results from a careful study of 150 young children in a slum in Chile. Mental development is seen to be related to the daily intake of animal protein.

Adolescent.   Children grow very rapidly during the year in which puberty is reached. The majority of girls are growing at their fastest rate since early infancy when they reach a point about six months before their first menstruation. After puberty, the rate of growth slows down, until it stops. The time of the growth spurt depends more upon the nutrition of the children than upon any other factors, since it occurs when a child reaches a certain weight [11]. (For Caucasian girls, the average weight at menarche is 46 kilograms.)

During the growth spurt, large quantities of nutrients are needed for building and transforming the body of a child into that of an adult. The average girl of 12 and boy of 14 need more food, and high quality food, than they ever needed before. Since the boy has farther to go to reach his mature size, he needs more food than the girl, and needs larger quantities for a longer time. However, Henry, Zach, Yvonne,

FIGURE 13-1   Percentage of mental normality and deficiency in preschool children with different animal protein intake (Gesell test). The animal calorie consumption was determined by a nutritional survey in every home, using the technique called quantitative trend of food consumption, with chemical analysis of sample of food consumed during a 7-day period.

Source: Figure 3, p. 113. Fernando E. Monckeberg. Nutrition and behavior. In David J. Kallen (ed.), *Nutrition, development and social behavior.* Washington, D.C.: U.S. Dept. of Health, Education, and Welfare Publication No. 73, 1973.

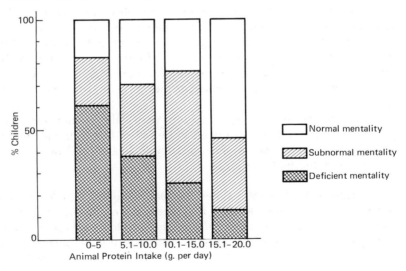

and Brenda are not "the average," just as no individual is. Each spurts, reaches puberty, and achieves mature status at a particular individual time. Zach grew 10 inches between ages 13 and 15; Henry grew six. Zach's mother complained that he made peanut butter sandwiches before she had finished the dinner dishes, whereas Henry waited until bedtime for his snack. Yvonne reached menarche at 11, Brenda at 14. Both are normal; neither is average.

As part of a study of the effects of mothers' employment, over 400 teen-age girls and boys were asked, "Did you have anything to eat this morning before school?" Eighty per cent of those with a nonemployed mother and 70 per cent of those with an employed mother answered *yes* [10a]. Therefore, 20 to 30 per cent of this sample of adolescents went to school without eating any food. The study also showed that more boys than girls ate before going to school.

Adolescent girls' nutrition is especially important. For the girl herself, of course, it is good to have a strong, beautiful, well-functioning body. In addition, her nutrition during adolescence is fundamental to her future performance in pregnancy and childbirth. Her baby will be healthier and better developed if she begins pregnancy with a mature body, well stocked with all the elements that go into building a baby. Her own nutrition will contribute to success in labor, delivery, and lactation.

Pregnant and Nursing Mothers. The nutrition of the fetus depends on the quality and quantity of food eaten by the woman carrying it and also on the reserves in her body at the beginning of pregnancy. An old wives' tale holds that the fetus will take what it needs from the mother, no matter what she eats. Although there is some truth in this notion, it is also partly wrong. The fetus has priority on certain elements, such as iron and ascorbic acid, but the mother has priority on other elements, such as iodine and vitamin A. Under conditions of scarcity, both will suffer, but with different deficiencies.

Until quite recently, it was customary for obstetricians to try to limit the pregnant woman's weight gain severely. Many women were urged to keep the gain to around 15 pounds. The Committee on Maternal Nutrition of the National Research Council now regards this practice as dangerous to the life and health of mothers and babies. The committee emphasizes an intake of the appropriate nutrients without curbing calories and with careful attention to the needs and condition of each individual [29].

The nursing mother requires even more calories than she did while she was pregnant. These calories also need to be rich in the nutrients that are the building blocks of the body. For instance, if calcium intake is inadequate, calcium will be drawn out of the mother's bones.

Pregnant Adolescent. When the requirements of adolescence and pregnancy are added together, the result is a real problem [16]. It is *possible* for a pregnant teen-ager to eat enough of the needed nutrients and to avoid useless and harmful foods, but very often, in reality, she does not. Studies of poor pregnancy outcome show two outstanding causes, poor nutrition and youth of the mother. Many of the very young mothers are poor girls who have had inadequate nutrition and other care throughout their lives, including their own prenatal lives. According to a nutritionist who has studied birth defects in relation to fetal impoverishment, the United States probably has more child marriages and pregnancies than any other nation in the world. In one year in the United States, 7,768 babies were born to mothers between ten and 14 years of age, a third of them to white girls, the rest to nonwhite. Two girls had each given birth to four children before the age of 14 [16]. During a recent year, there were 600,816 births to teen-age mothers, comprising 17 per cent of total births in the United States [32a, p. 18]. This represents a serious situation, when such a large proportion of infants face greater risks of death or deformity than would be the case if their mothers were older.

Old Age. When Craig telephoned Mrs. Baker, age 97, to tell her that the geriatric day care center would be closed because of the ice storm, she asked, "How will I get anything to eat?"

"Take some of the cans from your food shelf," Craig suggested, "Open them, warm up the food, and eat it."

"No, I won't," Mrs. Baker replied. "I just won't have anything to eat unless you take me to the day care center."

Mrs. Baker is extreme, in refusing to eat anything at all, unless the meal is served to her in a social setting. She insists upon living alone. She is probably starving to death. She has already suffered a spontaneous hip fracture. Many older people are like her to a lesser degree, eating far less than they need to maintain life and health. Their diets are usually deficient in both quantity and quality. Snack foods, such as bread, cookies, and tea are easy to prepare, relatively inexpensive and easy to eat. Proteins, minerals, and vitamins require more money, planning, and effort, in short, more *management*. An example of a nutritional problem of older people, especially older women, is bone loss, or *osteoporosis,* as its extreme form is called. Bone loss may result in loss of height, back pain, and easily broken bones. Many people suffering from osteoporosis have had a long-term diet deficient in calcium [9].

Insofar as nutrition determines the health level of the elderly, it is important in determining their whole life-style. In a long-range study of 1200 old people, half drawn from a California community and half from admissions to a psychiatric ward, it was evident that physical problems preceded mental ones for several years and that early retirement was often the result of poor health [31].

Threats to Adequate Nutrition

Families are called upon to meet the nutritional needs of members in various stages of development. The persons in the critical stages, as outlined previously, need extra care in the management of their food intake. Basically, though, good foods for one person are good for all, since the nutrients that build human bodies are fundamental. The management of nutrition is indeed a complex job, including: deciding how much money, time, and effort shall be spent on nutrition; planning menus, buying food; preparing food; serving food; keeping up to date on information about preparing food and nutrition; educating family members. Although homemakers doubtless do the best they can, malnutrition is one of the most serious problems confronting human beings. The outstanding reasons for its existence follow.

Poverty. By far the most important worldwide reason for the prevalence of malnutrition is the unavailability of food. Good management means making the best of what there is, even when resources are inadequate.

Ignorance and Lack of Skills. Many people do not know much about how bodies are built from nutrients, how to select foods that contain the nutrients, how to prepare them, and how to make amounts and combinations suitable to the various family members. In most parts of the world, girls learn nutrition management from their mothers, who learned it from their mothers. If a young woman has seen babies weaned from breast milk to tapioca gruel, then most likely she will give her baby tapioca gruel rather than cow's milk or pureed meat. In countries where the infant mortality rate is high, one of the chief causes of infant death is inadequate feeding. The mothers do not know how to bridge the gap between breast-feeding and the time when children can eat the family diet. Often, they make and present liquids that look like milk but contain mostly carbohydrates, with little or no protein and minerals. The same mistake is made by some families in vegetarian cults in North America.

Rejection of Scientific Knowledge. When religious or cultist systems of nutrition are followed, results may or may not be good for growth and development as defined by science. Many Hindu vegetarians pay careful attention to getting enough balanced protein, for example, through eating a large variety and special combinations of milk products and legumes. Vegetarianism in the United States and Canada has become popular with millions of young people and some not so young people. Many choose food for its spiritual, rather than its nutritional, value. Nutritionists are studying the practices of some of the vegetarians and measuring the results of these food practices on them and on their children [10].

Some of the most extreme cultists have been found to suffer from various deficiencies. The Vegan cult diet contains practically no vitamin B 12, but does provide enough folic acid. Since folic acid masks B 12 deficiency, Vegan members sometimes suffer irreversible degeneration of the spinal cord before they are aware of having anything wrong. The Zen macrobiotic diet has probably caused deaths and has certainly caused scurvy, anemia, emaciation, and loss of kidney function. This diet is especially damaging to pregnant and lactating women and their infants. Such a child was John, age 23 months, who was admitted to the San Francisco General Hospital because of starvation. His weight, 15½ pounds, was that of the average five-month-old baby. His behavior was at a developmental level of 10 to 12 months, and his skeletal development was at a one-year level. The hospital nutritionists devised a vegetarian diet that did not violate the parents' beliefs and during two periods of hospitalization brought John's weight up to 24 pounds. The father refused to come to the clinic at all and the mother refused to continue with the prescribed dietary practices. When last seen, John was again on the way to starvation and another baby was about to be born to his mother.

Macrobiotic cultists consider an abnormally small baby a blessing. Followers of Ohsawa reported him to have said, "'Walking later is better. The brain instead is growing. If a baby is too active walking, all his energy goes to his feet and not to his head'" [10]. Thus rickets, lethargy, and developmental retardation are regarded as desirable.

Fortunately some of the new vegetarians are willing to accept nutritional advice, even though it often comes after they and their children have suffered damage from deficiencies. An adequate vegetarian diet presents a greater management problem than does one that includes meat, but some vegetarians have accepted the challenge.

Affluence and Advertising. The opposite extreme from vegetarian cultists are those who eat junk foods and too much food. In North America, these people are much more numerous than the starving vegetarians; in fact, they are the mainstream.

The common dietary faults of the average American are too much sugar, too much fat, and not enough of certain minerals and vitamins. Calcium, iron, vitamin A, and ascorbic acid were the elements most frequently deficient, according to a government survey of households in the United States [32]. People eat sugar and fat because they like them, they are available, and they got used to eating this way in childhood. Soft drinks, gum, candy, and fried snacks crowd out the foods that would supply the lacking nutrients, such as vegetables, fruits, milk, and milk products.

Adding refined sugar to the diet serves no useful purpose. As well as providing calories totally lacking in building materials, sugar promotes the growth of cavities in the teeth. Keeping sugar out of the family food intake is a continuing management problem, beginning with the infant. Recently I (MSS) saw a salesman in a store giving lollipops to two toddlers. The mothers thanked him and seemed delighted to have their children sucking the candy. I was reminded of my experience with my first child. For her first two years, we had managed in such a way that she never tasted sugar as such. Then Susan came home from the next door neighbors in great excitement, saying that she had eaten *candy* and it was very good indeed. Since candy is everywhere, and generally socially accepted, parents need strong conviction of the importance of good nutrition in order to manage effectively. One way of coping with such problems is to live in a community of like-minded people, such as the communes where only "natural" foods are eaten. Another way is to serve only nutritionally valuable foods at home, while educating children as they grow. Then they know what they are choosing when they are on their own.

Advertising, especially on television, adds to the homemaker's difficulties in nutrition management. The shows present attractive pictures and intriguing comments on bubbling sweet drinks, crunchy, sugar-loaded cereals, gooey chocolate bars, and crisp, fat-encrusted chicken and potatoes. Desires for junk foods are stimulated in parents, children, everyone.

For the affluent, who can afford to buy what they choose; for the poor, whose money will not stretch to enough good food; and for the alienated, who seek spiritual benefits in deficient diets; the way to healthy bodies is through learning the facts of nutrition and then applying them.

EXERCISE AND REST

All animals have rhythms of activity and rest. As far as we can tell, only human beings have to plan their lives so as to carry out the rhythms. Marital harmony is affected by partners who work, play, and sleep at times not congenial to each other, by one or both being fatigued, irritable or lethargic, by one having tremendous, sustained energy while the other needs a frequent change of pace. When children are added to the family, rhythms become much more complicated. The disruption caused by the first baby is largely one of breaking the patterns of living already established by the parents. The hardest adjustment for many new parents is having to get up in the middle of the night and early in the morning.

Managing Activity and Rest

For the sake of health and satisfying family interaction, homemakers plan and direct the rhythms of family members. If one person did exactly as he wished at each moment, the result would be chaos for all. Good managers allow as much leeway as possible for each individual taking special needs into account, but keeping the

overall situation in mind. Communication between family members is important in the planning stage. Since a tired person feels grouchy, he may keep quiet or snap at others when the subject of rest and activity comes up. Therefore, it helps to be aware of one's own state and its influence on communication. A discussion of some of the needs peculiar to various positions in the family follows.

The Partners. If partnership is to develop, live, and grow, the couple need time alone together when both feel good. The honeymoon is traditionally a time to be alone together for sex, communication, and recreation. Since the need for such time continues throughout life, timing of family activities ideally includes regular privacy for the couple. In cultures where husband-wife roles are clearly defined, their need for regular times alone together is not so great. Since everyone knows what husbands and wives are supposed to do, there is less to talk over and less to decide. In Samoa, for example, one big *fale* (a beautiful, oval, one-room thatched house, open on all sides) shelters a couple, all of their children, perhaps nine or 12, a grandparent or two, and possibly other kin. Privacy and secrets must be impossible.

The structure of the time plan for a family is usually strongly influenced by the occupational system, by the demands of the husband's job, and the wife's, if she has one. Then decisions have to be made about when to start and stop all the activities about which choice seems possible. In trying to work, study, communicate, and have good times together, a young couple may deprive themselves of sleep and exercise, both of which are essential to health.

Infants. The person who comes closest to needing everything *his* way is the newborn baby. When he is hungry, he is very, very hungry, and totally dependent upon his caregiver to feed him. He moves from one state to another under the influence of his own physiological processes. He drowses, sleeps, wakens quiet and alert, and actively cries. The timing of good care fits what *he* needs, whether it be food, holding, rocking, washing, or letting him sleep. His mother and other caregivers have to adjust their own rest and activity patterns to his, but for just a little while.

By three or four months of age, most babies are beginning to fit into family rhythms, having stabilized their own bodily processes. When caregivers try to understand what the baby wants and needs and to meet his needs during the first year, the year-old baby tries to cooperate with them [2]. Parents can then make use of the budding of respect (see page 33) in order to make changes in timing that are more convenient for other family member's activity-rest rhythms.

Preschool child. Because the essence of this time of life is curiosity, exploration, imagination, and action, the preschool child gets very tired. Good management involves planning for alternating quiet play and active play, regular, nutritious meals and snacks, quiet before meals and bed time, bed before exhaustion, much outdoor play, and opportunities for large muscle exercise.

School-age Child. Relatively slow growth allows more leeway in meeting needs for rest and food, but going to school means hours of physical inactivity. Inactivity at home, too, results in insufficient stimulation for muscular development and coordination, for exercise of heart, lungs, and all that goes into fitness and stamina.

American children spend many hours watching television. They ride on buses instead of walking to school. We have evidence that they think of themselves as inactive. We recently asked 100 girls and 100 boys in each of five countries to draw "a picture of yourself and someone else, anyone you like, *doing something,* anything you like" [29a]. Pictures showing children engaged in games and sports were between 40 and 60 per cent of drawings in Australia, Canada, England, and New Zealand, but in the United States, they were only 15 per cent. Frequently, American children drew themselves and their friends "just standing." Figure 13-2 shows typical drawings.

For school-age children, family management includes regular daily hours of active play, much of it outdoors. Children also do some housework that contributes to the family. Among 1400 families in upstate New York, children between six and eleven worked, on the average, half an hour daily [34]. Children can take an active part in planning the use of time. In fact, unless parents and children plan together, it is hardly family management, but parental. Some families have regular meeting times when they talk over matters of concern. Some find that mealtime offers the right time and place for planning and deciding.

Adolescent. During their growth spurt, adolescents need more rest than they did as children, since growth makes heavy demands upon energy. Teachers and parents usually expect more work from adolescents than from children. Teen-agers contributed an hour of housework daily in the New York State study [34]. To complicate the picture, planning and deciding with teen-agers may be difficult because they are so involved in establishing their own identity and independence. The best insurance for effective family management at this point is a history of planning together throughout childhood. Parents can still learn better methods of communication, though. They will probably need them in order to keep defining family goals and planning ways of reaching them.

Relation of Exercise and Rest to Nutrition

Exercise stimulates bodily processes in such a way that the body can make full use of oxygen and of nutrients from food. Fitness and stamina develop as muscles, lungs, and heart are used to capacity. Exercise causes individual muscle fibers to increase in size and strength, building up the lean tissues, making bones more rugged and better mineralized and decreasing the more inert fat tissues. Even in adults, exercise increases the outpouring of the growth hormone that in turn mobilizes stored fat for fuel [17, pp. 180–185]. Thus, the body is built and rebuilt most efficiently as the organizing processes are called upon, and the building materials are available.

Me an My Little Sister

a   b

FIGURE 13-2   Drawings by 11-year-old girls. a: An American. b: A New Zealander.

During periods of rest that are alternated with exercise, repair and growth of cells are enhanced.

SHELTER AND CLOTHING

A place to live and covering for the body are basic human requirements. They involve continued management, since both serve many different needs and both cost much in money, time, and effort. Housing and clothing affect life style and sex-role behavior, as well as health. Social contacts and employment opportunities are affected by where a person lives and the quality of her home and apparel. Thus, mental health, as well as physical health, is a consideration in planning the use of money and other family resources for shelter.

Housing and Family Health

What people want and expect as to housing differs in different cultures and climates [4]. In Canada and the United States, families need protection from weather and marauders, privacy for all members, sanitation, facilities for cooking and eating, a place to keep things, and access to the community. Some people desire and some achieve much more, such as beauty, a view, a prestigious address. Many get much less, as do inhabitants of ghettos and rural slums. The most commonly held image of a house held by Americans is "a relatively new, single-family, one-story or split-level brick structure having three or more bedrooms, a bath and a half or more, central heating, and various other electrically operated pieces of equipment." A study of housing in Appalachia compared aspirations and situations of rural and urban families. Aspirations were similar to the American mainstream. The reality was that about two out of three of the houses occupied by the people in this study were structurally sound, four out of five had a bathroom, two out of five had central heating, and three out of five had window screens [24].

Health conditions are better in the Appalachian sample than for some dwellers in metropolitan slum areas, where criminals and rats are a constant threat to safety, lead paint is peeling, and many families have to share toilets. Such families are caught in a financial squeeze that keeps them badly housed. Racial and ethnic membership may make it difficult to find housing that would be open to others, even though such discrimination is outlawed. High-rise public housing projects present grave problems in carrying out basic family functions [30]. Elevators and stairwells are scenes of frequent attacks and robbery by residents as well as outsiders, by children, adolescents, and adults. Police are often reluctant to answer calls for help. Public health nurses, social workers, and medical personnel avoid the high-rise projects, especially after dark. Mothers worry constantly about the safety of their children, often devoting large amounts of time and energy to escorting them to school and watching them play. Thus, other homemaking and health care functions have to be curtailed in order to maximize protection. Since the source of the problem lies largely in the structure of the buildings, families tend to put their efforts into finding better places to live. They develop hostility toward the building itself and hence abuse it. Then it deteriorates and becomes even more unpleasant. Cold, impersonal relations between resident families are frequent. A truly satisfactory solution would have to come from the community, by constructing buildings appropriate to family living and by helping the families with the other problems that poor people are likely to encounter. Also needed are designers of buildings who understand people and families, their functions and needs. Well-designed high-rise buildings have worked out very well for low-income aged people as well as for the affluent. The U.S. Department of Housing and Urban Development has ceased to approve high-rise buildings for low-income families with children [23].

An attempt to end segregated housing for the poor has been made by an agency created by the Massachussetts State Legislature. Poor, middle-income, and affluent tenants live in the same building, in apartments of identical quality, each paying according to his income. A welfare family pays $57 a month for the same accommodations for which a family with $22,500 annual income pays $319. Tenants at all income levels have expressed satisfaction. As the director of the agency has pointed out, segregation by social class is new in the history of North America, and the historic picture was of farmers, merchants, craftsmen, and statesmen living near one another [12].

The following conclusions were presented in reviews of research on relationships between housing and health [16a; 22]. In living areas of high density, higher incidences of physical and mental pathologies are seen, including pneumonia, tuberculosis, gastrointestinal disorders, venereal disease, infant mortality, juvenile delinquency, mental disorders, and suicide. The incidence of tension-related diseases is related to high noise levels. Increased numbers of medical problems are likely to occur in people living where it is difficult to make meaningful social contacts. Psychiatric problems are likely to result from a forced change of residence, especially among people outside the mainstream of society.

Managing for Health. Legal and political action may be necessary in order to improve the housing situation for many, but whatever a family has to live in, good management contributes to health and harmony by making some improvements. Once we visited an Indian village where graduate students had been carrying on a project of teaching home management to the villagers. The students were checking to see which innovations had been retained by the homemakers, and by which homemakers. The innovations were two: a shelf on which to keep pots and pans instead of keeping them on the floor and a stove pipe to carry smoke from the cooking stove out through the roof, instead of having it discharged into the house. When visiting houses in the two sections of the village, we found that most of the caste homes (which were larger and sturdier), had pots and pans on the floor and smoke in the main room. Almost all of the homes with utensils on a shelf and smoke going out the roof were those of outcastes (or Harijans, as they are most politely named). It had seemed more worthwhile to the Harijan women, in their one-room huts, to manage with the innovations introduced by the students. Although poorer than the caste homemakers, they had provided a healthier family environment through the intelligent use of resources.

Innovation, invention, and do-it-yourself home projects are part of the American way of life. Often a rearrangement of storage and work space can do more to improve home operations than the purchase of space or gadgets. When age and sex roles are flexible and communication is good, then all family members can plan, decide, and carry out the construction and maintenance of housing facilities.

Clothing the Family

Like housing, clothing serves not only health needs but many other purposes as well. While recognizing the importance of clothing for self-esteem, communication, and esthetic enjoyment, we merely point out in this chapter that the protective function is basic and that family management must take account of it. In buying, making, and maintaining clothing, the factors of temperature, support, sanitation, and growth are all pertinent.

ILLNESS AND ACCIDENTS

Being sick or injured is a negation of being healthy. Although health is promoted by good nutrition, sufficient rest and exercise, adequate housing and clothing, the immediate causes of illness and accidents must also be controlled.

Figure 13-3 shows the extent to which the health of schoolchildren and adolescents is a problem, from their parents' point of view and from the findings of a health survey. The United States government conducted the survey on 7,119 children between the age of 6 and 11, and 6,768 youths between the age of 12 and 17, all of whom were representative of the population of that age. Parents of 19 per cent of the children were worried about some aspect of their children's health. The examining pediatricians found about 13 per cent of the children to have a significant abnormality. This represents 3.1 million children in the total population.

Infections

Two types of strategy are necessary for preventing infections; both require management. Caring for an ill patient involves more management and skills. Adults have to

FIGURE 13-3 Per cent of U.S. children in 1963–65 and youths in 1966–70 with significantly abnormal findings on survey examination and parent ratings of fair or poor health or health a worry, by age.

Source: Jean Roberts. Examination and health history findings among children and youths, 6–17 years. Washington, D.C.: U.S. Department of Health, Education, and Welfare, Vital and Health Statistics–Series II-No. 129 DHEW Publication No. (HRA) 74–1611, 1973, Figure 1.

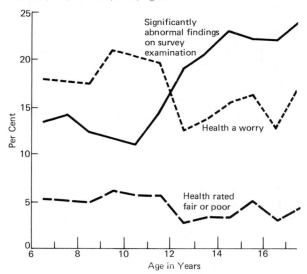

plan and carry out procedures for themselves and for the children and possibly old people for whom they care.

Building Immunity and Resistance. A healthy body can put up a stronger fight against most disease organisms than one weakened by poor nutrition, stress, insufficient rest, and/or lack of exercise. As we have just pointed out, it takes good home management to give all family members adequate nutrition and the like.

Immunization is required or recommended in the United States in order to prevent the following diseases: diphtheria, measles, mumps, poliomyelitis, rubella, tetanus, and whooping cough. Many communities provide free immunization programs for infants and young children, but parents have to plan to have it done. Middle- and upper-income parents also have to pay. A recent message to parents from the chief of immunization, National Center for Disease Control, warned that 40 per cent of all children between the ages of one and four are not adequately protected against polio, rubella, and measles [35]. The incidence of measles is increasing, as is the risk of polio. In Asia, Africa, and other parts of the world, additional immunizations are needed. Health management may include protection against smallpox, cholera, yellow fever, malaria, plague, and typhoid.

Preventing Invasion by Disease Organisms. The whole life style is pertinent to this topic. So is the particular spot in the world where a family lives. A family can live in a hookworm-infested area and yet prevent hookworm infection by wearing shoes. There may be amoebas in the water and on the vegetables, but amoebic dysentery can be avoided by boiling all drinking water, eating only freshly cooked food, and careful handwashing after toileting and before eating. Amoebas, and other intestinal parasites, hookworm, and the common cold are diseases that cannot be prevented by immunization. They have to be halted before they enter the body, and that is what cleanliness techniques do. When children grow up in a locality where such diseases are common, they learn from their parents how to manage. When adults move into the area of a health threat that is new to them, they must learn new management skills if they decide that it is worthwhile to prevent illness.

Venereal disease cannot be prevented by immunization, but only by keeping the organisms out of the body. Venereal diseases include all infections transmitted by sexual contact, but the best known are syphilis and gonorrhea. Because venereal disease has such far-reaching effects upon reproduction and health and because its spread depends upon interpersonal relationships and life-styles, we devote more space to it than to other diseases.

Figure 13-4 shows the incidence of reported cases of syphilis and gonorrhea in the United States, according to sex and age. During one year, over 91,000 cases of syphilis were reported, but the Public Health service estimates that about 500,000 have undetected syphilis. Gonorrhea is much more prevalent than syphilis, with a reported number over 767,000. Estimates of the actual incidence of gonorrhea are not available, since it has only recently been discovered that males, as well as females, can be symptomless while carrying the disease. A study of nearly

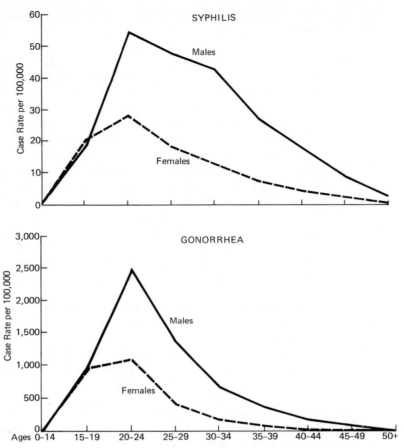

FIGURE 13-4 Incidence of venereal disease by age and sex of the United States civilian population. Case rates per 100,000.

Source: Metropolitan Life Co., *Statistical Bulletin,* 54 (Nov. 1973), p. 6. Reprinted by permission from the Metropolitan Life Insurance Company.

3,000 sexually active soldiers in the United States showed that 2.2 per cent had gonorrhea and of these, 68 per cent had no symptoms [15]. From the graphs in Figure 13-4, the greatest number of cases can be seen to occur in the late teens and early twenties, with males exceeding females after the early teens. The graphs probably reflect the numbers of sexual contacts typical of the various age groups, as well as ignorance and reluctance to get diagnosis and treatment.

Together, the reported cases of syphilis and gonorrhea were greater than the number of cases reported for all other reportable diseases. Venereal disease deaths were almost all caused by syphilis, the rate being three times greater for males than for females and five or six times greater for nonwhites than for whites [21].

Venereal herpes is a viral infection that is similar to the herpes disease more commonly known as cold sores. Persons who contract venereal herpes may be more likely to develop cancer of the cervix or prostate cancer [18], although medical opinion does not concur on this matter [19a]. Venereal herpes has not been proved to be dangerous to adults, but it is extremely dangerous to an infant born to an infected woman. A woman who contracts venereal herpes within a month of delivery should deliver her infant by caesarian section. Severe brain damage can result if an infant is born by normal delivery to an infected woman [18, 19a]. See Appendix E for symptoms and treatment of venereal disease.

Although the most certain way to avoid venereal disease is to have no sexual contact (intercourse or petting) with an infected person, strict monogamy is not acceptable to many people, and few have diagnostic examinations before beginning sex activity with a partner. The danger of infection is greatly reduced by using a condom, although the rash of syphilis is infectious to touch. A common misconception of young people is that contraceptive pills provide protection against venereal disease. On the contrary, although pills are highly efficient in preventing pregnancy, they greatly increase the chances of contracting gonorrhea and other vaginal infections, because pills make the vaginal secretions less acid.

Treating Illnesses. A decision that is often hard to make is whether to seek medical help for the illness of oneself or one's child. A homemaker often wonders whether the symptoms are serious enough to merit the price of a doctor and the effort of getting an appointment and going to the office or clinic. The more health knowledge and skills a parent has, the better she can manage this decision. When the illness is serious, or in need of specialized care, then it is important to get medical help and follow instructions. Family members feel concerned about and responsible for the health of family members. They consult one another as to how to treat illnesses and injuries, making extensive use of medicines that can be obtained without prescription. Americans do more self-medication than do families in countries where professional help is more available to all, such as in the United Kingdom and Yugoslavia [25].

Home nursing includes attention to nutrition. The body's reaction to stress is to break down some of its protein and other essential elements. Such stress can be caused by infections (especially gastrointestinal), surgery, accidents, and drugs. Therefore, the ill and recuperating patient needs extra protein, minerals, and vitamins [8]. And since rest aids in body building, it is also necessary for recuperation.

Prompt treatment for infections and other illnesses leads to quicker recovery and hence conserves the family resources of money, energy, and time. If the infection is venereal, prompt treatment is doubly important, since other people may be affected, too. When treated in the early stages, syphilis and gonorrhea are usually cured before they do serious damage. Any discomfort or unusual conditions in the genitals should be reported to a physician without delay. But what about symptomless venereal disease? Some mass screenings of college-age populations have recently been done. Sexually active persons of both sexes would be wise to have regular tests for syphilis and gonorrhea unless they have stayed exclusively with one partner who has also been monogamous.

Preventing Accidents and Injuries

Physical safety is an important consideration in planning where to live and in setting up and running a home. Are the community and neighborhood sites of violence and crime, polluted air, loud noise, or congested traffic? Is fire protection adequate and available? As mentioned previously, the physical features of the house may be safe or dangerous. Often a family has to balance one disadvantage against another, deciding which goal is more important. Table 13-2 shows trends in accident rates for children between five and 14, indicating a large increase in numbers of children hurt by motor vehicles. At all ages, boys had more fatal accidents than girls.

In planning space and home operations for maximum safety, the special characteristics of various family members are significant. For instance, because preschool-children are likely to be more impulsive and curious than older children, they need more protection from access to fires, machines, cleaning materials, medicines, garden tools, and trash. Because of poor eyesight, unsteadiness, and vulnerability to falls, older people need uncluttered passageways and handrails on steps and bath facilities. Safety in the kitchen is promoted by sturdy equipment, convenient storage arrangements, and work space planned to fit the tasks and the person performing

TABLE 13-2 **Mortality from Accidents at Ages 5-14, United States, 1960-61 and 1968-69**

	Accidents—Total			Motor Vehicle Accidents			All Other Accidents		
	Death Rate per 100,000			Death Rate per 100,000			Death Rate per 100,000		
Age and Sex	1960–61	1968–69	Per Cent Change	1960–61	1968–69	Per Cent Change	1960–61	1968–69	Per Cent Change
Total									
5–14	18.7	20.3	+9	7.7	10.0	+30	11.0	10.3	−6
5–9	18.9	20.4	+8	8.3	10.8	+30	10.6	9.6	−9
10–14	18.5	20.2	+9	7.1	9.2	+30	11.4	11.0	−4
Boys									
5–14	26.0	27.6	+6	10.2	12.8	+26	15.8	14.8	−6
5–9	24.0	26.2	+9	10.6	13.3	+26	13.4	12.9	−4
10–14	28.1	29.0	+3	9.8	12.2	+25	18.3	16.8	−8
Girls									
5–14	11.2	12.7	+13	5.2	7.1	+37	6.0	5.6	−7
5–9	13.6	14.5	+7	6.1	8.1	+33	7.5	6.4	−15
10–14	8.6	11.0	+28	4.3	6.1	+42	4.3	4.9	+14

Source of basic data: Reports of the Division of Vital Statistics, National Center for Health Statistics. Reprinted by permission from *Statistical Bulletin* of the Metropolitan Life Insurance Company (1973), **54**:12, p. 10.

them. If partners and children are flexible enough in sex roles and communication, all together may do better in planning and arranging for use of space, especially kitchen space.

In educating children for safety, parents' teaching and behavior are influential in many areas of life, including driving a car, wearing seat belts, walking in traffic, handling weapons, and engaging in sports, especially water sports. Basic attitudes of self-esteem and respect for the individual come through in the way adults take care of themselves and their children. Children most readily acquire the behavior patterns of parents who are consistent in what they say and what they do.

HEREDITARY AND GENETIC DEFECTS AND HANDICAPS

Family planning is a very basic foundation of health management, in fact so essential that we devote a chapter to it (See Chapter 14). Planning can prevent the birth of many children with hereditary disorders, but not all such children. At present, 6 per cent of infants are born with some sort of genetic defect. This incidence is increasing, as a result of modern medicine that makes it possible for children with various defects to grow up and reproduce. It is estimated that all human beings have twelve or more disadvantageous genes [13, p. 910]. When a handicapped child is born to a family or adopted into one, he brings special health management problems to be solved. Special arrangements are necessary if a family member has been disabled by a war injury, or has a speech defect or a metabolic problem.

Expert help is usually needed with such problems, in teaching methods of care and coping to the person affected and to the family. The treatment and teaching include what to do to help the person physically and educationally, how to manage a household with a handicapped member, and to deal with the social-emotional effects on all members of the family. Parents of handicapped children often feel guilt as well as sorrow. They are likely to isolate themselves from normal community contacts. People are usually helped by interaction with people who face the same problem. For this reason, there are associations of parents of retarded children, alcoholics, families of alcoholics, overweight people, single parents, and many other groups who have physical, mental, or social problems. Such groups supply opportunities for sharing, expressing, giving and receiving sympathy, understanding, and techniques for dealing with mutual problems. They are important, often essential, supplements to professional advice and treatment from physicians, psychotherapists, physical therapists, and social workers.

DRUGS

Drugs contribute to a tremendous health problem and at the same time, drugs are the means of relieving all sorts of illness and pain and of correcting bodily deficiencies.

Drugs are everybody's problem, not only the individual's and the family's but also the world community's. But here we are concerned with what families and individuals can do to preserve and promote the health of their members.

Medicines, especially pills, are very much a part of everyday life in the Western world, particularly in the United States. Young infants receive vitamins in drops and as soon as they can pick up bits of food and chew them, chewable vitamin pills are one of their daily pleasures and benefits. Adults toss down various food supplements and medications with breakfast and casually take a couple of aspirin tablets if bothered with a headache. Television commercials laud and illustrate a huge succession of pills, liquids, and sprays for all bodily parts from head to toes. A clear message is delivered every day, even every 20 minutes; solve your problems by swallowing or squirting something. It is not a very big jump for a 10 year old to 12 year old to accept a pill or a sniff from a friend who tells him it will make him feel great.

As with the other health problems discussed in this chapter, drugs pose the greatest threats to the person at times when growth is rapid. Those periods are prenatal life, infancy, and adolescence.

Prenatal Life and Infancy

The Thalidomide tragedy is well known throughout the world, since deformed children are growing up in several countries, and much publicity was given to their parents' attempts to secure reparations from the manufacturers of the medicine that caused prenatal damage. Obstetricians and health educators caution women to take *no drugs during pregnancy* except those approved by their doctors. Medical advice usually includes a warning that cigarette smoking is likely to harm the fetus by resulting in a smaller birthweight and possible premature birth. Infants born to heroin-addicted mothers showed withdrawal symptoms and disturbed sleep patterns, indicating that their central nervous systems had been affected by heroin [28].

The prenatal effects of mind-changing drugs have not been proven conclusively on human subjects, although there have been reports of brain damage resulting from LSD. Animal experiments, however, have yielded some evidence that should give pause to pregnant women. For example, pregnant mice were subjected to marijuana smoke at the rate of one daily cigarette for ten days. Their offspring were born with serious defects. About 20 per cent had cleft palates and defective jaws [19]. Surely abstinence from all drugs makes sense for pregnant women, since some noxious substances are known to cause damage in human embryos and many more have been demonstrated to be harmful to animals, and there are some with unknown effects.

At first glance, it might seem that there was little chance of infants ingesting drugs, and yet there are several ways in which they do. Breast-fed babies receive a share of the drugs taken by their mothers. Some drugs pass into the breast milk more readily than others. Since new medications are being constantly produced and prescribed, research can hardly keep pace enough to give information about all. The director of a poison control center gives this rule of thumb for judging whether to give a particular drug to a nursing mother: if $\frac{1}{15}$ or $\frac{1}{12}$ of the dose would not be suitable for a baby, then do not give the drug to the mother [3]. Existing evidence indicates that oral contraceptives, nicotine, and marijuana will be transmitted to the baby and that they are probably harmful. Moderate amounts of alcohol (one or two drinks a day) are thought not to hurt the baby. In prescribing medicine for a nursing mother, the physician needs to take great care to protect the baby, and if in doubt, he can consult a poison control center for the latest information.

Young children sometimes swallow pills, medicines, cosmetics, or cleaning materials that they find. The best management of such situations is *prevention*, through careful storage of harmful materials, as well as supervision of children.

Sometimes parents give drugs to their children, either because they do not believe that the substance is harmful to anyone or because they believe that children and adults should be treated alike. Parents have been known to share their "joints," LSD, or alcoholic drinks with their very young children. Such practices are likely to endanger the child's present health and set the stage for future habituation. The danger is greater in the case of some drugs, such as cocaine or LSD, than others. However, alcohol is highly dangerous for some individuals. Families that incorporate alcohol into a cultural or religious ritual teach their children to use it moderately. Such teaching, however, does not guarantee that the child will not become addicted.

Adolescence

Adolescence and perhaps the preceding year or two are the time of life when most people think of drug problems as pertinent. Looking for new experience and asserting their independence of adults, the preadolescent is likely to try cigarettes alcohol, marijuana, and other drugs. Where he goes from here depends upon many factors, including his self-esteem, his parents' behavior, his peers' behavior, and the availability of the various drugs.

Considering drugs (including alcohol and cigarettes) as a health management problem, the first thing for individuals and families to do is to get full information on the action of drugs that they use or consider using. Good communication patterns are very helpful in family discussions of this topic, on which many adolescents and parents have trouble talking with each other. Other tensions and conflicts are often reflected in an abuse of drugs. When one member of a family is habituated or addicted, it is likely that outside help is needed in order to solve the problems that led to it and to change present behavior patterns. Sources include professional therapy, groups, and individuals that have experienced the same problem, and combinations of these agents.

RECREATION

Recreation means continuing renewal of the person, in body, mind, and feeling. *Play,* the normal means of recreation, is any activity carried on with pleasure, for its own sake. Physical health is enhanced by active motor play, as in sports and outdoor games. Mental and emotional refreshment come from artistic creating and experiencing, social play, humor, and enjoyment of nature, as well as from sports and games.

Planning for recreation is part of health management, too. Family members have to take into consideration time, place, money, and everyone's abilities and preferences. Often play can be a part of more serious or humdrum processes. A creative act can transform a meal into recreation, something as simple as an interesting conversation, some jokes or funny stories, or a heart-shaped red gelatin dessert on Valentine's Day. In New Zealand, most families have easy access to a beach, camp grounds, skiing, bowling, cricket, and many more outdoor activities. Since all places of business are closed on Saturdays, couples and families often go on week-end expeditions. When getting acquainted with people, they often ask, "What are your sports?" Everyone is expected to enjoy some sort of outdoor exercise and to take part in it frequently. Americans may be headed in this direction, although they have been generally relatively sedentary. However, outdoor active recreation has had an impetus from the energy crisis, from renewed interest in fitness by health-conscious young adults, and from increased amounts of leisure time. This is not to say that

ROBERT J. IZZO

jogging for weight control is exactly play and recreation, but jogging is definitely exercise in the service of health. And perhaps those who jog will sometimes hike or play golf for fun.

At the same time that recreation is contributing to health, it can be strengthening the bonds of partnership, parent-child relations, sibling relations, and even kin relations. Mutual enjoyment, sharing, and cooperation of an experience result in positive feelings between the participants.

HEALTH SERVICES

No individual, couple, or family can possibly be self-sufficient in health care. Even residents of the Australian bush turn to the bush hospitals in time of need, getting advice by radio and emergency help by plane. Pitcairn Islanders, living in a cooperative community without modern medical facilities, fear appendicitis and infections brought by ships. The average North American has many health services available in the form of public health programs and health care. Voluntary agencies such as Planned Parenthood and the Cancer Society also offer care and education. Good health management includes taking advantage of the services needed for optimal health.

Positive Health Care

In order to stay free from illness and to function on a high level of energy and well-being, all the home health practices have to be supplemented by some professional services. Immunizations have already been mentioned. Regular physical examinations and dental examinations, with all appropriate laboratory tests, constitute positive care. It is not always easy to find a physician who takes a real interest in *keeping* a patient in optimal condition, since many are specialists in repairing one small portion of the body. In areas where doctors are scarce, they may be quite justified in thinking that their first responsibility is to sick people. In addition to the problem of finding a doctor who is interested in whole persons who are well, there is the cost of his services. Few insurance programs pay for positive health care, although there are some groups of doctors who offer comprehensive care. Tel-Med, an innovation of the medical society of San Bernardino County, California, is a way of helping families to help themselves. Anyone can dial a number, ask for and receive free, authoritative information on all sorts of medical and health problems.

Positive dental care is also somewhat elusive, but worth looking for. Even though twice-a-year cleaning and examination may seem expensive, they result in saving dollars, as well as teeth. When adolescents and young adults are first on their own financially, they are often tempted to neglect their teeth. Dental care seems to cost such a great deal of money, and the results of postponing it are not immediately apparent. The net result, however, is much greater expense, more time and pain (or *agomins*, as our family terms painful moments).

Free or inexpensive positive health care is offered to low-income families in some clinics in the United States, but more often available services are for emergencies rather than for keeping well. Immunization clinics are definitely a positive service. Some other affluent countries offer more. In New Zealand, a visit to a physician's office costs about 20 per cent of what it costs in the United States and prescriptions are filled free. All care in public hospitals, including surgery and childbirth, are free to patients. School dental clinics provide complete care for children's teeth. Of course, the government (taxes from the people) pays the doctor, pharmacist, hospital, dentist, and dental nurse. Income taxes are high, but the result is that all people can have health care when they need it.

Sanitation

Clean water has been taken for granted by most North Americans, but those who have had to boil drinking water will always appreciate the comfort and security of potable tap water; the same is true with milk. After having to boil milk before using it, pasteurized milk and powdered milk seem like the greatest luxuries. Modern industrialized nations ordinarily provide sanitation of milk, water, and foods through legislation, inspection, and taxes. Communicable diseases are controlled through both prevention and detection, isolation and treatment. Efforts are mounted against carriers, such as malaria mosquitoes and rabid animals. Garbage and trash are collected and disposed of. Public toilets are provided. In very poor countries, most of these amenities are either lacking or inadequate. Especially in very crowded cities, such as Calcutta and Jogjakarta, educated, wealthy people provide their own sanitation, whereas the poor have no choice.

Safe Streets

Pedestrians can walk along most North American streets without falling into holes, tripping over loose pieces of sidewalk, stumbling into the wares of a sidewalk shopkeeper, or slipping in fresh cow dung. However, an American strolling in a big city, especially at night, stands a greater chance than a Canadian of getting mugged, robbed, raped, and/or killed. Where bicycle riding is concerned, North Americans have a long way to go to equal the networks of safe paths provided in the Netherlands and other advanced European countries.

Nutrition

Although much remains to be done, North Americans have made efforts to feed people through a variety of programs. The school hot lunch program is one of the most important ones, since it reaches many children who need it tremendously. When breakfast is also given to hungry children, they benefit greatly, both physically and mentally. In some schools, only subsidized milk is given. Food stamps and surplus foods have been used to supplement the diets of the poor. There have been occasional programs to improve the intake of pregnant and nursing mothers. *Meals on Wheels,* a combined public and voluntary service, is invaluable to invalids and old people. Some schools, as well, provide meals for the aged.

Milk and milk products are subsidized by the New Zealand government. Everyone can afford generous quantities of these highly nutritious foods.

Education

Health education is a vital public health service, covering many different kinds of programs to all sorts of people. It cannot be done once and for all in the schools, although the foundation is laid by sound health courses in school. However, health sciences are constantly yielding new knowledge, requiring people to update their education.

Even more important, a person needs education on special topics at certain points in life. Sometimes the appropriate education can come from the family and a public program is not necessary, as with preschool children's sex education. At other times, public programs are the only way in which most will be reached, as in adolescents' education for family planning and venereal disease control. Education for childbirth and infant care is a necessity to prospective parents and new parents. Although a few may get sufficient education privately, the need for public services is great in this area. The greatest need is among single pregnant girls and adolescent parents. A recent social action program for this population includes health services along with educational programs [7]. Another great need is for adult education in regard to aging.

An expansion and revamping of nutrition education is needed in order to motivate people of all ages to eat what is good for life, growth, and health. Traditional nutrition education could be supplemented with teaching based on cultural food imagery and emotional play upon such themes as survival, minimizing suffering, parental love and duty, success, achievement, and beauty [5].

SUMMARY

In caring for one another, all family members can promote family health. Achieving and maintaining health requires management of family resources. Optimal health enhances all functions of the individual and contributes to group well-being. Health can be defined in terms of physical and behavioral characteristics.

Nutrition is important to health at all times but is critical in periods of rapid growth or change. During prenatal life, when the basic systems of the body are constructed, nutrition plays a vital role, especially in brain development. Birthweight is related to survival and absence of defects. Nutrition is also critical in the change-over from infancy to early childhood. The rapid growth and bodily reorganization of adolescence require large quantities of high-quality food. The nutrition of the adolescent girl has implications for her reproductive performance. When pregnancy is superimposed on adolescence, nutritional problems are great. Poverty is the most basic cause of malnutrition in the world, followed by ignorance and lack of skills. Many people in affluent societies eat large amounts of food that is devoid of nutritional value, promoting obesity and tooth decay. Advertising encourages the intake of sugar and fats.

Exercise and rest, in appropriate rhythms, are essential to health. Since consider-able management is involved in the establishment and maintaining of harmonious rhythms, family communication and decision-making are important. Needs are different at different stages of development. Exercise and rest articulate with each other and with nutrition, growth, and repair of tissues.

Shelter and clothing, necessary for protection, compete for family resources of money, time, and effort. Wants and expectations are geared to prevailing weather and sociocultural conditions. Inadequate housing causes grave problems of safety and interpersonal disruptions. Although good management cannot alleviate all such problems, it can minimize them.

Many illnesses and injuries can be prevented. Immunity to infection is built by good nutrition, rest, exercise, and protective immunizations. Many diseases can be prevented only by keeping the organisms from entering the body, which is accom-plished by sanitation and specific modes of personal cleanliness. Venereal disease, especially gonorrhea, is a growing threat to health. The treatment of illness requires knowledge and skills, and often professional help as well. Nutrition, rest, and prompt treatment are basic. Providing for physical safety is the joint responsibility of community and family, in which home management contributes adequate arrange-ment of space, safe operation of equipment, education, and supervision of children.

Family planning can prevent the propagation of many hereditary defects, but many families must cope with the reality of a handicapped child. Permanent injuries can be incurred at any time of life and thus a family may have an adult with needs for special care. Such a family usually needs to share its problems with understanding, and with helpful persons and groups.

Drugs are a health problem as well as an aid to health. Drugs pose particular problems during prenatal life, childhood, and adolescence. Although some problems may be prevented by good family management, established problems involving the use of drugs usually require outside help.

Recreation, or continuing renewal of the person, is achieved by all types of play. Outdoor games and exercise contribute especially to bodily growth and renewal.

Health services, of one sort or another, are provided by a community for its members. Family management determines the use made of these services. Positive care means trying to keep people in excellent health, not just treating them when they are sick or injured. Cost in money is often a determining factor in getting good care. Public health services include many kinds of sanitation, and provisions for

A FAMILY IS BASED ON HOME

safety, nutrition, and education. The existence and quality of such services depend heavily on prevailing financial and political situations.

REFERENCES

1. Ademowore, Adebayo S., Norman G. Courey, and James S. Kime. Relationship of maternal nutrition and weight gain to newborn birthweight. *Obstetrics and Gynecology,* 1972, **39,** 460–464.
2. Ainsworth, Mary D. Salter. The development of infant-mother attachment. In Bettye M. Caldwell and Henry Ricciuti (eds.). *Review of Child Development Research,* Vol. 3. Chicago: U. of Chicago, 1973.
3. Arena, Jay M. Contamination of the ideal food. *Nutrition Today,* 1970, **5:** 4, 2–8.
4. Belcher, John C. and Pablo B. Vasquez-Calcerrada. A cross-culture approach to the social functions of housing. *Journal of Marriage and the Family,* 1972, **34,** 750–761.
5. Berg, Alan. *The nutrition factor: Its role in national development.* Washington: The Brookings Institution, 1973.
6. Coursin, David. Maternal nutrition and the offspring's development. *Nutrition Today,* 1973, **8:** 2, 12–18.
7. Cromwell, Richard E. and Joan L. Gangel. A social "action" program directed to single pregnant girls and adolescent parents. *Family Coordinator,* 1974, **23,** 61–66.
8. Dairy Council. Nutrition in illness. *Dairy Council Digest,* 1969, **40:** 5, 25–28.
9. Dairy Council. Nutritional implications of osteoporosis. *Dairy Council Digest,* 1970, **41:** 5, 25–28.
10. Erhard, Darla. The new vegetarians. *Nutrition Today,* 1973, **8:** 6, 4–12.
10a. Feldman, Margaret and Harold Feldman. *Sexism in the family.* Ithaca, N.Y. Unpublished manuscript, 1974.
11. Frisch, Rose E. Weight at menarche: Similarity for well-nourished and undernourished girls at differing ages, and evidence for historical constancy. *Pediatrics,* 1972, **50,** 445–450.
12. Gallese, Liz R. Living together. *Wall Street Journal,* June 25, 1974.
13. Handler, Philip (ed.). *Biology and the future of man.* New York: Oxford U. P., 1970.
14. Horwitz, Abraham and Gerald D. LaVeck. Preface. In David J. Kallen (ed.). *Nutrition, development and social behavior.* Washington D.C.: U.S. Department of Health, Education and Welfare Publication No. 73, 1973.
15. Hunter, Handsfield H., Timothy O. Lipman, James P. Harnisch, Evelyn Tronca, and King J. Holmes. Asymptomatic gonorrhea in men: Diagnosis, natural course and prevalence. *New England Journal of Medicine,* 1974, **290,** 117–123.
16. Hurley, Lucille S. The consequences of fetal impoverishment. *Nutrition Today,* 1968, **3:** 4, 3–10.
16a. Kasl, Stanislav V. Effects of residential environment on health and behavior: A review (Report to the Bureau of Community Environmental Management, HSMHA, PHS, DHEW). New Haven: Yale University, 1972. (Mimeo)
17. Krogman, Wilton M. *Child growth.* Ann Arbor: U. of Michigan, 1972.
18. Leger, Richard R. Viral venereal disease is highly contagious and doesn't go away. *Wall Street Journal,* April 19, 1974.
19. Lynch, Vincent. Report to the New York State Committee on marijuana laws. Reported in the *New York Times,* October 18, 1970.
19a. McLaughlin, J.D. Personal communication. May 1975.

20. Metropolitan Life Insurance Company. Death rates in Canada lowest among married persons. *Statistical Bulletin,* 1973, **54:** *(August), 4–6.*

21. Metropolitan Life Insurance Company. Venereal diseases: Recent morbidity and mortality. *Statistical Bulletin,* 1973, **54:** 11, 5–7.

22. Michelson, William. *Man and his urban environment: A sociological approach.* Reading, Mass.: Addison-Wesley, 1970.

23. Montgomery, James E. Commentary on misconceptions about man-made space. *Family Coordinator,* 1974, **23,** 57–59.

24. Montgomery, James E. and Gracia S. McCabe. Housing aspirations of southern Appalachian families. *Home Economics Research Journal,* 1973, **2,** 2–11.

25. Pratt, Lois. The significance of the family in medication. *Journal of Comparative Family Studies,* 1973, **4,** 13–31.

26. Purvis, George A. What nutrients do our infants really get? *Nutrition Today,* 1973, **8,** 28–34.

27. Russell, Candyce S. Transition to parenthood: Problems and gratifications. *Journal of Marriage and the Family,* 1974, **36,** 294–301.

28. Schulman, C. A. Sleep patterns in newborn infants as a function of suspected neurological impairment of maternal heroin addiction. Paper presented at meetings of the Society for Research in Child Development, Santa Monica, California, 1969.

29. Shank, Robert E. A chink in our armor. *Nutrition Today,* 1970, **5:** 2, 2–11.

29a. Smart, Russell C. and Mollie S. Smart. Group values shown in preadolescents' drawings in five English-speaking countries. *Journal of Social Psychology,* 1975, **97:**1.

30. Spanier, Graham B. and Carol Fishel. The housing project and familial functions: Consequences for low-income urban families. *Family Coordinator,* 1973, **22,** 235–240.

31. Spence, Donald L. and Betsy C. Robinson. Patterns in retirement. In Frances Carp (ed.). *The retirement process.* Public Health Service Publication No. 178. Washington D.C.: Government Printing Office, 1968.

32. U.S. Department of Agriculture. *Dietary levels of households in the United States, Spring, 1965.* Hyattsville, Md.: Agricultural Research Service, 1968.

32a. U.S. Department of Health, Education, and Welfare. *Teen-agers: Marriages, divorces, parenthood, and mortality.* Rockville, Md.: National Center for Health Statistics. 1973.

33. Vore, David A. Prenatal nutrition and postnatal intellectual development. *Merrill-Palmer Quarterly,* 1973, **19,** 251–260.

34. Walker, Kathryn E. Household work time: Its implications for family decisions. *Journal of Home Economics,* 1973, **65:** 7, 7–11.

35. Witte, John. A complete guide to immunization. *Parents' Magazine,* 1973 (November), 35–36.

CHAPTER 14

family planning: getting it right

In this chapter, we discuss population policy and programs, methods of population and birth control, and pregnancy, and birth. Because population has reached a crisis point, hunger and mass starvation will most likely continue to be the world's most pressing problem. Most families in the world today are hungry, or cannot provide adequate nutrition for their members, or both. Technology for controlling death has far outstripped technologies for food production and controlling births. Awareness of the problems that face us is a small but important step toward meeting the crisis.

POPULATION

Good family management involves finding a balance between income and outlay of resources. In an expanding agricultural society, children past preschool age are resources for the family because their labors contribute to the income of the family. In such societies, family planning would involve having many children, even though frequent and closely spaced children take a toll on the mother's physical strength. Although children are resources in the sense that they are sources of love and emotional growth, they can no longer by regarded as sources of income. Raising a child in the United States from birth to the age of eighteen costs about $72,000 at today's prices. In poorer countries, the monetary cost of a child would be much smaller, but an extra child might be a relatively greater strain upon the already overtaxed resources of the family.

349

Factors Limiting Population Growth

A **fecund** woman (one capable of producing children) could theoretically have twenty or thirty children, and a few women have had as many as 15 or 20 children [6]. The average number of children per family is fortunately much smaller. Before the eradication of childhood killer diseases, it was necessary for a couple to have a large number of children in order to have two or three who survived until adulthood. However, it is not merely the decline in deaths from such diseases as malaria, smallpox, and scarlet fever that has caused an upsurge in population density in the past hundred years. Cultural factors play an important part in determining who will marry and when they will marry, which in turn plays a part in determining how many children will be born. For example, if celibacy (refraining from sexual relations) is

practiced by a fair proportion of a society, the number of children born in that society will be cut down. If women marry and begin sexual intercourse at age 30 rather than age 15, appreciably fewer children will be born. If widows are not allowed to remarry, they will be less likely to produce more children.

Cultural factors also influence how many children will be born, once conceived, or survive to adulthood, if born. The way a pregnant woman is cared for; the cultural taboos concerning what she may or may not eat; the way an infant is delivered, nursed, and weaned; the way the infant is housed and clothed; the treatment of infant diseases; whether or not infanticide is practiced; the relative importance of male and female children; all of these factors and more determine how many children, and of what sex, will survive.

In the ancient Greek city-state of Sparta, infants were exposed at birth to determine which would live and which would die; only strong infants would survive. In countries such as India where male children are prized more than female, male children are fed first, if there is not enough food to go around; the female children may not get enough to eat, and may be more likely to die. If a mother is unable to nurse her baby, she is more willing to pay another woman to nurse a male child than a female child, who may be fed on a mixture of flour and water. Poor Indian mothers seek medical care more readily for boys than for girls.

Population Growth

It has been estimated that between 600,000 B.C. and 6000 B.C., a period of 594,000 years, 12 billion human beings were born. Between 6000 B.C. and A.D. 1650, a period of 7,650 years, 42 billion people were born. And between A.D. 1650 and 1962, a period of 612 years, 23 billion people were born [10].

Another way of looking at the growth of world population is to consider how many people were alive on the earth in a particular year. Around 2,000 years ago, the world population was about 250 million. By 1600, the population had doubled to 500 million. Between 1600 and 1820, it doubled again to become 1 billion. In another hundred years (1920) it had doubled once more, to become 2 billion. In 1972, it was predicted that by 1975 the world population would be 4 billion. By the year 2000 if the 2 per cent growth rate continues, there will be well over 6 billion people on our planet: from 250 million to 6000 million in two thousand years. By 2050, at a 2 per cent growth rate, the world population theoretically will reach 15 billion, or its absolute limit [7].

Growth Rates. Growth rates represent the difference between birth rates and death rates for the world. In 1974, the world birthrate was 33 per 1000 population, and the death rate was 13. The difference between these figures is 20 per 1000 or a growth rate of 2 per cent per year. The death rate is expected to drop more; population stabilization, therefore, must come from declining birth rates.

Whenever the birthrate is around 20 (that is, 20 births per 1000 population), it means that fecund females are having, during their reproductive period, an average of slightly less than three children each. A birthrate of 40 to 45 means that fecund women are averaging eight to ten children; this rate is not unusual in some parts of the world. Developed countries have much lower birth rates: Sweden's birthrate in 1972 was 13.8 (per thousand population); Hungary's was 14.7 [5] Canada's was 15.5 in 1973, down from 15.9 in 1972 [12]. The United States has been experiencing a decline in birthrate, with 14.9 the lowest point at this writing having been reached in 1974. Figure 14–1 illustrates crude birthrates in the United States from 1933 to 1974. It shows the decline during the Depression years of the 1930s, the tremendous jump during the post-World War II "Baby Boom" years, and a gradual decline since.

Although national figures for China are not available, the birth rate in Shanghai in 1971 was reported to be six or seven per thousand population per year [26]. The figure was 5.9 for one district in Hangchow. The rate was 18 to 20 in one commune. Before 1949, China's birth rate was around 45. Another report on the birth rate in Shanghai shows a steady decrease from 33.45 to 5.42 during the years from 1960 to 1973 [31].

The Problem in the United States. Obviously, population is growing much more rapidly in the poorer nations of the world than it is in the United States and

FIGURE 14-1   U.S. crude birth rates from 1933 to 1973.

Source: Vital statistics of the U.S. 1968. Vol. 1. Natality Table 1-1. Monthly vital statistics report. Provisional statistics. Annual summary for U.S. 1973. Statistical abstract of the United States, 1973. Table No. 66 And Globe and Mail, Toronto, Oct. 2, 1974.

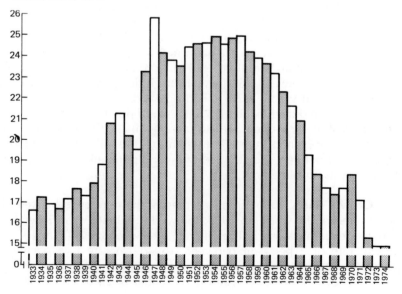

A FAMILY IS BASED ON HOME

other developed countries as Figure 14-2 indicates. The United States is blessed with land that is unusually rich in both agricultural lands and mineral wealth. Some people believe that the land could easily support a much denser population, that there is no real cause for concern yet.

However, the population of the United States comprises only 6 per cent of the world's population and uses about *half* of the world's resources. One more American, therefore, depletes many more resources and creates more waste than one more Ghanaian or Indian. The poorer nations of the world have a right to a higher level of living, but a higher level of living also means more consumption.

The population of the United States is still growing. It increased from 76 million in 1900 to 205 million in 1970, both from natural increase and from immigration. By 2013, at the replacement rate of two children per family, the population will be 300 million. If each family has three children, there will be 400 million people by 2013. Fortunately, the average desired number of children has declined from three to slightly over two [9].

In 1972, for the first time, the total fertility rate (the number of children women would have if they maintained the rate of 1972 throughout their reproductive years) fell under the magical Zero Population Growth rate of 2.11. Indeed in 1973, it fell to 1.9 children per woman. However, because of the relatively large numbers of young people in the United States, the population would still increase until well into the twenty-first century even without immigration. Tomas Frejka has calculated that

if fertility dropped immediately to an average of fewer than two children per family . . . and remained there, the United States population would nevertheless continue to grow

FIGURE 14-2   Birth rates (births per 1,000 population) by world areas, 1970.

Source: L. F. Bouvier and Everett S. Lee. The vital revolution. Unit No. 3 of population profiles. Washington, Connecticut: Center for Information on America, 1972.

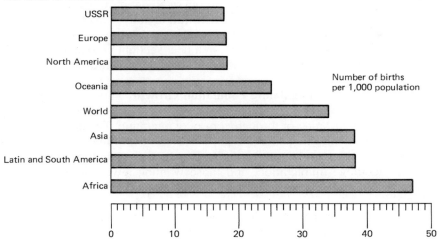

for at least another fifty years. . . . The United States population would reach its peak around the year 2020 and would be about 20 per cent larger than it is now, that is, about 247 million. . . . By the year 2050, . . . it would decline by 20 million persons and be in the order of 227 million inhabitants. [11, p. 166]

This *without* immigration!

Population Policies and Programs

Many nations in the world have recently recognized the gravity of their population problem. Numbers of citizens or subjects used to help to determine the strength of a nation, but unlimited numbers of people create more strain than strength. Some governments of the world give support to population planning, but this support varies in type and amount. A *policy* forms the guiding philosophy or underlying theory of *programs* that may or may not be carried out in reality. The effectiveness of both population policies and programs is under debate.

Reasons for Population Planning. In addition to the stark fact that mankind is pushing the global limits on maintaining life, population control is needed because it contributes to the health of individuals and families. Repeated, closely spaced childbearing not only taxes the mother's physical stamina, but, on the average, produces children of lower physical and mental quality. Some parents have the financial and emotional resources to provide adequately or generously for a large number of children, but most parents do not.

The problem of adequate resources for children is even more pressing in poor societies, where most people are hungry all the time. Inadequate nutrition during pregnancy results in a higher fetal and infant mortality rate, and smaller infants that are less developed mentally and physically at birth. Inadequate nutrition during the early years (both before and after birth) literally starves the brain. Drastically cutting the birthrate in the hungry nations would mean more food for the people who already exist, but as discussed in a later section, cutting the birthrate is not a simple matter. Furthermore, it alone will not solve the problem of world hunger.

Ways of Regulating Population Growth. There are only three ways in which population growth of a given area may be regulated: through alteration of the death rate, or birthrate, or through control of migration. The death rate has been drastically cut, causing a huge jump in population. The birthrate is less easily reduced, because it is much more an area of individual control. Countries that want more people can encourage immigration, and those wanting fewer can encourage emigration and forbid immigration.

Policies and their implementation. Birth, death, and migration can be implemented by governments in five ways. Governments can:

A Planned Parenthood clinic.

1. Communicate with people in order to influence their demographic behavior in the desired manner,
2. Provide services to effect the desired behavior,
3. Manipulate the balance of incentives and disincentives to achieve the desired regulation,
4. Shift the weight of social institutions and opportunities in the desired direction, and
5. Coerce the desired behavior through the power of the state [4, p. 2]

The extraordinarily low birth rates reported for the People's Republic of China, on page 352 are witness to the effectiveness of the Chinese policy, which seems to include all five of these methods of implementation. Reports form a social worker [26] and a pediatrician [3] give a picture of how the low birth rate is achieved and maintained. First and foremost is the unity of purpose of the Chinese people, who have a strong sense of mission for the good of their country.

In crowded areas of China, a low birth rate is understood as a means of promoting the general welfare by avoiding too great a drain on resources, by giving parents responsibilities they can shoulder and by freeing women to work. Not only are birth control education and services provided free of charge, but a woman medical worker calls on women once a month. Each woman chooses her own contraceptive method. After two children, many women choose tubal ligation (sterilization). Abortion is free on request of the woman but is used rarely. A third pregnancy is frowned upon. At the World Population Conference in 1974, the leader of the Chinese delegation explained China's policy of discouraging population growth in crowded areas and encouraging it in sparsely populated regions [30].

The change in social institutions that go along with the shift from a traditional to a modern society has a drastic effect upon the birthrate of a nation. Urbanization and industrialization influence the kinship system, values and beliefs, education, nutrition and sanitation, and the status of women [4]. These changes in social institutions reduce the birthrate, but slowly.

Incentives to raise fertility have been practiced in some developed countries, with uncertain results. Incentives to lower fertility are being used in some undeveloped countries, with some success but certainly not an overwhelming amount. Providing or forbidding services can have a major effect upon a country's population growth rate. Legal abortion was a major element in lowering Japan's postwar birthrate, and withdrawing legal abortion caused a dramatic temporary rise in Romania's birthrate. The recent withdrawal of the prohibition of abortion in the United States has probably reduced the birthrate by about 1.5 points [4].

In the United States, the official trend toward family planning did not begin until 1961 when President Kennedy called for U.S. aid to family planning programs in developing nations. In the mid-1960s, the U.S. Department of Defense began to support family planning for servicemen and their families. Programs were also started for the nation's poor. It was not until the end of the 1960s that the fact was publicized that the primary population problem in the United States is caused by the nonpoor, since they make up between 80 and 85 per cent of the population.

In 1972, President Nixon commissioned a report on population growth that made a number of important recommendations. The commission could not agree upon the policies that were needed to stabilize the population, and their recommendations probably did not go far enough [9]. Implementation of the suggestions of the commission has been scanty.

Evaluation of Family Planning Programs. As a general rule, family planning as a means of population control succeeds in countries that have low death rates and high levels of affluence, and fails in areas of poverty and high death rates. Industrialization, urbanization, the introduction of legalized abortion and sterilization, raising the status of women, and reducing unemployment and poverty all contribute to more effective family planning.

Perhaps more important than all these factors is the availability of birth control services to *women*. Only during the past few years has birth control been widely available to poor women, although the rich have had it for a long time. Since 1972, when services were provided to 2.6 million women in the United States, acceptance of family planning has exceeded all expectations [16]. Fertility rates have declined more rapidly among poor women than among those above the poverty level. Decreases in unwanted births have been greater among the poor. Middle- and upper-class people have apparently harbored a misconception that poor people conceived irresponsibly, whereas actually, the poor had little choice until birth control services were readily available to them. We wonder if this finding has implications for people in the poor countries of the world. Perhaps, like North American women, most women would welcome control over their own bodies and would not choose to have children if they could not care for them.

Many ethnic and national groups have a tradition of large families, and these traditions die hard, especially when it is outsiders who espouse having smaller families. We cannot be certain whether or not family planning programs will succeed in stabilizing the world population, and will therefore afford a better life for most people. The success of family planning programs in at least reducing population growth in nations approaching modernization indicates that there is some hope. It appears that in most societies, especially those that espouse a democratic philosophy, governments need to start with a soft-sell approach. This approach is even more necessary if families in that society have traditionally been large. Roman Catholic Costa Rica is succeeding in reducing its population growth rate through a voluntary family planning program that began privately in 1962, but did not receive official government endorsement until 1967. Oral contraceptives and intrauterine devices (explained later in this chapter) are used by many younger women in Costa Rica, and sterilizations are performed, although their availability is not openly advertised. The program is integrated with maternal and child health programs, placing the emphasis upon the family's well-being [13]. For both moral and practical reasons, this is where the emphasis should be.

BIRTH CONTROL

Through birth control, couples, but especially women, gain more control over their lives. In this section, we discuss birth control methods.

Decision Making

The question of whether or not to practice birth control is one that is left up to the individual in our society. If the decision is made to use some kind of birth control, the modern individual has a number of methods from which to choose. Religious, cultural, and medical factors will influence the decision as to which method is most suitable. There is no such thing as a perfect birth control method: the most statistically effective method may be dangerous medically to a particular person, or it may be objectionable on moral or other grounds. For some groups of people, any kind of birth control is immoral. For others, having more than two children is immoral. One should also realize that in order for a nonmedical method of birth control to be effective, it must be used every time that the erect penis is in or near the vagina. Occasionally, a pregnancy may result even when intercourse has not occured if the male ejaculates near the vaginal opening.

Since it takes two to make a baby, each partner to sexual intercourse has a responsibility to plan for birth control or the care of an infant should one result. Taking such responsibility requires communication and planning. A man should not assume that a woman is using contraceptives if she does not mention it. A woman should not assume that she cannot get pregnant, unless she knows for sure that she is sterile. Pregnancies can occur even with the safest methods of birth control. Marriage or abortion are not easy solutions if an unplanned pregnancy results.

Birth Control: Some Historical Methods

Many people today seem to think that the subject of birth control is relatively new. However, birth control was mentioned in Egyptian records dating back to 4,000 years ago, and it was discussed by the Greek philosophers 2,400 years ago. The earliest surviving records on birth control from India are about 1,600 years old. The first Chinese record of birth control is in a medical text written 1,300 years ago, although the idea is probably much older [15].

Some of the ancient contraceptives were more useful than others. Magic charms might be worn, or brews drunk from roots or leaves. The vagina might be washed out by means of a douche, or other substances such as pepper might be inserted in the vagina after coitus. More sophisticated methods included the forerunners of modern mechanical barrier methods: Egyptian women used plugs made of crocodile droppings; other people have used plugs made of seaweed, beeswax, cloth, and other substances. Aristotle recommended the use of oil of cedar or frankincense mixed with olive oil inserted in the vagina before intercourse.

Romans used the forerunner of the modern condom, which is a sheath placed over the penis to catch the ejaculate fluid. However, the first condom-like devices were used by women who placed a loose pouch made of animal membrane in their vagina. Condoms worn by men were probably a later invention, and it is not until 1844 when rubber was first vulcanized that the use of condoms became widespread [15].

"Natural" Methods

The most effective method of birth control is **abstinence.** This method is more widely practiced among the unmarried than the married, although certain religious groups have practiced abstinence. Gandhi, the political leader who fought for India's independence from the British, advocated abstinence as the solution to India's growing population problem, with disastrous results.

Continence like abstinence, is a method of birth control that requires no special devices. In this method, the male penetrates the vagina with his penis, but does not achieve orgasm or ejaculation. This method was practiced by the Oneida community in New York State in the midnineteenth century. It is not recommended medically, because male sexual release is not attained. When the individual is sexually aroused, his or her genitals become engorged with blood. When the individual has an orgasm, tension and blood buildup are released. If there is no release, painful congestion may result, sometimes known as "blue balls" or "lover's nuts," in the male. The female may also suffer from congestion, although she may obtain release through orgasm without fear of pregnancy. Another hazard of this practice is that it is possible for a woman to become pregnant even if her partner is capable of practicing continence. A few sperm may be contained in the preejaculatory fluid that may ooze from the end of the penis during sexual excitement. If these sperm are deposited in the vagina, it is possible that pregnancy will result.

Withdrawal (also called **coitus interruptus**) is similar to continence, except that the male withdraws his penis from the vagina just before he ejaculates. As with continence, sperm in the preejaculatory fluid may cause pregnancy. Another danger is that during orgasm the male's natural reaction is to thrust deeper into the vagina, not to withdraw. This method may cause considerable anxiety on the part of both partners, but especially the female, wondering whether the male will be able to withdraw in time. Out of 100 women whose partners use this method for one year, 22 will become pregnant [15]. For every 100 sexually active women using *no* contraceptives for one year, 80 will become pregnant [14].

Rhythm is the only method of birth control presently sanctioned by the Roman Catholic Church. The rationale behind the rhythm method is that a woman may become pregnant only a few days of each month, just before and just after she ovulates. Therefore, if she restricts intercourse to only her infertile days, she will not become pregnant. In theory, the rhythm method should work well, but unfortunately it is difficult to determine for sure when the fertile days are. If a woman's menstrual cycle is perfectly regular each month, she is more likely to succeed with the rhythm method. However, if a woman's periods are not regular, it is impossible to determine in advance when ovulation will occur. Even a woman whose periods are regular may ovulate early or late because of sickness or a change in routine.

A second method of determining the time of ovulation is by taking her temperature every morning before she gets out of bed. A day or two before ovulation, her temperature will rise about 0.6° F. When this occurs, she should refrain from sexual intercourse for three days. The temperature method is not foolproof, either, because illness or distress may also cause temperature fluctuations that have nothing to do with the presence or absence of ovulation [15]. For every 100 women who use the rhythm method for one year, approximately 38 will become pregnant [14]. More research needs to be done on the temperature method in order to determine its effectiveness.

Mechanical Methods. The **diaphragm** is a shallow rubber or synthetic rubber cup that is inserted into the vagina and fit over the cervix, preventing sperm from entering (see Figure 14-3). It ranges in size from about two to four inches in diameter, depending upon the size of the woman's internal organs. A flexible rubber-covered metal ring helps hold it in place. The diaphragm must be properly fitted to the individual woman by a physician or other trained medical person. The diaphragm must be used with a spermicidal (sperm-killing) jelly or cream, which is smeared around the edge of the diaphragm and placed in the center of the cup. Additional cream or jelly may be inserted into the vagina after the diaphragm is in place. The diaphragm must be inserted not more than two hours before coitus, and must be left in place for at least six hours afterwards. Properly inserted, the diaphragm may be left in place for 8 to 24 hours without causing discomfort.

Over the period of one year, among women who use the diaphragm every time there is a penile-vaginal contact, two or three out of 100 will become pregnant. Since diaphragm users occasionally fail to use the devices, the actual rate of pregnancies among diaphragm users is nine to 34 per hundred women per year.

The **condom** is a sheath worn on the penis that prevents the sperm from coming into contact with the female (see Figure 14-4.) It may be made of animal membrane, or more usually, very thin rubber. Almost as reliable as the diaphragm, the effectiveness of the condom may be increased by placing a small amount of spermicidal cream or jelly in it before it is put on, or by the woman's using contraceptive foam. Condoms are available in drugstores, and sometimes in vending machines in men's rooms. It is advisable to buy them only from drugstores, since the quality is probably higher. Condoms may deteriorate if exposed to heat; therefore, one should not keep them in a pocket or wallet next to the body.

Condoms may be reused. If they are the rubber kind, they should be washed after use, dried with a towel, powdered with talc, and rerolled. If they are made from animal membrane, they should be washed out and stored in rubbing alcohol. One should be sure to rinse condoms very carefully before reusing those stored in alcohol. Before reuse, condoms should be tested for holes by filling them with water.

It is important to leave a space at the end of the condom for the semen. If worn too snugly, the condom may burst. The male should withdraw after ejaculation so that the shrinking of the penis does not cause semen to leak out of the edge of the condom. For every 100 women whose partner uses condoms each and every time there is penile-vaginal contact for one year, 2.6 will become pregnant. This number may be reduced if contraceptive cream or jelly is used in conjunction with the condom. The actual rate for condom users is 15 pregnancies per 100 women per year [14].

Chemical Barriers. Chemical methods include the use of jellies and creams that are inserted into the vagina prior to intercourse, forming a barrier that both prevents sperm from entering the uterus and kills many of the sperm. The most effective

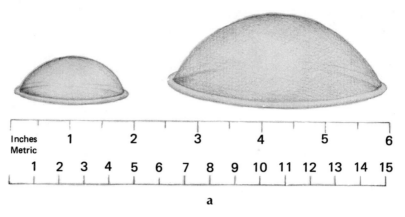

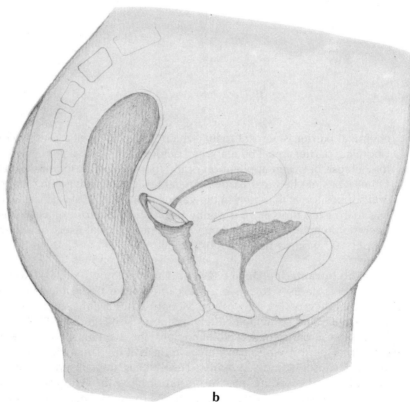

FIGURE 14-3   Diaphragms. a: Scale shown by ruler. b: Diaphragm in place.

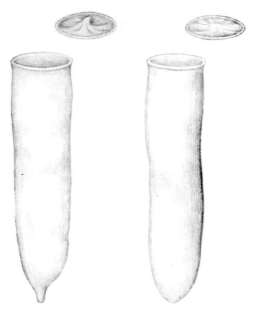

FIGURE 14-4   Condoms.

chemical barrier is aerosol foam, which is sold without a prescription in drugstores. Chemical barriers must be reapplied before each act of coitus. The length of time that may elapse between application of the foam and coitus varies with type and brand. Other types of chemical barriers are tablets that dissolve on contact with the vagina and suppositories that melt in the vagina. For every 100 women who use contraceptive foam each time there is penile-vaginal contact for one year, slightly over 3 will become pregnant. The pregnancy rate among actual users of contraceptive foam is 29 per 100 women per year [14].

The Intrauterine Device (IUD). The first known "IUDs" were pebbles placed in camels' uteruses to prevent the camels from being burdened by pregnancy or young while crossing the deserts. Modern IUDs are made of steel, plastic, or plastic and copper, and come in a variety of shapes (see Figure 14-5). The device is inserted by a doctor or trained technician into the woman's uterus, usually during her menstrual period when the mucus plug is thin. The cervix is slowly dilated; this process causes some cramping. The IUD is then inserted. There may be some cramping and bleeding after the insertion, and the IUD may be expelled from the uterus by means of muscle contractions. Many women experience no discomfort; others experience mild discomfort during their menstrual periods. For still others, pain may be severe at times. If the bleeding and pain become intolerable, a woman may have to have the device removed. However, if she is able to retain the device, it may remain in place for about two years.

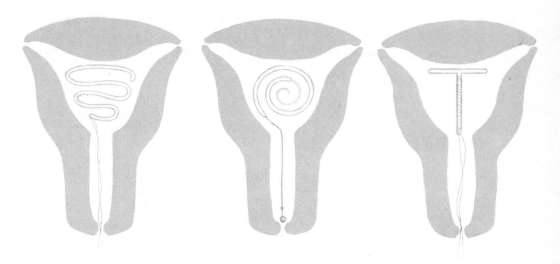

FIGURE 14-5   IUDs in place. Left to right: Lippes loop, coil, copper T.

IUDs have a small string that hangs down through the cervix, and may be felt by the women's fingers when she inserts them in her vagina. She should check each week to make sure that she can still feel the string.

It is not known exactly how IUD's work. Different shaped IUDs work better in different women. Popular kinds are the Lippes loop and the Saf-T-Coil. Recent tests have indicated that a device made of plastic and copper, and shaped like a T, may be more effective than the loop or Saf-T-Coil. At this writing the "copper T" is inserted in the United States only on an experimental basis, pending approval from the Food and Drug Administration. Out of every 100 women using IUDs who do not expel the devices, between one and three will become pregnant in one year. The longer a woman uses an IUD, the less likely she is to become pregnant [14].

Oral Contraceptives. Birth control pills have freed between 150 and 200 million women in the world from the fear of unwanted pregnancy. In the United States, there are about 18 million "Pill" users. There are three kinds of female oral contraceptives, all of which work by preventing ovulation, by making the uterine lining hostile to any fertilized ovum that "tries to implant," or both. Exactly how pills work is not completely understood; other factors as well may prevent pregnancy.

The most commonly prescribed pill is made of a combination of estrogen and progesterone. The first pill is taken on the fifth day of the menstrual period, and pills are taken for a total of 20 or 21 days. A few days after the last pill is taken, menstruation begins again.

The sequential pill is also taken for 20 to 21 days, beginning on the fifth day of the menstrual period. The first fourteen pills contain only estrogen, and the last six or seven contain estrogen and progesterone.

The "minipill," which is less effective than the combination pill, contains a small dose of progestin and is taken every day. The minipill is more effective in previous users of other oral contraceptives. Among women who have never used other oral contraceptives, the pregnancy rate is about 3.5 per 100 women per year, but among previous users of other oral contraceptives, the pregnancy rate is just under two.

Birth control pills should not be used without consultation with a doctor. The woman should ask the doctor for a complete physical examination, including a test for cervical cancer. If there is a history of breast cancer or blood clotting in the women's family, she should tell her doctor so that he can take the information into consideration. She *must* not use birth control pills if she has any history of blood clotting disease, breast cancer, undiagnosed genital bleeding, undiagnosed breast lumps, severe impairment of the liver or kidney, or any undiagnosed uterine mass [22].

The metabolic processes and nutritional requirements of normal women have been found to be affected by oral contraceptives [8]. In women taking oral contraceptives, requirements for vitamin B 6 were raised considerably and the level of vitamin A in the bloodstream was increased. The glucose tolerance level has been changed [32]. (Glucose tolerance refers to an individual's ability to metabolize carbohydrates, or starches and sugars. A woman who uses oral contraceptives has a higher blood glucose level than a woman who does not use oral contraceptives. Therefore, diabetics and other individuals with glucose tolerance problems should avoid using oral contraceptives.) Effects of oral contraceptives on metabolic processes are heightened in women who smoke [32].

A number of side effects are associated with the use of birth control pills. For most women, however, the side effects are minor. Some women become nauseous when they first begin to take pills. Others gain or lose weight. Some may have an increase in size and/or tenderness of their breasts. If a woman is troubled by side effects from the pill, she should consult her physician. When properly used, the combined type of birth control pill is the most effective method of birth control that is reversible. For every *thousand* women who use birth control pills for one year, between one and ten will become pregnant [14].

Sterilization. The most common kind of male and female sterilization uses the same technique: in both cases, the tubes through which the sex cells travel are severed and tied off, or burned. The male operation is called a **vasectomy,** and may be done in a doctor's office. Usually, the parts of the vasa deferentia that are in the scrotum are cut and each end is tied back upon the tube. A few stitches are all that is necessary to sew the slit in the scrotum. After the operation, the sperm can no longer escape from the testes, but are resorbed into the body. However, sterilization is not effective until the sperm stored outside of the testes are ejaculated, in a few weeks to a few months. Since sperm make up only a tiny fraction of the ejaculate fluid, it is impossible to detect the difference between the semen of a sterilized man from a fertile, nonsterilized man unless a microscope is used. The man does not have any impairment of his sexual functions, unless he is affected psychologically.

Because the woman's Fallopian tubes are located deep within her body, a **tubal ligation,** the female counterpart of a vasectomy, is harder to perform. There are several ways in which a tubal ligation may be done. If a woman has delivered a baby by means of Caesarian section, the tubes are readily available and may be cut and tied. Although this kind of sterilization is easiest for the doctor to perform, it has the highest failure rate. An incision may be made in the vagina, or in the abdomen, and the tubes cut and tied. Another method of severing the tubes is cauterization (burning). When this procedure is used, the tubes may be approached either through an incision in the abdomen, an incision in the vagina, or through the cervix. The third approach is not used in the United States, but the first two are commonly used in this country.

Although the chances of pregnancy are extremely small once one partner or the other has been sterilized (three women in 100,000 would become pregnant in a year if she or her partner had been sterilized [15]), sterilization is not ideal method for everyone because it is usually not reversible. Some skilled doctors claim that they may reverse a high proportion of vasectomies that they perform; others claim that vasectomies are not reversible. In the future, it may be possible to induce temporary sterility by surgically placing a gold and stainless steel valve in the vas deferens.

Tubal ligations are not reversible. Sterilization is the ideal method for the couple or individual who do not want any or any more children. Of course, it is important that the individual who is getting sterilized be satisfied with this method. If a man becomes worried that he will not be able to maintain an erection after he has been sterilized, his fears may cause him to fail. However, the vasectomy itself does not directly influence potency. Sterilization is one of the most popular methods of birth control among Americans over 30.

Injections. Progesterone injections given to women were approved by the Food and Drug Administration in 1973. Injections are given every three months. The theoretical effectiveness rate is under one pregnancy per 100 women per year, but the rate among actual users is much higher, between five and ten pregnancies [14].

Sub-skin Implants. A method which is still being tested is a small capsule containing progestin which is placed beneath the woman's skin. The capsule releases the hormone slowly, preventing pregnancy for a year.

Other Experimental and Future Methods. A new vaginal foam tablet available in some countries has been found to have a remarkably low failure rate of 3.2 pregnancies per 100 women per year [24]. Female contraceptive methods which are being considered are devices containing progesterone worn either in the vagina or as an IUD. Also being worked upon is hormonal regulation of ovulation, so that a woman would know exactly when her fertile period occurs. This method of birth control would be acceptable to the Roman Catholic Church, because it would be a rhythm method.

Reversible male contraceptives have been developed but are not marketed in North America because they have not yet been approved. Hormones that cause a temporary cessation of sperm production without causing negative side effects will give men the same kind of freedom from fear of pregnancy that women pill users now have. Two variations of a "male pill" have been developed independently in West Germany and at the University of Washington in Seattle [23]. Another experimental male contraceptive is a hormone that is given by injection once per month [19].

Douching: Not a Contraceptive. The myth still exists that douching (cleansing the vagina with water or water with other substance dissolved in it) is a form of birth control. Douching is not only too late to prevent pregnancy, it may actually harm the female's delicate tissues. A douche with carbonated soda may actually kill a woman, if the carbon dioxide dissolved in the liquid should enter the woman's bloodstream.

After-the-Fact Methods

A couple has intercourse with a condom, which bursts during coitus. What can they do then? The best thing to do is to call the woman's physician. Some doctors will prescribe what is called *"The morning after pill"*—a massive dose of estrogen taken over five days. The "morning after pill" must be taken within 72 hours after intercourse at the very latest, but preferably treatment should begin within 24 hours. It is a drastic measure that would not be safe for all women, and may cause severe nausea in others. It should not be repeated often.

Menstrual Extraction. Menstrual extraction is a method very similar to abortion, except that it is performed before a pregnancy is confirmed. The cervix is dilated, and the contents of the uterus are sucked out.

Abortion. A spontaneous abortion (also known as a miscarriage) is the termination of a pregnancy by natural causes. Usually, there is something wrong with the fetus when it is spontaneously aborted. Contrary to popular belief, a woman cannot bring on a miscarriage by falling down a flight of stairs or by taking hot and cold showers: if she has a spontaneous abortion after a fall, the abortion was not caused by the fall and would have happened anyway.

Abortions may, of course, be performed medically in order to interrupt a pregnancy that will be harmful to the woman, or that the woman does not wish to carry to term. As a birth control device, abortion is a last resort. As we have seen, no method of preventive birth control is completely foolproof: even sterilizations may prove to be ineffective in some cases.

Until the 1973 U.S. Supreme Court decision that struck down state laws prohibiting abortions before the twenty-fourth week, women in most of the United States could not get legal abortions. Desperate women have always sought abortions, whether or not they were legal or safe. A dramatic drop in maternal death rates in areas with liberal abortion laws indicates the value of medically supervised abortions.

Opponents to abortion believe that it is wrong to purposely terminate a pregnancy because it is taking a life. Those who believe that women have the right to choose whether or not to have an abortion believe that women have the right to control their own bodies, and that every child has a right to be wanted by its parents.

Abortions performed up to the twelfth week of pregnancy are safer and less expensive than those performed later. The preferred method for an early abortion is the suction method. The cervix is dilated, sometimes under general anesthesia and sometimes under local, by inserting a tapered metal rod into the cervix until the opening is large enough for a thin metal tube to be inserted. A vacuum pump is attached to the outer end of the tube, and the embryo and the lining of the uterus are gently sucked out. The entire operation including preparation takes about 15 to 20 minutes, and is usually accompanied by cramps. For up to two weeks after the abortion, a woman will have intermittent spotting or light bleeding.

After the twelfth week of pregnancy, the cost of the operation and the risk involved increase. Between the thirteenth and sixteenth weeks, there is a great risk of hemorrhage with suction and most doctors believe that the uterus is still too small for the late abortion method, saline abortion or "salting out." To perform an abortion by this method, the physician removes some of the amniotic fluid from the woman's uterus by inserting a needle through the abdominal wall, under local anesthesia. He replaces the fluid by a concentrated solution of salt water. The salt water kills the fetus, and labor usually begins within 12 to 48 hours. This method is generally considered to be safer between 21 to 24 weeks [2].

The decision to have an abortion is often a difficult one, involving complicated feelings and relationships. Counseling is highly desirable for the pregnant woman, her partner, and any of their family members who are involved with the problem pregnancy. Adequate abortion clinics provide emotional care and support before, during, and after the procedure. Women who choose not to have an abortion can seek help from organizations such as Birthright, which offers alternative methods of coping with problem pregnancies.

A 1975 Gallup survey indicated that three out of four Americans *favored* legalized abortion during at least the first three months of pregnancy, and that 22 per cent believed that abortion should be *illegal* in all circumstances [11a].

Infanticide

Plato and Aristotle approved of infanticide for limiting the population and eliminating deformed and diseased babies [18]. Infanticide was common in Europe during a period of rapid population growth, from 1750 to 1850. A higher death rate in girls results from the Indian practice of giving scarce food and other resources to boys before girls. Severe child abuse and neglect cause infant deaths in the United States, at present, but the killing of children is regarded with horror and infanticide is not considered as a method of population control. Many of the deaths from abuse and neglect could be prevented by a birth control policy that protected people from unwanted births.

REPRODUCTION

Sexual intercourse is the beginning of the whole sexual cycle, but only the beginning. Because conception does not *have* to follow intercourse, it is easy to lose sight of the fact that pregnancy, labor, birth, lactation, and care of the young are all steps in the process of reproduction, just as courtship, lovemaking, and impregnation are steps. The flow of events can be interrupted at any point. Contraception interrupts it by preventing sexual intercourse from causing pregnancy. Even when there is no planned interruption of the sexual cycle, there are many occasions on which the cycle is initiated but not completed. In this section, we discuss the sexual cycle that does move to completion. Having commented at length on sexual intercourse (see pages 99–102), we begin with pregnancy.

Pregnancy

After the sperm penetrates the egg, the fertilized egg descends the Fallopian tube to float in the uterus. The fertilized egg divides into two cells, then four, and continues to divide. After about a week, when the organism has become a ball of cells, it attaches itself to the wall of the uterus. Meanwhile, in the ovary at the spot from which the egg burst forth, the corpus luteum (yellow body) is developing. If the egg had left the uterus instead of attaching itself to the wall, the corpus luteum would have regressed and disappeared. When the developing egg implants in the lining of the uterus, however, the corpus luteum continues to develop in the ovary, producing the hormones of pregnancy and thus taking part in the development of the bodies of the woman and embryo.

Throughout the whole period of pregnancy, the woman's body performs three functions in addition to all that it does in the nonpregnant state. It nurtures the organism that is to become a baby, it prepares for giving birth, and it prepares for breast feeding the future baby. Although all three functions proceed without any conscious effort or knowledge on the part of the women, she is involved as a whole person. Pregnancy is an *experience,* different from all other experiences, just as each part of the sexual cycle is a unique experience. It has its own perceptions and emotions, strengths and vulnerabilities. Figure 14-6 shows the pregnant woman in the first, second, and third trimesters.

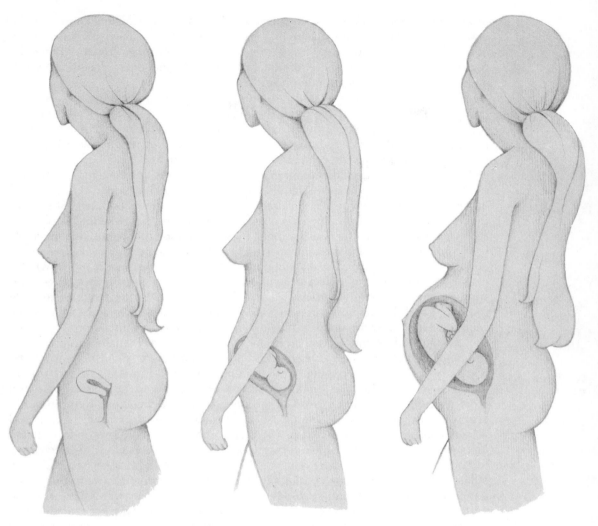

FIGURE 14-6   Three trimesters of pregnancy. Left to right: approximately one month, five months, and eight months.

Development and Experiences. The first trimester (three months) is a time of reorganizing and rebalancing bodily processes. The **embryo** is much too small (about 10 grams weight and 22 millimeters length at six weeks) to be a drain on her nutrients or a strain on her abdominal muscles and pelvic organs. Why, then, does the first stage of pregnancy often bring on a need for extra sleep and rest, emotional ups and downs, a finicky appetite and nausea? The best answer seems to be that the changeover of the body from nonpregnant to pregnant state requires considerable use of energy and resources. The nausea of pregnancy is most likely caused by the biochemical balance or imbalance that is typical at this time. The experience of the bodily state is probably similar to the experience of rapid growth during the pubescent growth spurt, when hormonal balances change, energy needs are great, and emotional reactions are often heightened.

The beginning of the second trimester usually marks a change in bodily functions and perceptions. At this time, the healthy pregnant woman feels well and vigorous. She looks pretty, with the "glow" of pregnancy. The changeover has taken place and her bodily systems have settled into their expanded functions that are basic to nurturing the fetus. (The embryo completed the structure of its basic systems at eight weeks and achieved the new name and status of **fetus.**) As the fetus increases in size, the woman's uterus grows larger. Early in the second trimester, the top of the uterus rises above the pelvis, making a little bulge in the abdomen. She looks pregnant, as well as pretty. The next important experience is **quickening,** feeling the fetus move. Of course, the fetus has been moving for a long time, but, floating freely in the amniotic fluid, the movements could not be felt. Only as the fetus grows big enough to push against the walls of the uterus can the pregnant woman feel what is inside her. At first it feels like a gentle fluttering. As the fetus grows bigger and stronger, pushing more vigorously against the uterine walls, the fluttering turns to squirming and thumping. Fetuses are individuals, just as infants and children are. Each fetus has its own pattern of moving and responding to stimulation.

By the end of the second trimester, the fetus is well finished as to bodily structures, but it must grow bigger and more mature before it will be ready to be born. The tasks of the pregnant woman during the third trimester are to carry an increasingly heavy load, to supply more and more nutrients, to remove more and more waste products, and to prepare for labor, birth, and lactation. Thus, all of her systems must work harder. Dramatic changes take place in some of them. Blood vessels and blood supply increase. The uterus and birth canal develop in size and functional capacities. Breast tissue increases and the breasts begin to secrete colostrum, the infant's first food. Many of the normal bodily changes require some adjustment, such as expanded clothing, more frequent urination, more rest, more bathing, and careful attention to eating enough of essential nutrients. And while bodily preparation for birth goes on spontaneously, psychological preparation is a matter of conscious effort and learning. During the third trimester, a North American woman has the option of taking a course that will teach her how to control her body and perceptions during the birth process (see pages 372–373). Since she has had little or no experience with birth and since the culture offers next to nothing in the way of preparation, this is her last chance to get ready for the enormous physical and emotional performance.

Sharing Pregnancy as Partners. Until quite recently, a husband was an object of pity and the butt of jokes as he waited nervously in the waiting room, excluded from his wife in the labor and delivery room. The stress of fatherhood is real. An

English study showed one in seven to nine suffering some symptoms in reaction to his wife's pregnancy, including nausea and expansion of the abdomen [29].

Americans and Canadians used to hold two strangely conflicting notions on the nature of pregnancy and childbirth. These were women's topics and women's business, to be discussed and performed by wives but not husbands. At the same time, childbirth was the province of male doctors, who were the real authorities and stars of the show. It was as though the obstetrician, not the mother, produced the baby. Although this situation still prevails for some women and men, it does not have to be so.

For couples who choose modern prepared childbirth, the man is an active participant in pregnancy and birth and the woman's performance is the center of interest. The doctor and nurses assist the mother to deliver the baby. When abnormal conditions occur, doctors diagnose and treat.

The first pregnancy brings new situations to the couple and requires them to grow and change by adapting to the new. The woman has experiences with her body that she can share through communication with her partner. Both are likely to have misgivings or fears or feel excitement and anticipation about the new roles and responsibilities that they are about to take on. Information about the developing embryo and fetus are interesting to both and make for strengthening the bonds between them. Although it is natural for the woman to be preoccupied with her perceptions and thoughts, her behavior may look like withdrawal from her partner, or a pushing aside. Her awareness and his understanding can serve as a bridge. So also does their joint planning for taking care of the child, both short term and long term.

Preparation for childbirth includes both expectant parents. Since the father can assist the mother at birth, he must learn along with her. As well as instruction in the processes and conduct of labor, prospective fathers are usually given a lesson or two in the special contributions of fathers to the heredity and development of the child. Childbirth preparation classes are held for groups of couples in about the same stage of pregnancy. Thus, they share one another's problems and anxieties, often finding reassurance and solutions. When the father is not available to share the pregnancy and birth, or does not choose to do so, the mother can still prepare herself and can even share it with another person. In the era before father participation, women were assisted by other women who *cared*. Nurses and midwives are worldwide helpers of women in labor.

Prepared Childbirth

Essentially, preparing for childbirth means learning about the physiology of labor and how to control and work with the natural processes. For this reason, it is sometimes called **natural childbirth.**

Different cultures have different ways of preparing individuals for childbirth.

First of all, there is the basic attitude and interpretation that permeates the culture [21]. Pregnancy is considered an illness by the Cuna Indians of Panama, where a pregnant woman consults her medicine man daily and takes medicine throughout labor. Some societies see pregnancy as a sign of strength and sexual adequacy. Many cultures, including Judeo-Christian, have interpreted birth as defiling and have required women to be purified afterwards, through religious ceremonies. The Puritans, like their English forebears, thought that labor pains were the cross that God placed upon women for Eve's sin and that woman's honor could be recovered by the bearing of children. A sixteenth-century English writer published this quotation, " . . . we are conceived in filth and uncleanness, born in sin and care and nourished with pain and labor" [25]. The fear, shame, and guilt built up by such beliefs would practically guarantee painful and difficult childbirth! Pain is minimized in societies where childbirth is regarded as a natural event with which women are equipped to cope. This is not to say that birth is painless in any society. It can be more or less so. Some individuals report experiencing no pain at all. Pain can be dealt with in different ways that minimize or maximize, that blot it from memory through amnesiacs, or that eliminate it from perception through drugs or psychological training. Modern Western culture has developed, in addition to drug-dependent methods, two main methods of controlling and sometimes preventing the pain of childbirth.

Read Method. Grantly Dick-Read, an English physician, began in 1914 to develop his theory and method of childbirth without fear. He believed that pain resulted from tension caused by fear and anxiety. Instead of working in harmony, the muscles of the uterus work against each other and abdominal muscles may also hold back the birth process. Therefore, the pregnant woman is taught details of her reproductive system, the anatomy and physiology involved in labor. She does exercises to promote physical fitness and learns relaxation and controlled breathing. She learns of the experiences of other women, trained in this method, who found birth a supreme experience. During labor, she uses skills she has acquired under the guidance and support of doctors and nurses trained in the Read method. Their confident expectations are important in maintaining her own control and freedom from tension-causing pain. Although drugs are used only minimally in the Read method, they are not forbidden. They are used when the woman or the doctor sees a real need. The Read method is commonly used in the United Kingdom today.

Lamaze Method. During the 1950s, Russian obstetricians applied the conditioning principles of Pavlov to childbirth. Lamaze brought the method to France and from there it spread to the rest of the Western world. The Lamaze method is now the most widely used method of preparation for childbirth in the United States and Canada.

Lamaze training is given during the last two months of pregnancy to a woman and the partner who plans to help her during labor. As in the Read method, they learn the anatomy and physiology of reproduction. Then the woman learns to perform breathing and mental concentration that control her brain activity in such a way that pain sensations are blocked out [28]. By strongly activating one area of the brain, other areas are rendered inactive and do not respond to incoming stimuli. Emotions influence bodily functioning, and fear produces changes that create pain during labor. Words act as stimuli to produce emotional states and can thus create fear and pain. Through teaching, words can be used to produce positive emotional states and to thus eliminate fear and pain. Anesthetics are used, if needed, but the need is minimal, since prepared women wish to retain control and experience the birth.

The LaLeche League International, an association devoted to the promotion of natural childbirth and breast feeding, disseminates this information in a pamphlet:

> childbirth . . . should not cause any discomfort that would be unwillingly borne by a normal, happy mother who has the cooperation and encouragement of her husband, wants her baby and fearlessly and lovingly welcomes its birth, is healthy in mind and body, is prepared in mind and body for the great event of birth, understands what is happening to her and to her baby during the process, knows how to relax during labor when this is needed, knows how to work with the forces of labor when this is needed, and has kindly and understanding support and encouragement from those who attend her in labor. [17]

Growing numbers of parents attest to the effectiveness of childbirth preparation, especially the Lamaze method. It is the standard birth method in the Soviet Union and China and is used in half the births in France [28, p. 253]. An American study contrasted women who followed the Lamaze method with a group who did not receive systematic psychological preparation. The outstanding findings were that the Lamaze group developed more positive attitudes toward pregnancy, had more positive experiences in labor and delivery, had less pain, and, after the birth of the baby, had more positive views of themselves. Husbands' participation during labor and presence during birth contributed greatly to wives' feelings of rapture. These wives perceived their husbands as strong and helpful, whereas wives in the control group often saw their husbands as weak and helpless [28].

The Birth Process. Labor is real muscular work, since it is the force that pushes the baby out of the mother's body. The first stage of labor serves to dilate, or open, the cervix, making a passageway out of the uterus into the vagina. The uterus contracts rhythmically, pushing the baby downward. At the same time, muscles surrounding the opening relax and are pulled upward, thus enlarging the opening. This stage lasts several hours, the length of time varying greatly from one woman to another and from one labor to another. As labor progresses, contractions become stronger and closer together. The traditional term for contractions is *labor pains*. Since contractions do not always hurt, and the word *pain* is likely to stimulate fear and pain, this word is not used by Lamaze and Read practitioners. During the first stage, the prepared couple put their knowledge into practice, breathing, relaxing, back-rubbing, and keeping up confidence and positive attitudes. The most difficult

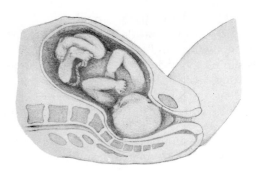

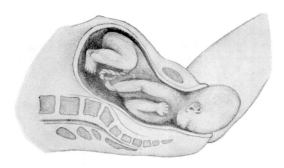

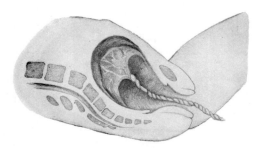

FIGURE 14-7   Three stages of labor.

time in most labors is the end of the first stage, when the cervix is enlarging to its full opening.

The second stage consists of pushing the baby out of the uterus, through the vagina and out of the mother's body. Now the mother feels like pushing, and her efforts help, whereas in the first stage, the uterine contractions are not under her conscious control. The prepared woman has techniques for breathing, bearing down and relaxing that she can exert precisely. The husband coaches, as for an athletic event, which indeed it is. Doctors and nurses direct them both, acknowledging the father as part of the team. As the baby emerges, the prepared mother feels a tremendous sense of achievement, even joy and rapture. Some women equate the experience with an orgasm. The father, acting in partnership at the birth, feels his own joy and catches the supreme emotion of the mother.

The placenta and membranes are expelled during the third stage, monitored carefully by the medical personnel but little noticed by the new parents. The traditional patient is usually anesthetised at this point, the father still in the waiting room. The prepared couple is ecstatically greeting their new baby and telling each other how wonderful they are and how much they love each other. The prepared-for baby, usually alert now, may be put to the mother's breast for a welcoming few drops of colostrum.

Obstetrical Assistance and Intervention. Having a baby is not a very risky venture as far as the mother's survival is concerned. Today, the United States maternal death rate is less than 4 in 10,000 live births, whereas in 1930, it was 67 in 10,000 [27]. Childbirth is safe because of good obstetrical care. Although the great majority of births are normal and *could* be conducted without a physician, not all emergencies are predictable. For the safety of mother and baby, it is best to have the knowledge, skills, and equipment of modern medicine available. Every pregnancy should be monitored and supervised so as to apply the best knowledge and judgment to nutrition and to any irregularities or problems.

Qualified midwives can take care of a normal pregnancy and birth, but medical doctors are needed in abnormal cases. The skills and knowledge derived from Lamaze or other such preparation are not substitutes for qualified medical personnel but are useful in cooperation with them. Although it is true that babies have been

A prepared mother, fully awake, greets her daughter who was born a few moments ago.

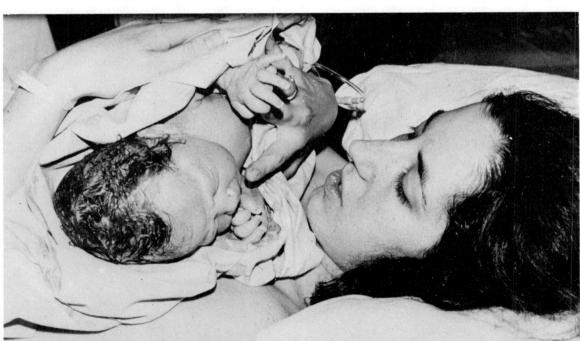

HALVAR LOKEN

born in taxis or at home without professional assistance, it is much safer for mothers and babies to use the advantages offered by modern medicine.

Drugs for Labor and Childbirth. Sedatives induce calm, drowsiness, or sleep; amnesiacs make the patient forget; analgesics reduce pain; general anesthetics induce unconsciousness; local anesthetics block the transmission of impulses through nerves. A wide range of drugs is used to accomplish these purposes at different times, in various women. Research on infants has indicated that excessive use of drugs is harmful to embryos and fetuses and that infants may suffer from the effects of drugs given prenatally. A recent review of the effects of drugs on the neonate concludes,

> there is enough evidence to date that obstetric anesthesia in any form involves an element of calculated risk to the infant. Without denying the great beneficial possibilities of analgesia and anesthesia, one should consider carefully the alternative of natural childbirth, by means of hypnosis or one of the various relaxation techniques, whenever the physical and emotional condition of the mother allows it. [1]

Obstetricians are aware of these findings. Their responsibility is to judge the type and amount of medication that is most beneficial to mother and infant. Although the patient can talk over these matters with her doctor, she must trust his judgment when she is in labor, since the obstetrician, not the patient, has the training and experience that qualifies him to decide. When a complication requires a painful procedure, such as surgery, the doctor orders an appropriate anesthetic. The use of Caesarian section, although not a normal birth, is of tremendous benefit to mother and infant in cases where it is needed. When an abnormal birth occurs, the mother cannot have the experience of controlling her body and delivering her child in full consciousness. It is fortunate, however, that she can go through the procedure with relative safety. She need not forego all preparation if a surgical birth is indicated. There is much to learn about the process of birth, getting ready for child care, and, if chosen, breast-feeding.

Beginning Parenthood

Prepared childbirth also means being prepared for beginning parent-child relationships. Simply being awake to greet the baby upon arrival is quite different from being deeply asleep from an anesthetic and pain-relieving drugs received throughout labor. When a woman has had a difficult birth and/or heavy medication, she may require a few hours or even longer to recover before beginning her new relationship with the baby. The newborn infant who has received minimal medication is usually alert and able to relax into normal sleep patterns. The infant who has experienced a difficult birth also requires a while to recover.

Traditional North American obstetrical practice has been to keep the new mother and baby apart except at regularly scheduled feeding times. Fathers and other persons could look at the baby through the glass windows of the nursery, where infants were kept in groups. Throughout most of the world, however, mothers and babies stay together, especially during the early days. In most societies, mothers carry young infants almost constantly and sleep with them at night. Today there are some hospitals in the Western world that allow mothers and infants to be together in a system called *rooming in*. Couples who have had prepared childbirth usually want to continue the close family relationships that they have started. And some parents who have had traditional births also see the advantage of getting acquainted with their baby under the guidance and protected atmosphere of the hospital.

Prepared childbirth and rooming in are closely associated with another practice that industrialized societies have almost discarded. *Breast-feeding* is done by only a minority of Americans, but its acceptance seems to be increasing. The decline of breast-feeding was caused by many factors, including the technology of artificial feeding, the tensions that depressed lactation in women, and the lack of social esteem for the practice. Today, new findings in nutrition and growth emphasize the physical benefits of human milk for human infants. Psychological studies indicate emotional benefits of breast-feeding to both mother and baby. Women's frank acknowledgement of sexuality includes recognition that breast-feeding is a stage in the sexual cycle and that it brings sensory gratification to the pair who participate in this symbiotic activity. Ethologists point out that sucking is attachment behavior, through which the infant builds the basis of a love relationship with his mother. Suckling is the reciprocal role, through which the mother strengthens her own attachment to the baby.

The mother and baby pictured on page 375 are here seen in a reciprocal relationship and mutual enjoyment.

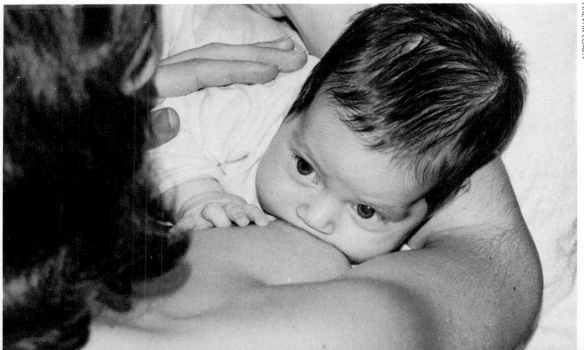

HALVAR LOKEN

Breast-feeding begins, of course, very soon after birth. A new mother has to learn how to help the baby to feed. The infant has rooting and sucking reflexes that are ready to go, but needs some help in positioning, keeping his nose free for breathing, bringing up air bubbles afterwards, and so on. An experienced nurse is of immeasurable help and comfort to the mother with a first baby.

Some women do not choose to breast-feed and some cannot. In times past, the only satisfactory solution for their infants was a wet nurse. Today the substitutes for human milk are safe and convenient. Bottle feeding also gives fathers a chance to feed their infants and thus to establish close relationships early. Older siblings, grandparents, and friends can also share in the baby's meals. When nursing mothers want to go out for recreation or work, bottles can be substituted for some of the feedings. Breast-feeding does not have to be exclusive, even in the early weeks when milk is the infant's only food.

A well run rooming-in program provides the new parents with help and guidance, along with the opportunity for both to be with the baby. Fathers come and go freely, taking care to wash their hands and to put on clean hospital gowns before touching the mother and baby. The baby can be fed when hungry, instead of by the clock, and the teacher-nurse can help the mother to interpret the baby's cries and actions. She also teaches diapering, bathing, and other baby care techniques. Since new mothers are usually tired from labor, they need extra rest in order to recover. When the mother sleeps, the nurse takes care of the baby. Rooming-in does *not* mean that the mother is in full charge, taking complete care of her infant.

The present custom in the United States is to send the mother and baby home three or four days after the birth. Before World War II, when obstetrical wards became too crowded, mothers rested in the hospital for ten days. They still do in New Zealand, and in some places, new mothers rest even longer in the hospital. Where the **couvade** is practiced, fathers rest too, since they share the experience of the mother just as much as they can. No matter whether a short or long rest period after birth is deemed correct, the new mother needs several weeks of extra support from someone, as she takes care of the baby, establishes her breast milk, and reorganizes her body. (The uterus takes six weeks to return to normal.) Many new fathers are able to give considerable help and support at this time. Grandmothers often come to help, also, especially if there are other children in the family. Some professional help is highly desirable, even if it is just for reassurance and advice. Often it is possible to have visits from a nurse who is skilled in promoting the adjustments of infants and their families.

SUMMARY   Family planning is a management problem at three levels, the family, the nation, and the world. Children must be balanced with the outlay of resources that they require. Excessive growth of the world's population has already resulted in famines and food shortages that will increase in severity. All nations and all families are affected. North America uses world resources at a highly disproportionate rate, whereas poor countries are severely deprived. From a family standpoint, excessive children deplete not only material resources but the mother's body as well, with negative effects upon children.

Population growth is regulated by births, deaths, and migration. Coercion is ordinarily used to control death and migration, but not birth. Many nations are now trying to influence births.

The use of birth control requires decision-making and management and results in giving people, especially women, more control over their lives. Methods that are reliable when properly used include mechanical, chemical, intrauterine, hormonal, and surgical. Rhythm has a high failure rate. Douching is not a contraceptive. Conceptions can be interrupted by immediate medication, menstrual extraction, and abortion. Early abortion performed by qualified personnel is safe and simple, although emotions are also involved. An adequate abortion includes counseling and emotional support. A later abortion is more difficult physically, emotionally, financially, and philosophically.

Infanticide, although strongly disapproved at present, has been used widely throughout space and time, and persists today, even in North America. Adequate birth control would prevent most infanticide.

Reproduction occurs when conception proceeds uninterrupted. The fertilized egg divides to form a ball of cells that implants in the lining of the uterus, grows into an embryo, and then into a fetus. The corpus luteum in the ovary that produced the egg directs the development of the pregnant woman's body. Her physical reorganization and development are focused on nurturing the embryo and fetus, preparing to give birth and preparing to breast feed. Her experience, which is different in each trimester, is absorbing and may result in some exclusion of the husband unless efforts to share are sincere.

A modern revolution in methods of conducting childbirth has given women more control over the process and has placed importance on the family interaction involved. The importance of medical skill and technology is acknowledged, since childbirth is a crisis and a tremendously complicated although normal event. Constructively handled, childbirth is a cooperative achievement between the parents, the infant, and the medical and hospital personnel. During the recovery period, kin and friends also play a part. Continuing support and education are needed by the new parents. Adequate programs are not readily available to meet this need in the United States, although some other countries do better.

REFERENCES

1. Aleksandrowicz, Malca K. The effect of pain relieving drugs administered during labor and delivery on the behavior of the newborn: A review. *Merrill-Palmer Quarterly,* 1974, **20:** 122–141.
2. Anonymous. Legal abortion: How safe? How available? How costly? *Consumer Reports,* 1972, **37,** 466–470.
3. Arena, Jay M. China's children. *Nutrition Today,* 1974, **9:** 5, 20–25.
4. Berelson, Bernard. An evaluation of the effects of population control programs. *Studies in family planning,* 1974, **5:** 1, 2–12.

5. Bouvier, Leon. Personal communication, 1974.

6. Bouvier, Leon and Everett Lee. The bearing of children. *Population Profiles, #5*. Washington, Ct.: Center for Information on America, 1972.

7. Bouvier, Leon and Everett Lee. The vital revolution: How did we get where we are now? *Population Profiles, #3*. Washington, Ct.: Center for Information on America, 1972.

8. Butterworth, Charles E. Interactions of nutrients with oral contraceptives and other drugs. *Journal of the American Dietetic Association*, 1973, **62,** 510–514.

9. Chilman, Catherine S. Public and social policy and population problems in the United States. *The Social Service Review*, 1973, **47,** 511–530.

10. Desmond, Annabelle. How many people have ever lived on earth? In Garrett Hardin, (ed.). *Population, evolution, and birth control*. San Francisco: Freeman, 1969.

11. Frejka, Tomas. *The future of population growth: Alternative paths to equilibrium*. New York: Wiley, 1973.

11a. Gallup, George. Three out of every four Americans support legal abortions. *Hartford Courant*. June 8, 1975.

12. *Globe and Mail*. 73 birth rate lowest ever across Canada. Toronto, October 2, 1974.

13. Gomez, B. Miguel and M. Vera Bermudez. *Country Profiles: Costa Rica*. New York: The Population Council, 1974.

14. Hatcher, R. A., C. C. Conrad, R. W. Kline, and F. L. Moorhead. *Contraceptive technology 1973–74*. Atlanta: Woodruff Medical Center, 1973.

15. Havemann, Ernest. *Birth control*. New York: Time-Life Books, 1967.

16. Jaffe, Frederick S. Public policy on fertility control. *Scientific American*, 1973, **229:** 1, 17–23.

17. LaLeche League International. *What is natural childbirth?* 9616 Minneapolís Ave., Franklin Park, Illinois.

18. Langer, J. W. Checks on population growth: 1750–1850. *Scientific American*, 1972, **226,** 93–100.

19. Maugh, Thomas II. 5-Thio-D Glucose: A unique male contraceptive. *Clinical Obstetrics and Gynecology*, 1974, **17,** 431.

21. Mead, Margaret and Niles Newton. Cultural patterning of perinatal behavior. In Stephen A. Richardson and Alan F. Guttmacher (eds.). *Childbearing: Its social and psychological aspects*. Baltimore: Williams & Wilkins, 1967.

22. Panzini, Marianne. Personal communication, 1974.

23. *People*. Contraceptives. 1974, **1:** 4, 33–34. Planned Parenthood International, London.

24. *People*. Contraceptives. 1974, **1:** 5, 38. Planned Parenthood International, London.

25. Schnucker, R. V. The English Puritans and pregnancy, delivery, and breast feeding. *History of Childhood Quarterly*, 1974, **1,** 635–658.

26. Sidel, Ruth. *Women and child care in China*. Baltimore: Penguin, 1973.

27. Swanson, Harold D. *Human reproduction*. New York: Oxford University Press, 1974.

28. Tanzer, Deborah and Block, Jean L. *Why natural childbirth?* New York: Doubleday, 1972.

29. Trethowan, W. H. Pregnancy symptoms in men. *Sexual Behavior*, 1972, **2:** 11, 23–27.

30. United Nations Fund for Population Activities. W.P.Y. Bulletin, 1974, No. 16.

31. Wray, Joe. How China is achieving the unbelievable. *People*, 1974, **1:** 4, 16–19. Planned Parenthood International, London.

32. Yeung, David. Personal communication. Guelph, Ontario, 1975.

CHAPTER 15

MONEY, WORK, ANd LAWS: UNAVOidABLE

The family system interacts with other systems in society, the economic and legal systems being two of the very important ones. The more a family can direct those interactions, the better it can function in other ways. The management of financial and legal affairs is an important part of the whole process of family management. Since individuals vary greatly in their economic values, family decisions can be hard to make.

No matter how carefully a person plans and manages, much depends on circumstances beyond her control. The individual has nothing to say about the part of the world where she is born and grows up, the education available to her, inflation, the ups and downs of the stock market, the deterioration of a neighborhood, property values, and so on. The more flexible and resourceful the person, the better she can adapt to change and make the best of what happens. It would be a mistake, however, to think that personal effort alone can make a great change in the individual's economic status, especially at the lowest levels. In North America and throughout the world, families vary enormously in financial resources and legal resources, which make significant differences in the options available to them.

FINANCIAL MANAGEMENT

A value system is abstract, but money, food, clothes, cars, and other goods are concrete. They can be seen, touched, counted, added, and subtracted. Family members can easily disagree over money and objects. Sometimes a quarrel over money really masks a conflict over something else that is too painful for the family members to face. It may often seem that money is the cause of hostility between husband and wife, parent and child, or brother and sister. But then solutions are often found without changing the amount of money or goods in question. Instead, expectations are changed, roles redefined, messages rephrased, listening improved, and joint goals developed. This is not to say that scarcity of money makes no difference to a family. Money is a resource, and resources are what are managed. But money is also a symbol invested with various meanings.

Meanings of Money

The significance of money for an individual or family depends first of all upon the level of needs being met. Then values determine meanings of money. Values, being products of the whole life experience, vary in time and space, between individuals and between families. Some examples of the meanings of money follow.

Survival. For people who are poor and living precariously, *survival* is the basic meaning of money. To an Indian sweeper and his family, money means eating *today*. To Abdul, a jewelry salesman in the Vale of Kashmir, it was the wherewithal to flee from the Chinese, whose attack he considered imminent. To the women who head one third of the black families in the United States, money is subsistence since most of these women live below the poverty level. More money than their present income would mean some freedom of choice as to where to live and how to take care of their children [10]. These women, like other poor people, realistically think that they have little control, power, or freedom of choice because survival has to be their first goal.

Security. Although most people agree that money gives security, some individuals are much more concerned than others with having enough money to last for the rest of their lives. To the generation that struggled through the Depression of the 1930s, money is likely to be important as security. Young mainstream North American adults had no experience with financial depressions during their childhood and adolescence. Conflict is practically inevitable when money means earning and saving to parents, but spending and enjoying to teen-agers.

Freedom of Choice. Even when people are as poor as the black women mentioned previously, cash in hand gives them some power and freedom of choice. They may not be free to buy steak, but they can go to the grocery store and select tunafish or chicken, a course of action generally preferred to receiving a package of food chosen by an agency.

Freedom of choice increases with affluence. As smaller proportions of family income are needed for the basic supports to life, more can be used as resources for reaching other goals. With a little more money than what is needed for subsistence, the poor family heads could have more control over where they live. They would

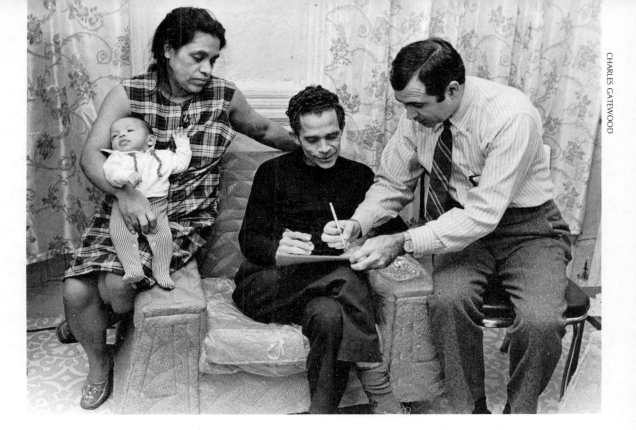

look for more comfortable quarters to rent. With additional funds they might buy a house, and this step would open up many choices for arrangements and making improvements in home management. Freedom to buy a house could mean having a wider choice of neighborhoods and schools. Money could mean all of this!

Children's freedom of choice is also affected by the amount of money available to them. At six or seven years of age, a universal time for transition into middle childhood, experiences with money and choice begin to form the child's foundations of money management.

Pleasure. Enjoy yourself! You can't take it with you! Money is only a means to an end, and that end is having a good time and making others happy, provided they have access to unlimited funds. Since few people are so affluent, the goal of *happiness today,* with money as the means, can precipitate financial crises and disasters.

Unimportance. Money does not matter. The Lord will provide, or someone else will. This meaning is similar to the meaning of money as pleasure, in that management does not enter significantly into the picture. One life-style in which this meaning is truly functional is that of the religious ascetic. The monk, the nun, and the holy beggar do not need to plan because money has no meaning for them and someone else does the managing and providing that sustains their lives. For a family, however, money cannot be stripped of significance, but it can be given more or less emphasis. When counterculture families choose a simple, rural, perhaps communal life style, they minimize the importance of money.

Power. Money can be the means of dominating other people. Money is power to the industrialist who enjoys managing a business empire, to the old person whose heirs are submissive in anticipation of future gain, and to the child who can buy treats for docile peers. Research suggests that in some cultures (but not others) high earnings increase a husband's decision-making power [19] and that the same is true for wives [14].

Prestige. Similar to power, but not identical, prestige means being recognized as important, being looked up to, being respected. When a person thinks of money as bringing prestige, he has to have some way of letting other people know that he has money. He can carry out conspicuous consumption or flashy spending, make well-publicized contributions to charity, and let the amount of his earnings be known. Prestige was found to be a key to satisfaction of highly paid executives, most of whom were dissatisfied with salaries of less than $50,000 [11]. At any income level, some persons try to gain prestige by buying things that will impress other people. One buys an expensive car, another clothing, another a color television, and another an elaborate barbecue. Living in a particular neighborhood, or going to an expensive college, may be a dominant goal. Often when buying for prestige reasons, people buy on time, go into debt, and otherwise strain their financial resources. Many women, suffering from low self-esteem, find that when they earn a good income from a job they gain prestige with other people and thereby think more of themselves.

Compensation. Although the ordinary meaning of compensation is pay for work done, money may also mean compensation for deprivation, jealousy, and other hurt feelings. The young woman who marries a rich old man gives up the possibility of marrying a young, vigorous husband, but is compensated by more luxurious support and the prospects of a large inheritance. The secretly unfaithful man buys presents for his partner. The neglected wife spends recklessly on clothes, makeup, and expensive furnishings, partly to make herself feel better and partly to punish her husband. She thus compensates herself for deprivation by him.

Self-Development. When growth of the individual personality is important, money may be looked upon as a means to this end. A person might use money to pay for taking courses, getting a degree, learning a skill or sport, taking a trip, purchasing books or materials for arts and crafts, or going to concerts and plays.

Defining Goals

Perhaps everyone uses money in all its meanings, but some people emphasize one or more meanings, and other people emphasize different ones. When making plans for spending, a couple or family needs to think about what money really means to them. The Campbell family had a passion for seeing new places. They decided that they would live in a very modest house and spend generously on travel. The Links, with the same income, stayed home year-round in a handsome house, equipped with all conveniences and many extras.

Unlike the Campbells and the Links, many couples do not agree readily on values, or what money means to them. Instead of working toward stated goals, they may conflict over how they should earn and spend. Jennie and Robert have lived from crisis to crisis throughout their married life. Generous, lovable, fun-loving Robert believes that money is for pleasure and that money is unimportant. Somehow, money will come, and somehow it does, through his occasionally frantic efforts and the help of friends and kin. Worrying, tense Jennie is torn between enjoying life with Robert and trying to find financial security. She keeps a secret savings account from which she bails out the family at the most critical moments. Jennie is always concerned about money. She and Robert have never been able to make a plan for managing their finances because money has different meanings for them. They have settled into tacit acceptance of disagreement. Neither is really satisfied, Jennie because she feels very insecure economically and Robert because he knows that Jennie feels this way.

Robert and Jennie demonstrate a financial problem that is really a management problem that is really a communication problem! (See Chapter 3, on communication.) The management of family finances begins in the beginning of the partnership and continues until the death of both. Therefore, the communications process goes on and on, and goals are constantly defined and redefined. If Jennie and Robert had started their marriage with a plan for spending and saving, their different interpretations of money would have been brought out into the open. They might have been able to discuss their differences, to understand each other's real feelings, and to work toward a compromise. They might even begin to do so now.

We are not suggesting that Jennie and Robert, or any other two people, could necessarily come to complete agreement on the meaning of money if they started from two very different interpretations. Attitudes toward money are the products of the whole personality, not just the result of logical thought. Almost any family with several children can illustrate this point. Take the Schulman family. From the age of five onward, each child received an allowance planned with the child to meet his ordinary spending needs. Sonya has always had money and a plan for spending and saving, making her income sufficient, no matter what its size. Jeb frequently borrowed from his sister, spending his allowance promptly. As a child, Jeb was an ingenious earner and today he receives a high salary. He owes over half the price of his handsome car. He is behind on his credit card payments. Of course, Jeb could

MONEY, WORK, AND LAWS: UNAVOIDABLE

learn to manage differently, to spend less, save and invest, *if he wanted to do so.* He could change his goals and also the way in which he used his resources. His goals may change if he falls in love, develops a partnership, works as a member of a couple to set up a home, and plans to have children. Jeb may never be as orderly as Sonya in his planning, but he could, with a communicating partner and pair goals, learn to seek information, to delay impulse spending, and to make decisions that use resources productively.

Somewhere during the process of becoming a couple, the topic of money can be explored in depth. Like mutual revelations about other important beliefs and attitudes, exchanging ideas on financial matters can be helpful in building the relationship or cutting it off after a few dates. If the pair continue into partnership, communication about finances grows more important. The partners and their children, if any, will set small and large goals throughout the life of the family. Marriage counselors and teachers often use inventories and questionnaires in order to help students, especially engaged couples, to explore their attitudes together. By comparing answers, they can see where they disagree on financial values and can then talk about their recognized problems [18]. The Premarital Questionnaire in Appendix A could be used to start an exploration of attitudes toward earning and spending. Another way for two people to begin communicating with each other as to financial goals is this: Each person should list five necessities and five luxuries; compare lists and discuss discrepancies.

Learning Needs at Different Stages

In applying the findings from their research on three-generation families, Hill and his associates [8] made some recommendations for training programs, focused on the special needs that they found typical of the following stages.

Newly Married. Many important decisions are made and patterns of management are set up during the transition from single to married life, the period of engagement, wedding, honeymoon, and early marriage. Many plans are made and risks are taken. Decisions are often less rational than those made by more seasoned couples. Newly marrieds could profit from instruction on *making plans more specific, searching for more information* before deciding, and *evaluating their decisions* more critically. They could also benefit from help in life-cycle management, or *long-term planning.* Thus, they would anticipate the demands of later stages and to some extent control the demands, as well as ways of meeting them. Perhaps most important, in controlling the demands, is controlling the number and spacing of children. Plans for meeting demands, of course, are concerned with earning, saving, investing, and upgrading earning capacities through education and training. Along with help in short-term and long-term planning and deciding would go training in communicating with each other and in maintaining beneficial kinship ties.

Child-Rearing Families. When children are young, parents are faced with all sorts of growth needs about which they may know very little. They have to *seek much information* and make many decisions as to how to use their resources. Needs of various family members have to be balanced. There are questions of when and how to involve children in making decisions. Decisions about jobs, careers, and housing have long-term consequences. Parents need help in *communicating with children* and in *including them in joint decisions and actions*. Parent education courses and study groups may meet this need. Expert help can be sought from insurance companies and consumption economists on questions of *financial management*.

Launching Period. One of the important functions of the parents of older adolescents and young adults is to help them to get educated and to enter the occupational system, and perhaps to settle into married life or its equivalent. At the same time, the parents are likely to be helping the grandparent generation. They must also make their own adjustments to *living without children at home* and to *future retirement*. Although many couples are experienced and expert in planning and decision-making at this point, some could profit from help in these areas. Most could use information and discussion with other people in similar situations on questions of *obligation to other generations* and sharing of problems and solutions.

Earning and Producing

Income is important to satisfaction! If any reader is doubtful of this, research shows that as income increases so does the homemaker's satisfaction with her level of living [7]. It is also no surprise to find that if she thought she had enough money, she felt good about it. Satisfactions connected with earning and producing include more than getting the money or things needed and wanted. Satisfactions depend on the meanings of money, as outlined in the first section of this chapter, and also upon the special interests, skills, tastes, and needs of the individuals involved. I (MSS) knit socks and sweaters and sew my own dresses because I enjoy producing these items. Since it would cost more to buy them than to make them, I am producing the equivalent of money. If my purpose were to make as much money as I could, however, I would do better to spend the time teaching or writing, instead of knitting and sewing. The satisfaction brought by my handwork makes it worthwhile, even though it represents a deplorable hourly wage.

The same could be said of a person's choice of jobs or of life style. Evelyn graduated with honors and a teacher's certificate, but she went to work and lived in a rural commune, where she earned no money and received only bed and board. Carlos turned down a promotion with a big raise because the new job would have required him to be away from home frequently. Being with Margarita and the children was more satisfying to him than the extra money, prestige, and power offered by the new position.

Income Is More Than Money. Economists define **real income** as "a flow of commodities and services available for the satisfaction of human wants and needs over a given period of time" [6, pp. 487–493]. Thus, a family might have a very comfortable real income even when its cash earnings were small. As Figure 15-1 shows, real income includes market income, goods, services, and social income. For example, Sue and Jack earn cash (part of their market income) by teaching and by selling maple syrup, hay, and lambs. They produce goods for their own use that include maple syrup, all the vegetables they eat, lamb to eat, flowers, Christmas trees for themselves and their friends, wood for the fireplaces, and some clothing. The services they perform include cooking, dishwashing, cleaning, laundering, child care, painting, carpentering, snow shoveling, and entertaining. The children, too, perform some services, such as table-setting, dishwashing, and emptying sap buckets during the sugaring season. The durable goods that they own are also producers of real income, since without their house, two cars, barns, farmland, tractor, freezer, washer, and so on, they would have to spend a great deal more cash in order to live as they do. Social income consists of facilities provided by the community or the environment, such as parks, schools, police protection, and libraries. Living in a rural area, Sue and Jack are limited in such facilities, but they have a county agent who helps them with farming problems, state parks, a good road that is plowed after snowstorms, and a free view of beautiful mountains. In addition to their money income from their salaries and the fringe benefits that go with their salaries, their **market income** also includes the products of *barter*. Both give services to a cooperative school, where other parents also give of their talents to all the children

FIGURE 15-1   Real income comes from many sources.

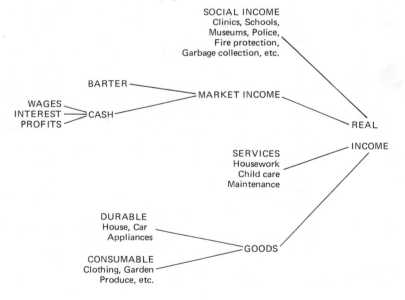

enrolled. They exchange goods and services with their neighbors, making deals on the use of land, barns, farm machinery, and labor.

Every family can identify some income that is not money. Many people do not realize that services are equivalent to money. If they did, then the housework that women do would be regarded more highly and people might feel more worthwhile for doing it. By estimating what it would cost to hire someone else to perform those services, investigators at Cornell University figured that when only the husband was employed outside, the household work of both was worth $8,800, of which $7,600 was contributed by the wife and $1,200 by the husband [4]. When the wife also had an outside job for fifteen hours or more weekly, her contribution through work at home was worth $6,200 and the husband's $1,300. Since estimates were based on 1967 prices, the amounts would be much greater today. And these were modest estimates. For example, pay for child care was figured at the rate of a low-paid worker rather than a skilled teacher, which many mothers are.

Community activities, such as a traveling circus, represent one form of social income.

Distribution of Income. The majority of North American families are in the middle-income brackets, unlike Asian majorities, who are very poor. The poor in the United States have been estimated as 12.5 per cent of the population, more than two thirds of whom are white [23]. About 40 per cent of the poor families were headed by women. A U.S. government definition of a poor family is one that must spend more than one third of its income on food, in order to meet a given minimum standard.

Income is distributed more evenly in countries with socialistic governments, such as New Zealand and the Scandinavian countries. Taxes are higher than in North America, reducing the incomes of the rich and increasing the social income of the poor. Even in these countries, as well as in Canada, the United States, and throughout the world, some families have more than others. Everyone has to come to terms with the limits of his resources and the fact that someone else has more. If he thinks he cannot make do with what he has, then he must figure out ways of increasing his income. He may learn another skill, add to present ones, move to a place with more opportunities, or work harder. When a family wants more income, the earning capacities of all members can be considered. The wife might earn the needed amount if the husband helped more at home. Eventually, though, each person and each family reaches a limit of moneymaking. If a family is to live with integrity, its members have to manage money effectively.

Influences on Income. The most effortless way to receive a large income is to inherit wealth and thus to receive income from investments. However, since no amount of good planning (except marrying an heir or heiress), makes inherited wealth available to most people, we turn our attention to more manageable influences. Or, if not manageable, it may at least help to understand them.

Occupation makes a big difference to income. The highest salaries are paid to top-level executives in big companies, sports "superstars," and a few entertainers. Considering average earnings, self-employed professionals, such as lawyers and physicians, earn the most and household workers earn the least.

Some jobs, such as teaching or working for most big companies, yield a steady income, whereas other kinds of work are paid unpredictably. Self-employed workers can rarely count on prompt, regular payment. The family supported by freelance writing, for example, will not be able to count on a certain weekly, monthly, or even yearly income. Their spending plans may have to be very flexible, with methods of lasting for periods with no income.

The *age* of the family head (a term used by the U.S. Bureau of the Census) is related to amount and timing of income [22]. In the U. S. population, when the head of the family was under 25, income was low. Income increased steadily to the 45–54 age bracket, after which it declined steadily to the lowest point of all, at 65 and over. This means that many older people are poor, often with fixed incomes from pensions or Social Security, or both. Inflation may be disastrous, changing the old person's economic status from moderate or low to extreme poverty.

Rise and fall of income varies with different occupations. Therefore, in making life-career plans, a couple would base them on what they can expect from their particular situation. A craftsman might reach his peak of earning at an age when a physician would be hardly beyond his lowest point. Professionals, especially the self-employed, reach earning peaks late in life and may taper off very little until well over the age of 65.

Sex and *race* differences in market income are well known. Women's average earnings have been less than men's, for the same work, at all levels of occupation. In one year, the average white woman earned $2,600 less per year than the average white man and $1,500 less than the nonwhite man [2]. Most disadvantaged of all, the average nonwhite woman earned $3,800 less than the average white man, $1,900 less than the nonwhite man, and $1,200 less than the white woman. Most of the nonwhite women, about 94 per cent, were black. Although it may seem that sex and race are not manageable in terms of changing them, federal law has already been changed in order to equalize opportunity and income for women and blacks.

Market income varies considerably from one state or province to another. In 1974 a U.S. government report indicated the highest cash income in Alaska, where the cost of living is also very high. Cash income was lowest in Mississippi. The Northeast region was highest, with the West and North Central region not far behind. The South's median income was considerably lower, but rising fast [23]. Ontario has a high average income, whereas the Maritime Provinces rank low.

National differences in market income are large, with Canada and the United States in a high bracket and the Third World in the low ranks. The monetary criterion for poverty in the United States would sound like great wealth to the average Asian. Sex and race differentials also vary from one national setting to another. It seems that Soviet and Chinese women are more equal to men in income than are North American and Western European women. When income is owned and managed by the whole group, as in a kibbutz, there is no chance for men to be paid more highly than women. Just as market income and its distribution are influenced by the ideology, politics, and resources of a nation, so also are the other parts of real income. The various parts of real income are balanced in different ways. Comparing New Zealand with the United States, market income is low but social income is high.

Life-career management for some families includes emigrating from their country of origin to another country, where the conditions of earning, producing, and consuming are more compatible with their values. In North America, everyone but American Indians and Eskimo can point to an ancestor, remote or recent, who did just that. When I (MSS) lived in New Zealand, I knew many people who had emigrated from Europe in order to establish a new level and balance of income and consumption.

Women Workers. Women work, whether they do it at home or on a paid or volunteer job. As the previous section showed, women's work at home is worth a substantial sum of money. If their volunteer activities were similarly evaluated, they would doubtlessly show the same. These facts should be taken into consideration when a couple are deciding whether they both should have paid jobs and whether both should be full-time. Although it is common for a woman to take a part-time job in order to supplement the family income, in the future it may become more acceptable for the man to take the part-time job and the woman the full-time position.

More and more women are convinced that they have a right to a permanent, interesting job with pay and status equal to that of men. At the same time, they expect to have marriage, and children if they choose to have them. This kind of occupational ambition makes quite a different home situation, as compared with that of the woman who works at an indifferent sort of job until she bears children, takes time out while the children are young, and goes back to the job market in order to earn the extra money that the family needs. A third type of situation is that of the woman being the chief or only earner in the family.

The first type, the career woman, gets the satisfaction of self-development, along with status, self-confidence, and a large (compared with other women's) paycheck. She can afford to buy help with the housework and child care, although it may be in the form of labor-saving devices, professional services, short-cut foods, and private schools, rather than a housekeeper. The problems of the career woman are largely pressures of time. There is not enough time to spend with her family and friends, to do all she thinks she should do in the house, to do volunteer work, and to enjoy hobbies and sports. Her husband may be proud of her and her greatest source of help and encouragement. Or he may feel diminished by her, especially if she makes more money than he does. If he is quite liberated from sex-role stereotypes, he may rejoice at her income as well as in her being an interesting and competent person. He, too, will experience time pressures. At the very least, he will have to make adjustments to her schedules. He may do more homemaking than the average husband.

Some career women choose part-time jobs in order to have time for childrearing and homemaking, often planning to resume full-time work when the children are older. In the past, these women have been discriminated against, denied promotions, raises, and fringe benefits, and were often paid at below the minimum rates. Progress is being made in protecting the rights of part-time workers, men as well as women. Some couples now hold two part-time jobs and share homemaking and childrearing.

If a woman chooses to work part time with little or no commitment to self-development through work, she may do so because she and/or her husband hold traditional sex-role concepts. If they agree, it probably works out to the satisfaction of both. Or she may not have the strength to cope with the combined demands of home and career. Some women carry very heavy loads at home. The minister's wife is expected to fill many social roles, and often on a slim income. The doctor's wife has to change plans at a moment's notice and often must do traditional men's work, such as home repairs and lawnmowing, along with the whole set of traditional women's jobs. The mother of many children or of a handicapped child must work much harder at home than does the average mother. Some women spend many hours doing volunteer work in the community. For all of these and other reasons, careers or even part-time jobs are not attainable for many women whose education and intelligence would be sufficient to do them.

The third type of female jobholder, the chief earner, works because she must. She may be a career woman, but more likely is in a low-level job. If she is lucky, her mother or another relative or friend helps at home. If not, she does two jobs, the one at home and the one at the factory, office, store, or school. This woman needs a great deal of social support, usually much more than she gets. If she is a mother, one of her worst problems is getting good day care for her young children and after-school care for older ones. Other problems include caring for sick children and getting health services, finding shortcuts to adequate meals, shopping, and getting rest and recreation.

The Working Couple. We consider it unfair for the full-time working woman to do the major part of the housework and child care and even more unfair if the man is working part time. In many cases, the man does not do an equitable share of work at home because he lacks homemaking skills. His early socialization did not include cooking, meal-planning, buying, dishwashing, cleaning, ironing, and mending. The learning of these skills may look too difficult, even to the man who is theoretically in favor of equality for the sexes. He may have always thought of these activities as lowly or simple and now it would be embarrassing to bungle in the kitchen or laundry. He might take two hours to prepare dinner and then have the meat done when the potatoes were still hard. It would have been easier to learn homemaking skills in high school, but they can be learned at any time. If a man wants to learn and a woman wants to teach him in a sharing way, it is not too difficult. Unfortunately, some women want to keep the key parts or most important parts of homemaking under their own control, allowing their men and children to do only the chore jobs, such as dishes, floor scrubbing, and garbage dumping. Then they themselves star at making gourmet dishes and flower arrangements.

Girls usually grow up with some notion of where they excel in homemaking tasks, what they like best, and what they dislike. A man may have to discover some strengths in homemaking, even though he is all too likely to think he does not like it and cannot do it. Starr does all the food shopping, getting satisfaction out of his ability to judge quality and values, and to keep track mentally of every cent he spends as he fills his basket. Rus is an expert on kitchen arrangements, having planned, modified, built, and arranged storage and use in the 16 houses in which he has lived his married life. Since many, even most, kitchens could be more convenient if rearranged, many husbands could make real contributions here. Especially if he is not accustomed to working in a kitchen, a man can look at the whole process with a fresh viewpoint. What is more, men, on the average (not all men), have more spatial ability than women, on the average (not all women), largely because of childrearing practices and probably partly because of genetics.

There is no perfect way of sharing work, since each person has strengths, weaknesses, and preferences. Each couple has to continually work out ways of sharing that seem fair to both and that give each person jobs that are satisfying as well as some that are unwelcome. In doing so, they show knowledge of and respect for each other. Working for the family is a way of expressing love, through care.

What shall we buy? How much shall we pay? Who will purchase what? These are decisions that have to be made, based on the family's goals. An overall plan, designed to fit the *real income,* has to answer these questions for both the short term and the long term. Policies cover general methods of procedure, such as that one person will be responsible for day-to-day decisions about buying food, but that the couple or the family will make joint decisions about large items, such as cars and furniture. A budget is a plan for spending and saving money. Since saving is usually done in order to have something to spend in the future, a budget is a way of allocating money and timing its use.

Budgeting. When a couple first establish a partnership and begin living together, they have to take some actions with money. If they plan to have children, their first long-term plan will probably be in regard to the money earned by the wife. They will realize that her salary will not be available for everyday living expenses after the first baby comes. Even if she goes back to work, it may be part time instead of full time. Therefore, they will use the money earned by her at present for saving or for capital outlays, perhaps a house, furniture, or education.

The necessity of allocating resources continues throughout all stages of life. The following procedures in budgeting are recommended by Gross, Crandall, and Knoll [6, pp. 554–577]: estimate funds available for spending, estimate expenditures, compare requirements and resources, review the plan as a whole. A year is a convenient time interval for planning, since some types of income and outgo occur on a yearly rather than a monthly or weekly basis. Detailed plans can be made by week, month, or pay period, more general plans for a year, and some plans for the whole family-life career. Indeed, some plans will even be made for the lineage family, but more likely by older families rather than younger.

When *estimating funds* available for spending, all sources should be included. Salaries and wages form the bulk of income for most people, but there may also be pensions, Social Security, disability payments, and interest from investments. We are assuming that the family budget reflects a partnership and that the couple pool what each earns, rather than thinking of any income as "my money." Since most family incomes fluctuate from year to year, the best estimate will probably not be exact. Overestimation of income leads to overspending. Therefore, it is better to err on the low side. The amount of weekly or monthly expenditures can then be calculated. If lump sums are expected, their timing should be noted.

Savings and credit can also be considered as available for spending, if deemed necessary. Since savings are usually accumulated for emergencies and long-term goals, there would have to be a careful assessment before spending them on daily living. Using credit means using goods or services now and paying in the future. Credit is, in effect, borrowing money, and charges are made for it just as interest is normally charged on any loan. Lenders are legally required to tell borrowers how much interest they are charging and what is the rate of interest, not just the lump sum. The borrower can then decide whether the extra cost of buying the car or television on credit is worth it. If a family decides to buy on credit, then its budget will have to include interest charges. If the family can wait to accumulate enough money for cash payments, or payment at the end of the month of purchase, it will be able to get along with lower expenditures.

There are some exceptions to the rule of saving by paying cash. Many sellers who accept credit cards or offer charge accounts do not give reductions for cash payment, even though it costs them more to have a customer charge an item than to have him pay cash. The result is that the customer can delay payment for a month or more without extra cost to himself. He actually has more money available to use. The drawback for many people is that they yield to impulse buying when the money does not have to be paid immediately. With strong-mindedness and careful planning, however, credit cards and charge accounts can be made to give a family financial flexibility without extra cost. Additional advantages include accurate records and protection in case of faulty merchandise. Therefore, credit must be included in considering funds available for spending. In order to open a charge account or obtain a credit card, an individual has to have a good credit rating, a way of showing that he is likely to pay his debts. A previous record of paying bills promptly is the quickest path to a good credit rating.

The *estimation of expenditures* is more complicated than estimating income, since it covers such a multitude of goods and services. One way to begin is to delay making a budget until a record of expenditures has been kept for a few weeks or months. Fixed items, of course, must be listed first and classified in terms of time: monthly items, such as rent and essential transportation, and yearly amounts, such as insurance and taxes. Debts must be paid on a regular schedule. Appendix C, on pages 497–499, is a form developed at Cornell University for organizing payments that must be made and relating them to expected income [24]. All promised payments are to be listed at the times when they must be paid. When the list of promised payments for each pay period is subtracted from the income expected, the remainder is what is available for other purposes. It may be more convenient to divide the promised payments differently, so as to even out the remainders from each pay period.

Remainders can then be divided into amounts needed regularly for food, clothing, personal allowances, recreation, education, contributions, savings, transportation, insurance, and miscellaneous. Some families will have additional categories. If a record of expenditures has been kept, amounts needed in each slot will be easy to estimate. If they add up to more than the remainder of income after deducting promised payments, some categories must be reduced.

Balancing the budget means working out a harmonious relation between requirements and resources. Upon adding both columns, if requirements exceed resources, then requirements have to be cut down or resources increased, or both. Relations between present and future must also be kept in some sort of balance. A disastrous, and not-too-infrequent solution to present imbalance, is heavy use of credit that piles up an even bigger load of requirements for the future. Sometimes

MONEY, WORK, AND LAWS: UNAVOIDABLE

present debt is offset by reduction of future requirements, as in buying a washing machine on credit in order to save paying a diaper service and making trips to a laundromat. A house mortgage is often an economical debt, the means of saving money that would have been spent in rent. A loan for further education is likely to result in a larger income.

Evaluating the budget means reviewing the whole plan from time to time, to see if it is satisfying family and personal needs in the best ways possible. As conditions change in the family and in the systems outside the family, changes in the budget are required. When a new baby is planned, or expected even if unplanned, all categories need adjusting, not only the cash expenditures but also the use of human resources or services. Likewise, when children grow up and the mother can spend more hours in a job, a complete reassessment of the flow of commodities and services is in order. A continuing question is that of sharing work in such a way that burdens and responsibilities are fair to all, to the couple and to the children. As we have already mentioned, the majority of working wives put in long hours of housework, often working many more daily hours than their husbands. This unfair situation occurs throughout the world, even in the Soviet Union and China, where women are supposed to be equal with men [1, p. 194]. On the other hand are families in which the husband works long and hard at a different job while the wife earns no market income and contributes few good and services. In a third type of family, partners share housework and child care in such a way that both can carry jobs outside. *The Two-Career Family* by Lynda Holstrom [9, pp. 87–94] discussed in detail the planning and actions of couples who manage this sort of life. In regard to budgeting, Holstrom points out, two-career couples think carefully about the ways in which they spend their time, realizing that they can and should purchase many services that will reduce time pressures. They fully understand the equivalence of the resources of time, money, goods, and services.

The budget can serve as the focus for communicating and deciding about all sorts of matters basic to satisfying family life. In coordinating the flow of commodities and services from resources into family action, family members have recurring chances to consider everyone's present and future needs.

Protection, Savings, and Investments

During times of crisis, a family has to call upon special ways of coping. A financial crisis occurs when there is not enough money to take care of present needs. Unemployment or illness can precipitate a financial crisis.

In an extended family or in closely knit communities, relatives or neighbors take care of the family in crisis. They give food, nursing care, shelter, or whatever is needed, even though they may share at some inconvenience and cost to themselves. The young man who was helper to our Indian cook had two younger brothers living with him, his wife, and his baby in a one-room shack. In justifying the large families

Discussing the ways in which they are spending their money, Jan and Joe try to agree on priorities. Good communication leads to success.

in Samoa, the father of 11 children explained, "Here, our children are our treasure. We don't put our money in banks but into our families."

North American nuclear families help their needy relatives, but not to such a great extent, and with less feeling of duty. There is a fairly strong feeling among young couples that they would like to stand on their own feet financially if they possibly can, although they would probably ask for help from their parents if they were in great need. Illness cannot cause a financial disaster in England, New

Zealand, and other places where medical and hospital services are underwritten by the government. Public assistance or welfare will provide a minimal support for North Americans who cannot earn or acquire money from private sources. Many people think that there is a stigma attached to welfare and most find the conditions of receiving it humiliating or at least annoying. They would prefer to receive unemployment insurance, sickness insurance, or some sort of support to which they feel entitled.

Savings, money set aside for future use, are used by some families to tide them over a period of crisis. Others borrow. An educational loan may be had for little or no interest while a student equips himself for a job that will enable him to repay the loan. A family may mortgage its house or put a higher mortgage on it in order to get money for an emergency. Since earnings tend to be small at the beginning of the occupational career and in the early stages of family life, savings are likely to be small or even nonexistent. The family with infants and preschool children is very vulnerable financially, because of greatly increased requirements and, possibly, decreased income. Insurance is a way of compensating for lack of savings and making sure that the family will have some income in the event of the death or disability of the chief breadwinner. *Term insurance,* or insurance that is renewed after a short term, is the cheapest way of buying financial protection for the beginning family. The younger the insured person, the less are his chances of dying, and the less is the cost of the insurance. Insurance can also be a way of saving at the same time that financial protection is offered, but it may not be the best way of saving. *Straight life insurance* pays the survivor a sum at the time the insured one dies, no matter how old he is. It costs more than term insurance because it is a way of saving, as well as a way of protecting the family. A young family may need high protection until the children are older or until the wife goes back to work. By analyzing and comparing the benefits and costs of term and straight life insurance, the family can see which plan would serve it better. If the family buys term insurance, it can also save in a bank account or in some other way, such as making payments on a house. Another way of buying straight life insurance that suits the young family is with step-rate premiums. In this plan, premiums are lowest in the beginning and highest at the end of the period.

As mentioned previously, buying a house can be a way of saving. Since part of the monthly payment on a mortgaged house is for interest, and part for repayment of the loan, it is important not to contract for too large an interest payment. A rule of thumb on how much to pay for a house is about two and one-half times the yearly income. This ratio varies, of course, with the real income, the earning potential of both members of the pair, size of the down payment, number of children, and the spending requirements of the family. As the mortgage is paid off, the family's equity in the house grows larger and as it maintains and improves it, the sale price is likely to go up. And all the time, the family has a place to live that costs less than rent. Thus, the amount invested in the house grows larger and the family has actually saved and even made money.

Many businesses and institutions now have retirement plans and ways of encouraging employees to save for emergencies and for their old age. Families who are covered by such plans are fortunate. Social Security, of course, offers some retirement income to most people, but not enough to live on comfortably. Most families want to save and try to save something beyond funds for emergencies. Those who start young are likely to save more since interest can be compounded and money grows. The problem of how to invest savings is beyond the scope of this book, except to point out that the study of investment is well worth the time and effort of anyone who can save a few dollars. Any bank offers free information and counsel on investments.

MANAGEMENT AND THE LAW

Since the law defines important rights and responsibilities for persons and families, it could be a resource to be used wisely. Legal knowledge is also a means to keeping out of trouble, by using it to plan and act within the law. The importance of law to families is illustrated by the Vanier Institute of Canada's selecting the subject of *the family and law* as one of its program priorities during 1974. Because its purpose is to strengthen and serve the family, the Vanier Institute called together a task force of lawyers, judges, educators, and social scientists. These experts investigated ways of changing Canadian law to make it more concerned with a broad range of human relationships and less limited to property questions.

Learning about Law

Since the United States has more laws and more lawyers than any other nation, the ordinary person is faced with a large task in simply learning what he needs to know about the law. The problem is aggravated by the differences in laws from one state to another and by the mobility of Americans. If opportunities to use the law are going to be equal, then everyone has to have access to a knowledge of law. The Bar Association of Wisconsin is demonstrating a program that would be valuable in all the states [13]. About 1,000 lawyers are voluntarily teaching courses in high schools. Students are learning the legal aspects of consumer behavior, family relations, marriage, divorce, academic rights, elections, and other topics. Since 41 states now confer adult privileges and responsibilities at 18 years of age, teen-agers find the law courses very salient. Family law can, of course, be learned by reading books on it. For example, a good resource for Americans is *The Time-Life Family Legal Guide*. (See references 5 and 21.) A helpful book for Canadians is *Canadian Women and the Law* [25].

To some extent, all laws are important to families because they regulate people's action, but some laws are especially important.

Marriage. Each province and state makes its own laws concerning marriage, specifying the ages of brides and grooms, with and without parental consent, period of waiting between getting a license and marrying, and conditions of common law marriage. The usual ages for marrying without parental consent are 18 and 21. When a difference is made between male and female, the most common specification is that women may marry at 18 and men at 21 [21, 25]. With parental consent, minimum ages for marriage vary from 13 for the bride and 14 for the groom in New Hampshire to 16 and 18 in most states. Some marriages of persons below the legal limits are permitted, especially if the girl is pregnant. Close relatives are not allowed to marry. Some states consider first cousins too close to marry, whereas others permit it. Until 1967, interracial marriages were forbidden in some states. In all but Maryland, Minnesota, Nevada, and South Carolina, blood tests for syphilis are required. The waiting period, between license and ceremony, varies from none to seven days, three days being the most usual period.

Almost any sort of ceremony can tie a legal knot, as long as the couple, who are legally free to marry, state their intention to take each other as husband and wife for life. Witnesses are required, one of whom is a clergyman or state official.

A *common law marriage,* in which there is neither license nor ceremony, is legal in twelve states and the District of Columbia: Alabama, Colorado, Georgia, Iowa, Kansas, Montana, Ohio, Oklahoma, Pennsylvania, Rhode Island, South Carolina, and Texas. The basic requirements of a common law marriage are that the couple be legally free to marry and that they agree to consider themselves husband and wife. In some states, another requirement is some sort of public acknowledgement or recognition of their status, such as registering in a motel as Mr. and Mrs., having a joint charge account, or simply telling their neighbors that they are married. With the current practice of living together before marriage, some couples are getting themselves legally married without intending to do so, as did Fern and Vern in Rhode Island. They lived together for only a month, with a sign on their door saying *Fern and Vern Stern*. Neither of them knew that they were really married, but when Fern left Vern and announced her engagement to Walter, Vern found out about the common law and informed Fern that she would have to divorce him before she could marry anyone else. Even if Fern had married Walter before Vern learned that she was legally his wife, the marriage to Walter would have been void.

There are legal and financial advantages and disadvantages to being married. These have been summarized for Canadians and, in general, the same is true for Americans and, in fact, for most people [25]. Marriage restricts the freedom of all participants, placing the main financial burden on the husband and limiting the mobility of the wife. More obligation for sexual faithfulness is placed on the wife than on the husband. Wives gain rights to support, inheritance, and, in the case of separation or divorce, alimony or maintenance. In a partnership or living together without legal marriage, neither person has any legal claim to sexual exclusivity. Children belong to the mother; the father cannot legally control their upbringing, education, or religion. If a man is proved to be the father, in Family Court, or if he agrees in writing that he is the father, then he must support his children.

Duties of Wives and Husbands. With the current rapid change in sex roles, some of the existing laws on duties of spouses are out of date and not usually invoked. For example, few people would support the law that says the husband may decide where they will live and that the wife must live with him. However, desertion for a certain period constitutes grounds for divorce.

Different states have different laws concerning the property of a married couple. Before marrying and moving to a new state, it is a good idea to find out what the laws are. For example, some states (Arizona, California, Idaho, Louisiana, New Mexico, Texas, and Washington) have community property laws, by which the couple jointly own everything that they acquire during their marriage.

Parenthood. An American couple has a right not to have children, but in the Republic of Ireland, as late as 1972, laws prohibited the importation and distribution of contraceptives [16]. The Irish situation was an exception, because most countries have been encouraging birth control; most have problems from rapidly increasing populations.

If a person enters into marriage with a secret intention of having no children, such concealment constitutes fraud and, therefore, is grounds for annulment. If one partner knows that the other wants no children and still goes ahead with marriage, then no fraud is involved.

Before 1965, some state laws forbade the use of contraceptives. Until the Supreme Court decision of 1973, only a few states permitted abortions unless the woman's health was being severely threatened by the pregnancy. In Canada, a legal abortion requires the approval of an abortion committee, consisting of three physicians. The United States Supreme Court has declared that states cannot legislate whether a woman could terminate her pregnancy during the first 12 weeks and that only limited control can be exerted on the conduct of terminations between 12 and 20 weeks. The issue is still a "hot" one, however, with various interest groups seeking to change both the federal and state jurisdiction over the individual's reproductive functions. Many people, especially women's liberation groups, believe that women should continue to have the right now given by the Supreme Court, the right to control their own bodies. Those working for restrictive abortion laws believe that every embryo has the right to become a baby. On the other hand, many champions of children's rights believe that every child should be wanted and loved by his parents and that, therefore, an unwanted pregnancy should be terminated. The perspective offered by cross-culture observations shows that these questions are viewed differently in various times and places. The legal use not only of abortion but of infanticide has been widespread in some societies. Such laws reflect the population needs of the country as well as the place of religion in the society and the particular religion that dominates.

Whether a country's laws give couples any choice as to whether they shall have children, other laws are applied to them when they do become parents. In most nations, the parents are required to register the birth, an act that serves the same function as a ceremony of acknowledging the child. Other legal requirements include giving basic care, food, clothing, housing, medical care, education, and protection from harm and injury. Parents are generally liable for willful damage done by their children, especially when they do not supervise their children sufficiently.

Since adoption laws are not uniform from state to state, persons involved in adoptions usually need information and advice from professionals. In arranging the adoption of children in the United States, the rights of two sets of parents have to be considered. The natural mother, of course, has a right to keep her child, and she must surrender that right without coercion in order to make the child adoptable. The natural father is rarely in the picture, since most adopted infants are born out of wedlock. However, if the father is married to the mother, he, too, must agree to surrender the child. There is some question as to whether unwed but acknowledged fathers should have rights to their children. Some states, including Illinois and Wisconsin, have established legal rights of unwed fathers. Before their infants can be placed for foster care or adoption, these fathers must give approval. When unwed fathers' rights are also considered, they, too, may be counseled and advised. For instance, in New York City, the Urban League's Adolescents' Maternity Program counsels the couple through pregnancy and until their baby is a year old.

The state tries to see that the mother has thought seriously about the consequences of giving up her child and that she (and possibly the father) really wants to do it. Some states (but not others) allow her to change her mind any time before the adoption becomes final, which may be six to 18 months. Although this arrangement protects the natural mother, it makes great hardships for adoptive parents. If the natural mother takes back her child, both baby and adoptive parents can suffer tremendously from the broken attachment. Adoptive parents have to comply with state and agency requirements before qualifying to receive a child from an agency. Then they must wait, often a long time, for a child to be offered. Then they go to court and file a petition for adoption. If the court approves the petition, they wait for one to 18 months for the adoption decree. At last the child is theirs and they have exactly the same obligations and privileges as other parents.

If a state issues a new birth certificate, as Rhode Island does, the adoptive parents are listed in the same way that biological parents are. This custom minimizes differences between adopted and biological children, but may lead to later problems if the child needs or wants to trace his heredity.

Childhood. As soon as a baby is born, he may be placed in one of two categories, legitimate or illegitimate. Some countries and some states (Arizona and Oregon) have eliminated all differences between the legal statuses of children born to married and unmarried parents, but in other places, certain differences hold.

Where there is any difference, the advantage is all on the side of being born to parents who are married to each other. In the United States and Canada, the unwed mother has legal custody of her child and she is required to support him and care for him. If she can prove paternity in court, then the father has to contribute to the child's support. Until recently, illegitimate children had no rights of inheritance from their fathers, but in a 1974 case, a New York State Surrogate Court gave the sole residue of her father's estate to an acknowledged out-of-wedlock daughter [3].

Juvenile courts were founded in the United States in 1899, in order to protect children and to help them solve problems that had involved them with the law. Children were to be spared publicity and the harsh punishments given to adults and to be rehabilitated so as to become good citizens. Although much has been accomplished by the juvenile courts, advocates for North American children today are criticizing the system. In many situations, children are denied the legal rights enjoyed by adults, basic rights such as having counsel when accused of a crime or misdemeanor. The U.S. Supreme Court has ruled that a minor must have a lawyer if he is to be tried for an offense that could result in his commitment to an institution [21, p. 82]. Parents and children should know this and insist upon the child's rights. Free counsel must be provided by the court if the parents cannot afford it.

Since young children cannot know their legal rights and stand up for them, they are often helpless when their parents abuse them. Less frequently, there are situations where other adults, sometimes teachers, abuse children. In the past, courts have been reluctant to move against parents, especially to take children away from them, without repeated and compelling proof of unfitness. Sometimes the process of proof is so prolonged that in the meantime, children are tortured and even killed. The law is moving toward safeguarding children's rights by the creation of children's advocates.

Since persons can now vote at age 18, that age, instead of 21, is sometimes considered the point of adulthood. A child is required to go to school until age 16. A child can be emancipated from his parents before 18 or 21 if they agree and he supports himself. However, if he leaves home without parental permission, they can ask the police to find the child and bring him home. If the parents file a complaint, however, the juvenile court conducts a hearing. The court may put repeaters in a state training school.

The Elderly. American law has little to say about the duties of adult children to their old parents. Although most states have some law that requires offspring to support their old, indigent parents and grandparents, details are not spelled out and enforcement rarely occurs. What is made clear is how to declare an old person incompetent to manage his business and/or his money, how to assume guardianship and how to commit him to an institution [21]. Children may act sincerely to protect old parents from their own failing powers or they may be trying to get control of a business, money, or estate. Sometimes they are trying to prevent an aged parent from remarrying and leaving money to a new spouse. In order to have a person declared incompetent and/or committed to an institution, most states require a court hearing, at which the person has a right to be represented by a lawyer. Sometimes the adult child does not need to take such initiative. The older person who realizes his own increasing incompetence can give over some of his control to someone he trusts. He can grant power of attorney, permitting another person or a bank or trust company to manage his finances.

When an elderly person is ill or immobilized, he may be literally in the power of his caretaker and unable to exercise his legal rights, even if he knows what they are. Even though the law tries to safeguard him, his welfare also depends on having people who love him, feel responsibility, and want to take care of him.

Marriage Dissolution. A marriage can be ended by annulment, legal separation, divorce, or death. When the court **annuls** a marriage, it says, in effect, that it never existed. A marriage is void or invalid from the beginning if it is contracted by a pair who are not legally allowed to marry. It can be voided by the court or declared invalid if one or both of the couple are under age, either is incapable of sexual intercourse, the marriage took place under duress, or lack of true consent or fraud has occurred. Examples of fraud are entering a marriage while pregnant by another man and hiding an unwillingness to have children.

Legal separation is an arrangement, affirmed by the court, in which spouses live apart, under specified conditions. Financial support, care of children, and division of property are usually worked out and formalized. When a person's religion forbids divorce, she can petition the court for "divorce from bed and board." The couple then are legally separated but not free to remarry.

Divorce is a permanent termination of a marriage that allows the two people to remarry legally. Although the United States has a worldwide reputation for a high divorce rate, it is by no means the highest. Egypt has four times as high a divorce rate, reflecting the influence of religion upon law [12]. Moslem men can divorce their wives by simply saying, "I divorce thee" three times. It is not that simple in the United States! It may be very complicated, with the different states having various laws, and different religions exerting their own particular pressures on their members and occasionally on the state and nation. As a matter of fact, Egyptians are now reviewing their divorce laws.

Although most states and nations require one spouse to prove the other wrong before the divorce can be granted, there is a trend toward facing the fact that in many cases, both persons want the divorce. No-fault divorce is being promoted as a way of making the best of a bad marital situation, preserving the dignity of husband and wife, and sparing the children as much discomfort as possible. By 1973, 14 states had legalized marital dissolution for marriages that have deteriorated beyond hope of restoration [17]. In other states, there are various grounds, of which adultery, cruelty, and lengthy separation are the most frequent. Most states have required a divorce applicant to have lived in the state for a certain length of time, from about six weeks to two years. Pressures are being mounted to change state residence requirements for divorce.

Where no-fault divorce is not available, an uncontested divorce is the method usually employed by a couple who agree to divorce. In some uncontested divorces, only one person wants it but the other does not wish to fight it. Although a divorcing person ordinarily hires a lawyer, some individuals in both Canada and the United States have successfully carried out their own uncontested divorces without hiring lawyers. Canadian magazines and newspapers have published guides to do-it-yourself divorce and in British Columbia, do-it-yourself divorce kits are sold [25, p. 63]. When one person contests the divorce, the procedure is more difficult and expensive. Lawyers' services are essential if the conflict is over financial arrangements, as it often is, or over custody of children. The fight may be long and bitter.

Custody of children is usually given to the mother, if she wants them and if the father does not prove her unfit to take care of them. Visiting privileges are usually awarded to the parent who does not get custody. Fathers are almost always required to contribute money to the children's support and often alimony to the wife, as well. If the wife remarries, alimony usually stops, but child support continues until the children are of age. If the husband defaults on alimony or child support payments, the wife can go to court in her home state for assistance, even if he has moved to another state. The "Uniform Reciprocal Support" law requires that the court in the husband's state get the payments from him.

Inheritance. Passing on property to heirs is a varied and complex business that plays a part in shaping family life, especially the lineage family. In highly socialistic or communistic countries, where the wider society is more important than family ties, tax laws may be structured so as to allow little inheritance. Where social income is extensive, a widow needs less market income in order to live and bring up children. If she can get a job that pays equally with men, and her children can go to a good day care center, then she will not need as much money from her husband as will the average young American widow. In a society where family lineage is important, inheritance customs and laws are such that the father can pass on some substance that will sustain the line. A common form of this arrangement is primogeniture, where the eldest son gets the biggest share, often the farm or the business. In noble and royal families, he inherits the title. No matter where one lives, there are legal regulations on inheritance that reflect the values of that particular society. A person is not free to do exactly as he wishes with his estate. He usually has to pay taxes and to leave a certain portion of the estate to the spouse and children. As with other laws, inheritance laws and taxes differ from one state to another, and family management includes learning what laws will apply.

Making out a *will* is an important way of caring for one's family. Failing to do so is financial and legal neglect. Although insurance and pensions can be made out to a spouse without a will, all other assets have to be included in wills in order to make sure that the desired plans are carried out. Young couples do not expect to die soon and they often think that they own so little that it is not worth making a will. No matter how little, though, the surviving spouse will get more of it and get it more easily if there is a will leaving assets to the spouse than if there is none. Joint property, of course, goes to the survivor, in any case. When a child is conceived, and as each change is made in the family, wills should be reviewed and changed to fit the new resources and goals. As in all the financial planning done in democratic family management, parents and children together have much to discuss in regard to inheritance plans. When children grow up and leave home, and parents are in the stage of financial recovery just before retirement, frank communication is very desirable. Both generations will benefit if they can talk over their financial needs, how they could help each other, and what the younger generation might expect eventually in the way of inheritance.

FINANCIAL AND LEGAL MANAGEMENT ARE RELATED

Laws regulate the ways in which money can be obtained and used. Good management involves operating within the laws, which in turn requires knowing what the laws are and how to stay within them. Some wealthy people have used the tax laws to their own great advantage, paying little or no income tax on huge incomes. In addition to using their own knowledge of the law, they were able to purchase even more expert knowledge from tax lawyers. In contrast, many disadvantaged people get into extreme financial difficulties because they do not take advantage of laws that would help them because they do not know how to go about using them.

The best time to learn about law and finance is early, before getting into trouble and while there are many years ahead for both short-term and long-term planning. If every child is to have an equal chance to learn and use this important body of knowledge, then it has to be available in school. Some of it could be integrated into courses on business law, history, current events, citizenship, consumer management, and family relationships. Participation of lawyers is urgently needed, since teachers are often not sufficiently expert. The Wisconsin Bar Association project is a demonstration of what can be done.

When people get into serious financial and legal trouble, the need to learn is obvious, but learning is not enough. When faced with mounting debts, clamoring creditors, and income insufficient for daily needs, a family may seek help from a financial counseling service. A survey [6, p. 561] of the characteristics of financially troubled families who filed bankruptcy or went to credit counselors showed that they were likely to be headed by men in their midthirties or younger, with several children, or by persons over 65. They were most frequently renters rather than home owners, blue-collar workers with low income and a recent history of decreased income or unemployment, in debt to the extent of two-thirds of their yearly income, owing financial institutions, department stores and medical debts most frequently, rent least often. Such a family may go for help to a consumer credit counseling service, where they can get advice on budgeting, including a plan for paying off debts, perhaps consolidating them. The service may also negotiate with the client's creditors. The Family Financial Crisis Clinic at California State University, Long

Beach, is an example of a free clinic that diagnoses, treats, and educates its clients to manage their affairs better in the future [15]. Spouses are encouraged to come together, to discuss and plan with the counselor. For couples with severe problems, many of whom think that they must file bankruptcy, this alternative is often workable: the wage earner's salary is paid to the court, which turns over to the client an amount to cover the budget worked out with the counselor. Then the court divides the rest among the creditors. The creditors cannot touch the assets that the debtor retains. Whether or not this court procedure is used, the emphasis of the clinic is on developing appropriate spending habits by all family members.

Getting Legal Help

There are times in the life of every person and every family when a lawyer is needed. Do-it-yourself legal jobs can be just as disastrous as do-it-yourself medical care. Marriage and parenthood ordinarily require no professional legal advice unless problems come up, but many other events and circumstances do. *When to Consult a Lawyer* has been summarized by the executive director of the Institute for Court Management, University of Denver Law Center [5]. He recommends that a lawyer be called: before signing an agreement involving a large sum or a long time; before settling an accident involving more than minor property damage; for a major domestic problem; and when implicated in any crime more serious than a traffic ticket. A person should have his *own* lawyer not one shared with others, if he is implicated with others in a criminal action or if the other party to a contract or dispute has a lawyer. His own lawyer will represent his interests only, whereas a shared attorney will have to choose between joint clients who have conflicting needs.

It is a good idea to have a family lawyer, just as it is to have a family doctor. When a person cannot afford a lawyer, he can consult the Legal Aid Society in some cities or he can ask the local Bar Association where to go for advice. When involved in criminal court action, the court will provide free counsel for anyone who cannot afford his own lawyer. In some urban areas, such as San Francisco, young lawyers are contributing their services to poor people who ordinarily have little access to legal expertise.

MARRIAGE CONTRACTS: A NEW DIRECTION IN FINANCIAL AND LEGAL MANAGEMENT

Many people are not satisfied with the ways in which current laws interpret relationships within a partnership. They are writing their own agreements, as marriage contracts. Such a contract can be purely informal, or it could be drawn up with the aid of a lawyer. Some couples think that the main benefit from such contracts is in the planning and evaluation involved, rather than in the possibility of coercing a partner to live up to the terms spelled out.

Personal marriage contracts represent a new custom that is a variation on an old one. In historic societies and in tribal cultures, the families and kin make the contracts, but now the two persons do it. A pilot research project indicates that contracts include a wide range of provisions, of which the major ones are: *economic,* the division and pooling of resources and income before and after marriage; *children,* whether to have them, responsibility for birth control, responsibility for care and support; *career-domicile,* relative importance of each person's career and what shall enter into choices regarding them; *relationships with others,* with friends, relatives, and sexual partners outside the marriage; *household responsibilities,* how work shall be shared; *evaluation, continuation and termination of contract* [20]. One purpose of the research project is to find out how many pairs, married and unmarried, are approaching partnership on a contractual basis.

SUMMARY

Money is a resource that people acquire in greater or lesser amounts. Satisfaction results from effectively managing what one has and accepting limits realistically. Money may serve as a symbol, sometimes masking the real meaning of a conflict. The various meanings of money include survival, freedom of choice, security, pleasure, unimportance, power, prestige, compensation, and self-development. Communication between family members is essential for defining economic goals and plans. The development of partnership requires some attention to money matters.

Research has identified what many families need to learn about financial management at different stages of the family life career. Newly married couples need instruction on specific planning, information seeking, evaluating decisions, and long-term planning. Childrearing families must learn to communicate with children, to include them in decision-making and to learn the technicalities of financial-career management. The family in the launching stages must clarify its obligations and functions in regard to helping younger and older generations and in making plans for retirement.

The processes of earning and producing can be satisfying in themselves. The product, whether it be money, goods, or services, is not the only thing that matters.

Real income includes market income, goods, services, and social income. Market income consists of money and the products of barter. Goods are both consumable and durable. Services include everything that family members do for each other and to build and maintain the home and property. Social income is what social groups, the community, state, and nation provide to all in the environment.

Distribution of money income varies with location, age, race, occupation, education, and sex. Nations differ greatly in size of income, distribution, and makeup of real income.

Many women work outside the home, as well as at home. Although the majority who hold jobs do so in order to earn money, self-development and satisfaction are also motivations. Barriers to cooperation and sharing of homemaking include outmoded sex-role restrictions, lack of skills, desire to control, and lack of effort to find new skills and build new strengths. A fair work arrangement indicates caring, an expression of love.

A budget is an orderly way of allocating resources for both short-term and long-term use. Setting up a budget is one of the important economic tasks of new partners. Maintaining it is a continuing responsibility. Both processes require identifying joint goals, making plans and decisions, acting, and evaluating. The welfare of the family is heavily dependent on the adequacy of financial management, as well as upon the size of real income.

Different ways of saving and investing are appropriate to different stages of family life. The essential function of insurance in the first stage is protection against the financial disaster of death or incapacitation of the breadwinner. Buying a house is a good way of saving for some young families.

Laws define the rights and responsibilities of people. Some laws have particular significance for families. In the United States, family law varies considerably from state to state. Since people move freely and often, they must be alert to differences and make efforts to learn the many laws that may affect them.

Marriage laws include minimum ages for marrying with and without parental consent, restrictions on blood relationships between spouses, health requirements, waiting requirements, and content of ceremony. Common-law marriage is legal in some states but not in others.

In most, but not all countries of the world, a couple has the right not to have children, in that they may use contraceptives. The right to terminate an unwanted pregnancy varies in time and place. Parents are generally required to acknowledge their child legally, which takes the form of birth registration in most industrialized societies. They must give the basic care of food, shelter, clothing, medical care, education, and protection from harm and injury. In case of adoption, the legal rights of natural and adoptive parents are spelled out by law.

The legal rights of children are being redefined. Juvenile courts, although founded for the benefit of children, sometimes deprive children of basic human rights as defined for adults. Young children are often helpless against parents and other adults who abuse them. The rights of the elderly, too, are not always sufficiently protected by the law, although courts regulate incompetency and commitment procedures.

Planning for death is an essential task of management for all adults, especially those responsible for children and other dependents. Insurance and wills should be discussed, planned, and arranged.

Dissolution of marriage is accomplished by annulment, legal separation, divorce, or death. The law defines the conduct of the first three. Financial arrangements and the rights of children are two of the main concerns.

Knowledge of law and economics is a great asset to family well-being. The sooner an individual begins to learn and use the knowledge the better for his personal and family careers. When in financial or legal trouble, outside help is usually needed in the form of counseling or legal advice. For those who cannot afford to pay a lawyer, free legal services are available in court cases and in some communities.

Through the use of personal marriage contracts, couples are spelling out agreements as to how their marriage and family living shall be conducted.

REFERENCES

1. Bardwick, Judith M. (ed.). *Readings on the psychology of women.* New York: Harper, 1972.
2. Dixon, Marlene. The rise of women's liberation. In Judith M. Bardwick (ed.). *Readings on the psychology of women.* New York: Harper, 1972.
3. Fraser, Gerald. Out-of-wedlock girl gets right to inherit from dead father. *New York Times,* January 27, 1974.
4. Gauger, William. Household work: Can we add it to the GNP? *Journal of Home Economics,* 1973, **65:**7, 12–15.
5. Graham, Fred R. and Ernest C. Friesen. The law. In John Dille (ed.): *The Time-Life family legal guide.* New York: Time-Life Books, 1971.
6. Gross, Irma H., Elizabeth W. Crandall, and Marjorie M. Knoll. *Management for modern families.* New York: Meredith, 1973.
7. Hafstrom, Jeanne L. and Marilyn M. Dunsing. Level of living: Factors influencing the homemaker's satisfaction. *Home Economics Research Journal,* 1973, **2,** 119–132.
8. Hill, Reuben. *Family development in three generations.* Cambridge, Mass.: Schenkman, 1970.
9. Holstrom, Lynda L. *The two-career family.* Cambridge, Mass.: Schenkman, 1972.
10. Jackson, Jacqueline J. Black women: The latent Cinderellas of American society. Speech at University of Rhode Island, Kingston, Rhode Island, March 4, 1974.
11. Lawler, Edward E. How much money do executives want? In Helena Z. Lopata (ed.). *Marriage and families.* New York: Van Nostrand, 1973.
12. *New York Times.* For every marriage in Egypt, two divorces. September 23, 1973.
13. *New York Times.* Wisconsin may be making Naders. March 10, 1974.
14. Oppong, Christine. *Marriage among a matrilineal elite.* London: Cambridge U. P., 1974.
15. Rader, Bonnie J. Law and reality: Financial counseling clinic. *Journal of Home Economics,* 1973, **65:**5, 10–13.
16. Robbins, John. Planned Parenthood—World Population report. New York: Planned Parenthood-World Population, 1972. (mimeo)
17. Robbins, Norman N. Have we found fault in no-fault divorce? *Family Coordinator,* 1973, **22,** 359–362.
18. Rolfe, David J. The financial priorities inventory. *Family Coordinator,* 1974, **23,** 139–144.
19. Safilios-Rothschild, Constantina. The study of family power structure: A review 1960–1969. *Journal of Marriage and the Family,* 1970, **32,** 539–552.
20. Sussman, Marvin B. Personal marriage contracts: Old wine in new bottles. Cleveland, Ohio: Institute on Family and Bureaucratic Society, Case-Western Reserve University, 1974. (mimeo)
21. Thompson, David S. and David G. Paulsen. The family. In John Dille (ed.). *The Time-Life family legal guide.* New York: Time-Life Books, 1971.

22. U.S. Bureau of the Census. Current population reports. Series P-60, No. 83, Table 3. July, 1972.
23. U.S. Department of Commerce. *We, the Americans: Our income.* Washington, D.C.: U.S. Government Printing Office, 1974.
24. Wiegand, Elizabeth. *Preview your spending.* Cornell Extension Bulletin 1143. Ithaca, N.Y.: Cornell University, 1968.
25. Zuker, Marvin A. and June Callwood. *Canadian women and the law.* Toronto: Copp Clark, 1971.

CHAPTER 16

THE CRISES OF RELATIONSHIPS

Problems and their solutions are part of everyday life, but some problems are more persistent and harder to solve than others. A **crisis** occurs when a sudden, highly significant change produces a situation that the person or family cannot handle effectively. The crisis requires the application of behavior patterns or resources that are not available. The person or group is in disequilibrium and thus to restore equilibrium, habitual modes of response must change quickly. Very often, because the resources at hand are insufficient for producing new responses, new sources of help, support, teaching, and problem-solving must be sought. The individual may turn first to his family or perhaps to a friend. The family in crisis may turn to friends or relatives or to another social institution, such as the church, school, or hospital. Because change in modern life is rapid, families in crisis often do not know how to get help. History and past experience are either not known or not adequate for this particular problem.

The stresses that lead to crises may originate within an individual (as in an illness), within a family (as in divorce), or outside the family (as in famine). Stresses can be physical or psychological or both.

A crisis represents a turning point for the individual or family. Persons in crisis are more likely to reach out for aid, because their own resources are not adequate for coping. A successful solving of the crisis, whether with help from the intervention of others or by working it through by oneself, can upgrade the individual or family interaction patterns. The newly formed behavior patterns may improve present ways of living. The experience may also prepare them to cope better with future crises. Failure to resolve the crisis can start a pattern of overlapping crises, or chronic problems.

CRISIS AND PROBLEM-SOLVING

The purposes of effective handling of a crisis and problem-solving are the same: to effect a change in behavior patterns that will allow the individual (or family) to continue living at an optimum level. The effective handling of some, but not all, crises will prevent them from turning into or precipitating chronic problems. Some life situations engender an environment that makes problem-solving difficult or impossible. The family with the severely handicapped child and the family living in poverty and under the oppression of racial discrimination will probably have very difficult times solving their problems effectively, if indeed they ever do. Some problems or crises when solved cease to be an influence on the individual's life: adjusting to a new community can be a crisis at one point in time, but once the adjustment is made, the crisis disappears. Other crises, such as the death of a loved one, become less severe with time, but the loved one can never be replaced. The chronic problem can be handled with more or less effectiveness: the stroke victim can give up all hope of living an interesting life or can find new ways to use his talents.

Steps in Crisis Resolution

In order for a crisis or problem to be solved, it must first be identified. The person who is in a sudden crisis situation is in a state of disorientation [12]. His behavior patterns have been upset and cannot be relied upon. Emotionally upset, he is likely to be influenced by fantasies and irrational stereotypes. His identification of the problem, therefore, may not be accurate. He needs to explore the reality-based issues of the problem and the hazards involved. As the problem is identified and explored, it can be broken up into smaller, more manageable "pieces." The individual needs to identify his goals, as well, which can be thought of as the inverse of the problem. If my problem is that I am unemployed, my goal is to find employment [14].

Actively seeking help, and accepting it when it is offered, can make crisis solution easier. A person also needs to attempt vigorously to master certain issues, while resigning herself to accepting other issues. If the crisis is the death of a loved one, the individual must accept that the person is gone permanently and cannot be replaced, but must learn to live without that person and to seek other relationships or behavior patterns to fill the void. However, feelings regarding the crisis need to be expressed: feelings of fear, loneliness, anger, guilt, and so on often accompany a crisis. Expressing these feelings helps to work them through. We explore this issue more thoroughly in the section on coping with death.

A crisis is exhausting, both mentally and physically. Although the person in a crisis needs adequate rest, he should not retreat into sleep as a means of escape [12]. In times of crisis, many people find it difficult to go to sleep.

Crisis Intervention. A person in crisis is most likely to turn to family or friends for support and help. If the other individuals are closely involved in the problem, however, their own feelings may be stirred up to the extent that they cannot be of much help in identifying the problem and searching for a solution. An uninvolved, trained person may be useful in this kind of situation.

One method of crisis intervention is the *decision counseling method* [29]. The *counselor* first helps the *helpee* (person in need of help) to delineate the problem. They then attempt to discover and explore the options that are open to them. A precise decision-making model is selected from among the options. The helpee then must attempt to carry out the decisions that are made. In another session, the counselor and helpee assess the outcome, and start over if the outcome was not satisfactory. The crisis intervention model just described is very similar to the steps of problem-solving discussed previously.

Coping with Chronic Problems. The person with chronic problems is in some ways less fortunate than the person with a sudden crisis. The intensity of a crisis makes the individual more likely to reach out for help and search for new solutions that may solve the problem. The person with chronic problems is locked into ineffective behavior patterns but is not jolted to look for alternatives. Attempts of well-meaning persons to intervene may be looked upon with suspicion. The person with chronic problems may feel that he had better not rock the boat: things are bad, but any change is as likely to make them worse as to make them better.

INDIVIDUAL DISRUPTION

Many family crises and ongoing problems are the results of impairments, disabilities, or disasters encountered by individuals. Because the individual changes in the roles he plays or because he cannot play normally expected roles, the other persons in the family must also change their ordinary modes of behavior. They change in the family roles they assume and in their interactions with the community. Successful crisis management and problem-solving can be defined from different points of view, or according to different value systems. For example, an old person becomes disabled. Instead of being able to take care of herself in her own apartment, she now needs to have her meals brought to her and to be helped from bed to bathroom and wheelchair. She might go to live in her daughter's home or in a publicly supported home for the aged. The first solution would be more acceptable to the old woman, but would require many changes in the behavior of all family members. Some of

them may think that the home for the aged would be the better arrangement. The community would approve of the daughter taking care of her mother and would consider it a good solution.

Individual disruption often has its cause within the family. Or it may be caused by precipitating forces from outside that are augmented within the family. Sometimes it is the family's interpretation of the individual's condition that determines whether or not it is a problem.

The following types of individual disruption are representative of those most frequently encountered. The list certainly does not include all possible problems.

Acute Physical Illness and Injury

When a person becomes ill or gets hurt, there is usually some discussion as to whether the problem can be handled within the family or whether outside aid is necessary. As pointed out in the chapter on health, self-medication, or family medication, is important in health care. When the illness or injury is severe, however, and the decision is to get outside help, then there is intervention from systems outside the family, a hospital, clinic, physician, or other healer. The family may also call for help from other sources, or it may only need to accept the offers of help that are quickly given.

An illustration of sources of support in the severe crisis of acute illness is given by the experiences of 345 urban men who had first heart attacks [18]. Because of the nature of the crisis, these men had all received medical treatment in hospitals. They were interviewed in the hospital and later, at home, as to the amount of help and support received from various sources. Almost half the subjects saw as "very helpful" the members of their own families of orientation (parents and siblings) and also their in-laws. Friends were next most helpful, ranking considerably higher than "other relatives." A large minority (28 per cent) saw their parents as not at all helpful, and 21 per cent saw their siblings in this way. Little use was made of community organizations after discharge from the hospital, 72 per cent saying that they contacted none. No significant differences between ethnic groups were seen. The investigators concluded that friends and neighbors were supplementary to family, rather than compensatory, and that the amount of help received from family and friends seemed to be related to the degree of social integration of the individual. In other words, the better the individual's social relationship before his crisis, the more aid he received.

The conclusions from this study of male heart-attack victims may not be entirely applicable to other situations. Even in this group, however, there was variation as to who helped and how much they helped. There may be differences related to the age and sex of the patient and the nature of the crisis. Other studies have shown the kin network to be of considerable help at times of illness.

In the first stages of an acute illness or injury of a member, the immediate family usually suspends ordinary operations to apply all efforts to relieving the threat. Often at such times, families find unusual strength and resources that they were not aware of possessing. In giving care to the loved one who is in danger, partners, parents, and siblings can reach heights of selflessness and generosity.

Chronic Physical Illness and Disability

Most acute illnesses progress into a milder stage that lasts for a while, perhaps for a very long time or forever. A permanent disability can occur anytime, as a result of an accident, disease, or war. Disabled war veterans suffer a precipitous change from vigorous fitness to being permanently handicapped. A disability may be present from birth. Dealing with a temporary impairment is, of course, different from integrating a permanently handicapped person into family living.

The "sick role" is a pattern of behavior expected of an ill person, varying with the nature and circumstances of the illness and with other roles played by the person. The sick person is generally regarded as needing special care and help, which he should accept in order to speed his recovery. Since he has diminished strength and is in need of extra nurture, the patient is relieved of some of his ordinary obligations and responsibilities. Immature behavior is tolerated, not only in children but also in adults. "He's like a big baby when he's sick." Sometimes patient and family do not agree on how the sick role should be played. Conflicts may arise over how much the patient should do for himself, whether he should stay in bed and take medicine.

In order to support one or more members in the sick role, a family has to make changes in the behavior of all members. One or more of the well members will take on the role of nurse, giving care that will help the sick one to recover. "Moral support," helping the patient to feel more cheerful and confident, is given by family and friends who offer evidence of love and concern by visiting, entertaining, and bringing offerings of flowers, food, books, and so on. In addition to offering the patient care, respect, response, and knowledge, family members must make additional adjustments to the illness. Someone has to take over the work that the patient would ordinarily do. When my (MSS) husband is sick, I often teach his classes. When I am sick, he does the shopping and cooking and answers my professional mail.

When an adult is sick for a long time, or permanently disabled, the family will most likely have to adjust to a lower income and to spending portions of its income on therapy, equipment, and other supports for the disabled member. If it is the father who is incapacitated, the mother may have to carry a paid job without much help with the housework and childrearing. Psychological adjustments to such situations are often difficult, not only for the person who cannot live up to the ordinary role expectations for his age and sex but also for the rest of the family, whose roles are also altered and who must often live within unusual constraints. There is also the problem of accepting the attitudes and behavior of other people, who regard the disabled and his family as different, inferior, or pitiable. When community supports are necessary, there are requirements of dealing with the clinic, the welfare department, the Veterans' Administration, and other bureaucracies that may add strains as they give help. And all too often, the assistance is not sufficient for completely satisfactory solutions.

Mental Retardation. Among the many kinds of disabilities that affect family life, mental retardation stands out as a particularly difficult one. A crisis is precipitated when a retarded or abnormal child is born, or when the condition is diagnosed. Expectations and behavior patterns must be changed on many levels. In an immediate context, the child needs care that is modified to suit her special needs. Special treatment and services may have to be sought and bought. Long-term planning may be even more difficult. The family's relationship to the community is likely to be affected.

The presence of a retarded child poses many questions in family management. One difficult decision is whether to keep the child at home or to put her in an institution for the retarded. It may also be possible to combine living at home with day care or day school. Sometimes foster home placements are made. In making such a decision, parents usually need counseling. In fact, they can hardly avoid it, since facilities for retarded children almost always have professional social work services as part of the program. However, the decision is the parents' responsibility. When a plan has been made for care and education, much additional planning remains to be done. Although many retarded children can eventually earn their living, they may need continuing help in managing their affairs. Some will not be able to earn their living. Parents realize that the child will probably outlive them. How will they provide for the child's supervision and care after their death? Only the most affluent can set up trust funds and arrange for paid guardians. Sometimes siblings and kin accept future responsibility for the child. Some families must rely on social institutions outside the family in order to provide future care.

In addition to the stress of caring for, obtaining services for, and making future provisions for the retarded child, families are subject to additional stress from the behavior of other people, and often from their own fears, guilt, and anxieties concerning the causes of retardation. Siblings, as well as parents, suffer from these social and emotional disturbances connected with the retarded member.

Families of retarded children have been studied in order to understand the nature of their peculiar stresses and their reactions to them [24]. The effects of home and institution were compared by studying, over the period of a year, the functioning of families who kept their retarded children at home and families whose retarded children were placed in institutions. Prior to institutionalizing their child, families functioned less adequately than the families who kept their retarded children at home. Since the former families felt more stress from their retarded children, it is hard to say whether the children were the cause of poorer functioning or whether the lower level of family functioning resulted in more difficult retarded children. More significant was the finding that over the year, the families with retarded children at home deteriorated. In this group the siblings appeared to suffer most. As far as the functioning of retarded children were concerned, no differences were found between those who were institutionalized and those who remained at home. In interpreting the results of this study, it would be easy to conclude that all retarded children should be sent to live in institutions. There are, however, other solutions that might turn out to be just as satisfactory for siblings and parents. A day care center offers enough support to some families.

Social interaction in 281 families with one or more retarded children was shown to be different from that of 754 families with normal children [45]. Interaction within the family, indicated by reading and talking with children, was less in families with retarded children. Such families visited less with people outside the immediate family, especially in the neighborhood. The results of this study suggest that parents of retarded children may be timid in making social advances or that neighbors may not be as friendly with these parents as with others. In either case, the study points up the value of an association for parents of retarded children. By socializing with families who have similar problems, interaction would be increased and families may also gain emotional support from one another.

Mental Illness

The family plays a crucial role in the prevention, causation, treatment of, and recovery from mental illness. Mental illness is a frequent result of crises that are not handled in positive, adaptive ways. The life histories of mentally disordered persons often show sudden deterioration after crises that were beyond the person's capacities [13, p. 201]. The disorder is actually a response to the problem, the best response that the person can make at the moment. During a crisis time, help in finding effective responses can make the difference between health and illness.

The causes of a mental illness can be physical, such as poisoning from lead paint or pellagra caused by a vitamin B deficiency. Some mental illness is genetically based. Severe developmental crises sometimes occur when individuals change from one stage of life to the next, as during adolescence. A role change can precipitate a crisis, as may the change into parenthood or widowhood. Disorders may result from the straining or breaking of family relationships, as in hospitalization, divorce, and death. Interpersonal problems can arise within the family, or outside of it. But no matter what the source of the basic cause of mental disorder, when one person suffers, so does the rest of the family. From that time onward the rest of the family also continues to be involved with the illness.

The significance of the family is recognized to some extent by psychiatric programs that include the families of patients who are undergoing treatment. In this situation, families are helped to understand the patient's illness and what they can do to promote his health. They may also discuss their own feelings and benefit from sharing with other families of mentally ill patients. Family therapy is different from programs that focus on one patient. In this new approach, the pathology is seen as a product of group interaction, as well as of individual disruption [1]. The family is regarded as a behavior system and not just a number of individuals. The adaptive responses of family members are strongly related to the ways in which the group functions as a whole. When psychiatric help is first sought, it is usually for one member of the family whom the others consider ill or disturbed. When the therapist talks over the problem with the whole family, he often finds that several or even all of the members are disturbed and that their difficulties are interlocking. Often, the problem has existed for some time, but was contained by some sort of balance in the family. When the equilibrium was upset, perhaps by the breakdown of one member, the others assumed that all their trouble was caused by the ill person.

It is easy to see how family therapy could be applied to conflicts between husband and wife or between parents and children. It also seems logical that it would help the family to understand a member who had been hospitalized and to integrate the recovering patient into the family in a healthy way. If family interaction contributed to the illness, then family interaction would have to change in order to support the members instead of tearing them down.

In solving problems of mental illness, persons and families usually need outside help. Although kin and friends can make big contributions in supportive roles, professional therapy is often crucial. Information on where to get help can be obtained from clergymen, physicians, public health nurses, community mental health clinics, councils of community services, and psychology departments of colleges and universities.

The prevention of mental health problems involves the whole society in many areas. This book is concerned with an essential aspect of mental health promotion, the development of loving families and of individuals who can communicate and act upon the love they feel.

Problems Centered in Children

In the course of growing up, almost every child shows some disturbed behavior. Often the problem behavior of a child would indicate mental illness if it occurred in an adult. It is the way in which the child resolves his crises that determines whether this particular period of disturbance leads him toward health or illness.

Personality growth, like intellectual growth, takes place through a series of transformations. The thinking of the preschool child is of a different quality from the thinking of the infant and of the school-age child. So is personality structured differently. In moving from one stage to another, the child reorganizes himself, going through a period of disequilibrium before he achieves a new kind of equilibrium. In periods of disequilibrium, he is upset in mind, body, emotions, and social interactions. That is, he goes through a crisis. The normal crises of growth are called developmental problems. Some of the ordinary ways of releasing tension or expressing disturbance at these times are temper tantrums, eating problems, bad dreams, bedwetting, thumbsucking, masturbation, lying, fighting, shyness, failure at school, untidyness, and stealing. The term *normal* does not mean that these symptoms of disturbance will be sure to go away if ignored but only that most children exhibit some of these behaviors at times of crises.

Children's crises also arise from disturbances within the family and outside it, in relationships with friends and school. The normal problem behaviors can be expressions of tension originating from such sources. Disease, accidents, and disasters also precipitate crises in children, as well as in adults.

Most of the crises of children are handled within their families, sometimes with the help of kin and friends. Some parents and siblings are more able than others to help a child master his problems. For example, two-year-old Ali began to cry frequently, threw his toys around angrily, and said *no* to whatever anyone asked him to do. His parents watched him more closely, talked over what they saw, and decided that Ali was often blocked in making decisions and doing what he wanted to do for himself. They reorganized the living room to make fewer restrictions necessary and also gave Ali some real but simple choices. Ali soon was able to organize himself better and played constructively, with infrequent need to express his anger and frustration. Gary's parents, when faced with the same situation, were very annoyed by his crying and felt that a two year old should learn to obey his parents. They tried ignoring Gary's behavior and then spanked him.

Some children are easier to live with than are other children because of their genetic makeup and its interaction with their environment. Whereas one child copes with developmental transitions with little strain, another has a hard time with each crisis. One child manages to play the roles expected of him by family, neighbors, and school, whereas another finds the roles incompatible. Relatively unskilled parents may get along well with an easy child, but are thrown into family chaos by a difficult one. Some talented parents, often aided by loving, insightful family members, can help difficult children to cope with crises in ways that produce healthy growth.

Services. In previous chapters, we discussed some of the supports that parents need in order to bring up children and to maintain a healthy family climate. Children's behavior problems and mental illnesses could be greatly minimized if families could get quick help with crises. When growth is monitored by health specialists, then small deviations can be detected and treated before they become serious. Pediatricians, family doctors, nurses, and child health clinics may serve in this capacity. Teachers and school psychologists may also, on occasion, perform this function. An example of very early successful crisis intervention is a case handled by a nurse in New Zealand [61]. Ray Taylor recognized a sudden behavioral and physical change in a nine-week-old infant as indicating a crisis caused by the mother's withdrawal. When the mother, guided by the nurse, restored her loving attention, in extra measure, the infant promptly recovered. Being very immature, the infant reacted as a whole to the threat. Because he was in a stage of rapid development, his reorganization and recovery were very swift. This case documents the importance of dealing with mental health problems at an early age and of having community support systems available to parents.

When children's problems are severe, therapy from specialists may be needed. Behavior modification is a method that attempts to change the child's troublesome behavior directly, without concern for its sources. Since the parents are usually the ones to apply the techniques, they must first modify their own behavior. In so doing, they often remove the source of the child's problem [40]. In other types of treatment, the therapist may work alone with the child. When this is done, the family also needs help in understanding and restructuring relationships. The sources of information on where to find help on children's problems is the same as the sources mentioned in the section on mental illness.

Drug Use and Addiction

In extreme stages of dependence on any drug, the individual is disrupted and his condition is certainly a problem to his family. Drug use is not a clear-cut behavior, however. I (MSS) feel that I need two cups of coffee in order to wake up completely in the morning, but I do not think of myself as a drug addict. Is a person alcohol-dependent if he looks forward greatly to a drink before dinner every night? What about the light smoker who cannot give up his daily consumption of ten cigarettes? Is a weekly marijuana party a sign of dependence? Surely drugs are an area where the definition of problem behavior is very salient. Definitions vary widely. The individual and his family may take a different view of drug use. The community may tolerate what the law forbids. Therefore, we confine the discussion to situations where the disrupting influence of drug use is obvious and acknowledged, although we recognize that more subtle problems also occur. It is also possible for people to use drugs without getting into difficulties. Examples include the moderate smoking of the Hunzas of Pakistan who may live to well over one hundred years, the ritualized moderate drinking in many cultures, and the religious use of hallucinogens by the Peyote Indians.

Drug use becomes problematic when it results in harm to body, mind, family relationships, and social behavior. Like all instances of individual disruption, family, kin, and community are also involved in causing the behavior, treating it, suffering from disturbed relationships, and establishing a new equilibrium. Since alcoholism is the most widespread drug problem, its treatment is probably more advanced than treatment of other types of drug abuse. The role of the family is clearly recognized in the treatment of alcoholism, particularly in terms of the husband-wife relationship. When the alcoholic is beginning to gain control of his drinking, changes occur in relationship with the spouse and a new balance must be achieved. Alcoholics Anonymous have a companion organization for the families of alcoholics, to which children, as well as spouses, belong.

Addiction to hard drugs, such as heroin, places an even greater strain on family relationships than does dependence on nicotine and alcohol. Because hard drugs are illegal, users may be socially stigmatized, prosecuted, and even imprisoned. In order to maintain themselves on hard drugs, many users commit crimes and thereby bring financial and legal disasters upon themselves and their families. Addicts and their families urgently need expert help in dealing with the addiction, the sources of its occurrence, the crises and chronic problems caused by it, and the establishment of healthy patterns of living. Research into methods of treating heroin addicts gives some information on the changes that methadone therapy made in the patients and their families [17]. Reports were obtained from the wives of 72 men who had remained for a year on the methadone program of the drug abuse research team. Of these wives, 22 had also been heroin addicts and were on methadone. Results showed that after entering the methadone program, regular employment and time spent with the family increased and sexual relations improved.

Persons seeking help with drug problems can get information from regular sources, as mentioned earlier. Such agencies and individuals will recommend groups, organizations, and therapists who specialize in the particular problem.

Aging

Aging is problematic in an industrialized society largely for two reasons. Most basic is the fact that in modern societies with good sanitation, nutrition, and health care, more and more people survive until old age. Another factor is the industrialized society's emphasis upon productivity: the individual's sense of self-worth is largely tied up in what he *does* rather than what he *is*. The retired person is likely to feel cast aside and worthless.

However, aging does have certain inherent problems that are largely culture-free. The body atrophies and becomes less resilient and resistant to disease. For example, bones become less dense and more likely to break; connective tissue becomes less elastic; the working capacity of the heart decreases; the nervous system deteriorates [8]. Many of these problems can be delayed by proper diet, rest, and exercise.

Some societies venerate age, equating it with wisdom. In spite of the various cultural revolutions in China, a positive value is still placed upon old age. However, a study of villages in India indicates that although respect for the aged is still espoused as an ideal, the reality in everyday life may be very different [30].

Although Western society worships youth, the age group of 40- to 60-year old holds a great deal of power [48]. People of this age control business, and have a great deal of influence in law, medicine, education, the financial world, and politics. In most cases, however, when the age of retirement comes at 65 or perhaps earlier, the individual often does not have a choice regarding his own retirement. Although it is illegal in the United States to fire a person because of his age, he need not be retained once he reaches the age of retirement.

Theories of Aging. Not all persons, of course, dread retirement. For some it provides a chance to increase activities in other areas, or take a rest. Two theories of aging stem from the debate concerning the value of continued activity in old age. Activity theory holds that the best adjusted people are those who remain active, and disengagement theory holds that adjustment is fostered by a mutual withdrawal of the older individual and society from each other. Research indicates that there is

some truth in each theory. It is customary for most people in our society to decrease their activities as they age; for some, this is associated with better adjustment. For others, remaining as active as possible fosters adjustment. Many persons regret the drop in role activity, but regard it as a natural part of aging, and are able to maintain their sense of self-worth [33].

Poverty and Aging. Both engagement and activity theories imply that the individual has a choice in her life-style. However, poverty is a fact of life for many of the elderly. Retirement almost always means a loss of income that is not adequately offset by pensions and Social Security. In 1969 the median income for all families in the United States was $9,596. For families headed by an elderly person, the median income was about half that amount, $4,985; the median income for older persons not living in families was only $1,813 [63].

424   A FAMILY IS BASED ON HOME

Services for the Elderly. As the numbers of aged persons increases in our society, their political power will also increase. The low birthrate at the present time indicates that the "baby boom" generation will continue to be a significant part of the population for many years to come. In recent years the elderly have gained more social income in the form of increased Social Security benefits, and Medicare and Medicaid. The study of gerontology is blossoming in medical schools and universities.

Many communities have programs that are designed specifically or primarily for the elderly. Meals On Wheels provides hot meals for shut-ins who cannot cook. Churches and other organizations provide hot lunches on the premises for the elderly at a nominal fee that may be waived in some cases. Transportation is provided to and from the meal center. Geriatric day care centers provide not only meals and transportation but social activities, nutritional education, health care, physical therapy, family counseling, and even legal advice. The geriatric day care center helps the old person in many ways, and in so doing helps the old person's family. If the old person lives alone, the center provides social contacts that may have been completely unavailable to her previously. If the old person lives with her family, the family is freed of responsibility of her care for a significant number of hours per week.

FAMILY DISSOLUTION

As we have seen, the problem or crisis of one family member invariably has an effect upon others in the family. Individual disruption causes at least some family disruption as other family members react and adjust to the individual's problem. The dissolution of a family through death, divorce, or desertion can be a major crisis, or it can be the solution to a long-term problem, or both.

Death

In our society, death has become increasingly associated with old age, as more and more people survive childhood and middle age. An individual may not lose a loved one until his parents die, when he himself is approaching old age. In our society a few generations ago, and in many preindustrial societies today, deaths in childhood are quite common. In some societies and historical periods, death was common in the middle years as well.

Approaching death can be a crisis for the family, and it also can be an individual crisis. Some individuals can predict the time of their own death with amazing accuracy, and persons who work with the aged may also have the capacity to predict death. Psychological changes independent of illness appear to occur several months before an aged person dies [42]. The hospitalized person, whether aged or not, may sense that he is dying, or may be told by his doctor that he is dying. Whether or not he accepts the reality of his impending death will determine the smoothness of his passage from life to death, and may have profound effects upon those whom he leaves behind. Some patients, when told they are dying, are able to use the remaining time to tie up the loose ends of their lives, get their wills in order, and say good-bye to and leave instructions for the surviving family members [25].

Grief Work. When a person is bereaved through death, his life is disrupted in a major way. In order to return to normal functioning, he needs to mourn. He must realize that the dead person is gone forever, and will never be replaced. His initial reaction to death is likely to be numbness and disbelief. Seeing the dead person, and going through the ritual of a funeral can facilitate this process of realization, but does not guarantee it.

The bereaved person is likely to have an alarm reaction: anxiety, restlessness, and the physiological accompaniments of fear [50]. He may wonder how he can go on living without the loved one. He may search for the dead person, expecting her to reappear at some point. He may have feelings of anger and guilt, anger toward those who press him toward premature acceptance of death, or anger at the loved one for abandoning him. He may feel guilt that he himself did not die. This is especially true for survivors of disasters. See Robert Jay Lifton, *Death in Life: Survivors of Hiroshima* [43]. The bereaved person may also have feelings of internal loss of self or mutilation. All meaning may go out of life [50].

Role Problems of Widowhood. A number of researchers have noted problems associated with role changes when an individual becomes widowed. The widowed individual acquires a new status, widow or widower instead of wife or husband. Because of higher mortality rates for men, the widow is less likely to be able to regain married status through remarriage. However, it appears that widowhood represents a more traumatic role change for the male than for the female [4, 6, 32]. The traditional female role, that of housekeeper and cook, continues after widowhood even though the widow no longer performs these tasks for her husband. The widower may be at a loss at doing these simple everyday tasks. The widow, however, does not escape role problems. For example, the widow whose husband took care of the couple's financial matters is likely to be at a loss concerning how to handle these affairs [44].

Coping with Widowhood. In modern societies, widowhood is primarily a problem of the aged. In 1970, there were 2.11 million widowers and 9.64 million widows, not counting those who remarried. Sixty-four per cent were 65 and over. The percentage of widowed persons in the United States has declined since 1900, but the years of survivorship have increased. Half of those widowed at 65 can expect to live 15 more years and one third can expect to live 20 years or more [32].

Widowhood represents both a crisis and a problem. When it occurs, its suddenness and intensity make it a crisis, and as the individual finds ways of coping, it becomes a problem. In some cases, widowhood represents a release for the widowed person from other problems.

One community has begun to meet the problems of widowhood through a widow-to-widow crisis intervention program. Soon after she is bereaved, the new widow is contacted by a woman who was widowed previously. The widow aide offers help to the new widow in adjusting to her situation. Not all widows want or need assistance, but the adjustment of many that do is facilitated by such a program [56].

The widowed often report that friends are embarrassed by their grief, and try to discourage their expression of it [44, 56]. Incompletion of grief work can lead to psychiatric problems in the bereaved [50]. Widows also report that they feel like "fifth wheels" socially; their married friends may also feel that the widow is a threat to the stability of their own marriages [44, 56].

How well the widowed person is able to adjust to his new roles and status depends upon the kind of person he is. Among women, ability to re-engage in society is associated with higher education and greater flexibility [44]. Among aged men, the problems of widowhood are compounded and perhaps superceded by feelings of uselessness brought on by retirement [6]. A major problem of widowhood is isolation, which theoretically can be reduced through increased interaction with the community or kin. Remarriage is another possibility, although it may bring problems of its own (see pages 214–216).

Death of a person other than a spouse, such as a child or parent, is also a family crisis. It involves role changes, and necessitates grief work. Because the death of a child in a modern society is relatively unusual, it may be especially stressful for family members.

Divorce

The attitude that marriage is more important than the individuals involved is changing in the United States, and other parts of the world as well, as evidenced by more liberal divorce laws and an increase in divorce. It is possible now to get not only marriage counseling but also divorce counseling. California, which led the way with no-fault divorce, has a system of conciliation courts that serve about 70 per cent of the state's population [21]. The purpose of the courts is not to save all marriages but to prevent unnecessary divorces. Marriage counseling becomes divorce counseling when a couple decides that reconciliation is no longer practical or possible. Divorce counseling seeks to lessen the pain and humiliation of divorce and to help all persons involved in it toward personal growth and adjustment [23].

Decision Making. Divorce is resorted to when the problems of a marriage make one or both partners determined to end the relationship. Only about 10 per cent of U.S. divorces are contested, indicating that usually both partners want the divorce [47]. The small number of contested divorces does not mean that persons who divorce approach it eagerly or without giving it considerable thought [7]. There is good evidence that divorce is not entered into lightly and that the decision to divorce is usually made slowly and reluctantly, generally taking around two years to be made, and sometimes up to ten or twelve years or more [19, 27].

Factors that enter into the decision of whether or not to divorce include whether or not the couple can afford the divorce financially, whether or not they are self-sufficient enough to make it on their own, the effect upon children who are involved, and what the couple's friends, neighbors, and family will think of them [9].

Divorce itself is expensive, and two households are more expensive to maintain than one. The wife who cannot support herself may be reluctant to seek divorce, especially in states where alimony is not granted. When one or both partners lack self-sufficiency, unhappy couples find themselves in a double bind: they cannot live together, but they are dependent upon each other in a maladaptive way and cannot live apart. We deal with the effect of divorce on children in a later section of this chapter, the *one-parent family* (see pages 430–432).

Divorce as a Crisis. The time of greatest crisis is usually when final separation occurs [23, 27]. However, the legal system complicates divorce, and the final divorce does not end the legal problems [53]. Problems involving child custody, alimony, or child support, and moving to a distant state may constitute recurring crises for those involved in divorce. Although gaining custody of the children may complicate one parent's adjustment, the other parent who is cut off from the children may experience more trauma [54].

Divorce Adjustment. As with widowhood, divorce necessitates coping behaviors on the part of those involved. The divorced person may need to mourn the death of this marriage before he can put his life back together again. Adjustment to divorce is helped by the approval of friends and family, by having divorced friends, and by starting new activities. A new definition of one's self-identity is needed. Adjustment is made more difficult by the fact that there are no role prescriptions to guide the behavior of ex-spouses in their interaction with each other [54].

Desertion

Desertion is the poor man's divorce. One spouse, usually the husband but in increasing numbers the wife, leaves against the will of the other spouse. In the case of husband desertion, the husband fails to support his wife and children. In a recent three-year period in Ontario, the number of deserted wives on family benefits almost doubled [20]. Usually, the deserting husband has a legal obligation to support his wife and children that the deserting wife does not have. In years past, few efforts were made by local courts to track down the deserting husband, but as it became apparent that deserted families placed a financial burden on the taxpayers because of increased public assistance payments, more efforts have been made to locate the absent fathers [57]. As the problem of deserting mothers becomes more well known, more attention will probably be given to it by researchers and the courts.

A private firm that specializes in finding missing persons reports that the number of female runaways whom they were hired to locate has increased dramatically. In the early 1960s they handled 300 cases of deserting husbands for every one wife, but in 1973 the ratio was about even, and in the last six months of 1973 the company was tracing more women than men. The typical runaway wife is 34 years old; she was married at 19, had a child within the first year of marriage and another 18 months later. She lives in the suburbs, and is "intelligent, concerned, and anxious to be more than a housewife" [10].

Desertion involves many of the same problems as divorce, but is made more difficult by the complete unavailability of the deserting partner. Unless the deserter wants to be found, as sometimes is the case, she is usually careful to cover up her tracks. The spouse left behind may have no idea why he was deserted and has no chance of receiving alimony or child support. Although divorced parents often do not try to explain to their children the reasons for the divorce, the deserted parent usually can give no explanation because he himself doesn't know what it is. The deserted spouse also cannot remarry until a divorce is secured.

Many deserting husbands are chronic deserters, returning for a time and then leaving again [31]. Furthermore, their own fathers were often themselves deserters [57]. It is not known whether deserting wives are likely to become chronic deserters. Some wives find life on the outside much more difficult than they had expected, but are afraid to return to their families because they do not want to go back to their old way of life [10].

One-Parent Families

By one-parent families, we mean those families that were originally intact, with parents married to each other, that have been broken by death, divorce, separation, or desertion. Unwed parenthood as a chosen life style is discussed in Chapter 17.

The percentage of divorces involving children, and the number of children involved in divorce, have both increased in the United States. In 1953, 45.5 per cent of divorces involved children; in 1962, 60.2 per cent did; and in 1969, 61.1 per cent of divorces involved children under 18 [15, 51] (see Figure 16-1).

One-parent families were 8.9 per cent of Canadian families in 1971 and 11.6 per cent of American families in 1972, showing an increase in both countries [55]. In the United States in 1971, 90 per cent of white children and 64 per cent of black children were living with their two parents. About nine million United States

FIGURE 16-1   Number of divorces each year and number of children involved in divorces in the United States.

Source: Alexander A. Plateris, *Divorces: Analysis of changes.* Washington, D.C. U.S. Dept. of Health, Education, and Welfare Publication No. (HSM) 73–1000, 1973.

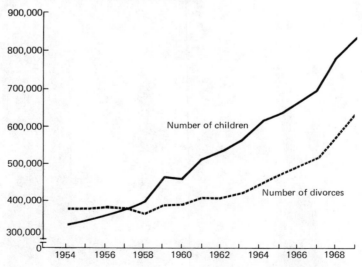

children are being raised by one parent, over eight million by mothers, and 800,000 of them by fathers [20]. Among female family heads, 27 per cent of the white and 54 per cent of the black were below the poverty line. Percentages of marital status of female family heads was as follows: never married, 20 black, 9 white; separated or divorced, 49 black, 41 white; widowed, 25 black, 44 white; husband absent, 5 black, 6 white [60a].

Children in the Single-Parent Family. Contrary to popular myths, broken homes are not always worse for children than unbroken homes. Although children from happy, unbroken homes tend to be better adjusted than children from broken homes, the worst adjustment is associated with intact, unhappy homes [38, 49].

Children need to be helped to adjust to separation from a parent through divorce or desertion. This task may be a difficult one for the remaining parent. Many parents fail to give their children any explanation of why they are divorcing and what the divorce will mean to them [7]. Children with the most negative reaction to divorce are those who had believed that theirs was a happy home [38]. These children especially need an explanation for the divorce. *My Dad Lives in a Down Town Hotel* [44a] and *Minoo's Family* [17a] are books that can help a young child to accept his parents' divorce and to feel more comfortable about it [44a]. These books and other books [41] that deal with children's emotional problems can assist parents in understanding their children and helping them with their disturbed feelings.

Children who lose a parent through death need to be able to express their grief and work through their feelings of loss, just as the bereaved spouse does. The bereaved parent who hides his sorrow and shock from his children is not helping himself or his children. A very young child who does not understand the permanence of death may continue to insist for quite some time that the dead parent will return. Although the explanation has to be suited to the maturity of the child, it should be what the parent believes. A book designed to help a child and his parents at the death of a loved one is titled *My Grandpa Died Today* [22].

The Parent's Adjustment. We have already discussed the adjustment of spouses to widowhood and divorce. The surviving parent has the same problems as a childless widow or divorcée, and also has problems that are specifically related to childrearing. The single mother usually has the problem of a limited income (if she receives alimony or child support), and needs time away from her children in order to earn money. She also needs to be able to maintain discipline, educate her children, and promote their healthy emotional growth. The single father also needs time to work and to care for his children. The myth that a single parent cannot raise a healthy child makes the parent feel anxious and guilty, and these feelings affect his ability to raise the children [11].

Although raising a family without a partner can be problematic, the divorced person who does not get custody has problems as well, especially if he wanted it. The parent without custody cannot be as large an influence upon his children's lives, and the children may become alienated from him, especially if the parent with custody is bitter about the divorce. Loneliness can be a problem for the parent without custody.

Solo Black Mothers. Black women, having suffered a double disadvantage of being both female and black, have developed strength and resources for coping with problems. An exploratory study of black, female heads of families found the typical subject not overwhelmed by her divorce and new single parenthood [50a]. Being used to working at home and on the job, she felt confident in her own resources. She used public assistance if necessary, but not day care. Nor did she find community agencies, except *Aid to Families of Dependent Children,* very helpful. Her mother, other relatives, or older children helped with babysitting. Younger mothers usually went out socially and had a good time, but older mothers could not find men friends. All but one of the women reported that there were men in the lives of their children, either relatives, friends, or the children's own fathers. All but one of the subjects could see some advantages in their present family situation.

Services for Disrupted Families

The family that is struggling to cope with the problems of family dissolution can get help from outside agencies. Some states provide compulsory or voluntary counseling before a divorce is granted. Mental health centers and family service agencies provide counseling, frequently with a sliding pay scale. Such agencies could also put the individual or family in touch with other help agencies in the community, such as the widow-to-widow program, or Parents Without Partners, Big Brothers, and Big Sisters. The family that belongs to a church can receive help from the clergy in coping with the death of a family member.

DISORGANIZATION AT ALL LEVELS

In discussing both individual and family disruption, it was apparent that each disruption has causes and effects at other levels. There are some disturbances that are hard to place at any particular level of organization, since they so fully involve individuals, families, and societies. Problems of this type include poverty, violence, economic crises, natural disasters, and moving. Since we discuss family finances in an earlier chapter, we do not discuss economic crises here.

Poverty

Being poor means not having enough to live on, not enough of what it takes to live in ways considered normal and adequate by the society in which one lives. The official United States definition of poverty is based on income. A family of four was poor in 1971 if its income was $4,140 or less [64]. About 25,600,000 persons, or 12.5 per cent, were living in poverty in the United States. In poor countries, the poverty line is much lower and a much larger percentage of the population lives in great need. In India, a family with $4,140 would be prosperous; most persons exist there on less than $100 annual income. The existence of greater misery in other nations does not make it any easier for North Americans who are hungry, cold, badly clothed, and blocked as to opportunities for earning enough income.

The problems of poor people are chronic, since they go on and on. Crises happen often as food runs out, the rent comes due, payments of income are held up, a family member becomes ill, another gets into trouble at school or with the police, the man of the family deserts, or an unwanted pregnancy occurs.

The responses and behavior patterns of poor people have common elements, because many of their efforts are directed toward survival in a harsh environment. However, many differences arise out of both individuality and culture. Cultural differences between India and North America are vast. Hinduism promotes acceptance through a belief in fate and hope of a better life in the next reincarnation. Among the very poor are beggars and sweepers, following in the occupations of their parents, knowing how to live and act as beggars and sweepers. Hinduism also encourages almsgiving in the rich and the not-so-poor. North Americans, in general, believe that success depends upon hard work and self-discipline, and that during his one life span, a person should make the most of his opportunities. Even so, the very poor are more likely to believe that success is due to luck or fate, rather than to hard work. Quite logically, the poor cherish toughness and endurance, qualities necessary for survival in the world of poverty. Characteristics of the urban poor in Western societies include: a large proportion of mother-centered families, high rate of desertion by men, belief in male superiority, fighting, physical punishment of children, wife-beating, early sex activity, and living together without marriage [34, p. 47].

The public has a generally negative attitude toward those people who must live on public funds. Furthermore, the recipients of public assistance tend to feel disparagement and hopelessness toward themselves [16, p. 7]. These negative attitudes contribute to the impotence of poor people, adding to the multitude of factors that prevent them from improving their socioeconomic status. Among people with low incomes, there are important differences between those who manage to live without public assistance and those who cannot, perhaps because of the low esteem in which welfare recipients are usually held. And among all low-income people, there are large individual differences in behavior, probably greater than differences between people who have moderate and high incomes.

Adaptations to Poverty. Among the very poor, much of the behavior that is adaptive to poverty is also behavior that prevents the achievement of higher financial and social status. Thus, they are caught in their efforts to survive, unable to develop strategies that would help them in the long run.

Most very poor people share the overall cultural high esteem for a stable marriage and childbirth within marriage. However, the ideal is not always achievable, and being unmarried is also acceptable. As expressed by a Harlem mother, "If you want somebody—oh, you *want somebody*—to help you—and there's the children and the rent—well maybe then it doesn't seem all that important whether you're married or not" [34, p. 10]. Similarly, poor people tend to regard out-of-wedlock births less negatively than do the affluent, but they still prefer that parents be married. Poor women, in general, would like a good marriage to a good man, but good men are hard to find and most men are seen as unpredictable, controlling, and difficult to understand. As one woman put it, "Men folks are rotten these days. You got to lick 'em to get along with them. You got to take so much off 'em" [34, p. 50].

Maladaptive behavior in childrearing methods is most serious, since poverty is perpetuated through this channel. During the past 15 years, many research studies have focused upon relations between the parent behavior and children's intelligence, learning, and achievement motivation. Physical care, including nutrition and control of illness, is often inadequate because parents lack both material resources and knowledge. Growth of children's bodies, and most important, their brains, is depressed by malnutrition and disease. Beginning in infancy, the teaching style of the parents, mostly the mother, is a vital influence on the child's personality and intelligence. The mother, or principal caretaker, arranges a stimulating, orderly, responsive environment or permits barren or chaotic surroundings. She encourages questions, exploration, and initiative, setting up situations where the child can succeed in choice-making, problem-solving, and creating, or she ignores him until he gets into trouble, when she punishes him or tells him to shut up. She gives out information, names objects, directions, numbers, and colors, reads stories, points out interesting events, takes the child on outings and trips, shows him how to act with friends, plays imaginative games, role plays, pretends, shows him how to help her, explains how to do things right and what went wrong, generalizes on a level that the child can understand, or she does not teach in these ways. The television is making too much noise, the light is dim, and the mother is too tired, too busy, or even absent. (Working mothers include 29 per cent of women with children under 3, 45 per cent of women with children under 6, and 57 per cent of women whose children are between 6 and 17 [65]. Among black women, 42 per cent of mothers of preschool-children were employed in 1972. Numbers of children with employed mothers have risen since then.) Although the affluent mother may be employed and still interact in these ways with her children, the poor mother has too much to do at home and too little support in doing it. She teaches that being good is being quiet, not talking back, not asking questions, and obeying the rules set by adults. These teachings make the child easier to live with at home and fit him for school *as it looks to the mother*. In reality, such a child goes to school without basic cognitive concepts; with language and social behavior inappropriate to the classroom; lacking in achievement motivation, curiosity, impulse control, and self-esteem.

Are race differences in behavior really only socioeconomic differences? Most childrearing studies have suggested that poverty is much more salient than race.

However, an analysis of *very poor* versus *moderately poor* mothers and children shows some differences that are more pronounced in the very poor [52]. The subjects came from several preschool programs in which mothers, as well as children, were taught. Mothers' attitudes and behaviors were measured before and after the educational programs. Child measures included IQs, IQ gains, and motivation. *Authoritarianism* was higher in black mothers than in white mothers. The difference increased among the very poor. Highly authoritarian mothers were likely to express approval of strictness and to have unrealistically high expectations for their children in school. (Other studies have found that poor black children's low achievement aspiration is expressed in statements of unachievable goals.) Highly authoritarian mothers less frequently expressed nurturance, as shown by meeting their children's needs, communicating, and sharing. After the mothers had finished the educational program, the white mothers decreased in authoritarianism and increased in egalitarianism. The black mothers did not change in mean scores on authoritarianism. Increases in egalitarianism appeared in mothers of girls, but not of boys. Egalitarianism in mothers was related to their children's IQ, IQ gains, and behavior leading to cognitive development. These results suggest that the black mothers, especially the poorest ones, were trying very hard to make their children obedient. In the dangerous life of the black ghetto, obedience to the mother has survival value, but in school and in the mainstream of North American life, a serious deficit results from the tactics through which the mothers taught their children obedience.

Better Solutions for the Poor. We have tried to show that dwellers in poverty have developed ways of meeting crises and solving problems that make survival possible but that perpetuate their poverty. The cycle of poverty is a cycle of the lineage family, in which each generation contributes to the entrapment of the next. Individuals, nuclear families, and lineage families are locked in. The community, on local, state, and national levels, has made attempts and is still trying to find the keys to freeing the poor and letting them join the mainstream. Many keys will be needed, because the solutions will have to be on many levels. The most important door to open is the economic one through which everyone has access to enough food and other materials that are basic to life. Although much is known about education and mental health, delivery of sufficient services remains problematic. Although we believe in assistance at all levels, we also believe that the most crucial time for intervention is in infant-mother interaction.

Violence

Physical force and the threat of force are used by persons and groups for controlling others. The armed forces of Rome, Britain, and the United States have been called peace-keeping, meaning that the threat they exerted served to control other nations. The strong father may never hit his children and yet control them because they know he could overpower them. Goode [26] says that force or the threat of force is used by all social systems, since it is one of the four major resources by which people can get others to do what they wish. The other three sets of resources are economic, prestige, or respect, and love, or friendship. The person with less force at his command will have to give more money, respect, and/or love in order to motivate another person to do what he wishes. Parental authority is backed by the force that parents can exert and also by social institutions that are themselves backed by force. The police, for example, will hunt for a delinquent child and the courts will apply restrictions and controls at the parents' request.

Violence involves the actual application of force, although force can be applied without violence. For instance, an adult picks up a child in order to prevent him from running into the street, or holds his arm as he is about to attack another child. Such restraining force is not violent. Violent behavior involves the use of physical force in order to hurt, destroy, or control. Suicide is the ultimate violent act of a person against himself. Within the family, violence takes the forms of fighting, beating, or slapping the wife or husband; spanking, beating, and otherwise abusing children; hitting, pinching, and biting siblings, and sometimes killing. Within a given year in New York City, 7 men were killed by their brothers, 2 women by their sisters, 11 sons and 13 daughters by their mothers, 5 sons and one daughter by their fathers, 40 women by their husbands, and 17 men by their wives [3]. Outside the family, illegal forms of violence include assault, murder, rape, gang fights, kidnapping, and hijacking, whereas legal forms include war and simulated violence in films, television, and other forms of communication. There are strong interrelationships in what happens within the family and in the whole of society. And yet, although North Americans admit the frequency of societal crimes, they are reluctant to face the existence and implications of family violence.

Constructive Aspects. Can anything good be said about violence in the home? Does a good fight clear the air? Some marriage counselors have suggested that fighting helps to preserve and strengthen a marriage [2]. But the sort of fighting they are talking about is not hitting and slapping, but being frank about thoughts and feelings, even though the immediate effect is hurtful. The fact remains, however, that husbands and wives do hit each other and their children. Such an act may make it clear that a crisis is occurring. The aggressor is hitting out because he does not know what else to do about the intolerable situation in which he finds himself. If the violence brings those involved face to face with their problem, then they may take the next step of looking for solutions. But as for hurting, destroying, and killing having any intrinsic value, it just does not make sense.

Catharsis through Violence. In their comprehensive book *Violence in the Family,* Steinmetz and Straus [59, pp. 14–16] discuss the myth that the acting out of aggression will minimize or prevent further violence. Since there is no scientific proof that this is so, the authors suggest that the myth is used in order to justify existing patterns of violence. In his research on the quarreling and fighting of marital partners, Straus found that verbal and physical abuse escalated over time and that instead of reducing physical aggression, verbal and symbolic expression increased it [60]. Although there is an emotional release of tension immediately after a fight, the long-term result is more fighting.

Learning and Unlearning Violent Behavior. Children learn patterns of aggressive behavior by seeing and experiencing it. Later, under certain circumstances, the child uses the forms of violence that he has learned. In one of the most pathological results of early experience with violence, parents abuse their children as they themselves have been abused. (Child abuse is discussed in Chapter 10, pp. 255–256).

A review of research on aggression control concludes that children can be helped to interpret frustrations through explanations and reasoning and that when violence is witnessed, it should be discussed and labeled *bad* [5]. Aggressive behavior should be neither reinforced nor ignored, but prevented or halted, explained, and disapproved. Punishment can be used to suppress instrumental aggressive behavior that has been established by rewards, but punishment will not eliminate responses that meet biological needs. This review also negates the notion of catharsis reducing violence.

Sex-role learning is another part of growing up that has implications for violence. Instrumental aggression is object-oriented, used for the purpose of getting a desired object or defending rights or territory. Hostile aggression is a response to a threat to self-esteem, directed toward the persons responsible for the threat. Young boys and girls (preschool, first grade, and second grade) showed no sex difference in instrumental aggression, but boys used more hostile aggression than girls [31]. This finding is consistent with the fact that boys are taught to be proud of themselves when they challenge, fight, and defend. When boys learn that to be male is to be tough, aggressive, and dominant, they are building a foundation for violence. Lower-class males especially are socialized to aggression by being taught that masculinity requires it. A new concept of males as human beings would contribute to a decrease of violence in future generations [66].

Reducing Violence. Can people change themselves, their families, and nations in such ways that they will do less hurting and more loving and giving? Could violence be eliminated, and controlling force used sparingly, in the service of order and justice? Since family and society interact so intimately in producing violence, any constructive programs must deal with both.

First of all, in the crisis of a violent episode, the participants need help, just as they do in any other crisis. An example of a source of help is the Family Crisis Unit of the New York City Police Department [3]. Police officers were trained to deal with crises of aggression in families and were made available 24 hours a day, to answer calls reporting family disturbances. When dealing with a case, an officer would prevent or stop violence, help the participants to calm down, seek the causes of the episode, and bring in the services of agencies that could help with long-term solutions. Not one homicide occurred in families that were previously contacted by the Family Crisis Unit. In other crises of violence, kin or friends may be able to intervene and assist until other help can be found. I (MSS) remember a neighbor of ours who knocked on our door at 2:00 A.M., saying that her husband was threatening to kill her. She spent the rest of the night with us and, in the morning, began the work of enlisting aid from social institutions.

A comprehensive program has been outlined by Steinmetz and Straus, recognizing the interaction of the individual, family, and society:

1. Poverty and its resultant frustration and powerlessness must be reduced.
2. Elimination of violent models of behavior that saturate our culture through the media, especially television. These models include violence in criminal punishment and international relations.
3. Preventing the birth of excessive children by providing contraceptive resources that will enable families to have no more than they want and can care for.
4. Education on childrearing and management of family conflicts.
5. Changes in the power structure of the family that will modify male dominance and extreme masculinity norms, thus reducing husband-wife conflict and competition, as well as men's frustrations and failure [59].

Moving

Geographical mobility is a fact of life in the United States. One out of five families moves each year (see Figure 16-2). The move itself represents a crisis point, but at least among the middle class, adjustment to moving is not difficult. Families who move frequently learn how to cope with the stresses of moving and are able to settle into a new community without much difficulty [39]. Wives who moved frequently reported that frequent moves did not diminish the number or quality of the social relationships that they had, but that they had grown in their skills of making close friends [35].

Children, however, appear to be more able to adjust to moving than do parents. Furthermore, children under the age of 11 generally have the easiest time adjusting. In one study, it was reported by mothers that 90 per cent of their children between the ages of 6 and 11 made friends easily in the new community, and 69 per cent of those between 11 and 18 years of age did [58]. Perhaps mothers' reports do not tell the whole story. An autobiography written by my (LSS) sister at age 11 expressed her grief at moving to a home in a new state. She told of her happy former life with a group of friends who had a bicycle club, a sewing club, and a Girl Scout troop. Then, she wrote, "My life was shattered. I had to leave everything." At age 10, I (LSS) was sick and miserable for the first two months after our move to India.

Adjustment to the new community is facilitated by the arrival of furniture and other familiar objects, by the return to a "normal" schedule, by friendly neighbors in

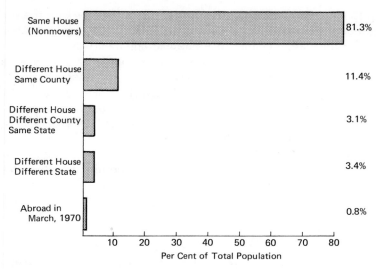

FIGURE 16-2   Mobility status of the population of the United States, March 1970 to March 1971.

Source: Statistical Abstract of the United States, 1973, p. 37.

the new neighborhood, and by the presence of familiar chain stores and restaurants in the new community [35].

Maladaptions to Moving. Unhappiness with moving is associated among middle-class wives with the wife's not taking part in planning the move. Persons with less income perceive their neighbors as being less helpful [35], and since neighbors play a significant role in whether the newcomers feel welcome or not, it is likely that adjustment is more difficult for persons with lower income.

Military families move frequently, usually without having a choice regarding where they are going or when. A study of military wives found that those who identified with military life were able to adjust easily to frequent moves, and that their children adjusted well. Women who did not want to be military wives did not adjust to moving. The researcher writes: ''Having been forced to move, they apparently experience the event as a major problem-ridden life crisis in the midst of an already wretched existence, cut off from and unable to reach out to informal or formal support'' [46].

The military families just described involved people from a lower-class background who were generally upwardly mobile socially. Indeed, geographic mobility is very much tied in with class mobility; a move to a new community is very often undertaken as an effort to raise the family's level of living. In reality, this may not occur, especially among the rural poor who go to the city in search of work [28]. Adjustment to moving for these families is made much more difficult because of the number and complexity of changes that they must make. They must change from rural to city living; they must learn new job skills; they lose the support of kin and neighbors; they must learn new management skills such as shopping and food storage in the city; they must learn how to find their way around a strange city; they are unaware of recreational and cultural opportunities such as libraries and museums, and they have left behind their rural pastimes.

For an aged person, being moved against her wishes may precipitate an earlier death. Patients in a home for the aged were more likely to die during the first year of their stay there; after the first year death rates stabilized. An eighty-year-old patient who had been there for ten years was no more likely to die than if she had been there two years. When an employees' strike forced the relocation of 57 patients, their mortality rate rose significantly for the first three months after relocation and then dropped to the earlier rates [37].

Disasters

Tornadoes, floods, earthquakes, fires involving large areas, plane crashes, shipwrecks, and acts of terror or violence against large numbers of people (such as the dropping of an atomic bomb on a city) are crises on a very large scale. Because of their intensity and the large number of people involved, they are called disasters. A whole community, including the usual help agents, may be destroyed or badly damaged during a disaster. An individual in a disaster may lose all of his personal possessions, including perhaps even his clothes; his loved ones may die or be badly injured; he himself may be injured. Friends may have all they can do to handle their own needs. Famine in a widespread area may also be seen as a disaster, although it lacks the suddenness that characterizes most disasters.

Phases of Disasters. Three overlapping phases of reaction to community disasters have been identified: (1) a period of impact, (2) a period of recoil, and (3) the posttraumatic period [62]. The first period is characterized by the impact of stress, and it continues until the stresses no longer operate. A tornado destroys a home in a matter of minutes; a flood may take hours or days. The period of recoil begins with the suspension of the initial stress. Further stresses may continue, but their intensity is not as great. After the flood has swept through the town, the waters remain high but do not flow as swiftly. In the posttraumatic period the stresses are more social in nature. During this period people begin to realize what the disaster means in terms of loss.

Psychological Reactions. During the impact period, reactions vary. Some individuals remain "cool and collected"; others experience states of confusion, paralyzing anxiety, and hysterical crying. About three-quarters of the survivors, however, are stunned and bewildered by the disaster. During the recoil period, most survivors seek shelter, sit or pace about, are in ambulances, or are telling someone about their

440   A FAMILY IS BASED ON HOME

experiences. At first, they are not very aware of what they are doing and exhibit dependent behaviors. Within one or two days, however, most survivors are unwilling to talk as freely as they were at the beginning of the recoil period [62].

During the posttraumatic period, many survivors have reactions of anxiety, fatigue, depression, recurrent dreams, and the like. Children are likely to be especially disturbed by disasters, fearing their return. Adults, as well, may find that they never completely get over the feelings of terror brought on by the disaster. Survivors are subject to "acute episodes of *symbolic reactivation* of their entire constellation of death anxiety and loss" [43, p. 485]. Survivors of Nazi concentration camps and of the atomic bombs dropped on Hiroshima and Nagasaki report an increased awareness of their own mortality. Those survivors who cannot complete their "grief work" are especially susceptible to mental disturbance [43].

SUMMARY   A crisis is a state of disequilibrium precipitated by a problem that has no ready solution. Future health and illness hinge upon the way in which the crisis is met. Intervention and support come from family, kin, friends, and community agencies. Chronic or ongoing problems do not have the same potential for growth-promotion, nor do they invoke such vigorous efforts at intervention and help. Many problems begin as critical and continue as chronic.

Personal disruption often results in crises for the family as well as for the individual. When a person gets injured or becomes ill, the family experiences a crisis, in which resources are mobilized and steps are taken to aid the afflicted individual. Professional medical help may be called in. During recovery and also in the case of chronically ill and disabled patients, the patient acts as a sick person and the family plays reciprocal roles. Kin, friends, and neighbors also have obligations.

Mental retardation, one of the most difficult of disabilities, places a heavy burden on the family. Demands on management skills and planning are great. The social life of the family is likely to be restricted. These families need community help in caring for the retarded child and association with families with similar problems.

Mentally ill persons are involved with their families in the causes for the disturbance, in the effects upon the family group, and in the family's potential for improving the mental health of all members. Often more than one person in a family is mentally disturbed. Family therapy is often necessary. Even if therapy is concentrated on the one patient, the whole family needs some supportive treatment. The same statements could refer to drug addicts.

Much of the problematic behavior of children is developmental, representing temporary ways in which the child deals with tensions caused by growing up. Sources of tension are within himself, the family, the school, and the community. Good management prevents problems from becoming serious. Severe problems require help from specialists, and even simple problems can be made easier by early intervention.

Aging brings physical problems that can be managed but not avoided. Emotional problems are magnified by societies that define old people as worthless and that condemn many old people to living in poverty. The person must get ready to die.

The dissolution of a family usually involves a crisis and chronic problems. Death brings a crisis of loss and grief and then the problems of taking on new roles and learning new skills. For the widowed, it is difficult to learn to cook or to take on financial and legal management while suffering loss, loneliness, and changed social relationships. Help comes from family, kin, friends, clergy, lawyers, bankers, and community organizations.

Problems of divorce occur before, during, and after the event. Since a severe breakdown in relationships, and often in self-esteem, is involved, considerable help is needed. Problems include emotional, legal, financial, and life management. Being deserted is often more difficult than being divorced, since settlements and solutions cannot be made with an absent person. Single-parent families need help in supplying the interactions and services that the missing member would ordinarily perform.

Poor people must put their main efforts into immediate survival. Very often, behavior that is necessary for survival is behavior that prevents the poor from improving their socioeconomic status. Likewise, an oppressed minority is likely to develop behavior that is adapted to present demands but maladapted to future change of status.

Violence, the use of force to hurt, destroy, or control, occurs in individuals, families, and society. Children learn violent behavior by experiencing it, observing it, and being permitted and encouraged to perform it. Although decrying family violence, North American society promotes it through the catharsis myth, masculinity norms, acceptance of the use of physical punishment on children, harsh punishment of criminals, war, depiction of violence in the media, and lack of support for family planning and parent education.

Moving disrupts a family to greater or lesser degree, depending upon the strength of the stresses and the resources available for restoring equilibrium. Survivors of disasters experience three phases; impact, recoil, and posttraumatic.

REFERENCES

1. Ackerman, Nathan W. and Stephen W. Kempster. Family therapy. In Alfred M. Freedman and Harold I. Kaplan (eds.). *Treating mental illness*. New York: Atheneum, 1972.
2. Bach, George R. and Peter Wyden. *The intimate enemy*. New York: Morrow, 1968.
3. Bard, Morton. The study and modification of intra-family violence. In Suzanne K. Steinmetz and Murray A. Straus (eds.). *Violence in the family*. New York: Dodd, 1974.
4. Berardo, Felix. Survivorship and social isolation: The case of the aged widower. *Family Coordinator*, 1970, **19,** 11–25.
5. Berkowitz, Leonard. Control of aggression. In Bettye M. Caldwell and Henry N. Ricciuti (eds.). *Review of child development research*, Vol. 3. Chicago: U. of Chicago, 1973.
6. Bock, E. Wilbur. Aging and suicide: The significance of marital, kinship, and alternative relations. *Family Coordinator*, 1972, **21,** 71–79.
7. Bohannon, Paul. *Divorce and after*. Garden City, N.Y.: Doubleday, 1970.

8. Bromley, D. B. *The psychology of human ageing.* Middlesex, England: Penguin, 1971.

9. Brown, Emily. Splitting or splicing: How should social work approach divorce? Paper presented at the Family Service Association-Child Welfare League Midwest Joint Conference, Omaha, Nebraska, April 1971.

10. Bruning, Fred. Wives run away to a failing dream. *Providence Sunday Journal,* March 31, 1974.

11. Burgess, Jane K. The single-parent family: A social and sociological problem. *Family Coordinator,* 1970, **19,** 136–144.

12. Caplan, Gerald. Emotional crisis. (Mimeo.) Also published in A. Deutsch and H. Fishbein (eds.). *The encyclopedia of mental health,* Vol 2. New York: Franklin Watts, 1963.

13. Caplan, Gerald. *Support systems and community mental health.* New York: Behavioral Publications, 1974.

14. Carkhuff, Robert R. *The art of problem-solving.* Amherst, Mass.: Human Resource Development Press, 1973.

15. Carter, Hugh and Paul C. Glick. *Marriage and divorce: A social and economic study.* Cambridge, Mass.: Harvard U.P., 1970.

16. Chilman, Catherine S. Families in poverty: Rates, associated factors, some implications. *Journal of Marriage and the Family,* 1975, **37,** 49–60.

17. Clar, June S., William C. Capel, Bernard Goldsmith, and Gordon T. Stewart. Marriage and methadone: Spouse behavior patterns in heroin addicts maintained on methadone. *Journal of Marriage and the Family,* 1972, **34,** 496–502.

17a. Crawford, Susan H. *Minoo's family.* Breslau, Ontario: Before We Are Six, 1974.

18. Croog, Sydney H., Alberta Lipson, and Sol Levine. Help patterns in severe illness: The roles of kin network, non-family resources and institutions. *Journal of Marriage and the Family,* 1972, **34,** 32–41.

19. Cuber, John and Peggy Harroff. *The significant Americans.* New York: Appleton, 1965.

20. Dullea, Georgia. U.S. Statistics show single-parent families growing 7 times as fast as 2-parent ones. Toronto: Globe and Mail, December 4, 1974.

21. Elkin, Meyer. Conciliation courts: The reintegration of disintegrating families. *Family Coordinator,* 1973, **22,** 63–71.

22. Fassler, Joan. *My grandpa died today.* New York: Behavioral Publications, 1971.

23. Fisher, Esther Oshiver. *Divorce—the new freedom. A guide to divorcing and divorce counseling.* New York: Harper & Row, 1975.

24. Fotheringham, John B., Mora Slekton, and Bernard A. Hoddinott. *The retarded child and his family: The effects of home and institution.* Toronto: Ontario Institute for Studies in Education, 1971.

25. Glaser, Barney and Anselm Strauss. Temporal aspects of dying as a non-scheduled status passage. In Bernice Neugarten (ed.). *Middle age and aging.* Chicago: U. of Chicago, 1968.

26. Goode, William J. Force and violence in the family. *Journal of Marriage and the Family,* 1971, **33,** 624–636.

27. Goode, William. *Women in divorce.* New York: Free Press, 1956.

28. Gottlieb, David and Anne Heinsohn. *America's other youth: Growing up poor.* Englewood Cliffs, N.J.: Prentice-Hall, 1971.

29. Hansell, Norris, Mary Wodarczyk, and Britomar Handlon-Lathrop. *Decision counseling method: Expanding coping at crisis in transit.* Northwestern University Medical School Department of Psychiatry Curricular Reprint No. 27, 1970.

30. Harlan, William H. The aged in three Indian villages. In Bernice Neugarten (ed.). *Middle age and aging.* Chicago: U. of Chicago, 1968.

31. Hartup, Willard W. Aggression in childhood: Developmental perspectives. *American Psychologist,* 1974, **29,** 336–341.

32. Harvey, Carol D. and Howard Bahr. Widowhood, morale, and affiliation. *Journal of Marriage and the Family,* 1974, **36,** 97–106.

33. Havighurst, Robert J., Bernice Neugarten, and Sheldon Tobin. Disengagement and patterns of aging. In Bernice Neugarten (ed.). *Middle age and aging.* Chicago: U. of Chicago, 1968.

34. Herzog, Elizabeth. *About the poor: Some facts and some fictions.* Children's Bureau Publication 451–1967. Washington, D.C.: U.S. Government Printing Office, 1968.

35. Jones, Stella. Geographic mobility as seen by the wife and mother. *Journal of Marriage and the Family,* 1973, **35,** 210–218.

36. Kephart, William. *The family, society, and the individual.* Boston: Houghton, 1972.

37. Knight, Aldrich C. and Ethel Mendkoff. Relocation of the aged and disabled: A mortality study. In Bernice Neugarten (ed.). *Middle age and aging.* Chicago: U. of Chicago, 1968.

38. Landis, Judson. The trauma of children when parents divorce. *Marriage and Family Living,* 1960, **22,** 7–13.

39. Landis, Judson and Louis Stoetzer. Migrant families: An exploratory study of middle-class migrant families. *Journal of Marriage and the Family,* 1966, **28,** 51–53.

40. LeBow, Michael. The behavior modification process for parent-child therapy. *Family Coordinator,* 1973, **22,** 313–319.

41. LeShan, Eda. *What makes me feel this way?* New York: Macmillan, 1972.

42. Liebermann, Morton. Psychological correlates of impending death: Some preliminary observations. In Bernice Neugarten (ed.). *Middle age and aging.* Chicago: U. of Chicago, 1968.

43. Lifton, Robert Jay. *Death in life: Survivors of Hiroshima.* New York: Vintage, 1969.

44. Lopata, Helena Z. *Widowhood in an American city.* Cambridge, Mass.: Schenkman, 1973.

44a. Mann, Peggy. *My dad lives in a downtown hotel.* New York: Doubleday, 1973.

45. McAllister, Ronald J., Edgar W. Butler, and Tzuen-Jen Lei. Patterns of social interaction among families of behaviorally retarded children. *Journal of Marriage and the Family,* 1973, **35,** 93–100.

46. McKain, Jerry Lavin. Relocation in the military: Alienation and family problems. *Journal of Marriage and the Family,* 1973, **35,** 205–209.

47. Monahan, Thomas. National divorce legislation: The problem and some suggestions. *Family Coordinator,* 1973, **22,** 353–357.

48. Neugarten, Bernice. The awareness of middle age. In Bernice Neugarten (ed.). *Middle age and aging.* Chicago: U. of Chicago, 1968.

49. Nye, F. Ivan. Child adjustment in broken and in unhappy, unbroken homes. *Marriage and Family Living,* 1957, **19,** 356–361.

50. Parkes, C. Murray. *Bereavement: Studies of grief in adult life.* New York: International Universities, 1972.

50a. Peters, Marie F. The solo black mother. Paper presented at meetings of the National Council on Family Relations. St. Louis, October, 1974.

51. Plateris, Alexander. *Divorces: Analysis of change.* Rockville, Md.: National Center for Health Statistics, 1973.

52. Radin, Norma and Paul Glasser. The utility of the Parental Attitude Research Instrument for intervention programs with low family incomes. *Journal of Marriage and the Family,* 1972, **34,** 448–458.

53. Robbins, Norman N. End of divorce—beginning of legal problems. *Family Coordinator,* 1974, **23,** 185–189.

54. Rose, Vicki and Sharon Price-Bonham. Divorce adjustment: A woman's problem? *Family Coordinator,* 1973, **22,** 291–297.

55. Schlesinger, Ben. The one-parent family in Canada: Some recent findings and recommendations. *Family Coordinator,* 1973, **22,** 305–309.

56. Silverman, Phyllis. Widowhood and preventive intervention. *Family Coordinator,* 1972, **21,** 95–102.

57. Skarsten, Stan. Family desertion in Canada. *Family Coordinator,* 1974, **23,** 19–25.

58. Smith, Ramona and Victor Christopherson. Migration and family adjustment. *Journal of Home Economics,* 1966, **58,** 670–671.

59. Steinmetz, Suzanne K. and Murray A. Straus. *Violence in the family.* New York: Dodd, Mead, 1974.

60. Straus, Murray A. Leveling, civility and violence in the family. *Journal of Marriage and the Family,* 1974, **36,** 13–29.

60a. Sudia, Cecelia E. An updating and comment on the United States scene. *Family Coordinator,* 1973, **22,** 309–311.

61. Taylor, Ray and Mollie S. Smart. Depression and recovery at nine weeks of age. *Journal of the American Academy of Child Psychiatry,* 1973, **12,** 506–510.

62. Tyhurst, J. S. The role of transition states—including disasters—in mental illness. Paper presented at the Symposium on Preventive and Social Psychiatry, Washington, D.C., 1957.

63. U.S. Bureau of the Census. *We, the American elderly.* Washington, D.C.: U.S. Government Printing Office, 1973.

64. U.S. Bureau of the Census. *We, the Americans: Our income.* Washington: U.S. Government Printing Office, 1973.

65. *Wall Street Journal.* Women with children. May 14, 1974.

66. Wolfgang, Marvin E. Violence and human behavior. In Kenneth O. Doyle (ed.). *Interaction: Readings in human psychology.* Lexington, Mass.: Heath, 1973.

Throughout the book, and especially in Part V, where we think about the future, we are concerned with people in other parts of the world. Family life in North America is and will be affected by what is happening to people elsewhere. We feel that we have to tell what we see, even though some of it is disturbing. When considering only the possibilities for improving the quality of North American home life and personal relationships, the future looks promising.

PART five

down the road and around the world

CHAPTER 17

dOWN THE ROAd ANd AROUNd THE WORLd

Before we think about the future of family life, we must first consider the future of human life. What happens in Africa and Asia affects North America, and vice versa. People everywhere are responding to pressures from changes in the physical and biological world. Figure 17-1 illustrates the extremes of underdevelopment and overdevelopment, and shows how human survival is threatened by food shortages and exploding populations. Already, in Third World countries, famine is a reality. Affluent nations, as well as poor ones, are continually menaced by environmental deterioration and violence.

On the whole, people in affluent nations live as though their lands of plenty were eternal. Middle-class adolescents and youth have known nothing else, but they will. Few have even thought of what it will be like to live in a world where millions of starving people beg for our aid and we do not have enough to feed them and ourselves [23].

No matter how dire the threats posed by the biological world or how upsetting the new ideology to the established order, human beings continue to live in families of one kind or another. In fact, the more difficult the world seems, the more a person feels in need of a few other people with whom he can work and love. The intimates who compose a family may be the common grouping of man, woman, and their children, or they may be one of many types of combinations. Most importantly, they meet each other's needs, especially emotionally. The needs to be met, and the ways of meeting them, are affected by the prevailing physical, biological, and social conditions.

Although human beings have made some terrible problems for themselves by interfering with the balance of nature, the large-scale bungling was possible because of flexible thinking, reasoning, and innovation. People are now applying these very

449

Japan Poisoning Itself—Take Heed, World

Nicholas Daniloff

TOKYO, May 19—(UPI)—Did you ever wonder what it would be like if one day there was too much pollution, too many people, too few resources in the world?

Take a close look at Japan.

Since World War II, Japan has been growing at a phenomenal rate. Japanese products are high class and famous. Japanese businessmen are everywhere. But in the process of developing—so envied by the less developed nations—Japan has literally been poisoning itself.

The Japanese environment agency has produced documents to show that serious and persistent pollutants have entered Japan's air, rivers, streams, bays, land—and even some mothers' milk. There are new diseases in Japan, caused by pollution and known nowhere else. Government figures list 8,737 officially recognized air pollution victims in 1972, and 728 water pollution victims.

The Japanese government today is waging what could turn out to be a life-and-death struggle to clean up the environment, and it is warning the rest of the world to take heed. . . .

The pollution problem is made all the more acute by the grim realities of Japan's geographic and demographic peculiarities.

Japan's population is 108 million, approximately half that of the United States. Yet the Japanese live on an island chain whose territory is slightly less than that of the state of California. . . .

When you visit Tokyo, it is not unusual to feel the acrid smog stinging your eyes, or irritating your throat. If you fly, or travel by train, you may notice a thin veil of greyish smog which obliterates some of those famous views of Mount Fuji. . . .

. . . The pollution crisis poses a number of tough questions for Japan—as for many other nations. What is the effect of industrial pollution on human health? What kind of government determination and social cooperation will it take to clean up? Perhaps more importantly, what will it cost, and will other crises along the way—such as the oil shortage—shake the country's determination?. . .

Source: *Providence Sunday Journal*, May 19, 1974. F–12.

FIGURE 17-1 These articles appeared side-by-side in a newspaper in 1974. The first article discusses the problems of Japan, a critically overdeveloped country. The second article discusses the problems of sub-Saharan West Africa, which is desperately underdeveloped. Is there any hope that the world will ever reach a level of uniform, optimum development?

human resources to solving their problems by developing new ways of interacting with each other. Even though physical and biological scientists continue to work in their areas, they, along with social scientists, recognize the need for widespread changes in human interaction. Many, but not all of the constructive changes in human interaction, will be in intimate, primary relationships. It is here that personalities are shaped and values created, in the arena known as family living.

And so we have come full circle from Chapter 1, where we examined the kinds of families that people live in. We have found that not everyone is living in a marriage or a family, as marriage and family have been defined in the past. Some persons are living in a variety of relationships in which they are emotionally close to

How Much Food Are Starving Africans Getting?

Larry Heinzerling

N'DJAMENA, CHAD, May 19—(AP)—Emergency drought relief operations in the famine zone of sub-Sahara West Africa are plagued by everything from armed bandits to bungling bureaucrats.

Nevertheless, relief officials stress that the bulk of hundreds of thousands of tons of food and other supplies being rushed to the region from abroad is reaching the millions of famished Africans who are almost totally dependent upon it for survival.

They complain bitterly, however, that corruption, soaring costs of transportation, tribal discrimination in food distribution, and a critical lack of facts are hampering the relief efforts. . . .

Many diplomats and relief workers interviewed across the Sahara say they fear critical reports on drought relief operations might adversely affect efforts to raise urgently needed funds and food in the United States and Europe.

They repeatedly underlined that the six-year drought in West Africa is a major disaster in which millions face possible starvation.

No matter what the problems, they said, massive inputs of food and other aid are desperately needed.

The countries worst hit by the savage dry spell range in a sub-Saharan arc through Mauritania, Senegal, Upper Volta, Mali, Niger, and Chad.

But the drought has crept south, striking crops and livestock in other countries including Gambia, Ghana, and Nigeria.

"These countries are among the poorest and most backward in the world," said one United Nations official. "We are not only fighting mass starvation but the whole syndrome of underdevelopment."

In one country, which a diplomatic source insisted should not be identified, foreign diplomats recently had to get together and demand action by procrastinating local government officials to organize nationwide food distribution.

With just three months to go before the rains, which every year wash out West Africa's primitive network of dirt roads, the government concerned had not yet planned food distribution in areas likely to be cut off.

A West German airlift is underway in Chad where armed antigovernment rebels, commonly called "bandits," have made it impossible to deliver food to some areas by road without an armed escort. . . .

Source: *Providence Sunday Journal,* May 19, 1974. F–12.

other people who are adults and/or children. They are not always related by blood or by law. The group usually performs several functions typical of families in the old sense. We call these new types of groups different forms of the family. The most common family form remains the nuclear family, a married man and woman and their child or children. Other traditional family forms, such as the extended family, also continue. Many innovative family forms are being tried, some on a large scale, some on a small scale. In North America, a large number of people are living in nontraditional styles, but it is very hard to find out just how many. It is said that when 7 to 10 per cent of a population practices an innovation, the custom becomes accepted by the mainstream of society [28]. Therefore, it is possible for the traditional mode to continue while other customs practiced by a small minority are also permitted.

Among family innovators, motivations vary from self-interest to sincere attempts to solve human problems. No matter what the reasons for the new family forms, all of them are potentially valuable as experiments in human relationships. They offer the means of learning more about human potential and the possibilities for restructuring modes of living. The main part of this chapter deals with family innovations in North America and ways in which family life could be supported and improved. But first we want to discuss the worldwide concern with equality and some orientations that are newly important in North American thought. These orientations are significant in family innovation.

NEW ORIENTATIONS TO LIFE

Many young adults, and some not-so-young ones have adopted new values and adapted old ones, based on different interpretations of reality and philosophies of life.

The Notion of Equality

Around the world, people are thinking about equality and feeling the effects of this heady idea. The *notion of equality* is operating in many contexts, including the following: equality among nations (one vote in the United Nations, equal respect, equal access to food and other resources); equality among races and ethnic groups (equal opportunities for education, jobs, housing, and respect); equality among classes (an adequate income for all, equal treatment by the legal and educational institutions); equality between age levels (children's right to be protected under the law to the same extent that adults are protected, adolescents' rights to meaningful work and a place in society, the rights of the aged to use their abilities productively and to have care and respect); equality between the sexes (in pay scale, job opportunities, education, politics, religion, law, and work within the home).

Time Orientation

The present is very important. Less emphasis is put on the future and the past. For other people, the change is to vast units of time, or even timelessness, rather than counting time in hours, days, and years. Existential philosophy has contributed to the present-orientation. This point of view has much to contribute to the improvement of family relationships, since it can mean cherishing each day, each encounter, each experience, and making them all as good as they can be. It implies shedding the burdens of inadequacies and guilt from the past, as well as the possibility of becoming different in the future. Although emphasis on the present has many positive influences on relationships and experiences, it also may take away from other aspects of life. Immediate gratification may prevent building long-term relationships and other investments, such as economic and educational ones.

Sources of Knowledge

Science is mistrusted, instead of being considered the fountain of wisdom that it once was. Part of the argument against science is along the lines of, "Look what a mess the world has got into through the use of science. The technology of war has been developed by science and yet the world's hunger cannot be appeased." People express horror of a computerized society, with surveillance of individuals and domination by an intellectual elite. (There are many others with an opposite view, who look forward to a technological society, the postindustrial era, where everyone is affluent, educated, and happily employed in interesting, nontaxing work.)

Instead of getting information from science and using its methods for exploring, some young people are turning inward to find knowledge through intuition, meditation, and drug-induced states. They also turn outward, in the opposite direction from science, to find reality and meaning in religion, mysticism, extrasensory perception, and charismatic leaders. A young friend recently explained to us, "Science is only a phase in human thinking. Man has lost the ability to receive revelation of truth from God, but he will regain it. We must take a time perspective of eons rather than years. We now have some revelations, through prophets."

At the same time, scientists and technologists are discovering and producing at a fast pace. Their products have revolutionized life through changes that continue. Scientists are also probing the sources of the mystics and prophets. Sometimes science fiction points the way to new knowledge. There is an open-mindedness that admits the possibility of learning from nonscientific sources.

Power versus Love

The reality of power is very obvious on the national level, in politics and war; within nations, in politics, revolution, and crime; between classes and races and sexes; and between persons within the family. On all these levels, people are questioning the morality of power and how to limit it. If people are to be equal in important ways, then one cannot overpower another. Actually, it is not new for religious leaders to look to love as a way of restricting power orientation, but the application to family life is new. Never have we had so many women questioning and challenging the right of men to control them through power. Nor have the rights of children ever been so clearly distinguished from the rights of adults over them.

Roles versus Individuality

Probably most people believe as we do, that roles are necessary as guides to behavior and expectations in daily life. A person would be paralyzed a good deal of the time if he had to have intimate knowledge of every individual before he could interact with him. In other social institutions, as well as in the family, many persons are objecting to having to play roles, however, because they feel too restricted in them.

Educational and Occupational Roles. Students have shown that they do not want their roles restricted to taking in what the teacher gives out. They want to be able to take part in making decisions as to what and how they learn. The more choice each student has, the less he must play a role and the more he can be a unique individual.

Factory workers do not want their roles restricted to tightening a nut or coming to work at a moment determined by the head office. They want to take part in planning what work shall be done, who shall do what, and when they shall do it. In plants where managers have cooperated thus with workers, the results have been generally excellent in terms of production and worker satisfaction. In making expanded, flexible role definitions, each worker had opportunities to feel creative and unique.

Gender Roles. Having commented already at length on this lively topic, we will now be brief. Women are rejecting the restrictions and burdens placed on them because of their being female. They want access to all kinds of work, equal pay for

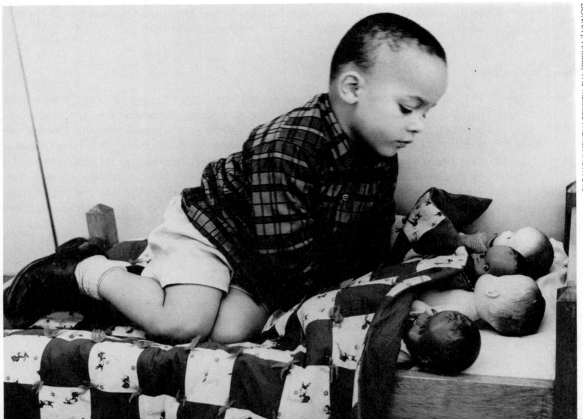

PHOTO BY DONNA J. HARRIS, THE MERRILL-PALMER INSTITUTE

equal work, free choice as to whether and when to bear children, and opportunities for true sharing in housework and childrearing. Men want equal access to the world of feeling, emotion, and self-expression that is largely denied them in the traditional masculine role. Men want free choice as to whether they may be dominant, aggressive and competitive, achieving and tough. Men and women both want to be primarily human beings who can choose their behavior from the range of human activities in which they are interested and talented.

Age Roles. The newly popular field of psychohistory reveals that age segregation has increased ever since the Middle Ages, when there was little difference between children and adults. Children and adults wore the same style of clothing, ate the same food, played games and took part in celebrations together, did similar work, and went to bed at the same time. This pattern holds true in most primitive societies. In industrial cultures, such as our own, children are different from adults in what they wear and eat, how they work and play, when they sleep, who takes care of them when they are sick, and in just about every aspect of their lives. The culture of childhood is separate from the culture of adulthood. Childhood, too, is differentiated into infancy, preschool, school age, adolescence, and youth. Adulthood is not quite so clearly categorized, but old age is definitely cut off from young and middle adulthood.

Youth and young adults are considered the most beautiful and attractive. Middle adults have the most power. People in other stages are objecting to having to play roles assigned to them. School-age children would like some choices in what they learn in school and how they spend their time. Adolescents would like to clear up many of the conflicts they experience from being defined as both dependent and independent. Old people do not want to be powerless, useless, and out of date. Middle-age adults would like release from some of the pressures and demands that come from being in the middle of the generations.

Definitions of infancy and the preschool years come from child development specialists. Since young children are not sophisticated enough to criticize the roles to which society assigns them, they have not raised objections. What research has shown is that the early years are very important in physical and mental development. Young children develop competencies through interaction with talented, responsive caretakers. The role of excellent caretaker (see pages 434–435) has been well defined by a number of researchers, of whom White is an example. Excellent caretaker is a very demanding role [35]. If a mother is expected to carry the whole role, she may opt against when she realizes what caring for a child would involve. (That is, if she has the freedom to choose or not choose this role.) Another possibility is that with men also free to choose, and not forced into rigid roles, a man and woman will share the demands of giving excellent care.

Emphasis on Sex

Sex is very important in North America. Many industries, especially advertising, thrive on sex ideology. Many people believe that everyone needs sexual intercourse in order to be healthy, or that everyone has a right to it. Evaluations of social life, friendship, family life, and marriage are highly weighted in sexual terms. Preoccupation with sexual expression diminishes the amount of time and energy spent on other pursuits, such as intellectual, cultural, artistic, athletic, and community service activities. With some people, sex is an all-consuming hobby and anything goes, as suggested by these excerpts from a report in *Newsweek:*

"Why should we be restricted from sleeping with half the human race?" asks one feminist lawyer. "But that doesn't mean we don't sleep with men, too" . . . In Paris, sexual experimenters from the international set make the his-and-her scene at Le-

Bronx. . . . Certainly few give a damn at LeJardin, an ultra-in gay discotheque in New York where the banquettes swarm with sexual permutations. "We have homosexuals, bisexuals, trisexuals," chuckles owner John Addison. [13].

Emphasis on Growth

Continued personal growth is highly valued. There is nothing unusual about recognizing that individuals develop as they grow older. Hinduism outlines five normal stages of life and Shakespeare mentioned seven. But modern thought, typified by Maslow [18] and Rogers [30], holds that the individual personality can grow continually, through creative problem-solving and honest human interaction. This idea is a central one in encounter groups and some kinds of therapy. It has obvious significance in a rapidly changing culture.

NEW MODES OF LIVING AND RELATING

Both the United States and Canada are made up largely of peoples from other countries. The United States was characterized as a "melting pot," but in recent years many groups have experienced an upsurge in ethnic pride. Canada has long recognized the existence of cultural pluralism within its boundaries, but this coexistence has not always been easy. Currently, the United States is recognizing that it is not a monolingual, monocultural nation.

There has always been pluralism in these nations, but attention is currently being focused upon the new family forms that are, in some cases, emerging, and becoming more visible in others. In this section we briefly describe contemporary family (and nonfamily) forms, none of which is really new, but that are becoming more prevalent. Many of these forms are changing rapidly, and it is impossible to determine how many people are directly involved with them. Some of these life-styles are temporary for large numbers of people, as indeed the nuclear family is a temporary life-style for many. Much of what we say is speculative.

Communes

In Chapter 1, we noted that communes are not new to the United States in this century, and that other countries have and are experimenting with this life-style. Communes vary tremendously in their purpose, size, and structure; the only generalization that applies to all communes is that they are cooperating groups of people committed to their group.

Communes have been categorized in a number of ways, two of which we mention here. Ramey [28] breaks down communes into three types, the *religious,* the *utopian,* and the *evolutionary* (see Table 17-1). Religious communes are characterized by strong leadership and a faith that binds the members to the leader and group. Utopian communes, although often consisting of alienated youth grouped together in an unstructured way, may instead have a tight structure and a strong leader. The evolutionary commune, in contrast to the other two types, is not aloof from society but represents a group of people who are committed to each other and to coping with today's society in a more successful way than they could manage on their own.

Additional ways of characterizing communes make distinctions between *rural* and *urban* communes, and *creedal* and *noncreedal* [3]. Urban communes are more prevalent and easier to start; all that is needed is a place to live and a group of people. Membership is often fluid. In many college and university towns, "co-ops" are an established way of life. Some urban communes are what Ramey calls evolutionary communes. For others, the urban commune represents a means for poor (although generally middle-class) young people to share their resources while they break away from their families.

The rural commune, by contrast, represents a "purer" type of commune, since it entails more isolation from the members' former environment, and a bigger change in life-style. The ideology of the rural commune stresses conservation and agriculture as a way of life. This attitude recognizes the reality of the wasteful, overdeveloped world. However, in the early stages of a rural commune, subsidization from benefactors or welfare is usually essential. Moving beyond this stage of dependence is difficult [3].

Sex roles in many rural communes are strongly traditional, not always happily so for women [11]. However, age roles are not characteristic of the rural commune. Children and adults are thought to have the same needs and abilities. Children are expected to contribute to the welfare of the commune through work that is the same as adult work, and are expected to solve their own problems. Adults tend to see themselves as "kids" [3].

Creedal communes are similar to Ramey's religious communes. They are

TABLE 17-1   Types of Contemporary Communes

Religious	Utopian	Evolutionary
Aloof from society	"Dropped out" from society	"Straight" jobs
Family oriented	Youth oriented	Many post-children
Highly structured	Loosely structured	Highly mobile
Self sustaining	Often relies on subsidization	High achievers
Authoritarian leader	"Do your own thing"	Opinion leaders
Work ethic	Sometimes revolutionary	Upper middle class
	Usually short-lived	

Source: James Ramey, Emerging patterns of innovative behavior in marriage. *The Family Coordinator,* 1972, **21,** 435–456.

organized around a formal structure of beliefs and have a strong leader. The Children of God and followers of the Guru Maharaj Ji are contemporary examples of the creedal commune, which has a long history on this continent. Creedal communes are generally more successful than noncreedal communes. Members of a noncreedal commune often share a set of unwritten beliefs and values, but are not so tightly bound together by these more loosely conceptualized beliefs.

The relative success of creedal communes, both historically and at the present time, indicates that when a group of people reject the structure and values of the larger society, they need to have a formalized set to replace them. A charismatic leader who sets forth this structure may provide the "glue" for a commune, as did John Humphrey Noyes, founder and leader of the Oneida Community established in 1848 in central New York State. The community lasted for about thirty years until the death of Noyes, and represents one of the most radical family experiments that this continent has seen. The community was based upon the values of economic communism, group marriage, sexual equality, and scientific breeding of children, and grew to include several hundred members. After puberty, much sexual freedom was allowed, although couples were not supposed to form attachments. An individual conveyed his desire for sexual relations with another member to the Central Committee, which decided whether or not to grant permission. Children were not to be conceived unless planned by the committee, and male continence was the form of birth control that was used [17].

We include this extremely brief description of one aspect of a nineteenth-century commune to show that radical family experiments are not limited to the present. Many other interesting examples could be given.

Group Marriage

The marriage of several people to each other, called a group marriage or multilateral marriage, has probably occurred since primitive times [10]. The Constantines, who are studying contemporary multilateral marriages, have found the average group to consist of four adults and three children. They have studied group marriages consisting of from three to six adult partners. Those who entered group marriages had been significantly motivated toward personal growth. Sex as a strong motivator was acknowledged by 18 per cent [7]. *The Harrad Experiment,* a popular novel of 1966, described the social-sexual development of three young women and three young men who made a multilateral marriage [29]. As can be seen from the novel and from research, a marriage involving four or six people is much more complex than one involving two people. Advantages include more people to love and be loved by, greater security, more interesting activities to share, and greater possibility of each person finding someone to share her many facets, less chance of monotony in sex and other aspects of life, and a sharing of work, economic responsibilities, and children. No doubt, many people have thought of a multilateral marriage, or some sort of group living as a possibility for making life more interesting, less lonely, and generally fuller.

The problems involved are so difficult that very few group marriages actually exist, or ever have existed. The first problem is finding suitable participants. _The Harrad Experiment_ shows the complexity of this problem by setting up a college in which young men and women are educated to prepare them for thinking through and carrying out new and different life-styles. Another problem is that there are no guidelines in the form of social roles, making it necessary to think out, discuss, and plan how each person shall behave. Although increased freedom is what the multilateral spouses want, there are times when it would be simpler and easier to know that Wife A really should do this and that Husband B really should do that. It is often hard enough to dovetail the needs, wishes, demands, interests, weaknesses, and strengths of two spouses and harder when their children enter the picture. Two or four more adults, with their individual characteristics, complicate the scene enormously. It is hard for everyone to love and enjoy everyone. Jealousy and conflicts are threats. Most likely, group marriage will continue among a small minority of people but will be too complicated for most people to manage.

Co-marital Sex

Consensual extramarital relationships, or co-marital sex, represents the flourishing of a type of relationship that has probably been practiced by a small number of persons in our society for many years. Havelock Ellis, one of the early sex researchers who lived from 1859 to 1939, had a version of a consensual extramarital sexual relationship with his wife Edith. Both Havelock and Edith had women lovers [4]. Today, consensual extramarital relationships involve lovers of the same and opposite sex for both husbands and wives [28a]. Co-marital sex has gained in popularity and practitioners, reflecting the increasing cultural emphasis on sex. It has gained impetus from the decline of the double standard and the blossoming of honesty and communication in marriage.

Swinging. The form of co-marital sex that first came to public attention is swinging (see Chapter 5, pages 130–131). Swinging involves mostly white suburban couples with above-average incomes and educations. The median age of swingers in one study was around 30 [2]; in another study the age range was 35–50 [36]. The numbers of swingers has not been determined, but a study using a probability sample of 579 married adults in a Midwestern university community found that 1.7 per cent of the respondents had participated in swinging, and that an additional 6.7 per cent said that they would if the opportunity arose [6]. Finding such a tiny proportion of participants and would-be participants in an upper-middle class community indicates that swinging is a phenomenon limited to a very small number of people. While swinging grew in the sixties and early seventies, there is some evidence that by the mid-seventies it was starting to decline [1a].

Swingers claim that swinging makes a positive contribution to their marriage, helping them to feel closer not only sexually but in other areas as well. Communication is said to be facilitated. A study of dropouts from swinging shows that not all who try swinging are satisfied with it. Problems involved, in order of prevalence, were jealousy, guilt, feeling a threat to the marriage, the development of outside attachments, boredom, and loss of interest, disappointment, divorce or separation, and wife's inability to "take it" [8]. Some couples who drop out of swinging do so because they form *intimate friendships* ("an otherwise traditional friendship in which sexual intimacy is considered appropriate behavior" [28, p. 436]) with other swingers [24]. Most other literature on swinging notes that emotional involvement of any kind is taboo because it is considered a threat to the marriage [3, 36].

Swinging reportedly makes a marriage more egalitarian [2, 6]. However, men initiate swinging much more frequently than do women [15]. Bartell found that men often "wanted out" sooner than did women, but Denfield [8] reports the opposite.

At any rate, the prevalence and significance of swinging cannot be determined accurately. Its emphasis upon purely recreational sex seems to us superficial and decadent.

Sexually Open Marriage. Sexually open marriage has been called intimate friendship by Ramey [28; 28a] and interpersonal swinging by Varni [33a]. Each term denotes a slightly different version of a co-marital sexual relationship. The most significant difference between sexually open marriage and swinging is that the former emphasizes friendship and emotional commitment, whereas the latter condemns it. Some persons in sexually open marriages have friendship circles that often include both spouses and singles as well [28a]. Others prefer not to participate as couples, but instead form friendships with individuals whom they see without the presence of their spouse, but with the spouse's knowledge and consent. Jealousy is not unknown for persons in sexually-open marriages, but couples in one preliminary study tended to see the stresses and conflicts as potentially growth-promoting. Wives especially were motivated to form intimate friendships by a desire for more emotional fulfillment than they could get from one person [17a].

Open Marriage

Co-marital sex as a life style is not as pervasive as one might think, considering the amount of attention it has received. Open marriage, a life style publicized by George and Nena O'Neill in their book by that name [20], has probably won more to its side than have swinging and sexually open marriage. All but one of our list of new orientations to life are reflected in the book *Open Marriage*. It is present-oriented, emphasized individuality, growth, and to some extent, sex. The O'Neills believe that " . . . open marriage is designed to strengthen the individual in the marriage . . . The children of open marriages will tend to be responsible, confident, self-reliant individuals" [21].

The open marriage model is characterized by eight guidelines. The most important is open and honest communication between the partners, and between each partner and others outside of the primary relationship, including the opposite sex. Co-marital sexual involvement is an option that the O'Neills do not consider to be a crucial issue. The larger context of the open relationship is much more important.

Living for now, another guideline, involves relating to oneself and one's partner in the present rather than in terms of the past or distant future. Equality between the spouses involves relating to one's mate as a peer, instead of seeing one's mate in terms of the traditional roles of husband and wife. In order to achieve identity, each spouse must develop her own potentials insted of living her life through her spouse or child. "Trust, growing through the utilization of these and other guidelines and based on mutuality and respect, creates a climate for growth. Liking, respect, sexual intimacy, and love grow through the dynamic interaction and use of these elements" [21].

We concur with the O'Neills on most of their guidelines; we differ with them on time orientation. Living for now is important in the emotional sense, but long-term planning and goals are important for family functioning, as we have tried to show in Chapter 13. We certainly do not endorse living solely for future economic gain, or thinking so much about the past and future that the present becomes unimportant. In my (MSS) marriage, I have committed myself to my husband until death parts us, and I believe that this kind of commitment strengthens marriage. I (LSS) am ambivalent about this kind of commitment, and although I hope to be with my husband until one of us dies, I prefer to think about the future in smaller pieces. In short, we believe that the future and the past each have their place in our lives: the past, to give perspective, and the future, to provide continuity and goals. But the present moment should be lived, not just endured.

Homosexuality

Many homosexuals have "come out," declaring that they, like other people, have the right to live in a life-style that gives them close, committed human relationships. They have been influenced by modern notions of equality, of individuality versus rigid role requirements, and of emphasis on sex and growth. Although attitudes in our society are becoming less hostile to him, the homosexual is still legally discriminated against in many countries including the United States and Canada. If the original reason for societal hostility was that homosexuals did not reproduce, then society should now welcome them. But outmoded attitudes linger on, often outliving the original rationale for them.

Many homosexuals have noted the stresses that accompany their sexual orientation [1, 12]. They are different; they are not allowed in some restaurants and hotels; they are forbidden to work for the government; they are discriminated against in jobs and housing; they are not allowed to claim the benefits of marriage. Living a double life is another strain on them. Some male homosexuals date women or marry in order to hide their sexual orientation and thereby avoid discrimination. The Lesbian also is under pressure to marry, although generally she is less suspect than the male if she chooses to live with a friend of the same sex.

"Coming out," or recognizing and ceasing to hide one's homosexuality, can lift the burden of living a double life but it means opening oneself up to the other pressures described. Many homosexuals from small towns feel unable to "come out," or may not even recognize that they are homosexuals. Some are desperately lonely, unaware that there are others like them. The city offers a degree of anonymity and tolerance that is not available in one's small home town. Cities, therefore, attract many homosexuals. The college campus also may offer a more tolerant atmosphere for homosexuals, as evidenced by "Gay" or "Homophile" groups, especially on larger campuses.

As we have noted previously, female homosexuality has been viewed as less harmful to society. Some Lesbians do not recognize their relationship as being homosexual. One author writes,

> I have known women who shared a flat together for years and slept in the same bed without the slightest suspicion that they were homosexuals. They were passionately devoted, but the overt expression never went beyond kissing and lying close together. . . . [5, p. 163]

As the gay scene continues to come out farther into the open, it is likely that one will hear more about changes in the homosexual world, both in terms of increases in promiscuity and increases in long-term relationships among homosexuals. However, the homosexual who wishes to enter a stable relationship does not receive the same support that a heterosexual does, and is, therefore, less likely to be successful [5]. The heterosexual who marries receives legal and social support. It is harder for him to get out of marriage than it is for the cohabitor to break a relationship, whether or not the cohabiting partners are of the same sex. When considering the degree of promiscuity among gays, one should keep in mind that homosexuals do not receive the kind of support for their relationship that even unmarried heterosexual partners do.

As a life-style, homosexuality entails special problems and difficulties. For some individuals, psychotherapy as an attempt to become heterosexual might be the best solution. For others, however, learning self-acceptance and respect for oneself as a homosexual is the only road to adjustment, a road made difficult by society's attitudes.

Cohabitation

Since we have already discussed cohabitation (Chapter 8, pages 212–214), we do not dwell upon it here. It is likely that it will become more common in the future, both as an "engagement" period and as a substitute for marriage, most likely as a substitute for legalized serial monogamy. In other words, persons who do not wish to become committed through marriage will live together instead. For some, living together will come before marriage as a kind of trial marriage, or the first step in a system of two-stage marriage. Others will choose living together because they do not think that they will ever want to marry. Some cohabitors will stay with their partners for as long as married persons do, and others will enter temporary relationships of varying lengths.

Singles

Most singles are probably people who have not married yet, but will at some time. Some were once married, but are now divorced or widowed. Many are looking for spouses or other partners, but other singles are homosexuals, and still others are heterosexuals who do not see marriage or any kind of committed relationship as a part of their future. The ranks of singles are swelling. In 1974, 40 per cent of women between 20 and 24 years of age were single (never married), in contrast to 28 per cent in 1960 [14a]. The "baby boom" generation is coming of age and waiting longer to marry. Other factors contributing to the rise in numbers of singles include the spiraling divorce rate and a trend against early remarriage after divorce [16].

Commercial interests have recognized the singles as a market. California leads the way in catering to singles, but it is not alone [19]. In many urban and suburban areas one can find singles apartment buildings, bars, clubs, dating systems, and publications. The publications indicate that many singles do not plan to stay that way, since many contain advertisements for mates.

The singles movement, if it can be called that, has significance in its legitimization of the single status as a chosen status for females as well as for males. Although the single status is not always freely chosen, those that have done so want to be free from pressure to marry by friends, family, and society. The bachelor has always been conceptualized as somewhat glamorous, but the spinster or "old maid" has not. The term *bachelor* is now being applied to women as well as to men. As with homosexuals, an overpopulated society has no legitimate criticism of a life-style that produces no babies.

Spousefree Parents

Some single parents, such as those heading what we have called one-parent families, lack a spouse because of divorce, death, or desertion. The unwed mother, by contrast, used to be thought of as a young girl whose partner did not marry her when she became pregnant. Today, more unwed mothers (and some unwed fathers) are choosing to keep and rear their children, but not to marry. For this reason, we call them "spousefree parents." They have chosen to be parents and to reject the role of spouse.

What has been written about spousefree parents is speculative in nature [25], and we feel free to speculate as well. We doubt that spousefree parenthood will ever become a choice of many people. Adoption by unmarried persons has long been much more socially acceptable than keeping one's biochild that was produced out of wedlock, and this will probably continue to be the case.

In favor of spousefree parenthood is that it is a life style, which, by our definition, is freely chosen. The pregnant woman may conceive on purpose, or she may decide to keep a pregnancy once she discovers it. However, if she tricks a man into impregnating her against his will, we consider this to be unethical. The man who is unaware of his parenthood will not suffer. However, the man who knows of his paternity may have feelings of guilt or a frustrated desire to play a fathering role to his child.

Certainly, it is better for a child to be brought up by one stable, caring individual than by two people who fight constantly or neglect the child. The woman who knows that her child will be better off without its father is wiser to raise the child singly than to marry the man just to "give her child a name" or a "father." (However, the child might be *best* off being adopted by a stable couple.) A woman who chose spousefree parenthood because she did not think her partner would make a positive contribution to her child's welfare is Donna Lake. She had been living with Mark for several years, and had almost married him once. He failed to come to their small church wedding, returning to town after a month. Later, they began living together once again, and it is then that Donna conceived,at the age of 23.

It was a difficult decision for Donna to make when she learned that she was pregnant. She had already decided that she and Mark should not stay together much longer. She left him, and returned to live with her family. She decided to keep her baby whom she named Tanya Lake. Donna says that she was amazed at her family's acceptance and support. Her widowed mother moved out of her bedroom and into a smaller bedroom, giving Donna and Tanya the master bedroom that each newborn child of the Lake's had shared with his parents. Donna's younger sisters and younger brother have enjoyed caring for Tanya. Her older brother and his wife live nearby. When Donna's sister-in-law wants to be a ''mother'' for a while, she walks over to Donna's mother's house and borrows Tanya for the day or night.

Donna's main source of income at this point is welfare, but she hopes to be able to move out of her mother's house within the next couple of years. She has a boyfriend, but no definite plans to marry.

We do not know how representative Donna is of spousefree mothers. The ideal situation for such a mother is to be able to earn enough money to support herself and her child, which Donna is not yet able to do.

Unwed fathers now have legal rights, as well as responsibilities, in relation to their children. Some unwed fathers want to become spousefree parents; that is, to have custody of their children and to raise them.

Childfree Families

Now that birth control is more reliable and available than it has been in the past, it is possible for couples to choose to remain childfree. In chapter 9, ''Parenthood,'' we discussed reasons for rejecting parenthood as a life style (see pages 240–246). As stated in that chapter, approximately ten per cent of married couples do not have children, about half of them by choice [34]. For a couple to remain childfree is becoming a more acceptable choice, partly because of a growing concern about overpopulation, but also because of a growing belief that people should not be forced into life styles against their will, and that it is bad for children to be raised by parents who do not want them. Childfree persons are choosing individuality rather than the roles of parents. Present-orientation is also obvious in their lack of concern over continuing to live through their children or in gaining comfort, pleasure, and security through adult children when they themselves are old.

The National Organization for Nonparents (NON) supports the right of couples to choose or not choose parenthood. It is not against having children, although it is against having large numbers of children. Letters written to the editor of its newsletter indicate that there is a real need for such an organization, since the pressure to have

A sign of things to come—men taking care of children. These liberated men, Dennis Meredith and Henry Biller, are already doing it.

children is still great. The organization provides a counterbalance against the pressures coming from parents, who wish to become grandparents, and friends who have children who think that "everybody should go through what we've had to go through, the good and the bad."

Friendly Divorce

Some partners agree to end their primary commitment to each other while maintaining a cooperative relationship. "Just Friends, Lovers No More" was the title of a song that expressed sadness and acceptance. Some sadness is inevitable at the breakup of such an important attachment, but much trauma is avoided when the severed pair maintain a degree of respect and care. Property is divided fairly and business matters are worked out with full communication. If there are genuine affectionate relationships with in-laws, they can be maintained.

Since we do not have information about large numbers of friendly divorces, we only describe some cases. The first is a report of a divorce ceremony; the other two concern the ways in which divorced friends worked out their relationships.

The divorce of Anne and Matt was reported in an article in the *Christian Century* [32]. The couple told their friends that they were going to be divorced and invited them to a party at which the occasion was marked by cutting a cake. The "Service of Dissolution of Marriage" was performed at the couple's home. Matt responded "I do" to the question, "Do you release her with your love and blessing, in gratitude for the part she has played in your life, in knowledge that her part in you will never be forgotten or despised, and in faith that in separation as well as in union, you are both held in the grace and unity of God?" Anne was then asked the same question. Formal announcements of the "amicable divorce" were later sent out (see Figure 17-2).

Amy and Andy were married while both were in college. When they graduated, Amy worked as a secretary while Andy went on for his M.A. As soon as he got a teaching job, they had two children in rapid succession. Three years later, Andy said he wanted to live alone; he felt stifled by family life. He loved Amy and the children, but wanted to be free to date other women and to be himself. After a few months, Andy and Amy agreed to a divorce, since Andy did not think that he wanted to live with her again. Andy paid a reasonable amount for the children's support. Amy got a job and found day care for the children. Andy goes to see Amy and the children about once a week. Sometimes they have dinner at Amy's; sometimes Andy takes them all out. Occasionally, he takes Amy out on a date. Amy's friends have asked her why she puts up with Andy's desertion from the husband role and his assumption of a merely friendly role. She has explained that it is good for the children to have contact with their father and that for her, this arrangement is better than nothing. Andy represents present-orientation, rejection of roles, and emphasis on his own growth.

Bonnie and Buzz were happily married for ten years, during which time he did well in a professional career and she was a homemaker and mother of three children. Bonnie, feeling bored and restless, joined a women's liberation group and gained enough support and self-confidence to go back to college for a degree. Soon she found a job and did extremely well. Threatened by Bonnie's success and her contacts with other men, Buzz wanted out of the marriage. Bonnie had tried at first to change her husband's traditional concept of masculinity and femininity, but, by now, she was convinced that her new life-style would not fit with his old one. Her role as his wife was too confining. She wanted to grow. He wanted her to stay as she was. They agreed that divorce was best but that they would continue to live near each other, since the children needed both of them. The children are based at Bonnie's house, but they go regularly to Buzz's. If Bonnie is going out for dinner, or away for a weekend, Buzz takes care of the children. They all spend Christmas and other family festival days together. The parents contribute equally to the economic support of the children, but each knows that the other would do more if necessary. Bonnie has turned down offers of better jobs because they would require moving away from Buzz. She would not separate the children from their father. Nor would she want to lose him as a partner in childrearing, even though he is no longer a partner in marriage.

Matthew and Anne Surrey
Announce

An Amicable Divorce
Their friends and relatives
Are invited not to take sides
And to keep in touch
With both of them.

For the time being still
Both at home at
1492 Columbus Circle
Middle City, Midwest

FIGURE 17-2 A Midwestern couple sent announcements of their amicable divorce to their friends and relatives.

Source: Mary M. Shideler, An amicable divorce. *Christian Century,* 1971, 88, 553–555.

Viability of Alternate Forms

The United States and Canada have always had some family forms other than the nuclear conjugal family. The number and proportion of people living in alternate family structures seem to be increasing. Although they will probably increase further, it is unlikely that nuclear families will be in the minority in the forseeable future. A large sample of students was drawn from seven universities, representing five regions of the United States [9]. When asked questions about their attitudes toward various new life-styles, 70 per cent said that they thought the traditional monogamous marriage the most fulfilling type of man-woman relationship. Two-stage marriage had the highest expression of favorable attitudes, 45 per cent. About one third had favorable attitudes toward cohabitation, communal living, and marriage between homosexuals. Only 6 per cent were favorable to group marriage and 13 per cent were favorable to extramarital sex with mutual consent. Lowest approval was given to extramarital sex without knowledge of mate.

True acceptance of pluralism in family living would require facilitating constructive human relationships in a variety of ways. A program to help nuclear families to be more successful need not penalize other kinds of families and could even assist them. If some of the strains on individuals and nuclear families can be alleviated, the benefits will spill over to the minority of family forms, too. Nonnuclear forms can be thought of not only as alternates but also as backups to the nuclear family.

STRENGTHENING FAMILY LIVING

A pluralistic nation is much harder to run than one with a homogeneous population and a monolithic political organization. Will North American political, legal, religious, and economic institutions be up to the challenge? The family now needs some strengthening, creative action from other social institutions, in addition to the efforts of individuals. The following are positive changes that would support creative family living. Some of the changes are already under way.

Economic Support

Enough food, clothing, and shelter are basic to satisfactory family life. North America has the resources necessary for meeting the physical needs of all its people but has failed in sharing and distributing. The family cannot solve this problem. The challenge could be met through combined efforts of government and industry. (North America cannot, however, meet basic needs of all the poor people in the world.)

Work-sharing and Choice of Jobs

Many of the strains on the nuclear family come from the way in which work is divided between husband and wife. The traditional way has been for the husband to go out to work while the wife stayed home and took care of the house and children. The husband earned money but the wife did not. Consequently, women's work was considered to be worth less than men's or even to be worthless. Even while working for long hours at a variety of tiring tasks, women held themselves in low esteem and said apologetically, "I'm just a housewife."

It was lonely for the woman, staying home with no adult company. With young children at home, mothers were very busy but often longed for an adult to talk with.

They envied their husbands out in the world of factory and office, enjoying the company of peers and doing worthwhile work. Men had their problems, too, since they were expected to produce, to get ahead, to make more money, and to gain more status. Some of them wanted to spend hours at home, see more of their children, and have more choice in how to spend their time.

Some women went out to work, and then more and more, as mentioned on pages 124–125, they cut down on some of the hours of housework, doing it faster, but still working an inordinate number of hours each day. On the whole, men did not give any more help to working wives than they gave to wives who stayed home.

Some men did help more at home. Some couples have worked out patterns of life in which drudgery is shared and special jobs fall to the person who likes them best and/or can do them best, without regard for whether society holds the work to be masculine or feminine. My (MSS) husband does our income tax report but our daughters do them for their families. The jobs considered most feminine are probably cooking and taking care of babies. A male friend of ours does both when his wife is at her part-time job. They purposely live near his place of work in order that he can share in the homemaking and child care. Both members of this partnership like their jobs and their work at home. This father has an exceptionally close and joyous relationship with his baby and two year old.

Androgyny is the term given to the style of life in which choice of work is determined by personal preference instead of sex stereotypes. "Open marriage" is also similar to androgyny. Rowe [31] describes androgyny as "permitting men to cry, to join the nurturant professions, to care for children and colleagues" and "permitting women to be assertive and financially independent and giving them wide career options." The Osofskys [22] define androgyny as "a society with no sex-role differentiation." These authors are not suggesting that men and women should be alike, but rather that every individual, man or woman, be allowed to choose from the full range of human behavior. When this concept is applied to family management, it means that resources are expanded. The partners and their children, or the group, have more possibilities for achieving their goals.

No matter how strongly a given pair or family may want to practice androgyny, they need cooperation from other social systems. Business, industry, and educational institutions can contribute flexible job definitions that permit workers more choice in timing and even in location. The present custom of penalizing part-time workers (usually women) could be eliminated by job-sharing. A job can be shared by any pair or group who can do the job. Husband-wife job sharing is satisfying to some couples. Some colleges have even come to realize that they get more for their money by hiring a couple to share a job [14].

Child Care and Homemaking Support Systems

Another strain could be relieved by giving parents (chiefly mothers) some help in caring for their children. If a mother is going to go out to work, someone must look after the children; but even if she is not employed outside the home, nobody can stand the strain and the boredom of being constantly on duty. A variety of child care services are essential in order to meet the variety of needs that North American families have. Some children require all-day care every day, others for a few hours a week. Children who go to school may need a place to go in the late afternoon. Kindergarteners may need lunch and care for half a day.

Child development specialists know how to conduct excellent programs that will be good for children's physical, mental, and emotional development. Growth-promoting programs have been demonstrated at all age levels and for children with various capacities and limitations. Delivery of these services is barred not by lack of knowledge but by lack of conviction that it should be done. Industry could do some of the job. During World War II, the Kaiser Company delivered excellent day care services to mothers who worked in the shipyards. Day care facilities are attached to factories in other countries, including Russia, China, and India. Schools could do some of the job and benefit older children at the same time. Some schools already run nursery schools as laboratories. Churches and community agencies also provide day care. Much more is needed, in order to have enough places for all and to provide care for children whose parents cannot afford to pay. We believe that the government should give leadership and that public funds should be used for young children, just as they are for the education of older ones.

Although affluent parents often buy household services or provide their own through androgynous life-styles, many women and almost all single parents must struggle with heavy household burdens. Child care centers could offer many aids in addition to supervising and educating children. The first nursery schools in England, around 1920, gave the children baths when they arrived. The Kaiser child care centers used to prepare a main dinner dish that the parents could take home with their children at night. Children at the University of Rhode Island nursery school are taken to have their teeth cleaned at the University dental clinic. An obvious service is that of washing and mending clothing and exchanging clothing as children outgrow what they have. Food and clothing services could serve a double purpose if schools and universities used services to children for teaching older boys and girls. Older children could then use their homemaking skills to be more helpful in their families.

Some other homemaking supports exist but are not widely available. Geriatric day care centers (pages 423–425) can keep an old person based at home without overburdening the family. Visiting homemakers help families in crises, as when the mother is ill, but there are not enough of them to go around. Visiting nurses help in crises of illness, but they cannot go to all the families who could benefit from their services. Working mothers and single fathers urgently need help in caring for their children when they are ill. Only a minute proportion of day care centers have facilities for taking care of sick children.

Another type of homemaking support needed by many families is help in home maintenance and improvement. The poor, the aged, and single-parent family heads need it most. When people can neither pay a skilled workman nor do it themselves, what are they to do with a leaky tap, a stopped-up toilet, a burned-out element, or a broken stair tread? Although education for homemaking would be a long-term solution, communities might maintain home rescue squads for immediate action. If students were required to give a year or two of service to nation and community immediately after high school, there would be personnel available. The young people themselves would also benefit from learning skills and from doing constructive work for others.

Recreational services are another child care support that could be expanded to benefit families more. Many children need a safe place to play and opportunities to learn motor skills, games, and hobbies. Much is already done by voluntary organizations, such as Scouts, and by churches and community houses, but much more is needed. Poor families urgently need space, equipment, and teachers or leaders to promote constructive play. Families also need opportunities to play together and to enjoy recreation as families. Many commercial interests work against free, available, simple neighborhood recreation. As with child care, the knowledge is available. There are competent community planners and recreation professionals, who could deliver the services if they were given the financial resources to do so.

Education for Human Living

Our fast-changing culture has not developed adequate ways of keeping up with its own newness. Some of our biggest problems come from not knowing how to communicate, relate, share, and care. In almost every spot in the family life cycle, people need to know more about how to realize their full human potential. We have to discard the notion that education begins in kindergarten and ends upon graduation from school or college. Lifelong, continuing education is a basic support to family living.

Throughout this book, we have advocated many educational measures. To summarize, we propose that everyone be educated in these areas: for self-understanding in terms of feelings, emotions, abilities, health, and growth; for communication; for planning and decision-making; for homemaking; about sex; about childbirth and childrearing; about marriage and its alternates; for changing and growing old. There are other fields of education, too, but what we are recommending here is in connection with personal and family life.

Some privately endowed institutions, such as the Merrill-Palmer Institute in Detroit and the Clara Elizabeth Fund, in Flint, Michigan, are designed for education for human living. Some universities, such as Utah State University, have cooperated with a wide variety of community organizations to establish family life education that reaches beyond the student body and into communities [33]. Industry (Radio Corporation of America) and a community organization cooperated to create a family development training project that educated all family members in both job and home skills. The operation transformed 400 of 728 deprived seasonal farm worker families into self-supporting families, tripling their average income [26]. Canada has an official association, the Vanier Institute, which could well be expanded in its scope and functions. Voluntary associations provide leadership and demonstrations. They include Child and Family Service Associations, the Child Study Association of America, the National Council on Family Relations, the Groves Conference, and the Association of Couples for Marriage Enrichment, founded by David and Vera Mace [17b]. If such institutions and projects could be multiplied and their efforts expanded, family living would be greatly strengthened. Since all people need education for human living, occasional programs are not enough and a systematic delivery system is needed.

Social Contacts

Social isolation is problematic to many members of nuclear families and to people living alone or in single-parent families. Many have moved away from kin and childhood friends. They need ways of finding friends and groups of congenial people. Church membership offers a path to sociability for those who accept it, but many people do not. Nor can everyone do volunteer work, join an interest group, or find enough friendship even if they do work and join. Continuing education will offer some opportunities for making friends, as will consciousness-raising groups. Family cluster programs, sponsored by the Unitarian Church, are useful to urban families as a way of creating a network of relationships that substitutes for absent kin, friends, and neighbors. Instead of supplying only individual friends, the system brings together groups that resemble the larger family. Participants reported that they experienced these benefits: Relationships that were intimate, honest, and real; awareness of goodwill in others; contact with children for childless people; children relating to adults and children outside their immediate families; understanding of how other families operate [27].

Legal Reform and Clarification

As pointed out in Chapter 15, there are confusing and outdated laws regarding the family, marriage, sex roles, and children. Although laws of necessity lag behind the latest thinking, they should be kept up to date as much as possible. For example, marriage in two steps could be legalized, institutionalizing what many couples are in fact doing. Legal reform would make laws more functional and easier to understand and to apply. More uniformity between the states is highly desirable, as well as more cooperation in administering the law. Members of the legal profession vary from very corrupt to highly moral and unselfish. Greater numbers of the latter are needed by all, but especially by poor families and minority group members. Equality before the law is a reality only when everyone has equal access to its power.

Health Services, Broadly Conceived and Delivered

Canada has moved faster than the United States in making excellent medical care available to a large part of the population. Once more the United States is in the position of having tremendous knowledge and technology but flawed delivery. Both nations have a long way to go in putting the emphasis on optimal health. There are, however, some group practices in which services are oriented to keeping patients well, with treatment for illness considered a backup. The maintenance of family health would give much strength to family living. Family-centered medical care would take into account the physical and mental health of the group. With such an aim, many hospital practices would be adapted to the needs of the family. For instance, loved ones would stay with ill patients, especially with children; family-centered childbirth practices would predominate; children would be able to keep in touch with hospitalized parents; play programs would minister to the emotional health of all children; and hospitals would be places where patients learned how to be healthy. All of this already exists in a few places, such as the McMaster Medical Centre in Hamilton, Ontario.

Counseling, encounter groups and other group therapy, individual psychotherapy, and all the mental health services that now exist would be made more available. Again, preventive work would keep people healthy. Crises would be fewer and intervention more effective.

Better physical and mental health services will come from the cooperation of professionals with each other and with government at all levels, community to federal. Consumers' organizations can exert constructive influences.

IN CONCLUSION

We believe that the nuclear family will continue to be the most prevalent form of the family in our society and throughout the world. Other forms of the family will continue to exist and to exert an influence on the nuclear family. Our society was founded because of the belief in individual freedom. Progress made by minority groups has shown that the ideals of freedom and individuality still exist and can be made more of a reality through human efforts.

We are encouraged by the human liberation movement, since we believe that men, women, and children have much to gain from an androgynous life-style. Although the changeover from traditional to less structured sex roles is a difficult process for many people, the change will mean that persons in the present and future generations will be able to grow more fully in ways that will develop individual potential and suit individual needs. It will not mean that the sexes will be the same, as some people fear. Rather, it will allow for a more varied population and a more interesting life.

We hope that individuals and families will be able to reach out to each other, both in good times and bad. The nuclear family cut adrift from the extended family and home town community needs new supports, as we have shown. Such families have the advantage of being able to choose friends out of a wider population than was possible in the past. However, many people need to learn how to make deep, satisfying friendships more rapidly than was necessary in the past. North America needs people who care for each other, who cooperate willingly, and who often put the needs of the group ahead of individual desires. Because of the amazing flexibility of human beings, such adaptations can be made.

SUMMARY The future of human life is threatened by food shortages, exploding populations, and environmental breakdowns. Even in affluent countries, family life and human relationships will be affected. Present life-styles and ideologies take little account of these facts.

New orientations to life include: equality, more emphasis on the present, and less emphasis on the past and future; looking beyond science or away from science for new knowledge; reassessment of the morality of power; rejection of role restrictions in favor of expanded individual freedom in education, occupations, sex membership, age levels; emphasis on sexual freedom and activity; emphasis on personal growth.

Pluralism in life-styles is a fact in North America. A variety of family forms exists. Communes, both old and new, include many different ways in which groups of people live together in commitment and cooperation. Main categories are religious, utopian, and evolutionary. Rural communes are among the minority of organizations in our society that are developing a mode of life compatible with the world's diminishing resources. Among the different types of communes, all of the previously mentioned new orientations to life are represented.

Group marriage is a rare and difficult but potentially rewarding life-style. Co-marital sex is extramarital sexual relations with one's spouse's consent. Sexually-open marriages involve co-marital sex with emotional commitment. Swinging is organized co-marital sex that is usually done without emotional involvement, for purely recreational purposes. Co-marital sex may be included in "open marriage" but is not the main feature of it. The basics of open marriage are equality, identity, trust, communication, respect, honesty, personal growth, and present-orientation.

Homosexuality is made difficult as a life-style because of social disapproval. Homosexuals do not do any harm to society, but discrimination against them continues, denying them many of the supports accorded to heterosexual partners. Cohabitation may serve as engagement or trial marriage or marriage within limited commitment. Numbers of singles are increasing and denigration of single females is decreasing. Spousefree parents are usually women who wish to be mothers but not wives. This life-style is fraught with difficulties, both economic and relational, for mother and child, but it is viable under favorable circumstances. Childfree families are partners who do not wish to become parents. Present orientation and role

freedom are involved. Friendly divorce dissolves the husband-wife relationship while preserving parent-parent and parent-child relations. The monogamous nuclear family is preferred by most people.

Family living, in alternate as well as nuclear families, could be improved by a variety of measures. Economic support would give all persons a minimally adequate standard of living. A realignment of work and jobs would enable women and men to use their full human potential. Such changes require efforts of couples to plan and carry out fair distribution of work at home and to plan ways in which both can pursue employment to which they are suited. Changes in business, industry, and employers are also crucial to permitting couples to develop an androgynous life-style.

Families need much support for child care, care of the aged and ill, and homemaking services in order to lighten the burdens of loneliness of nuclear families. Examples of such services already exist. The help of industry, government, and educational institutions is needed. Education for human living and relating should take place continually throughout life. Current programs are good but do not reach enough people, especially the poor.

Many family units are isolated and in need of close social relationships. Ways of finding friends and developing group friendships are needed. Family clusters are one answer.

Legal reform would benefit family life. Clarification, modernization, and available services are needed. Health services, both physical and mental, should be more inclusive, available, and positive.

We are optimistic about the development of loving cooperating and caring relationships in the nuclear family in North America. Contributions to the good life will also come from pluralism and freedom of choice. Canada and the United States need more individuals who concern themselves with what is good for society.

REFERENCES

1. Altman, Dennis. *Homosexuals: Oppression and liberation.* New York: Outerbridge and Dienstfrey, 1971.
1a. Anonymous. Avante-garde retreat? *Time,* Nov. 25, 1974. 101–103.
2. Bartell, Gilbert. *Group Sex: An eyewitness report on the American way of swinging.* New York: Signet, 1971.
3. Berger, Bennett, Bruce Hackett, and Mervyn Millar. The communal family. *Family Coordinator,* 1972, **21,** 419–427.
4. Brecher, Edward. *The sex researchers.* Boston: Little, Brown, 1969.
5. Chesser, Eustace. *Strange loves: The human aspects of sexual deviation.* New York: Morrow, 1971.
6. Cole, Charles and Graham Spanier. Co-marital mate-sharing and family stability. *Journal of Sex Research,* 1974, **10,** 21–31.
7. Constantine, Larry L. and Joan M. Constantine. Sexual aspects of group marriages. In Roger Libby and Robert Whitehurst, (eds.). *Renovating marriage.* Danville, Calif.: Consensus, 1973, 182–191.
8. Denfield, Duane. Dropouts from swinging. *Family Coordinator,* 1974, **23,** 45–49.

9. Edwards, Maxine and Nick Stinnett. Perceptions of college students concerning alternate life styles. *Journal of Psychology,* 1974, **87,** 143–156.

10. Ellis, Albert. Group marriage: A possible alternative. In Herbert A. Otto (ed.). *The family in search of a future.* New York: Appleton, 1970.

11. Estellachild, Vivian. Hippie communes. In Joann Delora and Jack Delora (eds.). *Intimate life styles: Marriage and its alternatives.* Pacific Palisades, Calif.: Goodyear, 1972, 332–337.

12. Fisher, Peter. *The gay mystique: The myth and reality of male homosexuality.* New York: Stein and Day, 1972.

13. Francke, Linda. Bisexual chic: Anyone goes. *Newsweek,* May 27, 1974, p. 90.

14. Gallese, Liz R. Two for the price of one. *Wall Street Journal,* April 19, 1974.

14a. Glick, Paul C. A demographer looks at American Families. *Journal of Marriage and the Family,* 1975, **37,** 15–26.

15. Henshell, Anne-Maire. Swinging: A study of decision-making in marriage. *American Journal of Sociology,* 1973, **78,** 885–891.

16. Jacoby, Susan. 49 million singles can't all be right. *New York Times Magazine,* February 17, 1974. 12, 13, 41+.

17. Kephart, William. Experimental family organization: An historico-cultural report on the Oneida Community. *Marriage and Family Living,* 1963, **25,** 261–268.

17a. Knapp, Jacqueline J. Co-marital sex and marriage counseling: Sexually open marriage and related attitudes and practices of marriage counselors. Unpublished PhD. dissertation, University of Florida, 1974.

17b. Mace, David R. (Ed.) Marriage enrichment. *Family Coordinator,* 1975, **24,** 131–170.

18. Maslow, Abraham. *Toward a psychology of being.* New York: Van Nostrand, 1962.

19. Moran, Rosalyn. The singles in the seventies. *In* Joann Delora and Jack Delora, (Eds.) *Intimate life styles: Marriage and its alternatives.* Pacific Palisades, Calif.: Goodyear, 1972. 338–344.

20. O'Neill, Nena and George O'Neill. *Open marriage: A new life style for couples.* New York: Avon, 1972.

21. O'Neill, Nena and George O'Neill. Open marriage: its implications for human service systems. *Family Coordinator,* 1973, **22,** 449–456.

22. Osofsky, Joy D. and Howard J. Osofsky. Androgyny as a life style. *Family Coordinator,* 1972, **21,** 411–418.

23. Paddock, William and Elizabeth Paddock. *We don't know how.* Ames, Iowa: Iowa State University Press, 1973.

24. Palson, Charles and Rebecca Palson. Swinging in wedlock. in Helena Z. Lopata, (Ed.) *Marriages and families.* New York: Van Nostrand, 1973.

25. Pattison, Joyce. Single motherhood, a new life style: Implications for the personal freedom of the mother, father, and child. Paper presented at the annual meetings of the National Council on Family Relations, October, 1973. Toronto.

26. Porter, Gwendolyn H. The family training concept. *Family Coordinator,* 1974, **23,** 171–174.

27. Pringle, Bruce M. Family clusters as a means of reducing isolation among urbanites. *Family Coordinator,* 1974, **23,** 175–179.

28. Ramey, James W. Emerging patterns of innovative behavior in marriage. *Family Coordinator,* 1972. **21,** 435–456.

28a. Ramey, James W. Intimate friendship: Logical outcome of rejecting monogamy. *Family Coordinator,* 1975, **24,** in press.

29. Rimmer, Robert H. *The Harrad experiment.* New York: Bantam, 1966.
30. Rogers, Carl R. *On becoming a person.* Boston: Houghton, 1961.
31. Rowe, Mary P. That parents may work and love and children may thrive. In James Harrell and Peggy Pizzo (Eds.) *Child Care Reprints IV: Employed mothers.* Washington, D.C.: Day Care and Child Development Council of America.
32. Shideler, Mary M. An amicable divorce. *Christian Century,* 1971, **88,** 553–555.
33. Skidmore, C. Jay and Jay D. Schvaneveldt. Reaching the community through a family life conference. *Family Coordinator,* 1974, **22,** 465–471.
33a. Varni, Charles. cited in James Ramey, Intimate friendship: logical outcome of rejecting monogamy. *Family Coordinator,* 1975, **24,** in press.
34. Veevers, J. E. Factors in the incidence of childlessness in Canada: An analysis of census data. *Social Biology,* 1972, **19,** 266–274.
35. White, Burton L. and Jean C. Watts. *Experience and environment—Major influences on the development of the young child.* Vol. I. Englewood Cliffs, N.J.: Prentice-Hall, 1973.
36. Ziskin, Jay and Mae Ziskin. *The extra-marital sex contract.* Los Angeles: Nash, 1973.

appendixes

appendix A
PREMARITAL QUESTIONNAIRE

A couple contemplating marriage or a marriage-type relationship should spend time discussing values and goals. The Premarital Questionnaire provided here as a supplement to the text of *Families: Developing Relationships* can help this important process by raising a number of relevant issues.

Instructions: Each partner should have a copy of the questionnaire. Additional copies may be available from your instructor.

In the left column are questions to be answered either by checking the appropriate column or columns at the right, by writing in "yes" or "no," or by writing in a short answer, where appropriate.

You and your partner should each fill out one of these forms, without consulting each other or discussing the questions until you have finished. When finished filling out the forms, go over each question, reading your answers in turn, and discussing those that are problematic.

Place an O in the column or columns to show who did this task in your family of orientation (the family in which you grew up). *Place an X* in the column or columns to show who will do this in your family of procreation (the new family that you and your partner are forming). *Note:* If more than one person did or will do a particular task, indicate all of the people who shared the responsibility.

Place an O in the column or columns to show who did this task in your family of orientation. Place an X in the column or columns to show who will do this task in your family of procreation.	Wife	Husband	Child	Other	Outside paid help	No one
Paid work Who 1. works for pay, full time?						
2. works for pay, part time?						
Unpaid work, in and around home: *Care of the home* Who 3. washes the dishes?						
4. puts away the dishes?						
5. plans the meals?						
6. cooks the meals?						
7. does cooking such as baking bread or preparing other staples?						
8. plans the shopping list?						
9. does the food shopping?						
10. puts food away after the shopping trip?						
11. cleans the refrigerator?						
12. cleans the oven?						
13. vacuums or sweeps?						
14. washes floors?						
15. washes windows?						
16. dusts?						

Place an O on the column or columns to show who did this task in your family of orientation. Place an X in the column or columns to show who will do this task in your family of procreation.	Wife	Husband	Child	Other	Outside paid help	No one
17. picks up commonly used rooms such as the living room?						
18. picks up privately used rooms such as individual bedrooms?						
19. washes clothes?						
20. puts away clean clothes?						
21. mends clothing?						
22. irons clothing?						
23. sets the table before meals?						
24. clears the table after meals?						
25. does minor repairs of plumbing?						
26. does minor repairs of furnishings?						
27. does minor repairs of appliances?						
28. does or is responsible for major household repairs?						
29. takes care of the garbage and trash?						
30. If hired help is used, who does the hiring, firing, and supervising?						
Care of the yard Who 31. cuts the grass?						
32. shovels the snow?						
33. takes care of the garden?						

Place an O in the column or columns to show who did this task in your family of orientation. Place an X in the column or columns to show who will do this task in your family of procreation.	Wife	Husband	Child	Other	Outside paid help	No one
Care of yard, continued						
34. rakes leaves?						
Care of car or other vehicle Who						
35. sees that it has sufficient gas and oil?						
36. cleans the exterior (or takes it to a carwash)?						
37. cleans the interior?						
38. sees that it is serviced or kept in good repair?						
Care of pet Who						
39. feeds it?						
40. exercises it?						
41. disposes of waste?						
42. brushes, washes, etc.?						
Financial management Who						
43. decides the family budget?						
44. pays the bills?						
45. makes major purchasing decisions?						
Choosing a home or place to live Who						
46. decides whether to live in a rural, suburban, or urban environment?						
47. chooses the actual dwelling?						

Short answer: answer *yes* or *no,* or fill in with your answer, as appropriate, for questions 48–51.

Children, planning and care of.

48. Do you want to have children? _____

49. Will you use contraceptives? _____

    If yes, what kind? _____

    If yes, whose responsibility is
    the use of contraceptives? _____

50. If you want children, do you want
    natural, adopted, or both? _____

51. Would you want to terminate an unwanted or unplanned
    pregnancy with an abortion? _____

    If you want children:

52. when do you want to start your family?

    _____

53. will husband be present at birth of child(ren)? _____

54. do you believe in day care for infants? _____
    for small children? _____

Place an O in the column or columns to show who did this task in your family of orientation. Place an X in the column or columns to show who will do this task in your family of procreation.	Wife	Husband	Child	Other	Outside paid help	No one
Child care: Who cares for infant and toddler? 55. diapers?						
56. feeds?						
57. bathes?						
58. plays with?						
59. disciplines?						
60. gets up at night with?						
61. tends when sick?						

Place an O in the column or columns to show who did this task in your family of orientation. Place an X in the column or columns to show who will do this task in your family of procreation.	Wife	Husband	Child	Other	Outside paid help	No one
Child care, continued. Who care for preschool child? 62. feeds?						
63. bathes?						
64. puts to bed at night?						
65. teaches skills?						
66. takes care of child's toys? (organizes, puts away, etc.)						
67. disciplines?						
68. gets up at night with?						
69. takes care of when sick?						
70. plays with?						
Who cares for school-age child and teen ager? 71. sees that the child is fed and bathed?						
72. plays with and/or supervises activities?						
73. helps with homework?						
74. disciplines?						
75. takes care of when sick?						

Answer the following questions by writing in *yes, no,* or a short answer.

76. At what age will children be given household work responsibilities? _____

77. Will children be given an allowance? _____

    If yes, how much? _____

        at what age? _____

78. Will children be given formal religious instruction? _____

If yes, by whom and at what age? _____

79. Will you instruct your children about sex? _____

    If yes, at what age? _____

        who will do it? (mother, father, other?) _____

80. How will you express affection to your children? _____

    _____

    Will your way of expressing affection change as the children grow up?

    _____

81. Do you believe in physical punishment?

    If no, what kind of punishment do you think is appropriate?

    _____

Marital relationship

82. If your marriage becomes unbearable and cannot be saved, would you consider
    divorce? _____

83. How do your parents show affection for each other?

    _____

    How will you show affection for your spouse?

    _____

    After children are born, will you display affection
    for each other in front of the children? _____

84. How frequently do you expect to have sexual relations with your spouse? (times per
    week) _____

85. What kind of recreational activities will you engage in, without your spouse?

    _____

86. What kind of recreational activities will you engage in, with your spouse?

    _____

Outside relationships

87. Who will decide which other couples will be your friends?

    _____

88. Who will decide who each spouse's same-sex friends will be? _____

89. Will each spouse have friends of the opposite sex who are not necessarily the other
    spouse's friends?

    _____

90. If yes to 89, will these friends be strictly on a work or professional level? _____

91. If no to 90, will physical intimacy be a part of these relationships? _____

92. If yes to 91, will limits be placed upon the amount of physical intimacy? _____

93. Will friendships with members of the opposite sex be kept secret from the other spouse?

    _____

Religion

94. Do you attend church or temple? _____

    If yes, which one? _____

          how often? _____

95. Do you expect your spouse to attend church or temple?

    If yes, the same as yours? _____

    How often? _____

96. Do you celebrate religious holidays?

    If yes, which ones?

_____

    How do you celebrate?

_____

Work (These questions apply to you and your spouse, not to people in general.

97. How do you feel about the wife working outside of the home after children are born?

_____

98. How do you feel about the wife earning more than the husband?

_____

99. How do you feel about the husband working for pay on a part-time basis only, or being a full-time house-husband?

_____

100. Whose career should come first? _____

Miscellaneous

101. How often will you visit your parents? (times per week, month, or year) _____

102. How often will your parents visit you?

_____

103. How much money will you give to charity? _____

104. How much time will you spend working for community organizations? _____

105. Where would you go for help if you had personal problems, marital problems, or problems with a child? (check appropriate answer or answers)

    [   ] counselor (individual, marriage, or child therapist)

    [   ] clergyman

    [   ] friend

    [   ] medical doctor

    [   ] relative

    [   ] I would try to read about the problem

    [   ] consult no one.

106. Rearrange the following items in terms of their importance, most important first. First, order them in the way that you would like your spouse to feel. Do this even if you have no intention to change your spouse.

Then, order them the way that you feel.

	Spouse	Self
A. Devotion to your country		
B. Family (including having children)		
C. Personal growth of self as an individual		
D. Religion		
E. Work or career		
F. Your relationship as a couple.		

appendix B

basic sex

PRENATAL DEVELOPMENT

Conception

Of the millions of **sperm** that flow from the father, only one fertilizes the mother's single egg. The sperm and egg provide materials that combine to make a unique individual, unlike anyone who has ever been born before. The individual's uniqueness is possible because of the possible combinations of genetic material from the mother and father.

Each cell of a human body, with the exception of the sex cells (sperm and ova) contains a total of 46 **chromosomes.** Chromosomes contain **genes,** tiny codes that determine how the individual will develop from one cell into a large organism containing billions of cells. Of these 46 chromosomes, two determine the sex of the individual. From the mother's ovum comes an X chromosome (so called because when viewed under a microscope it looks like an X); from the father's sperm comes either an X chromosome, which results in a female child, or a Y chromosome, resulting in a male child.

When a sperm penetrates an egg, 22 chromosomes plus one X or Y chromosome from the father unite with 22 chromosomes plus one X chromosome from the mother in a unique new cell that will divide and subdivide to become a new individual. Seventy-two hours after conception, the individual consists of a ball of 32 cells; after four days it is a hollow ball of about 90 cells. This hollow ball of cells normally attaches itself to the mother's **uterus,** where it will spend the next nine months.

Embryo and Fetus

During the next period of development, the individual is called an **embryo.** It develops a face, neck, arms, legs, fingers, toes, functioning internal organs, and some bone calcification. The head end develops faster than the tail end. At the end of eight weeks, with the basic structures laid down, the individual begins to look human. It is given a new name, **fetus,** which it keeps until it is born and becomes an infant (baby). During the third month of prenatal life, the first month of the fetus, the organism becomes differentiated as male or female. Other bodily systems also become more complex. At the age of five months, the fetus is about half as long as it will be at birth. At the age of seven months, it has a good chance of living outside the mother, should the fetus become an infant prematurely.

Basic Sexual Anatomy

Male. The most obvious difference between a male and female baby is, of course, the difference between the external genitals: the boy has a **penis** and **testes,** and the girl has a **vulva** (see Figures B-1, B-2). The penis is a complicated organ made of three cylinders of erectile tissue, two of which are nearly alike* and lie next to each other. The third cylinder lies beneath the two, and contains the urethra, the tube that at separate times carries urine, and in mature males ejaculate fluid or **semen** (the liquid that contains the male sex cells). The head or **glans** of the penis is also made of erectile tissue, but it is more richly endowed with nerves, making it extremely sensitive to touch. When the penis is flaccid (not erect), the head is covered by a loose ring of skin known as the **foreskin.** When the penis is erect, the foreskin pulls back to allow the sensitive head to receive the greatest stimulation.

All males are born with a foreskin, but it may be removed surgically in an operation called **circumcision.** This operation is performed ritually upon Jewish and Muslim boys, but may be performed routinely in some hospitals for "medical reasons." Actually, there is considerable difference of opinion as to whether or not circumcision has medical merit. It is true that it is harder to keep the uncircumcised penis clean, as a smelly substance called *smegma* forms under the foreskin if it is not drawn back and carefully washed daily. If left too long, the foreskin may stick to the glans. Opponents of circumcision claim that the individual can be taught to wash routinely, and that unnecessary surgery is never advisable.

Behind the penis is the **scrotum,** a loose sack of skin that contains a pair of testes. When it is mature, each testis is usually about an inch and a half long and an inch in diameter and ovoid in shape. From before the boy is born until the end of his life, the testes produce testosterone, the hormone that before birth literally makes him male. Should he lose his testes before reaching puberty, he will not develop into a normal adult male, but will instead be a *eunuch.* A eunuch retains a high voice, does not develop bodily hair, and is, of course, sterile. In the mature male, the testes also produce the male sex cells, **sperm.**

Sperm is made in the seminiferous tubules, tiny tubes within the testes. However, it is not

*It is not unusual for one of these cylinders to be slightly larger than the other, making the penis curve slightly.

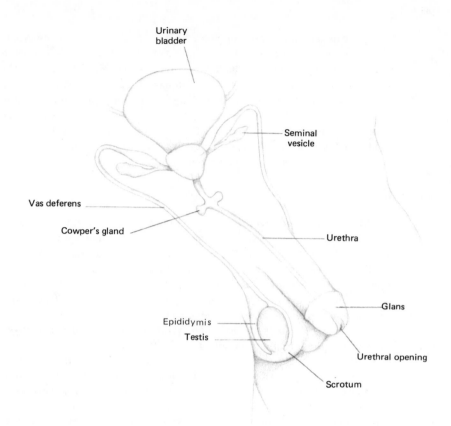

Urinary
bladder

Seminal
vesicle

Vas deferens

Cowper's gland

Urethra

Glans

Epididymis

Testis

Urethral opening

Scrotum

FIGURE B-1   Genital system of circumcised male.

yet mature when it is produced, and spends from two to four weeks in the **epididymis** or *collection tube,* during which time it becomes activated. The sperm is made of three parts: a head, containing the genetic material (chromosomes), which are the male contribution to the new life; a midsection, which produces chemicals that allow the sperm to convert materials in the seminal fluid into energy; and a tail section, for propulsion.

From the epididymis, the sperm is pushed into the body cavity via the **vasa deferentia** (singular *vas deferens*), a pair of tubes about eighteen inches long that loop up around the urinary bladder and then down to the **ampulla,** an enlargement in the vas deferens, which serves as a storage place. After the ampulla are several glands that produce the largest part of the fluid that contain the sperm: first, the *seminal vesicles,* and then the *prostate gland.* Below the prostate gland are two Cowper's glands, which produce an alkaline substance during sexual excitement that neutralizes any urine that may still be in the urethra.

Female. The female's external genitals are called the **vulva.** The vulva consists of the **mons veneris,** a small mound of fatty tissue located over the pubic bone; the **labia majora,** or outer lips, which when parted reveal the **labia minora,** or inner lips. The **clitoris,** the most sensitive part of a female's anatomy, is located where the inner lips join. It resembles a very tiny penis, although the urethra does not open through the clitoris, but is located instead below the clitoris in the **vestibule.** The clitoris does, however, have a glans and a tiny foreskin that, like the male's, should be carefully pulled back for a daily washing. Smegma may form around the clitoris and under the foreskin, eventually causing painful adhesions.

Into the vestibule opens the urethra, and also the **vagina** or birth canal. The newborn female may have a **hymen** or maidenhead, a fold of tissue that partly or completely covers the vagina. The thickness and appearance of this tissue varies widely from individual to individual: some females are born without one; others are born with one so elastic that it easily stretches out of the way during sexual intercourse. For other women, the hymen is so thick and tough that it must be removed surgically prior to sexual intercourse; for still others, the hymen

FIGURE B-2 Female genital system. A: External genitals. B: Varieties of hymens. C: Internal genital system.

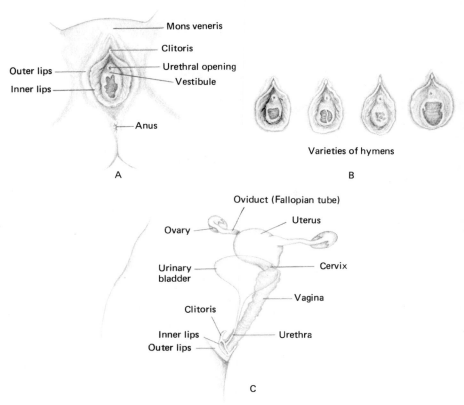

may be broken easily through manual manipulation or even through strenuous exercise. Although the absence of a hymen has historically been taken as proof that a girl is not a virgin, its absence or presence *proves* nothing.

The vagina is a tube made of extremely elastic muscle. It is the passageway from outside of the female's body to her **uterus,** a small, pear-shaped organ that is capable of stretching to hold a baby. The end of the uterus, the **cervix,** sticks down slightly into the vagina. The cervix is made of rings of strong muscle that dilate (open) when it is time for a baby to be born. At other times, the cervical opening is tiny and protected by a plug of mucus.

At the upper end of the uterus are two **Fallopian tubes** or **oviducts,** each of which opens into the uterus at one end, and at the other end forms finger-like projections reaching toward one of two **ovaries,** the female gonads or sex glands. A female is born with about 500,000 **ova,** (eggs, female sex cells), all that she will ever produce, unlike the male, who produces about a million sperm daily, once he matures sexually. The female does not release any ova until she reaches sexual maturity, about twelve or fourteen years after she is born.

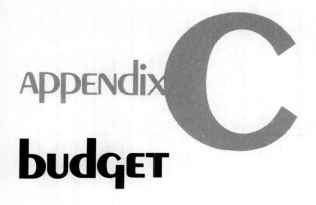

appendix C
budget

Source: Reprinted by permission from Elizabeth Wiegand, *Preview your spending.* Cornell Extension Bulletin 1143, Ithaca, New York: New York State College of Home Economics.

RECORD OF PROMISED PAYMENTS

1. Write in the column on the left side the various things you have agreed to pay for in the next 12 months. Your list may include such payments as house rent, car loan, insurance, or phone service, as well as payroll deductions such as social security, health insurance, or taxes. List only those things you have actually promised to pay for. Do *not* list the food, clothing, toll calls, or haircuts you hope to buy. You are not committed to pay for these things *yet*.

2. At the top of the next 12 columns write the names of the months, beginning with the month when you are making this record; for example, March, April, May.

3. Fill in the amount which is due in the column when you agreed to pay it. For example, life insurance: March $46, Sept. $46.

4. When you have recorded all the year's promised payments, add up each column and write the totals on the last line.

Promised payments												
Total promised payments												

MONTHS OR PAY PERIODS

RECORD OF ESTIMATED INCOME

1. In the first column list the kinds of income you expect to receive: gross wages or salary, commissions, interest on savings accounts, dividends, sale of products. Do not include children's earnings unless they will be spent for the family as a whole.

2. At the top of the next 12 columns write the names of the months.

3. Now try to estimate your income for each month. If you work or sell irregularly, your estimates may be difficult to make.

4. When you have written in the amounts, add up each column.

5. Copy the monthly totals of promised payments from above onto this Record.

6. Subtract the total promised payments from the total estimated income and you will know the sum to be available each month for other wants and needs.

Kinds of income	MONTHS OR PAY PERIODS											
Total estimated (gross) income												
Total promised payments												
Income available for other uses												

Can You Divide Your Income Better?

Now study your completed Records of Promised Payments and Estimated Income. You may want to shift some payments from a month having heavy expenses to one with light expenses or larger income. Insurance premiums and church and charitable pledges are fairly easy to shift. Or you can level large payments by paying monthly or quarterly. During some months you may prefer to keep unpledged income high—around Christmas or vacation time, for example.

If you are wondering about new borrowing or credit buying, a glance at your present load of promised payments will indicate when you could begin and how long payments need to last, depending on the size of installment you feel you could assume. Or you may simply decide that additional debt is unwise this year.

If your Preview helps you to know what income you will receive and the way you have divided a chunk of it, it has proved to be a valuable tool. Keep it handy; refer to it often.

appendix D
a daily food guide

Milk group (8-ounce cups)

2 to 3 cups for children under 9 years
3 cups or more for children 9 to 12 years
4 cups or more for teen agers
2 cups or more for adults
3 cups or more for pregnant women
4 cups or more for nursing mothers

Meat group

2 or more servings. Count as 1 serving:

2 to 3 ounces lean, cooked beef, veal, pork, lamb, poultry, fish—without bone
2 eggs
1 cup cooked dry beans, dry peas, lentils
4 tablespoons peanut butter

Vegetable-fruit group (½ cup serving, or 1 piece fruit, etc.)

4 or more servings per day, including:

1 serving citrus fruit, or other fruit or vegetable as a good source of vitamin C, or 2
servings of a fair source
1 serving, at least every other day, of a dark-green or deep-yellow vegetable for vitamin A
2 or more servings of other vegetables and fruits, including potatoes

Bread-cereals group

4 or more servings daily (whole grain, enriched, or restored). Count as 1 serving:

1 slice bread
1 ounce ready-to-cook cereal
½ to ¾ cup cooked cereal, corn meal, grits, macaroni, noodles, rice, or spaghetti.

Source: A daily food guide, *Consumers All,* Yearbook of Agriculture, 1965, U.S. Department of Agriculture, Washington, D.C., 1965, p. 394.

APPENDIX E

VENEREAL DISEASE

A venereal disease is a disease spread by sexual contact. Gonorrhea and syphilis are what most people mean when they say "V.D.," but there are other diseases as well, some dangerous and others merely irritating. In this appendix we briefly describe the more common venereal diseases. For more comprehensive coverage, we refer the reader to the *VD Handbook,* available for 25 cents from the address listed in the footnote.* (An excellent discussion of birth control, the Birth Control Handbook, is also available for the same price.) The *VD Handbook* explains not only the symptoms and treatments of the various diseases but also the history of the diseases.

GONORRHEA

Gonorrhea is the disease that is largely responsible for the V.D. epidemic. Although it is curable by penicillin (and other drugs for those who must not use penicillin), recently strains of gonorrhea that are resistant to treatment have evolved. The person who treats herself with nonprescribed penicillin may use the wrong type of the drug, or may stop taking the drug before all of the organisms that cause the disease have been killed. The surviving organisms are the strongest of those that caused the infection. The disease progresses in the infected individual, who passes the hardy strain of gonorrhea on to others through sexual contact.

*VD Handbook/Birth Control Handbook
P.O. Box 1000, Station G
Montreal 130, Quebec

502

Transmission of Gonorrhea

The organism that causes gonorrhea can be transmitted only through sexual intercourse, including vaginal, anal, or oral-genital intercourse. Outside of the body, it dies almost immediately. A man has a 20 to 50 per cent chance of contracting gonorrhea from one act of intercourse with an infected partner; a woman has a more than 50 per cent chance after one act of vaginal intercourse with an infected man [2].

Symptoms of Gonorrhea

Although many men first notice symptoms of gonorrhea within three to five days after exposure to it, asymptomatic (lacking symptoms) gonorrhea is becoming more common among men [1]. Symptoms may appear as soon as one day or as late as two weeks after exposure [2]. When symptoms appear in the male, he first has a thin, clear discharge seeping from the opening of his penis. After a day or two the discharge becomes heavy and creamy. It is usually white but may be yellow or yellow-green. The tip of the penis becomes swollen, with the lips of the urethral opening standing out from the glans. Urination is painful or causes a burning sensation and may become difficult.

If treatment is delayed for more than a few days, the infection spreads up the urethra, and may eventually invade the prostate gland and the epididymis, or the symptoms of gonorrhea may seem to go away. If untreated, however, the man can still spread the disease to his sexual partners. The untreated man may also become sterile.

Most women who contract gonorrhea experience no symptoms at all for the first weeks or months of their disease. Before the disease is discovered, permanent damage may be done to the Fallopian tubes, causing sterility. Some women, however, do notice a change in the vaginal secretions from the normal clear or white to a yellow-green or greenish color. The gonorrheal discharge is rarely noticeable unless another infection is present at the same time [2].

Complications of Gonorrhea

If left untreated, gonorrhea can cause severe pain and infection in both men and women. Damage to the reproductive system is not reversible, and sterility results. In women who have had such damage, the likeliness of an ectopic pregnancy (pregnancy that occurs outside of the uterus, in the Fallopian tube or abdominal cavity) is greatly increased. Fertilization occurs in the Fallopian tubes. If the tubes are partially blocked by scar tissue from the gonorrheal infection, the fertilized egg cannot pass to the uterus and develops elsewhere instead. Eventually, the area hemorrhages and the woman experiences severe pain and internal bleeding. If she does not receive immediate medical attention, she may die.

Treatment of Gonorrhea

The best treatment for gonorrhea is penicillin, given in injections in the buttocks. The *VD Handbook* discusses which types of penicillin are most and least effective in the treatment of gonorrhea. Tetracycline is the best treatment for persons who are allergic to penicillin [2].

Prevention of Gonorrhea

The condom is the best means of preventing transmission of the disease, but it is not 100 per cent effective [2]. Many birth control clinics include a test for gonorrhea as a part of a routine checkup. VD clinics test for gonorrhea and other venereal diseases, often without charge. Routine checks for gonorrhea and syphilis are important for sexually active persons, especially women. However, it should be emphasized that increasing numbers of men are contracting gonorrhea without the warning symptoms.

SYPHILIS

Although syphilis is not as widespread a disease as gonorrhea, it is more serious because of the extensive damage that it can do when untreated. It may affect any of the body's organs when in the late stage. The diagnosis of syphilis is difficult because symptoms at various stages resemble the symptoms of other diseases [2].

Transmission of Syphilis

Syphilis is highly contagious for about the first year of the disease, if untreated. It is most commonly passed from one person to another through vaginal, anal, or oral-genital inter-course. It can travel from one partner to the other through the intact skin of the sexual organs. A man wearing a condom can contract syphilis from his partner, "since the organism can enter at the junction of the penis and the rest of the body" [2, p. 29]. The syphilitic rash is also highly contagious. Within a few hours after the organisms enter the body, they are carried by the bloodstream to all parts of the body.

Stages and Symptoms of Syphilis

Primary Syphilis. Around three or four weeks after exposure to syphilis (or as early as ten days or late as three months), a chancre or sore appears on the body at the point of entry of the organism. On a man it is usually on the glans of the penis, but it may be elsewhere. A woman who has had vaginal intercourse usually does not notice the chancre, since it usually develops on her cervix or vaginal walls. Many women, therefore, are not aware when they have primary syphilis unless informed by their sexual partners.

When the chancre first appears, it is a dull red bump about as large as a pea. The bump's surface becomes eroded, and the chancre becomes a dull red, open sore that may be covered by a scab. The chancre does not hurt, and does not bleed easily. It may have a rubbery pink border. If left untreated, the chancre heals by itself within one to five weeks after its appearance [2].

Secondary Syphilis. The infected person continues to infect his sexual partners, even when symptoms do not exist. The disease usually progresses to its second stage about six months after exposure, when a skin rash develops. The rash is extremely contagious to other people. It may not be obvious or may not appear at all. Nevertheless, the syphilitic person is still able to infect others.

Latent Syphilis. If secondary syphilis is not treated, it may become dormant or hidden for many years. About a year after the initial infection, the individual is no longer infectious to others, with one exception. A pregnant woman passes the disease to her fetus.

Late Syphilis. A number of years after exposure, the untreated individual may develop a number of complications, including heart disease, blindness, paralysis, insanity, and other serious complications.

Treatment of Syphilis

A complete physical examination should be given to persons who believe that they may have syphilis. If sores or a rash exist, fluid taken from them are examined under a microscope. For years, blood tests have been given routinely to persons applying for marriage licenses in most states. Such a test is required in all but two states.

As with gonorrhea, the first choice in antibiotics to treat syphilis is penicillin (though a different type than the type used to treat gonorrhea), and the second choice is tetracycline.

VENEREAL HERPES

A venereal disease extremely dangerous to an infant born by normal delivery to an infected woman is venereal herpes. Unless born by caesarian section, such infants are likely to suffer severe brain damage [3].

The organism that causes herpes is similar to the virus that causes cold sores. The disease may be spread through sexual contact, although such contact with an infected individual does not always result in infection, and persons who have avoided sexual contact may become infected [4].

Symptoms of Herpes

In the male, small blisters usually occur on the outside of the penis or in the urethra. In a female, the blisters may be external, but are usually on the cervix or vaginal walls. Although they may be painful, the blisters are often not noticeable. The blisters break down, becoming eroded sores.

Treatment of Herpes

A person who develops herpes sores should wash the infected area, if it is external, with soap and water. A cream such as zinc oxide ointment may be applied as a salve. The sores will disappear in two weeks to a month.

OTHER VENEREAL DISEASES

Both men and women may develop irritating genital diseases that may be spread through sexual contact or other means (such as a washcloth) as well. These diseases may be confused with gonorrhea and often develop in conjunction with it. In the male, the disease is known as *urethritis* (inflammation of the urethra), and in the female, *vaginitis* (inflammation of the vagina). The affected area burns or itches, and there may be an abnormal discharge from the male's urethra or female's vagina. Females may have itching or burning sores on the clitoris, inner lips, vestibule, cervix, or vagina. Urethritis and vaginitis are caused by a number of different organisms, and treatment for the different organisms varies. Therefore, medical examination and diagnosis are essential.

CONCLUSIONS

Venereal diseases are usually spread by sexual contact, and vary in severity from being merely annoying to causing severe injury or death. Ignorance is the biggest factor in the spread of venereal disease, which is reaching epidemic proportions. The person who believes that he or she is infected with any kind of venereal disease should seek immediate medical attention and should inform his sexual partners when a disease is confirmed. Sexual contact should be avoided until the disease is cured.

By law, all information regarding the patient's condition is kept confidential. In all states but Wisconsin, it is unlawful for authorities to inform parents that their children, minor or otherwise, have a venereal disease. Most states have free VD clinics. To find out the laws and availability of clinics in a particular state, the reader should contact the state health service.

REFERENCES

1. Altman, Lawrence K. Some gonorrhea in men lacks sign. *New York Times,* January 20, 1974.
2. Cherniak, Donna and Allan Feingold. *VD Handbook.* Montreal: Handbook Collective, 1972.
3. Leger, Richard R. Viral venereal disease is highly contagious and doesn't go away. *Wall Street Journal,* April 19, 1974.
4. McLaughlin, J. D. Personal Communication. May, 1975.

appendix F

glossary

Adolescence—Socially defined time of life, beginning with a biological event (pubescence) but ending when adulthood begins.

Ambisexual—See bisexual.

Ampulla—Enlargement in vas deferens in which sperm are stored.

Annulment (of marriage)—Declaration by the court or church that a valid marriage between two particular persons never existed.

Attachment—An enduring tendency to seek the presence of and to make and keep contact with a particular other.

Basic conflict—Conflict over basic values.

Behavioral modification—The gradual changing of response patterns through the planned use of reinforcements.

Bisexual—An individual who is sexually attracted to members of both sexes.

Bond—A tie that exists when a value of the individual is felt by him to be fostered by association or interaction with another person or group.

Caste—Unit of stratification in a society wherein individual mobility is not allowed.

Cervix—End of the uterus that opens during the labor process.

Chromosome—A body within the cell carrying the material of heredity. Each egg and each sperm carries twenty-three chromosomes.

Circumcision—Surgical removal of the foreskin on the penis (or on the clitoris, in the case of the female).

Class—Unit of stratification in a society in which individual mobility is allowed.

Climacteric—See menopause.

Clitoris—The female homolog of the penis; the most sensitive part of female anatomy.

Cohabitation—The state of an unmarried, heterosexual couple sharing a bedroom.

Coitus—Sexual intercourse.

Co-marital sex—Extramarital sexual relationships based on mutual agreement of spouses.

Communication—The sending and receiving of messages in a social context through the use of words and nonverbal behavior.

Congruent message—A message conveyed through the use of words and nonverbal cues, both of which give the receiver the same meaning.

Conjugal family—Nuclear family in which the husband-wife relationship is of primary importance.

Connotative meaning—The implied meaning of a word; its emotional overtones.

Consanguine family—Family held together by ''blood'' ties.

Control—The setting of limits; curtailing child's autonomy; demanding compliance.

Correlation—When two conditions or events vary together.

   Positive correlation—When one variable increases, so does the other.

   Negative correlation—When one variable increases, the other decreases.

Couvade—Practice among some peoples in which a man, preceding the birth of his child, imitates the mother's pregnancy, the birth of the child and recovery from giving birth. He complains of, and probably experiences, labor pains.

Crescive bond—A growing bond.

Crisis—That which occurs when a sudden, highly significant change produces a situation that cannot be handled effectively.

Demographic information—Vital statistics, such as birthdate, place of birth, marital status, nationality of parents.

Denotative meaning—The meaning of a word as defined in the dictionary, devoid of emotional overtones.

Embryo—The unborn individual, prior to the eighth week after conception.

Empathy—Ability to accurately perceive another's feelings, without forgetting that the feelings are the other's and not one's own.

Epididymis—Collection tube, located in the testis, through which sperm pass after they are produced in the seminiferous tubules.

Extended family—A family consisting of two or more nuclear units living in one home.

Fallopian tubes—Tubes through which ova pass from the ovaries to the uterus.

Family career—A series of experiences of a particular type that begin at one time and end at another, such as the marital career and the parent-child career.

Family development—The changes that take place in a nuclear family during the span of its existence. The changes that take place as a family continues, generation after generation.

Family life cycle—Processes of family development that repeat in one generation after another.

Family of orientation—The family consisting of an individual's parents and siblings.

Family of procreation—The family consisting of an individual's spouse and children.

Fecund—Capable of producing children.

Fetus—The unborn individual, from the eighth week after conception until birth.

Foreskin—Loose ring of skin covering the glans of an uncircumcized penis (or clitoris, in the case of the female).

Gender identity—The conviction that one is a boy (man) or girl (woman).

Gender role—Behavior patterns that are culturally acceptable as sex-appropriate.

Gene—The functional unit of heredity, a segment of a chromosome.

Generativity—An investment of oneself and one's resources in the development of the next generation; a caring for ongoing creativity.

Genitalia—Sex organs.

Glans—The knob-like head of the clitoris, in the case of the female, or penis, in the case of the male.

Gonads—Sex glands (see also *ovary, testis*).

Heterosexual—An individual who is attracted to and possibly has sexual relations with members of the opposite sex.

Homogamy—Like marrying like.

Homosexual—An individual who is attracted to and possibly has sexual relations with only members of the same sex.

Hymen—Fold of tissue partly or completely sealing the vagina of most virgins.

Incongruent message—A verbal message accompanied by nonverbal cues that do not give the same meaning.

Infant—The human young from birth to two years of age.

In love—Includes feelings that accompany attachment behavior, efforts to attain and keep proximity to the loved one, and sexual response.

Kin—Relatives, both "blood" relatives and those acquired through marriage or legal adoption.

Kinship web—The particular pattern of connections with kin that each nuclear unit establishes and maintains.

Labia majora—Outer lips of the vulva.

Labia minora—Inner lips of the vulva, joining at the clitoris.

Legal separation—Agreement, affirmed by a court, for a married couple to live apart under specified conditions.

Lesbian—Female homosexual.

Lineage family—The family over generations.

Management—The setting of goals and the process of organizing, directing, and using resources in order to reach those goals.

Marital success—Although sometimes used to mean the same as "marital happiness," in this book marital success refers to undivorced marriages.

Market income—Barter and cash.

Masturbation—Sexual stimulation, usually referring to self-stimulation.

Matrilineal family—Family headed by a female; descent is traced through the female line.

Menarche—First menstruation.

Menopause—Cessation of menstruation.

Menstruation—Sloughing off of blood-rich uterine lining.

Mons veneris—Small mound of fatty tissue over the pubic bone.

Negative reinforcement—An event followed by a response that terminates the event or that makes its recurrence less likely.

Nuclear family—Father, mother, and children.

Nurturant socialization—Care and teaching of another (usually an infant or child) that nurtures. The implication of nurturant socialization is love.

Nurture—To promote the development of, by providing nourishment, support, encouragement, and so forth.

Orgasm—Peak of sexual excitement.

Ovaries—Female gonads that produce ova in the mature female before menopause and hormones through her lifetime.

Oviducts—See Fallopian tubes.

Ovulation—Release of an ovum by the ovary.

Ovum (*plural* **ova**)—Egg, female sex cell.

Pair-bond—Special kind of attachment between two people who sees themselves as a couple.

Partnership love—A mutual love, consisting of being in love, care, responsibility, respect, and knowledge.

Patrilineal family—Family, headed by a male; descent is traced through the male line.

Penis—Male sex organ.

Polyandry—Marriage of one woman to more than one man.

Polygamy—Marriage of one individual to more than one spouse. (See also *polyandry* and *polygyny*.)

Polygyny—Marriage of one man to more than one woman.

Positive reinforcement—An event that increases the probability that a certain response will recur.

Prenatal—Before birth.

Propinquity—Closeness in terms of space. When applied to partner selection, it means people tend to marry those who live close to them.

Prostate gland—A gland surrounding the neck of the bladder and urethra in the male.

Puberty—Period of development at which sexual maturity is reached.

Puberty rites—Ceremonies that mark the passage from child to adult status.

Pubescence—Series of bodily changes preceding puberty, lasting about two years.

Punishment—That event that makes a person hurt or unhappy.

Quid pro quo—(literally, "something for something") Reciprocal behavior patterns that develop when two people associate closely with one another over a period of time.

Real income—Goods, services, social income, market income.

Rite de passage—Ceremony that marks an important period or change in a person's life.

Role—Behavior expected of a person who occupies a position. Roles are reciprocal (mother-daughter), and an individual has many roles (mother, teacher, wage-earner, friend, daughter, etc.).

Romantic love—Love based on a complex of beliefs, attitudes, and values including mystery, uniqueness, influence of fate, beauty, symbols, and jealousy.

Scrotum—Loose sack of skin located behind the penis and containing the testes.

Semen—Sperm-containing fluid.

Seminal vesicles—Paired structures opening into the urethra in the male.

Sense of integrity—Feeling of belonging in time and space, and in one's personal and social relationships; a conviction that one's life is meaningful, and an absence of any strong desire to have lived it differently.

Sense of intimacy—The capacity for knowing another person deeply and allowing oneself to be known deeply in a mutual relationship.

Sexually open marriage—Marriage of individuals who grant each other permission to have sexual and emotional relationships with others.

Sibling—Brother or sister.

Social income—Facilities provided by the community or environment, such as parks, schools, police protection, libraries.

Socialization—The process of learning a society's culture: values, behaviors, attitudes, knowledge, skills.

Sperm—Male sex cells.

Spousefree parent—An unmarried person who chooses to become a parent.

Status, ascribed—A status that a person acquires by right, as opposed to earning it. A child born to a king is a prince or princess. By contrast, one must earn the nonascribed status of doctor.

Structure of a family—Pattern of positions and roles in the family.

Sympathy—"Feeling with" another person; feeling the same as another, and (in contrast to *empathy*) not recognizing a difference between the feelings of other and self.

Testis (*plural:* **Testes**)—Male gonad or sex gland that produces both sperm and hormones.

Testosterone—A hormone produced by the testes in males, and by the adrenal gland in both sexes. It is the predominantly male hormone.

Urethra—Passageway from the bladder to the urethral opening, conducting urine in both female and male. In the male, the urethra also carries semen.

Uterus—The hollow organ in the female in which the young develops during gestation.

Vagina—Female organ of sexual intercourse; also *birth canal*.

Vas deferens (*plural:* **vasa deferentia**)—Tubes that carry the sperm from the testes to the base of the penis.

Vestibule—Area between the clitoris and the vaginal opening.

Virgin—A male or female not experienced in having coitus.

Vulva—External female sex organ, consisting of the mons veneris, labia minora and majora, clitoris, vestibule, and vaginal opening.

Wet dream—Ejaculation of semen during sleep.

author index

Entries in *italics* refer to pages on which bibliographic references are given.

Ackerman, N. W., 419, *442*
Adams, B. N., 268, *271*
Ademowore, A. S., 321, *347*
Adler, A., 283, *297*
Ainsworth, M. D. S., 32, 33, *52, 53,* 73, *79,* 329, *347*
Aldous, J., 87, *104*
Aldridge, D., 195, *199*
Aleksandrowicz, M. K., 376, *379*
Alexander, J., 238, 247, *249*
Alexander, J. F., 311, *316*
Altman, D., 462, *477*
Ames, E. W., 11, *24*
Andersen, E., 255, *271*
Anderson, S., 212, 213, 214, *220*
Andres, D., 72, *79*
Anspach, D. F., 278, *298*
Apoko, A., 281, *297*
Apple, D., 286, *297*
Ard, B. N., 68, *78*
Arena, J. M., 341, *347,* 355, *379*
Arnott, C., 204, *219*
Aronson, E., 150, *171*

Bach, G. R., 69, *78,* 436, *442*
Bahr, H., 426, *444*
Bain, J. K., 234, *250*

Bakan, D., 91, 92, *104*
Bales, R., 211, *220*
Balswick, J., 113–16, *138*
Barber, K. E., 195, *199*
Bard, M., 436, 437, *442*
Bardwick, J. M., 396, *410*
Bartell, G. D., 123, 130, *136,* 460, 461, *477*
Baumrind, D., 72, *79,* 257, *271,* 313, *316*
Bayer, A., 191, *199*
Beach, F. A., 15, *24,* 30, *52,* 95, 99, *104,* 106, 107, 129, *136,* 227, *249*
Beckwith, L., 264, *271*
Bee, H. L., 264, *272*
Beecher, E., 460, *477*
Belcher, J. C., 331, *347*
Bell, R., 114, 117, *136*
Berardo, F., 426, *442*
Berelson, B., 355, 356, *379*
Berg, A., 345, *347*
Berger, B., 458, 461, *477*
Berger, D., 206, *219*
Berger, S., 280, *299*
Berkowitz, L., 437, *442*
Bermudez, M. V., 357, *380*
Bernard, J., 215, 216, *219*
Berscheid, E., 150, 151, *171*
Bigner, J. J., 278, 283, *297*

513

Biller, H. B., 86–88, *104*, 258, 264, *271*
Birdwhistell, R. L., 55, 61, *78*
Block, J. H., 87, *104*
Block, J. L., 373, *380*
Blood, R. O., 118, *137, 157, 171,* 205, 211, 218, *219, 220*
Bock, E. W., 218, *219,* 426, 427, *442*
Bohannon, P., 427, 431, *442*
Bohn, C. J., 231, 235, *249*
Boll, E. S., 278, 281, 282, *297*
Bolton, C. D., 170, *171*
Bortner, R. W., 231, 235, *249*
Bossard, J. H. S., 278, 281, 282, *297*
Boston Woman's Health Book Collective, 132, 133, *136*
Bouvier, L., 350–52, *380*
Bowlby, J., 32, *53*
Boyd, R. R., 286, *297*
Brickman, P., 259, *272*
Briggs, K., 187, *200*
Britton, J., 65, *78*
Broderick, C., 96, *104,* 157, 160, *171*
Brody, J., 123, *136*
Bromley, D. B., 423, *443*
Brown, C. T., 61, 62, 74, 75, 77, *78*
Brown, E., 428, *443*
Brownfield, E. D., 63, *79*
Bruning, F., 429, 430, *443*
Bryan, J. H., 259, 260, *271, 272*
Buerkle, J., 117, *136*
Burchinal, L. G., 195, *199*
Burgess, E., 118, *136,* 175, *199,* 205, *219*
Burgess, J. K., 431, *443*
Burr, W. R., 233, 234, *249*
Busse, P., 257, *271*
Busse, T. V., 257, *271*
Butler, E. W., 419, *444*
Butterworth, C. E., 364, *380*
Byrne, D., 43, *52,* 148, 150, 151, *171*

Callwood, J., 399, 400, 405, *411*
Cannon, K. L., 109, 115, 116, 118, *136,* 205, *221,* 234, *250*
Capel, W. C., 423, *443*
Capellanus, A., 45, *52*
Capetta, M., 191, 192, *200*
Caplan, G., 414, 419, *443*
Carkhuff, R. R., 414, *443*
Carlier, A., 44, *52*
Carpenter, G., 116, 117, *136*
Carter, H., 165, *171,* 430, *443*
Carter, L. M., 217, 218, *221*

Catton, W. R., 145, *171*
Cavior, N., 150, *171*
Chancellor, L. E., 195, *199*
Chaskes, J., 114, *136*
Chesser, E., 463, *477*
Cheung, Y. M., 81, *104,* 123, *136*
Chilman, C. S., 11, 13, *24,* 88, *104,* 353, 356, *380,* 433, *443*
Christensen, H. T., 109, 114–117, *136,* 192, 195, *199,* 206, *219*
Christopherson, V., 438, *445*
Cicirelli, V. G., 280, *297*
Clar, J. S., 423, *443*
Clark, A. B., 292, *297*
Clellan, F. A., 106, 107, 130, *137*
Cohen, J., 238, 247, *249*
Cole, C., 460, 461, *477*
Collard, R. R., 284, *297*
Combs, R. H., 151, *172*
Conrad, C. C., 359–65, *380*
Constantine, J. M., 459, *477*
Constantine, L. L., 459, *477*
Consumer Reports, 367, *379*
Conte, H., 44, *53*
Corrales, R., 68, *79*
Courey, N. C., 321, *347*
Coursin, D., 321, *347*
Cox, F. D., 96, *104*
Cozby, P., 145, *173*
Crandall, E. W., 315, *316,* 388, 394, 406, *410*
Crawford, S. H., 431, *443*
Cromwell, R. E., 345, *347*
Croog, S. H., 416, *443*
Crouse, B., 197, *199*
Cuber, J. F., 69, *78,* 175, *199,* 428, *443*
Cutler, B., 69, *78*
Cutright, P., 194, 196, *199,* 205, *219,* 242, *249*

Dairy Council, 325, 337, *347*
Danzger, B., 253, *272*
Davis, K. E., 115, *137,* 181, *199,* 214, *220*
Davis, P., 117, *136*
Dawson, J. L. M., 81, *104,* 123, *136*
Day, B., 196, *199*
DeFee, F. F., 275, *297*
DeForest, E., 71, *79*
deLissovoy, V., 191, 200
Denfield, D., 461, *477*
Demos, J., 266, *271*
Depner, C., 129, *138*
Desmond, A., 351, *380*
Deutscher, I., 216, *219*

Dion, K. L., 41, *52*, 150, 151, *171*
Dixon, M., 391, *410*
Dobring, A., 187, *200*
Dokecki, P. R., 150, *171*
Doten, D., 154, 155, *172*
Douey, J., 150, *173*
Duchowny, M. S., 253, *271*
Dullea, G., 428, 431, *443*
Dunsing, M. M., 387, *410*
Duvall, E. M., 17, *24*, 197, *200*, 291, *297*
Dyer, W., 69, *78*

Edwards, M., 469, *478*
Ehrhardt, A. A., 81, 86, *104, 105*
Ehrlich, C., 206, *219*
Eiduson, B. T., 238, 241, *249*
Elder, J. F., 279, *297*
Elkin, M., 427, *443*
Ellis, A., 459, *478*
Emmerich, W., 266, 267, *271*
Epstein, A., 124, *136*
Erhard, D., 326, 327, *347*
Erikson, E. H., 36, 38, 39, *53*, 113, *136*, 290, *297*
Estellachild, V., 458, *478*

Fagot, B. I., 88, *104*
Farber, B., 282, *298*
Farley, F. H., 275, *298*
Farrell, W. H., 91, *104*
Fassler, J., 431, *443*
Feldman, H., 17, *24*, 234, 236, *250*, 324, *347*
Feldman, M., 17, *24*, 324, *347*
Ferreira, A. J., 309, 310, *317*
Ferrell, M. M., 84, *105*
Field, S., 208, *220*
Figley, C. R., 205, *221*, 234, *250*
Fish, K. D., 88, *104*
Fishel, C., 332, *348*
Fisher, E. O., 427, 428, *443*
Fisher, P., 462, *477*
Ford, C. S., 15, *24*, 95, 99, *104*, 106, 107, 129, *136*
Fotheringham, J. B., 418, *443*
Francke, L., 457, *478*
Fraser, G., 403, *410*
Frejka, T., 354, *380*
Friedan, B., 125, 126, *136*, 239, *250*
Friesen, E. C., 399, 407, *410*
Friis, H., 286, *299*
Frisch, R. E., 97, *104*, 323, *347*
Fromm, E., 33, 38, 39, *53*
Furstenberg, F. R., 153, *172*

Gallese, L. R., 333, *347*, 471, *478*
Gallup, G., 117, *136*, 367, *380*
Gangel, J. L., 345, *347*
Gauger, W., 389, *410*
Gebhard, P. H., 102, *105*, 112, 132, *137*
Gelles, R., 255, *272*
Gibran, K., 50, *53*
Gibson, G., 293, *298*
Gifford-Jones, W., 132, *137*
Gil, D. G., 255, *272*
Gillespie, D., 211, *219*
Glaser, B., 426, *443*
Glasser, P., 435, *445*
Glenn, N., 217, *219*
Glick, P. C., 10, *24*, 165, *171*, 190, 192, 196, 197, *200*, 215, 216, *219*, 222, *250*, 430, *443*, 464, *478*
Goldsmith, B., 423, *443*
Gomez, B. M., 357, *380*
Goode, W. J., 128, *137*, 428, 435, *443*
Gordon, A. I., 166, *172*
Gordon, M., 44, *53*
Gordon, T., 72, *79*
Gottlieb, D., 439, *443*
Gould, R. E., 119, *137*
Graham, F. R., 399, 407, *410*
Green, R., 123, *137*
Gregg, C., 109, 114, 115, *136*, 206, *219*
Griffitt, W., 43, *52*, 150, *172*
Gross, I. H., 315, *316*, 388, 394, 406, *410*
Gurin, G., 208, *220*
Gusdorf, G., 75, *79*

Hackett, B., 458, 461, *477*
Hafstrom, J. L., 387, *410*
Hager, D., 116, *139*
Haley, J., 76, *79*
Hamblin, R., 118, *137*
Hammond, B., 111, *137*, 157, *172*, 205, 211, 219, *220*
Handler, P., 339, 341, *347*
Handlon-Lathrop, B., 414, *443*
Hanks, C., 35, *53*
Hansell, N., 414, *443*
Harlan, W. H., 423, *444*
Harris, T., 72, *79*
Harrison, N., 111, *137*
Harroff, P. B., 69, *78*, 175, 199, 428, *443*
Hartley, R. E., 126, 130, *137*
Hartup, W. W., 437, *444*
Harvey, C. D., 426, *444*
Hatcher, R. A., 359–65, *380*

Havemann, E., 358, 359, 365, *380*
Havighurst, R. J., 424, *444*
Hays, W. C., 287, *298*
Hawkins, J., 207, *220*
Heath, L. L., 234, *250*
Heer, D., 211, *220*
Heinsohn, A., 439, *443*
Henshell, A-M., 461, *478*
Henze, L., 203, 213, *220*
Herman, R. D., 160, *172*
Herzog, E., 433, 434, *444*
Hetherington, E. M., 88, *105*
Hetzel, A., 191, 192, *200*
Hickey, L. A., 290, *298*
Hickey, T., 290, *298*
Hicks, M., 203, 204, 206, 209, 217, *220*
Hill, R., 232, *250*, 270, *272*, 292, *298*, 307, 309, 313, 314, *316*, 386, *410*
Hillsdale, P., 164, *172*
Himelstein, P., 275, *297*
Hobart, C. W., 69, *79*, 109, 114, 116, *137*
Hoddinott, B. A., 418, *443*
Hoffman, L. W., 232, *250*
Hogan, R., 33, *53*, 73, *79*
Hohn, R. L., 233, *250*
Hollingshead, A. B., 165, *172*
Holstein, C. E., 258, *272*
Hornick, J., 113–16, 118, *137*
Horwitz, A., 323, *347*
Houlihan, N. B., 157, *172*
Howard, D., 206, *220*
Huang, L. J., 109, 116, *137*, 214, *220*
Hudson, J., 203, 213, *220*
Hugins, W., 258, *272*
Hultsch, D. F., 231, 235, *249*
Humphreys, L., 122, *137*
Hunt, D., 266, *272*
Hunt, M., 130, 131, *137*
Hunter, H. H., 335, *347*
Hurley, J. R., 233, *250*
Hurley, L. S., 324, 325, *347*
Hutt, C., 81, 82, 84, *105*, 123, *137*
Hutt, S. J., 123, *137*

Ibsen, C. A., 295, *298*
Illsley, R., 223, *250*

Jackson, D. D., 54, 57, *79*, 182, 197, *200*
Jackson, J. J., 211, *220*, 270, *272*, 382, *410*
Jacob, T., 312, *316*
Jacoby, S., 464, *478*
Jaffe, F. S., 357, *380*

Jankowski, J. J., 263, *273*
Jensen, M. S., 123, *138*
Johnson, V., 99, 101, 102, *105*, 132, *138*
Jolly, A., 9, *24*, 30, 35, *53*, 70, *79*
Jones, S., 438, 439, *444*

Kaats, G. R., 115, *137*
Kahana, B., 288, *298*
Kahana, E., 288, *298*
Kando, T., 128, *137*
Kannin, E., 206, *220*
Kantner, J., 114, 116, *137*
Kaplan, H. S., 100, *105*
Karlins, M., 197, *199*
Karlsson, G., 69, *79*
Kasl, S. V., 333, *347*
Katz, R., 63, *79*
Keller, H., 55, *79*
Kempster, S. W., 419, *442*
Kenkel, W., 151, *172*
Kephart, W., 151, *172*, 430, *444*, 459, *478*
Kertesz, A., 83, *105*
Khatri, A. A., 11, *24*
Kime, J. S., 321, *347*
King, C. D., 234, *250*
King, K., 113–16, *138*
Kinsey, A., 102, *105*, 112, 118, 132, *137*
Kinzer, N. S., 229, 246, *250*
Klausner, W., 69, *79*
Klemer, R. H., 206, *220*
Kline, R. W., 359–65, *380*
Klobus, P., 295, *298*
Knapp, J. J., 461, *478*
Knight, A. C., 440, *444*
Knoll, M. M., 315, *316*, 388, 394, 406, *410*
Koch, H., 278, 282, *298*
Kogan, B., 120, 121, *137*
Kohlberg, L., 258, *272*
Komarovsky, M., 69, *79*, 118, 128, *137*
Krogman, W. M., 330, *347*
Kuhlen, R., 157, *172*

Ladner, J., 111, *137*, 157, *172*
LaLeche League International, 373, *380*
Landers, D. M., 275, *298*
Landis, J. T., 291, 292, *298*, 431, 438, *444*
Landis, M. G., 291, 292, *298*
Langer, J. W., 367, *380*
Lau, T. S., 81, *104*, 123, *136*
LaVeck, G. D., 323, *347*
LaVoie, J. C., 73, *79*, 258, *272*
Lawler, E. E., 384, *410*

Laws, J. L., 202, *220*
LeBow, M., 422, *444*
Lederer, W. J., 57, 64, *79*, 182, 197, *200*
Lee, E., 350, 351, *380*
Lee, P. C., 88, 90, *105*
Leger, R. R., 337, *347*
Lei, T-J., 419, *444*
LeShan, E., 431, *444*
Levine, S., 416, *443*
Levinger, G., 209, *220*
Lewis, O., 152, *172*
Liberman, D., 280, *299*
Liebermann, M., 425, *444*
Lifton, R. J., 426, 441, *444*
Lipetz, M., 214, *220*
Lipman, A., 218, *220*
Lipson, A., 416, *443*
Lobsenz, N., 213, *220*
Locke, H. J., 69, *79*, 175, *199, 200*
London, O., 148, 151, *171*
Long, R., 109, 115, 116, 118, *136*
Lonner, T. D., 18, *24*
Looft, W. R., 73, *79*, 258, *272*
Lopata, H. Z., 426, 427, *444*
Lorenz, K. Z., 30, *53*
Lott, B. E., 228, *250*
Lozoff, M., 109, 114, 115, 126, *138, 159, 172*
Luckey, E. B., 234, *250*
Lunneborg, P. W., 280, *298*
Lynch, V., 340, *347*
Lyness, J., 214, *220*

Mace, D. R., 474, *478*
Macklin, E., 203, 213, *220*, 291, *298*
Macorory, B., 167, *172*
McAllister, R. J., 419, *444*
McCabe, G. S., 332, *348*
McClain, D., 148, *173*
McCormick, T., 167, *172*
McDonald, C., 245, *250*
McGinnis, R., 167, *172*
McGlone, J., 83, *105*
McIntire, W., 206, *220*
McKain, J. L., 439, *444*
McKain, W., 196, *200*
McLaughlin, J. D., 337, *347*
Madsen, C., 67, *79*
Mann, P., 431, *444*
Martens, R., 275, *298*
Martin, C. E., 102, *105*, 112, 118, 132, *137*
Maslow, A., 174, *200*, 457, *478*
Mason, G., 150, *173*

Masters, W., 99, 101, 102, *105*, 132, *138*
Matteson, R., 73, *79*
Maugh, T., 366, *380*
Mayo, J., 125, *138*
Mead, M., 35, 47, *53*, 144, *172*, 210, *220*, 372, *380*
Mead, R. D., 232, *250*
Mealiea, W. D., 275, *298*
Mehrabian, A., 59, *79*
Meissner, H. M., 192, *199*
Melton, A. M., 100, *105*
Mendkoff, E., 440, *444*
Meredith, D., 87, *104*
Metropolitan Life, 224, *250*, 286, *298*, 318, 336, *348*
Michelson, W., 327, 333, *348*
Midlarksy, E., 259, *272*
Milhhoj, P., 286, *299*
Millar, M., 458, 461, *477*
Miller, B. C., 109, *138*
Miller, S., 68, *79*
Mindel, C. H., 287, *298*
Mirande, A., 116, *138*
Mitchell, E., 90, *105*
Monahan, T. P., 166, *172*, 195, 196, *200*, 215, *220*, 427, *444*
Money, J., 86, *105*
Montgomery, J. E., 217, 218, *221, 332, 348*
Moorhead, F. L., 359–65, *380*
Moran, R., 464, *478*
Moreau de St. Mary, M., 154, *172*
Morgan, E. S., 47, *53*
Moskin, J. R., 246, *250*
Mumaw, C. R., 306, *316*
Murdock, G. P., 16, *24*
Murstein, B. I., 151, 169, *172*

Nass, G., 206, *220*
Navran, L., 69, *79*
Neugarten, B. L., 287, 289, *298*, 423, 424, *444*
New York Times, 165, *172*, 197, *200*, 399, 404, *410*
Newcomb, T. M., 150, *172*
Newton, N., 372, *380*
Nichols, R., 306, *316*
Norton, A. J., 190, 192, 196, 197, *200*, 215, 216, *219*
Novgorodoff, B. D., 150, *172*
Nowili, S., 150, *172*
Nye, F. I., 431, *444*

O'Leary, V., 129, *138*
Olive, H., 277, *298*
Olson, D., 209, *220*
O'Neill, G., 130, *138*, 461, 462, *478*
O'Neill, N., 130, *138*, 461, 462, *478*
Oppong, C., 18, *24*, 384, *410*
Orthner, D., 207, *220*
Osofsky, H. J., 471, *478*
Osofsky, J. D., 253, *272, 471, 478*

Paddock, E., 449, *478*
Paddock, W., 449, *478*
Palson, C., 130, *138*, 461, *478*
Palson, R., 130, *138*, 461, *478*
Pam, A., 44, *53*
Panzini, M., 364, *380*
Parke, R. D., 72, *79*
Parkes, C. M., 426, 427, *444*
Parsons, T., 211, *220*
Patterson, G. R., 88, *104*
Pattison, J., 464, *478*
Patty, R. A., 84, *105*
Paulsen, D. G., 399, 400, 403, *410*
Paynter, M., 306, *316*
Pedersen, F. A., 263, *273*
Perlman, D., 109, 114, 118, *138*
Peterman, D. J., 212–14, *220*
Peters, M. F., 432, *444*
Peters, S., 155, *172*
Planned Parenthood International, 365, 366, *380*
Plateris, A., 189, 195, 196, *200*, 214, 216, *221*, 430, *444*
Platt, M., 203, 204, 206, 209, 217, *220*
Pleck, J., 124, 129, *139*
Plonk, M. A., 306, *316*
Plutchik, R., 44, *53*
Pohlman, E., 233, *250*
Pomeroy, W. B., 102, *105*, 112, 118, 132, *137*
Porter, G. H., 473, *478*
Porter, S., 185, *200*
Prabhu, P. H., 48, *53*
Pratt, L., 207, 209, 211, *221*, 313, *316*, 337, *348*
Prentice, N. M., 258, *272*
Price, D. Z., 306, 310, *316, 317*
Price-Bonham, B., 428, *445*
Prince, A. J., 167, *172*
Pringle, B. M., 474, *478*
Providence Journal-Bulletin, 166, *173*, 195, *199*
Purvis, G. A., 322, *348*
Pytkowicz, A. S., 264, *272*

Rader, B. J., 407, *410*
Radin, N., 435, *445*
Radl, S., 242, *250*
Ramey, C. T., 264, *273*
Ramey, J. W., 13, *24*, 130, *138*, 451, 458, 460, 461, *478*
Rebelsky, F., 35, *53*
Reeves, K., 148, 151, *171*
Reiss, I. L., 16, 22, *24*, 41, *53*, 108–10, 112, 113, 116, 117, *138*, 169, *173*
Reitz, W., 150, *173*
Renne, K. S., 205, 207, *221*, 234, *250*
Reusch, J., 76, *79*
Ridley, C. A., 204, 212–14, *220, 221*
Rimmer, R. H., 459, *479*
Robbins, J., 401, *410*
Robbins, N. N., 404, *410, 428, 445*
Roberts, A., 148, *173*
Robinson, B. C., 325, *348*
Robinson, I., 113–16, *138*
Rogers, C. R., 50, *53, 174, 200, 457, 478*
Rogoff, M., 235, *250*
Rohner, R. P., 253, *272*
Rolfe, D. J., 386, *410*
Rollins, B., 205, *221*, 234, *250*
Roper, B. S., 234, *250*
Rose, V., 428, *445*
Rosenberg, B. G., 167, *173*, 253, *272*, 278–80, 282, 283, *298, 299*
Rosenberg, G. S., 278, *298*
Rosenblatt, P., 145, *173*
Rosenthal, E., 165, *173*, 195, *200*
Rosenzweig, S., 81, *105*, 121, *138*
Ross, D. M., 89, 90, *105*
Ross, S. A., 89, 90, *105*
Rossi, A. S., 235, *250*
Rothman, D. J., 44, *53*
Rothman, S. M., 44, *53*
Rowe, M. P., 471, *479*
Rubenstein, J. L., 263, *273*
Rubin, Z., 43, 49, *53*
Russell, C. S., 226, 227, 235, *250*, 318, *348*

Sabagh, G., 69, *79*
Safilios-Rothschild, C., 209, 211, *221*
Santrock, J. W., 280, *299*
Satir, V., 60, *79*
Scanzioni, J., 183, *200*
Schacter, S., 275, *298*
Schaeffer, E. S., 265, *272*
Schlesinger, B., 13, *24*, 430, *445*
Schnucker, R. V., 372, *380*

Schooler, C., 275, *298*
Schroder, H., 197, *199*
Schuham, A. I., 310, *317*
Schulman, C. A., 340, *348*
Schulz, D., 175, *200*
Schvaneveldt, J. D., 473, *479*
Scott, J. F., 296, *298*
Seamans, B., 102, *105*
Sears, R. R., 284, *299*
Seligson, M., 186, *200*
Serbin, L., 89, *105*
Shanas, E., 286, *299*
Shank, R. E., 324, 330, *348*
Shideler, M. M., 468, *479*
Sidel, R., 247, *250,* 355, *380*
Siegelman, M., 257, *272*
Silverman, P., 427, *445*
Sindberg, R., 148, *173*
Singh, L., 232, *250*
Skarsten, S., 428, 430, *445*
Skidmore, C. J., 473, *479*
Slekton, M., 418, *443*
Smart, M. S., 234, *251, 258, 272,* 330, *348,* 421, *445*
Smart, R. C., 234, *251, 258, 272,* 330, *348*
Smircich, R. J., 145, *171*
Smith, D., 153, *173*
Smith, H. E., 11, *24*
Smith, R., 438, *445*
Smith, W. M., 156, *173*
Sorensen, R. C., 114, 116, 122, *138*
Spanier, G., 201, *221,* 332, *348,* 460, 461, *477*
Spence, D. L., 18, *24,* 325, *348*
Spitzer, S., 118, *138*
Sprey, J., 174, *200*
Staples, R., 111, 116, *138,* 211, *221*
Stass, A. W., 49, *53*
Staub, E. A., 259, *272,* 279, *299*
Stayton, D. J., 33, *53,* 73, *79*
Stefaniak, D., 150, *171*
Stehouwer, J., 286, *299*
Steinmetz, S. K., 436, 438, *445*
Sternglanz, S. H., 90, *105*
Steward, D., 264, *272*
Steward, M., 264, *272*
Stewart, C., 114–16, 128, *139*
Stewart, C. T., 423, *443*
Stewart, M. K., 88, *105*
Stinnett, N., 217, 218, *221,* 252, 257, *273,* 469, *478*
Stoetzer, L., 438, *444*
Stolz, L. M., 252, 266, *273*

Stratton, J., 118, *138*
Straus, M. A., 70, 75, *79,* 183, 200, 436–38, *445*
Strauss, A., 167, *173,* 426, *443*
Stroup, A., 194, *200*
Stuart, I. R., 196, *200*
Sudia, C. E., 13, *24,* 431, *445*
Sullivan, J. A., 167, *173*
Sussman, M. B., 408, *410*
Sutton-Smith, B., 123, *138,* 167, *173,* 253, 272, 278–80, 282, 283, *298, 299*
Swanson, H. D., 375, *380*

Talley, S., 257, *273*
Tanner, J. M., 98, *105*
Tanzer, D., 373, *380*
Taylor, R., 421, *445*
Teevan, J., Jr., 116, *138*
Teismann, M., 181, *200*
Terman, L. M., 205, *221*
Thomes, M. M., 69, *79*
Thompson, D. S., 399, 400, 403, *410*
Time, 460, *477*
Tobin, S., 424, *444*
Toronto Globe and Mail, 222–24, *250,* 352, *380*
Townsend, P., 286, *299*
Tresemer, D., 124, 129, *139*
Trethowan, W. H., 371, *380*
Troll, L. E., 268, *273,* 285, 286, *299*
Turner, R., 179, 180, *200*
Tyhurst, J. S., 440, 441, *445*

Udry, J. R., 16, *24*
Uhr, L. M., 201, *221*
United Nations, 286, *299,* 356, *380*
U.S. Bureau of the Census, 390, *411,* 424, 433, *445*
U.S. Department of Agriculture, 327, *348*
U.S. Department of Commerce, 390, 391, *411*
U.S. Department of Health, Education, and Welfare, 325, *348*

Van Riper, C., 61, 62, 74, 75, 77, *78*
Vandenberg, S. G., 165, *173*
Varni, C., 461, *479*
Vasquez-Calcerrada, P. B., 331, *347*
Veevers, J. E., 240, 243, *251,* 466, *479*
Vener, A., 114–16, 128, *139*
Veroff, J., 208, *220*
Vincent, C. E., 166, *173*
Vore, D. A., 322, *348*
Vygotsky, L. S., 74, *79*

Wackman, D., 68, 69, 78, *79*
Wadsworth, B., 46, *53*
Wake, F. R., 117, *139*
Walker, K. E., 204, *221,* 330, *348*
Wall Street Journal, 434, *445*
Waller, W., 156, *173*
Wallin, P., 118, *136,* 205, *219*
Walster, E., 150, 151, *171*
Walster, G. W., 150, 151, *171*
Walters, J., 252, 257, *273*
Walters, R. H., 72, *79*
Warren, J., 292, *297*
Watson, J. S., 263, *273*
Watts, J. C., 264, *273,* 456, *479*
Wedderburn, D., 286, *299*
Weinstein, K. K., 287, 289, *298*
Weiss, R. S., 238, *251*
Welter, B., 46, *53*
Wenger, M., 206, *219*
Wheeler, E. W., 37, *53*
White, B. L., 264, *273,* 456, *479*
Whitehurst, R. N., 167, *173*
Whiting, B., 125, *139,* 268, *273,* 275, *299*

Wiegand, E., 395, *411*
Willis, F. N., Jr., 49, *53*
Winter, W. D., 309, *317*
Witte, J. A., 335, *443*
Wodarczyk, M., 414, *443*
Wohlford, P., 280, *299*
Wolfe, D., 211, 218, *219*
Wolfgang, M. E., 437, *445*
Wolinsky, A. L., 88, 90, *105*
Worchel, P., 150, *171*
Wray, J., 352, *380*
Wyden, P., 69, *78,* 436, *442*

Yarrow, L. J., 263, *273*
Yeung, D., 364, *380*
Yue, F., 81, *104,* 123, *136*

Zimmerman, C. C., 15, *24*
Ziskin, J., 460, 461, *479*
Ziskin, M., 460, 461, *479*
Zolotow, C., 90, *105*
Zuker, M. A., 399, 400, 405, *411*

index of subjects

Abortion, 366–67, 401
Abstinence, sexual, 108–10
Abuse of children, 255–56, 403
Accidents, 338–39
Adaptation, 55–57
Adjustment
  divorce, 428
  illness, 417
  marital, 69–70
Adjustment and communication, 69–70
Adolescence, 237
Adolescent, 323–24, 330, 341
Adoption, 237–38, 402
Adult children, 237, 268–70
Adversaries, 282–84
Advertising, 42–43, 327–28
Affluence, 327–28
Agency, 91–92
Aggression, 258, 436–38
Age restrictions, 455–56
Aging, 132–35, 216–18, 423–25
Alcoholism, 422
Alternate families, 247
Altruism, 259
Ambisexuality, 118–19
Anal stage, 85
Androgyny, 471
Anger, 74–75
Annulment, 404

Anxiety, 74–75
Arranged marriage, 48
Assortative mating, 165–66
Astrology, 19, 167–68
Attachment, 29–35, 311
  behavior, 35, 38, 49–50
Attraction, 43–44
Authoritarian parents, 313
Authoritative parents, 312
Authority, 312

Bargaining, 181–82, 211–12
Basic sex, 492–96
Behavior modification, 421–22
Bereavement, 426–27
Birth, 192–94
  process, 371–75
  rates, 222–23
Birth control methods, 357–68
  abortion, 366–67
  chemical barriers, 360–62
  continence, 359
  coitus interruptus, 369
  historic, 358
  infanticide, 367–68
  intrauterine, 362–63
  mechanical, 360
  "natural," 358–59
  oral, 363–64

521

Birth control methods (*cont.*)
 rhythm, 359
 sterilization, 364–65
Bisexuality, 118–19
Black feminism, 125
Bonds, 178–81, 184
Brain, 321–22
 organization, 81–83
"Breaking up," 164
Breast feeding, 377–78
Broken family, 11
Budget, 497–99
Budgeting, 395–96
Bundling, 154–55

Care, 32–33, 35–36, 38–39, 311, 318, 393, 417
 behavior, 29–31
Career, family, 18
Caregiving, 255
Caste, 20–22
Casual sex, 47
Catharsis, 436–37
Child nurse, 280–81
Childbirth, 371–75
Childcare programs, 471–72
Childfree families, 466–67
Childlessness, 239–43
Childrearing, 71–73
 as family management, 312–13
 maladaptive, 434–35
Children
 and marital satisfaction, 205
 intended number of, 223–24
 marital problems centered in, 420–22
Chronic problems, 414
Clarification of messages, 65
Class, 208, 264
 social, 20–22
Clothing, 472
Codes of communication, 67–68
Cognitive theory, 92
Cohabitation, 203, 212–14, 291, 463–64
Co-marital sex, 130–31, 460–62
Commitment, 159–62
Common law marriage, 400
Communal family, 11, 13
Communes, 296, 457–59
Communication, 54–79, 131, 184, 305, 307, 310–11, 396
 defensive, 311
 nature of, 57–63
 problems in, 63–65

supportive, 311
 tactile, 70
Communion, 91–92
Community support systems, 420–22, 425, 432
Companionship, 207–208, 275–78
Compensation, 384
Competence, 264–65, 284
Computer dating, 147–48
Conception, 492
Concern with overpopulation, 243
Condoms, 360
Conflict, 182–84
 and communication, 69
Congruent messages, 58–59
Conjugal family, 9–10, 16
Connotative meaning, 60–61
Consanguine family, 11
Consciousness raising, 125–26
Contraception, 132, 163
 See also Birth control
Contraceptives, 401
Contracting-family stage, 17
Contracts, marriage, 407–408
Control, through communication, 76–77
Cooperation, infant, 33
Courtly love, 45
Credit, 394–96
Crises, 197, 412–22
 financial, 396–99
Crisis resolution, 414
Crushes, 96
Cultural differences, 94–95
Custody of children, 405
"Cute response," 35
Cycle, family, 18

Daily food guide, 500–501
Dating, 153–59
 computer, 147–48
Dating–rating complex, 156–57
Death, 425–27
Decision-making, 309–11
Defining a relationship, 76
Denotative meaning, 60–61
Dental care, 343–44
Dependence, 270
Desertion, 428–30
Deterrents to reproduction, 240–43
Developmental approach, 17–18
 problems, 420
Diaphragm, contraceptive, 360

Diets, unscientific, 326
Difficulties of parenthood, 244–46
Disadvantages of parenthood, 240–46
Disagreements, handling of, 69
Disasters, 440–41
Discipline, 72–73, 260–65
Discovery of others, 75
Disease prevention, 335–37
Disorganization, family, 432–41
Divorce, 189–99, 215–16, 404–405, 427–28
    counseling, 427
    friendly, 467–69
Dominance, 311
Double standard, 108–10, 153
Douching, 366
Dramatic play, 35
Drug use, 422–23
Drugs, 339–40
    for labor and childbirth, 376

Early childhood, 236
Early marriage, 291–92
Earning and producing, 387–93
Education for human living, 473–74
Educational programs, 315
Effective communication, 63–65
Electra complex, 85
Embryo, 369, 493
Empathy, 63–64
Engagement, 161–62, 194–95
Equality, 452
Evaluation, 308
Evolution of love, 29–31
Exercise, 328–30
Expanding-family stage, 17
Expense of childrearing, 241–42
Extended family, 11–12, 396–97
Extramarital sex, 95, 129–30
Eye contact, in love, 49

Family
    career, 18
    childfree, 466–67
    communal, 13
    communication in, 65–73
    conjugal, 9–10
    consanguine, 9–10
    cycle, 18
    development, 17–18
    dissolution, 425–32
    extended, 11–12
    forms, 450–52, 457–70

    homosexual, 14–15
    lifetime, 17
    lineage, 17–18, 313–15
    management, 162
    matrilineal, 11–12
    nuclear, 9–11
    of orientation, 5
    one-parent, 13–14, 432
    patrilineal, 11
    person-oriented, 66
    policy, 245–46
    status-oriented, 66
    structure, 8–15
    therapy, 419–20
Fathers, 34–35, 87, 264
Fears concerning parenthood, 242–43
Feelings in communication, 62–63
Female
    puberty, 96–98
    sexual anatomy, 495–96
    sexual response, 100–102
Feminism, 125, 126, 155
Fetus, 370, 493
Fictive kin, 295
Financial
    counseling, 406–407
    management, 381–99
    needs, 386–87
Food guide, 500–501
Fraternal societies, 296
Fraud, 404
Friendly divorce, 467–69
Friends and coworkers in love career, 36
Functions of families, 15–17

Gender role, 177–78, 280
    learning, 84–92, 123–24, 437
Genetic defects, 339
Genital stage, 85
Glossary, 508–512
Goals, 266, 310–11, 385–86
Going steady, 160
Gonorrhea, 502–504
Grandparents, 285–90
Group marriage, 459–60
Growth, 320–24, 457
Guilt, 112

Handicaps, 339
Happiness, 215–16
Harem, 12

Health, 207, 315–45
  education, 345
  planning, 162
  practices, 313
  services, 343–45, 475
Helping, 259
Hereditary defects, 163
Herpes, venereal, 505–506
Heterosexual love, 50
Heterosexuality, 118–19
Hindu view of love, 47–48
Home circle of love career, 34–35
Homemaker, 306–13
  support systems, 471–72
Homogamy, 164
Homosexual
  family, 14–15
  weddings, 188
Homosexuality, 118–22, 462–63
Honesty in communication, 66–67
Hormones, 84, 120
Hostility, 437
Housework, 241
Housing, 331–33
Human liberation, 8, 90–92, 129

Identity, sense of, 36, 113
Ignorance, 326
Illegitimacy, 402–403
Illness, 334–38
  mental, 419–20
  physical, 416–18
Immortality, 230
In-laws, 290–93
Income, 204–205
  distribution of, 390
  influences on, 390–91
  market, 388–90
  real, 388–90
  social, 390
Incongruent messages, 58–59
Individual differences in sexual response, 102–103
Individual disruption, 414–25
Individualism, 50–51
Individuality, 454–56
Ineffective communication, 63–65
Infant, 32, 320–23, 340–41
Infanticide, 13
Infatuation, 37
Infant–mother love, 31–34
Inferiority, 283

Infidelity, 113
Influence of children, 234–37, 252–53
Immunity, 335
Injury and disability, 416–18
Innovations, 451–52
Insurance, 398
Integrity, sense of, 290
Intended number of children, 223–24
Interaction of partners, 178–85
Intergeneration relationships, 290–93, 313–15
Interpersonal attraction, 148–50
Intimacy, 38–39
  and communication, 70

Jealousy, 181, 282–84
Job satisfaction, 204
Juvenile courts, 403

Kama Sutra, 47–48
Kibbutz, 13
Kin, 10, 88, 293–96
Knowledge, 38–39, 311

Lactation, 324
Lamaze method of childbirth, 372–73
Language, 54–55
Latency, 85
Laws, concerning families, 400–406
Learning, 278–80
Legal
  help, 407
  management, 399–410
  reform, 464
  separation, 404
Life style, 309
Lifetime family, 17–18
Liking vs. loving, 44
Lineage family, 17–18, 313–15
Living together, 203
Love, 7, 29–53, 115, 178, 307, 318, 393, 453
  career, 31–39
  for the Puritans, 45–46
  for the Victorians, 46
  in India, 47–48
  in the ancient world, 44–45
  in the South Seas, 46–47
  in the West, 44–46
  marriage, 48
  regulation of, 49–50
  romantic, 41–43
Lovers, 33–39
  and spouses circle in love career, 36–39
  in various cultures, 39–48

Machismo, 229
Male, puberty, 98–99
    sexual anatomy, 493–94
    sexual response, 99–100
Malnutrition, 320–23
Management
    financial, 381–99
    household, 303–15, 319, 333
    legal, 399–410
Marital adjustment, 69–70
Marital problems centered in children, 420–22
Marital stability, 188–98
Marriage
    contracts, 407–408
    group, 459–60
    open, 461–62
    preparation for, 162
    stability, 191–98
    typology, 175–76
Masturbation, 95–96
Matchmaking, 145–48
Matrilineal family, 11–12
Media, 90
Menarche, 96–98
Menopause, 132–34
Mental illness, 419–20
Mental retardation, 418–19
Middle years, 292–93
Military families, 439–40
Mixed matches, 165–66, 195–96
Modeling of behavior, childhood, 262
Money, meanings of, 382–84
Monogamy, 95
Moral development, 258–65, 313
Mortality, 318, 320
Mortgages, 398
Mothers, 87–88, 264
Mourning, 426
Moving, 438–40
Mutuality, 38, 50–51

National Organization for Nonparents (NON), 243
Natural childbirth, 371–73
Needs, financial, 386–87
Negative reinforcement, 261–62
Neglect, 255–56
Neighborhood circle of love career, 35–36
Newborn, 32
No-fault divorce, 404–405
NON, 243

Nonlistening, 64–65
Nonsocial system, 19
Nonverbal communication, 57–58, 253–54
Nuclear family, 9–11
Nurturance, 257–58
Nutrition, 320–28, 344–45
    infant, 320–23
    prenatal, 320–23

Obedience, infant, 33
Obstetrical assistance, 375–76
Oedipus complex, 85
Old age, 325
One-parent family, 10, 11, 13–14, 430–32
Oneida Community, 13
Open marriage, 461–62
Oral stage, 85
Orgasm, 88, 100–102
Orientation, family of, 5

Pair-bonded, 38, 160
Parent–child career, 233–37
Parent education, 268
Parental
    growth, 235–37
    influence, 254–56
    role, 229
    teaching, 263–65
Parenthood, 222–51, 376–78
    as crisis, 226
Parents, 86–90, 144
    single, 238, 432
    spousefree, 464–66
Partner
    esteem, 206
    interaction, 178–85
    love, 38–39
    selection, 143–71
    selection, theories of, 166–70
Partnerhood, 174–221
    and pregnancy, 370–71
Partnership, 43
Patrilineal family, 11–12
Peers, 116
Permanence of marriage, 163–64
Permissiveness-with-affection, 108–10
Permissiveness-without-affection, 108–10
Person-oriented family, 66
Personality, 257–58
Phallic stage, 85
Planned communication, 68–69
Planning, 303–15, 394–99

Polyandry, 12–13
Polygamy, 12–13, 95
Polygyny, 12–13
Population, 349–57
    growth, 350–54
    policy and program, 354–59
Position in family, 8–9
Postmarital sex, 131
Poverty, 424, 426, 432–35
Power, 209–12, 217–18, 311–12, 384, 453
Pre-engagement, 161
Pregnancy, 324–25, 368–71
    and partnerhood, 370–71
    premarital, 111
Premarital questionnaire, 483–91
Premarital sex, 95, 108–18, 205–206, 340–41
Prenatal
    development, 320–23, 340–41, 492–93
    sexual differentiation, 80–81
Preparation for marriage, 162
Prepared childbirth, 371–73
Preschool child, 329
Prestige, 384
Primates, 9
Problem-solving, 308
Problems in communication, 63–65
Processing of feelings, 73–74
Procreation, family of, 5
Propinquity, 145
Protection, 280–82
Psychoanalytic theory, 85
Puberty, 96–99
    rites, 107
Punishment, 72, 261–62

Quasi-kin, 294

Read method of childbirth, 372
Reality, representations of, 59–60
Reasoning, 72, 260–61
Reasons for childbearing, 228–33
Reciprocity, 174, 182
Recreation, 342–43
Regulation of love, 49–50
Reinforcement, 261–62
Rejection, of children, 233, 257–58
Rejection of parenthood, 239–43
Religion and love, 47–48
Religious societies, 296
Remarriage, 196, 214–16
Rematching, 164
Reproduction, 368–75

Resources, 267
Respect, 33–36, 38–39, 68–69, 311
Response, 311
Responsibility, 36, 38–39
Rest, 328–30
Retardation, 282
Retirement, 423–24
    plans, 399
Revolution, sexual, 114–16
Rewards, 261–62
Rite de passage, 187
Rivalry, childhood, 282–84
Role, 8–9, 76, 209, 454–56
    strain, 128
Roles and communication, 65–66
Romantic love, 41–43, 45–47
Rooming in, 377–78
Rules of love, 45

Safety, 338–39, 344
Sanitation, 344
Satisfaction, 217–18
Satisfactions of parenthood, 227–33
Savings, 398
School age, 236
School-age child, 330
Science, 326–27, 453
Self concept, 99
Self development, 384
Self esteem, 68, 73, 118, 126, 134–35, 206, 235, 307, 423
"Senior Panic," 17
Sex, 492–96
    after loss of partner or separation, 131
    as bond, 181
    as value, 456–57
    differences, 81–83
    education, 92–94, 99, 163
    play, 35
    ratio, 81–82
    therapy, 50
Sexual anatomy, 493–96
Sexual behavior, 94–99
Sexual development
    abnormalities, 81
    prenatal to puberty, 80–104
    puberty to old age, 106–36
Sexual experience, 205–206
Sexual response, 99–103
Sexual revolution, 114–16
Sexual standards, 108–14, 130–31
Sexually open marriage, 130–31, 461

Sibling relationships, 274–90
Siblings, influence of, 88
  in love career, 35
"Sick role," 417
Single parents, 238, 432
Singles, 464
Social learning theory, 85–90
Social stratification, 20–22
Social systems, 19–20
Socialization, 16, 54–55, 86–90,
  256–62
Societal regulation of love, 49–50
Spending, household, 394–96
Spousefree parents, 13, 238, 464–66
Spouses, 33–39
Stability, 55–57
Stages of labor, 374
Standards, sexual, 108–14, 130–31
Status, 229
Status-oriented family, 66
Strengthening family living, 470–75
Structure of family, 8–15
Sub-skin implants, contraceptive, 365
Support, 231–32
  to parents, 246–68
Swinging, 460–61
Sympathy, 63–64
Syphilis, 504–505
Systems, family, 18–22

Tax laws, 406
Tactile communication, 70
Teachers, 88–89
Television, 90
Tension release, 74–75
Theories of partner selection, 166–70
Therapy, family, 419–20
Time orientation, 452

Transsexuality, 123
Treatment, 337–38
Trends in family living, 449–76
Two-step marriage, 144

Unconditional love, 35
Uniqueness of families, 22–23
Upper-class extended family, 12
Utopian societies, 296

Values, 6, 266, 305–308, 405, 452–57
Vegetarian diet, 326
Venereal disease, 112, 163
  gonorrhea, 502–504
  herpes, venereal, 505–506
  syphilis, 504–505
Verbal communication, 57–58
Vicarious satisfaction, 232–33
Violence, 70, 435–38
Virginity, 48

Weddings, 185–88
Widowhood, 131, 215, 426–27
Will, legal, 405–406
Women workers
  career woman, 392
  chief earner, 393
  part-time, 392
Women's movement, 124–29
Work, 203
Workers, 454
Working
  couples, 393–94
  wives, 204
Work-sharing, 470–71
World-wide problems, 449–51

Young marriages, 192–93